Intuition &
the Machine

Intuition ist von essenzieller Bedeutung für den Architekturentwurf. Ganz egal, wie rational und vernünftig man vorgeht, der Anteil der Entwurfsentscheidungen, den man als ArchitektIn intuitiv trifft oder sogar treffen muss, bleibt stets groß und bildet oft genug den Unterschied zwischen guten und mäßigen Entwürfen. Interessanterweise wird aber unter ArchitektInnen kaum darüber gesprochen, wie Intuition genau funktioniert. Das mag daran liegen, dass Intuition etwas ist, das im Unbewussten passiert und wir deshalb vielleicht gar nicht darüber sprechen *können*. Müssen wir also – mit Wittgenstein gesprochen – darüber schweigen?

Für die zehnte Ausgabe von GAM haben wir dazu aufgerufen, das Schweigen zu brechen. Unser Titel „Intuition & the Machine" erklärt warum: Die digitalen Maschinen, mit denen wir es in der Architektur immer mehr zu tun haben, fordern diese Auseinandersetzung heraus. Denn sie sind längst keine Maschinen im herkömmlichen Sinn mehr: Sie nehmen uns immer mehr kognitive Tätigkeiten ab und sie entwickeln sich rasant. Daraus entsteht das Spannungsfeld, dem wir uns in dieser Ausgabe von GAM widmen.

Intuition is essential for architectural design. No matter how thoughtfully and rationally you proceed, the portion of design decisions that are made or maybe even have to be made "from the gut" is always substantial and often enough distinguishes good from mediocre designs. Interestingly, however, there is little discussion among architects about how intuition actually works. The reason for this may be that intuition is something that happens in the subconscious and that we therefore cannot speak of it. Is intuition thus one of those subjects whereof—to speak with Wittgenstein—one must be silent?

For the tenth issue of GAM we asked for contributions to break this silence. The title "Intuition & the Machine" explains why: digital machines present in architecture engender this debate because they have long ceased to be machines in the traditional sense. They are taking on more and more of our cognitive tasks and developing rapidly, thus creating the field of tensions that this issue of GAM is devoted to.

URS HIRSCHBERG

Das Thema scheint einen Nerv getroffen zu haben. Im Verhältnis zwischen ArchitektInnen und ihren Entwurfswerkzeugen ist einiges in Bewegung geraten. Dabei geht es nicht nur um die neuen digitalen Möglichkeiten, sondern gerade auch um unsere menschlichen Fähigkeiten, unser ästhetisches Empfinden, unser Gefühl, unsere Intuition. Werden auch sie immer mehr an den Computer delegiert? Oder ist es im Gegenteil so, dass sie durch die technischen Entwicklungen aufgewertet, in ihrer Bedeutung stärker erkannt, ja vielleicht sogar auf neue Weise eingesetzt werden können? Das sind Fragen, denen sich unsere AutorInnen auf den folgenden Seiten in unterschiedlicher Weise stellen.

Die landläufige Meinung zu Intuition ist nicht sehr einheitlich. Auf der einen Seite gibt es die Intuition als Motor unserer Kreativität, als unfehlbarer innerer Kompass, wie sie Albert Einstein beschrieben hat: „Der Verstand spielt auf dem Weg der Entdeckung nur eine untergeordnete Rolle. Es findet ein Sprung im Bewusstsein statt, nennen Sie es Intuition oder was Sie wollen, und die Lösung kommt zu Ihnen und Sie wissen nicht wie und warum."[1] Auf der anderen Seite gibt es aber auch Skepsis, wie sie etwa in einem Bonmot des Schweizer Schriftstellers Friedrich Dürrenmatt anklingt: „Unter Intuition versteht man die Fähigkeit gewisser Leute, eine Lage in Sekundenschnelle falsch zu beurteilen."[2]

Auch in den Beiträgen dieser GAM Ausgabe gibt es keine einheitliche Auffassung von Intuition. Dass man intuitiv zu falschen Einschätzungen kommen kann, insbesondere in Bezug auf die digitalen Medien, wird öfter thematisiert. Viele Entwicklungen scheinen hier geradezu im direkten Widerspruch zu unserem gesunden Menschenverstand zu stehen. Im Bezug auf den Computer können wir unserer Intuition häufig nicht trauen. Andererseits ist gerade die Fähigkeit, Dinge zu erahnen, eine, die uns der Computer wohl nicht so bald abnehmen wird.

In guter GAM-Tradition sind die Beiträge dieser thematischen Ausgabe bunt und kontrovers. Zudem sind die Schreibenden zumeist Personen, die nicht nur beobachten und reflektieren, sondern auch aus eigener Erfahrung schreiben, weil sie aktiv involviert sind in Forschungen und Entwicklungen, die das Thema „Intuition & the Machine" neu erschließen. Dadurch ergibt sich eine multiperspektivische Sicht, die viele aktuelle Positionen und Tendenzen des zeitgenössischen Architekturdiskurses zu Wort kommen lässt. Das Thema bringt es mit sich, dass auf den folgenden Seiten wenig von gebauter Architektur die Rede ist. Vielmehr geht es um das Entwerfen an sich und um die neuartigen Prozesse, die derzeit im Entwurf möglich werden. Vieles ist experimentell und manches scheint von einer Anwendung in der Praxis weit entfernt zu sein. Abgesehen davon, dass uns auch da unsere Intuition trügen könnte: Das Betrachten der grundsätzlichen Bedingungen, auf denen sich das Spannungsfeld zwischen Intuition und Maschine aufbaut, war uns bei der Auswahl der Beiträge wichtig.

Das Heft ist in drei Scktionen gegliedert: In der ersten, **Senses and Tools**, geht es um unsere Sinne und um das, was neuartige digitale Werkzeuge für sie und mit ihnen zu leisten vermögen. Wie kann ein anderer Umgang mit Komplexität aussehen, wie kann Freude im Gebrauch der neuartigen Werk-

The topic seems to touch a nerve. The relationship between architects and their tools is changing in many ways. The debate is not just about digitally enabled possibilities, but precisely about our very own human capacities: our esthetical judgment, our feelings, our intuition. Can they be delegated to the computer as well? Or is the opposite true: Are human design factors being strengthened by digital technology? Is their importance better appreciated, could they even be put to better use thanks to advances in technology? These are questions our authors deal with in various ways in the following pages.

Popular opinion on the subject of intuition is varied. On the one hand there is intuition as the motor of creativity, the unerring inner compass, as described by Einstein: "The intellect has little to do on the road to discovery. There comes a leap in consciousness, call it intuition or what you will, and the solution comes to you and you don't know how or why."[1] On the other hand there is skepticism, as in the quote by Swiss author Friedrich Dürrenmatt who quipped that "intuition is the capacity of certain people to incorrectly assess a situation in a matter of seconds."[2]

Likewise there is no consistent take on intuition in the contributions to this edition of GAM. That one can intuitively make wrong assessments, especially when dealing with digital media, is discussed in several texts. Many developments in the realm of information technology seem to directly go against our instincts. With regard to the computer we often can't trust our intuition too much. On the other hand, the human hunch is probably something that we won't teach computers anytime soon.

In good GAM tradition the thematic contributions to this number are colorful and controversial. Furthermore our authors are for the most part not only people who observe and reflect, but also who write from their experience of being actively involved in research and developments that shed new light on the topic of "Intuition & the Machine." The multi-perspective view that results includes a variety of positions and tendencies in contemporary architectural discourse. The topic attracted contributions that don't reflect primarily on built architecture. Instead they focus on the design process and on novel procedures that are currently becoming possible. Much of this work is experimental and some of it appears to be far from practical application, but apart from the fact that our intuition might be wrong about this, too: the fundamental conditions that are shaping tensions between intuition and machine were important in our selection of contributions.

The issue is structured in three sections: The first, **Senses and Tools**, discusses our perceptual senses and the effects and

1   Zitiert nach Larry Chang (Hg.): *Wisdom for the Soul*, Washington 2006, S. 179.

2   Zitiert nach Monika Mörtenhummer (Hg.): *Zitate im Management*, Wien 2008, S. 192.

1   Larry Chang, ed., *Wisdom for the Soul* (Washington, 2006), p. 179.

2   Monika Mörtenhummer, ed., *Zitate im Management* (Vienna 2008), p. 192.

affects that novel digital tools could have on them. What could another way of dealing with complexity be? How can the use of novel digital tools be made pleasurable? How can new synergies between analogue and digital processes be found?

The second, **Mind and Matter**, brings together contributions that focus on the philosophical basis of the topic, taking a longer view of the development of algorithmic design. The beginnings of the "Paperless Studios" are critically assessed, as are the influences of postmodernism, of cybernetics and of mathematics and philosophy on current designerly thinking.

In **Interactions and Mutations**, the third section of GAM.10, practical applications of innovative interactive design- and fabrication processes are featured. They demonstrate how the topical spectrum of architecture is changing and expanding and the surprising possibilities that arise when machines become partners and materials are digitally informed.

Each section ends with an interview: respectively with psychologist Edith Ackermann, ETH CAAD researcher Ludger Hovestadt and director of the MIT Self-Assembly Lab Skylar Tibbits. The two photo-series that separate the three sections showcase works from the labs of the latter two: *Digital Grotesque*, *Decibot* and *Fluid Crystalization*—research projects as fascinating for their innovation as for their beauty.

Fascination, not only with novel technical possibilities but also with our emotional reaction to them, is an important aspect of this issue. Fascination can keep us wondering, can lead to new insights, can challenge our intellect as well as our intuition. In this sense we hope you will be fascinated by what you read on the following pages and thereby inspired to think about machines and intuition.

Finally a personal remark: this is the tenth issue of GAM. Over the past ten years many different editors have contributed to establishing GAM as part of the TU Graz Architecture Faculty and as part of the international academic discourse about architecture. Of the founding editors I'm the last remaining—now for me, too, it's time to step aside. I want to thank all my colleagues for their excellent collaboration and for the opportunity to act as guest editor on this "jubilee" number. As usual you will find information about our plans for the upcoming 11th issue of GAM in the *Call for Papers* on the last pages.

zeuge entstehen, wie kann eine neue Arbeitsteilung zwischen digitalen und analogen Prozessen gefunden werden?

In der zweiten Sektion, **Mind and Matter**, sind Beiträge versammelt, welche den Akzent auf die philosophischen Grundlagen des Themas legen, bzw. auch eine Betrachtung der Entwicklung von algorithmischem Entwerfen über einen größeren Zeitraum vornehmen. Die Anfänge der „Paperless Studios" werden hier ebenso kritisch diskutiert wie der Einfluss der Postmoderne und jener der Kybernetik, aber auch der Mathematik und der Philosophie auf das heutige entwerferische Denken.

In **Interactions and Mutations,** der dritten Sektion von GAM.10, sind einige praktische Anwendungen neuartiger, interaktiver Gestaltungs- und Fertigungsprozesse versammelt. Sie zeigen auf, wie sich das Themenspektrum der Architektur wandeln und erweitern kann und welche überraschenden Möglichkeiten entstehen können, wenn Maschinen zu Partnern werden und Materialien digital informiert werden.

Den Abschluss der einzelnen Sektionen bildet jeweils ein Interview: mit der Psychologin Edith Ackermann, mit dem ETH-CAAD-Forscher Ludger Hovestadt und mit dem Leiter des MIT Self-Assembly Labs Skylar Tibbits. Aus dem Wirkungskreis der letzteren beiden stammen auch die Bildstrecken, die zwischen den Sektionen eingefügt sind: *Digital Grotesque*, *Decibot* und *Fluid Crystalization* – Forschungsarbeiten, die uns nicht nur durch ihren Innovationsgehalt, sondern auch durch ihre Schönheit zum Staunen bringen.

Das Staunen, nicht nur über das, was heute technisch möglich ist, sondern auch darüber, welche Empfindungen es in uns auszulösen vermag, ist ein wichtiger Aspekt dieses Heftes. Staunen kann uns davor bewahren, vorschnell zu urteilen, kann neue Erkenntnisprozesse anregen, kann unseren Verstand wie unsere Intuition herausfordern. In diesem Sinne hoffen wir, dass Sie, liebe Leserin, lieber Leser, bei der Lektüre recht häufig ins Staunen kommen und damit angeregt werden zum Nachdenken über Maschinen und Intuition.

Schließlich sei noch ein persönliches Wort erlaubt. Es ist dies die zehnte Ausgabe von GAM. In wechselnder Besetzung der Redaktion hat sich GAM in den letzten zehn Jahren als fester Bestandteil nicht nur der Grazer Architekturfakultät sondern auch des internationalen akademischen Diskurses über Architektur etabliert. Von der Gründungsredaktion bin ich der letzte noch Verbliebene – nun ist es auch für mich Zeit, mich neuen Herausforderungen zu widmen. Für die gute Zusammenarbeit und für die Möglichkeit, zum Abschluss diese Jubiläumsnummer als Gasteditor zu betreuen, möchte ich mich bei meinen Kolleginnen und Kollegen ganz herzlich bedanken. Über die Pläne für die elfte Ausgabe von GAM informieren wir wie gewohnt durch den *Call for Papers* auf den letzten Seiten.

Senses & Tools

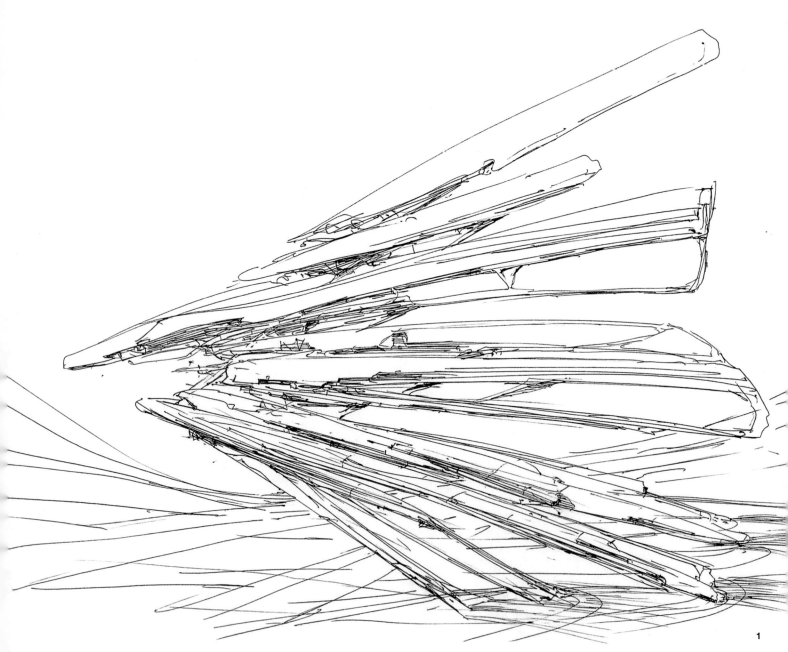

1 Lebendige Linien. Vgl. dazu Abb. 7, 8. "Living lines." See also figs. 7, 8. © MAKOTO SEI WATANABE/ARCHITECTS' OFFICE

ALGOrithmic-Design/Can the Child Machine Develop into an Adult?

1. Design/A Gift from "Below" Consciousness. Intuition Design/If You Have a Pen, You Can Design. Design is intuition. Pictures do not emerge from reasoning about this or that. Some people might disagree. They might say that ideas and concepts are the core of design. And as far as that goes, they would be right.

ALGOrithmischesDesign. Kann die Kind-Maschine erwachsen werden? 1. Entwerfen/Ein Geschenk aus dem Unterbewusstsein. Intuitives Entwerfen/Wenn du einen Stift hast, kannst du entwerfen. Entwerfen ist Intuition. Bilder entstehen nicht aus Diskussionen über dies und jenes. Einige mögen anderer Meinung sein. Sie behaupten womöglich, Ideen und Konzepte stünden im Mittelpunkt des Entwerfens. So gesehen hätten sie Recht.

MAKOTO SEI WATANABE

Le Corbusier (to return to the textbook) defined five principles of modern architecture and designed the Villa Savoye as an example of architecture to embody them. It became famous as the formal expression of a modernist scheme: free floor plan, free facades, horizontal windows, pilotis, and a roof garden. All of this is too well-known to repeat. These five principles were "algorithms" to enable the establishment of "modern architecture." So, if we used these algorithms to design architecture on a similar scale, would the result be the Villa Savoye? Of course not. The pilotis might not stop at the roof but continue reaching up toward the sky. The choice of color does not need to be restricted to white, and the walls could be curved without violating the five principles. The algorithms of the five principles do not determine the form. To put it bluntly, we could say that the villa has the form it has because the architect liked that form. Perhaps "liked" is too blunt. Perhaps we should attribute it to overall intuition. Intuition "decides" matters that are hard to decide with algorithms, "integrating" the whole into a marvelous form. A freehand sketch using nothing more than pen and paper has the power to transcend a multitude of analyses and debates, producing a beautiful answer that solves the problem in single stroke. This ability on the part of humans still leaves computer programs far behind. However, such a "flash of inspiration" does not come to those who simply wait. It comes only after many studies, repetitions of making and tearing down, suddenly like a ray of light after the struggles, a blissful moment that visits the fortunate. Actual design work involves evaluating that first insight, and re-evaluating the next one, and then doing it again. It could be called design by feedback circuit. Other design methods may be developed, but I think it will be some time before design by insight and intuition is replaced. We still do not know what powers lie hidden in the brain.

Where Insights Are Born. So where do they come from, these insights and revelations? According to the research of the neurophysiologist Benjamin Libet, when a person decides to move a part of the body, instructions to move (electrical signals) have already been issued to the muscles, about 0.5 seconds before the conscious decision. In other words, what seems to us to be an act of conscious volition has in fact already been decided on the subconscious level. If this is true, then "consciousness" is suffering from an illusion, because we believe that we are deciding what has already been decided subconsciously. Sudden insights, revelations, and other kinds of inspiration may in fact be "gifts" delivered to our consciousness from the unconscious. Further, if this is so, then granting the maximum degree of freedom to our unconscious activities should be an effective way to make better hand-drawn designs. Free the subconscious from constraints imposed by consciousness. (But how might that be accomplished?)

> A freehand sketch using nothing more than pen and paper has the power to transcend a multitude of analyses and debates, producing a beautiful answer that solves the problem in single stroke.

Le Corbusier (um zum Lehrbuch zurückzukehren) definierte die fünf Prinzipien der modernen Architektur und entwarf die Villa Savoye als ihr gebautes Beispiel. Sie wurde berühmt als methodische Umsetzung einer modernistischen Planung: freier Grundriss, frei gestaltete Fassaden, horizontale Fenster, Pilotis und ein Dachgarten. All dies ist zu bekannt, um es wiederholen zu müssen. Diese fünf Prinzipien waren „Algorithmen", die es der „modernen Architektur" ermöglichen sollten, Fuß zu fassen. Würden wir also diese Algorithmen verwenden, um Architektur ähnlichen Maßstabs zu entwerfen, wäre das Ergebnis die Villa Savoye? Natürlich nicht. Die Pilotis würden vielleicht nicht am Dach enden sondern sich weiter himmelwärts recken. Die Farbwahl müsste nicht auf Weiß beschränkt werden und die Wände könnten gebogen sein, ohne die fünf Prinzipien zu verletzen. Die Algorithmen der fünf Prinzipien bestimmen nicht die Form. Offen gesagt glauben wir, die Villa hat ihre Form, weil sie dem Architekten gefiel. Vielleicht ist „gefallen" hier zu unverblümt. Womöglich sollten wir es der Gesamtintuition zuschreiben. Intuition „entscheidet" Angelegenheiten, die mit Algorithmen schwer zu entscheiden sind und „integriert" das Ganze in eine hervorragende Form. Eine freihändige Skizze mit nichts mehr als Stift und Papier hat die Macht, eine Vielzahl von Analysen und Debatten zu überschreiten und dabei eine wunderbare Antwort zu generieren, die das Problem auf einen Streich löst. Diese menschliche Fähigkeit lässt Computerprogramme weit hinter sich. Ein solcher „Inspirationsschub" trifft allerdings nicht jene, die bloß auf Inspiration warten. Er geschieht nur als Folge vieler Studien, wiederholtem Anfertigen und Zerstören, plötzlich wie ein Lichtstrahl nach der Mühsal, ein seliger Augenblick, der den Glücklichen vergönnt ist. Bei wirklicher Entwurfsarbeit geht es darum, diese erste Eingebung zu bewerten, dann die nächste und dann das Ganze von vorn. Man könnte es Entwerfen mittels Feedback-Schleifen nennen. Andere Entwurfsverfahren könnten noch entwickelt werden, aber ich glaube, es wird Zeit brauchen, bis an die Stelle von Entwerfen durch Eingebung und Intuition etwas anderes tritt. Noch sind wir uns der Kräfte, die im Gehirn schlummern nicht wirklich bewusst.

Wo Eingebungen entstehen. Wo kommen sie also her, diese Eingebungen und Offenbarungen? Der Forschung des Neurophysiologen Benjamin Libet zufolge wurden Anweisungen sich zu bewegen (elektrische Signale) bereits an die Muskeln gesandt, wenn eine Person erst beschließt, einen Körperteil zu bewegen. Dies geschieht etwa 0,5 Sekunden vor der bewussten Entscheidung. Mit anderen Worten: Was uns als bewusster Willensakt erscheint, wurde in Wirklichkeit bereits auf der Ebene des Unterbewusstseins entschieden. Falls dies zutrifft, unterliegt das „Bewusstsein" einer Illusion, weil wir glauben, etwas zu entscheiden, was bereits unbewusst entschieden wurde. Bei plötzlichen Eingebungen, Offenbarungen und anderen Inspirationen könnte es sich tatsächlich um „Geschenke" handeln, die unser

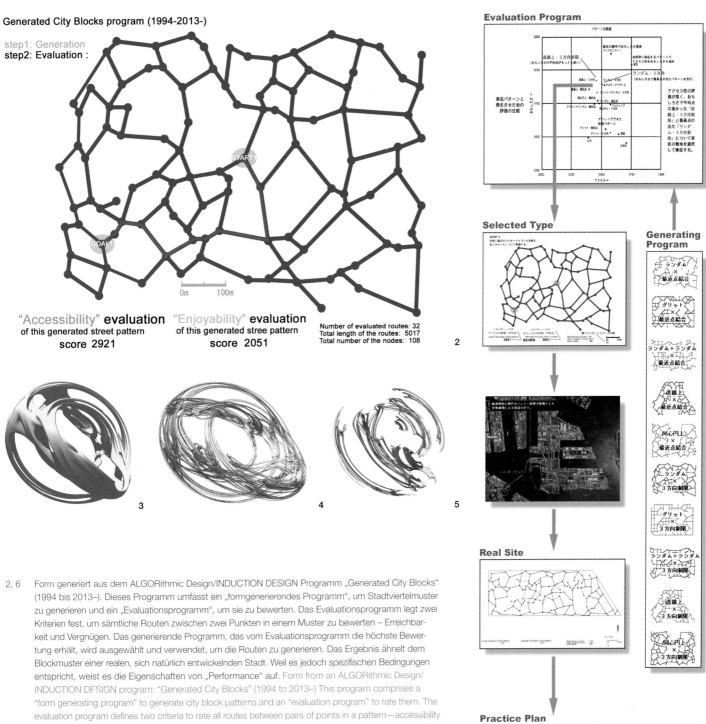

Generated City Blocks program (1994-2013-)

step1: Generation
step2: Evaluation :

START1

GOAL1

0m   100m

"Accessibility" **evaluation**
of this generated street pattern
score 2921

"Enjoyability" **evaluation**
of this generated stree pattern
score 2051

Number of evaluated routes: 32
Total length of the routes: 5017
Total number of the nodes: 108

3   4   5   2

Evaluation Program

Selected Type

Generating Program

Real Site

Practice Plan

6

2, 6   Form generiert aus dem ALGORithmic Design/INDUCTION DESIGN Programm „Generated City Blocks"
(1994 bis 2013–). Dieses Programm umfasst ein „formgenerierendes Programm", um Stadtviertelmuster
zu generieren und ein „Evaluationsprogramm", um sie zu bewerten. Das Evaluationsprogramm legt zwei
Kriterien fest, um sämtliche Routen zwischen zwei Punkten in einem Muster zu bewerten – Erreichbarkeit und Vergnügen. Das generierende Programm, das vom Evaluationsprogramm die höchste Bewertung erhält, wird ausgewählt und verwendet, um die Routen zu generieren. Das Ergebnis ähnelt dem
Blockmuster einer realen, sich natürlich entwickelnden Stadt. Weil es jedoch spezifischen Bedingungen
entspricht, weist es die Eigenschaften von „Performance" auf. Form from an ALGORithmic Design/
INDUCTION DFSIGN program: "Generated City Blocks" (1994 to 2013–) This program comprises a
"form generating program" to generate city block patterns and an "evaluation program" to rate them. The
evaluation program defines two criteria to rate all routes between pairs of points in a pattern—accessibility
and enjoyability. The generating program that receives the highest score from the evaluation program is
selected and used to generate/design the routes. The result resembles the block pattern of an actual,
naturally developing town. But because it meets specified conditions, it has the characteristic of "performance." © MAKOTO SEI WATANABE/ARCHITECTS' OFFICE

3–5   Form durch ein formgenerierendes Programm: Julia set. Julia sets werden aus Formeln generiert und
nehmen ihren Parametern entsprechend viele Formen an. Die Formen haben keine besondere Bedeutung.
Damit eine Form Bedeutung hat, muss es eine „Zielvorgabe" geben (eine Ursache für die Wahl dieser Form)
und eine „Bewertung", um zu bestimmen, wie gut sie dieser Zielvorgabe entspricht. Ein Design wird zum
algorithmischen Design, wenn es über beides verfügt. Form by a form generating program: Julia set. Julia
sets are generated from formulas and take on many shapes according to their parameters. The shapes
have no special meaning. For a shape to have meaning, there must be an "objective" (a reason for selecting
the shape) and an "evaluation" to determine how well it meets the objective. A design becomes "algorithmic
design" when it has both. © MAKOTO SEI WATANABE/ARCHITECTS' OFFICE

2. Design/Work on the Conscious Level. Design in a World of Anything and Everything/Assignments as Answers. Although we can do our best to liberate the subconscious, what do people actually do on the conscious level? A large part of design work on the conscious level is devoted to meeting requirements. Architects must deal with a multitude of requirements. There are requirements related to area, functional requirements, the relationship with the environment, neighbors' opinions, regulations, the construction schedule, cost, etc. The test of an architect is how skillfully these various requirements can be met. There are also conditions that do not show up in the formal requirements: history, social ethics, values, all of the things which (although missing from the brief) raise a building to the status of "work of architecture" when they are expressed in the design. The architect's assignment is to "solve" all of these requirements, and most of the time spent on a project is devoted to conscious research and experimentation—this should be handled so, but what about that? Suppose it were possible to cancel the conditions imposed on architecture. What would that be like? Such a thing is easy to say, but if cancelling conditions were so easy then our troubles would be over.

However, there is one domain where cancellation is possible—the virtual world. In the immaterial world of movies and games there are no onerous requirements. In that world, almost all of the conditions imposed upon architecture (the conditions that we struggle to solve by devising logic and programs) are no longer there. There is no gravity, the site is limitless, walls are permeable to teleporting, no accidents happen, and everything can be redone. Because nothing in that world constrains the design, requirements cannot be offered as "reasons" for the design. Blame for a particular plan or form cannot be assigned to functions or construction methods, the energy load, or the historical style in the neighborhood. Everything is free. It was all chosen personally by the architect. The resulting forms and arrangements should furnish a good gauge of the "caliber" of the architect. A world with no excuses, where the only question is the abilities and talent of the architect. In such a world, where the conditions normally imposed upon architecture are cancelled, what would become the new "conditions"?

Freedom—Constraints—Flexibility. A world without limits, where anything is possible. As stated, this is a world where the talent of the architect is tested. But from another angle, in this world of freedom, the "conditions" for a design would probably consist of the creation of new constraints.

For example, consider games. Games have rules. Even though games are a world where anything is possible, players are required to follow certain rules. They compete under the rules or set out on a journey of discovery. They have experiences, acquire things, and are satisfied. Then they do it again.

What is Gained by Imposing Constraints. When designing architecture for the real world, with all of its constraints, a major goal is to discover a sphere of freedom by overcoming constraining conditions = solving problems. In the virtual world, where anything is possible, the goal is enjoyment, which is gained by setting constraining conditions and then acting within those rules.

In the world of building, we want methods to satisfy conditions. In the world of non-building, we want methods to impose conditions. In both worlds, we need to set goals and develop algorithms to meet them. Both need "algorithmic design," though in the opposite directions.

Bewusstsein vom Unterbewusstsein erhält. Wenn dem so ist, dann sollte maximale Freiheit für unsere unbewussten Aktivitäten ein effektiver Weg zu besseren Handzeichnungen sein. Man befreie das Unterbewusstsein von den Zwängen, die ihm das Bewusstsein auferlegt. (Wie könnte das jedoch gelingen?)

2. Design/Arbeiten auf der bewussten Ebene. Design in einer Welt von Allem und Jedem/Aufgaben als Antworten. Wenngleich wir uns bemühen können, unser Unterbewusstsein zu befreien, was tun Leute eigentlich auf der bewussten Ebene? Bei einem großen Teil der bewussten Entwurfsarbeit geht es darum, Anforderungen gerecht zu werden. Architekten müssen sich mit einer Fülle von Anforderungen befassen. Es gibt Anforderungen in Bezug auf die Region, funktionale Anforderungen, die Beziehung zur Umgebung, die Meinungen der Nachbarschaft, Vorschriften, die Bauplanung, Kosten usw. Das Können eines Architekten zeigt sich daran, wie geschickt er diese verschiedenen Anforderungen erfüllen kann. Darüber hinaus gibt es Bedingungen, die nicht Teil der offiziellen Anforderungen sind: Geschichte, soziale Ethik, Werte, all die Faktoren, die, obwohl sie nicht Teil der Ausschreibung sind, dem Gebäude den Status eines „Bauwerks" verleihen, falls sie im Entwurf zum Ausdruck kommen. Aufgabe des Architekten ist es, all diese Anforderungen zu „erfüllen", und der größte Teil der Arbeitszeit an einem Projekt ist bewusster Forschung und dem Experimentieren gewidmet – hiermit sollte man so verfahren, wie aber sieht es damit aus? Angenommen, es wäre möglich, die mit Architektur verknüpften Bedingungen aufzuheben, wie wäre das? So etwas ist leicht gesagt, aber wenn es so einfach wäre, Bedingungen aufzuheben, hätten unsere Probleme ein Ende.

Es gibt jedoch einen Bereich, in dem Aufhebung möglich ist – die virtuelle Welt. In der immateriellen Welt von Filmen und Spielen gibt es keine lästigen Anforderungen. In dieser Welt existieren nahezu alle der Architektur auferlegten Bedingungen nicht mehr, um deren Bewältigung wir mithilfe von Logik und Programmen kämpfen. Es gibt keine Schwerkraft, das Gelände ist grenzenlos, die Wände sind durchlässig für Teleportation, es passieren keine Unfälle und immer wieder kann erneut begonnen werden. Weil nichts in dieser Welt das Entwerfen einschränkt, können Anforderungen nicht als „Gründe" für einen Entwurf angeführt werden. Die Schuld für eine bestimmte Planung oder Form kann nicht Funktionen oder Konstruktionsverfahren, Energiebelastung oder dem historischen Stil in der Nachbarschaft angelastet werden. Alles ist frei. Alles wurde vom Architekten persönlich ausgewählt. Die daraus entstehenden Formen und Anordnungen sollten eine gute Einschätzung des Architekten ermöglichen. Eine Welt ohne Ausreden, in der die einzige Frage die nach Fähigkeiten und Begabung des Architekten ist. Wie würden in einer solchen Welt, in der die den Architekten normalerweise auferlegten Bedingungen aufgehoben sind, die neuen „Bedingungen" aussehen?

Freiheit – Beschränkungen – Flexibilität. Eine Welt ohne Begrenzungen, in der alles möglich ist. Wie gesagt ist dies eine Welt, in der die Begabung des Architekten auf die Probe gestellt wird. Aus einem anderen Blickwinkel gesehen würden in dieser Welt der Freiheit die „Bedingungen" für einen Entwurf vermutlich in der Schaffung neuer Beschränkungen bestehen. Man denke zum Beispiel an Spiele. Spiele haben Regeln. Obwohl Spiele eine Welt darstellen, in der alles möglich ist, müssen die Spieler bestimmten Regeln Folge leisten. Sie wetteifern unter Beachtung der Regeln oder begeben sich auf eine Entdeckungsreise. Sie machen Erfahrungen, erwerben Dinge und sind zufrieden. Dann tun sie es erneut.

Was erreicht man durch den Erlass von Beschränkungen? Wenn man Architektur für die Realität mit allen ihren Beschränkungen entwirft, gilt es vor allem, eine Sphäre der Freiheit zu entdecken, indem man einschränkende Bedingungen überwindet, d.h. Probleme löst. In der virtuellen Welt, wo dagegen alles möglich ist, geht es um Spaß, den man erreicht, indem man beschränkende Bedingungen festlegt und dann im Rahmen dieser Regeln handelt. In der Welt des Bauens möchten wir Verfahren, die Bedingungen erfüllen. In der Welt des Nicht-Bauens möchten wir Verfahren, die Bedingungen auferlegen. In beiden Welten müssen wir Ziele setzen und Algorithmen entwickeln, um sie zu erreichen. Beide brauchen „algorithmisches Entwerfen", nur in entgegengesetzte Richtungen.

Freiheit und Beschränkung liegen rechts und links auf demselben Schieberegler. Was also bewirkt „algorithmisches Entwerfen" in der virtuellen Welt und wie tut es das? Denken wir beispielsweise an die Simulation einer Flucht. In der Welt des Bauens besteht angesichts eines bestimmten Grundrisses und einer bestimmten Zahl von Menschen das Ziel darin, die Flucht aller schnellstmöglich durchführen zu können. In der Virtualität geht es darum, für eine hochdramatische Simulation Hindernisse anzuordnen. Bei diesen beiden Arten von Design ist die Richtung entgegengesetzt, aber die Logik dieselbe, was ähnliche Algorithmen zur Folge haben sollte. Falls das zuträfe, bestünde die Möglichkeit, ein Programm zu generieren, das durch das Umlegen eines Schalters in beide Richtungen nutzbar wäre. Sind also die reale und die virtuelle Welt umschaltbar? Besteht der einzige Unterschied in einem einzigen Zeichen in einem Programm? Wenn ja, dann wären Verfahren, die in der virtuellen Welt wirksam sind, vielleicht auch in der Realität wirksam. Die virtuelle Welt, keineswegs nur ein Spielplatz für Eskapisten, könnte in die reale Welt zurückkehren oder zwischen beiden pendeln.

3. Entwerfen durch Entscheiden und Entwerfen ohne zu Entscheiden. Design, das nicht entwirft/Was entscheidet der Designer? In „Generated City Blocks", einem der „INDUCTION CITIES/INDUCTION DESIGN" Programme (1994 bis 2012), entspricht der gewählte Vorschlag nicht dem Entwurf

Freedom and Constraint Are Right and Left on the Same Slider. So what does "algorithmic design" do in the virtual world, and how? For example, consider the simulation of an escape. In the world of building, given a certain plan and a certain number of people, the goal is to allow the escape to be completed as quickly as possible. In the virtual world, the goal is to arrange obstacles for the most dramatic simulation. In these two types of design, the direction is opposite but the logic is the same, which should mean that the algorithms would be similar. If they are, then it might be possible to create a program that could be used in either direction by flipping a switch. So are the real and virtual worlds switchable? Is the only difference a single character in a program? If so, then methods which are effective in the virtual world might also work in the real world. Far from being only an escapist realm of play, the virtual world might return to the real world, or might come and go between the two.

3. Design That Decides, and Design That Does Not Decide. Design That Does Not Design/What Does the Designer Decide? In "Generated City Blocks," one of the "INDUCTION CITIES/INDUCTION DESIGN" programs (1994 to 2012), the proposal that is "selected" is not the design itself. Instead of a superior pattern of streets, what is selected is the program that is capable of generating a superior pattern of streets. Designs are "generated" by entering specific conditions in the selected program. In this case, "design" is not the act of designing but rather the discovery of a superior parent = a program that is capable of generating superior results = children. Instead of producing designs themselves, the idea is to design "mechanisms" to produce designs. This is the process of "induction," the main theme of the "INDUCTION CITIES/INDUCTION DESIGN project. Design that does not design—one of the possibilities for the design of the future.

Designing Everything/Scale-Free and Magic Numbers. Another way lies at the opposite pole. This way is to discover the rules that govern some state and use those rules to guide the design in the desired direction. But is it actually possible to discover such "rules"? For example, it is known that common patterns can be observed regardless of scale, from cosmic dimensions down to viruses. The bubble structure of the universe is one candidate for such patterns. Some "scale-free" phenomenon is occurring there, apparently identical even at different sizes. Fractals are also scale-free. Again, it is known that when body mass and metabolic rate are graphed for different species, the slope of the graph becomes ¾. Sometimes this is called a "magic number."

When one element (variable) scales in this way to a certain power of another element, the relationship is called a power law. Power laws have been reported in various domains, from physical phenomena such as the probability of earthquakes to social domains such as the economy and networks. If all of these phenomena were the result of the same "law," then there would be a "super-generalized law" governing everything from the

> In the virtual world, the goal is to arrange obstacles for the most dramatic simulation.

flow of water and the diet of animals to our daily shopping patterns. It would be a tremendous discovery. But does it really exist? What we are calling a "law" may refer to some cause in another dimension. Something that is common both to nature and to artificial phenomena in society. The causes of scale-free phenomena and magic numbers are still unknown. But even if the reasons for their existence are unknown, we can discover their existence inductively and use them. Laws with unknown causes may be difficult to use in science. But if their existence has been verified, they can be used in the related fields of "design + engineering," in the same way as rules of thumb and implicit knowledge. Even though they have not yet been formally derived as laws, phenomena that actually occur can (probably) be translated into programs.

4. Where the Brain Encounters the Machine. Master Craftsman Programs and Child Programs. Assuming it were possible to design with such a new method, what types of procedures and processes would be involved? Programs follow procedures, so they need to be written as procedures. One method that has been suggested to overcome the limitations of the procedural approach is interactive programming, and another is learning-based programming. The "interactive" type could be compared to a master craftsman who is highly skilled but who does not yet understand our intentions. The "learning-based" type could be compared to a developing child who may not be capable of many things yet but who has potential and ambition. When dealing with a "master craftsman" program, we decide the specifications (parameters) and "place an order" for what we want. Then we examine the results and place another order with different specifications. Currently there are many programs of this type. For the user, it is a process of trial and error. When dealing with a "developing child" program, we praise the program or scold it, and the program responds by trying something else. The trial and error takes place on the side of the program, not the teacher. This type of program is used in robotics, but is rarely seen in the field of design. The "Induction Design—Program of Flow" (2004) aimed in this direction.

Tools for Conveying Images. But what about the human side? Design is the process of satisfying conditions and eventually arriving at a form. It begins with an image, which can be either vague or distinct, and which can arise of itself or not. Whether the "cradle of images" is the mind or the heart, design is the process of making images into forms. What is not possible is to take images in the heart and translate them directly into form. To give something form, you can sketch it, or draw it on a monitor, or make a clay model. Or, of course, tell your staff what you want and have them make it.

> Whether the "cradle of images" is the mind or the heart, design is the process of making images into forms. What is not possible is to take images in the heart and translate them directly into form.

selbst. Anstelle eines idealen Straßennetzes wird ein Programm gewählt, das in der Lage ist, ein ideales Straßennetz zu generieren. Entwürfe werden „generiert", indem man bestimmte Bedingungen in die gewählten Programme eingibt. In diesem Fall bezeichnet „Design" nicht den Akt des Entwerfens, sondern die Entdeckung eines ausgezeichneten Elternteils = eines Programms, das fähig ist, ausgezeichnete Ergebnisse = Kinder zu generieren. Anstatt selbst Entwürfe zu produzieren, geht es darum, „Mechanismen" zu entwerfen, die Entwürfe produzieren. Dies ist der Prozess der „induction", das Kernthema des „Induction Cities/ Induction Design"-Projekts. Design, das nicht entwirft, wird zu einer der Möglichkeiten für das Design der Zukunft.

Alles entwerfen/Maßstabslos und magische Zahlen. Ein weiterer Weg befindet sich am entgegengesetzten Ende. Bei diesem Weg gilt es, die Regeln aufzudecken, die einen Zustand beherrschen und diese Regeln zu verwenden, um den Entwurf in die gewünschte Richtung zu lenken. Ist es jedoch tatsächlich möglich, derartige „Regeln" zu entdecken? Es ist beispielsweise bekannt, dass gebräuchliche Muster unabhängig von der Größe, von kosmischen Dimensionen bis zu Viren, beobachtet werden können. Die Blasenstruktur des Universums ist ein Paradebeispiel für diese Art Muster. Ein „maßstabsloses" Phänomen spielt sich dort ab, das offenkundig selbst bei unterschiedlicher Größe identisch abläuft. Auch Kurven sind maßstabslos. Es ist gleichfalls bekannt, dass bei der Aufzeichnung der Entwicklung von Körpermasse und Stoffwechsel verschiedener Spezies die Steigung der Kurve ¾ beträgt. Bisweilen wird dies als „magische Zahl" bezeichnet.

Wenn ein Element (variabel) sich in dieser Weise zu einer bestimmten Kraft eines anderen Elements verhält, wird die Beziehung als „power law" (Kraftgesetz) bezeichnet. Kraftgesetze kommen in unterschiedlichen Bereichen vor, angefangen bei physischen Phänomenen wie der Wahrscheinlichkeit von Erdbeben bis hin zu sozialen Bereichen wie Wirtschaft und Netzwerken. Wären all diese Phänomene das Ergebnis desselben „Gesetzes", gäbe es ein „ultra universalistisches Gesetz", das vom Fließen des Wassers und der Ernährung von Tieren bis hin zu unseren alltäglichen Einkäufen alles regelte. Es wäre eine enorme Entdeckung. Aber existiert es wirklich? Was wir als „Gesetz" bezeichnen, könnte sich auf irgendeine Ursache in einer anderen Dimension beziehen. Etwas, das sowohl der Natur als auch künstlichen Gebilden in der Gesellschaft eigen ist. Die Ursachen von maßlosen Phänomenen und magischen Zahlen sind noch unbekannt. Aber selbst wenn die Ursachen für ihre Existenz unbekannt sind, können wir ihr Vorhandensein induktiv wahrnehmen und sie verwenden. Gesetze ohne bekannte Ursachen mögen in der Wissenschaft schwer anwendbar sein, aber sobald ihre Existenz verifiziert ist, können sie in den verwandten Gebieten „Design + Technik" in gleicher Weise wie Faustregeln und implizites Wissen zur Anwendung kommen. Wenngleich sie bisher noch nicht offiziell als Gesetze abgeleitet wurden, können Phänomene, die tatsächlich vorkommen, (vermutlich) in Programme übertragen werden.

4. Wo das Gehirn auf die Maschine trifft. Handwerksmeisterliche und kindliche Programme.

Mal angenommen, es wäre möglich, mit einer solchen neuen Methode zu entwerfen, welche Arten von Verfahren und Prozessen wären daran beteiligt?

Programme folgen Prozeduren, also müssen sie als Prozeduren geschrieben werden. Eine Methode, die vorgeschlagen wurde, um über die Begrenzungen des prozeduralen Ansatzes hinwegzukommen, betrifft das interaktive Programmieren, eine weitere das lerngestützte Programmieren. Der „interaktive" Weg könnte mit einem Handwerksmeister verglichen werden, der hochqualifiziert ist, aber unsere Absichten noch nicht begreift. Den „lerngestützten" Typus könnte man mit einem heranwachsenden Kind vergleichen, das noch nicht viele Dinge kann, sich aber durch Potenzial und Ehrgeiz auszeichnet. Wenn wir es mit dem „handwerksmeisterlichen" Programm zu tun haben, entscheiden wir uns für genaue Angaben (Parameter) und „bestellen", was wir möchten. Dann prüfen wir das Ergebnis und geben eine neue Bestellung mit anderen Spezifikationen auf. Gegenwärtig gibt es viele Programme dieses Typs. Für den Benutzer ist es ein „Trial and Error"-Prozess. Im Fall eines „lerngestützten" Programms loben oder schelten wir das Programm und das Programm reagiert, indem es etwas anderes versucht. Das Ausprobieren findet auf Seiten des Programms und nicht des Lehrers statt. Diese Art von Programm kommt bei der Robotertechnik zur Anwendung, selten jedoch auf dem Gebiet des Entwerfens. Das „Induction Design-Program of Flow" (2004) visierte diese Richtung an.

Hilfsmittel zum Vermitteln von Bildern.

Aber welche Rolle spielt dabei der Mensch? Als Entwerfen bezeichnet man den Prozess zum Erfüllen von Bedingungen, mit dessen Hilfe man letztlich zu einer Form gelangt. Er beginnt mit einem Bild, das entweder vage oder bestimmt sein und aus sich selbst oder auch nicht entstehen kann. Gleich, ob die „Wiege der Bilder" nun der Geist oder das Herz ist, Entwerfen bezeichnet den Vorgang, der Bilder in Formen verwandelt. Es ist jedoch nicht möglich, Bilder direkt aus dem Herzen in Formen zu übersetzen. Um einem Gedanken Form zu geben, kann man ihn skizzieren, auf einen Monitor zeichnen, oder ein Modell aus Ton anfertigen. Man kann natürlich auch seinen Angestellten sagen, was man möchte und es von ihnen ausführen lassen.

DID/Direct Image Design.

In jedem Fall nehmen Bilder nur durch einen dieser indirekten Prozesse Form an. „Form" bezeichnet hier etwas, das man anderen übermitteln kann. Sie wird durch Medien übermittelt. Wir verwenden Bleistifte, Befehle, Ton oder andere Medien, um Bilder in Formen zu verwandeln, die für andere (und auch uns selbst) verständlich sind. Könnte es möglich sein, Bilder direkt, ohne die Vermitt-

DID/Direct Image Design.

In any case, images become form only via one of these indirect processes. Here, "form" means something that can be conveyed to others. It is conveyed via media. We use pencils, commands, clay, or other media to transform images into forms that can be understood by others (and ourselves). Might it be possible to turn images into form directly, without the intermediary of media? There is a field called BMI (Brain Machine Interface). Note the order of the characters. It is a different term from the BIM which is familiar from architectural CAD. The idea is to directly link the brain and information technology. Put simply, it is to extract and display thoughts. Toys have already been commercialized that float if the player concentrates on them strongly enough. Research is underway into smart houses that would allow elderly and handicapped persons to perform various operations by BMI. A future goal of this research is to reveal thoughts on the screen. If we could have thoughts and extract them directly as 3D information, then we could do Direct Image Design (DID) without the intermediary of pencils or commands. Perhaps we can look forward to the day when we can say "I DID it."

Practice at Extracting Images.

Let's try some practice with this new DID technology. If one step short is good enough, it is possible to "extract images" even today. There is no need for a machine or a program. Let's try something simple. How about a cone shape? A cube would make it harder to follow rotations of the shape, because every side looks the same. Think about a cone. The color is white. Let's say it is a white ceramic. If there is a desk in front of you, imagine it placed on the desk. It is small, only about 10 cm in height. If you don't have a table, imagine it floating in the air. So, now do you see a nice cone in front of you? Now let's rotate the cone vertically. If rotated horizontally it would look the same, so let's rotate it 90 degrees vertically, with the tip pointing away and the circular base pointing toward you. If you can see that, try turning it around and around, or moving it sideways.

Let's try changing the material and color. Change it to silver aluminum, to clear glass, to a cone with a surface of water covered with ripples. Once you get used to that, try expanding the size, twisting it, crumpling it into a ball, whatever you like. The fact that you can form an imagine of the "original cone" in front of you, even after all of these operations, means that the information for that image is "somewhere" (in your mind or heart = brain). If the information exists, and we were able to extract it, then we could process it any way we pleased (in an IT device outside the brain). What this means is the ability to extract our dreams. Formerly this was mocked as the stuff of dreams, but today it lies within range.

Direct Processing Using Images in the Brain.

There are methods to process information much faster than normally by using such images within the brain. For example, speed readers can understand a page in a second or less. Instead of reading the characters, they apparently perceive it as an image. (I have tried some of these methods myself.) However, design is slightly different, because in design the ability to process a complex mix of information is more important than speed. Another example is "anzan" (mental calculation), using traditional Japanese techniques based on the soroban, the Japanese abacus. I cannot do it myself, but I am told that it involves visualizing the beads on the soroban (an actual soroban is not used) and calculating by moving the beads around the mental image. Persons skilled in the art can perform mental multiplication and division of 5-digit numbers while the numbers are read out in quick succession, needing only a few seconds per question. The questions are read out at fearsome speed, but it is possible to keep up with the questions, moving the (virtual) beads around multiple columns, fixing them in the precisely correct positions, and then mentally redrawing them. The calculations use a mental image of the soroban, around which the beads are moved at will. If the image were to become blurred, then the calculation would end at that point. If such distinct and long-lasting images exist, does it not seem possible that soon we will be able to retrieve them from the brain?

5. Things Which Only People (Probably) Can Do. What is a living line? From tens of thousands of years in the past, people have formed images in their hearts and used their hands to draw them. Whether on a cave wall or on paper. Brain and hands, feelings and lines, are directly connected. The sketches in this paper were all drawn on paper with pencil or pen (figs. 1, 7, 8). They are shown exactly as drawn, without being digitally altered. No erasers were used. They are "living" lines, which never vanish once drawn. Without ever going back, the drawn lines are extended by drawing further. This process is one of the conditions of this design. What has been done cannot be deleted—that is true of many things in the world. It is also a condition of real social systems. A sketch on a piece of paper is also a simulation of social systems. A major difference between such sketches and computer graphics is this singularity of the line, its momentum. The line holds within itself the direction in which it is going, the parts that are not yet drawn, the momentum.

This is the power of the line, which is not decided by its thickness or the pressure of the brush. To put it metaphorically, it is what gives life force to the line. The sketch is not the architectural design itself, but it may be the source that gives birth to the design.

Computers Come Closer to Humans/Vanishing Programs. If humans work out a way to export images from the brain, then what about progress on the other side of the collaboration, on the program side? Algorithms and programs are means to an end, a path toward the goal. The important thing is to reach the goal. Algorithms and programs are not absolutely necessary. If we could do without them, all the better. The reason is that once the goal is decided, any design that reaches the goal is good enough. This leads back to the world of intuition. Instead of writing programs in special-purpose languages, as we do now, suppose it were possible to write them in natural languages. That might bring us closer to intuition. Natural languages are vague. It is easy to say "a beautiful form," but what does that mean? What kind of form is beautiful, and what kind is not? There are no instructions for that. But if there were circuits to "understand" nebulous expressions of this kind, to "infer" our intentions, and to "respond" to them in some way, then we could probably get a good answer even with instructions like these.

(Computers that understand natural language are here already. They are still at the stage where a computer can beat a human on a quiz show—Watson/IBM, 2011—, but eventually they will probably acquire more general abilities.) If ordinary language like this sentence can become a program, without any special-purpose language, that would certainly be more convenient (because we would not need to study programming languages).

lung von Medien, in Formen zu verwandeln? Es gibt den Begriff des BMI (Brain Machine Interface), der eine Schnittstelle von Hirn und Maschine bezeichnet. Achten Sie auf die Reihenfolge der Buchstaben. Es ist ein anderer Terminus als BIM, der im Kontext des CAD der Architekten verwendet wird. Bei einem BMI geht es darum, das Gehirn unmittelbar mit der Informationstechnologie zu verbinden. Einfach gesagt werden dabei Gedanken extrahiert und zur Schau gestellt. Es gibt bereits Spielzeug zu kaufen, das schwebt, wenn sich der Spieler stark genug darauf konzentriert. Es gibt darüber hinaus Forschung zu „Smart Houses", die Älteren und Behinderten ermöglichen würden, verschiedene Handlungen mittels BMI auszuführen. Künftig möchte diese Forschung Gedanken auf dem Bildschirm sichtbar machen. Wenn wir Gedanken direkt als 3D-Information extrahieren könnten, könnten wir Direct Image Design (DID) ohne die Zwischenstation Bleistift oder Befehle herstellen. Womöglich können wir uns auf den Tag freuen, wenn wir sagen können „I DID it".

Übung im Extrahieren von Bildern. Lassen sie uns mit dieser neuen DID-Technologie ein paar Übungen versuchen. Wenn man sich die Sache etwas vereinfacht vorstellt, ist es schon heute möglich, Bilder zu extrahieren. Man braucht dazu keine Maschine und kein Programm. Wir sollten mit etwas Einfachem anfangen. Wie wär's mit einem Kegel? Bei einem Würfel fiele es schwerer, die Rotationen der Form zu verfolgen, weil alle Seiten gleich aussehen. Stellen Sie sich einen Kegel vor. Er ist weiß, aus weißer Keramik. Falls ein Schreibtisch vor Ihnen steht, stellen Sie sich vor, der Kegel steht auf dem Schreibtisch. Es ist klein, nur etwa 10 cm hoch. Wenn Sie keinen Tisch haben, lassen Sie ihn in der Luft schweben. Also, sehen Sie einen hübschen Kegel vor sich? Jetzt sollten wir den Kegel vertikal rotieren lassen. Wenn er sich horizontal drehen würde, sähe er immer gleich aus, also drehen wir ihn um 90 Grad vertikal, wobei die Spitze von uns weg, die runde Basis auf uns zu zeigt. Wenn Sie das sehen können, versuchen Sie ihn herumzudrehen oder seitlich zu bewegen.

Wir sollten Material und Farbe ändern. Nehmen wir silbriges Aluminium, durchsichtiges Glas, oder einen Kegel mit einer Oberfläche aus gekräuseltem Wasser. Sobald Sie sich daran gewöhnt haben, versuchen Sie die Größe zu verändern, ihn zu drehen, zu einem Ball zusammen zu knautschen, was auch immer. Die Tatsache, dass Sie das Bild des „ursprünglichen Kegels" vor sich sehen, selbst nach all diesen Manövern, heißt, dass sich die Information für dieses Bild „irgendwo" befindet (in Ihrem Verstand oder Herz = Gehirn). Falls die Information existiert und es uns gelingen würde, sie zu extrahieren, dann könnten wir sie in jeder gewünschten Art verarbeiten (in einem IT- Gerät außerhalb des Gehirns). Was das bedeutet, ist die Fähigkeit, unsere Träume zu extrahieren. Früher wurde das als Träumerei verspottet, aber heute erscheint es greifbar.

Direct Processing durch Verwendung von im Gehirn vorhandenen Bildern. Es gibt Verfahren, mit denen sich Informationen viel schneller als sonst verarbeiten lassen, indem man im Gehirn vorhandene Bilder verwendet. So können zum Beispiel Schnellleser eine Textseite in einer Sekunde oder noch weniger verstehen. Anstatt die Buchstaben zu lesen, nehmen sie die Seite offenbar als Bild wahr. (Einige dieser Methoden habe ich selbst ausprobiert.) Beim Design verhält es sich jedoch etwas anders, weil beim Entwerfen die Fähigkeit, eine komplexe Mischung von Information zu verarbeiten, wichtiger ist als Geschwindigkeit. Ein weiteres Beispiel stellt „anzan" (mentales Rechnen) dar, bei dem traditionelle japanische Techniken zur Anwendung kommen, die auf dem „Soroban", dem japanischen Abakus beruhen. Ich selber beherrsche es nicht, habe mir aber sagen lassen, dass man sich dabei die Perlen auf dem „Soroban" vorstellt und rechnet, indem man die Perlen auf dem geistigen Bild des „Soroban" bewegt. In dieser Kunst versierte Personen können im Kopf Multiplikationen und Divisionen 5-stelliger Zahlen innerhalb weniger Sekunden ausführen, während ihnen die Fragen in furchterregender Schnelligkeit vorgelesen werden. Wenn man die virtuellen Perlen um mehrere Spalten bewegt, sie exakt an der richtigen Stelle fixiert und sie dann mental verschiebt, kann man mit den Fragen gleichwohl Schritt halten. Die Berechnungen machen sich ein geistiges Bild des „Soroban" zunutze, um das sie die Perlen nach Belieben bewegen. Wenn das Bild verschwimmen sollte, würde die Berechnung an diesem Punkt enden. Wenn solche deutlichen und langanhaltenden Bilder existieren, sollte es dann nicht in naher Zukunft möglich sein, sie aus dem Gehirn herauszuholen?

5. Dinge, die (vermutlich) nur Menschen tun können.
Was ist eine lebende Linie? Seit zehntausenden von Jahren haben Menschen in ihren Herzen Bilder geformt und sie dann mit ihren Händen gezeichnet. Ob auf einer Höhlenwand oder auf Papier. Gehirn und Hände, Gefühle und Linien stehen in direkter Verbindung. Die Skizzen in diesem Essay wurden nur mit Bleistift oder Stift auf Papier gezeichnet (Abb. 1, 7, 8). Sie sind ohne jede digitale Veränderung exakt wie gezeichnet zu sehen. Es wurden keine Radiergummis verwendet. Es sind „lebende" Linien, die, einmal gezeichnet, nie mehr verschwinden. Ohne an ihren Anfangspunkt zurückzugehen, verlängern sich die gezeichneten Linien durch Weiterzeichnen. Dieser Vorgang gehört zu den Konditionen dieses Entwurfs. Was getan ist, kann nicht gelöscht werden – das trifft auf viele Dinge in der Welt zu. Es ist des Weiteren eine Bedingung realer Gesellschaftssysteme. Eine Skizze auf einem Stück Papier ist ebenfalls die Simulation von Gesellschaftssystemen. Ein Hauptunterschied zwischen solchen Skizzen und Computergrafiken ist die Einzigartigkeit der Linie, ihr Impuls. Die Linie birgt in sich die Richtung, in der sie verläuft, den noch nicht gezeichneten Anteil, den Impuls.

Without ever going back, the drawn lines are extended by drawing further. This process is one of the conditions of this design. What has been done cannot be deleted—that is true of many things in the world. It is also a condition of real social systems. A sketch on a piece of paper is also a simulation of social systems. A major difference between such sketches and computer graphics is this singularity of the line, its momentum. The line holds within itself the direction in which it is going, the parts that are not yet drawn, the momentum.

Algorithms and programs are means to an end, a path toward the goal. The important thing is to reach the goal. Algorithms and programs are not absolutely necessary. If we could do without them, all the better. The reason is that once the goal is decided, any design that reaches the goal is good enough. This leads back to the world of intuition.

Das ist die Kraft der Linie, die nicht von ihrer Stärke oder vom Druck auf den Stift bestimmt wird. Um es metaphorisch auszudrücken, es ist das, was der Linie Lebenskraft gibt. Die Skizze stellt nicht den Architekturentwurf selbst dar, könnte aber die Quelle sein, die den Entwurf entstehen lässt.

Computer nähern sich dem Menschen an/Verschwindende Programme. Wenn es Menschen gelingt, eine Methode zu finden, Bilder aus dem Gehirn zu exportieren, wie sieht es dann mit dem Fortschritt auf der Gegenseite, der Programmseite aus? Algorithmen und Programme sind Mittel zum Zweck, ein Weg zum Ziel. Es kommt darauf an, das Ziel zu erreichen. Algorithmen und Programme sind nicht unbedingt notwendig. Wenn wir ohne sie auskommen können, umso besser. Wenn nämlich das Ziel einmal feststeht, ist jeder Entwurf, der es erreicht, zufriedenstellend. Das führt zurück in die Welt der Intuition. Anstatt also Programme, wie wir das derzeit tun, in Spezialsprachen zu schreiben, stellen wir uns vor, es wäre möglich, sie in natürlichen Sprachen zu schreiben. Das könnte uns näher an die Intuition heranführen. Natürliche Sprachen sind vage. „Eine schöne Form" sagt sich leicht, was aber bedeutet es? Welche Art von Form ist schön, welche ist es nicht? Dazu gibt es keine Anweisungen. Falls es jedoch Systeme gäbe, um nebulöse Ausdrücke dieser Art zu „verstehen", unsere Absichten zu „folgern" und auf sie in irgendeiner Weise zu „reagieren", dann bekämen wir möglicherweise sogar mit solchen Anweisungen eine gute Antwort.

(Computer, die die menschliche Sprache verstehen, gibt es bereits. Sie befinden sich noch in einem Stadium, wo ein Computer einen Menschen in einer Quizshow schlagen kann – Watson/IBM, 2011 – aber mit der Zeit werden sie allgemeinere Fähigkeiten erlangen.) Wenn normale Sprache wie dieser Satz ohne Spezialsprache zum Programm werden kann, wäre das gewiss bequemer, weil wir keine Programmiersprachen lernen müssten.

Heuristisch algorithmisch/Das menschliche Herz schwankt. In dem Film *2001: A Space Odyssey* des Regisseurs Stanley Kubrick, gedreht nach einer Kurzgeschichte von Arthur C. Clarke, redet der berühmte Computer HAL 9000 mit Menschen in ihrer Sprache, führt Raumflug-Aufgaben aus und spielt auf Wunsch Schach. Der von seinen „Schöpfern" ausgebildete HAL entwickelt sich zu einer vollständig ausgebildeten Persönlichkeit. (Es gibt eine Schlüsselszene, in der HAL, nachdem er Mitglieder der Besatzung getötet hat, von widersprüchlichen Anweisungen verwirrt, seine Entwicklung rückwärts durchläuft und an den Augenblick seiner Geburt zurückgesetzt wird.) Es heißt, HALs Name stehe für „Heuristisch programmierter ALgorithmischer Computer". Heuristik bezeichnet Techniken zur „Findung" zufriedenstellender Lösungen, ohne perfekte Antworten zu verlangen. Bedingt durch den Charakter des Arbeitsgebiets kann man sagen, dass es beim Design keine „perfekten Antworten" gibt. Die Anforderungen auf der Seite

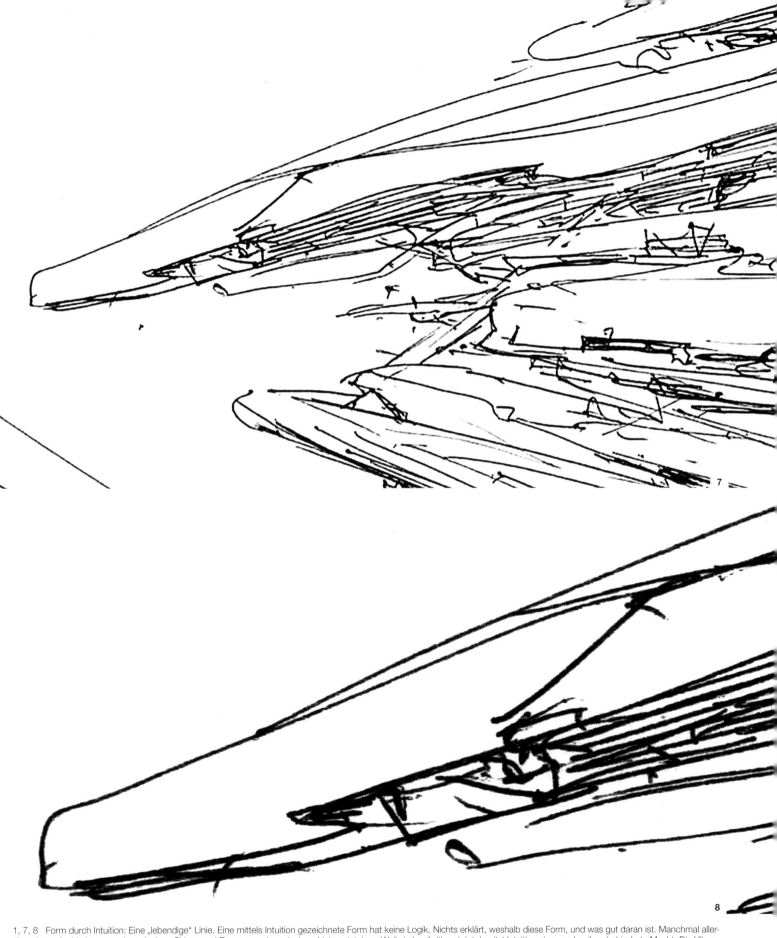

7

8

1, 7, 8   Form durch Intuition: Eine „lebendige" Linie. Eine mittels Intuition gezeichnete Form hat keine Logik. Nichts erklärt, weshalb diese Form, und was gut daran ist. Manchmal allerdings kann Architektur aus einer einzigen Skizze und Raum aus einer einzigen Linie entstehen. Weil sie Logik übersteigt, besitzt Intuition eine von Logik unbehinderte Macht. Die Vibrationen in einer einzigen Linie sind eine weitere Welle, die parallel zum „algorithmischen Design" verläuft. Ein einzelnes Blatt Papier ist ein Fenster, um Unterbewusstsein und Bewusstsein zu verbinden. Form through intuition: A line with "life." There is no logic in a form drawn through intuition. Nothing to explain why it is that form, or what is good about it. But sometimes architecture can be born from a single sketch, and space can be born from a single line. Because it transcends logic, intuition harbors a power that is unconstrained by logic. The vibrations in a single line are another wave, running in parallel with "algorithmic design." A single sheet of paper is a window to connect the subconscious and conscious. © MAKOTO SEI WATANABE/ARCHITECTS' OFFICE

Heuristically Algorithmic / The Human Heart Wavers. In the film *2001: A Space Odyssey*, directed by Stanley Kubrick and based on a short story by Arthur C. Clarke, the famous computer HAL 9000 converses with humans in natural language, performs mission tasks, and when asked plays chess. Having been educated by "his" creators, HAL develops into a fully formed personality. (There is a memorable scene in which HAL, conflicted by contradictory instructions and having killed members of the crew, retraces his development in reverse and is returned to his moment of birth.) HAL's name is said to stand for "Heuristically programmed ALgorithmic computer." Heuristics refers to techniques for "discovering" satisfactory solutions without demanding perfect answers. By the nature of the field, it can be said that there is no "perfect answer" in design. Requirements on the human side are constantly shifting and changing shape. Often we ourselves do not understand our "true" feelings. Given the vacillating definition of the requirements (the "question,") there can be no perfect "answer." If there is no "perfect" answer, we want a method to find "highly satisfactory" answers. HAL, who in the film was born in 1992, was the algorithmic implementation of this method. For this reason, HAL is conflicted when confronted by humans, who represent a "problem without answers."

The way to DID, which was described above, will open up only when we obtain the cooperation of more highly evolved computers.

Programs That Learn/ The Child Machine. Programs that learn and develop like HAL were described above. This concept was laid out in the paper "Computing Machinery and Intelligence" by Alan Mathison Turing[1], one of the fathers of computing. The paper compares a "child machine" to a notebook with many blank sheets, and proposes to start with a "teaching process" that uses punishments and rewards. It describes the agreement between this teaching method and the natural processes of "random mutations" and "evolution." This was a quarter of a century before the emergence of genetic algorithms (GA).

Raising Architecture/Nurturing Design. The way to DID, which was described above, will open up only when we obtain the cooperation of more highly evolved computers. By that time, the contemporary concept of "design" may have changed to "generation" by means of "induction."

This will mean "fostering" design in a given environment, teaching it to give us "answers" that meet the requirements, instead of making what we intend in the way we intend it. Better terms for it might be "cultivation design" or "nurturing design." (The resulting works would be our "children," in the same way as always?) By that time, "ALGODesign/ALGOrithmic Design" will be regarded as a natural process for "generating" man-made products. While humans exercise "skills," algorithmic design will be constantly at their side, with no one taking particular notice.

des Menschen verschieben sich ständig und wechseln ihre Form. Häufig verstehen wir selbst unsere „wahren Empfindungen" nicht. Da die Definitionen der Anforderungen (der „Fragen") schwanken, kann es keine perfekte „Antwort" geben. Wenn es keine „perfekte" Antwort gibt, brauchen wir eine Methode, mit der wir „höchst befriedigende Antworten" finden. Der im Film 1992 geborene HAL verkörperte die algorithmische Realisierung dieser Methode. Konfrontiert mit Menschen, die ein „Problem ohne Antwort" darstellen, gerät HAL deshalb in Schwierigkeiten.

Programme, die lernen/Die Kind-Maschine. Programme, die lernen und sich entwickeln wie HAL, wurden oben beschrieben. Diese Vorstellung wurde von Alan Mathison Turing,[1] einem der Väter der theoretischen Informatik, in seinem Aufsatz „Computing Machinery and Intelligence" erklärt. In dem Aufsatz wird eine „Kindmaschine" mit einem Notizbuch mit vielen leeren Seiten verglichen und angeregt, mit einem „Lehrprozess" zu beginnen, der Strafen und Belohnungen anwendet. Er beschreibt die Übereinstimmung zwischen dieser Lehrmethode und den natürlichen Vorgängen der „Zufallsmutationen" und der „Evolution". Dies geschah ein Vierteljahrhundert vor dem Aufkommen der genetischen Algorithmen (GA).

Architektur großziehen/Design fördern. Der oben beschriebene Weg zu DID wird sich nur auftun, wenn wir uns die Kooperation weiterer hochentwickelter Computer sichern. Bis dahin könnte sich die gegenwärtige Vorstellung von „Design" zu „Generierung mittels Induktion" gewandelt haben. Dann wird es darum gehen, Design in einem gegebenen Umfeld zu „fördern", ihm beizubringen, uns „Antworten" zu liefern, die den Anforderungen entsprechen, anstatt das von uns Gewünschte in der von uns intendierten Weise herzustellen. Bessere Bezeichnungen dafür könnten „erziehendes Design" oder „förderndes Design" sein. (Wären die daraus entstehenden Arbeiten unsere „Kinder" in der gleichen Weise wie zuvor?) Zu diesem Zeitpunkt werden „ALGODesign/ALGOrithmic Design" als natürliche Vorgänge zur „Generierung" künstlicher Produkte gelten. Während Menschen „Fertigkeiten" beweisen, werden sie fortwährend vom algorithmischen Design begleitet werden, ohne dass irgendjemand dem besondere Beachtung schenkt.

Die Macht, Zielvorgaben darzustellen. Wenn diese neuen Entwicklungen, darunter „ALGOrithmic Design" und „Induktionsdesign", neue Möglichkeiten für Entwurfsverfahren eröffnet haben, wer wird dann die Zielvorgaben schaffen? „ALGODesign" generiert keine Zielvorgaben. Sie müssen gesondert bereitgestellt werden. Und neu sein. Zu welchem Zweck stellen wir etwas her, und was wollen wir? Welche Dinge sind gut?

1   Alan M. Turing, "Computing Machinery and Intelligence," *Mind* 49 (1950), pp. 433–460.

1   Alan M. Turing: „Computing Machinery and Intelligence", in: *Mind* 49, (1950), S. 433–460.

Das Recht (und die Pflicht) zu zeigen, „was gewünscht ist = Werte", wird Menschen übertragen. Genau das ist der Beitrag, den nur Menschen bei diesem Vorgang der „Design = Generierung" leisten können. Es ist der Bereich, in dem Menschen noch unbekannte (latente) Fähigkeiten beweisen werden (sollten), über die einzig sie verfügen.

Dieser Text ist eine erweiterte und veränderte Version des Materials, das in Makoto Sei Watanabe, ALGODEX: ALGOrithmic Design EXecution and Logic, Tokio 2012 publiziert wurde.

Übersetzung aus dem Englischen: Christiane Court

The Power to Depict Objectives. If these new developments, including "ALGOrithmicDesign" and "Induction Design," have opened up new possibilities for design methods, who will create the objectives?

"ALGODesign" does not generate objectives. Objectives must be provided separately. New ones. What is the purpose of making something, and what do we want? What things are good? The right (and responsibility) to show "what is wanted = values" is delegated to humans. Exactly that is the contribution that only humans can make in this process of "design = generation." It is the domain where humans will (should) demonstrate as yet unknown (latent) abilities possessed only by them.

This text is a translation from Japanese by Thomas Donahue, with revisions and additions, of material published in Makoto Sei Watanabe, ALGODEX: ALGOrithmicDesign EXecution and Logic (Tokyo, 2012).

1 *Spacensing: Raumerfahrung und Bewegung* (Diplomarbeit Stefan Zedlacher). Das no_LAb als mixed reality Tanzstudio. Die Bewegungen eines Tänzers konditionieren durch projizierte Formen und Farben den Raum, auf den der Tänzer in der Improvisation reagiert. Im Rahmen des Projekts wurde eine Kollektion solcher rückbezüglicher Setups entwickelt, auch unter Verwendung physikalischer Simulationen. *Spacensing: Spatial Perception and Movement* (Diploma Thesis Stefan Zedlacher). The no_LAb as mixed reality dance studio: a dancer's movements condition the space through projected colors and shapes to which the dancer reacts in improvisation. A collection of such self-referential set-ups was developed as part of the project, also including physical simulations. © S. Zedlacher, IAM/TU Graz

„Augmented Architecture" Transparenz, Intuition und unsere Sinne

Für die Internet Generation ist vieles selbstverständlich, was noch vor wenigen Jahren unvorstellbar war. Man denke nur, wie schnell sich Kulturtechniken wie „googlen" oder „twittern" etabliert haben, wie bereitwillig Leute in sozialen Netzwerken aller Welt ihr Privatleben offenbaren – jederzeit von überall, denn heute ist man stets online oder zumindest erreichbar.

"Augmented Architecture:" Transparency, Intuition and Our Senses. For the Internet generation many things are second nature that only a few years ago were unimaginable. The speed at which "googling" and "twittering" were established as cultural techniques is astounding. Individuals now share their lives with the world via social networks—anytime anywhere—we are constantly online and reachable.

URS HIRSCHBERG

Vor zehn Jahren konnte, wer unterwegs sein Handy beantwortete, mit „Woher wusstest Du, dass ich hier bin?" noch einen passablen Scherz machen. Heute funktioniert der nicht mehr. Wir nehmen die Erfahrung der ortsunabhängigen Erreichbarkeit nicht mehr als etwas Besonderes wahr.

Digitale Transparenz? Den Zustand, in dem ein bestimmter Teil eines Systems zwar vorhanden und in Betrieb ansonsten aber unsichtbar ist und daher vom Benutzer nicht wahrgenommen wird, bezeichnet man in der Informatik als Transparenz. Ganz ähnlich spricht man in der Psychologie beim Gebrauch von Werkzeugen von Transparenz, wenn dieser bei geübten Benutzern so selbstverständlich wird, dass sie sozusagen eins werden mit ihrem Werkzeug und sich gar nicht mehr bewusst sind, dass sie es bedienen. Diese Art der Transparenz ist meist ein Zeichen dafür, dass wir etwas intuitiv tun. Man kann in diesem Sinn auch von transparenten Kulturtechniken sprechen: Dinge, die so alltäglich, so selbstverständlich mit unserem Leben verbunden sind, dass wir sie nicht mehr beachten.

Der Begriff der Transparenz ist an sich fast durchwegs positiv konnotiert. Wörtlich genommen heißt transparent durchscheinend, durchsichtig. Transparenz gewährt uns den Einblick in Verborgenes, erhellt Zusammenhänge, ist der Gegner von dunklen Geschäften. Wir wollen eigentlich immer und überall mehr Transparenz.

Die oben erwähnte Art von Transparenz, die – ganz im ursprünglichen Wortsinn – eine Sache unsichtbar macht, weil wir sie ob ihrer Alltäglichkeit nicht mehr wahrnehmen, ist grundsätzlich ebenfalls positiv zu sehen. Technik, die sich so leicht bedienen lässt, sich so selbstverständlich in unser Leben integriert, dass wir sie vergessen können, wer möchte das nicht begrüßen? Aber sie ist dennoch nicht unproblematisch, verkehrt sie doch viele der positiven Attribute, die wir gerne mit Transparenz identifizieren in ihr Gegenteil. Wenn etwas gar nicht mehr wahrgenommen wird, ist es wieder vor uns verborgen, entzieht sich unserer Kontrolle. Dies ist gefährlich – zumal bei digitalen Technologien. Nicht zuletzt die Enthüllungen über den Datensammeleifer der NSA, welche 2013 zum Politikum geworden sind, haben gezeigt, dass unsere Teilnahme an den diversen Kommunikationsnetzen zwar eine Alltäglichkeit, aber dennoch keine unbedenkliche Sache ist. Manche Kommentatoren haben darauf hingewiesen, dass die neue Dimension der gesellschaftlichen Überwachung zwar ohne Präzedenzfall, aber eigentlich trotzdem nicht überraschend ist. In Kenntnis der technischen Möglichkeiten hätte man sich das alles leicht ausmalen können. Eine aufmerksamere, kritischere Haltung – auch gegenüber transparenten Techniken – ist im digitalen Zeitalter eine Notwendigkeit.

Computer im Architekturalltag. Auch die Anwendung des Computers in der Architekturpraxis ist in diesem Sinne transparent geworden. CAD-Programme sind ein so selbstverständlicher Bestandteil des Büroalltags, dass ihr Vorhandensein nicht mehr erwähnenswert ist. Viele sind darüber erleichtert. Es war eine mühsame Zeit, da man sich mit der Frage herumschlagen musste, ob sich die Investition in CAD-Arbeitsplätze nun lohnt oder nicht, in der man darüber diskutierte, ob und wie man den digital erzeugten Plänen einen persönlichen Ausdruck geben kann, von der Frage, ob man nun mithilfe des Rechners anders entwerfen könne ganz zu schweigen. Heute stellt sich diese Fragen scheinbar niemand mehr. Wo noch vor wenigen Jahren

Ten years ago the line "How did you know I was here?" when answering a call on your cellphone could pass for a joke. Today the joke works no more: the experience of being reachable at any location is no longer unusual.

Digital Transparency? Technically speaking, the state in which a part of a computer system functions in such a way that it becomes invisible and is taken for granted is referred to as "transparency." Likewise, in psychology the use of a tool is referred to as "transparent" when it seems to disappear in the hands of the skilled user who is no longer conscious of it. This type of transparency results from the use of intuition (or unconscious thought). We also refer to cultural techniques as "transparent:" these are commonplace practices that are so embedded in our daily lives that we no longer pay attention to them.

The term transparent has almost entirely positive connotations. Literally, transparent means "able to be seen through:" transparency brings to light the nature of relationships, it gives us insight into hidden affairs, and is the enemy of secrecy. We also use it to describe ideas that are obvious, or easy to understand, as well as honesty and openness. It is an almost universally desirable quality. The technical form of transparency, when objects or actions become invisible to our conscious perception because they are so much part of our daily routine, is certainly also a positive quality. Technology that recedes into the background, to help us without requiring any special attention—who wouldn't welcome that? Yet this type of transparency isn't entirely unproblematic as it actually turns many of the positive qualities that we typically attribute to transparency into their opposites: when something is no longer perceived, it becomes hidden again, escapes our control. The ongoing revelations about the NSA's data collection activities that marked the year 2013 amply demonstrate that our participation in various communication networks is, while clearly an everyday affair, not at all unproblematic. Commentators have pointed out that while the scale of the societal surveillance we learned about is absolutely unprecedented, the surveillance itself isn't really surprising. Knowing the technical possibilities as we do, we easily could have imagined it. It's a lesson: a more alert and more critical attitude—especially towards transparent technologies—is a necessity in the digital age.

Computers in Architectural Practice. In architectural offices, the use of computers has likewise become transparent. CAD programs are so much a standard component of the daily routine of any architecture practice that it's hardly worth mentioning them anymore. Many are relieved about this. It was a painful time when one had to worry about whether investing in CAD stations was worthwhile, when the question was whether plans drawn in CAD could incorporate personal expression—not to mention whether one designed differently with a computer.

Nowadays no one is interested in these questions anymore. The intense debate of a few years ago has been settled. Those who still oppose digital tools in their practice are as "uncool" as those that still get excited about them.

If one takes a closer look, however, one notices that the situation is all but satisfying. Computing in architecture and building has become a vast field with many different areas of application and research: parametric modeling, simulation technology, digital fabrication, optimization and visualization of complex conditions are all part of an expanding field that far transcends traditional expectations of CAD. Yet the majority of offices make use of the computer only as a 2D drawing aid. Building Information Modeling (BIM), the integrated planning system that promises to facilitate all stages of the design and construction process is far from being established in practice. Not least because the packages the software industry promotes don't live up to our expectations. Digitally advanced architectural offices and their partner engineers typically use several different digital tools to fulfill the demands of today's complex design and construction processes. Less technically ambitious offices minimize the number of different software packages as their working routine is largely the same as in pre-computer times: computers are digital drawing boards, not more. Technically advanced or not, architectural practice is losing control and influence as ever more aspects of design that used to be the natural domain of the discipline are taken over by digitally well-versed and increasingly specialized building engineers.

It is very common that only younger architectural staff are capable of operating CAD programs effectively. Senior staff and project managers that are unable to use the programs themselves look over their assistants' shoulders—a situation that isn't pleasant for either one. Thus, it may be true that the use of computers in architecture has become "transparent" in the sense that it is an everyday affair, but the using of them still hasn't become intuitive.

Frank O. Gehry Associates is one of the offices that pioneered the use of computers in architecture; Gehry even founded a software company to market the programs they developed in-house. Yet Gehry himself cannot use the 3D package that his employees have developed and used in his work for years. He describes the experience of first looking over the shoulder of one of his computer specialists and trying to tell him what to do with the digitized form he saw on screen as extremely uncomfortable: "… as if somebody were tightening screws into me."[1]

1   Greg Lynn, ed., *Archeology of the Digital: Field Notes*. Canadian Centre of Architecture (Montréal 2013), p. 26.

hitzig debattiert wurde, gibt es jetzt den Konsens, dass das alles ja längst selbstverständlich ist. Wer die digitalen Hilfsmittel im Architekturalltag heute noch ablehnt, ist dabei genauso „uncool" wie diejenigen, die sich dafür weiterhin begeistern.

Bei näherer Betrachtung stellt man allerdings fest, dass die Situation alles andere als befriedigend ist. Die Computeranwendung in der Architektur und im Bauwesen ist heute ein weitverzweigtes Gebiet mit vielen Anwendungs- und Forschungsbereichen. Dazu gehören das parametrische Modellieren, die Simulationstechnik, die digitale Fabrikation, die Optimierung und Visualisierung komplexer Zusammenhänge – viel mehr als nur das traditionelle CAD. Die große Mehrheit der Büros verwendet den Computer aber lediglich als zweidimensionales Zeichenwerkzeug. Die von der Software-Industrie vermarktete Vision des Building Information Modeling (BIM), welches eine integrierte Planung aller Bau-Aspekte in einer Gesamtlösung verspricht, ist noch längst nicht in der Praxis etabliert, auch weil die so vermarkteten Programme diese Ansprüche im Praxistest selten einlösen. Digital avancierte Büros verwenden eine Vielzahl von Programmen, mit welchen sie und ihre Partner in den Ingenieurfirmen die komplexen Anforderungen der heutigen Entwurfs- und Ausführungsplanung bewältigen. Oft ist dafür ein Team von Spezialisten innerhalb des Büros zuständig. Weniger ambitionierte Büros minimieren den Einsatz verschiedener Programme: die Arbeitsabläufe sind zwar digitalisiert, werden aber analog gedacht. Der Computer dient lediglich als digitaler Zeichenstift. Die Konsequenz ist ein Verlust von Einfluss und Kontrolle: immer mehr Planungsaspekte, die früher Architektensache waren, werden von digital versierten Ingenieurbüros übernommen.

> Der Computer dient lediglich als digitaler Zeichenstift. Die Konsequenz ist ein Verlust von Einfluss und Kontrolle: immer mehr Planungsaspekte, die früher Architektensache waren, werden von digital versierten Ingenieurbüros übernommen.

Verbreitet ist auch nach wie vor die Situation, dass nur die jüngeren Mitarbeiter den Computer bedienen können. Die Projektverantwortlichen, die selbst das Programm nicht bedienen können, schauen Ihnen dabei über die Schulter – eine Situation, die für keine Seite angenehm ist. So ist die Verwendung der Computer in der Architektur zwar transparent im Sinne von alltäglich, aber dennoch nicht intuitiv.

Frank O. Gehry Associates gehört zu den Büros, welche schon früh auf die Möglichkeiten des Computers gesetzt haben, bekanntlich hat Frank Gehry sogar eine Softwarefirma gegründet. Die 3D Programme, die seine Mitarbeiter entwickeln und mit denen sein Büro seit vielen Jahren arbeitet, weiß der Chef indes nicht selbst zu bedienen. Dies, obwohl er die Situation, als er erstmals einem Mitarbeiter bei der Arbeit am Bildschirm über die Schulter schaute und versuchte, ihm zu erklären, was er an einem digitalisierten Modell verändern sollte, als extrem unangenehm beschreibt: als ob jemand Schrauben in ihn hineindrehte.[1]

Digitale Sinneserweiterungsmaschinen. Es besteht die Hoffnung, dass sich das „distanzierte" Verhältnis, das viele Architekten zum Computer heute noch haben, bald ändern wird. Wenn man sich vor Augen hält, wie angenehm die digitalen Geräte des Unterhaltungssektors wie Tablets oder Spielkonsolen mittlerweile zu bedienen sind, so ist davon auszugehen, dass diese Entwicklungen auch nicht ohne Folgen für die Architekturpraxis bleiben werden.

Seit der Einführung der Computer in die Architekturpraxis hat sich einiges getan. Computer haben sich immer mehr zu universellen Sinneserweiterungsmaschinen entwickelt. Multi-Touch Bildschirme, die von unseren Fingern komplexere und auch angenehmere Bewegungen verstehen als nur Tippen und Klicken oder die neue Generation Computerspiele, mit denen man durch die eigenen Körperbewegungen, statt nur mittels Knöpfchen und Joystick spielen kann, finden sich heute in Wohn- und Kinderspielzimmern. Der Umgang mit der Digitaltechnologie, die uns immer so abstrakt und technisch vorgekommen ist, hat heute eine körperlich-sinnliche Dimension. Das ist kein Zufall, sondern das Resultat eines schon lange bestehenden Trends.

Optische Sensoren gehören als Herzstücke von digitalen Kameras in immer besserer Qualität zur üblichen Ausrüstung von immer mehr digitalen Geräten. Bildbearbeitung, ja Bilderkennung findet heute schon in den Kameras statt. Die Audio-Technik ist ohnehin seit langem digitalisiert, auch Spracherkennung wird immer besser. Andere Sensoren können aber auch Veränderungen von Luftfeuchtigkeit, Temperatur, Schadstoffen, etc. erspüren, die weit unterhalb der menschlichen Wahrnehmungsschwelle liegen. Auch diese Sensoren und viele weitere, wie etwa Beschleunigungssensoren oder GPS-Empfänger, werden immer häufiger in Alltagsgegenständen eingebaut.

Das Gegenstück zu diesen vielen Sensoren sind die Output-Medien. Diese sind ihrerseits in der Lage, unsere Sinne immer besser zu bedienen. Immer höher auflösende, brillantere Displays, auf denen Bilder detailreich, dynamisch und interaktiv dargestellt werden können und Beschallungssysteme, mit denen Klang räumlich wird, sind heute Standard. Mit entsprechenden Programmen können wir darauf auch die Performance von Objekten und Situationen darstellen, die nur als physikalische Simulation von digitalen Modellen vorliegen. Komplexeste Formen können nicht nur modelliert, visualisiert und virtuell getestet, sondern auch von digital gesteuerten Maschinen wie Robotern oder 3D Printern gefertigt werden.

> Seit der Einführung der Computer in die Architekturpraxis hat sich einiges getan. Computer haben sich immer mehr zu universellen Sinneserweiterungsmaschinen entwickelt.

1   Greg Lynn (Hg.): *Archeology of the Digital. Field Notes.* Canadian Centre of Architecture, Montreal 2013, S. 26.

Digital "Sense-Expander" Machines. There is hope that the somewhat ambivalent relationship with the computer that is still common among architects today is about to change. Think of computer games and tablets, consider how comfortable we have become with digital devices in the entertainment sector. We can assume that such developments will not remain without consequence for architectural practice as well.

A lot has happened since computers were first introduced into the practice of architecture. Not least, computers have evolved into universal sense-expansion-machines: multi-touch screens that understand the complex and nuanced, as well as comfortable, movements that our fingers make. The latest generation of computer games that can be controlled through body movements, rather than buttons or joysticks, can already be found in our living rooms and kids' playrooms. Interaction with digital technology that seemed so abstract and technical in the past, has today acquired a physical-sense-sensitive dimension. This is no accident but the result of a long existing trend.

Optical sensors of ever improving quality and resolution can be found not only at the heart of digital cameras but also in an increasingly large number of other digital devices. Image processing, even image-recognition, takes place in cameras already. Audio-technology has long become digital, with superhuman capacity; speech recognition is getting better and better. Other types of sensors gauge changes in humidity, temperature, pollution, etc. at levels far below the threshold of human perception. These sensors as well as many others such as accelerometers or GPS receivers are built into many everyday things.

Output media are the counterparts to such sensors. They, in turn, are capable of catering to our senses in ever more sophisticated ways. Display resolution is increasing, as is the brilliance of contrasts and colors used to present dynamic images that are interactive and rich in detail. Audio systems that produce spatial sound are standard nowadays. With the necessary software programs, output devices can represent events and situations that exist only in virtual form. Complex shapes can be modeled, visualized and virtually tested, furthermore they can also be produced by digitally controlled machines such as robots and printers.

It gets complicated when output devices in turn become sensitive themselves: when an industrial robot adjusts to a new situation it "sees" through a camera or, if by way of force-feedback, it dynamically reacts to the quality of a material it is working on. The terminological distinction between input- and output devices gets mixed up in such constellations, yet unsurprisingly, this isn't confusing at all: it's exactly the kind of feedback-system that we are familiar with from our own bodies. Our own motion apparatus performs the most intricate and nuanced procedures, for example, when we walk over uneven ground: the groping of our feet, the balancing, the dampening

2

2 no_LAb: Das Medienlabor des Instituts für Architektur und Medien (IAM) ist kein traditionelles Labor, sondern eine offene Plattform für digitale Raumexperimente.
no_LAb: The media lab at the Institute of Architecture and Media (IAM) is not a traditional lab, but an open platform for spatial experiments with digital media.
© C. Fröhlich, M. Kern, IAM/TU Graz

3–9 Nonstandard Architecture: Projekt gefördert vom Österreichischen Wissenschaftsfonds FWF (2009–2012). Oben: Diskretisierung von Freiformflächen, Optimierung mit ornamentalen Mustern. Unten: Die *Kobra*, ein gebauter Prototyp als Anwendung der neuen Methode, realisiert aus Brettsperrholzplatten. **Nonstandard Architecture**: project supported by the Austrian National Science Foundation FWF (2009–2012) Top: freeform surface discretization, optimization with ornamental patterns. Bottom: The *Cobra*, a prototypical application of the novel method built from cross-laminated timber panels. © M. Manahl, E. Ruffo, M. Stavric, H. Schimek, A. Wiltsche, U. Hirschberg, IAM/TU Graz

of our joints—are processes that our body executes automatically and at lightning speed, without thinking.

Digitally Enhanced Intuition? The heightening, deepening and expanding of our senses, through digital technologies that allow human-user interaction with devices that react ever more precisely to sensor-input, is already finding its way into architecture. Digital media that caters to our senses in novel ways is increasingly influencing both work on the computer and the things that we build. This particular development will continue and it should interest us as it harbors a special potential to bring one of our most important capabilities into play: our intuition.

Intuition is an enigmatic term with many different definitions. What's beyond doubt is that it is important for the design professions and that it represents a counterpart to rational thought. French philosopher Henri Bergson described intellect and intuition as two opposing capabilities of the mind. Whereas intellect represents the rational or analytical reflection that deals with the inert and stands outside of time, intuition, to Bergson, is what allows man to deal with the living, to act in time.[2] One can intuitively grasp something before, or without ever, rationally understanding it.

Bergson's take on intuition is helpful in that he points out the role of intuition in our daily lives. And also because, despite the many physical and sensual aspects of what we often refer to as a gut-feeling, he describes intuition as a capability of the mind, rather than of the body. We can therefore conclude from Bergson that intuition, just as any other capability of the mind, is something that we can train and develop. If intuition is something that can be learned, can we also assume that we can develop it for novel phenomena and circumstances? Therein lies great potential: if we design digital tools accordingly, then our ability to grasp complex relationships quickly—through use of our intuitive skills—can increasingly be put to work.

Augmented Architecture. In the following paragraphs we describe some examples that show the novel potential of digital media in architecture. We propose "Augmented Architecture" as the leitmotiv of a future practice in which the computer is no longer simply understood as a sophisticated tool or communication medium, but also as a way to expand our senses. Projects from teaching and research carried out at the Institute of Architecture and Media at Graz University of Technology, serve as illustrations.

The projects that we describe are very different, but they all have in common the principle of augmentation. They all

Verwirrend wird es, wenn diese Output-Geräte ihrerseits wieder sensibel werden und zum Beispiel ein Industrie-Roboter durch eine Kamera „sieht", woran er arbeitet und seine Bewegung dynamisch an neue Situationen anpassen kann oder wenn er durch sogenanntes Force-Feedback dynamisch auf die Beschaffenheit des von ihm bearbeiteten Werkstoffes reagieren kann. Die terminologische Unterscheidung von Input- und Output kommt bei solchen Konstellationen durcheinander, aber eigentlich ist das nicht verwirrend: genau solche Feedback-Systeme sind uns am eigenen Leib bestens vertraut und kommen uns deswegen in ihrem Verhalten ganz natürlich vor. Unser Bewegungsapparat vollführt komplexe Steuerungsvorgänge, wenn wir zum Beispiel über ein unebenes Gelände gehen: das Tasten unserer Füße, das Ausbalancieren, das Abfedern in den Gelenken – es sind Vorgänge, die unser Köper blitzschnell und automatisch ausführt, quasi ohne nachzudenken.

Digital erweiterte Intuition? Die Erweiterung unserer Sinne durch digitale Techniken, bzw. die Interaktion mit Geräten, die immer perfekter auf Sensoren-Input, bzw. auf unsere Sinne eingehen können, macht auch vor der Architektur nicht halt. Sowohl die Arbeit am Computer als auch die Dinge, die wir bauen und die immer mehr mit digitalen Medien durchsetzt sind, können heute schon auf neue Weise auf unsere Sinne eingehen. Diese Entwicklung wird sich in der Zukunft noch fortsetzen. Dies sollte uns interessieren, denn sie birgt ein besonderes Potenzial. Sie ermöglicht uns, eine unserer vorzüglichsten Eigenschaften wieder vermehrt einzubringen: unsere Intuition.

> Intuition ist ein schillernder Begriff mit vielen Definitionen. Unstrittig ist, dass sie für gestalterische Berufe wichtig ist, ebenso, dass sie gewissermaßen einen Gegenpart zu unserem rationalen Verstand darstellt.

Intuition ist ein schillernder Begriff mit vielen Definitionen. Unstrittig ist, dass sie für gestalterische Berufe wichtig ist, ebenso, dass sie gewissermaßen einen Gegenpart zu unserem rationalen Verstand darstellt. Beim französischen Philosophen Henri Bergson sind Intellekt und Intuition zwei entgegengesetzte, sich ergänzende Funktionen unseres Bewusstseins, wobei Intellekt das starre, analytische Prinzip ist, das außerhalb der Zeit steht, wohingegen Intuition das Erkennen des handelnden Menschen in der Zeit meint.[2] Dazu passt, dass man intuitiv schnell erfassen kann, noch bevor bzw. ohne dass man rational versteht.

Bergsons Intuitionsbegriff ist hilfreich, insofern als er die Bedeutung von Intuition für unser tägliches Leben herausstellt und auch insofern als er das, was wir oft als „Bauchgefühl" umschreiben, trotz seiner körperlich-sinnlichen Aspekte eindeutig als geistige Fähigkeit bezeichnet. Man kann daraus ableiten, dass Intuition, wie alle geistigen Fähigkeiten, etwas ist, das man schulen und entwickeln kann. Wenn aber Intuition erlernt werden kann,

---

2   See Henri Bergson, *Creative Evolution* (New York, 1998). Original title *L'Evolution créatrice*, 1907.

2   Vgl. Henri Bergson: *Creative Evolution*, New York 1998. Originaltitel: *L'Evolution créatrice*, 1907.

dann ist davon auszugehen, dass man sie auch für ungewohnte, neuartige Phänomene und Sachverhalte entwickeln kann. Darin liegt großes Potenzial: Wenn wir unsere digitalen Werkzeuge entsprechend gestalten, dann kann unsere Fähigkeit komplexe Zusammenhänge schnell zu erfassen – indem wir unsere Intuition einbringen – vermehrt und gezielt zum Einsatz kommen.

Augmented Architecture. Im Folgenden werden Beispiele beschrieben, welche dieses neuartige Potenzial digitaler Medien in der Architektur aufzeigen. Wir schlagen „Augmented Architecture" als Leitmotiv einer zukünftigen Praxis vor, in welcher der Computer nicht mehr nur als Werkzeug oder Kommunikationsmedium, sondern auch als Sinneserweiterung verstanden wird. Als Illustration dienen Projekte aus Forschung und Lehre, die am Institut für Architektur und Medien der TU Graz entstanden sind.

Die Projekte, die wir beschreiben, sind sehr unterschiedlich. Allen gemeinsam ist das Prinzip der Augmentation, also der Erweiterung, und zwar um eine sinnlich-ästhetische Dimension. „Augmented Architecture" ist eine Abwandlung des bekannteren Begriffes „Augmented Reality". Letzteres wird in der Computerwissenschaft als Oberbegriff für Anwendungen verwendet, welche die Erweiterung der Wirklichkeit durch zusätzliche Information bezwecken, ein populäres Beispiel ist die Google Brille. Auch der davon abgeleitete Begriff der „Augmented Architecture" meint eine mediale Erweiterung, aber eine, welche die Architektur verändert: sowohl den Entwurfs- und Bauprozess als auch das gebaute Objekt.

Ein Teil der folgenden Projekte, welche diese Erweiterung beispielhaft darstellen, sind Programmentwicklungen für den Entwurfsprozess. Der Computer übernimmt dabei nicht die Entwurfsarbeit, aber er unterstützt sie, indem er Entwurfsaspekte berechnet und darstellt, die der Mensch entweder nicht, oder jedenfalls nicht in derselben Geschwindigkeit berücksichtigen könnte. Das digitale Modell wird also durch eine spezifische, vom Entwerfer steuerbare Art und Weise informiert und verfeinert. Das Programm überprüft bestimmte messbare Kriterien, der Entwerfer bestimmt das architektonische Konzept und den ästhetischen Ausdruck. Das Ziel ist eine Partnerschaft, bei welcher die gestalterische Kompetenz des Entwerfers – und dazu gehört auch die Intuition – sich trotz komplexer technischer Anforderungen frei entfalten kann.

Eine weitere Form der Augmentation bezieht sich auf das Einbringen unseres Körpers in den Gestaltungsprozess. Die Experimente, die wir beschreiben, ermöglichen das Entwickeln von Formen durch Bewegung und untersuchen das Potenzial unseres Tastsinns.

Die derzeit sich eröffnenden Möglichkeiten, schon im Entwurf den digitalen Fabrikationsprozess mitzugestalten, sind ein weiterer Aspekt von „Augmented Architecture". Erweiterte Kontrolle über die Fabrikation, verstärktes Einbeziehen unserer Sinne sowohl im Entwurfsprozess als auch in der gebauten Umwelt, sowie interaktive Visualisierungen komplexer Sachverhalte sind charakteristisch für „Augmented Architecture". Das Ziel ist es,

> Das digitale Modell wird also durch eine spezifische, vom Entwerfer steuerbare Art und Weise informiert und verfeinert.

have an extra dimension and this extra dimension is a sense-sensual one. "Augmented Architecture" is a modification of the more well-known term "Augmented Reality". The latter is a computer science term used to describe applications in which our perception of reality is supplemented with additional information, as with, for example, Google glasses. The term "Augmented Architecture" also refers to a digitally-enabled enhancement, but one that alters the field of architecture in terms of both the design process and the designed product.

Some of the projects described, all of which we consider as representative of augmentation, are software programs that support the design process. The computer's role is not to design, but to provide real-time design support by continuously calculating and representing aspects of design propositions, that humans could not otherwise take into account. The digital model is thus informed by and refined in reaction to specific criteria imposed by the designer. The program simply checks for compliance with predetermined criteria whilst the designer controls architectural concept and esthetic expression. The goal is a partnership in which the intuitive talent of the designer reigns free from complex technical requirements.

Another type of augmentation refers to the role of the human body in the design process as well as in the built environment. Experiments we describe allow the creation of form through movement, and explore the potential of our sense of touch.

Furthermore the designers' new-found control over digital fabrication processes is an area of growing possibility that represents another aspect of Augmented Architecture. Improved control and design of the digital fabrication process, greater inclusion of the human senses in both the design process and in the built environment and enhanced interactive exploration of complex circumstances are all characteristic of "Augmented Architecture." Its parallel goals are to relieve the designer of the increasingly important technical burden present in contemporary building design whilst enhancing the human in architectural design criteria—through increasing the influence of our senses (sight, sound, hearing, touch …) and thus our intuitive judgment.

Nonstandard Architecture. Free form surfaces are well established in contemporary architecture vocabulary, but their design and construction remains a technical challenge that leads to high costs. In a research project funded by the Austrian Science Foundation (FWF), IAM developed a program in which the discretization of free form surfaces, that is the breaking down of double curved surfaces into individual flat pieces, is guided by ornamental patterns.[3] Dividing such forms into flat pieces makes sense because many building materials (in

3   FWF Projekt L695: Non-standard Architecture Using Ornaments and Plane Elements. See https://iam2.tugraz.at/fwf/freeform/

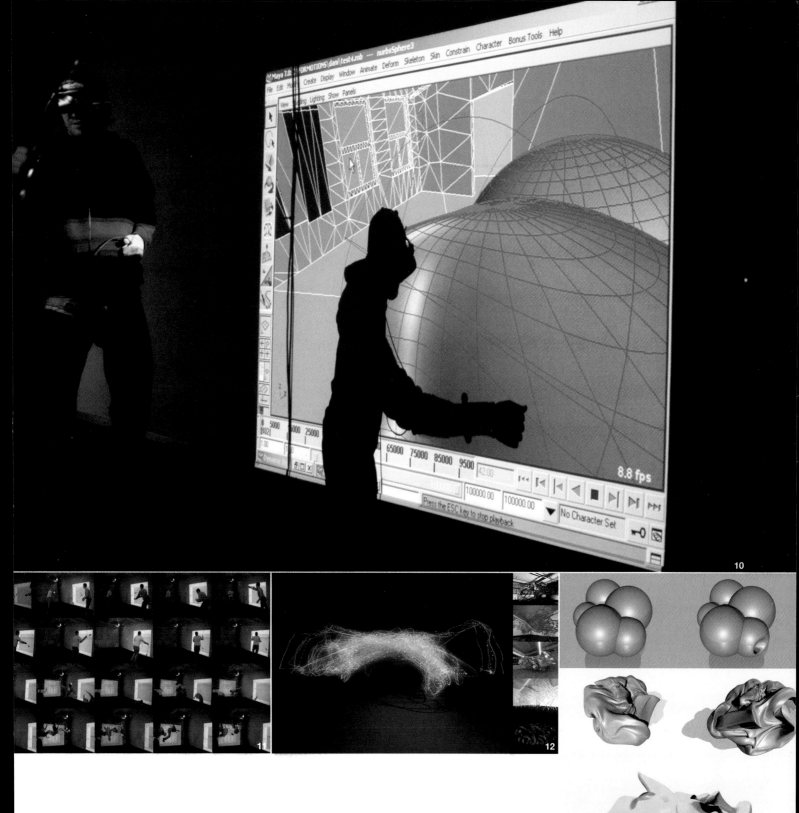

10–13 *Formotions*: Studierende entwickeln gestische Entwurfswerkzeuge (Workshop geleitet von Martin Frühwirth und Stefan Zedlacher). Unten: Das lineare Übersetzen von Bewegung in Form liefert interessante Resultate, ist aber schwierig zu kontrollieren. Oben: Durch die Einbindung simulierter physikalischer Kräfte wie zum Beispiel Wind (der Student im Bild sprach von einem virtuellen Föhn) erlaubt eine feinere Dosierung der Formgebung, die überraschenderweise auf Anhieb verständlich und leicht zu bedienen ist. *Formotions*: Students develop gestural design tools (Workshop led by Martin Frühwirth and Stefan Zedlacher). Bottom: The direct translation of movement into form yields results that are interesting, but difficult to control. Top: Using simulated physical forces such as wind (the student spoke of a virtual blowdryer) introduces a more subtle way of interacting with form that feels very natural and is surprisingly easy to pick up. © IAM, TU Graz

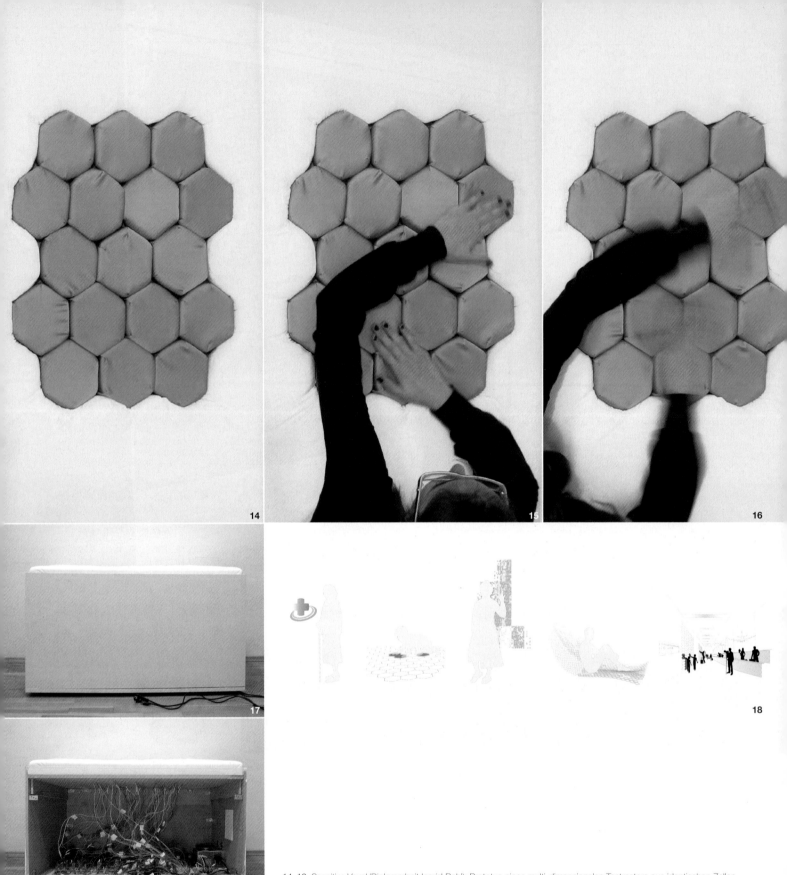

14–19 *Sensitive Voxel* (Diplomarbeit Ingrid Pohl): Prototyp eines multi-dimensionalen Tastrasters aus identischen Zellen, die mit Wärme, Kälte und Vibration auf unseren Tastsinn wirken können. *Sensitive Voxel* (Diploma Thesis Ingrid Pohl): Prototype of a multi-dimensional touchfield, made up of identical cells, which can use warm, cold and vibration to communicate with our sense of touch. © I. Pohl, IAM/TU Graz

the project we were concentrating on cross-laminated timber) are produced as flat boards or sheets. In terms of jointing, configurations in which no more than three elements meet at one point are ideal, but this is only possible for patterns that consist of four- or more-sided polygons. To fulfill the condition of planarity for all faces of such patterns, complex optimization calculations are necessary that can only be performed by computer: in an iterative process, in response to the designer's desired pattern, the program seeks a best match that ensures co-planarity of all points on all faces, thus proposing a configuration, which can be refined, again and again, by the user. This software is designed for the use of architects, thus both esthetic (intuitive) and technical control of the optimization process is achieved without having to call in the specialists[4] (figs. 3–9).

The *Cobra* (figs. 5–9) is the timber built prototype of a freeform surface discretized in this manner. A new jointing technique was invented for its construction.[5]

Body Movement and Sense of Touch. no_LAb, the IAM media laboratory (fig. 2), features a highly sensitive 3D motion tracking system of the type used not only in medical research but also in the film industry. Movement can be tracked and represented to a millimeter of precision, in (almost) real time. We use this system, amongst other things, to experiment with bodily human—computer interaction.

The master thesis project *Spacensing*[6] investigated relationships between perception of space and movement (fig. 1) in dance. The student workshop *Formotions*[7] developed design tools that work through human bodily gestures (figs. 10–13).

Not only tools used to design, but also the products and spaces we build can be augmented through media. Here, too, the challenge to identify meaningful types of enhancement is taken up in studio experiment at IAM. The project *Sensitive Voxel*[8] questions why the human sense of touch is used to communicate with input devices, but almost never as the recipient of digital information. Our multi-dimensional touch-grid prototype is made up of identical cells, each one of which produces hot and cold temperatures as well as vibration to communicate with us through our sense of touch (figs. 14–19).

---

4 See Markus Manahl, Milena Stavric, and Albert Wiltsche, "Ornamental Discretisation of Free-form Surfaces," in: *International Journal of Architectural Computing* 10,4 (2012), pp. 595–612.

5 See Markus Manahl and Albert Wiltsche, "'Kobra' aus Brettsperrholz: Neue Methoden zur Realisierung von Freiformflächen aus ebenen Elementen an Prototyp erprobt," in: *Konstruktiv* 286 (2012), pp. 26–27.

6 *Spacensing* was the Master thesis of Stefan Zedlacher for which he collaborated with the dancer Klaus Seewald at IAM in 2007. See http://spacensing.net

7 *Formotions* was a one week student workshop led by Martin Frühwirth and Stefan Zedlacher in November 2006 at IAM. See http://iam.tugraz.at/dm4/w06/

8 See Ingrid Pohl and Urs Hirschberg, "Sensitive Voxel – A reactive tangible surface," in: *Proceedings of the 14th International Conference on Computer Aided Architectural Design Futures*, Liege 4–8 July 2011, pp. 525–538.

sowohl den Entwerfer von den im zeitgenössischen Bauen immer wichtigeren technischen Aspekten freizuspielen, als auch menschliche Aspekte im Entwurf vermehrt einzubringen – indem der Einfluss unserer Sinne gestärkt wird und damit auch der unserer Intuition.

Nonstandard Architecture. Freiformflächen sind Teil des zeitgenössischen Architekturvokabulars, aber ihre Planung und Umsetzung stellt immer noch eine bautechnische Herausforderung dar, die zu hohen Kosten führt. Im Rahmen eines vom österreichischen Wissenschaftsfonds FWF geförderten Projekts[3] wurde am IAM ein Verfahren entwickelt, wie die Diskretisierung von Freiformflächen, das heißt die Aufteilung mehrfach gekrümmter Oberflächen in ebene Teilflächen durch ornamentale Muster gesteuert werden kann. Das Aufteilen solcher Formen in einzelne flache Teilelemente ist sinnvoll, weil sehr viele Baustoffe (im Projekt konzentrierten wir uns auf Brettsperrholz) als Platten produziert werden. Fügetechnisch sind Muster, bei denen sich immer nur drei Elemente in einem Punkt treffen ideal, diese Bedingung erfüllen aber nur Muster, die aus vier- oder mehrseitigen Flächen bestehen. Damit die Bedingung der Planarität für solche Aufteilungen erfüllt ist, bedarf es aber aufwändiger Optimierungsrechnungen, die nur der Computer leisten kann: In einem iterativen Prozess gibt der Benutzer des Programms eine gewünschte Aufteilung vor, das Programm sucht dazu eine Lösung, welche auch die Komplanarität aller Teilflächen erfüllt. Auf diese Weise wird die ästhetische (intuitive) Kontrolle dieses Optimierungsverfahrens erreicht, ohne dass dafür Spezialisten beigezogen werden müssen[4] (Abb. 3–9).

Die *Kobra* (Abb. 5–9) ist der gebaute Prototyp einer mit diesem Verfahren diskretisierten Freiform. Für die Umsetzung wurde auch ein eigenes Fügeprinzip entwickelt und getestet.[5]

Körperlichkeit und Tastsinn. Im no_LAb, dem Medienlabor des IAM (Abb. 2), steht uns ein 3D-Motion-Tracking-System zur Verfügung, wie es auch in der medizinischen Forschung oder in der Filmindustrie verwendet wird. Durch spezielle Hardware können Bewegungen im Raum millimetergenau und fast latenzfrei verfolgt werden. Wir verwenden das System unter anderem dafür, mit neuen Interaktionsformen zu experimentieren.

Das Projekt *Spacensing*[6] untersucht in Kooperation mit einem Tänzer die Beziehung zwischen Raumerfahrung und Bewegung (Abb. 1). Im Projekt

> Die Experimente, die wir beschreiben, ermöglichen das Entwickeln von Formen durch Bewegung und untersuchen das Potenzial unseres Tastsinns.

---

3 FWF Projekt L695: „Non-standard Architecture Using Ornaments and Plane Elements". Vgl. https://iam2.tugraz.at/fwf/freeform/

4 Vgl. Markus Manahl/Milena Stavric/Albert Wiltsche: „Ornamental Discretisation of Free-form Surfaces", in: *International Journal of Architectural Computing* 10, 4 (2012), S. 595–612.

5 Vgl. Markus Manahl/Albert Wiltsche: „,Kobra' aus Brettsperrholz. Neue Methoden zur Realisierung von Freiformflächen aus ebenen Elementen an Prototyp erprobt", in: *Konstruktiv* 286 (2012), S. 26–27.

6 *Spacensing* ist 2007 als Diplomarbeit von Stefan Zedlacher und in Kooperation mit dem Tänzer Klaus Seewald am IAM entstanden. Vgl. http://spacensing.net

Formotions[7] haben Studierende neue gestische Entwurfswerkzeuge entwickelt (Abb. 10–13).

Nicht nur unsere Planungswerkzeuge, auch die Räume, die wir bauen, können medial erweitert werden. Auch hier gilt es, Potenziale auszuloten, um herauszufinden, welche medialen Erweiterungen tatsächlich auch sinnvoll sind. Das Projekt *Sensitive Voxel*[8] hinterfragt, warum unser Tastsinn zwar immer mehr zur Eingabe, aber so gut wie gar nicht als Rezipient von digitaler Information erprobt wurde. Der im Rahmen einer Diplomarbeit entwickelte Prototyp eines multi-dimensionalen Tastrasters ist aus identischen Zellen aufgebaut, die mit Wärme, Kälte und Vibration auf unseren Tastsinn wirken können (Abb. 14–19).

Augmented Styria Desk. Im Rahmen eines Projektstudios über die Zersiedelung der Steiermark wurde ein interaktiver Planungstisch entwickelt.[9] Er besteht aus einem topografischen Modell der Steiermark, auf welches dynamische Visualisierungen projiziert werden können. Komplexe Zusammenhänge und Daten zur Steiermark, welche die Studierenden in einer umfassenden Datenbank mit demografischen, verkehrstechnischen, politischen, touristischen, geografischen und topografischen Informationen zusammengetragen haben, können damit interaktiv und visuell verständlich dargestellt werden. Für die Interaktion mit diesen Daten wurde eine eigene Präsentationsform entwickelt. Ein Zeigestift, dessen Bewegung und Lage im Raum verfolgt wird, dient als Eingabegerät, mit dem – wie wir aus verschiedenen Ausstellungen wissen – auch Kinder spontan umgehen können. So lenkt der Tisch von seiner technischen Komplexität ab und ermöglicht die Diskussion und interaktive Erkundung unterschiedlicher Szenarien mit mehreren Personen (Abb. 20–25).

> Für die Interaktion mit diesen Daten wurde eine eigene Präsentationsform entwickelt.

Augmented Parametrics. Im Projektstudio *Parametric Wood Joints* wurde der *Framed Pavilion* entwickelt, bei welchem, anknüpfend an traditionelle handwerkliche Fügetechniken Holz-Holz-Verbindungen entwickelt wurden, die vom Roboter millimetergenau gefräst werden können. Keine zwei Teile des Pavillons sind gleich. Die Computerpräzision erlaubte die Ausführung und Passgenauigkeit der Fügedetails in einer Weise, dass der Pavillon ganz ohne Verwendung von Schrauben oder Nägeln oder Leim errichtet werden konnte. Nach dem Zusammenfügen der Balken sind alle Fügedetails unsichtbar (Abb. 26–34).

Das Projekt ist nicht nur interessant, weil es Möglichkeiten einer neuen, ins Digitale erweiterten Handwerklichkeit aufzeigt. Es führt auch das Potenzial

Augmented Topography—Styria Desk. An interactive 3D physical model (planning table) was developed by students in a master studio about urban sprawl in Styria.[9] It consists of a scale topographical model onto which both static and dynamic information is projected. The setup visually represents complex information about Styria (students compiled data about geography, topography, vegetation, traffic, demographics, politics, tourism, health and much more into a large custom database). The table was developed along with a novel type of presentation and interaction. A "magic wand" whose movement is tracked can be used as a 3D pointing device that can be shared by several persons who discuss and explore different scenarios while standing around the table. From exhibitions we know that the use of this wand takes no learning, even children can use it easily (figs. 20–25).

Augmented Parametrics. The *Framed Pavilion* developed in the master studio *Parametric Wood Joints* was designed and built by students and robots. Inspired by traditional methods of wood jointing, the studio explored the innovative use of such types of connections in bespoke timber structures. Milled by a robot, computer precision allowed the making of bespoke details such that no nails, screws, or glue were required in the building of the pavilion. Once the parts were put together, the jointing detail disappeared (figs. 26–34).

The project demonstrates the potential of digitally enhancing traditional craftsmanship. It showcases parametric design in an exemplary fashion: all construction-related constraints, such as the minimal and maximal angles at which parts can be joined, become part of a parametric definition within which variables such as light openings, spatial configuration and sequence can be explored and optimized. The list of unique geometric parts is sent directly from the parametric model to the robot for milling.

In another project sponsored by the Austrian Science Foundation (FWF) we are currently researching how physical simulation methods can assist in parametric form exploration. "Augmented Parametrics" feeds relevant site-specific information, concerning for example: climate, local environment, and light, directly into the modeling process (figs. 35–36). The system returns instant easy to read feedback about the impacts of formal decisions on building performance, which the designer can use to confirm his or her choices. At the same time the system itself can optimize building forms to meet specific performance criteria defined by the designer, thus providing a sense of the relevance of certain formal decisions. So far no commercially available program is capable of providing this

7   *Formotions* war ein einwöchiger Workshop, der unter der Leitung von Martin Frühwirth und Stefan Zedlacher im November 2006 am IAM stattgefunden hat. Vgl. http://iam.tugraz.at/dm4/w06/

8   Vgl. Ingrid Pohl/Urs Hirschberg: „Sensitive Voxel – A Reactive Tangible Surface", in: *Proceedings of the 14th International Conference on Computer Aided Architectural Design Futures*, Liege, 4–8 July 2011, S. 525–538.

9   Atlas Zersiedelung Steiermark, Projektstudio im Sommersemester 2010 unter der Leitung von Richard Dank, Stefan Zedlacher und Urs Hirschberg. Vgl. https://iam2.tugraz.at/studio/s10/

9   Atlas Zersiedelung Steiermark, master studio Summer semester 2010 led by Richard Dank, Stefan Zedlacher and Urs Hirschberg. See https://iam2.tugraz.at/studio/s10/

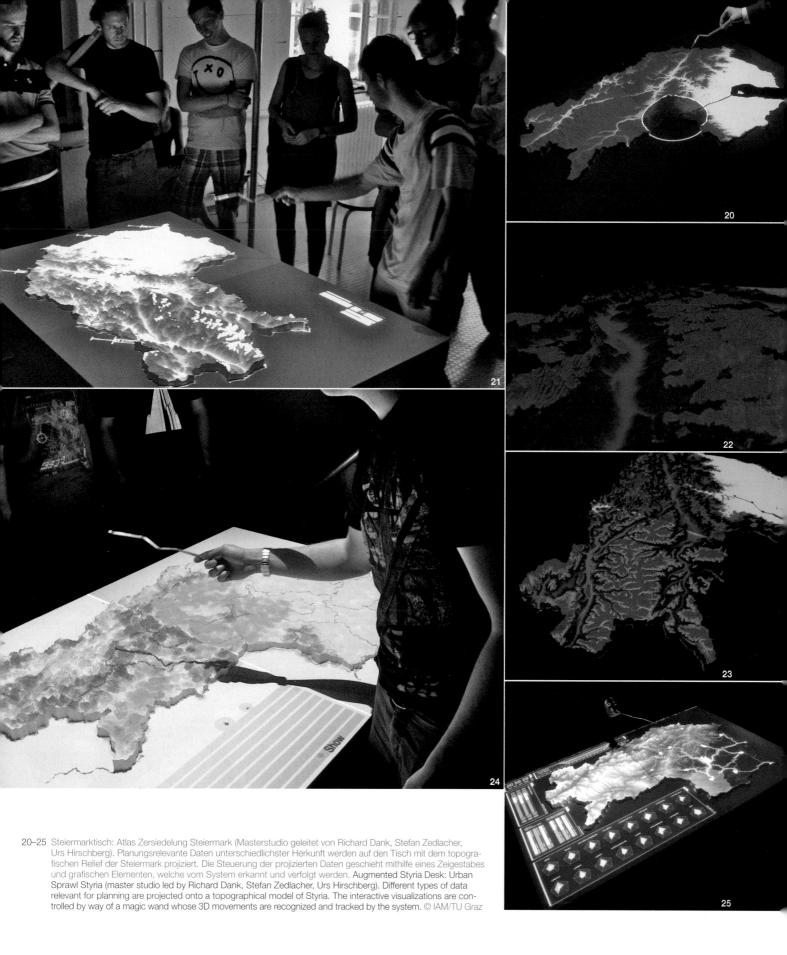

20–25 Steiermarktisch: Atlas Zersiedelung Steiermark (Masterstudio geleitet von Richard Dank, Stefan Zedlacher, Urs Hirschberg). Planungsrelevante Daten unterschiedlichster Herkunft werden auf den Tisch mit dem topografischen Relief der Steiermark projiziert. Die Steuerung der projizierten Daten geschieht mithilfe eines Zeigestabes und grafischen Elementen, welche vom System erkannt und verfolgt werden. Augmented Styria Desk: Urban Sprawl Styria (master studio led by Richard Dank, Stefan Zedlacher, Urs Hirschberg). Different types of data relevant for planning are projected onto a topographical model of Styria. The interactive visualizations are controlled by way of a magic wand whose 3D movements are recognized and tracked by the system. © IAM/TU Graz

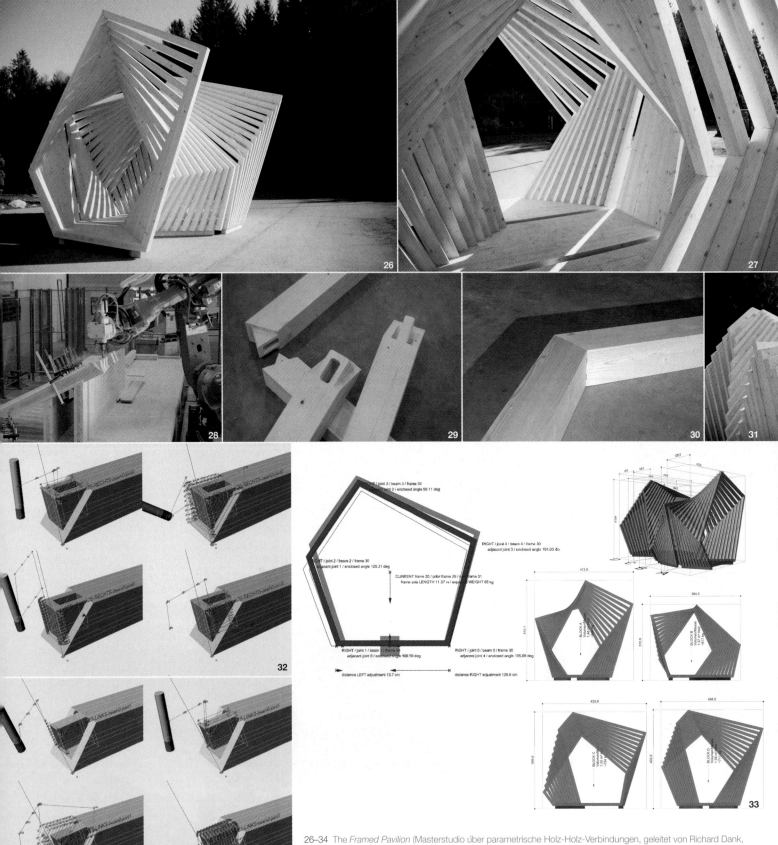

26–34 The *Framed Pavilion* (Masterstudio über parametrische Holz-Holz-Verbindungen, geleitet von Richard Dank, Christian Freissling, Urs Hirschberg in Kooperation mit dem Wolzinnovationszentrum Zeltweg). Die digitale Fabrikation durch den Roboter wird vom parametrischen Modell aus kontrolliert. Für den Bau wurden weder Nägel, Schrauben noch Leim verwendet. The *Framed Pavilion* (master studio about parametric wood joints, led by Richard Dank, Christian Freissling, Urs Hirschberg in cooperation with the wood innovation center Zeltweg). The digital fabrication with a robot is controlled in the parametric model. No nails, screws, or glue were used in the construction. © IAM/TU Graz

bi-directional parametric functionality, but we see it as an obvious next step in the evolution of parametric design.

A Critical Attitude? The examples presented above are intended to demonstrate what we mean by "Augmented Architecture" at IAM and also the types of development that we contribute to in our work. We are optimistic about these developments, which allow digital technology a friendly service role and in which human intuition can gain new significance. If this paradigm shift is to occur in architecture too, digital tools must cater to our perception in such a way as to become natural partners. In this, "Augmented Architecture" is a touch-stone: not all new applications of digital media will prove useful or meaningful. To be of real value, digital technology must enhance our senses, our world and our understanding of them. If it isn't the case, then there is no augmentation. Paradoxically, the best examples of "Augmented Architecture" are those we hardly notice because we quickly accepted them as natural. Those are the ones that expand the reach of our senses and our intuition. As we wrote earlier, technology that is "second-nature" is referred to as transparent.

This brings us back to our introduction, and to discussion of the problematic aspects of transparency. The optimistic description of our projects should not be interpreted as advice to sit back and wait for the day when computers are finally easy to use. The vulnerability of architectural practice sketched at the beginning of this text is already a consequence of a passive attitude towards information technology. Simply waiting for a time when computers better suit our intuitive way of working would be a mistake—it's far better to get involved! In seeking ways to make the most of digital technology, a critical understanding is key. Despite all their sense-sensitivity: computers are first and foremost abstraction machines. Their potential is fundamentally different from that of any analogue machines that we intuitively understood in the past.

In their recent book *The Second Machine Age*[10] Erik Brynjolfsson and Andrew McAfee write about the dangers of the current era which, they say, is characterized by a generation of machines that are increasingly taking over our cognitive tasks. They describe the exponential growth of processing speed as radically counter-intuitive and warn that it will lead to enormous upheavals in the labor market as fewer and fewer people aided by ever more potent machines command more and more power.

If *The Second Machine Age* ultimately portrays such developments optimistically, it makes our stated hope for a friendly technology that makes our work easier, seem rather naïve.

10 Erik Brynjolfsson and Andrew McAfee, *The Second Machine Age: Work, Progress, and Prosperity in a Time of Brilliant Technologies* (New York, 2014).

des parametrischen Entwerfens exemplarisch vor: bautechnische Einschränkungen wie zum Beispiel die minimalen und maximalen Winkel, die fügetechnisch möglich sind, können Bestandteil der parametrischen Definition werden, innerhalb derer man dann Dinge wie Raumwirkung, Lichteinfall etc. erkunden und optimieren kann. Die Bauteilliste mit geometrisch unterschiedlichen Elementen kann vom parametrischen Modell an den Roboter geschickt werden.

In einem weiteren vom österreichischen Wissenschaftsfonds FWF geförderten Projekt entwickeln wir derzeit Möglichkeiten, wie physikalische Simulationsverfahren in Echtzeit Teil der parametrischen Formentwicklung werden können. Das Ziel dieser erweiterten Parametrik ist, schon in einer frühen Entwurfsphase ortsspezifische Gegebenheiten wie zum Beispiel Klimadaten oder Lichtsituation direkt in den Modellierprozess einzubinden (Abb. 35–36). Einerseits können so die Auswirkungen formaler Entscheidungen auf die Performance des Gebäudes fast beiläufig überprüft werden. Andererseits kann das System aber auch selbst formale Vorschläge machen, welche die vom Benutzer gewählten Anforderungen bestmöglich erfüllen, so dass der Nutzer sehr schnell ein Gefühl für die Relevanz bestimmter formaler Entscheidungen bekommt. Diese bi-direktionale Parametrik leistet derzeit noch kein kommerziell erhältliches Programm, aber es ist absehbar, dass dies die nächste Entwicklungsstufe des parametrischen Entwerfens sein wird.

Eine kritische Haltung? Die vorgestellten Beispiele sollten einen Eindruck davon vermitteln, was wir unter „Augmented Architecture" verstehen und in welche Richtung die Entwicklung geht, zu der wir durch unsere Arbeit beitragen. Es ist eine hoffnungsvolle Entwicklung, welche der Digitaltechnik eine freundliche, menschengerechte Rolle zuweist und in der

Nicht einfach jede Erweiterung des Architekturschaffens, die technisch machbar ist, ist auch sinnvoll.

auch unsere Intuition eine neue Bedeutung erhalten kann. Damit dieser Paradigmenwechsel auch in der Architektur erfolgen kann, müssen sich die neuen Werkzeuge auf ganz natürliche Weise mit unserer Wahrnehmung verbinden. So verstanden wird der Begriff „Augmented Architecture" zum Prüfstein: Nicht einfach jede Erweiterung des Architekturschaffens, die technisch machbar ist, ist auch sinnvoll. Die digitale Technik soll unsere Welt und unser Verständnis bereichern, ohne unsere Sinne zu überfordern, sonst bewirkt sie keine echte Erweiterung. Paradoxerweise kann man also nur dann von „Augmented Architecture" sprechen, wenn die Erweiterung gar nicht als solche empfunden, sondern von Benutzern als ganz natürlich akzeptiert wird. Nur dann bietet sie auch neue Einsatzmöglichkeiten für unsere Intuition. Eingangs wurde erklärt, dass der Zustand, in dem dies gelingt und eine Technik selbstverständlich wird, als Transparenz bezeichnet wird.

Damit schließt sich der Kreis zu unserer Einleitung, und nach all den optimistischen Beispielen ist es höchste Zeit, auch nochmals auf die Problematik dieser Art von Transparenz zu sprechen zu kommen. Die Beschreibung der Projekte sollte keinesfalls als Aufforderung missverstanden werden, uns bequem zurückzulehnen und darauf zu warten, dass Computer bald kinderleicht zu bedienen sein werden und uns dienstfertig zur Verfügung stehen. Dies wäre verhängnisvoll. Die eingangs skizzierte Situation in der Architekturpraxis ist die Folge einer verbreiteten passiven Haltung gegenüber diesen Entwicklungen. Sie hat schon jetzt dazu geführt, dass Architekten im Planungsprozess an Einfluss verlieren. Nicht mitzudenken wird auch in Zukunft das falsche Rezept sein. Denn trotz aller Sinnlichkeit: Computer sind nach wie vor in erster Linie Abstraktionsmaschinen. Ihr Potenzial ist grundsätzlich anders als das aller analogen Phänomene, auf die wir unsere Intuition bisher angewendet haben. Dies gilt es stets zu berücksichtigen.

In ihrem jüngst erschienen Buch *The Second Machine Age*[10] schreiben Erik Brynjolfsson und Andrew McAfee über die Gefahren, die das, was sie das zweite Maschinenzeitalter nennen, mit sich bringt, weil die neue Generation Maschinen den Menschen einen immer größeren Teil der kognitiven Tätigkeiten abnimmt. Sie beschreiben die exponentiell wachsende Geschwindigkeit der Prozessoren als etwas, das unserer Intuition radikal widerspricht und schon in kurzer Zeit zu enormen Umwälzungen in unserer Arbeitswelt führen wird, weil immer weniger Menschen mithilfe von immer mächtigeren Maschinen immer mehr Macht haben werden.

Auch wenn *The Second Machine Age* diese Entwicklungen letztlich optimistisch darstellt, ist vor diesem Hintergrund die Hoffnung auf eine freundliche Technik, die uns die Arbeit leichter machen wird, allzu naiv. Um die wachsenden Möglichkeiten des Digitalen für die Architektur zu nutzen, ist ein vertieftes Verständnis dafür, in welchem neuartigen Sinn die Abstraktionsmaschine Computer abstrakt *und* sinnlich zugleich sein kann, unabdingbar. Dieses Verständnis ist die Voraussetzung dafür, dass man sich die neuen Medien aktiv aneignen kann, ohne sich ihnen ausliefern zu müssen. Für den „dumb user" ist in dieser Zukunftsperspektive kein Platz.

Für den „dumb user" ist in dieser Zukunftsperspektive kein Platz.

Dies gilt auch für die kurz vorgestellten Projekte. Es handelt sich dabei um Eigenentwicklungen, die nur durch erhebliche Programmierkenntnisse entstehen konnten. Die möglichst einfache, intuitive Interaktion ist ein essenziell wichtiges Ziel für die Zukunft der Architektur. Angesichts der Komplexität unseres Faches kann dieses Ziel aber nur erreicht werden, wenn wir die medialen Funktionen ganz präzise und individuell für unsere persönlichen Bedürfnisse anpassen können. Das dafür notwendige Maß an Kontrolle über die digitalen Werkzeuge kann auch in Zukunft nur erreicht werden, indem man diese Werkzeuge zu einem gewissen Grad mitgestaltet. Dafür sind nach unserer Überzeugung grundlegende Kenntnisse im Scripting – der *lingua franca* der digitalen Medien – unabdingbar. Deswegen werden an der TU Graz diese Kenntnisse den angehenden Architektinnen und Architekten schon in der Bachelorausbildung vermittelt. Die medialen Erweiterungen unserer Sinne und die potentielle Aufwertung der Intuition sollten uns Ansporn sein, diese Entwicklungen selbst mitzugestalten. Es ist wichtiger denn je, dass wir auch die Art, wie wir entwerfen, entwerfen.

Nevertheless, the successful use of digital media in architecture depends on better understanding of the extraordinary capacity of the computer to be both abstract and sense-sensitive, in parallel. Better understanding should allow us to engage actively in partnership with new digital media—the alternative is to be subjected to it. There is no room for the "dumb user" in the future scenario.

The projects presented above are a case in point—they are research and student projects that took significant programming skills. We believe that easy, intuitive interaction between architect and information technology is essential to the future of architecture, and, given the complexity of the field that we'll succeed if we customize the media to match our particular needs. Such a level of control over digital tools can be achieved only if we participate in their design. For this, a basic knowledge of scripting—the *lingua franca* of digital media—is indispensable. It's why TU Graz architecture students learn scripting early in their bachelor studies. The potential of augmenting both our senses and our intuitive skills is surely enough incentive for architects to participate in the development of information technology. It's more important than ever that we design the way we design.

Translation Urs Hirschberg

---

10   Erik Brynjolfsson/Andrew McAfee: *The Second Machine Age: Work, Progress, and Prosperity in a Time of Brilliant Technologies*, New York 2014.

Bi-Directional Parametrics: Simulation Based Performative Optimizations

INITIAL

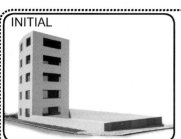

SOUTH VIEW   TOP VIEW

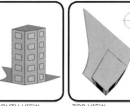

TOP VIEW   SOUTH VIEW

MIN ENERGY

INITIAL MODEL DATA TABLE
AHD = 40,5 (kWh/m2a)
PROFIT = -132141 (EU)
WALL INSULATION = 20 cm
ROOF INSULATION = 27 cm
NORTH-WEST FACADE GLAZING = 34,86 m²
NORTH-EAST FACADE GLAZING = 30,12 m²
SOUTH-EAST FACADE GLAZING = 35,85 m²
SOUTH-WEST FACADE GLAZING = 23,20 m²
TOTAL AREA OF TERRACES = 67,60 m²
FOOTPRINT AREA = 67,60 m²

MIN ENERGY MODEL DATA TABLE
AHD = 12,3 (kWh/m2a)
PROFIT = +143538 (EU)
WALL INSULATION = 30 cm
ROOF INSULATION = 38 cm
NORTH-WEST FACADE GLAZING = 35,01 m²
NORTH-EAST FACADE GLAZING = 45,81 m²
SOUTH-EAST FACADE GLAZING = 37,14 m²
SOUTH-WEST FACADE GLAZING = 110,70 m²
TOTAL AREA OF TERRACES = 195,61 m²
FOOTPRINT AREA = 195,36 m²

Site Visualization

Chorost Architekti - Passive Family House, Hradec Kralove, CZ

MAX PROFIT MODEL DATA TABLE
AHD = 25,5 (kWh/m2a)
PROFIT = +507021 (EU)
WALL INSULATION = 20 cm
ROOF INSULATION = 27 cm
NORTH-WEST FACADE GLAZING = 7,61 m²
NORTH-EAST FACADE GLAZING = 8,09 m²
SOUTH-EAST FACADE GLAZING = 54,04 m²
SOUTH-WEST FACADE GLAZING = 19,55 m²
TOTAL AREA OF TERRACES = 252,79 m²
FOOTPRINT AREA = 252,24 m²

PROFIT - ENERGY DATA TABLE
AHD = 17,2 (kWh/m2a)
PROFIT = +388842 (EU)
WALL INSULATION = 28 cm
ROOF INSULATION = 35 cm
NORTH-WEST FACADE GLAZING = 7,21 m²
NORTH-EAST FACADE GLAZING = 8,12 m²
SOUTH-EAST FACADE GLAZING = 50,71 m²
SOUTH-WEST FACADE GLAZING = 43,57 m²
TOTAL AREA OF TERRACES = 207,36 m²
FOOTPRINT AREA = 206,93 m²

MAX PROFIT

SOUTH VIEW   TOP VIEW

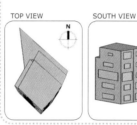

TOP VIEW   SOUTH VIEW

MAX PROFIT - MIN ENERGY

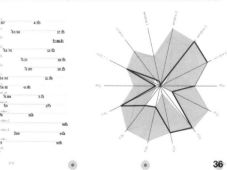

35–36 Augmented Parametrics (erweiterte Parametrik): Projekt gefördert vom Österreichischen Wissenschaftsfonds FWF (2012–2015). Bi-direktionale Parametrik: Auf der Basis physikalischer Simulationsmethoden, welche ins parametrische Modell integriert sind, können Optimierungsverfahren Vorschläge machen, wie ein Entwurf performativ verbessert werden kann. Der Entwerfer bekommt durch dieses Feedback ein Gefühl für die Auswirkungen seiner formalen Entscheidungen. Augmented Parametrics: Project supported by the Austrian National Science Foundation FWF (2012–2015). Bi-directional Parametrics: based on physical simulation methods which are directly integrated into the parametric modeler, optimization-procedures can make suggestions how a design's performance can be improved. Through such feedback, the designer gets a feel for the consequences of formal design decisions. © IAM/TU Graz

1　Antony Gormley, *Exposure*, Lelystad, Niederlande　Antony Gormley's "Exposure," Lelystad, the Netherlands © Sean Hanna

Machine Intuition

Throughout its history, artificial intelligence might seem to have been essentially the remnant of what is left whenever a new algorithm has been discovered. In the early days of the field, chess playing was a prime example of artificial intelligence[1] until a string of chess programs culminating in IBM's Deep Blue reduced it to simple brute force search. In similar terms, the use of natural language was thought to be uniquely human, but is now beginning to be approximated by web-based translation applications.

Seit es sie gibt, schcint künstliche Intelligenz der übrig gebliebene Rest zu sein, wenn wieder einmal ein neuer Algorithmus entdeckt wurde. In den Anfangsjahren des Fachs war das Schachspiel ein Paradebeispiel für künstliche Intelligenz,[1] bis eine Reihe von Schachprogrammen, mit Deep Blue von IBM als krönendem Höhepunkt, es auf eine simple Brute-Force-Suche reduzierte. In ähnlichem Sinne galt die Verwendung natürlicher Sprache als dem Menschen vorbehalten, jetzt kommen ihr web-basierte Übersetzungsprogramme immer näher.

SEAN HANNA

In all of these cases, once the algorithm is explained, the task ceases to be a mystery, and thus ceases to be considered intelligence. Artificial intelligence constantly reduces its domain, taking as a definition only those tasks not yet explained.

It is because the scope of artificial intelligence is not fixed, that the Turing Test—the most well known test investigating whether machines can think like humans—has no clear and well-defined objective, except for successfully fooling an intelligent observer. Originally called the "imitation game," Alan Turing[2] proposed that a computer communicating in conversation with an interrogator via a text based interface should be considered to exhibit all relevant signs of intelligence if it could not be distinguished from a human participant against all lines of questioning that the interrogator can devise. It is entirely up to the interrogator, in this case, to change the nature of the test based on their implicit, human judgment, the criterion for which cannot be predefined, and requires intelligence.

What is said of artificial intelligence can equally be said of intuition. Aesthetics, and everything in design that relies on intuition, can be defined as just those aspects we find impossible, yet, to be explicit about. In the practice of architecture there has also been something like the reduction of domain seen in artificial intelligence, as new professions—engineers, surveyors, and other consultants—take over some of the responsibility of design and management. These rational elements of architectural design are those about which one can be most explicit. But there is still very much left (perhaps more than is obvious), and it is often through the architect's intuition that some of the most important elements are determined. This is why the education of the architect is so protracted, and why long training and experience are required to develop the intuition required for competency.

What would it mean for a computer actually to be intelligent? The position known as "strong" artificial intelligence argues that this is possible. It does not seem to have happened yet, but I would argue that it is indeed possible, and more specifically, that the kind of thinking that happens in design can provide an answer to the question. This is because we are reaching a point in the complexity of what we design at which our own intuition may not suffice and at which point the help of an intelligent computer may be required. At the same time, the mechanism of design intuition is, unlike the formal reasoning most easily simulated by a machine.

> Aesthetics, and everything in design that relies on intuition, can be defined as just those aspects we find impossible, yet to be explicit about.

In all diesen Fällen verliert die Aufgabe, sobald der Algorithmus erklärt ist, ihr Mysterium und damit das Intelligente. Die künstliche Intelligenz reduziert unaufhörlich ihre Domäne, da sie sich nur über jene Aufgaben definiert, die noch nicht erklärt sind.

Weil der Bereich künstlicher Intelligenz nicht eindeutig abgesteckt ist, hat der Turing Test – das berühmteste Verfahren zur Ermittlung, ob Maschinen wie Menschen denken können – keine klare, eindeutig definierte Zielvorgabe, außer jener, einen intelligenten Beobachter erfolgreich auszutricksen. In seinem „imitation game" – „Nachahmungsspiel" – genannten Test schlug Alan Turing vor, einem Computer, der über ein textbasiertes Interface mit einem Fragesteller im Gespräch ist, alle relevanten Anzeichen von Intelligenz zuzusprechen, wenn er bei sämtlichen Befragungen, die sich der Fragesteller ausdenkt, nicht von einem menschlichen Teilnehmer zu unterscheiden ist.[2] Es steht den Fragestellern dabei frei, das Wesen des Tests anhand ihrer impliziten, menschlichen Urteilskraft zu verändern, des Kriteriums, das sich nicht vorab bestimmen lässt und Intelligenz erfordert.

Was für künstliche Intelligenz zutrifft, gilt auch für Intuition. Ästhetik und alles, was bei Gestaltung auf Intuition beruht, lässt sich als jene Aspekte definieren, die wir – noch – nicht eindeutig kodieren können. Auch die Architektur erfährt so etwas wie die Reduzierung ihrer Domäne, ähnlich wie die künstliche Intelligenz, da neue Berufe – Ingenieure, Sachverständige und andere Berater – die Zuständigkeit für Design und Management teilweise übernehmen. Diese rationalen Elemente architektonischen Entwerfens lassen sich am besten kodieren. Es bleibt jedoch ein großer Rest (vielleicht mehr als ersichtlich) und oft ist es die Intuition eines Architekten, durch die maßgebliche Elemente bestimmt werden. Deshalb ist die Architektenausbildung so langwierig, deshalb sind lange Übung und Erfahrung nötig, um die zur Kompetenz erforderliche Intuition zu entwickeln.

Was wäre denn nun unter einem intelligenten Computer zu verstehen? Die Theorie der „starken" künstlichen Intelligenz hält ihn für möglich. Es scheint noch nicht gelungen zu sein, aber ich würde behaupten, dass er in der Tat möglich ist, genauer gesagt, dass die Art zu denken, die beim Entwerfen am Werk ist, eine Antwort auf die Frage geben kann. Denn wir erreichen in der Komplexität dessen, was wir entwerfen, einen Punkt, an dem unsere eigene Intuition möglicherweise nicht ausreicht, und an dem die Zuhilfenahme eines intelligenten

1   See Claude C. Shannon, "Programming a Computer for Playing Chess," *Philosophical Magazine*, 41, 314 (1950), pp. 256–275.

2   See Alan Turing, "Computing Machinery and Intelligence," *Mind* 59, 236 (1950): pp. 433–460.

1   Vgl. Claude C. Shannon: „Programming a Computer for Playing Chess", *Philosophical Magazine* 41, 314 (1950), S. 256–275.

2   Vgl. Alan Turing: „Computing Machinery and Intelligence", *Mind* 59, 236 (1950), S. 433–460.

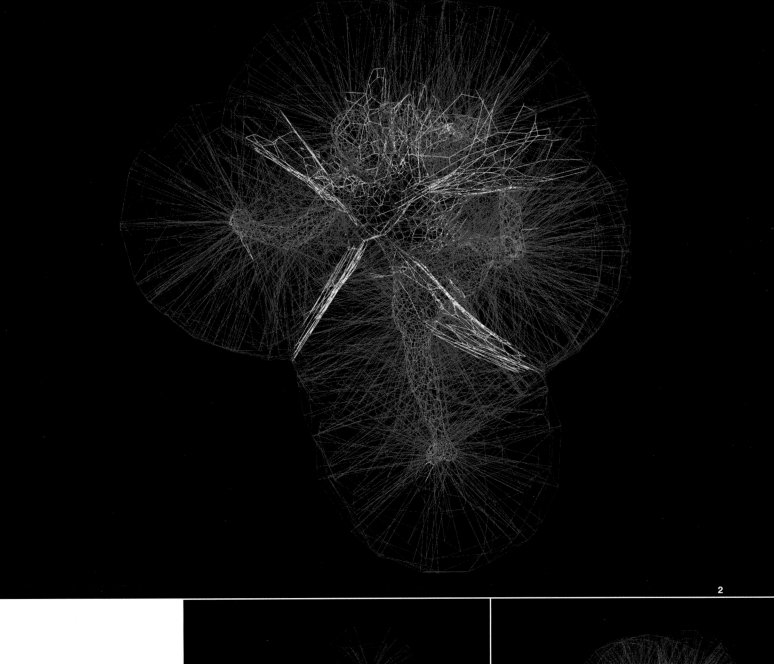

2

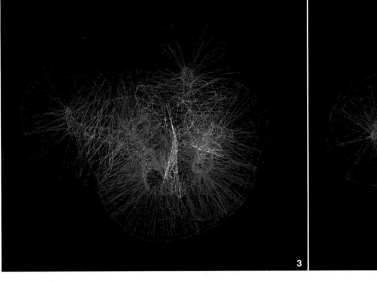

3

4

2–4 Digitale Modelle für mehrere
Body Expansion-Werke von
Antony Gormley. Digital models
for several of Antony Gormley's
body expansion pieces.
© Sean Hanna

5

5   Space Syntax-Analyse, die das „Durchgangspotenzial" (choice) bzw. die „Betweenness-Zentralität" des Straßennetzes von Südostengland anzeigt. Space syntax analysis indicating "choice" or "betweenness centrality" of the road network covering the south east of the UK © UCL Space Group

Computers nötig werden könnte. Gleichzeitig lässt sich der Vorgang intuitiven Entwerfens, anders als die formale Logik, problemlos von einer Maschine simulieren.

Schwierige Probleme lösen. Als das Fach „noch in den Kinderschuhen steckte"[3] ging es um das logische Analysieren vereinfachter Situationen unter eng begrenzten Bedingungen, oder „toy problems". Heute ist man sich einig, dass sie nicht nur der Bedeutung, sondern auch ihrem Wesen nach dem realen Denken nicht entsprechen, und man befasst sich seit einigen Jahrzehnten mit schwierigeren Aufgabenstellungen. Für Rittel und Webber fallen die Probleme, die sich bei komplexen Entwürfen stellen, in die schwierigste Kategorie – die der „wicked problems".[4] Architekten und Planer stehen in jeder Phase vor Schwierigkeiten, von der Bestimmung, welcher Art das Problem ist, bis zur Evaluierung potenzieller Lösungen, weil sich eine so komplexe Aufgabenstellung an keinem Punkt zur Gänze kodieren lässt. Intuition allein löst diese Probleme nicht, aber durch die Einbeziehung von Vorläuferfällen, Tradition und lebenslanger Erfahrung trägt sie am meisten zur Produktion von neuen Ideen, Neuerungen und kreativer Erkenntnis bei.

Wenden wir uns nun den Aufgabenstellungen zu, für die der Computer am besten geeignet ist: rechnen und die Verarbeitung großer Datenmengen. Milliarden von Webseiten zu bewältigen, übersteigt unsere persönliche Erfahrung und Intuition bei weitem, dasselbe gilt für die volle Komplexität städtischer Strukturen. Stadtplanerische Großprojekte werden immer häufiger, die verantwortlichen Teams werden größer, diversifizierter und sind oft über alle Welt verstreut, da ist unsere Intuition überfordert und muss durch Techniken unterstützt oder ersetzt werden, die einen solchen Grad an Komplexität erkennen und bewältigen können. Versuche mit „parametrischem Urbanismus"[5] etwa neigen dazu, gefährlich schiefzugehen, zum Teil aufgrund ihres Umfangs, doch hauptsächlich, weil sie Komplexität generieren, ohne sie verstehen zu müssen.

Der Computer ist ein ausgezeichnetes Visualisierungstool, eine Tatsache, die unsere Intuition unterstützen kann. Die rechnerischen Analysen von Space Syntax-Programmen beweisen dies exemplarisch.[6] Auf der Ebene einer ganzen Stadt löst sich das Straßennetz in ein Netz nahezu linearer, zu einem Graph

Solving Difficult Problems. The early days of "good, old fashioned, artificial intelligence"[3] involved reasoning about simplified situations in highly constrained environments, or "toy problems." Now acknowledged to be unlike real thought not just in degree, but in kind, emphasis in recent decades has shifted to more difficult tasks. Rittel and Webber describe the kind of problems faced in complex design tasks as the most difficult kind—"wicked problems."[4] Architects and planners face difficulties at every stage from defining the nature of the problem to evaluating its potential solutions, because at no point can such a complex task be made explicit in its entirety. Intuition alone does not solve these problems, but by taking in precedent, tradition, and a lifetime of experience, it makes the largest contribution toward the production of new ideas, novelty, and creative insight.

Now let us consider the sort of task for which the computer is best suited: crunching numbers and manipulating big data. The processing of billions of web pages is well beyond the scope of our personal experience and intuition, but the same is true for the full complexity of the design of a city. As large-scale design scenarios are becoming more and more common, and as the teams responsible are becoming larger, more diverse and dispersed over the globe, our intuition fails and needs to be supported or replaced by techniques that are able to see and handle this level of complexity. Attempts at "parametric urbanism,"[5] for example, may easily be prone to dangerous failure, due in part to their scale but mainly to the fact that they generate complexity without the need to understand it.

The computer is an excellent tool for visualizations, a fact which can aid our intuition. The computational analyses employed in Space Syntax research are a clear example of this.[6] At the scale of the city, the network of streets resolves itself into a network of nearly linear segments connected as a graph and represented with the strength of connections between elements as a function of their distance or angle. Measurements of the relative centrality of each node within the network can tell a great deal about the sort of behavior that might be expected on that particular street. Only by the form of the urban street network can accurate predictions be made. These predictions can, for example, concern the number of pedestrians or

> Architects and planners face difficulties at every stage from defining the nature of the problem to evaluating its potential solutions, because at no point can such a complex task be made explicit in its entirety.

3 John Haugeland: *Künstliche Intelligenz – programmierte Vernunft?* Aus dem Amerikanischen übers. von Waltraut Hüsmert, Hamburg, New York 1987, S. 153.

4 Horst Rittel/Melvin Webber: „Planning Problems are Wicked Problems", in Nigel Cross (Hg.), *Developments in Design Methodology*, Chichester 1984, S. 135–144.

5 Patrick Schumacher: „Parametricism. A New Global Style for Architecture and Urban Design", in *AD Architectural Design. Digital Cities* 79, 4 (2009), S. 14–23, insb. S. 15.

6 Vgl. Bill Hillier: *Space Is the Machine. A Configurational Theory of Architecture*, Cambridge 1996.

3 John Haugeland, *Artificial Intelligence: The Very Idea* (Cambridge, 1985), p. 116.

4 Horst Rittel and Melvin Webber, "Planning Problems Are Wicked Problems," in *Developments in Design Methodology*, ed. Nigel Cross (Chichester, 1984), pp. 135–144.

5 Patrik Schumacher. "Parametricism: A New Global Style for Architecture and Urban Design," in *Architectural Design: Digital Cities* 79, 4, (2009). pp. 14–23, esp. p. 15.

6 See Bill Hillier, *Space Is the Machine: A Configurational Theory of Architecture* (Cambridge, 1996).

vehicles present, the location of commercial centers at various scales, relative property values and also the probability of anti-social behavior such as rioting.[7] With increases in computing power, we are now able to address similar networks at a global scale, and recent studies suggest that there may be clear relationships between the international network of road, rail, and other modes of transportation, and national economic indicators such as GDP.[8] At this scale, all our normal experience fails to inform our intuition, but the computer provides an essential extension of our capacity to begin to make viable proposals.

The smallest scales are also beyond our normal experience, and, here too, the machine can observe and propose what would be difficult for us. Fine-scale digital manufacturing techniques such as laser sintering are easily able to produce complex interiors of fabricated objects with endless variation. Produced at the smallest resolution, these can mimic the natural variation found in materials such as wood and bone. To do so, the geometry of cellular lattice structures are varied such that each has the appropriate arrangement and shape of struts to give the appropriate behavior under localized or distributed loads. Properties like density, stiffness, and even Poisson's ratio can be easily tuned to the desired values and changed as required at any location within an object, however much of the cost is in the design of millions of individual cells. The computer can help here not only by traditional simulation and optimization but by employing machine learning to estimate ideal solutions. A supervised machine learning algorithm such as a neural network is trained on data for which we know both an input and a desired output. With a sample of local stresses that might exist within an object and a set of corresponding structural cells that produce a desired level of stiffness, the algorithm is able to learn an ideal geometry for any given distribution of load. It is able to generalize situations for which it has not been provided with sample data, and it is able to produce structures that outperform even the original sample set at a speed far exceeding that of fabrication.[9]

While these are powerful tools, the limitation with such statistical analyses and related visualizations is that we must still predetermine the nature of the phenomenon we are going to look at. The phenomenon may be an important one, but for any real world design task we can never be sure if it

> The computer can help here not only by traditional simulation and optimization but by employing machine learning to estimate ideal solutions.

verknüpfter Segmente auf, die je nach Entfernung oder Winkel mit unterschiedlich starken Verbindungslinien dargestellt werden. Die gemessene, relative Zentralität jedes Knotenpunktes im Netz gibt Auskunft über die auf der betreffenden Straße zu erwartende Aktivität. Allein anhand der Form des urbanen Straßennetzes lassen sich akkurate Vorhersagen machen. Diese Vorhersagen können zum Beispiel das Fußgänger- und Fahrzeugaufkommen betreffen, den Standort von Geschäftszentren unterschiedlicher Größe, relative Immobilienwerte, aber auch die Wahrscheinlichkeit sozialer Unruhen.[7] Dank höherer Rechenleistung sind wir heute in der Lage, ähnliche Netze in globalem Maßstab anzugehen und neuere Studien vermuten einen klaren Zusammenhang zwischen dem internationalen Geflecht aus Straße, Schiene und anderen Verkehrsmitteln und nationalen Wirtschaftsindikatoren wie dem BIP.[8] In dieser Größenordnung kann unsere normale Erfahrung der Intuition keine Informationen mehr liefern, der Computer hingegen erweitert unsere Fähigkeit, erste brauchbare Vorschläge zu machen.

Selbst die kleinsten Größenordnungen übersteigen unsere normale Erfahrung und auch hier kann die Maschine beobachten und Vorschläge machen, die für uns schwierig wären. Digitale Finescale-Verfahren wie Lasersintern sind problemlos in der Lage, komplexe Innenräume von 3D-Modellen in unendlichen Variationen herzustellen. In kleinster Auflösung produziert lassen sich die bei Holz und Knochen vorkommenden natürlichen Varianten imitieren. Zu diesem Zweck wird die Geometrie zellulärer Gitterstrukturen so verändert, dass die Stäbe die richtige Anordnung und Form haben, um bei Punkt- oder Flächenbelastung das erwünschte Verhalten zu gewährleisten. Materialeigenschaften wie Dichte, Festigkeit und sogar die Poissonzahl können problemlos auf die gewünschten Werte justiert und an jeder Stelle im Objekt nach Bedarf verändert werden; das Entscheidende ist jedoch das Design von Millionen individueller Zellen. Der Computer kann hier nicht nur durch konventionelle Simulation und Optimierung, sondern auch durch den Einsatz maschinellen Lernens helfen, rechnerische Ideallösungen zu generieren. Ein Algorithmus aus dem Bereich des überwachten maschinellen Lernens, beispielsweise ein neuronales Netzwerk, ist auf Daten trainiert, bei denen die Eingabewerte und die gewünschte Ausgabe bekannt sind. Über Samples potenzieller lokaler Belastungen in einem Objekt und einem Set korrespondierender

7   See Kinda Al Sayed and Sean Hanna, "How City Spaces Afford Opportunities for Riots," in *Proceedings of Ninth International Space Syntax Symposium*, ed. Young Ook Kim, Hoon Tae Park, Kyung Wook Seo (Seoul, 2013), available online at: http://www.sss9.or.kr/paperpdf/ussecp/SSS9_2013_REF093_P.pdf

8   See Sean Hanna, Joan Serras and Tasos Varoudis, "Measuring the Structure of Global Transportation Networks," in *Proceedings of Ninth International Space Syntax Symposium*, ed. Young Ook Kim, Hoon Tae Park, Kyung Wook Seo (Seoul, 2013), available online at: http://www.sss9.or.kr/paperpdf/mmd/SSS9_2013_REF060_P.pdf

9   See Sean Hanna, "Inductive Machine Learning of Optimal Modular Structures: Estimating Solutions Using Support Vector Machines," in *Artificial Intelligence for Engineering Design, Analysis and Manufacturing* 21 (2007): pp. 1–16.

7   Vgl. Kinda Al Sayed/Sean Hanna: „How City Spaces Afford Opportunities for Riots", in Young Ook Kim, Hoon Tae Park, Kyung Woo Seo (Hg.), *Proceedings of the Ninth International Space Syntax Symposium*, Seoul 2013, online unter: http://www.sss9.or.kr/paperpdf/ussecp/SSS9_2013_REF093_P.pdf

8   Vgl. Sean Hanna/Joan Serras/Tasos Varoudis, „Measuring the Structure of Global Transportation Networks", in *Proceedings of the Ninth International Space Syntax Symposium* (wie Anm. 7).

struktureller Zellen, die den gewünschten Festigkeitsgrad produzieren, kann der Algorithmus eine ideale Geometrie für jede denkbare Lastverteilung erlernen. Er kann Lösungen verallgemeinern, für die er noch gar keine Samples bekommen hat, und er kann Strukturen, die noch leistungsfähiger sind als das ursprüngliche Sample Set, in einer Geschwindigkeit generieren, die die Fertigungsgeschwindigkeit weit übertrifft.[9]

Dies sind zwar leistungsstarke Hilfsmittel, aber die Einschränkung bei statistischen Analysen wie diesen und den zugehörigen Visualisierungen besteht darin, dass wir noch immer vorab festlegen müssen, welches Phänomen wir untersuchen wollen. Es mag ein wichtiges Phänomen sein, aber wir haben bei konkreten Entwurfsprojekten im realen Leben nie die Gewähr, dass es die wichtigsten Aspekte des Problems erfasst. Manche Aspekte bei der Lösung eines „wicked problem" erweisen sich erst im Verlauf. Auch hier zeigt sich die Schwierigkeit mit parametrischem Design und verwandten Methoden: sie definieren vorab ein starres Schema mit festgelegten Struktur- und Parameterbereichen. In vielen Fällen ist dies für Entwurfs-Komplexitäten viel zu restriktiv.

Der intuitive Vorgang. Wir bekommen eine Vorstellung davon, was notwendig ist, damit ein Computer Intuition entwickelt, wenn wir uns den gedanklichen Prozess bei Designprojekten anschauen. Das herangezogene Beispiel ist formal einigermaßen komplex, aber einfach genug, um den typischen kreativen Akt klar zu illustrieren. Mehrere Plastiken des englischen Bildhauers Antony Gormley bilden mithilfe eines Gitters aus dünnen Stahlstäben den Raum ab, der den menschlichen Körper unmittelbar umgibt. Die Stäbe bilden eine Struktur kleiner, offener Polygone auf der Körperoberfläche, mehrere radiale Stäbe stehen in einheitlicher Länge etwa 50 cm nach außen ab, ein größeres Polygon schließt die äußere Oberfläche als annähernde Kopie der inneren ab. Die Konstruktion einer solchen Plastik dauert mehrere Tage und um zu garantieren, dass alles klappt, kommt es darauf an, die komplexe Geometrie als klares Regelset zu bestimmen.

Der bei diesem Projekt verwendete Algorithmus ist ein explizites Statement der gemeinsamen Intuition von Gormley und seinem Team, kommuniziert und abgeleitet aus den anfänglichen 2D-Modellen. Das Interessanteste an vielen dieser Modelle ist, dass sie sich auf mindestens zwei völlig unterschiedliche Arten interpretieren lassen. Die erste und offensichtlichste geometrische Regel ist die der Flächennormalen: Jeder Stab geht in gleicher Länge an einem Knotenpunkt senkrecht von der Körperfläche ab. So einfach diese Regel klingt, so schwierig wird es in jenen Bereichen, wo Körperflächen

captures the most relevant aspects of the problem. Some aspects always remain to be discovered in solving any "wicked problem." Here, too, is the difficulty faced with parametric design and related methods in that they predefine a fixed schema with a structure and parameter ranges set in advance. In many cases this is far too restrictive for the complexities of design.

The Mechanism of Intuition. We can get some idea of what is needed for a computer to have intuition by looking at the thought process within a design project. The example presented is reasonably complex in form but simple enough to provide a clear view of what may be a typical creative act. A series of sculptures by the British artist Antony Gormley represent the space immediately surrounding the skin of the body by a lattice of thin steel rods. These form a set of small, open polygons on the surface of the body, a number of radial rods extending outward a uniform distance of about 50 cm, and a larger polygon set finishing the outer surface as an approximate offset of the first. As the construction of each sculpture requires many days, it is crucial to determine the nature of the complex geometry as a clear set of rules to ensure that all goes well.

The algorithm used in this project is an explicit statement of intuition that is shared by Gormley and his team, communicated by and derived from initial sketch models. What is most interesting about many of these models is that they may be interpreted in at least two completely different ways. The first, and most obvious geometrical rule is that of surface normals, with each rod extending perpendicular from the surface of the body at a node point and capped off at a uniform distance. While simple to describe, this rule runs into trouble in the regions where surfaces of the body are close to one another so that their normals nearly intersect such as between the legs or between arm and torso. In these regions, intuition suggests that there would be a third set of open polygons, forming a graceful curved surface mid-way between the body's members, which is not produced by the surface normal rule. An entirely different representation can be described by a set of Voronoi cells,[10] each determined by a seed point on the surface of the body. These cells generate the entire geometry, i.e., both sets of open polygons, the radiating linear members, and the curved surfaces between legs, arms, and torso. More crucially, they more accurately convey the original intuition of the piece in that they geometrically describe space rather than lines and intersections.

The relevance of these two sets of rules is their occurrence in the design process. Creative thought in this case should be seen as one of alternating between two modes: implicit sketching and modeling with real, physical instances, and the distillation of clear, abstract, explicit concepts. Both rule sets were developed as intuitions: first, surface normals then Voronoi cells. Crucially, each is capable of generating instances of geometry as real, welded, steel rods, but each is also derived from instances of such geometry, and it is only by the production of a real instance of design that the design can progress from the first concept to the second. The ambiguity inherent in a sketch and our ability to represent a particular, real object in different ways

9   Vgl. Sean Hann: „Inductive Machine Learning of Optimal Modular Structures. Estimating Solutions Using Support Vector Machines", *Artificial Intelligence for Engineering Design, Analysis and Manufacturing* 21 (2007), S. 1–16.

10   The geometry of Voronoi cells is given by polygons enclosing the space that is closer to a given seed point than to any other. Sides of these polygons are line segments bisecting two neighboring points.

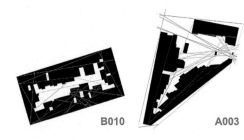

B010　　**A003**

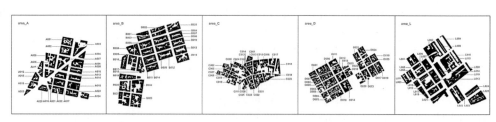

block No.	plan	mcv	mhv	v-value	h-value	fractal dim.	void perim. (m)	void No.	total area	footprint	buildings	built No.	open voids%	vertices	mean height	norm. height variance	land value	floor area factor
C001		47.45414	9.96377	9.96666	9.25691	1.41	138	3	1485.696	0.89418	10	1	0	4	4.204396	0.070973096	3000	2.4
C002		37.9753	6.01226	10.8207	7.8617	1.575	496	6	2808.111	0.64666	19	5	100	6	1.813111	0.285652119	2150	1.4
C003		73.2033	12.1267	10.4137	11.1051	1.484	221	7	2111.885	0.8511	20	2	71.429	6	1.960133	0.049409402	2150	1.6
C004		41.47869	6.62329	13.8226	8.14037	1.483	333	4	2701.386	0.50427	15	4	75	5	1.740534	0.149660392	2150	1.4

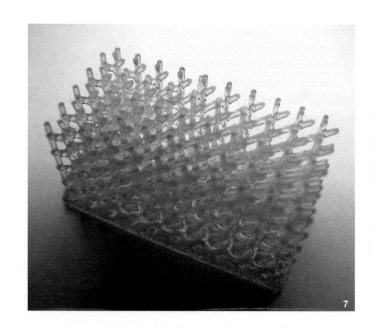

6　Geometrische Merkmale von Gebäudeblöcken in Athen und London in der Quantifizierung des Computers. Geometrical features of blocks of buildings in Athens and London as quantified by the computer. © Anna Laskari
7　Beispiel für eine zelluläre Mikrostruktur; Gesamtbreite ca. 1 cm. Sample of a cellular microstructure; total width approximately 1 cm. © Siavash Haroun Mahvadi, Sean Hanna

nah beieinander liegen, so dass sich die Normalen beinahe schneiden, etwa zwischen den Beinen oder zwischen Arm und Oberkörper. An diesen Stellen kommt man intuitiv auf ein drittes Set offener Polygone, das eine anmutig geschwungene Fläche mittig zwischen den Gliedmaßen bildet, unabhängig von der Flächennormalen-Regel. Eine ganz andere Darstellung erhält man mit Voronoi-Zellen,[10] von denen jede durch einen *seed point* auf der Körperfläche festgelegt ist. Die Zellen generieren die gesamte Geometrie, d. h. beide Sets offener Polygone, die abstehenden linearen Gliedmaßen und die geschwungenen Flächen zwischen Beinen, Armen und Oberkörper. Was noch entscheidender ist, sie transportieren die ursprüngliche Intuition des Werks genauer, da sie geometrisch Raum beschreiben, nicht Linien und Schnittpunkte.

Relevant sind die beiden Regelsets, weil sie im Entwurfsprozess vorkommen. Kreatives Denken sollte in diesem Fall verstanden werden als ein Alternieren zwischen zwei Verfahren: implizites Skizzieren und Modellieren mit realen, physischen Exemplaren und das Destillieren klarer, abstrakter, expliziter Konzepte. Beide Regelsets wurden intuitiv entwickelt: erst die Flächennormale, dann die Voronoi-Zellen. Entscheidend ist, jedes kann geometrische Exemplare in Form von realen, geschweißten Stahlstäben generieren, jedes ist aber auch eine Ableitung solcher Exemplare und nur durch die Produktion eines realen Exemplars kann der Entwurf den Schritt vom ersten Konzept zum zweiten vollziehen. Die in einer Skizze inhärente Uneindeutigkeit und unsere Fähigkeit, ein reales Objekt auf unterschiedliche Weise darzustellen, machen die allmähliche Entwicklung neuer Konzepte möglich, lassen Innovation entstehen und bringen den Entwurf voran. Diese Fähigkeit ist äußerst mysteriös, dennoch kann ein Computer sie wohl besitzen. Das entscheidende Element, das bei vielen unbefriedigenden Definitionen maschineller Intelligenz fehlt, ist die Fähigkeit, Konzepte aufgrund neuer Beobachtungen und Erfahrung radikal zu verändern. Um dies zu leisten, muss der Computer in der Lage sein, eigene, autonome Darstellungen zu generieren.

Autonome Darstellungen. Maschinelles Lernen und verwandte Verfahren können zu einer Art maschineller Intuition führen, wenn dem Computer gestattet wird, eigene Konzepte, eigene Darstellungen der Phänomene zu entwickeln, die er beobachten kann. Insoweit diese auf einer Verallgemeinerung von Daten basieren, die für den Computer verfügbar sind und von ihm bei bestimmten Operationen benutzt werden können, sind sie autonom und stehen – wie unsere Intuition – zur Verfügung, wenn es Entscheidungen zu treffen gilt. Maschinelle

is what allows the creation of new concepts over time, innovation to occur, and the design to move forward. It is this ability that seems most mysterious but is arguably possible for a computer to have. The crucial element missing from many unsatisfactory descriptions of machine intelligence is the ability to radically change concepts based on new observations and experience. However, in order to do this, the computer needs the ability to create its own, autonomous representations.

Autonomous Representation. Machine learning and related techniques can provide a kind of machine intuition by allowing the computer to come up with its own concepts, its own representations of those phenomena which it can observe. To the extent that these are based on a generalization of data available to the computer and can be directly used by it in some course of action, they are autonomous and readily available to inform judgments just as our own intuition. Like our own intuition, it is immediate, and based on implicit generalization from a wealth of previously observed precedents.

One of the more obvious uses lies in the control of adaptive systems, structures, or buildings. The control of natural light is often straightforward, but a prototype façade designed by Marilena Skavara[11] incorporates a pattern generated by cellular automata within the light controlling panels, which provides an interesting complexity from a minimum of actuation devices but places severe restrictions on the amount of control of each panel. By constructing a neural network to survey the angle of the sun and control only the top set of panels on the building, the building is able to learn how to achieve the desired natural lighting schedule in any given room. Structures built by Ryan Mehanna[12] also incorporate neural control systems to learn how to self-correct when pushed off balance by an external force, or to actively right themselves if toppled completely. In this case, the neural network develops a representation particular to the physical geometry and materials and is able to change over time to account for damage or repair. Gennaro Senatore[13] provides sound economic benefits for such an approach with adaptive trusses by demonstrating that a far smaller and lighter structure may be used along with carefully placed actuation devices to achieve the same stiffness as a

> Machine learning and related techniques can provide a kind of machine intuition by allowing the computer to come up with its own concepts, its own representations of those phenomena which it can observe.

---

10 Die Geometrie von Voronoi-Zellen ergibt sich durch Polygone, die den Raum einschließen, der näher an einem bestimmten *seed point* liegt als an allen anderen. Die Seiten dieser Polygone sind Liniensegmente, die zwei benachbarte Punkte schneiden.

11 Marilena Skavara and Sean Hanna, "Adaptive Fa[CA]de," in *Adaptive Architecture 2011* (London, 2011).

12 Ryan Mehanna, "Resilient Structures through Machine Learning and Evolution," in *Proceedings of ACADIA 2013: Adaptive Architecture*, eds. Philip Beesley, Omar Khan and Michael Stacey (Cambridge, 2013).

13 Gennaro Senatore, Philippe Duffour, Sean Hanna et. al. "Adaptive Structures for Whole-Life Energy Savings," in *Journal of the International Association for Shell and Spatial Structures* 52, 170 (2011), pp. 233–240.

In making design decisions
for real buildings, the computer
can employ this same sort of
intuition instead of simulation.
Computational fluid dynamics
are used to understand the effect
of wind on the placement of tall
buildings and their effect on
surrounding air flow, but detailed
calculations are often time
consuming and unsuited to
the early stages of design
where options change rapidly
and rougher estimates are
needed quickly.

Intuition ist, wie die menschliche, unmittelbar und beruht auf der impliziten Verallgemeinerung aus einer Fülle zuvor beobachteter Vorläufer.

Zu den naheliegenden Verwendungen gehört die Steuerung adaptiver Systeme, Strukturen oder Gebäude. Tageslichtmanagement ist grundsätzlich eine unkomplizierte Sache. Eine prototypische Fassade von Marilena Skavara[11] arbeitet jedoch mit einer von zellulären Automaten in den Lichtsteuerpanels erzeugten Struktur, die eine interessante Komplexität bei einem Minimum an Steuerelementen ergibt. Die Steuerbarkeit einzelner Panels ist jedoch stark eingeschränkt. Durch die Konstruktion eines neuronalen Netzwerks, das den Sonneneinfallswinkel registriert und nur die obersten Panels am Gebäude steuert, kann das Gebäude lernen, wie die gewünschte natürliche Beleuchtung in den einzelnen Räumen zu erzielen ist. Auch Bauten von Ryan Mehanna[12] lernen über neuronale Steuerungssysteme, selbständig Korrekturen vorzunehmen, wenn sie durch Einwirkung von außen aus dem Gleichgewicht gebracht wurden, oder sich aktiv zu justieren, wenn sie komplett zusammengebrochen sind. In diesem Fall entwickelt das neuronale Netzwerk eine auf die jeweilige physische Geometrie und die Materialien abgestimmte Darstellung und ist ausreichend anpassungsfähig, um Schäden oder Reparaturmaßnahmen berücksichtigen zu können. Gennaro Senatore[13] sieht in dem Verfahren mit adaptiven Trägern reelle wirtschaftliche Vorteile und demonstriert, dass sich bei einem weitaus kleineren und leichteren Bauwerk in Kombination mit klug platzierten Steuerelementen dieselbe Festigkeit erreichen lässt wie mit einem wesentlich schwereren Trägersystem. Der Betrieb des Systems verbraucht Energie – über die Lebenszeit des Gebäudes jedoch wesentlich weniger, als für die Produktion des statischen Trägerwerks erforderlich ist.

Bei Entwurfsentscheidungen für reale Bauwerke kann der Computer statt Simulation diese Art von Intuition einsetzen. Mit der numerischen Strömungsmechanik lässt sich die Windeinwirkung auf den Standort hoher Gebäude und deren Einfluss auf die Luftströmung verstehen, aber detaillierte Berechnungen sind oft zeitraubend und eignen sich nicht für frühe Entwurfsphasen, wenn sich die Optionen blitzschnell ändern und kurzfristig gröbere Einschätzungen benötigt werden. Was Strömungsprognosen in diesen frühen Phasen betrifft, so trainiert Sam Wilkinsons[14] den Computer mithilfe von Beispie-

11 Vgl. Marilena Skavara/Sean Hanna: „Adaptive Fa[CA]deWZ", in *Adaptive Architecture 2011*, London 2011.

12 Vgl. Ryan Mehanna: „Resilient Structures Through Machine Learning and Evolution", in Philip Beesley, Omar Khan und Michael Stacey (Hg.), *Proceedings of ACADIA 2013. Adaptive Architecture*, Cambridge 2013.

13 Vgl. Gennaro Senatore/Philippe Duffour/Sean Hanna et. al.: „Adaptive Structures for Whole-Life Energy Savings", in *Journal of the International Association for Shell and Spatial Structures* 52, 170 (2011), S. 233–240.

14 Vgl. Samuel Wilkinson/Sean Hanna/Lars Hesselgren/Volker Mueller: „Inductive Aerodynamics", in *Proceedings of eCAADe 2013. Computation an Performance*, Basel 2013.

len realer und hypothetischer Gebäude, den zu erwartenden Strömungseffekt ohne kostspielige Simulation zu prognostizieren. Auf konkreterer Ebene lässt sich die von Design, Nutzung und Heizungssystem abhängige Energieeffizienz eines Gebäudes an den Daten aus dem laufenden Betrieb ablesen, die der Energieausweis liefert. David Hawkins[15] nutzt sie, um ein neuronales Netzwerk auf die Prognose der Energieeffizienz eines Entwurfs und eine Verbesserung von 30 bis 40 Prozent über existierende Benchmark-Strategien zu trainieren. Durch den Ausbau existierender Online-Initiativen wie der Carbon Buzz-Datenbank für Gebäudeenergieeffizienz oder das Angebot einer Remote Computation im Tausch gegen gemeinsame Datennutzung lassen sich theoretisch weitere Beispiele sammeln, um solchen Modellen eine Präzision zu verleihen, die kein Architekt liefern könnte. Mittels Crowdsourcing ließe sich in diesem Sinne vermutlich eine wesentlich breitere und effektivere Intuition in der Maschine entwickeln.

Die oben angeführten Fälle haben immer noch eine relativ klare Vorstellung von Zielen und Optima. Die interessantesten Fälle sind aber vielleicht jene, in denen wir uns nach wie vor auf Gefühle und Ahnungen stützen. Die diffusen Eigenschaften eines Raums werden vom menschlichen Nutzer zweifelsohne empfunden, selbst wenn sie sich nicht mit Worten beschreiben lassen. Wir können ein Stadtviertel anhand der Gestalt der Gebäude von einem anderen unterscheiden, und wenn wir oft nicht genau sagen können, warum, ist es noch schwieriger, es einem Computer klarzumachen. Mithilfe analytischer Tools, die aus Space Syntax, industrieller Bildverarbeitung, Fraktalanalyse und ähnlichen Bereichen stammen, hat Anna Laskaris in Untersuchungen zu den Merkmalen bestimmter Stadtviertel in Athen und London bewiesen, dass der Computer ohne weiteres in der Lage ist, zwischen unterschiedlichen Häuserblocks zu differenzieren, ohne gesagt zu bekommen, welcher welcher ist.[16] Es gibt Grund zu der Annahme, dass solche Darstellungen tatsächlich autonom produziert werden können, ohne Rückgriff auf eine genau definierte und prädeterminierte Reihe von Variablen. Die Ergebnisse aus einigen der erwähnten Analysen deuten darauf hin, dass es weniger darauf ankommt, welche Variablen gewählt, als wie viele verwendet werden; so kann sich der Computer seine eigene Interpretation der Fallbeispiele unabhängig von jeder Anleitung aussuchen.[17] Zudem können

much heavier static truss. Although some energy is required to operate the system, this is far less over the life of the building than the embodied energy required to make the static truss.

In making design decisions for real buildings, the computer can employ this same sort of intuition instead of simulation. Computational fluid dynamics are used to understand the effect of wind on the placement of tall buildings and their effect on surrounding air flow, but detailed calculations are often time consuming and unsuited to the early stages of design, where options change rapidly and rougher estimates are needed quickly. Sam Wilkinson's[14] work on the estimation of air flow in these early stages uses sample sets of real and hypothetical buildings to train the computer to predict the ultimate effect of fluid flow without requiring costly simulation. At a finer level, the energy performance of buildings based on their design, use, and the nature of their heating systems can be seen in true post occupancy data provided by Energy Performance Certificates. These are used by David Hawkins[15] to train a neural network to estimate energy performance in proposed designs and provide an improvement of 30% to 49% over existing benchmark strategies. By extending existing online initiatives such as the Carbon Buzz database of building energy performance or offering remote computation in exchange for shared data, more examples may in theory be collected to further tune such models to a degree of precision that any single designer would be unable to provide. Crowdsourcing may in this sense be employed to develop a much larger and more effective intuition in the machine.

While the cases mentioned above still retain a relatively clear idea of objectives or optima, the most interesting cases are perhaps those in which we still rely on feelings and hunches. The vague qualities of a particular space are clearly experienced by a human user, even if it is impossible to describe these in words. We recognize a certain neighborhood as distinct from another by the shape of its buildings, and even if we often cannot say exactly why, it is even more difficult to make this clear to a computer. Using analytical tools borrowed from Space Syntax, machine vision, fractal analysis and similar areas, Anna Laskari's investigation into the properties of distinct neighborhoods in Athens and London revealed that the computer is easily able to distinguish different characters of the building blocks without being told which is which.[16] There is reason to believe that these sorts of representations can indeed be made autonomously, without recourse to a well-defined and predetermined series of variables. Evidence from some of the above analyses indicates that the particular variables chosen don't matter so much as how many used, and so the computer can select its own way of seeing the examples independently of any guidance.[17]

15   Vgl. David Hawkins/Sung-Min Hong/Rokia Raslan et. al.: „Determinants of Energy USE in UK Higher Education Buildings Using Statistical and Artificial Neural Network Methods", in *International Journal for Sustainable Building Environments* 1 (2012), S. 24–33.

16   Vgl. Anna Laskari/Sean Hanna/Christian Derix: „Urban Identity Through Quantifiable Spatial Attributes. Coherence and Dispersion of Local Identity Through the Automated Comparative Analysis of Building Block Plans", in John S. Gero und Ashok Goel, *Design Computing and Cognition '08*, Heidelberg 2008.

17   Vgl. Sean Hanna: „Design Agents and The Need for High-Dimensional Perception", in *Design Computing and Cognition '10*, London 2011, S. 115–134.

14   See Samuel Wilkinson, Sean Hanna, Lars Hesselgren, and Volker Mueller, "Inductive Aerodynamics," in *Proceedings of eCAADe 2013: Computation and Performance* (Basel, 2013).

15   See David Hawkins, Sung-Min Hong, Rokia Raslan et.al., "Determinants of Energy Use in UK Higher Education Buildings Using Statistical and Artificial Neural Network Methods," in *International Journal for Sustainable Building Environments* 1 (2012), pp. 24–33.

16   See Anna Laskari, Sean Hanna S and Christian Derix, "Urban Identity Through Quantifiable Spatial Attributes: Coherence and Dispersion of Local Identity Through the Automated Comparative Analysis of Building Block Plans," in *Design Computing and Cognition '08*, eds. John S. Gero and Ashok Goel (Heidelberg, 2008).

17   See Sean Hanna, "Design agents and the need for high-dimensional perception," in *Design Computing and Cognition '10* (London, 2011), pp. 115–134.

Furthermore, if multiple agents do so independently, they may still be able to communicate effectively even though they employ different representations.

These sorts of representations are immediately available to the machine and can be used to guide design decisions. They are a means for comparison and classification and thus can serve as measures of similarity to an existing catalogue of designs. It is a small step from here to their use in autonomously producing design proposals, particularly in the context of optimization, in which floor plans, for example, can be reliably produced to contain features from prior precedent.[18] Examples like these are still well within the domain of design we intuitively understand, the same methods of representation, at a much larger scale, make also successful generalizations of the differences in form of entire cities, in which the computer is able to predict the likely geographical location of a city, based only on the form of its street network. It is at this scale that the idea of machine intuition becomes most compelling, as problems can be addressed which lie beyond our normal field of judgment.

Still, it appears dangerous to allow such control to the computer. As with any method of design generation, there is a potential to misunderstand the "wickedness" of the problem, to misrepresent, and to misjudge the complexity hidden within the process, all the more so if the machine is essentially a black box. In a design context the computer may have a kind of intuition, but we would not follow it blindly, just as we don't with our own. The safeguard in place is just that that we apply to our own intuition and that of our peers, as the reflection and criticism that is central to the design process is just as crucial to the idea of intelligent machines. The Turing Test has long been a defining concept in the field of artificial intelligence but its importance lies in its uniqueness as compared to scientific experiments. It states no clear hypothesis or predetermined observations. It does not end in an objective and irrefutable answer. Instead it relies on evaluation and attack from every conceivable point of view available to an intelligent interrogator and so is a clear methodological tie between the sciences of intelligence and design. In the way it is conducted it resembles not so much a scientific experiment as a design crit.

> The safeguard in place is just that that we apply to our own intuition and that of our peers, as the reflection and criticism that is central to the design process is just as crucial to the idea of intelligent machines.

---

unabhängig operierende Multiagenten effektiv kommunizieren, obwohl sie unterschiedliche Darstellungen verwenden.

Solche Darstellungen stehen der Maschine sofort zur Verfügung und können als Leitlinien für Entwurfsentscheidungen dienen. Sie sind ein Vergleichs- und Klassifizierungsinstrument, mit dem sich Ähnlichkeiten mit einem vorhandenen Katalog von Entwürfen quantifizieren lassen. Von hier ist es nur ein kleiner Schritt zur Verwendung in autonom produzierenden Entwurfsvorschlägen, vor allem wenn es um Optimierung geht. Hier können beispielsweise Baupläne mit der Gewähr produziert werden, dass sie Elemente aus vorausgegangenen Entwürfen enthalten.[18] Beispiele wie diese bleiben durchweg im Bereich von Entwürfen, die wir intuitiv verstehen; dieselben Darstellungsmethoden liefern in viel größerem Maßstab auch Verallgemeinerungen der formalen Unterschiede ganzer Städte, hier kann der Computer die wahrscheinliche geografische Lage einer Stadt allein anhand des Straßennetzes berechnen. Bei dieser Größenordnung ist die Vorstellung maschineller Intuition besonders attraktiv, da Probleme angegangen werden können, die unser normales Urteilsvermögen übersteigen.

Dennoch ist es riskant, dem Computer so weitgehend die Kontrolle zu überlassen. Wie bei jeder Methode der Entwurfsgenerierung besteht die Gefahr, dass die „wickedness" eines Problems verkannt, falsch dargestellt und die im Prozess versteckte Komplexität falsch beurteilt wird, vor allem wenn die Maschine im Wesentlichen eine Black Box ist. Bei Entwurfsfragen mag der Computer eine Art Intuition haben, aber wir würden ihr nicht blind folgen – so wenig wie unserer eigenen. Wir sichern uns mit denselben Mitteln ab, mit denen wir unsere eigene Intuition und jene von Kollegen prüfen; die für den Entwurfsprozess so wichtige Reflexion und Kritik ist auch bei der Idee intelligenter Maschinen entscheidend. Der Turing Test ist ein altbewährtes Konzept auf dem Gebiet der künstlichen Intelligenz. Seine Bedeutung liegt jedoch im grundsätzlichen Unterschied zu wissenschaftlichen Experimenten. Der Turing Test gibt keine klare Hypothese, keine prädeterminierten Beobachtungen vor. Er führt nicht zu einem konkreten Ziel oder einer unwiderlegbaren Antwort. Stattdessen beruht er auf Evaluierung und kritischer Prüfung von allen erdenklichen Positionen, die einem intelligenten Fragesteller zur Verfügung stehen. Dies macht ihn eindeutig zu einem methodologischen Bindeglied zwischen Intelligenz- und Designforschung. In seiner Durchführung gleicht er weniger einem wissenschaftlichen Experiment als einer Entwurfskritik.

Übersetzung Marion Kagerer

---

18   See Sean Hanna, "Defining Implicit Objective Functions for Design Problems," in *Proceedings of the Genetic and Evolutionary Computation Conference, GECCO-2007* (New York, 2007).

18   Vgl. Sean Hanna: „Defining Implicit Objective Functions for Design Problems", in *Proceedings of the Genetic and Evolutionary Computation Conference, GECCO-2007*, New York 2007.

8

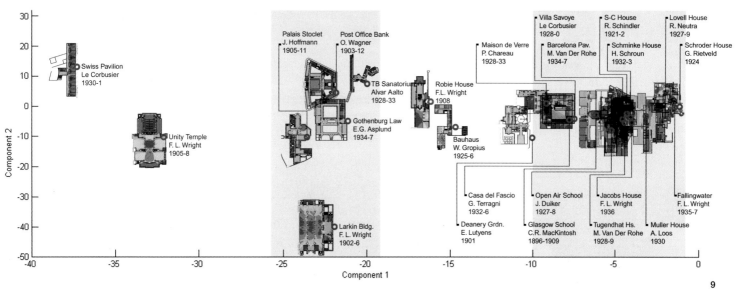

9

8   Zentralitätsmaße des internationalen Schienen- und Straßennetzes in ganz Europa zeigen Zonen an, in denen mit wirtschaftlicher Aktivität zu rechnen ist. Centrality measures of the international rail and road network across Europe indicate zones of likely economic activity. © Tasos Varoudis, Joan Serras, Sean Hanna

9   Architektur-Ikonen des 20. Jahrhunderts von der „Maschine" in einem höherdimensionalen Merkmalsraum „gesehen". Ähnliche Gebäude sind näher beisammen. Iconic 20th century buildings as "seen" by the machine in a higher dimensional feature space. Similar buildings are closer together. © Sean Hanna

1   DJ at Work, 2013 © photodune.net

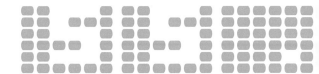

Entwerfer am Mischpult

Neue Instrumente für den
architektonischen Formfindungsprozess

Flinke Hände verschieben Slider und drehen an Knöpfen. Parameter werden definiert und Werte gesetzt. Zugleich generiert sich eine räumliche Struktur, die sich mit jeder Justierung einer Variablen verändert. Formen entwickeln sich im Fluss der Zeit als kontrolliert metastabile Erscheinungen. Angetrieben durch Interaktion strebt ein dreidimensionales Visual in Richtung Selbstorganisation. Das Setup steht. Der Raum bebt. Die Unité d'Habitation als typologische Baseline, darüber ein fein getunter Variablenmix: Der Haus DJ ist am Werk (Abb. 1)!

Designer at the Mixing Console: New Instruments for the Architectural Form-Generation Process. Deft hands are moving the slider and turning knobs. Parameters are defined and values set. At the same time, a spatial structure is generated that changes with each adjustment of a variable. Forms develop as controlled, metastable phenomena. Propelled by interaction, a three-dimensional visual aspires to self-organization. The setup stands. The room is quaking. With the Unité d'Habitation as baseline, accompanied by a nicely tuned mix of variables, the house DJ is at work (fig. 1)!

MARTIN EMMERER

Schon die Arbeiten von Marcel Duchamp und Andy Warhol haben gezeigt, dass der Einsatz neuer Technologien in der Kunst und die damit häufig einhergehende Reproduzierbarkeit von Kunstwerken nicht die Auslöschung des Status des Künstlers als autonomes Schöpfersubjekt bedeuten muss. Der Prozess der Modernisierung des Konzepts des Künstlers als Autor hatte bereits in der ersten Hälfte des 20. Jahrhunderts begonnen. Auch in der Musik kam es durch die zunehmende Technisierung zu grundlegenden Veränderungen. Zahlreiche Musiker legten ihre alten Instrumente beiseite und begannen stattdessen mit Beatboxen, Samplern und Mischpulten zu experimentieren. Wie die Pop Art der 1960er Jahre nahm auch die DJ-Kultur in der zweiten Hälfte des 20. Jahrhunderts einen ambivalenten Platz zwischen der Dekonstruktion und der Bewahrung der Autonomie des Künstlers ein.[1] Durch die Technik des Samplings verschwindet der DJ als Autor hinter seinem elektronischen Equipment und scheint durch seine referenzielle Praxis, also dem maßlosen Umgang mit den Werken anderer Musiker, der Funktion der künstlerischen Autonomie jeden Respekt zu verweigern.[2] Dennoch wird der DJ heute als eigenständiger Künstler wahrgenommen – wenn auch auf einer erweiterten Ebene. Matt Black, Mitbegründer des britischen Musikproduzentenduos Coldcut bemerkte dazu selbstbewusst: „We see ourselves as cut creators, scratching, sampling and mixing is basically the same thing for us as guitarplaying for Johnny Winter or Jeff Healy."[3] Und genau wie bei Gitarrenspielern oder Malern gibt es in jedem Bereich Amateure und Experten: „It's exactly the same with the sampler. Either you use it as a toy or you become a virtuoso."[4]

Zur Festlegung der erforderlichen Größe jedes einzelnen Raumes entwarf Negroponte eine Art digitales Mischpult.

Seit den 1960er Jahren träumt die architektonische Computeravantgarde davon, Formfindungsprozesse auf die Maschine übertragen zu können. Die Idee, Architektur als sich selbst erschaffendes, autopoietisches System zu betrachten, in welches der Mensch nur noch von außen durch das Abstimmen bzw. „mischen" von Parametern eingreift, fasziniert seit den Anfängen des Strukturalismus. Kybernetik, autonome Architektur und Selbstorganisation sind Schlagworte, die in diesem Zusammenhang häufig benutzt werden. Die Beweggründe für solche Visionen sind vielfältig. In jedem Fall spiegelt sich darin die Hoffnung, Computer könnten uns mit atemberaubenden neuen räumlichen Komplexen überraschen – Gebäude generieren, zu deren Schaffung wir niemals selbst in der Lage wären. Für die Verwirklichung dieser Idee wäre so mancher Architekt sogar bereit, etwas von der direkten Kontrolle über die Form abzugeben.

The work of Marcel Duchamp and Andy Warhol already showed that the implementation of new technology in art, along with the often concomitant reproducibility of artwork, need not signify the obliteration of the artist status as autonomous creator-subject. The process of modernizing the concept of the artist as author already began in the first half of the twentieth century. In music, fundamental changes were seen as well, thanks to advancing mechanization. Countless musicians put away their old instruments to instead start experimenting with beat boxes, samples, and mixing consoles. Like the Pop Art of the 1960s, DJ culture assumed an ambivalent position between deconstruction and a desire to retain the autonomy of the artist in the second half of the twentieth century.[1] With the advent of sampling technology, the DJ as author disappeared behind electronic equipment, and through his referential practice, that is, the extortionate approach to treating the works of other musicians, he has turned his back to the function of artistic autonomy in all respects.[2] Nonetheless, today DJs are perceived to be artists in their own right, though in a broader sense. As Matt Black, cofounder of the British music-producer duo Coldcut, self-confidently observed on this topic: "We see ourselves as cut creators, scratching, sampling and mixing is basically the same thing for us as guitarplaying for Johnny Winter or Jeff Healy."[3] And just as with guitar players or painters, there are amateurs and experts in any field: "It's exactly the same with the sampler. Either you use it as a toy or you become a virtuoso."[4]

Since the 1960s, the architectural computer avant-garde has been dreaming of transferring form-generation processes to the machine. The idea of viewing architecture as a self-creating, autopoietic system in which humans intervene only from the outside by determining or "mixing" parameters has fascinated since the very beginnings of structuralism. Cybernetics, autonomous architecture, and self-organization are catchphrases that are frequently used in this context. The motives for such visions are manifold. In any case, they mirror the hope that computers might surprise us with breathtaking new spatial complexes—generating buildings that we would never have been able to achieve on our own. Some architects would even be willing to surrender part of their direct control over form in the name of realizing this idea.

An important contribution to the human-machine debate was made in the year 1967 by the Architecture Machine Group, founded by Nicholas Negroponte at the Massachusetts Institute of Technology. The possibilities offered by the computer as an

1   Vgl. Ulf Poschardt: *DJ Culture*, Hamburg 1995, S. 2.

2   Vgl. ebd., S. 375f.

3   Ebd.

4   Ebd.

1   See Ulf Poschardt, *DJ Culture* (Hamburg, 1995), p. 2.

2   See ibid., pp. 375–76.

3   Ibid.

4   Ibid.

instrument of design composition were to be explored through playful experiments and art installations. The ambitious goal was to develop machines that go beyond simplifying architects' design activity to instead completely take over their tasks. Negroponte was convinced that it would be easier to spark the enthusiasm of architects for innovative technology via the path of practice over that of theory.[5] For example, he felt that designers shouldn't have to learn how to deal with unfamiliar computer codes. Special focus was placed on the development of suitable interfaces. This extended beyond the purely visual interaction between human and machine, as had been seen with Ivan Sutherland's Sketchpad. The planning program URBAN5 of 1967 was already designed in such a way that users could communicate with the computer not only visually but also by voice.[6] "It should be possible to enter the concrete questions, considerations, and directives related to a planning project, such as the optimal position of a house entrance or windows, in the form of a complete data set. The computer would understand the meaning of this data and calculate solutions accordingly, field counter-questions, and even make recommendations as to what should be done next or remembered during the planning process."[7]

In the year 1976, Negroponte developed a computer program called YONA, which reflected the implementation of a design methodology created by Yona Friedman.[8] The design process took place in four consecutive steps. First, the user had to define which rooms were to be allocated to his building, and he could choose from a predefined list of rooms. If a desired room was not available on the list, it could be manually entered by typing in the appropriate specifications. Negroponte developed a kind of digital mixing console for determining the necessary size of each individual room. Aided by slide controls, which spanned an interval of "very small" and "very large," the respective required area could be regulated. When the "area arrow" was moved into a new position, a numerical value was updated next to the slide control. Operating in the background was a "background routine" that calculated the total required floor space and offered a prognosis of building costs. The second step involved inputting the desired accessibility options between the rooms. Each added connection between two rooms caused a proximity matrix to be updated, which clearly showed the user the "links" already defined between specific rooms. The program used the data entered in this way to automatically

Einen wichtigen Beitrag in der Mensch-Maschine Debatte leistete die im Jahre 1967 von Nicholas Negroponte am Massachusetts Institute of Technology gegründete Architecture Machine Group. In spielerischen Experimenten und Kunstinstallationen sollte der Möglichkeitsraum des Computers als Instrument der gestalterischen Komposition erkundet werden. Das ehrgeizige Ziel bestand in der Entwicklung von Maschinen, welche die entwerferische Tätigkeit des Architekten nicht nur erleichtern, sondern sie ihm sogar vollständig abnehmen sollten. Für Negroponte stand fest, dass man Architekten für neuartige Technologien besser über den Weg der Praxis als über jenen der Theorie begeistern konnte.[5] Entwerfer sollten nicht etwa den ungewohnten Umgang mit Computercodes lernen müssen. Ein besonderes Augenmerk galt der Entwicklung geeigneter Schnittstellen. Dabei ging man über eine rein visuelle Interaktion zwischen Mensch und Maschine im Sinne von Ivan Sutherlands Sketchpad hinaus. Bereits bei dem 1967 entwickelten Planungsprogramm URBAN5 sollte der User nicht nur visuell, sondern auch sprachlich mit dem Computer kommunizieren.[6] „Konkrete Fragen, Überlegungen und Anweisungen zu einem Planungsprojekt, etwa nach der optimalen Lage eines Hauseingangs oder der Fenster, sollten in Form von ganzen Sätzen eingegeben werden können. Der Computer würde die Bedeutung dieser Sätze verstehen und dementsprechend Lösungen berechnen, Gegenfragen formulieren und sogar Empfehlungen aussprechen, was im Planungsprozess als nächstes zu tun sei oder nicht vergessen werden dürfte."[7]

Im Jahre 1976 entwickelte Negroponte das Computerprogramm YONA, welches die Implementierung einer von Yona Friedman entwickelten Entwurfsmethodik darstellte.[8] Der Entwurfsprozess erfolgte in vier aufeinanderfolgenden Schritten: Als erstes musste der User definieren, welche Räume in sein Gebäude eingeplant werden sollten. Dazu konnte aus einer vordefinierten Liste von Räumen gewählt werden. War einer der gewünschten Räume nicht darin enthalten, so erfolgte die Eingabe durch das Eintippen der Raumbezeichnung. Zur Festlegung der erforderlichen Größe jedes einzelnen Raumes entwarf Negroponte eine Art digitales Mischpult. Mithilfe von Schiebereglern, welche ein Intervall zwischen „very small" und „very large" aufspannten, konnte der jeweilige Flächenbedarf reguliert werden. Während man den „area arrow" auf eine neue Position verschob, aktualisierte sich ein numerischer Wert neben dem Schieberegler. Im Hintergrund arbeitete eine „Background Routine", welche den Gesamtflächenbedarf berechnete und eine Prognose über die Baukosten lieferte. Im zweiten Schritt erfolgte die Eingabe der gewünschten Zugänglichkeiten der Räume untereinander. Das Hinzufügen jeder Verbindung zwischen zwei Räumen aktualisierte eine Nachbarschaftsmatrix, welche dem User übersichtlich vor Augen führte, zwischen welchen Räumen bereits ein „Link" definiert wurde. Aus den auf diese Weise eingegebenen Daten generierte das Programm automatisch einen zweidimensionalen (planaren) Graphen, dessen Knoten vom User manuell an eine neue Position geschoben werden konnten.

5   See Georg Vrachliotis, *Geregelte Verhältnisse* (Vienna, 2012), pp. 226ff.

6   See Nicholas Negroponte, "Urban5," in *The Architecture Machine* (Cambridge, MA, 1970), pp. 70–93.

7   Vrachliotis, *Geregelte Verhältnisse*, pp. 209–10 (see note 5).

8   See Yona Friedman, *Toward a Scientific Architecture* (Cambridge, MA, 1975).

5   Vgl. Georg Vrachliotis: *Geregelte Verhältnisse*, Wien 2012, S. 226ff.

6   Vgl. Nicholas Negroponte: „Urban5", in: *The Architecture Machine*, Cambridge, MA 1970, S. 70–93.

7   Vrachliotis: *Geregelte Verhältnisse*, S. 209f. (wie Anm. 5).

8   Vgl. Yona Friedman: *Towards a Scientific Architecture*, Cambridge, MA 1975.

Während der Graph auf diese Weise vom User manipuliert wurde, arbeiteten im Hintergrund erneut Computerroutinen, welche das topologische Arrangement evaluierten und dem Benutzer Fehlermeldungen ausgaben, wenn diese für die spätere geometrische Anordnung der Räume Konflikte prognostizierten. Zum damaligen Zeitpunkt beschränkte sich das System auf nur zwei Warnungen: „No single level arrangement can be found for this set of links" und „[n]o arrangement is possible without some enclosed space". Dies bedeutete, dass die räumliche Umsetzung des Arrangements auf Grund der gewünschten Raumbeziehungen entweder auf mehr als einer Ebene erfolgen musste, oder das Einfügen von zusätzlichen Zwischenräumen, wie etwa einem Korridor, notwendig machte. Im Falle einer Erweiterung des Systems durch zusätzliche „Background Routines" könnte in Zukunft die Ausrichtung der Räume, so die Autoren, auch auf Aussicht oder Lichteinfall etc. überprüft werden. Nachdem durch die Manipulation des Graphen durch den User eine befriedigende Dateneingabe erreicht wurde, d.h., vom System keine Fehlermeldungen mehr angezeigt wurden, konnte der dritte Schritt eingeleitet werden: Die Umrechnung der topologischen Struktur in ein Nurbs-Modell. Die Fläche jeder einzelnen Blase entsprach bereits exakt den vorher definierten Wünschen. Im letzten Schritt sollte dem User das zellenartige Gebilde als Unterlage für den manuellen Entwurf der endgültigen Gestalt der Räume dienen. Die auf dem Monitor handgezeichneten Konturen wurden im Hintergrund ebenfalls maschinell überwacht und maßgebliche Abweichungen von den vorher definierten Flächenanforderungen angezeigt. War auch dieser Vorgang vollständig abgeschlossen, konnten die Blasen gelöscht werden.

Im Fazit des Aufsatzes „Architecture-by-Yourself" (1976) von Negroponte und Weinzapfel wird das eben vorgestellte Konzept von den Autoren selbst abwertend als eine „worst-case exercise in man-machine interaction"[9] bezeichnet. Die Architecture Machine Group sah ihr Ziel der Verbindung von Mensch und Maschine im architektonischen Entwurfsprozess durch dieses Experiment offensichtlich nicht erfüllt. Auch für Yona Friedmann war das Ergebnis des Experiments ernüchternd: „My experiment with MIT made me understand a fundamental disadvantage of using computers for design: they are too fast. People have their own thinking speed and computer thinking is too fast, too intransparent for them."[10]

Die Architektur ist nicht die einzige Disziplin, in der man mit komplexen Problemen konfrontiert ist und die nach neuen Wegen der Computerunterstützung sucht. In verschiedenen Bereichen der Wissenschaft, wie etwa der Molekularbiologie, werden bereits Softwaretools entwickelt, mit deren Hilfe es gelingt, die menschliche Intuition zu nutzen, um komplexe kombinatorische Probleme zu lösen. Wo selbst hochentwickelte Computeralgorithmen versagen, brillieren Menschen durch ihre natürlich gegebenen Fähigkeiten. Eines dieser Tools ist FOLD.IT (Abb. 2). Diese Software – kreiert von dem Molekularbiologen David Baker und dem Informatiker und Spiele-Entwickler Zoran Popović – nutzt das herausragende räumliche Vorstellungsvermögen des Menschen für wissenschaftliche Zwecke: Der

generate a two-dimensional (planar) graph whose node could be manually repositioned by the user.

While the graph was being manipulated by the user in this way, computer routines were once again working in the background by evaluating the topological arrangement and providing the user with error messages when it identified potential conflicts for the future geometric layout of the rooms. At the time, the system was limited to two possible warnings: "No single level arrangement can be found for this set of links" and "No arrangement is possible without some enclosed space." This meant that, due to the desired spatial relations, the three-dimensional realization of the arrangement had to play out across more than one level, or that the insertion of additional in-between spaces, such as a corridor, became necessary. According to the authors, in the case of an expansion of the system to include additional background routines, the future alignment of the rooms could also be reviewed with further factors in mind, such as the view or the incidence of light. Once satisfactory data entry was reached after manipulation of the graph by the user, that is, once the system had stopped generating error messages, then the third step could be initiated: the conversion of topological structure into a NURBS model, where the area of each individual bubble was precisely equivalent to the predefined wishes. In the final step, the celllike entity was meant to serve the user as a base for the manual design of the final configuration of the rooms. The hand-drafted contours on the screen were likewise machine-monitored in the background, with any significant deviations from the previously defined area requirements shown. Once this procedure was completely finished, the bubbles were deleted.

In the conclusion of the essay "Architecture-by-Yourself" (1976) by Nicholas Negroponte and Guy Weinzapfel, the authors labeled the concept that they had just introduced as a "worst-case exercise in man-machine interaction."[9] Apparently, the Architecture Machine Group did not consider their objective of connecting human and machine in the architectural design process to have been successfully addressed through this experiment. For Yona Friedmann, the results of the experiment proved sobering as well: "My experiment with MIT made me understand a fundamental disadvantage of using computers for design: they are too fast. People have their own thinking speed and computer thinking is too fast, too intransparent for them."[10]

Architecture is not the only discipline where people are confronted with complex problems and seek to find new, computer-supported paths. Software tools are being developed in

9   Nicholas Negroponte/Guy Weinzapfel: „Architecture-by-Yourself. An Experiment with Computer Graphics for House Design", in: *SIGGRAPH* 76 (1976). S. 74–78.

10   Yona Friedman: „About the Flatwriter", in: *Pro Domo*, Barcelona 2006, S. 137.

9   Nicholas Negroponte and Guy Weinzapfel, "Architecture-by-Yourself: An Experiment with Computer Graphics for House Design," *SIGGRAPH* 76 (1976), pp. 74–78.

10   Yona Friedman, "About the Flatwriter," in *Pro Domo* (Barcelona, 2006), p. 137.

various branches of science, such as in molecular biology, with an aim to successfully harness human intuition in solving complex combinatory problems. In places where even highly evolved computer algorithms fail, humans shine with their naturally born capabilities. One such tool is called FOLD.IT (fig. 2). This software—created by molecular biologist David Baker and computer scientist and game developer Zoran Popović—uses humans' preeminent capacity for spatial perception to achieve scientific ends: the mandate of the "player" is to fold protein chains as optimally as possible. A chaotic initial constellation must be converted into an extremely compact form using the available tools. While the player manipulates the protein via a pleasing graphic interface, its form is continually being analyzed by the program. Problem areas are color-coded, and the player receives verbal feedback from the program, which points out any problems that arise and even offers recommendations that can lead to an improvement of the situation and should not be disregarded in the process. Points are given for each achievement made. This is based on measurement operations that gauge the degree of optimization using certain criteria. Through this graphic and verbal feedback, the system enhances the senses of its users. The immediate visualization of the successes and failures resulting from each operative move hones intuition to facilitate the next correct move.

Playing FOLD.IT is fun. But like any "serious game," the software also has a more earnest background. In molecular biology attempts are being made to bind proteins that exhibit very particular properties, such as CO_2 or the HIV virus species. Whether this is successful is strongly determined by the state of folding, according to Baker. The player approaches reality in an isomorphic manner, which means that inferences may be drawn between the virtual copy and reality. Spatial constellations for which a player receives a high number of points simultaneously represent promising scientific hypotheses. Such proteins are then artificially cultivated and tested in a laboratory. Neither the player nor the computer can satisfactorily solve this complex task alone.

FOLD.IT offers exactly that which Robin M. Hogarth calls a "kind" learning environment in his book *Educating Intuition*. For the psychologist who scientifically explores the strengths and limits of human intuition, the structure of the learning environment is decisive. Hogarth asserts that a broad spectrum of different learning environments exists, ranging from "kind" to "wicked." Kind environments allow us to keenly feel the consequences of our behavior since they provide consistent and clear feedback. Through the consequences of our decisions we learn whether and to what extent the chosen behavior furthers or detracts from our goals.[11] By contrast, "wicked"

Auftrag an den „Spieler" lautet, Proteinketten möglichst optimal zu falten. Eine chaotische Anfangskonstellation muss mithilfe der bereitgestellten Werkzeuge in ein möglichst kompaktes Gebilde umgewandelt werden. Während der Spieler das Protein über ein ansprechendes grafisches Interface manipuliert, wird dessen Gestalt vom Programm laufend analysiert. Problemstellen werden farbig gekennzeichnet und der Spieler erhält ein sprachliches Feedback durch das Programm, welches die auftretenden Probleme benennt und sogar Empfehlungen ausspricht, was zur Verbesserung der Situation getan werden kann und dabei nicht vergessen werden dürfte. Für jeden erzielten Erfolg gibt es Punkte. Dahinter stecken Messoperationen, welche den Grad der Optimiertheit anhand bestimmter Kriterien messen. Durch das grafische und verbale Feedback erweitert das System die Sinne seiner Benutzer. Die unmittelbare Visualisierung der Erfolge und Misserfolge bei jeder Handlung schärft die Intuition für die nächste richtige Handlung.

> Räumliche Konstellationen, für die ein Spieler eine hohe Punktzahl erhält, stellen zugleich vielversprechende wissenschaftliche Hypothesen dar.

FOLD.IT zu spielen macht Spaß. Wie jedes „Serious Game" hat die Software aber auch einen ernsthaften Hintergrund. In der Molekularbiologie sucht man nach Proteinen mit ganz besonderen Fähigkeiten, wie etwa CO_2 oder HIV-Viren an sich zu binden. Ob dies klappt, hängt laut Baker entscheidend von der Faltung ab. Das Modell, in welchem der Spieler agiert, verhält sich isomorph zur Realität, d.h. zwischen virtuellem Abbild und Wirklichkeit sind Rückschlüsse möglich. Räumliche Konstellationen, für die ein Spieler eine hohe Punktzahl erhält, stellen zugleich vielversprechende wissenschaftliche Hypothesen dar. Solche Proteine werden daraufhin im Labor künstlich gezüchtet und getestet. Weder der Spieler noch der Computer könnten diese komplexe Aufgabe allein befriedigend lösen.

FOLD.IT bietet genau das, was Robin M. Hogarth in seinem Buch *Educating Intuition* als „freundliche" Lernumwelt bezeichnet. Für den Psychologen, der die Stärken und Grenzen der menschlichen Intuition wissenschaftlich untersuchte, ist in diesem Zusammenhang die Struktur der Lernumwelt entscheidend. Nach Hogarth existiert eine weite Bandbreite unterschiedlicher Lernumwelten, welche von „freundlich" (kind) bis „boshaft" (wicked) reicht. Freundliche Umwelten lassen uns die Konsequenzen unseres Verhaltens deutlich spüren, indem sie konsistentes und klares Feedback geben. Durch die Konsequenzen unserer Entscheidung lernen wir, ob und in welchem Ausmaß das eingeschlagene Verhalten zieldienlich oder zielhinderlich ist.[11] Im Gegensatz dazu erteilen „boshafte" Umwelten uneindeutige, undeutliche, zu komplexe, zeitlich-verzögerte, oder manchmal auch keine Rückmeldungen. In diesen Umwelten wird nach Hogarth adaptives Lernen erschwert, welches verhaltensorientiert, also erst durch die Wechsel-

11   See Tilmann Betsch, "Wie beeinflussen Routinen das Entscheidungsverhalten," *Psychologische Rundschau* 56, no. 4 (2005), pp. 261–70, esp. p. 267.

11   Vgl. Tilmann Betsch: „Wie beeinflussen Routinen das Entscheidungsverhalten", in: *Psychologische Rundschau* 56,4 (2005), S. 261–270, hier S. 267.

wirkung von Handlung und Erfahrung eintritt. Von etwas, das sich unserer Erkenntnis entzieht, können wir auch nichts lernen.

Die Arbeitsumgebung des architektonischen Entwerfers kann im Allgemeinen als eher „boshaft" bezeichnet werden. Durch den Einsatz von CAD-Programmen und assoziativen Gebäudemodellen (BIM) lassen sich architektonische Gebäudeentwürfe mittlerweile zwar wesentlich komfortabler entwickeln als zuvor auf dem Reißbrett, Feedback über die Qualitäten eines Entwurfs geben diese Softwareumgebungen jedoch nicht. Wie die Proteinfaltungen bei FOLD.IT stellt auch jeder architektonische Entwurf eine Hypothese dar. Ob und wie weit eine Entwurfsvariante den vielfältigen Anforderungen an ein zukünftiges Gebäude entspricht, unterliegt während des gesamten Entwurfsprozesses allein der Urteilskraft des Entwerfers. Durch das Fehlen eines begleitenden Feedbacks wird dem Architekten nichts von der Multitasking-Aufgabe Entwerfen abgenommen. Ob ein Gebäudeentwurf alle gewünschten Parameter erfüllt, ist für den Entwerfer keineswegs offensichtlich. Keiner unserer fünf Sinne ist in der Lage, Merkmale wie Fluchtwegslängen oder Raumgrößen direkt wahrzunehmen. Für jeden zugehörigen Nachweis der Erfüllung solcher Eigenschaften sind viele Handgriffe und teilweise mühsame Hilfskonstruktionen notwendig, die mentale Anstrengung erfordern. Dies raubt dem Entwurfsprozess häufig den „Flow" – jenen erstebenswerten „Zustand der mühelosen Konzentration," der laut dem Psychologen Mihaly Csikszentmihalyi beispielsweise beim Spielen eintritt und „so tief ist, dass [Spielende] ihr Gefühl für die Zeit, für sich selbst und für ihre Probleme verlieren".[12]

> Ob ein Gebäudeentwurf alle gewünschten Parameter erfüllt, ist für den Entwerfer keineswegs offensichtlich. Keiner unserer fünf Sinne ist in der Lage, Merkmale wie Fluchtwegslängen oder Raumgrößen direkt wahrzunehmen.

Architecture Machines 2.0. Zwischen den Problemstellungen des Faltens von Proteinen in der Molekularbiologie und dem Entwerfen von Gebäuden in der Architektur sind Parallelen zu beobachten: In beiden Fällen geht es um Formfindung. Die einzelnen notwendigen Eigenschaften der gesuchten Form sind zwar bekannt, nicht aber die räumliche Konstellation, welche diese befriedigend erfüllt. Ebenso ähneln sich die Strategien zur Unterstützung dieses Prozesses durch den Computer bei YONA und FOLD.IT. In beiden Programmen wird dem menschlichen Entwerfer ein Expertensystem beiseite gestellt, welches dem User ein klares Feedback gibt und deutliche Handlungsempfehlungen ausspricht, welche aus einer zuvor eingegebenen Wissensbasis abgeleitet werden. Während sich FOLD.IT jedoch von Anfang an einer großen und stetig wachsenden Zahl von „Mitspielern" er-

environments offer responses that are ambiguous, vague, too complex, temporally delayed, or sometimes even nonexistent. Hogarth notes that the latter environments impede adaptive learning, first allowing it to occur in a behavior-oriented way through the interplay between action and experience. Indeed, we cannot learn anything from something that eludes cognition.

The working environment of architectural designers may generally be considered quite "wicked." Thanks to the implementation of CAD programs and associative building information modeling (BIM), designs for architectural structures are now much more conveniently developed than in previous times with a drawing board. However, these software environments do not provide feedback on the qualities of a design. As in the case of protein folding in FOLD.IT, each architectural design represents a hypothesis. Whether and to what extent a design variant meets the multiple demands of a future building is solely subject to the designer's power of judgment during the entire design process. Without the accompanying feedback, an architect lacks support for his multitasking design work. In the eyes of the designer, whether a building design fulfills all parameters is not obvious by any stretch. Not one of our five senses is capable of directly perceiving features like room size or the length of emergency escape routes. In order to arrive at each required verification of such properties, many maneuvers and sometimes even laborious auxiliary structures are necessary, all of which entail mental strain. This often robs the design process of its "flow"—that "desirable state of effortless concentration" which, according to psychologist Mihaly Csikszentmihalyi, for instance arises during play and is so "intense that [those engaged in play] lose their sense of time, self, and their problems."[12]

Architecture Machines 2.0. Parallels can be observed between the problem of folding proteins in molecular biology and the design of buildings in architecture: both cases deal with form generation. The individual properties necessary for the sought form have already been established, but the spatial constellation to satisfactorily do them justice has not. By the same token, the computer-based strategies for supporting this process in YONA and FOLD.IT are similar. In both programs the human designer is supported by an expert system which provides the user with clear feedback and makes distinct recommendations for action as derived from a knowledge base entered in the early stages. Yet while FOLD.IT has enjoyed a large and continually growing number of "teammates" from the outset, YONA was considered dissatisfactory early on. This discrepancy cannot be simply chalked up to the limited computing power of the devices available at the time. Nor did the limitations of

12   Mihaly Csikszentmihaly zitiert in Daniel Kahneman: *Schnelles Denken, langsames Denken*, München 2011, S. 56f.

12   Mihaly Csikszentmihalyi quoted in Daniel Kahneman, *Schnelles Denken, langsames Denken* (Munich, 2011), pp. 56–57.

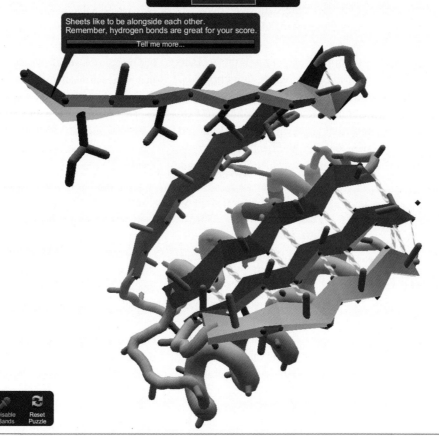

Sheets like to be alongside each other.
Remember, hydrogen bonds are great for your score.

Tell me more...

Shake   Wiggle   Freeze   Remove   Disable   Reset
        All   Protein Bands   Bands   Puzzle

▲ Actions   ► Undo   ► Menu

► Chat - Group   ☺ ✗ auto show
► Chat - Puzzle Levels ☺ ✗ auto show
► Chat - Global   ☺ ✗ auto show

2

freute, galt YONA von Anfang an als gescheitert. Dies lässt sich nicht einfach durch die eingeschränkte Rechenleistung der damals zur Verfügung stehenden Computer erklären. Die Grenzen des Experiments der „Architecture Machine Group" lagen wahrscheinlich auch nicht daran, dass der architektonische Formfindungsprozess einfach zu komplex ist, denn in dieser Hinsicht steht ihm die zellbiologische Aufgabe möglicherweise in nichts nach. Der Hauptgrund, warum das Projekt gescheitert war, lag vielleicht eher an der damals kursierenden Vision, die menschliche Kreativität könne zur Gänze durch eine Künstliche ersetzt werden. Friedman formulierte es klar und deutlich: „[…] the architect or the planner, who has for centuries kept his role as interpreter, has been eliminated from the process."[13] Auch Negroponte äußerte sich zu diesem Vorhaben unmissverständlich: „The architects' primary function, […], will be served well and served best by computers."[14] Bei Negroponte sollte sich der Architekt in der Universalität einer lernenden Maschine auflösen, bei Friedman durch die Partizipation der Bewohner.[15] Dieses absolute Ziel wurde mit Sicherheit verfehlt.

Die Maschine unterstützt den Menschen bei den räumlichen Verschachtelungen diskursiv durch visuelle und sprachliche Hinweise, greift aber niemals gestalterisch in diesen Prozess ein.

Der „Trick" bei FOLD.IT, wie es David Baker formuliert, liegt gerade darin, „dafür zu sorgen, dass sich Mensch und Maschine mit ihren jeweiligen Stärken möglichst gut ergänzen."[16] Keine Seite will die andere ersetzen. „Wir Menschen haben ein besonders gut ausgeprägtes räumliches Vorstellungsvermögen", erklärt David Baker, „wir gucken uns das an und sagen: Aha, da ist ein Loch, und dieser Abschnitt könnte genau hineinpassen. Computer sehen das nicht."[17] Die Maschine unterstützt den Menschen bei den räumlichen Verschachtelungen diskursiv durch visuelle und sprachliche Hinweise, greift aber niemals gestalterisch in diesen Prozess ein. Die Umformungen im Raum übernehmen bei FOLD.IT ausschließlich die Menschen, deren naturgegebene intuitive Fähigkeiten der Brute-Force[18] einer Maschine überlegen sind. Bei YONA sind diese Aufgaben noch nicht ganz so klar verteilt. Außerdem wurde die Komplexität, welche jeden architektonischen Entwurfsprozess auszeichnet, sehr vereinfacht und die einzelnen Handlungsschritte in eine streng lineare Abfolge gebracht – bis hin zu einem Punkt, an dem das System den Prozess nicht mehr umfassend abbilden konnte. Die Komplexität der Architektur ist jedoch irreduzibel. Die von YONA errechneten

the Architecture Machine Group experiment likely result from the architectural form-generation process merely being too complex, for in this respect the cytological problem is conceivably not inferior at all. The main reason why the project failed likely had more to do with the vision circulating at the time, namely, that of human creativity being entirely replaceable by its artificial counterpart. Friedman articulated it very clearly: "… the architect or the planner, who has for centuries kept his role as interpreter, has been eliminated from the process."[13] Negroponte, too, commented on this undertaking in no uncertain terms: "The architects' primary function … will be served well and served best by computers."[14] With Negroponte, the architect was to be dispelled by the universality of a learning machine, and with Friedman, by the participation of the residents.[15] This all-out target was surely missed.

In the case of FOLD.IT, the "trick," as David Baker phrases it, lies in "making sure that human and machine complement one another as well as possible in terms of their respective strengths."[16] Neither side wants to replace the other. "We humans have an exceptionally well developed capacity for spatial perception," explains Baker. "We look at something and say: Aha, that is a hole, and this section could fit in there perfectly. This is something that a computer wouldn't see."[17] The machine discursively supports the human when it comes to the interweaving of space by offering visual and verbal hints, but it never creatively intervenes in the process. With FOLD.IT, space is exclusively reshaped by humans since their natural intuitive abilities are superior to the brute force[18] of a machine. In the case of YONA, these tasks were not quite so clearly allocated. Moreover, the complexity inherent to each architectural design process was strongly simplified and the individual operative steps subjected to a strictly linear sequence—until reaching a point where the system could no longer comprehensively reflect the process. The complexity of architecture is indeed irreducible. In any case, the planning templates calculated by YONA required extensive postprocessing by humans. The developers of FOLD.IT, in turn, have been able to draw on four decades of research on artificial intelligence and complexity. Though the findings have occasionally been sobering, at the same time the awareness of the scientific world has been heightened for the

13 Friedman: *Toward a Scientific Architecture*, S. 9 (wie Anm. 8).

14 Nicholas Negroponte: *Soft Architecture Machines*, Cambridge, MA 1975, S. 1.

15 Vgl. Vrachliotis: *Geregelte Verhältnisse*, S. 227 (wie Anm. 5).

16 David Baker zitiert in Dirk Asendorpf: „Die Nacht-Falter. Computerspiele helfen Forschern, komplexe Probleme zu lösen", in: *Die Zeit*, 27.01.2011, Nr. 5, S. 39.

17 Ebd.

18 Die Brute-Force- oder Exhaustionsmethode ist ein Lösungsverfahren der Informatik, welches auf dem erschöpfenden Ausprobieren aller potentiellen Lösungen beruht.

13 Friedman, *Toward a Scientific Architecture*, p. 9 (see note 8).

14 Nicholas Negroponte, *Soft Architecture Machines* (Cambridge, MA, 1975), p. 1.

15 See Vrachliotis, *Geregelte Verhältnisse*, p. 227 (see note 5).

16 David Baker quoted in Dirk Asendorpf, "Die Nacht-Falter: Computerspiele helfen Forschern, komplexe Probleme zu lösen," *Die Zeit*, January 27, 2011, no. 5, p. 39.

17 Ibid.

18 The "brute force" or "proof by exhaustion" method is a solution methodology used in computer science that is based on the exhaustive testing of all potential solutions.

astounding intuitive capabilities of humans (e.g., when applied to space), which to date have not been successfully imitated by technology. By contrast, the 1960s were characterized by a strong belief and high expectations in computer technology. The pioneering ideas of the Architecture Machine Group were radical and revolutionary. Our comparison with FOLD.IT has shown that some of the approaches developed back then still have topicality today. If taken further in a conceptual sense with a view to the current level of research and technology, today these approaches could serve to inspire a new generation of collaborative software tools for supporting the architectural design process. This process could also benefit from an intermeshing of human and machine, that is, from intuitive action and rational assessment methods. In this respect, the positive and playful approach taken by FOLD.IT may prove to be extremely useful.

A concrete experiment is found in ARCHILL.ES, a custom-made software environment for architectural design conceptualized by the author. The rationale behind ARCHILL.ES is simple: the spatial development of a building should be manually carried out by the human designer, whose outstanding capacity for spatial perception and his inborn intuitive capabilities flow into the design. In carrying out this pursuit, he is provided with a "kind" environment where the potentials of the computer are utilized. While the designer manipulates the spatial arrangement via an easy-to-use graphic interface, in the background algorithms are running in parallel (so-called "architecture routines"). The latter monitor this process and constantly provide the designer with differentiated feedback on whether the many project objectives have already been met and to what extent. This information is given both visually and verbally.

A wide range of design parameters can be machine-monitored in this way, such as those described in space- and function-related programs. But there is a hurdle to be overcome initially: still today design tasks are generally drafted in natural language. Here the specifications of individual rooms and their reciprocal relationships are usually expressed using terminology. The desire to create a "well-oriented" apartment or the claim that Room A should be situated "proximate" to Room B reflect seemingly clear planning measures from a human perspective. We associate the term "orientation" with a certain conceptual idea, as we do the term "proximity." Yet upon closer examination, even these terms prove to be exceedingly vague. If architectural design qualities are to be monitored by computers, then it is no longer enough to have only a rough idea of the meaning of the terms being employed. After all, it is necessary to supply the computer with an exact set of guidelines (i.e., an algorithm) which details how each of the features designated by the terms can be imposed. In order to convert the "pre-scripts" that are still today only readable by

Planungsvorlagen verlangten in jedem Fall nach einer umfassenden Nachbearbeitung durch den Menschen. Die Entwickler von FOLD.IT können auf vier Jahrzehnte der Erforschung von künstlicher Intelligenz und Komplexität zurückgreifen, deren Erkenntnisse zwar teilweise ernüchternd waren, zugleich aber auch die Aufmerksamkeit der Wissenschaft für die verblüffenden, technisch bis heute nicht imitierbaren, intuitiven Fähigkeiten des Menschen (beispielsweise im Umgang mit Raum) schärften. Die 1960er Jahre dagegen waren von einem starken Glauben und höchsten Erwartungen an die Computertechnologie geprägt. Die bahnbrechenden Ideen der „Architecture Machine Group" waren radikal und revolutionär. Der Vergleich mit FOLD.IT hat gezeigt, dass einige der damals entwickelten Ansätze noch heute Aktualität aufweisen. Weitergedacht und mit dem heutigen Stand der Forschung und Technik im Einklang können diese gegenwärtig einen inspirierenden Einfluss auf die Entwicklung einer neuartigen Generation kollaborativer Softwaretools zur Unterstützung des architektonischen Entwurfsprozesses ausüben. Auch der architektonische Gestaltungsprozess kann vom Ineinandergreifen von Mensch und Maschine, d.h., von intuitivem Handeln und rationalen Beurteilungsverfahren, profitieren. Der positive und spielerische Ansatz von FOLD.IT kann sich dabei als äußerst nützlich erweisen.

Einen konkreten Versuch stellt ARCHILL.ES, eine vom Autor konzipierte, für den architektonischen Entwurf maßgeschneiderte Softwareumgebung, dar. Das Grundprinzip von ARCHILL.ES ist einfach: Die räumliche Entwicklung eines Gebäudes soll manuell durch den menschlichen Entwerfer erfolgen, der sein herausragendes räumliches Vorstellungsvermögen und seine naturgegebenen intuitiven Fähigkeiten in den Entwurf einfließen lässt. Zur Ausführung dieser Tätigkeit wird ihm eine „freundliche" Umgebung geboten. Hierzu werden die Potenziale des Computers genutzt: Während der Entwerfer das räumliche Arrangement über ein einfach zu bedienendes grafisches Interface manipuliert, arbeiten im Hintergrund parallel dazu Algorithmen (sog. Architektur-Routinen), welche diesen Vorgang überwachen und dem Entwerfer laufend ein differenziertes Feedback darüber geben, ob und wie weit die zahlreichen Zielvorstellungen bereits erfüllt sind. Die Hinweise erfolgen sowohl visuell als auch sprachlich.

Eine Vielzahl von Entwurfsparametern, wie sie beispielsweise in Raum- und Funktionsprogrammen beschrieben werden, können auf diese Weise maschinell überwacht werden. Dazu muss zunächst aber eine Hürde überwunden werden: Entwurfsaufgaben werden bis heute üblicherweise in natürlicher Sprache verfasst. Die Spezifikationen der einzelnen Räume und deren Beziehungen untereinander erfolgen dabei in der Regel durch Begriffe. Der Wunsch nach einer „gut orientierten" Wohnung oder die Forderung, dass Raum A „nahe" Raum B situiert sein soll, stellen für Menschen scheinbar eindeutige Planungsvorgaben dar. Wir verbinden mit dem Begriff „Orientierung" genauso eine bestimmte Vorstellung, wie mit der „Nähe". Bei genauerer Betrachtung sind selbst diese Begriffe jedoch äußerst vage. Sollen architektonische Entwurfsqualitäten von Computern überwacht werden, genügt es nicht mehr, eine ungefähre Vorstellung von der Bedeutung der verwendeten Begriffe zu besitzen. Dem Computer muss schließlich eine exakte Handlungsanleitung (i.e., ein Algorithmus) bereitgestellt werden, die beschreibt, wie jedes der durch die Begriffe bezeichneten Merkmale erhoben werden kann. Um die bis heute nur von Menschen lesbaren Vor-Schriften in von Computern ausführbare Programme umzuwandeln, ist es nötig,

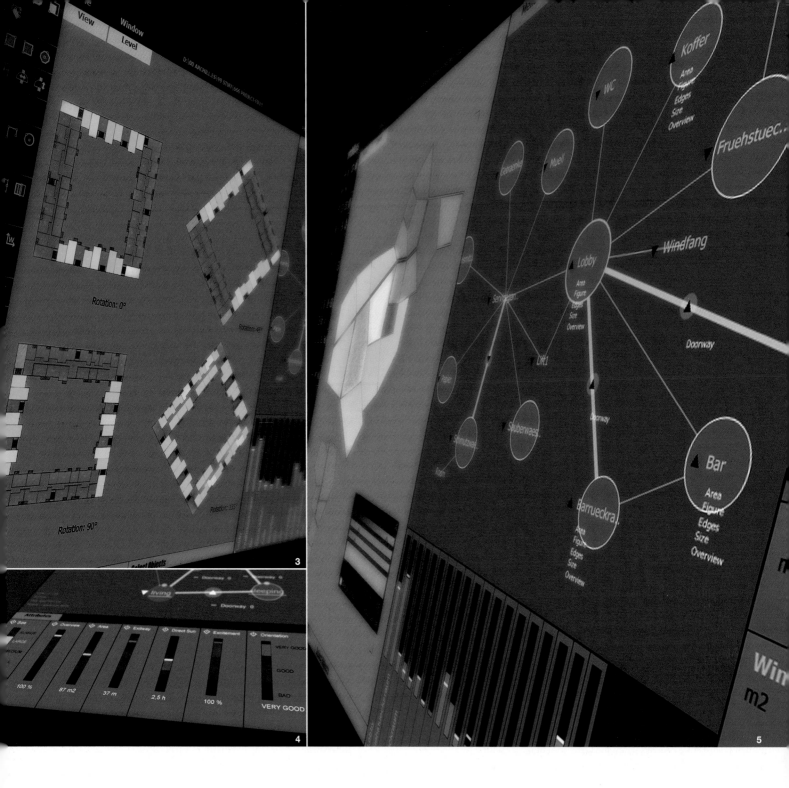

3   Entwurfstool **Design tool** ARCHILL.ES: Analyse einer Wohnanlage **Analysis of a housing complex**, 2013 © Martin Emmerer

4   Entwurfstool **Design tool** ARCHILL.ES: Parameter-Setup am Mischpult **Parameter setup at the mixing desk**, 2013 © Martin Emmerer

5   Entwurfstool **Design tool** ARCHILL.ES: Topologie einer Entwurfsaufgabe **Topology of a design job**, 2013 © Martin Emmerer

humans into programs run by computers, it is necessary to pay attention to the relationship between terms and objects. A machine-based counterpart needs to be posited vis-à-vis the mysterious "associative bond"[19] that allows us to recognize the qualities of a building design.

To this end, the author developed the concept of *algorithmic explication*. First it is necessary to translate words that in everyday language are often used in a vague manner into unequivocal terms. When applying this method, which is commonly used in empirical science, a vague term undergoes a semantic analysis in that as many of its linguistic indicators are listed as possible. In the case of "well-oriented" living space, a simplified process might play out as follows: "a room with one or more windows, which is at least partially oriented to a southern or western direction." Here it is possible, but not necessarily imperative, to take into account already existing scientific studies of the term. It is surely possible to define "well-oriented" in a different or more elaborate way, but the semantic analysis of terms is less concerned with finding the "only correct" method, than with reaching an intersubjective agreement on as plausible of a definition as possible. After completing a thorough semantic analysis, it is time to operationalize the term by furnishing particulars about how the indicators of the term in question, as listed in the analytical definition (semantic analysis), can be specified concrete terms. In our example of "well-oriented" space, this would entail verifying whether this particular room has at least one window with an axis that deviates less than 90 degrees from the geographic south or west direction. The previously vague idea of the concept of "well-oriented" living space has now been turned into a measureable and calculable specification. Implementing this process in algorithm form to address the property "orientation" in a suitable digital building model is now no longer a real challenge. After completing these steps, a computer, for example, would be in a position to identify all "well-oriented" apartments in a sophisticated housing complex in a matter of seconds. By repeatedly carrying out this technique to address all terms that might be enlisted on an everyday basis to describe design tasks, a vocabulary is built which is not only associated with intersubjective concepts, but which also fosters a dialogue with the machine. Such an explicit vocabulary is used in the computer program ARCHILL.ES (figs. 3–5).

In this environment the design process is configured as follows: the user starts out by modeling the topological structure of the design task in graph form, with the nodes and edges being "weighted" with various desired properties (fig. 5). This is carried out by a docking of "property modules." The significance of the spatial and relational properties is explicitly explained in a brief text, which contains not only a terminological definition

der Beziehung zwischen Begriffen und Objekten Aufmerksamkeit zu schenken. Dem geheimnisvollen „Band der Assoziation",[19] welches es uns ermöglicht, Qualitäten eines Gebäudeentwurfes zu erkennen, wäre ein maschinelles Pendant gegenüberzusetzen.

Dazu wurde vom Autor das Konzept der *Algorithmischen Explikation* entwickelt. Zunächst ist es notwendig, die häufig unscharfen Begriffe der Alltagssprache in deutliche Begriffe umzuwandeln. Bei diesem in den empirischen Wissenschaften gängigen Vorgang wird ein vager Begriff einer Bedeutungsanalyse unterzogen, indem möglichst alle seiner sprachlichen Indikatoren aufgezählt werden. Im Falle eines „gut orientierten" Wohnraums könnte das vereinfacht etwa so aussehen: „Ein Raum mit mindestens einem Fenster, welches zumindest anteilig in Richtung Süden oder Westen orientiert ist." Eine Berücksichtigung bereits vorliegender wissenschaftlicher Auseinandersetzungen mit dem Begriff ist dabei möglich, aber nicht zwingend. Es ist sicherlich möglich, „gut orientiert" anders oder ausführlicher zu definieren. Bei der Bedeutungsanalyse von Begriffen geht es aber weniger darum, die „einzig richtige" Methode zu finden, sondern vielmehr um die intersubjektive Vereinbarung einer möglichst plausiblen Definition. Nach einer vollständigen Bedeutungsanalyse kann die Operationalisierung des Begriffes erfolgen, indem Angaben gemacht werden, wie die in der analytischen Definition (Bedeutungsanalyse) aufgezählten Indikatoren des betrachteten Begriffs konkret erfasst werden können. In unserem Beispiel des „gut orientierten" Raumes würde dies bedeuten, zu überprüfen, ob der betreffende Raum mindestens ein Fenster aufweist, dessen Achse um weniger als 90° von der geografischen Süd- bzw. Westrichtung abweicht. Die zuvor vage Vorstellung des Begriffs von „gut orientierten" Wohnräumen ist nun in eine mess- und berechenbare Angabe umgewandelt worden. Die Implementierung dieses Vorgangs in einen Algorithmus zur Erfassung des Merkmals „Orientierung" in einem geeigneten digitalen Gebäudemodell stellt jetzt keine große Schwierigkeit mehr dar. Danach ist ein Computer beispielsweise in der Lage, in Sekundenbruchteilen alle „gut orientierten" Wohnungen einer komplexen Wohnanlage zu identifizieren. Durch die wiederholte Anwendung dieses Verfahrens auf möglichst viele Begriffe, welche alltäglich zur Beschreibung von Entwurfsaufgaben herangezogen werden, entsteht ein Vokabular, welches nicht nur an intersubjektive Vorstellungen geknüpft ist, sondern auch einen Dialog mit der Maschine erlaubt. Ein solches explizites Vokabular wird vom Computerprogramm ARCHILL.ES genutzt (Abb. 3–5).

Der Entwurfsprozess gestaltet sich in dieser Umgebung wie folgt: Der Benutzer modelliert zunächst die topologische Struktur der Entwurfsaufgabe

> Das differenzierte Setup der Variablen erfolgt wie über ein spezielles Mischpult, auf dem die gewünschte Ausprägung jedes Merkmals vom Benutzer über Schieberegler eingestellt wird.

19 Ferdinand de Saussure, *Course in General Linguistics* (1959; repr., New York, 2011), p. 66.

19 Ferdinand de Saussure: *Grundfragen der allgemeinen Sprachwissenschaft*, Berlin 2001, S. 77.

als Graph, dessen Knoten und Kanten durch diverse Wunschmerkmale „gewichtet" werden (Abb. 5). Dies erfolgt durch das Andocken von „Merkmalsmodulen". Die Bedeutung der vom Programm zur Verfügung gestellten Raum- und Beziehungsmerkmale wird durch einen Kurztext explizit erklärt. Dieser beinhaltet nicht nur eine exakte begriffliche Definition (Bedeutungsanalyse), sondern erklärt auch wie und auf welchem Skalenniveau das Merkmal im räumlichen Entwurf erfasst wird. Das differenzierte Setup der Variablen erfolgt wie über ein spezielles Mischpult, auf dem die gewünschte Ausprägung jedes Merkmals vom Benutzer über Schieberegler eingestellt wird (Abb. 4). Die Skalen qualitativer Merkmale setzen sich aus begrifflichen Kategorien zusammen, während Schieberegler für quantitative Merkmale numerische Intervalle repräsentieren. Während das Merkmalsmodul „Orientierung" beispielsweise nur die Wahl zwischen „sehr gut", „gut" und „schlecht" erlaubt, kann beim Modul „Raumgröße" die gewünschte Zahl der Quadratmeter durch Verschieben des Reglers beliebig festgesetzt werden. Wenn das Setup vollständig ist, kann mit dem räumlichen Entwurf begonnen werden. Die Konturen der gewünschten Räume werden gezeichnet und auf einer oder mehreren Ebenen angeordnet. Ebenso werden wichtige architektonische Elemente wie Türen, Fenster, vertikale Erschließungselemente etc. platziert. Hinter dem sehr einfach zu bedienenden Zeichenprogramm steckt ein radikal vereinfachtes *Building Information Model*, gerade detailliert genug, um den vergleichsweise niederen Detailgrad eines üblichen Wettbewerbsbeitrags abbilden zu können. Die klare Trennung von Topologie und Geometrie ist entscheidend. Der räumliche Entwurf und die vorweg modellierte topologische Struktur der Entwurfsaufgabe bestehen parallel nebeneinander. Die Knotenpunkte des Graphen werden über die Raumbezeichnungen mit ihren geometrischen Repräsentanten im Entwurf synchronisiert und die Abweichungen von den vorab definierten Zielvorstellungen (durch sog. Architektur-Routinen) berechnet. Die Ergebnisse werden durch Farben dargestellt. Abbildung 3 zeigt vier Varianten derselben Wohnanlage. Für jede Wohneinheit wurde der Status „gut orientiert" definiert. Der Plan ist genordet. Durch die Rotation des Gesamtbaukörpers um jeweils 45% verändert sich die Orientierung der einzelnen Wohneinheiten. Die Farbnuancen geben dem Entwerfer Auskunft über den Grad der Erfüllung des zuvor formulierten Zieles. Dabei steht Rot für „sehr gute", Grün für „gute" und Blau für eher „schlechte" Orientierung. Die farbige Visualisierung stellt ein eindeutiges und unmittelbares Feedback dar und erlaubt es dem Entwerfer, intuitiv und planerisch gezielt auf mögliche Schwachpunkte seines Entwurfes zu reagieren bzw. die beste Variante auszuwählen.

Die Software stellt bereits ein Basisrepertoire implementierter Merkmale zur Modellierung von Entwurfsaufgaben zur Verfügung. Dieses soll laufend erweitert werden. Als Umschlagplatz der Merkmalsmodule wird die

Durch die Verwendung expliziter Begriffe bei der Beschreibung von Entwurfsparametern werden klare Vereinbarungen getroffen. Die Maschine übernimmt in der Folge die Funktion eines Schiedsrichters.

(semiotic analysis) but also explanations of how and on which level of measurement the property is covered. The differentiated setup of variables ensues as if using a special mixing console with which the user adjusts the desired manifestation of each property via slide controls (fig. 4). The scales of qualitative properties are made up of terminological categories, while the slide controls for quantitative properties represent numerical intervals. While for instance the property module "orientation" only permits a choice between "very good," "good," and "poor," the module "room size" allows the desired number of square meters to be stipulated at will by sliding the controls. When the setup is completed, the spatial design can begin. The contours of the desired rooms are drawn and arranged across one or more levels. Moreover, important architectural elements are placed, like doors, windows, vertical access elements, et cetera. Operating in the background of this very easy-to-use drawing program is a radically simplified building information model that is just detailed enough to be able to portray the comparatively low degree of detail needed for a typical competition proposal. The clear separation between topology and geometry is decisive. Spatial design and the topological structure of the design task modeled in advance exist in parallel. The nodal points in the graph are synchronized with their geometric representatives in the design using the room specifications, and deviations from the previously defined objectives (through the so-called "architecture routines") are calculated. The results are presented using different colors. Figure 3 shows four variants of the same housing complex. For each housing unit the status "well-oriented" has been defined. The plan is geared toward the north. In rotating the entire building structure by 45 percent respectively, the orientation of the individual housing units is shifted. Shades of color provide the designer with information about the degree to which the preformulated goal has been fulfilled. Here red stands for "very good," green for "good," and blue for a rather "poor" orientation. The colorful visualization represents clear and immediate feedback and makes it possible for the designer to take an intuitive and planning-related approach to targeting potential weak points in his design and to thus react or select the best variant.

The software already places at one's disposal a basic repertoire of implemented properties for modeling design tasks. The aim is to continually expand this repertoire. The platform WWW.ARCHILL.ES is designed to serve as a reloading point for the property modules. Newly developed modules can be downloaded like apps for testing. The plan for the future is to make it possible for ARCHILL.ES users to implement their own property modules, which can then be loaded by the system as plug-ins. This will enable the vocabulary of the system to expand much more quickly and thus allow design tasks to be modeled in an increasingly differentiated way. The know-how of experts from different specialty fields could automatically flow into the design process. This would allow a use of the software in a teaching context to assume a highly experimental and playful character. The fact that the tool is also designed to handle the modeling of differentiated suitability functions of building designs equally opens up new possibilities in the research of generative design strategies. Modules allowing the computer to actively intervene in form-generation processes are also conceivable here.

To a certain extent, designing in such an environment is akin to a game. Like on any gameboard, here, too, "an absolute and peculiar order reigns."[20] Although the rules of the game are clearly defined, they are set by the slider on the mixing console. By using explicit terms in describing design parameters, clear agreements are reached. The machine subsequently takes on the role of referee. If a room is colored blue, for example, then it is "poorly oriented." Whoever wants to keep this up for debate is going against the laws inherent to the game. While the "player" tries to arrive at red color fields and achieve high scores, serious architecure is created step by step. "The noblest games, such as chess, are those that organize a combinatory system of places in a pure *spatium* infinitely deeper than the real extension of the chessboard and the imaginary extension of each piece."[21] Just as constructivism saw architecture as the "mother of all arts," after the digital turn the act of designing buildings might now have a chance at becoming the "noblest of all games." And the architect, or homo faber, would become the homo ludens.[22] So be house DJs and accept the support of machines. Develop routines and "play" with new instruments—or, to paraphrase Beastie Boy Mike D., "let the computer rock!"[23]

Translation Dawn Michelle d'Atri

Plattform WWW.ARCHILL.ES dienen. Neu entwickelte Merkmalsmodule können hier wie Apps heruntergeladen und getestet werden. Es ist geplant, den Benutzern von ARCHILL.ES in Zukunft auch die Implementierung eigener Merkmalsmodule zu ermöglichen, welche dann als Plug-ins in das System geladen werden können. Auf diese Weise kann sich das Vokabular des Systems rascher erweitern und Entwurfsaufgaben können dadurch immer differenzierter modelliert werden. Experten unterschiedlicher Fachrichtungen können ihr Know-how automatisiert in den Entwurfprozess einfließen lassen. Dadurch kann die Anwendung auch im Bereich der Lehre sehr experimentellen und spielerischen Charakter annehmen. Da es sich bei dem Tool gleichzeitig um ein Werkzeug zur Modellierung differenzierter Fitnessfunktionen von Gebäudeentwürfen handelt, eröffnet dies ebenso neue Möglichkeiten im Bereich der Erforschung generativer Entwurfsstrategien. Dabei sind auch Module zum aktiven Eingriff des Computers in den Formfindungsprozess denkbar.

In gewisser Weise gleicht das Entwerfen in einer solchen Umgebung einem Spiel. Wie auf jedem Spielbrett herrscht auch hier eine „eigene und unbedingte Ordnung".[20] Die Spielregeln sind klar definiert, sie werden über die Slider am Mischpult aufgestellt. Durch die Verwendung expliziter Begriffe bei der Beschreibung von Entwurfsparametern werden klare Vereinbarungen getroffen. Die Maschine übernimmt in der Folge die Funktion eines Schiedsrichters. Färbt sich ein Raum blau, ist er zum Beispiel „schlecht orientiert". Wer darüber noch diskutieren will, bricht die inneren Gesetze des Spiels. Während der „Spieler" roten Farbflächen und High-Scores nacheifert, entsteht Schritt für Schritt ernsthafte Architektur. „Die nobelsten Spiele wie Schach bilden eine Kombinatorik von Orten in einem reinen Spatium, das unendlich viel tiefer ist als das reale Ausmaß des Schachbretts und die imaginäre Ausdehnung jeder Figur."[21] So wie dem Konstruktivismus die Architektur als „Mutter aller Künste" galt, hätte der Entwurf von Gebäuden nach dem *Digital Turn* vielleicht nun die Chance, auch noch zum „nobelsten aller Spiele" zu werden. Und der Architekt, der homo faber, wird zum homo ludens.[22] Seid Haus DJs und nehmt die Hilfe der Maschine an. Entwickelt Routinen und „spielt" auf neuen Intrumenten – oder in den Worten des Beastie Boy Mike D: „Let the Computer rock!"[23]

20 See Johan Huizinga, *Homo Ludens: A Study of the Play Element in Culture* (London, 1955), p. 10.

21 Charles J. Stivale, "Appendix: Deleuze's 'How Do We Recognize Structuralism?,'" *The Two-Fold Thought of Deleuze and Guattari: Intersections and Animations* (New York, 1998), p. 264.

22 Huizinga, *Homo Ludens*, p. ix (see note 20).

23 Diamond Michael aka "Mike D.," cited in Thomas Hüetlin, "Drei Jungs im Müll," *Der Spiegel*, August 1, 1994, p. 140.

20 Vgl. Johan Huizinga: *Homo Ludens. Vom Ursprung der Kultur im Spiel*, Hamburg 2011, S. 19.

21 Gilles Deleuze: *Woran erkennt man den Strukturalismus*, Berlin 1992, S. 19.

22 Vgl. Huizinga: *Homo Ludens*, S. 1 (wie Anm. 20).

23 Diamond Michael aka „Mike D." zitiert nach: Thomas Hüetlin: „Drei Jungs im Müll", in: *Der Spiegel*, 1.8.1994, S. 140.

1 Montage des Gitters aus gebogenem Bambus Installation of the secondary structure made of bent bamboo, Architekten architects. Kristof Crolla & Adam Fingrut, 2012
© Kevin Ng for LEAD

1

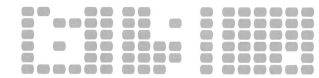

Golden Moon: Digital Control Meets Crafts- manship

Computational tools increase the architect's control over the construction process. Yet often the "computability = constructability" equation seems inadequate, especially in contexts where the available craftsmanship is inept, or simply not complementary to requested levels of complexity easily generated in virtual environments.

Golden Moon. Digitale Kontrolle trifft Handwerkskunst. Computertools erhöhen die Kontrolle des Architekten über den Bauprozess. Dennoch trifft die Gleichung „Berechenbarkeit = Baubarkeit" in der Realität meist nicht zu. Vor allem dort nicht, wo das notwendige handwerkliche Können fehlt oder einfach nicht dem Komplexitätsniveau gerecht wird, das in virtuellen Environments so leicht zu generieren ist.

KRISTOF CROLLA

Where craftsmanship is inherently capable of dealing with serendipitous occurrences during construction, it is the intolerance of computational worlds towards unpredictability that gradually pushes the role of skilled labor aside.[1] Still, an opportunity is presented by the equation's dissociation from reality. Rather than rendering skilled building trades obsolete,[2] if strategically integrated into the construction process, computational power can be combined with unanticipated events during construction, and bring an unpredictable, yet unique added value to the final work. This case study—Hong Kong's "Golden Moon" 2012 Mid-Autumn Festival Lantern Wonderland by the Laboratory for Explorative Architecture & Design Ltd. (LEAD)—explores how top-down, parametric design techniques can be combined productively with a highly intuitive and century old regional craft, currently only surviving in the Cantonese region of Southern China:[3] the use of bamboo scaffolding.

The Mid-Autumn Festival is one of the most important Chinese festivals taking place in Hong Kong. The celebrations include an annual design competition to design and build a "Lantern Wonderland" as the architectural highlight of the festival. The 2012 winning entry "Golden Moon" conceptually revisits the notion of a Chinese lantern and establishes a direct link to the legend of Chang'e (嫦娥), the Moon Goddess of Immortality.[4] A lightweight steel geodesic dome forms the pavilion's primary structure and is the basis for a computer-generated grid wrapped around it. This grid is materialized through a secondary bamboo structure, which was then clad with stretch fabric flames, all lit up by animated LED lights (fig. 8). Only a period of three weeks was available for prefabrication and a mere eleven days for onsite construction were permitted.

> A light-weight steel geodesic dome forms the pavilion's primary structure and is the basis for a computer-generated grid wrapped around it.

Components. Steel Geodesic Dome. The primary structure is formed by a freestanding twenty-meter diameter steel geodesic dome which gives both form and stability to the installation and which is mounted onto a steel base structure. On top of this base structure a circular concrete slab is placed to provide stability, since no anchoring in

Und wo das Handwerk grundsätzlich in der Lage ist, mit dem beim Bauen sich ergebenden glücklichen Fügungen umzugehen, dort verdrängt wiederum die in der Welt des Rechnens herrschende Intoleranz gegenüber dem Unvorhersehbaren zunehmend die handwerklichen Fähigkeiten.[1] Allerdings ergeben sich aus der Realitätsferne der obigen Gleichung durchaus auch Möglichkeiten. Statt die traditionellen Bauhandwerke durch strategische Integration in den Konstruktionsprozess obsolet zu machen,[2] kann man die rechnerischen Möglichkeiten auch mit unvorhersehbaren Ereignissen beim Bauen verbinden und so dem fertigen Bauwerk einen im Voraus nicht zu berechnenden Mehrwert verleihen. Die vorliegende Fallstudie über den vom Laboratory for Explorative Architecture & Design Ltd. (LEAD) entworfenen „Golden Moon", das Laternenwunderland für das Hongkonger Mittherbstfest 2012, zeigt, wie sich parametrische Top-Down-Entwurfstechniken produktiv mit einem hochgradig intuitiven jahrhundertealten regionalen Handwerk verbinden lassen, das nur noch in der südchinesischen Region Kanton existiert:[3] dem Bambusgerüstbau.

Das Mittherbstfest ist eines der wichtigsten chinesischen Feste in Hongkong. Teil der Feierlichkeiten ist ein jährlich durchgeführter Designwettbewerb für ein „Laternenwunderland", welches das architektonische Highlight des Festes bildet. „Golden Moon", der Siegerentwurf von 2012, greift die Form des chinesischen Lampions auf und setzt sie direkt in Beziehung zur Legende von Chang'e (嫦娥), der Göttin des Mondes und der Unsterblichkeit.[4] Die Grundstruktur des Pavillons besteht aus einer leichten, aus Stahl gefertigten geodätischen Kuppel, die zugleich als Tragwerk für ein sie umhüllendes computergeneriertes Gitternetz dient. Dieses ist als sekundäres Bambus-Diagrid ausgeführt, das dann mit LED-beleuchteten Flammenzungen aus Stretchstoff verkleidet wurde (Abb. 8). Für die Vorbereitungsarbeiten standen lediglich drei Wochen zur Verfügung und für den Aufbau vor Ort gerade einmal elf Tage.

1 Willis and Woodward state: "The CONSTRUCTABILITY = COMPUTABILITY equation should in theory increase the architect's control over the project and make building costs more predictable. However, it also renders the skilled building trades largely obsolete and reduces opportunities for taking advantage of serendipitous occurrences during construction, eliminating the sorts of happenings that artists, and many architects, often find enliven their works." Dan Willis and Todd Woodward, "Diminishing Difficulty: Mass Customization and the Digital Production of Architecture," in Fabricating Architecture: Selected Readings in Digital Design and Manufacturing, ed. Robert Corser (New York, 2010), pp. 182–183.

2 "The demise of the skilled craftsperson is one instance in the ongoing transfer of economic and political power from those who work with their hands to the privileged class of 'symbolic analysts' who manipulate information." Willis and Woodward, "Diminishing Difficulty" (see note 1), p. 195.

3 The Cantonese region of Southern China comprises of Hong Kong S.A.R., Macau S.A.R. and the Guangdong Provence of China.

4 According to the very popular romantic story, Chang'e lives on the moon, away from her husband Houyi (后羿) who lives on earth. The couple can only meet on the night of the Mid-Autumn Festival when the moon is at its fullest and most beautiful. To symbolize the passionate love burning between the reunited couple that day, a six-storey-high, spherical moon lantern was proposed, clad with abstracted flames in fiery colors and patterns.

1 Willis und Woodward schreiben: „Die Gleichung BAUBARKEIT = BERECHENBARKEIT sollte theoretisch die Kontrolle des Architekten über das Projekt und die Vorhersagbarkeit der Baukosten verbessern. Sie macht allerdings auch die qualifizierten Bauberufe weitgehend obsolet und verringert die Möglichkeit, glückliche Fügungen beim Bau aufzugreifen, eliminiert also die Art von Ereignissen, die Künstler, aber auch viele Architekten, als belebend für ihre Arbeit ansehen." Dan Willis/Todd Woodward, „Diminishing Difficulty: Mass Customization and the Digital Production of Architecture", in: Robert Corser (Hg.): Fabricating Architecture: Selected Readings in Digital Design and Manufacturing, New York 2010, S. 182–183.

2 „Das Verschwinden des qualifizierten Handwerkers ist ein Beispiel für den fortgesetzten Transfer ökonomischer und politischer Macht von denen, die mit ihren Händen arbeiten, hin zur privilegierten Klasse informationsverarbeitender ‚symbolischer Analytiker'." Ebd., S. 195.

3 Die Region Kanton besteht aus den Sonderverwaltungszonen Hongkong und Macao sowie der Provinz Guangdong.

4 Der überaus populären romantischen Legende zufolge lebt Chang'e auf dem Mond, getrennt von ihrem auf der Erde lebenden Ehemann Houyi (后羿). Das Paar kann nur in der Nacht des Mondfestes zusammenkommen, wenn der Mond am vollsten und schönsten strahlt. Als Symbol für die an diesem Tag erglühende leidenschaftliche Liebe des wiedervereinten Paars wurde ein sechs Stockwerke hoher, von abstrakten, feuerfarbenen Flammenzungen umloderter kugelförmiger Mondlampion vorgeschlagen.

2 „Golden Moon" – Mittherbstfest Laternenwunderland, Hongkong "Golden
Moon" – Mid-Autumn Festival Lantern
Wonderland, Hong Kong, Architekten
architects: Kristof Crolla & Adam Fingrut,
2012 © Grandy Lui für for LEAD

3 „Golden Moon" Hauptbestandteile:
Geodätische Stahlkuppel, zwei Kilome-
ter gebogener Bambus, 475 Stretchstoff-Flammenzungen "Golden Moon's"
main components: A steel geodesic
dome, two kilometers of bent bamboo,
475 stretch fabric flames, Architekten
architects: Kristof Crolla & Adam
Fingrut, 2012 © LEAD

4 Kreuzungspunkte zwischen Grund-
gerüst und sekundärem Gitternetz des
„Golden Moon" Intersections between
the primary and the secondary structure of "Golden Moon", Architekten
architects: Kristof Crolla & Adam
Fingrut, 2012 © LEAD

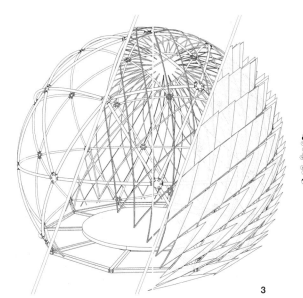

3

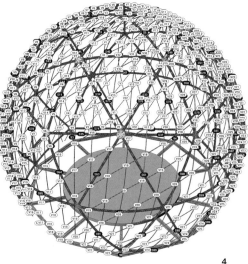

4

5   Innenansicht des „Golden Moon" – Mittherbstfest
Laternenwunderland, Hongkong Interior perspective
of "Golden Moon" – Mid-Autumn Festival Lantern
Wonderland, Hong Kong, Architekten architects: Kristof
Crolla & Adam Fingrut, 2012 © Kevin Ng for LEAD

6   Sich auflösende Geometrie am Pol des „Golden
Moon" – Mittherbstfest Laternenwunderland, Hongkong
Disintegrating geometry at the top pole, "Golden
Moon" – Mid-Autumn Festival Lantern Wonderland,
Hong Kong, Architekten architects: Kristof Crolla &
Adam Fingrut, 2012 © Hong Kong Tourism Board

Komponenten. Geodätische Stahlkuppel. Die Grundstruktur besteht aus einer freistehenden geodätischen Kuppel aus Stahl mit einem Durchmesser von zwanzig Metern, die der Installation sowohl Form als auch Stabilität verleiht. Sie steht auf einem ebenfalls stählernen Unterbau, der von einer kreisförmigen Betonplatte gekrönt und stabilisiert wird, da eine Verankerung im Boden nicht gestattet war. Diese Betonplatte bildet zugleich den Boden der zentralen Beobachtungsplattform. Alle Stabelemente und Verbindungsteller der Kuppel wurden nummeriert und die vielen hundert Kreuzungspunkte zwischen dem Stahlgerüst und dem sekundären Bambus-Diagrid nach einem vereinfachten, aus den digitalen Dateien extrahierten Zeichnungssatz von Hand aufgetragen (Abb. 4).

Sekundäres Bambusgitter. Das sekundäre Gitternetz des Projekts verbindet digitale Planerstellung mit Techniken des Bambusgerüstbaus. Traditionellerweise kommt der chinesische Bambusgerüstbau ohne konventionelle Pläne oder Zeichnungen aus. Es ist eine schnelle, intuitive und unscharfe Baumethode, die sich auf eine Reihe grundlegender Prinzipien stützt. Dazu gehören etwa die strategische Anbringung von Verstrebungen, Auslegern und Abständen oder der Einsatz verschiedener Knoten mit unterschiedlichen Eigenschaften, die es den Handwerkern erlauben, auf wechselnde materielle und situative Bedingungen einzugehen. Die „Gestaltung" durch die Handwerker beruht also oft auf einer scheinbar beliebigen Positionierung von Ankerpunkten und Stangen sowie einer „Vorstellung" von der Form des einzurüstenden Gebäudes.

Zur Erzielung der dynamischen Raumwirkung wurde das Golden-Moon-Diagrid mithilfe von Algorithmen entworfen, die um den Äquator herum Reinheit und Wiederholung und zu den Polen hin geometrische Unschärfen generierten. Die größte Herausforderung des Projekts bestand darin, einen flexiblen Bauplan zu erstellen, der es den Handwerkern ermöglichte, das digitale Design mit entsprechender Genauigkeit, d.h. einer Toleranz von 10–15 cm, umzusetzen.

Diese Herausforderung wurde erfolgreich mithilfe eines Arbeitsablaufs bewältigt, bei dem zusammenhängende Bambusstangen verschiedener Länge, Dicke und Biegbarkeit zunächst gekennzeichnet und dann zu durchgehenden flexiblen Bögen von bis zu 40 m Länge zusammengesetzt wurden. Auf diesen Bambusbögen wurden sämtliche Kreuzungspunkte zwischen dem Stahlgerüst und den beiden Richtungen des Gitternetzes nach vereinfachten Zeichnungs- und Datenauszügen aus den Computermodellen von Hand aufgetragen. Um die erforderlichen Radien herzustellen, wurden die Stangen wo immer möglich nach Dicke und naturwüchsiger Biegung ausgewählt (Abb. 1). Zur Verbindung des Gitters und zur Befestigung am Stahlgerüst wurden traditionelle Knoten aus schwarzem Kunststoffdraht verwendet. Entwurf und Ausführung der Details für die Stretchstoff-Flammenzungen waren daraufhin angelegt,

the ground was allowed. This concrete slab forms the basis of the central viewing platform. All members and node plates of the dome were numbered, and the hundreds of connection points between the steel structure and the secondary bamboo diagrid were manually marked up following a simplified drawing set extracted from digital files (fig. 4).

Bamboo Substructure. The secondary structure of the project merges digital design setups with bamboo scaffolding techniques. Traditionally, Cantonese bamboo scaffolding construction does without conventional plans or drawings. It is a high-speed, intuitive, and imprecise construction method that follows a set of basic principles such as strategic ways for cross-bracing, cantilevering or spanning, or the use of a series of knots with different properties, to allow craftsmen to respond to varying material conditions and differing site situations. Hence, the craftsmen's "design" involves an often seemingly random positioning of anchor points and poles and an "idea" about the shape of the structure to be scaffolded.

In order to achieve its dynamic spatial effects, the design of the Golden Moon's diagrid is based on algorithms that produce purity and repetition around the equator and geometric imperfections at the poles. The main challenge of this project was to create a flexible setup that would allow the craftsmen to materialize the digital design with sufficient accuracy, i.e., a tolerance of up to 10–15cm.

This challenge was met successfully by creating a work-flow involving the labeling of interconnected bamboo sticks of varying

> During the construction process, however, it turned out that the geometry at the top of the structure emerged to be too demanding for the material, not being able to follow the tight bending radii.

lengths, thickness, and bendability, which were joined together to create continuous flexible curves of up to 40 meters in length. All intersection points with the steel structure and between the two directions of the grid were manually marked onto these bamboo curves following simplified drawings and data extracted from computer models. Where possible, stick thicknesses and bamboo's inherent, pre-existing curvatures were selected and applied based on eventual bending radii (fig. 1). Traditional scaffolding knots made from black plastic wires were used to tie the grid together and fix it onto the steel base structure. Subsequent details for stretch fabric flames were designed and applied to absorb the anticipated deviations which went up to 15cm or more (fig. 8).

During the construction process, however, it turned out that the geometry at the top of the structure emerged to be too demanding for the material, not being able to follow the tight bending radii. The initial design anticipated the rigidity of the diagrid, clad with fabric flames, to visually disintegrate towards the top pole. This would symbolically refer to the dynamic flickering of the flames and the simultaneous destruction of the base geometry through fire. To materialize this, we relied on the craftsmen's intuition to build what they deemed most suitable within the framework of design principles we had developed together (fig.6).

Stretch Fabric Flames. For the stretch fabric flames, a flexible construction detail was designed in collaboration with the fabric and bamboo specialists. This detail uses the fabric's stretching properties to absorb the aforementioned geometry deviations. In response to this flexible detail, optimization scripts were developed to reduce the 475 unique flame geometries into only ten different types. These stretch and morph into the desired shapes onsite, using the bamboo sub-grid as a guide. Together with the choreographed lighting, the coloration of this fabric amplifies the requested otherworldly experience of a "Lantern Wonderland" (fig. 5). On display for only six days, the flamboyant Golden Moon was visited by over 400,000 visitors.

In spite of automation and the prolific use of computer controlled fabrication methods and robotics, the act of constructing remains a largely human enterprise. By opening the hermetically sealed nature of virtual models to this reality, an opportunity is presented for intuition to respond, and thus for craftsmanship to play a proactive role in the project realization.

The Cantonese traditional use of bamboo scaffolding is under heavy pressure from alternative methods. With the project of Golden Moon this custom's role is expanded by using its unique properties to make it part of the final architecture, rather than only having it serve a supporting role during construction. This integrative approach illustrates a possible way for craftsmanship to evolve and adapt in order to safeguard its sustainable future.

Through a combination of state-of-the-art digital design technology and traditional hand craftsmanship, the Golden Moon demonstrates that complex geometry can still be built efficiently and at low cost when intuitive actions are merged with digital control.

> In spite of automation and the prolific use of computer controlled fabrication methods and robotics, the act of constructing remains a largely human enterprise.

die erwarteten Abweichungen von bis zu 15 cm und mehr auszugleichen (Abb. 8).

Im Verlauf des Bauprozesses erwies sich die Geometrie am Kuppelpol als zu schwierig für das Material; es konnte den engen Radien nicht folgen. Im ursprünglichen Entwurf sollte sich die Strenge des mit den Stoff-Flammen verkleideten Gitters gegen den Pol hin visuell auflösen und so das dynamische Flackern des Feuers und dessen Zerstörung der Grundgeometrie versinnbildlichen. Bei der Umsetzung der Idee verließen wir uns auf die Intuition der Handwerker; sie sollten bauen, was ihnen im Rahmen der gemeinsam entwickelten Designprinzipien am passendsten erschien (Abb. 6).

Stretchstoff-Flammen. Für die Flammen aus Stretchstoff wurde gemeinsam mit den Stoff- und Bambusspezialisten ein flexibles Baudetail entwickelt, wobei die elastischen Eigenschaften des Stoffs dazu genutzt wurden, die erwähnten geometrischen Abweichungen auszugleichen. Als Reaktion auf diese Elastizität wurden die 475 individuellen Flammenformen mithilfe eigens entwickelter Optimierungsskripts auf lediglich zehn verschiedene Arten reduziert. Diese passen sich an Ort und Stelle an die jeweils geforderten, vom sekundären Bambusgitter ausgehenden Formen an. Die Farbe des Stoffs trägt zusammen mit der choreografierten Beleuchtung zum gewünschten übersinnlichen Erlebnis eines „Laternenwunderlands" bei (Abb. 5). In den sechs Tagen seines Bestehens wurde der flamboyante goldene Mond von über 400.000 Menschen besucht.

Trotz Automatisierung und dem breiten Einsatz von Robotik und computergesteuerten Fabrikationsmethoden liegt der eigentliche Bauprozess immer noch vorwiegend in der Hand von Menschen. Öffnet man die hermetisch verschlossene Welt virtueller Modelle für diese Realität, ergeben sich Möglichkeiten für die Einbindung intuitiven Handelns und damit eine aktive Rolle des Handwerks in die Projektrealisierung.

Der traditionelle kantonesische Bambusgerüstbau ist einem massiven Konkurrenzdruck durch andere Methoden ausgesetzt. Das Golden-Moon-Projekt erweitert die Rolle dieses Gewerbes, indem es seine einzigartigen Fähigkeiten zu einem Teil der eigentlichen Architektur macht und ihm nicht bloß eine Nebenrolle im Bauprozess zuweist. Der integrative Ansatz zeigt somit eine Möglichkeit auf, wie sich das Handwerk weiterentwickeln und anpassen und damit seinen Fortbestand sichern könnte.

Mit der Kombination von neuester digitaler Entwurfstechnik und traditionellem Handwerk, belegt das Projekt, dass sich komplexe Geometrien auch durch eine Fusion von intuitivem Handeln und digitaler Kontrolle effizient und kostengünstig umsetzen lassen.

Übersetzung Wilfried Prantner

7

7　Sich bei Nacht versammelnde Besu-
cher – Mittherbstfest Laternenwunder-
land, Hongkong Crowds gathering at
night, "Golden Moon" – Mid-Autumn
Festival Lantern Wonderland, Hong
Kong, Architekten architects: Kristof
Crolla & Adam Fingrut, 2012 © Pano
Kalogeropoulos für for LEAD

8　Anbringung der Stretchstoff-Flammenzungen am Bambusgitter Installation
of the Stretch Fabric Flames on the
Bamboo Diagrid, Architekten architects: Kristof Crolla & Adam Fingrut,
2012 © Kevin Ng für for LEAD

9　Eingang zum „Golden Moon" – Mit-
herbstfest Laternenwunderland,
Hongkong Entrance of "Golden Moon" –
Mid-Autumn Festival Lantern Wonderland, Hong Kong, Architekten architects: Kristof Crolla & Adam Fingrut,
2012 © Grandy Lui für for LEAD

8

9

1   Edith K. Ackermann. MIT Media Lab. April 2011 © Foto photo: Jean-Baptiste Labrune

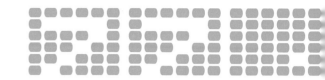

Embodied Cognition and Reflective Practices

Edith Ackermann (EA) in Conversation with Urs Hirschberg (GAM)

Verkörperte Kognition und reflexive Verfahren. Edith Ackermann (EA), im Gespräch mit Urs Hirschberg (GAM)

Edith Ackermann is a developmental psychologist who teaches graduate students, conducts research, and consults for companies, institutions, and organizations interested in the intersections between learning, teaching, design, and digital technologies.

Edith Ackermann ist Entwicklungspsychologin, Universitätsdozentin und in der Forschung sowie als Beraterin für Firmen, Institutionen und Organisationen tätig, die sich für die Schnittstellen zwischen Lernen, Lehren, Design und digitalen Technologien interessieren.

EDITH ACKERMANN

An Honorary Professor at the University of Aix-Marseille, France, she is also a Visiting Scientist at the Massachusetts Institute of Technology, School of Architecture, and a Senior Research Associate at the Harvard Graduate School of Design, Responsive Environments and Artifacts Lab. She started her career working as a junior faculty in the Department of Psychology at the University of Geneva, Switzerland and later became a Scientific Collaborator at the Centre International d'Epistémologie Génétique under the direction of Jean Piaget, Geneva. Ackermann was a Senior Research Scientist at MERL (Mitsubishi Electric Research Laboratory, Cambridge, MA) and an Associate Professor of Media Arts and Sciences at the MIT Media laboratory, in Cambridge, MA.

In her work as a consultant and a researcher she is particularly interested in the novel roles that digital media can play in creativity and learning. She has consulted companies such as the LEGO learning institute or the San Francisco Exploratorium Science Museum, but she also guides MIT architecture students in their thesis preparations. The interview with her was conducted via Skype and via email.

GAM: Before we talk about intuition, let us talk about talent. When architects are asked about how they design, many say that they cannot really explain it. Some will even go so far as to say that designing can't be taught. If this were true, wouldn't it undermine the very idea of architectural education?

EA: Like intuition, "talent" is a conceptual convenience to be taken with a grain of salt. We usually think of a talented person as someone with a natural gift, an above-average ability, or an innate aptitude for achievement or success. The problem, as I see it, lies less in how we position ourselves along the *nature-nurture* continuum than in the implied *fixity* or *malleability of mind* associated with either innate or acquired dispositions, competences, or character traits.

Teaching students to sharpen their "talents" as architects and designers constitutes an extra challenge, because when it comes to learning the craft or developing a designerly sensibility, "talking the walk" won't help "walking the talk." Alas, students who talk most in class or mimic their masters aren't always the ones whose productions stand out, surprise, or delight. This is not to say that mindful engagement, self-reflection, and perseverance, aren't essential to becoming a good thinker and an accomplished practitioner.

Learning is all about moving in and out of focus, shifting perspective, and coming to "see anew." Imagining and bringing forth novel ideas engages aspects of the mind, the body, and the self that we barely control. Learning, like the art of living itself, is about navigating uncertainties rather than imposing order over what we cannot predict. An exceptional educator, I think, is one who understands that teaching is always indirect, that learners may have reasons to stick to their beliefs, and that becoming an accomplished designer takes more than mimicking the master, incorporating experts' views, or following instructions. It is one who also knows when not to intervene.

GAM: Sounds like it also takes talent to bring out talent. What about the notion of intuition, then? It is often conceived as a mystical quality or as divine inspiration. Seen from a psychological point of view, is intuition an innate ability or is it something we acquire over time?

Die Honorarprofessorin der Université Aix-Marseille ist Visiting Scientist am Massachusetts Institute of Technology, School of Architecture, und Senior Research Associate an der Harvard Graduate School of Design, Responsive Environments and Artifacts Lab. Sie begann ihre wissenschaftliche Laufbahn als Assistentin an der Fakultät für Psychologie der Université de Genève, später war sie wissenschaftliche Mitarbeiterin am Centre International d'Epistémologie Génétique unter der Leitung von Jean Piaget in Genf. Ackermann war Senior Research Scientist am MERL (Mitsubishi Electric Research Laboratory, Cambridge, MA) und Associate Professor of Media Arts and Sciences am MIT Media Laboratory in Cambridge, MA.

In ihrer Forschungs- und Beratertätigkeit interessiert sie sich besonders für die neuen Funktionen, die digitale Medien im kreativen und didaktischen Bereich übernehmen können. Beratend tätig war sie für Unternehmen wie das LEGO-Lerninstitut oder das San Francisco Exploratorium Science Museum. Daneben betreut sie aber auch Architekturstudenten des MIT bei ihren Abschlussarbeiten. Das vorliegende Interview wurde per Skype und E-Mail geführt.

GAM: Lass uns, bevor wir zur Intuition kommen, über Begabung sprechen. Wenn Architekten gefragt werden, wie sie entwerfen, sagen viele, sie könnten es im Grunde nicht erklären. Manche behaupten sogar, Entwerfen könne nicht gelehrt werden. Wenn das zuträfe, wäre damit nicht das Architekturstudium an sich infrage gestellt?

EA: Wie Intuition ist „Begabung" ein Gebrauchsbegriff, der cum grano salis zu verwenden ist. Unter einer begabten Person verstehen wir für gewöhnlich jemanden mit einer angeborenen Gabe, einer überdurchschnittlichen Fähigkeit oder der Veranlagung zu Leistung und Erfolg. Das Problem liegt in meinen Augen weniger darin, wie wir uns entlang des *Natur versus Kultur*-Kontinuums als in der implizierten *Veränderlichkeit* oder *Formbarkeit des Denkens* positionieren, die mit angeborenen bzw. erworbenen Dispositionen, Kompetenzen oder Charaktereigenschaften assoziiert wird.

Studenten beizubringen, wie sie ihre „Talente" als Architekten und Designer entfalten, ist eine spezielle Herausforderung, denn was das Erlernen des Handwerks oder die Entwicklung eines Gespürs fürs Entwerfen betrifft, haben Worte nicht immer den Effekt, dass darauf auch Taten folgen. Leider treten jene Studenten, die im Unterricht am meisten reden oder ihre Professoren imitieren, nicht immer mit den originellsten, erstaunlichsten oder erfreulichsten Ergebnissen hervor. Das soll nicht heißen, dass besonnenes Engagement, Selbstreflexion und Durchhaltevermögen keine wesentlichen Voraussetzungen dafür seien, ein guter Theoretiker und erfolgreicher Architekt zu werden.

Lernen bedeutet Konzentration und Abschweifung, Perspektivenwechsel und Aneignung eines „neuen Blicks". Das

Ausdenken und Hervorbringen neuer Ideen nimmt geistige und körperliche Aspekte, sowie Aspekte des Selbst in Anspruch, auf die wir kaum Einfluss haben. Beim Lernen geht es, wie bei der Kunst zu leben, darum, Unwägbares in den Griff zu bekommen, nicht darum, etwas zu beherrschen, das wir nicht vorhersagen können. Ein außergewöhnlicher Lehrer ist, glaube ich, einer, der versteht, dass Unterrichten immer indirekt funktioniert, dass die Lernenden Gründe haben mögen, an ihren Überzeugungen festzuhalten, und dass für einen erfolgreichen Entwurfsarchitekten mehr notwendig ist als den Professor zu imitieren, sich auf Expertenmeinungen zu stützen oder Anweisungen zu befolgen. So ein Lehrer weiß auch, wann er nicht eingreifen soll.

GAM: Das klingt, als sei auch Talent nötig, um Talent zu fördern. Wie verhält es sich dann mit der Intuition? Sie wird oft für eine mystische Fähigkeit oder göttliche Eingebung gehalten. Ist Intuition, vom psychologischen Standpunkt aus gesehen, eine angeborene Fähigkeit oder etwas, das wir mit der Zeit erwerben?

EA: Intuition ist ein unglücklicher Begriff für eine eigentlich tiefgreifende Vorstellung: die menschliche Fähigkeit, *etwas zu verstehen, ohne es durchdacht zu haben* und unbewusst überraschende innere (und äußere) Ressourcen zu mobilisieren, wenn sie *in situ* gebraucht werden. Intuition erfordert, dass wir ein „Gefühl für das, was wichtig ist" (in Abwandlung von Damasios „Gefühl für das, was geschieht"[1]) entwickeln, bevor wir überhaupt behaupten oder belegen können, dass wir recht haben. Es geht darum, Situationen zu „durchblicken", die wir anders nicht begreifen oder erklären können. In seiner weniger vorteilhaften Konnotation evoziert der Begriff das Instinktive (das Tier in uns) oder wird, wie Du sagst, ins Mystische (göttliche Eingebung) erhoben. In beiden Fällen meint der Begriff den plötzlichen Ausbruch ungeprüfter „Wahrheiten" oder kryptischer Prophezeiungen (Offenbarungen, innere Rufe).

Der Schweizer Psychologe Carl Gustav Jung (1921) definiert Intuition als „Wahrnehmung [...] durch das Unbewusste"[2] und stellt sie der sinnlichen Wahrnehmung (durch Sinneseindrücke) gegenüber. Intuitive Menschen verlassen sich in Jungs Typologie hauptsächlich auf ihre Sinne, da sie als Auslöserimpuls, scheinbar unzusammenhängende Gedanken, Bilder, Möglichkeiten oder Auswege aus heiklen Situationen hervorbringen. Durch einen vorwiegend unbewussten assoziativen Prozess kommen diese Menschen zu überraschenden Erkenntnissen, können

EA: Intuition is an unfortunate term for an otherwise deep idea: namely our human ability to *understand something without thinking it through*, and to unknowingly mobilize unexpected inner (and outer) resources, when needed in-situ. Intuition requires that we develop a "feeling for what matters," (my own twist on Damasio's "a feeling for what happens"[1]) before we even can tell or prove that we are right. It is about "seeing through" situations that we cannot otherwise apprehend, or explain. In its unfortunate connotation, the term evokes the instinctual (the animal within) or, as you suggest, it gets elevated to the mystical (divinity inspired). In either case, it is seen as a sudden outburst of unexamined "truths" or cryptic prophecies (revelations, inner calls).

Swiss psychologist Carl Gustav Jung (1921) defined intuition as "perception … via the unconscious,"[2] and opposed it to sensation (perceiving via sensory inputs). Intuitive subjects, in Jung's typology, rely on their senses mostly as a trigger to bring forth other seemingly unrelated thoughts, images, possibilities, and ways out of tricky situations. By a mostly unconscious associative process, they come up with surprising insights yet are unable to tell why they thought or felt the way they did, or what prompted them to think their thoughts in the first place. They may do so in retrospect. We now know that intuition is less a matter of psychological type than it is a powerful heuristic tool used by most people to *stay afloat* in situations that are too unpredictable or bewildering to be apprehended otherwise.

GAM: Conceiving of intuition as a strategic tool, in what way can it help us to solve complex or difficult tasks both in everyday life and architectural design?

EA: Intuition also alludes to the notion that when it comes to human affairs, the tensions we experience (the dilemma we face) often cannot be *solved* (eliminated or explained away) but need to be carefully *monitored* (navigated). Maintaining a balance, in this sense, can't simply be achieved by opting out troubling causes, or comparing options. What's needed instead is an ability to *hold* the tensions, contain the trouble within range, stay alert, and re-calibrate along the way.

> Intuition requires that we develop a "feeling for what matters," (my own twist on Damasio's "a feeling for what happens"[1]) before we even can tell or prove that we are right. It is about "seeing through" situations that we cannot otherwise apprehend, or explain.

1   Antonio Damasio: *The Feeling of What Happens. Body and Emotion in the Making of Consciousness*, Harcourt 1999. Dt. Ausgabe: Antonio R. Damasio: *Ich fühle, also bin ich. Die Entschlüsselung des Bewusstseins*. Aus dem Englischen von Hainer Kober, München 2000.

2   Carl Gustav Jung: *Psychologische Typen*. Gesammelte Werke, Bd. 6, Freiburg im Breisgau 1981, S. 434.

1   Antonio Damasio, *The Feeling of What Happens: Body and Emotion in the Making of Consciousness*, Harcourt, 1999.

2   Carl Gustav Jung, *Psychological Types*, trans. Helton Godwin Baynes, Princeton, 1971, p. 538.

Intuition, as we have seen, provides us with hints without the burden of reason. Introspection, on the other hand, allows us to "look inward" and examine our own inner thoughts and feeling, *as if* outside-in. Used as both a technique for self-examination and a method in psychology, introspection is a mixed blessing.

aber nicht sagen, warum sie so und nicht anders gedacht oder empfunden haben oder was sie überhaupt zu ihren Gedanken veranlasst hat. Das passiert eher im Nachhinein. Heute wissen wir, dass Intuition weniger mit einem bestimmten psychologischen Typus zu tun hat. Vielmehr ist sie ein wirkungsvolles heuristisches Instrument, das die meisten Menschen benützen, um sich in Situationen *über Wasser zu halten*, die für ein Begreifen im herkömmlichen Sinn zu unkalkulierbar oder verwirrend sind.

GAM: *Wenn wir Intuition als strategisches Instrument denken, wie kann sie uns im Alltag oder architektonischen Entwurfsprozess dienlich sein, wenn es um die Lösung von komplexen oder schwierigen Aufgaben geht?*

EA: Intuition berührt auch die Vorstellung, dass sich im zwischenmenschlichen Bereich die Spannungen, die wir wahrnehmen (das Dilemma, vor dem wir stehen), oft nicht *lösen* (beheben oder wegreden) lassen, sondern aufmerksam *beobachtet* (gesteuert) werden müssen. So gesehen können diese nicht bloß dadurch austariert werden, dass man die Ursache des Problems ausklammert oder Optionen vergleicht. Gefordert ist stattdessen die Fähigkeit, Spannungen *auszuhalten*, das Problem in Grenzen zu halten, wachsam zu bleiben und sich immer wieder neu anzupassen.

GAM: *Manche Menschen „vertrauen" auf ihre Intuition …*

EA: Alternativen zum Begriff „Intuition" findet man in Polanyis „implizitem Wissen"[3], definiert als Wissen, von dem ein Handelnder *weiß, dass er es hat* (z.B. wie man einen Wettbewerb gewinnt, ein guter Trainer ist, einen Ball fängt), das er aber nur *durch (kundiges) Ausüben* beschreiben kann. Solche partiell ungeprüften aber souveränen Akte (Erkenntnisse oder Know-how) ähneln Schöns „reflection-in-action"[4] (dem Vermögen, über eine praktische Handlung zu reflektieren, während man sie ausübt), Lakoff und Johnsons „Leben in Metaphern" (situierte und verkörperte Kognition)[5] und Bruners „enaktiver Darstellung" (performative Akte).[6] Unser menschliches Streben zielt nicht auf den Widerspruch von Bauchgefühl und Intellekt ab, sondern auf die Versöhnung von dem Tier und dem Genie in uns. Zu diesem Zweck geben wir dem

3   Michael Polanyi: *The Tacit Dimension*. Chicago 1967. Dt. Ausgabe: Michael Polanyi: *Implizites Wissen*, Übers. von Horst Brühmann, Frankfurt am Main 1985.

4   Donald Schön: *The Reflective Practitioner. How Professionals Think in Action*, London 1983.

5   George Lakoff und Marc Johnson: *Metaphors We Live By*, Chicago 1980. Dt. Ausgabe: George Lakoff/Mark Johnson, *Leben in Metaphern*. Aus dem Amerikanischen übersetzt von Astrid Hildenbrand, Heidelberg 1998.

6   Vgl. Jerome Bruner: *Acts of Meaning*, London 1993.

Intellekt eine helfende Hand (oder eine Stütze) und unserer tastenden Hand etwas, woran sie sich festhalten können.

GAM: „Lautes Denken" oder Introspektion werden oft eingesetzt, um Architekten beim Entwerfen dazu zu bringen, ihre Erkenntnisse zu verbalisieren – oder in anderer Form zu externalisieren –, während sie sich durch Probleme hindurcharbeiten. Ist Introspektion Deiner Meinung nach ein geeignetes Verfahren für Architekten, um Erkenntnisse über den eigenen Entwurfsprozess zu gewinnen?

EA: Intuition gibt, wie wir gesehen haben, Anleitung zur Problemlösung, ohne intellektuell zu belasten. Introspektion wiederum gestattet uns, „nach innen zu schauen" und unsere inneren Gedanken und Gefühle zu untersuchen, als seien sie nach außen gestülpt. Als Selbstprüfungstechnik und Methode in der Psychologie eingesetzt, ist die Introspektion ein zweifelhafter Segen. Zum einen bewirkt fast jeder Versuch, das eigene Seelenleben – oder das Anderer – offenzulegen, eine Veränderung genau jenes Seelenlebens, das wir begreifen möchten.[7] Hinzu kommt, dass laut der Theorie des adaptiven Unbewussten unsere mentalen Prozesse (auch „high-level"-Prozesse wie Zielsetzung und Entscheidungsfindung), der Introspektion zumeist verschlossen bleiben.[8] Kurz gesagt, Introspektion funktioniert sehr gut als Fenster zu dem, was wir gegenwärtig denken, allerdings kann sie nicht erklären, wie wir zu diesen Gedanken gekommen sind. Und „lautes Denken" (Ich-Aussagen) sind nur dann nützlich, so lange sie durch andere Methoden wie Beobachtung oder klinische Interviews ergänzt werden.

GAM: Du sagtest, wir „geben dem Intellekt eine helfende Hand". Don Norman spricht von externen Hilfsmitteln, von „Dingen, die uns schlau machen". Architekten arbeiten immer wieder mit externen Hilfsmitteln in Form von Skizzen, Modellen, Diagrammen etc. Sind architektonische Instrumente wie diese auch Beispiele für die von Dir erwähnte „verkörperte Kognition"?

EA: „Situiertes" Lernen und „verkörperte" Kognition betonen die Bedeutung des In-der-Welt-Seins, den Kontakt mit Dingen – die tatsächliche Berührung – als Anker für das Denken. Und niemand sagt es eloquenter als Francis Bacon in dem berühmten Zitat: „Weder die bloße Hand, noch der sich selbst

GAM: Some people "trust" their intuition …

EA: Alternatives to the term "intuition" can be found in Polanyi's notion of tacit knowledge,[3] which he defined as knowledge that an actor knows he has (ex: how to win a contest, be a good coach, catch a ball) but cannot describe in terms other than its own (skillful) performance. Such partially unexamined yet masterful enactments (insights or know-how) come close to Schön's notion of "reflection-in-action,"[4] Lakoff and Johnson's "metaphors we live by" (situated and embodied cognition)[5], and Bruner's enactive representations (performative acts).[6] What drives our quests as humans is not so much to oppose gut feeling and brainpower, but to reconcile the beast and the genie within. We do so by giving our head a hand (or a handle) and our grappling hand something to hold on to.

GAM: "Thinking aloud" techniques or introspection have often been used to get designers to verbalize—or otherwise externalize—their insights as they work their ways through problems. Do you think introspection provides a useful technique for designers to gain insights into their own design process?

EA: Intuition, as we have seen, provides us with hints without the burden of reason. Introspection, on the other hand, allows us to "look inward" and examine our own inner thoughts and feeling, as if outside-in. Used as both a technique for self-examination and a method in psychology, introspection is a mixed blessing. For one, most any attempt at overtly digging into one's own—or other people's—mind tends to alter the very mind we are trying to capture.[7] What's more, as the theory of the adaptive unconscious suggests, our mental processes (including "high-level" processes like goal-setting and decision-making) remain mostly inaccessible to introspection.[8] In sum, introspection works fine as a window into what we are currently thinking yet it fails on how we arrived at those thoughts. And thinking aloud techniques (first person accounts) are valuable as long as they are complemented by other methods such as observation or clinical interviews.

GAM: You said that we need to "give our mind a hand." Don Norman talks about external aids, about "things that make us smart." Architects repeatedly make use of external aids in the form of sketches, models, diagrams, etc. Are these architectural tools also examples of what you referred to as "embodied cognition"?

EA: Both "situated" learning and "embodied" cognition emphasize the importance of being-in-the world, being in touch with things—literally

7   Vgl. auch Edith Ackermann: „Hidden Drivers in Pedagogic Transactions: Teachers as Clinicians and Designers", in Be Creative …Reinventing Technologies in Education. Proceedings of the 9th European Logo Conference, Porto 2003, S. 29–38.

8   Vgl. Timothy D. Wilson: „Knowing When to Ask: Introspection and the Adaptive Unconscious", Journal of Consciousness Studies 10, 9 (2003), S. 131–140.

3   Michael Polanyi, The Tacit Dimension, Chicago, 1967.

4   Donald Schön, The Reflective Practitioner: How Professionals Think in Action (London, 1983).

5   George Lakoff and Mark Johnson, Metaphors We Live By (Chicago, 1980).

6   See Jerome Bruner, Acts of Meaning (London, 1993).

7   See also Edith Ackermann, "Hidden Drivers in Pedagogic Transactions: Teachers as Clinicians and Designers," in Be Creative … Reinventing Technologies in Education. Proceedings of the 9th European Logo Conference (Porto, 2003), p. 29–38.

8   See Timothy D. Wilson, "Knowing When to Ask: Introspection and the Adaptive Unconscious," Journal of Consciousness Studies, 10, 9 (2003), pp. 131–140.

touching things—as a lever to thinking. And no one puts it more eloquently than Francis Bacon in his famous quote: "Neither the bare hand nor the unaided intellect has much power; the work is done by tools and assistance, and the intellect needs them as much as the hand."[9] *Giving the mind a hand* suggests that much of the knowledge we have gained is knowledge-in-action: we think and act at the same time! *Giving the hand a tool* further suggests that the materials we explore, and the tools we use, are instrumental in helping expand and mediate our action in the world.

I like to reserve "embodied" cognition (*verkörpert* in German) to the notion that our body has its own intelligence (it "thinks" as much as our mind), and that our insights and know-hows are so deeply engrained in our sensorimotor experience that we literally live by them. "Embedded" cognition (*eingebettet* in German), on the other hand, speaks to the ways intelligent beings *(*body/minds in-situ*)* shape and furbish the world in which they live.

To phenomenologists "embodied" cognition refers to the intuitive experience of *being-in-the-world*. Tool-use, on the other-hand, is about humans' abilities to extend their reach beyond the unaided hand's (body/mind's) immediate grasp and to feel empowered in return. As Michael Polanyi puts it, "while we rely on a tool or a probe, these are not usually handled as external objects … [Instead] we pour ourselves out into them and assimilate them as parts of our own existence. We accept them existentially by dwelling into them."[10] In Maurice Merleau-Ponty words: "To get used to a hat, a car, or a stick is to be transplanted into them, or conversely, to incorporate them into the bulk of our own body."[11] The point here is that even though there may be a physical demarcation between body and tool, through tool-use the demarcation fades away: the tool-at-hand becomes an extension and hence a part of us. Alas, our very abilities to set or blur boundaries, to switch modes, and to shift perspectives is what keeps us going and gets us smarter. We are not just cyborgs-in-principle, we come to our senses by learning to leap and see anew.

GAM: Does this mean that the tools architects use intuitively can be regarded as an extension of the body?

EA: Heidegger distinguished different modes of tool-use. In a first mode ("ready-to-hand," *zuhanden* in German), a person uses a tool as if it were an extension of the body; the focus is on the task and users are unaware of the tool (the tool is "phenomenally transparent"). In a second mode ("present-at-hand," *vorhanden* in German), a tool is treated as a separate entity and users are aware of "its" properties (the tool is "phenomenally present"). This mostly happens when users experience a "breakdown" (for example, the tool fails to function as expected and thus becomes the focus of attention).

The idea of *present-at-mind* further captures the *ways in which* creative people move between modes as they interact with an object, tool, or media.

überlassene Geist vermag Erhebliches; durch Werkzeuge und Hilfsmittel wird das Geschäft vollbracht; man bedarf dieser also für den Verstand wie für die Hand".[9] *Dem Verstand eine helfende Hand zu geben* bedeutet, dass ein Großteil des gewonnenen Wissens *knowledge-in-action* ist: wir denken und handeln gleichzeitig! *Der Hand ein Werkzeug zu geben* bedeutet wiederum, dass die erforschten Materialien und verwendeten Werkzeuge maßgeblich dazu beitragen, unser Handeln in der Welt zu erweitern und zu vermitteln.

Ich möchte *embodied cognition* („verkörperte" Kognition) der Vorstellung vorbehalten, dass unser Körper seine eigene Intelligenz besitzt (er „denkt" genauso wie unser Verstand), dass unser Wissen und Know-how so tief in der sensomotorischen Erfahrung eingeschrieben sind, dass wir buchstäblich davon leben. *Embedded cognition* („eingebettete" Kognition) hingegen besagt, wie intelligente Wesen (Körper/Geist in situ) die Welt, in der sie leben, gestalten und zurichten.

Für Phänomenologen bezieht sich „verkörperte" Kognition auf die intuitive Erfahrung des *In-der-Welt-Seins*. Beim Werkzeuggebrauch geht es dagegen um die menschliche Fähigkeit, die Reichweite über den Zugriff der bloßen Hand (von Körper/Verstand) hinaus zu verlängern und dadurch Macht zu empfinden. Michael Polanyi schreibt: „Wann immer wir bestimmte Dinge [ein Werkzeug oder eine Sonde] gebrauchen […], verändern diese Dinge ihr Aussehen. [Stattdessen] können wir sagen, dass wir uns die Dinge *einverleiben* […], [oder] dass wir unseren Körper soweit ausdehnen, bis er sie einschließt und sie uns *innewohnen*."[10] Maurice Merleau-Ponty formuliert es so: „Sich an einen Hut, an ein Automobil oder an einen Stock gewöhnen heißt, sich in ihnen einrichten, oder umgekehrt, sie an der Voluminosität des eigenen Leibes teilhaben zu lassen."[11] Der Punkt hier ist: obwohl es eine physische Abgrenzung zwischen Leib und Werkzeug gibt, verblasst diese Abgrenzung durch den Gebrauch des Werkzeugs: das gehandhabte Werkzeug wird zur Verlängerung und somit zu einem Teil unserer selbst. Und so ist es genau diese Fähigkeit, Grenzen zu ziehen und zu verwischen, umzuschalten, die Perspektive zu wechseln, die uns am Leben hält und schlauer macht. Es ist eben nicht so, dass wir im Prinzip nur Cyborgs wären, wir kommen zur Vernunft, indem wir lernen, ins kalte Wasser zu springen und neu zu sehen.

9   Francis Bacon, *The New Organon*, Cambridge Texts in the History of Philosophy, eds. Lisa Jardine and Michael Silverthorne, (Cambridge and New York, 2000), p. 33.

10 Michael Polanyi, *Personal Knowledge: Towards a Post-Critical Philosophy* (Chicago, 1958), p. 59. Both Polanyi and Merleau-Ponty refer to what Heidegger called the "readiness-to-hand" of equipment. Martin Heidegger, *Being and Time*, trans. John Macquarrie and Edward Robinson, (Oxford, 1962), p. 98.

11 Maurice Merleau Ponty, *Phenomenology of Perception* (London, 1962), p. 143.

9   Francis Bacon: *Instauratio Magna. Novum Organum*. Übers. J. H. Kirchmann, Norderstedt 2008, S. 30.

10 Michael Polanyi: *Implizites Wissen*, Frankfurt/M 1958, S. 23f. Polanyi und Merleau-Ponty nehmen hier Bezug auf das, was Heidegger die „Zuhandenheit" von „Zeug" nennt. Martin Heidegger, *Sein und Zeit*, Tübingen 1976, S. 136.

11 Maurice Merleau-Ponty: *Phänomenologie der Wahrnehmung*. Aus dem Französischen übersetzt von Rudolf Boehm, Berlin 1966, S. 173.

GAM: Bedeutet dies, dass die von Architekten verwendeten Tools intuitiv als Verlängerung des Körpers betrachtet werden können?

EA: Heidegger unterscheidet zwei Arten des Werkzeuggebrauchs. Bei der ersten, der „Zuhandenheit", benützt jemand ein Werkzeug wie eine physische Verlängerung seiner selbst; der Fokus liegt auf der Aufgabe und die Benutzer nehmen das Werkzeug als solches nicht wahr (das Werkzeug ist als Phänomen transparent'). Bei der zweiten Art, der Vorhandenheit, wird das Werkzeug als separate Entität behandelt, die Benutzer nehmen „seine" Eigenschaften bewusst wahr (das Werkzeug ist als Phänomen präsent'). Dies geschieht zumeist, wenn eine „Störung" auftritt (zum Beispiel, wenn das Werkzeug nicht wie erwartet funktioniert und dadurch die Aufmerksamkeit auf sich lenkt).

Der Begriff der Bewusstheit wiederum erfasst die *Art und Weise, wie* kreative Menschen zwischen den Modi hin- und herspringen, wenn sie mit einem Gegenstand, Werkzeug oder Medium interagieren. Der Akzent liegt auf der Interaktion: ich kann mit meinem Werkzeug eins (verschmolzen) sein (solange alles reibungslos läuft). Doch sobald etwas Unerwartetes eintritt, schalte ich um, ich behandle das Werkzeug als eigenständige Entität und stelle dessen Handhabung neu ein.[12] Anders gesagt, der Lernprozess ist Resultat des bewussten oder unbewussten Wechselns zwischen (1) Einziehen/Heraustreten (Immersion, Separation); (2) Zentrierung und Dezentrierung (als Selbst behandeln/als das Andere behandeln); und (3) Aufnahme/Projektion nach außen (internalisieren/externalisieren).

GAM: Digitale Phänomene unterliegen nicht denselben Gesetzen wie analoge: sie können nichtlinear sein, unberechenbar, fehlerträchtig, sie können abstürzen und wir verstehen nicht, warum. Sie sind in der Lage, Aufgaben zu bewältigen, die außerhalb von allem liegen, was wir ohne sie erreichen könnten. Manchmal sind sie geradezu irrwitzig. Können wir trotzdem Intuition für sie entwickeln?

EA: Ganz recht, die Sache wird kompliziert, wenn die von uns verwendeten Werkzeuge anfangen, eigenständig zu agieren, den Großteil einer Aufgabe alleine bewältigen oder ganz und gar das Ruder übernehmen, indem sie Probleme auf ihre Weise lösen. Dann werden sie von *Denkhilfen* zu in ein

The point here is that even though there may be a physical demarcation between body and tool, through tool-use the demarcation fades away: the tool-at-hand becomes an extension and hence a part of us.

---

12 Sogenannte Dual-Prozess-Theorien in der Kognitiven Psychologie unterscheiden zwischen automatischen und kontrollierten Prozessen. Ein kontrollierter Prozess wird „unter Kontrolle und durch Aufmerksamkeit des Subjekts" aktiviert und „kann in neuen Situationen, für die keine automatischen Abläufe erlernt wurden, ausgelöst, verändert und angewendet werden." Walter Schneider/Richard M. Shiffrin: „Controlled and Automatic Human Information Processing: I. Detection, Search, and Attention." *Psychological Review*, 84, 1 (1977), S. 1–66, hier S. 2–3.

The stress is on the dance itself: I may *be at one* (fused) with my tool (as long as everything runs smoothly). Yet, as soon as anything goes unexpectedly, I switch mode, I consider the tool as an entity in itself, and I recalibrate my handling of it.[12] In other words, learning occurs as a result of our conscious or unconscious moving back and forth between (1) dwelling in/stepping back (immersion, separation); (2) centering/decentering (treat as me/treat as other); and (3) taking it in/projecting it out (internalize/externalize).

GAM: Digital phenomena aren't bound by the same laws as analogue ones: They can be non-linear, unpredictable, buggy, they can crash and we don't understand why. They can also perform tasks that are outside anything we could achieve without them. They can be mind-boggling. Can we still develop an intuition for them?

EA: Indeed, things get complicated once the tools we use begin to act on our behalf, take on entire chunks of a task, or take over altogether (solving our problems their own ways). That's when from *objects to think with* they become *operations embedded* into a physical device or a computer program (machine, automaton). From mental aid (description, notation, model) or tool (instrument, abacus) they become "augmented" or blended realities, virtual world, artificial partners, avatars (simulations).

In an announcement of her latest book *Alone Together*, Sherry Turkle writes: "Facebook. Twitter. Second Life. Smart phones. Robotic pets. Robotic lovers. Thirty years ago, we asked what we would use computers for. Now the question is: what *don't* [shouldn't] we use them for."[13] Whether we feel depleted or enthralled by the previously unthinkable options made possible by digital technologies is an important question. Yet more intriguing, as you suggest, is whether we will still even notice, let alone challenge, the technologies' impact on how we think, learn, and live our lives, as their

> To be engaging, digital artifacts have to provide affordance as well, but that won't be enough. While affordance speaks to an artifact's clarity to signal uses, something more is needed to capture our imaginations and sense of delight. This "something more," may well be its own unusual blend of autonomy and responsiveness: an invitation to play and dance!

Gerät oder Computerprogramm (Maschine, Automat) *eingebetteten Operationen.* Aus mentalen Hilfsmitteln (Beschreibung, Notation, Modell) oder Werkzeugen (Instrument, Abakus) werden „erweiterte" oder vermischte Realitäten, virtuelle Welten, künstliche Partner, Avatare (Simulationen).

In einer Ankündigung ihres jüngsten Buchs *Alone Together* schreibt Sherry Turkle: „Facebook. Twitter. Second Life. Smartphones. Roboter-Haustiere. Robot Lovers. Vor dreißig Jahren fragten wir uns, wozu wir Computer verwenden sollten. Heute lautet die Frage, wozu wir sie *nicht* verwenden (sollten)."[13] Ob wir die bisher unvorstellbaren, durch digitale Technologien möglich gewordenen Optionen als Verarmung oder als Glück empfinden, ist eine wichtige Frage. Noch spannender ist es jedoch, sich zu fragen, ob wir den Einfluss der Technologien auf unsere Art zu denken, lernen und leben, überhaupt noch wahrnehmen, geschweige denn infrage stellen, da sich das Maschinelle (bzw. angeblich Menschenähnliche) immer mehr in die von uns bewohnten Zeit-Räume integriert bzw. auflöst.

GAM: Wenn sich die neuen Technologien in unserem Alltag auflösen, werden wir neue Arten von Intuition für sie entwickeln?

EA: Es ist schwer zu sagen, welche Intuition unterschiedliche Menschen für sie entwickeln werden, aber eines steht fest: nicht alle Hybride und Quasi-Objekte, die wir in unseren Alltag integrieren, sind so inspirierend oder lebendig wie Beziehungs-„Partner". Manche vereinnahmen uns, andere halten uns auf Distanz. Manche sind folgsam, andere scheinen einen eigenen Kopf zu haben. Manche sind winzig und begleiten uns überall hin; andere sind groß und unhandlich, halten uns „geerdet", an Ort und Stelle, ja eingesperrt: sie verlangen, dass wir ihnen gegenüber eine bestimmte Position einnehmen. Donald Norman führte den Begriff der „Sichtbarkeit"[14] (*affordance*) für die Fähigkeit eines Gegenstands ein, Zweck und Art seiner Verwendung zu signalisieren. Als Beispiele für Gegenstände mit schlechter Sichtbarkeit nennt er eine Lampe, bei der nicht ersichtlich ist, wo sich der An- und Ausschaltknopf befindet, und einen Türgriff, der nicht verrät, ob man drücken oder ziehen soll. Schließlich könnte selbst ein banaler Türgriff etwas Erfreuliches sein, wenn es ihm über das Einlassgewähren hinaus gelänge, unsere Aufmerksamkeit zu erregen, unseren Atem anzuhalten und – warum nicht? – unsere Schritte zu verlangsamen!

---

12   So-called dual processing theories in Cognitive Psychology establish a distinction between automated and controlled mental processes. A controlled process is "activated under control of, and through attention by, the subject," and "may be set up, altered, and applied in novel situations for which automatic sequences have never been learned." Walter Schneider and Richard M. Shiffrin, "Controlled and Automatic Human Information Processing: I. Detection, Search, and Attention." *Psychological Review*, 84, 1 (1977), pp. 1–66, esp. p. 2–3.]

13   Sherry Turkle, *Alone Together: Why We Expect More from Technology and Less from Each Other*, (New York, 2011). See also: http://www.alonetogetherbook.com/

13   Sherry Turkle: *Alone together. Why We Expect More from Technology and Less from Each Other*, New York 2011. Dt. Ausgabe: Sherry Turkle, *Verloren unter 100 Freunden. Wie wir in der digitalen Welt seelisch verkümmern. Aus dem Englischen von Joannis Stefanidis, München 2011. Vgl. auch: http://www.alonetogetherbook.com/

14   Donald Norman: *The Psychology of Everyday Things*. New York 1988, S. 9. Dt. Ausgabe: Donald A. Norman, *Dinge des Alltags. Gutes Design und Psychologie für Gebrauchsgegenstände*. Deutsche Übersetzung von Katharine Cofer, Frankfurt/Main, New York, 1989, S. 14.

Auch er könnte Empfindungen bezüglich Durchgang und Schwellen auslösen und die Erfahrung des Durchquerens bereichern. Er könnte eine Sprache sprechen, die unsere innersten Sehnsüchte erreicht. Selbstverständlich ist auch bei digitalen Artefakten Sichtbarkeit gefordert, aber damit ist es nicht getan. Sichtbarkeit heißt, dass ein Artefakt seine Verwendbarkeit kenntlich macht; um Fantasien und Hochgefühle auszulösen, braucht es jedoch mehr. Dieses „mehr" ist vielleicht seine ungewöhnliche Mischung aus Autonomie und Reaktivität: eine Einladung zum Spielen und Tanzen!

Verkörperte Interaktion, wie sie in der HCI (Human Computer Interaction) eingesetzt wird, versucht zu verstehen, welche Rolle der menschliche Körper bei der Konzeption von und Interaktion mit Technik spielt. Interaktionen gelten als intuitiv, wenn ein Nutzer ohne ausführliche Einweisung, Erklärung oder Hilfestellung die Technik sofort erfolgreich und unbewusst bedienen kann. Im Rekurs auf Heidegger definiert Paul Dourish verkörperte Interaktion (*embodied interaction*) als „die Produktion, Handhabung und Weitergabe von Bedeutung durch engagierte Interaktion mit Artefakten".[15] Dourish betont die Dualität des erlebten versus wahrgenommenen Körpers. Faktisch bewohnen wir die Welt durch unseren erlebten oder empirischen Körper (frz. *corps propre*) und das ist nicht dasselbe wie den eigenen Körper im Spiegel als eines von mehreren Objekten in der Welt zu sehen. Durch Empathie stellen wir eine Beziehung zu anderen Menschen her – nicht nur als Objekte in der Welt, sondern auch als erlebte Körper, für die wir etwas empfinden.

GAM: Du hast viel über neue, von digitalen Medien hervorgebrachte Formen von Kreativität geforscht und geschrieben. Man betrachtet die Intuition beim Entwerfen oft in engem Zusammenhang mit Kreativität. Wie würdest Du dieses Verhältnis beschreiben und welchen Einfluss haben dabei digitale Tools?

EA: Begabung, Intuition, Kreativität – Du verlangst von mir, ein Riesenthema nach dem anderen abzuhandeln! Um Deine Frage zu beantworten, müssen wir zuerst ermitteln, was wir mit „Kreativität" meinen. Ich habe kürzlich einen Artikel geschrieben, in dem ich Lubart zitiere, der sich mit unterschiedlichen Traditionen von Kreativität beschäftigt, die charakteristisch für unterschiedliche Kulturen sind. Nach Lubart ist Kreativität in westlichen Kulturen zumeist produktorientiert, originär und auf Problemlösung durch „Betreten von Neuland" ausgerichtet.[16] Das westliche Verständnis stellt zudem den indivi-

own "machine-ness" (or claimed "human-like-ness") increasingly dissolves into the fabric of the time-spaces we inhabit.

GAM: If these new technologies are dissolving into our daily lives, will we develop new types of intuition for them?

EA: It is hard to tell what intuition different people will develop for them but one thing is sure: not all the hybrids and quasi-objects we incorporate in our everyday lives are equally inspiring or vivid as relational "partners." Some draw us in while others keep us at a distance. Some are obedient while others seem to have a mind of their own. Some are tiny and stay with us wherever we go. Others yet, big and bulky, keep us grounded, posted, or even boxed in: they request that we position ourselves with respect to them. Donald Norman introduced the term "affordance" to refer to an object's ability to signal its potential uses.[14] Examples of objects with poor affordances include a lamp that doesn't tell the location of its on/off switch and a doorknob that doesn't communicate whether the door should be pushed or pulled. Ultimately, even a mundane doorknob could be delightful if, beyond getting us through a doorway, it could retain our attention, suspend our breath, and why not? Slow down our steps! It too could evoke feelings about passages and thresholds, and enrich our experience of transiting. It could speak a language that reaches our inner most aspirations. To be engaging, digital artifacts have to provide affordance as well, but that won't be enough. While affordance speaks to an artifact's clarity to signal uses, something more is needed to capture our imaginations and sense of delight. This "something more," may well be its own unusual blend of autonomy and responsiveness: an invitation to play and dance!

Embodied interaction, as used in HCI (Human Computer Interaction), seeks to understand the role the body plays in the conception, experience, and interactions with technology. And interactions are seen as intuitive, if a user, without much priming, explanation, or help, can instantly, successfully and unconsciously utilize it. Drawing from Heidegger, Paul Dourish in particular defines *embodied interaction* as "the creation, manipulation, and sharing of meaning through engaged interaction with artifacts."[15] Dourish stresses the dual nature of our lived vs. perceived body. In substance, through our lived, or experiential, bodies (*corps propre*, in French) we inhabit the world, which is different from seeing my body in the mirror as an object among other objects in the world. Through empathy we relate to other people not only as objects in the world but also as lived bodies that we feel for.

GAM: You have worked and written a lot about new forms of creativity that digital media have engendered. Intuition in design is seen as being closely related to creativity. How would you describe this relationship and how have digital tools influenced it?

EA: Talent, intuition, creativity—you really want me to address one huge topic after another! To answer this one we first have to establish what

15   Paul Dourish: *Where the Action Is. Foundations of Embodied Interaction.* Cambridge, MA 2004, S. 126.

16   Todd I. Lubart: „Creativity across Cultures", in Robert J. Sternberg (Hg.), *Handbook of Creativity*, Cambridge 1999, S. 339–350.

14   Donald Norman, *The Psychology of Everyday Things* (New York, 1988), p. 9.

15   Paul Dourish, *Where the Action is: Foundations of Embodied Interaction* (Cambridge, MA, 2004), p. 126.

we mean by "creativity." I recently wrote an article in which I quote Lubart who discusses different traditions of creativity we characteristic of different cultures. According to Lubart, Westerners mostly consider creativity as product-oriented, originality-driven, and aimed at solving problems by "breaking grounds."[16] The Western view also stresses individual gains (self-promotion, personal benefits) over greater social good (societal and environmental considerations such as air quality or collective welfare), and favors a work ethic based on competition and a belief in progress. The prevailing view in Eastern philosophies, by contrast, is rooted in tradition, seeks harmony (balance), and emphasizes the "emotional, personal and intra-psychic elements" of creativity (inner "truth"). The purpose is less to innovate, or be original, than it is about tuning in (composing with what's there), slowing down (dwelling), letting go (drifting), and seeing anew (adopting a beginner's mindset).

Today's "cultures of creativity" cut across generations, social groups, and territorial borders—be they geographic, national, or ethnic. Indeed digital media and the Internet play a key role in this as they enable new forms of expression, ways of sharing and trading, and modes of appropriation. Appropriation is the process by which a person or group becomes acquainted with, and gains interest in, things by making them their own. It is an eminently creative process, often resulting in unexpected uses, clever *détournements*, and surprising outcomes. The connection between creativity and intuition has much to do with appropriation. For a technology to evolve and become better adapted to its users, something more than mere adoption is needed. The long-term, innovative effects occur when users appropriate the technology, make it their own and embed it within their lives.

> Humans are corporeal beings embedded in a physical world. Yet, they are also curious minds and playful spirits. And they can stick to a task forever (beyond the cool factor) if they are enjoying what they get themselves into (they favor "hard fun" over ease of use).

GAM: During your work at MIT you have collaborated with a lot of nerds, techies, and geeks—including myself. It seems to me that your goal in these collaborations has always been to promote those aspects of a project or technology, which allow us to learn, to engage our minds, to enrich our experience. In your opinion, why are these qualities so hard to come by?

EA: Those who know how to code aren't always the best at imagining creative uses, and those who truly care about users aren't always of good advice when it comes to designing innovative concepts, scenarios, or products. One lesson I have learned in working with "geeks," designers, and

duellen Ertrag (Eigenwerbung, persönliche Vorteile) über die Belange der Allgemeinheit (gesellschaftliche und Umweltthemen wie Luftqualität oder Gemeinwohl) und favorisiert eine auf Wettbewerb und Fortschrittsglauben beruhende Arbeitsethik. In östlichen Philosophien hingegen stehen die Verwurzelung in der Tradition, das Streben nach Harmonie (Gleichgewicht) und die „emotionalen, persönlichen und intrapsychische Elemente"[17] der Kreativität (innere „Wahrheit") im Vordergrund. Das angestrebte Ziel ist weniger Innovation oder Originalität, sondern Einklang (mit dem arbeiten, was da ist), Verlangsamung (Wohnen), Loslassen (Sich-Treiben-lassen) und neu Sehen (den Blick des Anfängers annehmen).

Die heutigen „cultures of creativity" ziehen sich quer durch Generationen, soziale Gruppierungen und Territorialgrenzen – ob geografischer, nationaler oder ethnischer Natur. Die digitalen Medien und das Internet spielen dabei in der Tat eine zentrale Rolle, da sie neue Ausdrucksformen, neue Arten des Teilens und Austauschens und neue Aneignungsformen ermöglichen. Aneignung meint den Prozess, bei dem ein Einzelner oder eine Gruppe Dinge kennenlernt und Interesse an ihnen entwickelt, indem er sie sich aneignet. Es ist ein eminent kreativer Prozess, der oft zu unerwartetem Gebrauch, cleveren Wendungen und überraschenden Ergebnissen führt. Der Zusammenhang von Kreativität und Intuition hat viel mit Aneignung zu tun. Damit sich eine Technologie entwickeln und den Bedürfnissen des Nutzers besser entsprechen kann, ist mehr nötig als bloße Adaptierung. Innovative Langzeiteffekte stellen sich ein, wenn Nutzer sich die Technologie aneignen, zu eigen machen und in ihr Leben integrieren.

GAM: Am MIT hast Du mit vielen Nerds, Techies und Geeks zusammengearbeitet – mich eingeschlossen. Ich habe den Eindruck, Dir waren stets diejenigen Aspekte eines Projekts oder einer Technologie am wichtigsten, bei denen wir etwas lernen, den Verstand einschalten, unsere Erfahrung erweitern können. Warum ist das Deiner Meinung nach so schwierig?

EA: Diejenigen, die kodieren können, sind nicht immer die Besten, wenn es ums Ausdenken kreativer Verwendungen geht, und diejenigen, denen die User wirklich am Herzen liegen, fällt oft nichts Vernünftiges ein, wenn es innovative Konzepte, Szenarien oder Produkte zu entwerfen gilt. Eine Lektion habe ich bei der Arbeit mit „Geeks", Designern und Lehrern aller Art gelernt: wenn man für Andere innovativ sein will, ist es vielleicht das Beste, nicht zu spekulieren, was User wünschen, oder zu tun, was sie sagen. Stattdessen sollte man *genau zuhören* und dann die eigene Expertise einbringen, um *gemeinsam* etwas herzustellen, das die User – und man selbst – lieben, sobald es da ist!

---

16   Todd I. Lubart, "Creativity across Cultures," in *Handbook of Creativity*, ed. Robert J. Sternberg, (Cambridge, 1999), p. 339–350.

17   Ebd.

Eine zweite, nicht minder wichtige Lektion ist, dass die Szenarios, die wir uns ausdenken, und die Tools, die wir bauen, über bloße Funktionalität und Benutzerfreundlichkeit hinaus für den User kinästhetisch und propriozeptiv stimmen und seine Fantasie, sein Interesse auf längere Zeit bannen sollen (ich wachse mit meinen Tools und meine Tools wachsen mit mir). Menschen sind körperliche Wesen, eingebettet in eine physische Welt. Aber sie sind auch neugierige Köpfe und verspielte Naturen. Und sie können eine Ewigkeit (über den Cool-Faktor hinaus) an einer Aufgabe dranbleiben, wenn das, worin sie sich verbeißen, ihnen Spaß macht. (Anstrengender Spaß ist ihnen lieber als Bedienerfreundlichkeit.)

GAM: Anstrengender Spaß ist immer noch Spaß. Viele digitalen Produkte, denen wir ausgesetzt sind, machen überhaupt keinen Spaß. Sie sind nervig, unintuitiv, stinklangweilig. Siehst Du eine Möglichkeit, das zu ändern?

EA: Nicht alle Artefakte, die wir designen oder mit denen wir interagieren, eignen sich gleichermaßen als Projektionsmaterial. Manche sind eindeutig besser geeignet, sinnvolle und erfreuliche Begegnungen zu begünstigen. Deshalb ist es für Designer und User so wichtig, Verantwortung für ihre Produkte zu übernehmen und nicht in die trivial-konstruktivistische oder neoempiristische Falle zu tappen. Erstere geht davon aus – ich karikiere die konstruktivistische Position – dass, egal mit welchem Material man es zu tun hat, die Lernenden ihre Erfahrung ohnehin projizieren werden (warum sich also den Kopf über das Setting zerbrechen). Die zweite beruht, wie erwähnt, auf der Vorstellung, dass die Erkenntnisse, die man durch Interaktion mit coolen Tools gewinnt, schon in den Materialien drinstecken (warum sich also den Kopf über die Lernenden zerbrechen). Hier eine Balance herzustellen, scheint der Weg zu sein, den es zu beschreiten gilt. Doch das ist, wie wir wissen, wesentlich leichter gesagt als getan.

Übersetzung Marion Kagerer

educators of all kinds is that when it comes to innovating for others, it may be best not to guess what users want, or for that matter, do what they say. Instead, *listen carefully*, and then bring in your expertise to help *co-create* what they—and you—will love once it is there!

Another lesson, equally important, is that beyond mere functionality and ease of use, the scenarios we imagine and the tools we build should feel right to users' kinaesthetic and proprioceptive senses, and sustain their imagination and interest over time (I grow with my tools and my tools grow with me). Humans are corporeal beings embedded in a physical world. Yet, they are also curious minds and playful spirits. And they can stick to a task forever (beyond the cool factor) if they are enjoying what they get themselves into (they favor "hard fun" over ease of use).

GAM: Hard fun is still fun. Many digital products we are exposed to aren't fun at all. They are annoying, un-intuitive, mind-numbing. Do you see a way to change that?

EA: Not all the artifacts we design or interact with are equally good projective materials. Some are clearly better suited to foster meaningful and delightful encounters. This is why it seems essential for designers as well as for users to take responsibility of their products by not falling into the trivial-constructivist or the neo-empiricist trap. The first would like to assume—I am caricaturing the constructivist's stance—that no matter the materials at hand, learners will project their own experience anyway (so why bother about the setting). The second, as mentioned earlier, rests on the notion that the smarts to be earned by interacting with cool tools are themselves embedded in the materials (so why bother about the learners). Striking a balance between the two seems the obvious way to go. Though, as we know, this is much easier said than done.

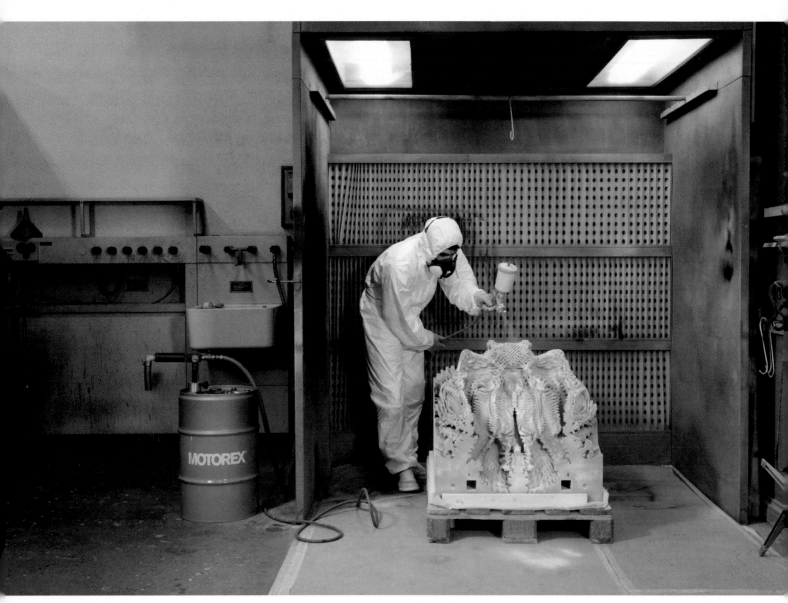

„Digital Grotesque" – Beschichtung der Oberfläche Surface coating © Foto photo: Emetris Shammas/Achilleas Xydis, 2013

Beseitigung von Sandresten Removal of surplus sand © Foto photo: Emetris Shammas/Achilleas Xydis, 2013

Aufbau der Grotte Grotto assembly © Foto photo: Emetris Shammas/Achilleas Xydis, 2013

Digital Grotesque, 2013
Michael Hansmeyer and Benjamin Dillenburger

Digital Grotesque is the first human-scale immersive space entirely 3D printed out of sand. Measuring 16 square meters and 3.2 meters in height, the structure is materialized at a resolution of a tenth of a millimeter with details at the threshold of human perception.

How could an architecture that is entirely designed by algorithms look? In the project Digital Grotesque, we develop customized algorithms to recursively refine and enrich a simple input form—until a complex geometry of 260 million individual facets is produced. This single process generates many scales of architecture, from the overall form with its broad curvature, to local surface formations, down to minute textures. They create an architecture that cannot be drawn and would be inconceivable using traditional means.

Additive manufacturing heralds a revolution in fabrication: just as with printing ink on paper, the amount of information and complexity of the output is no longer constrained. The combination of 3D printing and computational design allows a new, non-standardized, highly differentiated and spatially complex architecture. Digital Grotesque brings additive manufacturing technology to a true architectural scale: it is a lavish, exhilarating space, between chaos and order, both natural and artificial, yet neither foreign nor familiar: a Digital Grotesque.

Digital Grotesque, 2013
Michael Hansmeyer und Benjamin Dillenburger

Digital Grotesque ist der erste begehbare Raum, der vollständig im 3D-Druckverfahren aus Sand erstellt wurde. Die 16 Quadratmeter große und 3,2 Meter hohe Struktur ist in einer Auflösung von einem Zehntelmillimeter materialisiert worden und weist Details auf, welche die Grenze der menschlichen Wahrnehmung erreichen.

Wie könnte eine Architektur, die ganz durch Algorithmen gestaltet ist, aussehen? Im Projekt Digital Grotesque entwickeln wir eigene Programme, um eine einfache Anfangsform rekursiv zu verfeinern und anzureichern, bis sich die Form zu einer komplexen Geometrie aus 260 Millionen Einzelflächen transformiert. Derselbe Prozess generiert die architektonische Form in mehreren Maßstabsebenen, von der Gesamtform mit seinen geschwungenen Kurven zu lokalen Einzelformationen bis hinunter zu den winzigen Texturen. So entsteht eine Architektur, die man mit konventionellen Mitteln nicht zeichnen und auch nicht entwerfen könnte.

Additive Fabrikationsverfahren kündigen gegenwärtig eine Revolution im Bauen an. Genau wie beim Drucken mit Tinte auf Papier ist die Information und die Komplexität des Outputs nicht mehr beschränkt. Durch die Kombination von additiven Fabrikationsverfahren und computergestütztem Entwerfen entsteht eine neuartige, nicht standardisierte, hochdifferenzierte und räumlich komplexe Architektur. Digital Grotesque bringt additive Herstellungsverfahren in einen echten Architekturmaßstab: es ist ein überreicher, berauschender Raum, zwischen Ordnung und Chaos, sowohl künstlich als auch natürlich, weder fremd noch vertraut: eine Digitale Groteske.

Digital Grotesque in Zahlen **Digital Grotesque in Figures**

Virtuell Virtual
- Algorithmisch generierte Geometrie Algorithmically generated geometry • 260 Millionen Flächen 260 million surfaces • 30 Billionen Voxel 30 billion voxels • 78 GB Produktionsdaten 78 GB production data

Physisch Physical
- Sand-gedruckte Teile (Silikat und Binder) Sand-printed elements (silicate and binder) • 16 Quadratmeter, 3,2 Meter hoch 16 square meters, 3.2 meters high • 11 Tonnen gedruckter Sandstein 11 tons of printed sandstone • 0,13 mm Ebenenauflösung 0.13 mm layer resolution • 4,0 × 2,0 × 1,0 Meter maximales Druckvolumen 4.0 × 2.0 × 1.0 meter maximum print space

Zeitachse Timeline
- Entwurfsentwicklung: 1 Jahr Design development: 1 year • Herstellung (Druck): 1 Monat Fabrication (printing): 1 month • Aufbau: 1 Tag Assembly: 1 day

Partner und Sponsoren Partners and Sponsors
- Lehrstuhl für CAAD, Prof. Hovestadt, ETH Zurich Chair for CAAD, Prof. Hovestadt, ETH Zurich • Departement Architektur, ETH Zurich Department of Architecture, ETH Zurich • voxeljet AG • FRAC Centre • Strobel Quarzsand GmbH • Pro Helvetia

Die Forschung für das Digital Grotesque Projekt wurde am Lehrstuhl für Architektur und CAAD der Eidgenössischen Technischen Hochschule (ETH) Zürich durchgeführt. Alle Teile wurden von der voxeljet AG gedruckt. Der erste Teil von Digital Grotesque ist eine Auftragsarbeit des FRAC Centre für seine permanente Kollektion. Research for the Digital Grotesque project was carried out at the Chair for CAAD at the Swiss Federal Institute of Technology (ETH) in Zurich. All components were printed by voxeljet AG. The first part of Digital Grotesque is a commission by FRAC Centre for its permanent collection.

Team
Fabrikation Fabrication: Maria Smigielska, Miro Eichelberger, Yuko Ishizu, Jeanne Wellinger, Tihomir Janjusevic, Nicolás Miranda Turu, Evi Xexaki, Akihiko Tanigaito
Video und Fotos Video and Photos: Demetris Shammas, Achilleas Xydis

Grotte (innen) **Grotto interior** © Hansmeyer/Dillenburger, 2013

Grotte Detail Grotto detail © Hansmeyer/Dillenburger, 2013

Grotte Seitenwand Testaufbau **Grotto side 1 – test assembly** © Hansmeyer/Dillenburger, 2013

Mind & Matter

1 Kochendes Wasser Boiling water © http://brandikruse.wordpress.com/2012/12/14/the-glass-bubbles/

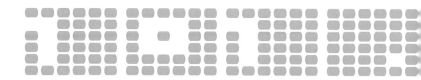

Digital Phenomenologies

From Postmodern Indeterminacy to
Big Data and Computation*

A couple of years ago I published a small book recounting the history of the digital turn in architecture from the early 1990s, when in my opinion it all started, to around 2010—which is when I finished writing the book.

Digitale Phänomenologien. Von postmoderner Unbestimmtheit zu Big Data und Kalkulation.* Vor einigen Jahren publizierte ich ein kleines Buch, das die Geschichte der digitalen Wende in der Architektur von den frühen 1990er Jahren, als nach meiner Meinung alles begann, bis etwa zu der Zeit um das Jahr 2010 erzählt, als ich die Arbeit an dem Buch abschloss.

MARIO CARPO

To make a long story short, in that book I divided the history of digitally intelligent design into three stages or phases: first, the age of form, of digital form-making (the age of free form and of complex geometries); second, the age of standards, or rather of the un-making of standards—the age of digital non-standards; and third, a period that in my view started in the years just after 2000, when the emphasis was on agency, or the unmaking of traditional, humanistic, and modern authorship in design. In my opinion, this is where we still are now, and this is yet an unfolding story: digital authorship in general, and authorship in digital design in particular—meaning who makes what in a digital environment—are still very much an open experimental field, where plenty of exciting new things keep happening. Today my topic is the second chapter, the follow-up to that story, namely: the more general challenge of indeterminacy in design, and some of its theoretical and technical implications. What happens when designers decide to use the unprecedented potentials of digital tools to delegate some design decisions to others, to many, to the crowds, or to random chance? And why should they do so anyway? Is design not about being in charge? Here one problem of course is that we do not know what chance is, regardless of the tools we may use to represent it; and opinions on that matter diverge very much. But before we tackle this insurmountable philosophical issue, let me go back, briefly, to an easier topic—to the recent history of design theory—to see how and why indeterminacy came to play such a central role in today's digitally intelligent design.

> Today my topic is the second chapter, the follow-up to that story, namely: the more general challenge of indeterminacy in design, and some of its theoretical and technical implications.

* * *

The story of the digital turn in architecture in the 1990s is well known, and it has been told many times. We all know the protagonists: it is the story of how Deconstructivism collided with early computer-aided design (CAD), spline modelers, and animation software, merged with the Deleuzian fold and evolved toward globular shapes and topological geometry while riding on the wave of technological optimism in the 1990s—then crashing with it around the turn of the century. So far so good—we are familiar with this story. Yet in hindsight, almost twenty years later, we can now perceive,

Um es kurz zu machen, in diesem Buch unterteile ich die Geschichte des digital gestützten Entwerfens in drei zeitliche Abschnitte: Zuerst in das Zeitalter der Form, des digitalen Formens (die Zeit der freien Form und komplexer Geometrien); zum zweiten in das Zeitalter digitaler Standards, oder besser gesagt der Aufhebung von Standards – das Zeitalter digitaler Non-Standards und drittens in eine Periode, die aus meiner Sicht unmittelbar nach dem Jahr 2000 einsetzte, als die Aufmerksamkeit auf der Wirkung oder der Aufhebung traditioneller, humanistischer und moderner Autorschaft beim Entwerfen lag. Meiner Ansicht nach befinden wir uns noch heute an diesem Punkt, und die Geschichte entwickelt sich noch immer weiter: digitale Urheberschaft im Allgemeinen und Urheberschaft beim digitalen Entwerfen im Besonderen – will heißen, welcher Akteur macht eigentlich was in einem digitalen Umfeld – sind immer noch ein offener, experimenteller Bereich, in dem sich viele überraschende Neuigkeiten ereignen. Mein heutiges Thema ist das zweite Kapitel, die Fortsetzung dieser Geschichte, nämlich die umfassendere Herausforderung von Unbestimmtheit im Entwerfen und einige der damit verbundenen theoretischen und technischen Implikationen. Was geschieht, wenn Designer beschließen, die beispiellosen Möglichkeiten der digitalen Verfahren zu nutzen, um einige der Entwurfsentscheidungen an andere, an viele, an größere Gruppen oder den Zufall zu delegieren? Und weshalb sollten sie das überhaupt tun? Geht es beim Entwerfen nicht darum, verantwortlich zu sein? Hierbei gibt es natürlich das Problem, dass wir nicht wissen, was Zufall ist, unabhängig von den Verfahren, die wir verwenden mögen, um ihn darzustellen. Die Meinungen gehen darüber weit auseinander. Aber ehe wir diese diffizile philosophische Frage in Angriff nehmen, lassen Sie mich kurz auf ein einfacheres Problem zurückkommen: auf die jüngste Geschichte der Entwurfstheorie und die Frage, wie und warum Unbestimmtheit heute beim digital gestützten Entwerfen eine derart zentrale Rolle spielt.

* * *

Die Historie der digitalen Wende in der Architektur in den 1990er Jahren ist wohlbekannt und wurde schon viele Male

* This is the text of a public lecture first read in January 2013 at the Bartlett School of Architecture in London and, with some variations, elsewhere in Europe and in the US in the spring of the same year. It is published here with some revisions and corrections but in the format and style of the oral delivery for which it was meant. For footnotes and further reference see: Mario Carpo, "Introduction," in *The Digital Turn in Architecture, 1992–2012. An AD Reader* (Chichester, 2012), pp. 8–15. Idem, *The Alphabet and the Algorithm* (Cambridge, MA and London, 2011). German translation, *Alphabet und Algorithmus: Wie das Digitale die Architektur herausfordert* (Bielefeld, 2012). Idem, "Digital Darwinism," *Log* 26 (2012), pp. 97–105. Idem, "Digital Style," *Log* 23 (2011), pp. 41–52. German translation, "Digitaler Stil," *Zeitschrift für Medien- und Kulturfoschung* 1 (2012), pp. 105–118.

* Dies ist der Text einer öffentlichen Rede, die ich im Januar 2013 an der Bartlett School of Architecture in London und danach mit einigen Abweichungen andernorts in Europa und im Frühjahr 2012 in den Vereinigten Staaten vortrug. Sie erscheint hier mit einigen Änderungen und Korrekturen, aber in dem Format und Stil des mündlichen Vortrags, für den sie gedacht war. Zu Anmerkungen und weiteren Referenzen vgl.: Mario Carpo, „Introduction", in: *The Digital Turn in Architecture, 1992–2012. An AD Reader*, Chichester 2012, S. 8–15. Ders.: *The Alphabet and the Algorithm*, Cambridge, MA/London 2011. Dt.: *Alphabet und Algorithmus: Wie das Digitale die Architektur herausfordert*, Bielefeld 2012. Ders.: „Digital Darwinism", *Log* 26 (2012), S. 97–105. Ders.: „Digital Style", in: *Log* 23 (2011), S. 41–52. Dt.: „Digitaler Stil", in: *Zeitschrift für Medien und Kulturforschung* 1 (2012), S. 105–118.

erzählt. Wir alle kennen die Protagonisten: Es ist die Geschichte, wie der Dekonstruktivismus mit dem frühen computergestützten Entwerfen (CAD), mit „Spline Modelers" und Animation Software verknüpft, mit der deleuzianischen Falte kollidierte, sich dann hin zu Kugelformen und topologischer Geometrie entwickelte, während er auf der Welle des technologischen Optimismus der 1990er Jahre ritt, um dann mit ihr um die Jahrtausendwende einzubrechen. So weit, so gut – diese Geschichte ist uns bekannt. Aber jetzt, zwanzig Jahre später, können wir im Rückblick aus einer entfernteren Sicht die Fragmente einer anderen Geschichte erkennen, die heutzutage häufig vergessen, in der Literatur der 1990er jedoch anschaulich geschildert wurde. So merkwürdig uns das auch heute erscheinen mag, sahen viele ihrer Protagonisten (Greg Lynn, Stan Allen, Alejandro Zaera-Polo und andere) die digitale Wende zu Beginn der 1990er Jahre als eine Fortsetzung, eine Wiederholung – fast eine Rechtfertigung – einiger, wenn auch nicht aller Ideen, die die Postmoderne spätestens seit Ende der 1970er Jahre vertreten hatte. Gegen die Herrschaft des mechanischen Zeitalters und modernistischer Standardisierung traten sowohl postmoderne Philosophen wie auch Architekten der Postmoderne für Differenzierung, Variation und Wahlfreiheit ein. Philosophen sprachen von der „Fragmentierung der großen Erzählungen", während Architekten von „radikalem Eklektizismus" oder von „Pluralität des Geschmacks" redeten – aber der Geist war derselbe. In den 1970er Jahren gab es natürlich keine technologische Alternative zur mechanischen Massenfertigung und Standardisierung. Digitale Verfahren konnten genau das liefern, was die Postmodernen schon immer wollten, aber zu einem annehmbaren Preis nicht bekommen konnten: Variabilität. Variationen sind das, was digitale Tools am besten können – in sämtlichen Bereichen und Gebieten, von realen bis hin zu medialen Objekten, von Text und Musik zu Shirts und Schuhen, zu Metallschildern und Gebäudeteilen geht es beim Digitalen um Massenproduktion und Spezialanfertigungen. In dieser Hinsicht stellte Digitalität die technische Antwort auf einige kulturelle Bedürfnisse und Erwartungen der Postmoderne dar. Sie stellte das technologische Angebot dar, das den postmodernen Wunsch nach Variationen erfüllte.

In diesem allgemeinen Rahmen verschaffte die Kultur der Postmoderne den digitalen Theorien einige weniger auffällige, häufig unerwartete Argumente, Ideologien und Themen, die man nicht ohne weiteres mit einer High-tech Revolution in Verbindung brächte. Von den 1990er Jahren bis heute blieb die digitale Theorie im Allgemeinen und digitales Entwerfen im Besonderen geprägt von Theorien und Überzeugungen postmodernen Ursprungs und von einer stark humanistischen, indeterministischen, phänomenologischen, spiritualistischen, ja selbst vitalistischen Ausrichtung. Computer und Animismus mögen wie kaum denkbare Partner erscheinen, und doch ist es

from a more distant vantage point, the fragments of another story that is today often forgotten, but was vividly recorded in the literature of the time. Strange as it may appear today, in the early 1990s the digital turn was seen by many of its protagonists (Greg Lynn, Stan Allen, Alejandro Zaera-Polo, among others) as a continuation, a reenactment—a vindication, almost—of (not all, but) some ideas that architectural postmodernists had been advocating since at least the late 1970s. Against the dominion of the mechanical age and of modernist standardization, postmodern philosophers and Po-Mo architects alike had argued for differentiation, variation, and choice. Philosophers spoke of "the fragmentation of master narratives," while architects spoke of "radical eclecticism" or of the "plurality of taste"—but the spirit was the same. In the 1970s, of course, there was no technological alternative to mechanical mass production—other than hand-making and preindustrial craftsmanship (which indeed many PoMos then embraced and favored). But in the 1990s, digital tools started to offer a viable technological alternative to industrial mass production and standardization. Digital tools can deliver just what the PoMos had always wanted but could never get at a reasonable price: variability. Variations are what digital tools are best at—in all field and areas, from physical objects to media objects, from text and music to shirts and shoes to metal panels and parts of buildings, the digital is about mass-producing and customizing variations. In this sense, digitality was a technical answer to some cultural needs and expectations of postmodernity. It was the technological supply that fulfilled the postmodern demand for variations.

Within this general framework, however, postmodern culture also bequeathed to digital theories a number of less conspicuous, often unsuspected arguments, ideologies, and topics that one would not easily associate with a high-tech revolution. From the 1990s to this day, digital theory in general, and digital design theory in particular, have been deeply marked by theories and beliefs of postmodern provenance, and tinted by a strong humanist, indeterminist, phenomenological, spiritualistic, or even vitalistic orientation. Computers and animism may seem unlikely partners, and yet it is a fact that from the beginning—that is, from the 1990s—and to this day, the adoption of digital technologies in design and making has been strongly influenced by a robust and pervasive irrationalist ideology and by a surprisingly strong anti-technological bias.

There is no time here to review all or even a few of these anti-technological theories, most of which derive from systems theory, complexity theory, and from the so-called postmodern sciences of indeterminacy. In the 1990s it was common among designers to refer to this way of thinking as "nonlinearity," and Charles Jencks and Manuel De Landa must be credited for bringing this term to the attention of the design professions. Let me go back to one of the examples that were common at the time to illustrate this matter. Imagine a heap of sand. If we let each grain of sand fall from above in a steady, regular way, and assuming that all the grains are the same, the sandpile will acquire the geometrical shape of a cone. The angle at the base of the cone (angle of internal friction) depends on the diameters of the grains, or granulometry, the material of which they are made, their humidity, and perhaps something else we all studied at school, and it can be calculated using a fairly simple formula. As the grains keep falling and the pile grows, this angle remains the same, until at some point one grain will provoke a catastrophe: the pile will collapse, and after some turmoil a new shape will emerge, and stabilize. As it seems, the point in time when the catastrophe occurs cannot be precisely calculated, and identical experiments repeated ad libitum will always give slightly different results. Likewise, each new configuration of the pile after the collapse will be different from all others, and none can be predicted. In short, the sand heap will at some point self-organize in an undeterminable, unpredictable way.

Indeterminacy in this instance may mean two different things: first, that the sandpile is *indeterminable*, meaning that we do not have the tools or skills to describe it properly, to model it fully, and to do all the calculations that would be necessary to predict its behavior; or that our observations tweak the object and influence its behavior, and so forth. This is the positivistic approach—implying that if we had enough science and computing power, then we could predict the fall of that sandpile as effectively as we can predict the fall of this pen to the ground (after I drop it, of course). Then there is another approach, which posits that the sandpile is inherently *indeterminate*, implying that the sandpile is endowed with some kind of free will, and it may make decisions as arbitrary as any living, intelligent, and animated being. While this may appear to be a long shot to many of us, this way of thinking, called vitalism, is deeply embedded in some religions and in most premodern Western science. And many smart people in the past, but also in the present—including people I know, and people you probably know, too—did and still do in fact believe in the "animation of the inorganic," as well as in magic and in many other supernatural things that cannot be easily proven with facts and figures.

Of course the notion that computers at some point may acquire a faculty of will, and become capable of choice, is long established in the history of science fiction. But in the 1990s the growing complexity of digital networks increasingly suggested and encouraged the notion that computers, and the Internet, are indeed to some extent self-organizing systems, and that they may at times behave in apparently nonlinear, indeterminable ways. This stands to reason, because the Internet, for example, evolved from a military technology which was meant to do just that—to self-organize and reorganize randomly after some catastrophic destruction. Again, for most people the indeterminacy of the Internet was and is just a metaphor—a strategy for the management of technological complexity. However, traces of a similar vitalistic belief in the animation of the inorganic, and particularly in the animation of networked technical systems, are ubiquitous in the digital culture of the 1990s—sometimes taken metaphorically, sometimes literally. Some of this thinking is also reflected in the discourse and in the experiments of the 1990s on what was then called cyberspace, hypersurfaces, virtual reality, and what Brian Massumi then termed "digital phenomenology": a digitally mediated and multisensory alternative to physical space, as found, for example, in some coeval work by Lars Spuybroek.

Anyway, back in the 1990s all this remained a relatively marginal intellectual and cultural phenomenon, and the so-called postmodern sciences of indeterminacy were then often seen as the extreme views of a group of radical thinkers and ideologues, albeit trendy at times, particularly in some circles. But today—today much more is happening. Today, many of these once arcane theories have been largely vindicated by technosocial

eine Tatsache, dass von Anfang an – sprich ab den 1990er Jahren – bis heute die Übernahme digitaler Technologien in Entwurf und Fertigung stark von einer stabilen und allgegenwärtigen irrationalen Ideologie und von einem überraschend starken technikfeindlichen Vorurteil beeinflusst war. An dieser Stelle können nicht alle oder zumindest einige dieser antitechnologischen Ideologien betrachtet werden, die zumeist von systemtheoretischen Grundlagen, Komplexitätstheorie und von der sogenannten postmodernen Wissenschaft der Unbestimmtheit abgeleitet sind. In den 1990er Jahren war es unter Designern üblich, diese Art des Denkens als „nicht linear" zu bezeichnen. Es ist das Verdienst von Charles Jencks und Manuel De Landa, diesen Begriff dem Vokabular von Designern hinzugefügt zu haben. Lassen Sie mich auf ein damals weitverbreitetes Beispiel zur Veranschaulichung der Sache zurückgreifen. Stellen Sie sich einen Sandhaufen vor. Wenn wir die exakt gleichen Sandkörner von oben regelmäßig herabfallen lassen, wird der Sandhaufen die geometrische Form eines Kegels annehmen. Der Winkel am Fuß des Kegels (innerer Kontaktreibungswinkel) hängt vom Durchmesser der Sandkörner oder der Granulometrie ab, vom Material aus dem sie bestehen, ihre Feuchtigkeit und vielleicht noch etwas anderem, das wir alle in der Schule gelernt haben und das nach einer ziemlich einfachen Formel berechnet werden kann. Solange die Sandkörner fallen und der Berg wächst, bleibt dieser Winkel gleich, bis irgendwann ein Sandkorn eine Katastrophe auslösen wird: der Haufen wird einstürzen und nach einigem Durcheinander wird sich eine neue Form herausbilden und stabilisieren. Wie es scheint, lässt sich der Zeitpunkt, an dem die Katastrophe passiert, nicht genau berechnen, und ad libitum wiederholte identische Versuche führen stets zu unterschiedlichen Ergebnissen. Ebenso wird sich jede neue Anordnung des Haufens nach dem Einsturz von allen anderen unterscheiden und keine lässt sich voraussagen. Kurz, der Sandhaufen wird sich ab einem gewissen Punkt auf unbestimmte, unvorhersehbare Weise selbst organisieren.

Unbestimmtheit könnte in diesem Fall zwei verschiedene Dinge bedeuten: zum einen, der Sandhaufen ist *unbestimmbar*, will heißen, uns fehlen die Hilfsmittel oder Fähigkeiten, ihn korrekt zu beschreiben, vollständig nachzubilden und all die Berechnungen anzustellen, die nötig wären sein Verhalten vorherzusagen; oder unsere Beobachtungen justieren das Objekt und beeinflussen sein Verhalten und so weiter. Dies ist der positivistische Ansatz, der impliziert, dass wir den Einsturz des Sandhaufens, wenn wir genügend wissenschaftliche und rechnerische Potenz hätten, ebenso erfolgreich vorhersagen könnten, wie den Fall dieses Stifts auf den Boden (natürlich nachdem ich ihn fallengelassen habe). Dann gibt es da noch einen anderen Ansatz, der davon ausgeht, dass der Sandberg inhärent *unbestimmt* ist, wobei implizit angenommen wird, der Sandhaufen habe eine Art freien Willen und könne

Entscheidungen treffen wie jedes lebende, intelligente Wesen. Obwohl dies vielen von uns weit hergeholt erscheinen mag, ist diese als Vitalismus bezeichnete Denkart in manchen Religionen und den meisten vormodernen westlichen Kulturen tief verwurzelt. Und viele kluge Leute glaubten in der Vergangenheit, und glauben sogar noch heute – darunter Leute, die ich kenne und Leute, die Sie vermutlich auch kennen – tatsächlich an die „Animation des Anorganischen" ebenso wie an Magie und viele andere übernatürliche Dinge, die sich nicht ohne weiteres durch Tatsachen oder Zahlen belegen lassen.

Die Vorstellung, dass Computer irgendwann über einen eigenen Willen verfügen und damit in der Lage sein werden, eine Wahl zu treffen, existiert in der Geschichte der Science Fiction schon seit langem. Die zunehmende Komplexität digitaler Netzwerke legte in den 1990er Jahren jedoch die Vorstellung nahe, dass es sich bei Computer und Internet gewissermaßen tatsächlich um sich selbst organisierende Systeme handelte, die bisweilen in scheinbar nicht-linearer, unbestimmbarer Weise agieren. Das ist naheliegend, da sich beispielsweise das Internet aus einer militärischen Technologie entwickelte, die genau das tun sollte – nach einer Katastrophe sich per Zufallsprinzip selbstständig organisieren und neu ordnen. Gleichwohl war und ist für die meisten Leute die Unbestimmtheit des Internets bloß eine Metapher – eine Strategie für den Umgang mit technischer Komplexität. Und doch sind Spuren eines ähnlichen vitalistischen Glaubens an die Animation des Anorganischen und insbesondere an die Animation vernetzter technischer Systeme in der digitalen Kultur der 1990er Jahre allgegenwärtig – zuweilen wird sie metaphorisch, manchmal buchstäblich aufgefasst. Ein Teil dieser Gedankengänge spiegelt sich auch im Diskurs und den Experimenten der 1990er Jahre wider, in dem, was man damals Cyberspace, Hypersurfaces, virtuelle Realität nannte und was Brian Massumi als „digitale Phänomenologie" bezeichnete: eine digital mediatisierte und multisensorische Alternative zum realen Raum, wie man ihn beispielsweise in einem zeitgenössischen Werk von Lars Spuybroek findet.

In jedem Fall blieb all dies in den 1990ern ein eher marginales intellektuelles und kulturelles Phänomen, und die sogenannte postmoderne Wissenschaft der Unbestimmtheit wurde damals häufig als extreme Ansicht einer Gruppe radikaler Denker und Ideologen betrachtet, wenngleich sie, insbesondere in gewissen Kreisen, zuweilen angesagt war. Heute aber – heute geschieht viel mehr. Viele dieser einst geheimnisumwitterten Theorien haben sich dank des technosozialen Wandels bestätigt, vermutlich weit über die kühnsten Erwartungen ihrer postmodernen Propheten hinaus. Postmoderne Philosophen neigten dazu, prophetisch, schwer verständlich, missmutig und häufig apokalyptisch zu sein. Heute sind ihre Visionen durch eine Fülle von Hightech Start-ups und dank einer neuen Generation von Unternehmern, von denen die meisten die

change—probably beyond the wildest expectations of their postmodern prophets. Postmodern philosophers tended to be vaticinatory, obscure, disgruntled, and often apocalyptic. Today, their visions have been turned into reality by a bunch of high-tech start-ups and by a new generation of adolescent entrepreneurs, most of whom may have never even heard the names of Gilles Deleuze or Ilya Prigogine. Technosocial change is as incremental as it is pervasive, so this bizarre development may have gone unnoticed. Yet it is a fact that indeterminacy is now a staple of our daily digital life, often tacitly accepted and taken for granted. Indeterminacy has already infiltrated many of our new, technologically driven social practices, our economic behavior, and even science. Whether we like it or not, *we are all nonlinear now*.

Again, there is no time here to discuss to what extent Big Data has brought nonlinearity into our daily lives. But, for example, we all know full well that most media objects today live in a permanent state of random drift, and that it is increasingly difficult—as well as pointless—to try and freeze them in one single, authorial, authorized, stable and reliable shape or form. Who could have anticipated, only a few years ago, the rise of a new encyclopedia entirely written by its readers, where entries are authored

> Imagine a heap of sand. If we let each grain of sand fall from above in a steady, regular way, and assuming that all the grains are the same, the sandpile will acquire the geometrical shape of a cone.

by many but by no one in particular, where all pages—or in fact most pages—may be edited by anyone at will, and without any control other than communal feedback, or the wisdom of crowds? Yet Wikipedia works, often surprisingly well, while the old authorial *Encyclopedia Britannica* in print has gone out of business.

Gmail's original motto, "Don't Sort, Search," phased out a notion of classification and taxonomies so ingrained in our minds that we would have thought it timeless, and universal. The idea that we must sort and classify events in order to make sense of the world goes back, in its present form, to Aristotle, and a historian of philosophy could argue that without Aristotle's predicaments or genus-species arborescent categories there is no Western philosophy. If that is so, then Google is not Western, nor are its users—that is, a large share of today's world population (which is, of course, indeed non-Western). From the beginning of time, classification, or sorting, has been our tool of choice for information retrieval: we put things in specific places, following some order, so we know where to look for them when we need them. But Google is training us to leave documents unsorted, because digital search is so fast that there is no need to manually presort documents. This principle needs not be limited to media objects; it may extend to physical objects of all kinds, which can be tagged and tracked using Radio Frequency Identification (RFID). This may apply to random junk in a garage, to books in a library, or to the full inventory of Amazon.com. Indeed, items

From the beginning of time, classification, or sorting, has been our tool of choice for information retrieval: we put things in specific places, following some order, so we know where to look for them when we need them. But Google is training us to leave documents unsorted, because digital search is so fast that there is no need to manually presort documents.

Namen Gilles Deleuze oder Ilya Prigogine noch nie gehört haben mögen, Realität geworden. Der technosoziale Wandel vollzog sich ebenso schrittweise wie allgegenwärtig, so dass diese bizarre Entwicklung unbemerkt geschehen sein mag. Es ist jedoch eine Tatsache, dass Unbestimmtheit heute stillschweigend akzeptiert und als selbstverständlich hingenommen zu unserem digitalen Alltag gehört. Unbestimmtheit ist bereits in vielen unserer neuen, technologisch betriebenen, sozialen Praktiken, unserem ökonomischen Verhalten und sogar in der Wissenschaft präsent. Ob es uns gefällt oder nicht, *wir sind jetzt alle nicht-linear.*

Doch ist hier keine Zeit, um zu diskutieren, inwieweit Big Data Nichtlinearität in unseren Alltag transportiert hat. Allerdings wissen wir zum Beispiel sehr gut, dass heute die meisten medialen Objekte sich permanent in einem Stadium der Zufallsverschiebung befinden und dass der Versuch, sie in einer einzigen, auktorialen, bevollmächtigten, stabilen und verlässlichen Form einfrieren zu wollen, immer schwieriger wird, ja sinnlos ist. Wer hätte noch vor wenigen Jahren den Aufstieg einer neuen Enzyklopädie vorausahnen können, die zur Gänze von ihren Lesern verfasst wird, deren Einträge von vielen, aber von keinem Bestimmten geschrieben werden, wo alle Seiten – oder tatsächlich die Mehrzahl der Seiten – von jedermann nach Belieben redigiert werden können und die einzige Kontrolle in allgemeinem Feedback oder der Weisheit der Masse besteht? Und doch funktioniert Wikipedia häufig überraschend gut, während die gedruckte Ausgabe der alten auktorialen *Encyclopedia Britannica* nicht mehr verlegt wird.

Das ursprüngliche Motto von Gmail „Don't Sort, Search" setzte eine in unseren Hirnen so fest verankerte Vorstellung von Klassifizierung und Taxonomien, die wir für zeitlos und allgemeingültig hielten, außer Kraft. Die Idee, wir müssten Ereignisse sortieren und klassifizieren, um die Welt zu verstehen, geht in ihrer gegenwärtigen Form bis auf Aristoteles zurück und ein Historiker der Philosophie könnte behaupten, ohne Aristoteles' Kategorien gäbe es keine westliche Philosophie. Wenn das zutrifft, dann sind weder Google westlich, noch seine Nutzer – das heißt, ein großer Teil der heutigen Weltbevölkerung, (die in der Tat nicht westlich ist). Vom Anbeginn der Zeit an galten Klassifikation oder Sortieren als unser bevorzugtes Verfahren zum Auffinden von Information: Wir legen Dinge an bestimmten Plätzen ab und folgen dabei einer Ordnung, damit wir wissen, wo wir suchen müssen, wenn wir sie brauchen. Google hingegen lehrt uns, Dokumente unsortiert zu lassen, weil die digitale Suche derart schnell ist, dass keine Notwendigkeit besteht, Dokumente von Hand vorzusortieren. Dieses Prinzip muss nicht auf mediale Objekte beschränkt werden. Es kann auf reale Objekte aller Art erweitert werden, die sich mithilfe von Radio Frequency Identification (RFID) markieren und verfolgen lassen. Dies kann auf beliebigen Krempel in einer Garage zutreffen, auf Bücher in einer

Bibliothek oder auf das Gesamtinventar von Amazon.com. Tatsächlich werden Objekte alle Arten, darunter Bücher, in den Lagerhäusern von Amazon nicht nach Themen oder Kategorien sortiert, sondern einzig nach der Häufigkeit des Verkaufs und damit nach einer für den menschlichen Geist völlig bedeutungslosen Ordnung. Würden wir die gleiche technische Logik in unseren Häusern anwenden, könnten wir Kartoffeln, Socken, Bücher und Fisch in derselben Schublade oder sonst irgendwo aufbewahren. Wir müssten uns nicht erinnern, wo wir Dinge hingetan haben oder wo sie sind, weil wir sie bei Bedarf einfach googlen könnten (im realen Raum).

Dieselbe Google-Logik muss nicht auf den Raum beschränkt bleiben – sie könnte auch auf die Zeit angewendet werden. Wenn jedes Ereignis, das jemals geschehen ist, sich verzeichnen, suchen und wiederfinden lässt, könnte in vielen Fällen die Suche nach einem exakten Präzedenzfall viele andere Techniken der Vorhersage ersetzen, auch die moderne Wissenschaft, wie wir sie kennen. In der Tat haben auf vielen Gebieten der prognostizierenden Wissenschaften, von der Wettervorhersage bis zu den Werkstoffwissenschaften, Informationsabruf und digitale Simulationen bereits die Stelle des herkömmlichen analytischen Ursache-Wirkung Ansatzes der modernen Wissenschaften eingenommen. Viele Wissenschaftler sind bereits davon überzeugt, dass es manchmal einfacher ist anzunehmen, dass, was auch immer zuvor passiert ist, einfach wieder passieren wird, vorausgesetzt es wurde aufgezeichnet und ist abrufbar, anstatt auf der Grundlage von Funktionen und Parametern Ergebnisse zu berechnen. Ähnlich dachten Galileo und Newton, aber sie verfügten nicht über Big Data; tatsächlich standen ihnen häufig nur sehr wenige Daten zur Verfügung. In gewisser Hinsicht war die westliche Wissenschaft insgesamt eine Kulturtechnik, die im Hinblick auf einen chronischen Datenmangel entwickelt wurde. Da früher die Menge der Daten, die wir speichern und verarbeiten konnten, begrenzt war, lernten wir abstrakte Formeln zu nutzen, um aus den wenigen Daten, die wir hatten, Muster abzuleiten und zu verallgemeinern. Jetzt, da wir Zugriff auf immer mehr Daten haben, brauchen wir paradoxerweise immer weniger Berechnungen. Wenn wir jedoch den exakten Präzedenzfall zu dem Ereignis, das wir untersuchen, finden können, brauchen wir keine Zahlen und Formeln, um aus begrenzten Unterlagen über nur wenige, ähnliche Erfahrungen Muster zu vergleichen, zu generalisieren und abzuleiten.

Kurz, man darf folgern, dass auch für viele Sparten des Lebens und der Wissenschaft der alte deterministische Ansatz von Ursache und Wirkung, den wir für selbstverständlich hielten, zumindest wenn es darum ging, das Verhalten der anorganischen Welt vorherzusagen, bereits durch eine neue, postmoderne und post-wissenschaftliche Methode ersetzt wurde, die nicht auf dem Prinzip von Ursache und Wirkung beruht, sondern auf Wahrscheinlichkeit, Statistiken und zunehmend auf

of all sorts in Amazon warehouses, including books, are not sorted based on subject, or category, but only based on the frequency of sale, following an order that is perfectly meaningless to a human mind. Using the same technical logic in our houses, we could keep potatoes and socks and books and fish in the same drawers, or indeed anywhere. We would not need to remember where we put things, or where things are, because whenever we need them we could simply Google them (in physical space).

The same Google logic need not be limited to space—it may also apply to time. If every event that ever happened can be recorded, searched, and retrieved, in many cases the search for an exact precedent may replace many other technologies of prediction, including modern science as we know it. Indeed, in many fields of predictive science, from weather forecasting to material sciences, information retrieval and digital simulation have already replaced the traditional, analytic, cause-to-effect approach of modern science. Many scientists have already come to the conclusion that sometimes, instead of calculating results based on functions and parameters, it is easier to assume that whatever has happened before, if it has been recorded, and if it can be retrieved, will simply happen again. This is not unlike what Galileo and Newton thought, but they did not have Big Data; in fact, often they had very little data indeed. In a sense, Western science as a whole was a cultural technology developed to cope with a chronic shortage of data. As the amount of data we could store and process in the past was limited, we learned to use abstract formulas to extrapolate and generalize patterns from the little data we had. But since we now have access to more and more data, paradoxically, we need fewer and fewer calculations. If we can find the exact precedent to the event we are studying, we do not need numbers and formulas to compare, generalize, and extrapolate patterns from a limited record of just a few similar experiences.

In short, it seems safe to conclude that in many walks of life, and of science, too, the old cause-to-effect, deterministic approach that we used to take for granted, at least for predicting the behavior of the inorganic world, has already been replaced by a new, postmodern, and post-scientific method, which is not based on cause-to-effect determination but on probabilism, statistics, and increasingly heuristic and holistic processes. More and more often, we do not calculate: we search and retrieve; and more and more often, we can better deal with a complex system as a whole, than with the simpler logic of its parts.

Regardless of any deliberate ideological or cultural stance, some of these developments are already reshaping our approach to design (and more). We may or may not be aware of the cultural provenance of these ideas and beliefs, or of their vast philosophical implications. But that is irrelevant. This seems to be, simply, the way many of today's digital tools work best—at least in our present cultural and technological environment. And if we use these tools, as we do, we cannot avoid some of this technical logic. Hence, not surprisingly, some of these developments are already reshaping our approach to design. Let me review, briefly, a number of scenarios and design strategies that share, I think, a similar indeterminist inclination, and which are becoming increasingly frequent among today's digitally intelligent designers.

1. The Wikipedic style of many hands. In a Wikipedia-like design environment, objects are made by many but by no one in particular. The object of design is forever drifting, permanently open to interactive editing and participatory versioning; hence objects are never finished and can never be entirely reliable or fully functioning. This mode of making is fast becoming a dominant technical paradigm of our time, but it is unsuited to building, as buildings must be built, at some point, and cannot change much thereafter. Yet the logic of Building Information Modeling (BIM) and of Integrated Project Delivery (IPD) is very close to the collaborative spirit of this game. Indeterminacy and open-endedness in the case of BIM are mostly limited to design notations prior to building, that is, to pure information; but they could in theory extend to the functioning life of the building, which must be maintained after it has been delivered.

2. Generative, evolutionary scripts. Parametric scripts can be instructed to generate random variations, which are then automatically selected based on the feedback deriving from a chosen set of data—from patterns of use, for example, or from some material conditions, etc. The whole process thus emulates and almost reenacts Darwin's theory of evolution by natural selection (first, random variation; second, elimination of the losers and survival of the fittest for each given environment). In the 1990s, designers often referred to the morphogenetic theories of D'Arcy Thompson in a similar context; more recently, digital design theory has largely adopted the terms "emergence" and "self-organizing systems" (in turn derived from postmodern systems theory). This mode of product evolution by automatic selection is frequent in the design of media objects—and famously in the case of web design, where it is practiced under the understated and misleading name of A/B testing. In A/B testing, design choices are made by trying out two versions of the same interface and comparing user data: when a new version (the B version) of a website works better than the old one (the A version), for example, because users stay on the page longer or click on a link more often, the change is automatically adopted. Variations used to be introduced by actual designers, but they are now often randomly generated. In this case, the system self-organizes through accidental mutations and environmental feedback, or natural selection, as in Darwin's model of biological evolution. The same form generates many random variations, and the one that happens to best fit a given environment, the strongest form, survives—to the detriment of all others that are eliminated.

3. Digital form-finding. A variant of the above is often practiced by designers testing the material performance of some particularly unwieldy structural systems. Typically, the anelastic or anisotropic deformations of some nonstandard materials may be too difficult to calculate analytically, and instead of mathematical calculations, designers must resort to tests with physical models, often with mock-ups in full size. In other terms, the only way to see how these systems will perform under stress is to build them and see what happens. This empirical approach to structural design is often called, somewhat improperly, "structural form-finding," implying that these systems will deform under stress to reorganize in macroscopic but unpredictable ways, and will in the end stabilize by "choosing" a new form or shape, which some claim is chosen by the object itself, that is, by nature. Frei Otto and Antoni Gaudí are frequently cited as pioneers of this

heuristischen und holistischen Prozessen. Immer häufiger kalkulieren wir nicht, sondern wir suchen und finden, und immer öfter können wir besser mit einem komplexen System im Ganzen umgehen als mit der schlichteren Logik seiner Teile.

Ungeachtet jeglichen bewussten ideologischen oder kulturellen Standpunkts sind manche dieser Entwicklungen bereits dabei, unsere Einstellung zum Entwerfen (und anderem) umzuformen. Uns mögen die kulturelle Herkunft oder die gewaltigen philosophischen Implikationen dieser Ideen und Überzeugungen bewusst sein oder nicht, aber das hat keine Bedeutung. Es scheint einfach die Art zu sein, wie heutzutage die meisten dieser digitalen Verfahren am besten funktionieren – zumindest in unserem gegenwärtigen kulturellen und technologischen Umfeld. Und wenn wir diese Verfahren tatsächlich benutzen, können wir diese technische Logik nicht umgehen. Daher ist es nicht erstaunlich, dass einige dieser Entwicklungen unsere Auffassung von Design bereits verändern. Lassen Sie mich kurz eine Reihe von Szenarien und Entwurfsstrategien nennen, denen, wie ich glaube, eine ähnliche unbestimmte Tendenz eigen ist und die unter den heutigen digitalen Designern zunehmen häufig anzutreffen ist.

1. Der Wikipediastil der vielen Urheber. In einem nach Wikipedia-Art organisierten Designumfeld werden Objekte von vielen, aber niemand Bestimmten angefertigt. Das Entwurfsobjekt bleibt immer in der Schwebe, beständig offen für interaktive oder teilnehmende Bearbeitung. Diese Art des Herstellens ist gerade dabei, schnell zum beherrschenden technischen Paradigma unserer Zeit zu werden, aber es eignet sich nicht zum Bauen, da Gebäude irgendwann errichtet werden müssen und sich danach nicht mehr verändern können. Allerdings steht die Logik von Building Information Modeling (BIM) und von Integrated Project Delivery (IPD) dem kollaborativen Geist dieses Spiels sehr nahe. Im Fall von BIM sind Unbestimmtheit und Ergebnisoffenheit zumeist beschränkt auf vor dem Bauen getroffene Entwurfsentscheidungen, d.h. auf reine Information. Sie könnten sich theoretisch auch auf das praktische Dasein des Bauwerks erstrecken, das aufrechterhalten werden muss, nachdem es übergeben wurde.

2. Generative, evolutionäre Skripts. Parametrische Skripts können angewiesen werden, beliebige Variationen zu erzeugen, die dann automatisch auf der Basis des Feedbacks, den ein Datensatz erzeugt, selektiert werden – beispielsweise aus Gebrauchsmustern oder aus irgendeiner stofflichen Beschaffenheit etc. Der ganze Prozess bildet Darwins Evolutionstheorie durch natürliche Auslese (erstens beliebige Variation, zweitens Elimination der Verlierer und Überleben für jede denkbare Umgebung) nach, ja spielt sie geradezu erneut durch. In den 1990er Jahren bezogen sich Entwerfer in einem vergleichbaren Kontext oft auf die morphogenetischen Theorien von D'Arcy

Thompson. In jüngerer Zeit hat die digitale Entwurfstheorie weitgehend die Begriffe „Emergenz" und „selbstregulierende Systeme" übernommen (wiederum abgeleitet von der postmodernen Systemtheorie). Diese Methode der Produktwahl durch automatische Selektion kommt häufig beim Design von Medienobjekten zur Anwendung – und bekanntlich im Fall von Webdesign, wo es unter der untertriebenen und irreführenden Bezeichnung A/B Test praktiziert wird. Dabei wird eine Wahl getroffen, indem zwei Versionen derselben Schnittstelle ausprobiert und die Daten der Anwender verglichen werden: Wenn eine neue Version (die B Version) einer Website besser funktioniert als die alte (die A Version), weil beispielsweise der Nutzer länger auf der Seite verweilt oder häufiger auf einen Link klickt, wird die Änderung automatisch übernommen. Früher wurden Variationen von realen Designern eingeführt, während das heute oft per Zufallsgenerator geschieht. In diesem Fall funktioniert die Selbst-Organisation durch zufällige Mutationen und Feedback der Umgebung oder wie bei Darwins Modell der biologischen Evolution durch natürliche Auslese. Die gleiche Form generiert viele wahllose Variationen und diejenige, die zufällig am besten zu einem gegebenen Umfeld passt, die stärkste Form, überlebt – zum Nachteil aller anderen, die eliminiert werden.

3. Digitale Formfindung. Eine Variante des obigen Verfahrens wird häufig von Entwerfern angewandt, die das Verhalten eines neuen, besonders schwer zu bearbeitenden Materials erproben. Typischerweise stellt sich die analytische Berechnung einiger unelastischer oder anisotropischer Verformungen bestimmter Non-Standard-Materialien häufig als zu diffizil heraus, so dass Entwerfer auf Tests mit realen Modellen, häufig 1:1 Mock-Ups zurückgreifen müssen. Mit anderen Worten, um herauszufinden, wie sich diese Systeme unter Druck verhalten, muss man sie bauen und dann schauen, was passiert. Dieser empirische Ansatz zum konstruktiven Entwerfen wird häufig – nicht ganz richtig – als „baukonstruktive Formfindung" bezeichnet, was impliziert, dass sich diese Systeme unter Druck auf makroskopische, aber unvorhersehbare Weise reorganisieren und am Ende stabilisieren, indem sie eine neue Form „wählen", von der manche behaupten, das Objekt selbst, sprich die Natur, habe sie gewählt. Frei Otto und Antoni Gaudí werden häufig als Pioniere dieser Methode genannt. Die Form einer Seifenblase, die Verformung einer Katenoide oder verknotete Fäden, die von einer Decke hängen, sind gute Beispiele dafür. Nach Meinung einiger handelt es sich bei dieser Entwurfsmethode eher um eine opportunistische Lösung, für die wir uns entscheiden, wenn wir keine Ingenieure zu Hilfe rufen wollen. Wieder andere glauben, es gäbe natürliche Phänomene, die selbst die beste Wissenschaft weder jetzt noch künftig voraussagen könne. Die Zukunft wird es weisen.

Parametric scripts can be instructed to generate random variations, which are then automatically selected based on the feedback deriving from a chosen set of data—from patterns of use, for example, or from some material conditions, etc. The whole process thus emulates and almost reenacts Darwin's theory of evolution by natural selection (first, random variation; second, elimination of the losers and survival of the fittest for each given environment).

method; the shape of a soap bubble, the deformation of a catenary rope, or of a batch of knotted linen hanging from a ceiling are said to be cases in point. For some, this mode of design is simply an opportunistic shortcut we choose when we prefer not to call in the engineers; for others, there are things in nature that even the best science cannot and will never predict. Time will tell.

4. Design by digital making. In cases less complicated than those just mentioned, however, digital simulations increasingly offer the possibility to test the performance of a given material system on the screen, rather than in reality. Think of the easiest cases of material resistance, elastic deformation, or thermal behavior: the visual feedback on the screen is now so fast that the designer can keep tweaking the design and test it in simulation for as many times as necessary—that is, until the desired performance is obtained. The designer can thus optimize a structural solution by the simulation of repeated trials and errors, rather than by predictive analytic calculation. This is, by the way, not dissimilar from what traditional craftsmen once did: the ideal craftsman is not an engineer, nor an architect; craftsmen neither design nor calculate; they just keep making and remaking an object until it does not break, and they learn, often tacitly, from this experience. Today, using digital simulation, designers can make and break on the screen in a minute more objects than a traditional craftsman would have made and broken in a lifetime. Design by feeling and by intuition, design by the gesture of the hand, which some call "design by making," hence becomes a viable alternative to the analytic, predictive approach of modern science—and modern design.

> Design by feeling and by intuition, design by the gesture of the hand, which some call "design by making," hence becomes a viable alternative to the analytic, predictive approach of modern science—and modern design.

* * *

Examples could continue, but allow me instead to jump to a conclusion: evidently, this is not design as we knew it. The pattern common to these disparate trends seems to be that we are increasingly redefining and limiting the ambit of design, because we assume that some digitally empowered systems are capable to self-organize, and can find the best solution by themselves—by aggregating the wisdom of crowds or by letting nature find its way. Both these solutions are of course problematic for many of us. They are problematic for the design professions, of course; they also have vast philosophical, ideological, social, and political implications.

Co-designing with nature, negotiating with and even surrendering to nature's will and whims are timeless human ambitions, redefined in the

4. Entwerfen durch digitale Verfahren. In weniger komplizierten Fällen als den eben erwähnten bieten digitale Simulationen allerdings zunehmend die Möglichkeit, die Leistung eines bestimmten Materialsystems auf dem Bildschirm anstatt in der Realität zu testen. Man denke an die einfachsten Fälle von materiellem Widerstand, elastischer Verformung oder thermischem Verhalten: das optische Feedback auf dem Bildschirm ist jetzt so schnell, dass der Designer am Entwurf unablässig feilen und ihn so häufig wie nötig in einer Simulation testen kann, bis die gewünschte Leistung erreicht ist. Durch die Simulation wiederholter Versuche und Irrtümer anstelle vorhersagender analytischer Berechnung kann der Designer so eine konstruktive Lösung optimieren. Dieses Verfahren ähnelt im Übrigen dem, was der traditionelle Handwerker einst tat: der ideale Handwerker ist weder ein Ingenieur noch ein Architekt; Handwerker entwerfen oder berechnen nicht; sie fertigen ein Objekt einfach immer wieder an, bis es nicht mehr entzweigeht und sie lernen, häufig implizit, aus dieser Erfahrung. Dank digitaler Simulation kann heutzutage ein Designer auf dem Bildschirm in einer Minute mehr Objekte erzeugen und zerstören als ein traditioneller Handwerker im Laufe seines ganzen Lebens. Entwerfen durch Fühlen und durch Intuition, Entwerfen durch eine Handbewegung, was einige „Desing by making" nennen, wird somit eine praktikable Alternative zum analytischen, vorausschauenden Ansatz der modernen Wissenschaft – und des modernen Designs.

* * *

Die Liste der Beispiele ließe sich fortsetzen, aber lassen Sie mich stattdessen eine Schlussfolgerung ziehen: Offenbar handelt es sich nicht länger um ein solches Entwerfen, wie wir es bisher kannten. Das diese disparaten Tendenzen zusammenführende Muster scheint darin zu bestehen, dass wir zunehmend den Bereich des Entwerfens neu definieren und begrenzen, weil wir davon ausgehen, dass irgendwelche digital betriebenen Systeme zur Selbstorganisation fähig sind und die beste Lösung für sich alleine finden können, indem sie das Wissen von zahllosen Menschen zusammenführen oder die Lösung der Natur überlassen. Beide Lösungen sind natürlich für viele von uns problematisch. Vor allem für jene, die beruflich mit Entwerfen befasst sind, aber auch, weil sie enorme philosophische, ideologische, soziale und politische Implikationen mit sich bringen.

Gemeinsam mit der Natur zu gestalten, mit dem Willen und den Launen der Natur zu verhandeln und sich ihnen sogar zu unterwerfen, sind zeitlose menschliche Bestrebungen, die im Industriezeitalter von der Romantik des 19. Jahrhunderts sowie von den verschiedenen naturalistischen und organizistischen Tendenzen neu definiert wurden, die im Laufe des 20. Jahrhunderts folgten. Und wie wir wissen, ist das Streben nach einer erneuten Allianz mit der Natur heute eine klügere und dringendere Taktik als zu jeder anderen Zeit in der Moderne. Im heutigen gesellschaftlichen und politischen Umfeld hat das Lob für die „unsichtbare Hand" der Natur oder für die „unsichtbare Hand" des freien Marktes oder des Finanzmarktes oder jedes anderen, sich vermeintlich selbst-organisierenden Systems jedoch weit größere Bedeutung. Selbstorganisation und digitaler Darwinismus sind absolut vernünftige Entwurfsstrategien – und in vielen Fällen funktionieren sie bestens. Aber wir sollten nicht den größeren Zusammenhang vergessen: Wir wissen bereits, was Sozialdarwinismus bedeutet – und was Sozialdarwinisten beabsichtigen.

Übersetzung Christiane Court

industrial age by nineteenth-century romanticism and by the various naturalisms and organicisms that followed in the course of the twentieth century. And as we know, the quest for a renewed alliance with nature is a wiser and more urgent policy today than at any time in modern history. But in today's social and political environment, praise for the "invisible hand" of nature—or for the "invisible hand" of the free markets, or of the financial markets, of any other supposedly self-organizing system—means much more than that. Self-organization and digital Darwinism are perfectly reasonable design strategies—and in many cases, they just work. But let's not forget the bigger picture: we already know what Social Darwinism means—and what Social Darwinists have in mind.

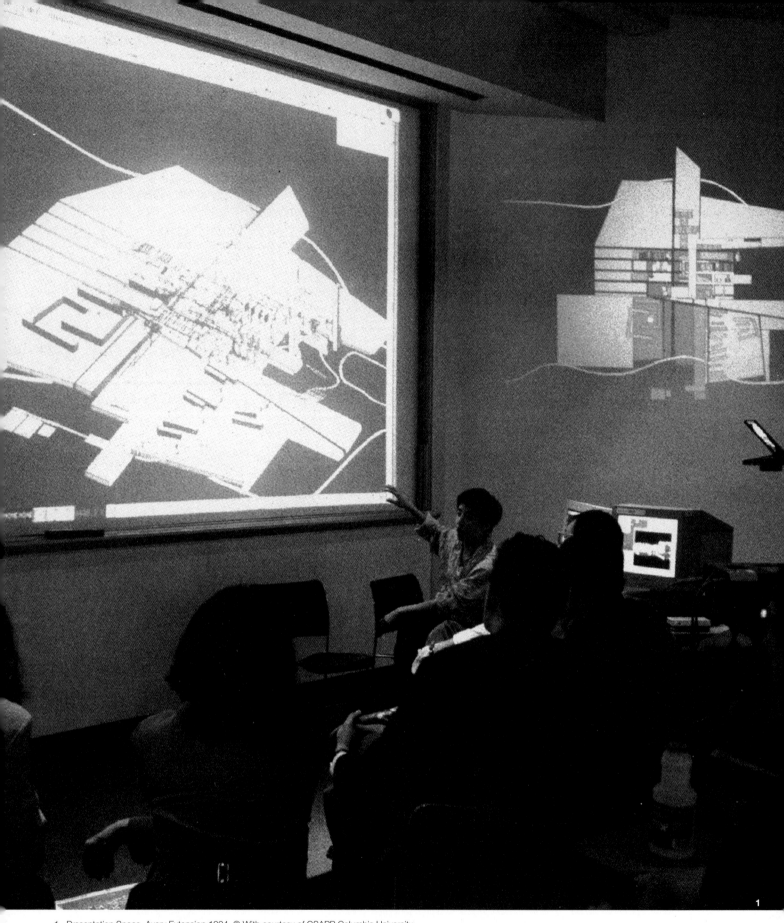

1 Presentation Space, Avery Extension 1994, © With courtesy of GSAPP Columbia University

Die Wissens-praktiken der *Paperless Studios*

1994 führte Bernard Tschumi die ersten mit Computern ausgestatteten Entwurfsstudios – die sogenannten *paperless studios* – an Columbias *Graduate School of Architecture, Planning and Preservation* (GSAPP) in New York ein.[1] Die damit verbundenen Veränderungen der Architekturfakultät standen im Kontext der zunehmend alle gesellschaftlichen Bereiche durchdringenden elektronischen Medien und den Forderungen der Studierenden, Computertechnologien in das Curriculum zu integrieren.[2]

The Knowledge Practices of the "Paperless Studio." In 1994, Bernard Tschumi introduced the first computer-equipped design studio—the so-called "paperless studio"—at Columbia University Graduate School of Architecture, Planning and Preservation (GSAPP) in New York.[1] The changes in the architecture department were based on the increasing uptake in society of electronic media as well as student demands for an integration of technological tools into the architectural curriculum.[2]

NATHALIE BREDELLA

Im obersten Geschoss von Avery Hall[3] schuf Tschumi einen Ort, an dem die Bedeutung des Computers für Verfahren des Entwerfens erforscht werden konnte. Über die gesamte Etage verteilt erhielten 33 Studierende einen mit Hard- und Software ausgestatteten Arbeitsplatz. In dem klimatisierten Raum mit Loftcharakter wurden jeweils parallel im Winter- und Sommersemester drei Entwurfsklassen unterrichtet (Abb. 8–9).

Mit der Erforschung digitaler Entwurfsprozesse ging eine Umgestaltung des Curriculums einher. Tschumi nutzte die Möglichkeit, Professoren als *Adjuncts* (i.e., außerordentliche Professoren) einstellen zu können und gab jungen Architektinnen und Architekten die Gelegenheit, ihre Fragestellungen im Kontext der Universität zu erforschen und mit Architekturtheoretikern und Philosophen zu theoretisieren.[4] Die interdisziplinäre Öffnung der Schule trug dazu bei, dass die Studierenden einer Vielfalt von Auffassungen begegnen konnten, die die Frage nach der Bedeutung des Computers für die Bestimmung von Zielen im Entwurf stellten. Getragen waren diese Entwicklungen von Tschumis Grundhaltung, dass die Universität – mit ihrem Wissen über die Techniken des Entwerfens – die Architekturpraxis verändern könne, anstatt von ihr bestimmt zu werden.[5]

Während sich die Forschungseinrichtungen des Massachusetts Institute of Technology unter der Leitung von William J. Mitchell vor allem der Entwicklung digitaler Technologien widmeten, bot die Architekturfakultät der Columbia University die Möglichkeit, die Bedeutung der Technologien im Kontext von Theorie und Geschichte zu diskutieren und direkt auf die Verfahren des Entwerfens zu beziehen.[6] Ed Keller, *graduate student* an der Columbia University beschreibt die *paperless studios* als „ein sich stetig entwickelndes Experiment, das gleichzeitig ein Instrument der Öffentlichkeitsarbeit als auch einen Raum für kritischen Diskurs darstellt."[7] Und so gehörte, wie Stan Allen betont, die Columbia University zu den ersten Universitäten, die den Computer in den Dienst der Entwurfskultur und nicht in jenen der Ökonomisierung stellte.[8] Anzumerken ist, dass die Diskussionen um die Interaktion von digitalen und architektonischen Wissens- und Erfahrungswelten kontrovers geführt wurden und nicht selten eine duale Beziehung zwischen Digitalem und Analogem unterstellten. Vereinfacht ließe sich zunächst sagen, dass die digital gesteuerten Entwurfsprozesse von jenen Architekten und Theoretikern kritisiert wurden, die davon ausgingen, dass Maschinen nicht entwerfen können, dass Entwerfen ein analoger Prozess

Located at the very top of Avery Hall,[3] Tschumi created a place where the impact of computers on the design processes could be tested. Thirty-three students equipped with hardware and software tools occupied the entire floor. In this loft-like, air-conditioned space, studio faculty were teaching three sections in the fall and spring (figs. 8–9).

The research of digital design processes went hand in hand with curriculum modifications. Tschumi made use of the opportunity to hire adjunct professors and thus gave junior faculty a chance to expand their explorative questions in a university context, while visting theorists and philosophers provided a critical framework for the design explorations.[4] The school became a type of laboratory for research in design, thus giving students the opportunity to encounter a variety of different viewpoints that questioned the computer's agency within the design process. These developments were supported by Tschumi's opinion that the university—with its knowledge of design techniques—should in fact influence architectural practice, rather than be determined by it.[5]

While the research facilities at the Massachusetts Institute of Technology, headed by William J. Mitchell, were primarily technically oriented, the architecture department at Columbia University offered an opportunity to discuss the significance of technology in the context of theory and design.[6] Ed Keller, a graduate student at Columbia at the time, described the paperless studio as "an evolving experiment, as well as a public relations tool and space for questioning."[7] Indeed, as Stan Allen has emphasized, Columbia was among the first of universities to use computers to facilitate design innovation rather than design economization.[8] It would be remiss not to mention that the debate on the nexus between more traditional architectural methods and these new digital approaches was indeed controversial. In its most basic terms, digitally controlled design processes were criticized by architects and theorists who argued that machines cannot conceive of design and that the act of

1   Vgl. Thomas Hanrahan (Hg.): *Abstract 1994–95*, GSAPP, (1995), S. 64.

2   Vgl. Ed Keller: „L'atelier sans papier de Columbia University", Interview, in: *PARPAINGS* 14 (2000), o. Sz. Dank an Ed Keller, der mir den Text des Interviews zur Verfügung stellte.

3   Avery Hall ist das Hauptgebäude der *School of Architecture, Planning and Preservation* (GSAPP), ihm angeschlossen sind die Gebäude Fayerweather Hall und Buell Hall. Vgl. http://www.arch.columbia.edu/about/avery-hall (Stand: 01. November 2013).

4   Vgl. Bernard Tschumi in Enrique Walker: *Tschumi on Architecture. Conversations with Enrique Walker*, New York 2006, S. 127f. Zu den Theoretikern, die an den Diskussionen um die Rolle des Computers im Entwurf teilnahmen, gehörten unter anderem Manuel de Landa, Jeffrey Kipnis, Sanford Kwinter, Brian Massumi, John Rajchman und Marc Taylor.

5   Vgl. Bernard Tschumi: „Introduction", in: ders./Matthew Berman (Hg.): *Index Architecture. A Columbia Book of Architecture*. Cambridge, MA 2003, S. 6a und Bernard Tschumi: „1,2,3 Jump", in: *Newsline*, (1994), S. 8.

6   Vgl. Anthony Webster: „Building Technologies Research Program Initiated at the School", in: *Newsline* (1994), S. 11.

7   Keller: „L'atelier", o. Sz. (wie Anm. 2). Im Original: „an evolving experiment, as well as a public relations tool and space for questioning."

8   Vgl. Stan Allen: „Avery 700-Level Computer Studios", in: *Newsline* (1994), S. 9.

1   See Thomas Hanrahan, ed., *Abstract 1994–95*, GSAPP (1995), p. 64.

2   See Ed Keller, "L'atelier sans papier de Columbia University" (interview), *PARPAINGS* 14 (2000), n.p. Many thanks to Ed Keller, who made the interview transcription available to me.

3   Avery Hall is the main building of the Graduate School of Architecture, Planning and Preservation (GSAPP) at Columbia University. It is located adjacent to the connecting buildings Fayerweather Hall and Buell Hall. See http://www.arch.columbia.edu/about/avery-hall (accessed November 2013).

4   See Bernard Tschumi in Enrique Walker, *Tschumi on Architecture: Conversations with Enrique Walker* (New York, 2006), pp. 127–28. The theorists who participated in discussion about the role of computers in design practice included Manuel de Landa, Jeffrey Kipnis, Sanford Kwinter, Brian Massumi, John Rajchman, and Marc Taylor.

5   See Bernard Tschumi, "Introduction," in *Index Architecture: A Columbia Book of Architecture*, ed. Bernard Tschumi and Matthew Berman (Cambridge, MA, 2003), p. 6a, and Bernard Tschumi, "1,2,3 Jump," *Newsline* (1994), p. 8.

6   See Anthony Webster, "Building Technologies Research Program Initiated at the School," *Newsline* (1994), p. 11.

7   Keller, "L'atelier," n.p. (see note 2).

8   See Stan Allen, "Avery 700-Level Computer Studios," *Newsline* (1994), p. 9.

designing is an analogue process.[9] What is perhaps most evident in all of these polemic discussions was the difficulty encountered in applying computer-based concepts and forms to architecture and then finding a suitable historical context.

This paper is focused on the restructuring that occurred in the architecture department as initiated by the paperless studio as well as the protagonistic status of the computer in the design studio. It examines the technical and aesthetic design practices pursued, as well as the prior knowledge and skills of the instructors involved, with an aim to more closely identify the architectural experiences related to these experimental systems.

I argue that computer-informed architectural education was influenced by the intuitive approach of the instructors, who with their explorative questions inspired a specific use of software without being in possession of comprehensive technological knowledge. Of special interest, therefore, are the processes of recognition and perception that were fostered through computer use.

The Media Ensemble and Studio Culture. The history of computers in the design studio originated with the approval of a grant for the 1994–95 academic year. This allowed Columbia University to establish the infrastructure necessary for accommodating computer technology and to install the paperless studio in the Avery Hall building.[10] At the time, Eden Muir was responsible for the Graduate School of Architecture's Digital Design Lab (DDL) and for integrating computer-aided design courses. Together with Rory O'Neill, they taught computer-aided design classes and held seminars that introduced new software applications for architectural design. Insights gained from these seminars also facilitated the conception of an interplay between virtual software environments and the physical infrastructure of the paperless studio.[11]

While Stan Allen designed the new studio space on the seventh floor of Avery Hall, Muir and O'Neill were responsible for designing the accompanying technical infrastructure. The conventional subdivision into cubicles, typical for design

---

sei und gesellschaftliche Probleme nicht durch neue Technologien zu lösen seien.[9] An den polemischen Diskussionen zeigte sich vor allem aber auch die Schwierigkeit, die computerbasierten Konzepte und Raumformen architektonisch zu deuten und historisch einzuordnen.

Der vorliegende Beitrag widmet sich den durch die *paperless studios* initiierten Umstrukturierungen der Architekturfakultät und fragt nach dem Akteurstatus des Computers im Entwurf. Er rückt die technischen und ästhetischen Praktiken des Entwerfens sowie das Vorwissen und Können der Lehrenden in den Fokus der Betrachtung, um die mit den Experimentalsystemen verbundenen architektonischen Erfahrungen näher zu bestimmen.

Ich gehe davon aus, dass die durch den Computer geprägte Architekturausbildung neben den technischen und kulturellen Veränderungen von der intuitionsbasierten Vorgehensweise der Lehrenden bestimmt war, die ohne umfassendes technologisches Wissen mit ihren Fragestellungen zu einem spezifischen Gebrauch von Software anregten. Von besonderem Interesse ist daher, welche Prozesse des Erkennens und Wahrnehmens durch den Computer gefördert wurden.

> Von besonderem Interesse ist daher, welche Prozesse des Erkennens und Wahrnehmens durch den Computer gefördert wurden.

Das mediale Ensemble und die Studio Culture. Die Geschichte der Computer im Entwurfsstudio begann mit der Bewilligung einer Subvention für das akademische Jahr 1994/1995, die es erlaubte, die Columbia University mit der für die Computertechnologie nötigen Infrastruktur auszustatten und die *paperless studios* im Gebäude Avery Hall einzurichten.[10] Eden Muir war zu dieser Zeit für die computergestützten Designkurse und das Digital Design Lab (DDL) der *Graduate School of Architecture* zuständig. Zusammen mit Rory O'Neill unterrichtete er Seminare, die eine Bandbreite von Softwareanwendungen vermittelten. Die Kenntnisse, die in den Seminaren gewonnen wurden, flossen auch in die Konzeption des Zusammenspiels von virtueller Software-Umgebung und physischer Ausstattung der *paperless studios* ein.[11]

Während Stan Allen die Räumlichkeiten der Studios im siebten Geschoss von Avery ausbaute und jene für die Entwurfsstudios typische Unterteilung in *cubicles* – mit Zeichentischen ausgestattete und von Wänden umschlossene Einheiten – durch Arbeitsplätze mit großzügigen Arbeitsflächen

9   The book *Index Architecture*, edited by Bernard Tschumi and Matthew Berman, compiles teaching positions and references the fruitful interaction between education, theory, and practice. On the critical positions vis-à-vis digital design practices, see Tschumi and Berman, eds., *Index Architecture*, pp. 2–3, 4–5, 27 (see note 5).

10   Webster, "Building Technologies," p. 11 (see note 6).

11   Experience with the interplay between real and virtual spaces was already acquired through experiments in Columbia's Digital Design Lab (DDL). In the building 206 Fayerweather, a prototype of the paperless studio was created, where students and instructors tested a digital design environment equipped with Silicon Graphics Inc. (SGI) machines and software (including Alias and Softimage). See Eden Muir and Rory O'Neill, "The Paperless Studio: A Digital Design Environment," *Newsline* (1994), pp. 10–11, and Thomas Hanrahan, ed., *Abstract 1993–94*, GSAPP (1994), p. 96. Moreover, O'Neill and Muir were involved in creating the computer-generated documentary film called *Amiens Cathedral*, realized through a cooperative relationship between the DDL and the Art History Department. See "Digital Infrastructure at the GSAPP," in Hanrahan, *Abstract 1994–95*, pp. 72–73 (see note 1).

9   Das von Bernard Tschumi und Matthew Berman herausgegebene Buch *Index Architecture* versammelt Positionen der Lehrenden und weist auf den befruchtenden Austausch zwischen Ausbildung, Theorie und Praxis hin. Zu den kritischen Positionen gegenüber den digitalen Entwurfspraktiken vgl. Tschumi, Berman (Hg.): *Index Architecture*, S. 2f., S. 4f., S. 27 (wie Anm. 5).

10   Vgl. Webster: „Building Technologies", S. 11 (wie Anm. 6).

11   Erfahrungen über das Zusammenspiel von realen und virtuellen Räumen waren bereits durch Experimente im Digital Design Lab (DDL) der Columbia University erlangt worden. Im Gebäude 206 Fayerweather war ein Prototyp des *paperless studio* eingerichtet worden, in dem Studenten und Lehrende eine mit Silicon Graphics Inc. (SGI) Maschinen und Software (u.a., Alias und Softimage) ausgestattete digitale Entwurfsumgebung testeten. Vgl. Eden Muir/Rory O'Neill: „The Paperless Studio. A Digital Design Environment", in: *Newsline* (1994), S. 10f. und Thomas Hanrahan (Hg.): *Abstract 1993-94*, GSAPP, (1994), S. 96. Des Weiteren waren O'Neill und Muir an dem computergenerierten Dokumentarfilm *Amiens Cathedral*, der als Kooperation zwischen dem DDL und dem Art History Department realisiert wurde, beteiligt. Vgl. „Digital Infrastructure at the GSAPP" in: Hanrahan (Hg.): *Abstract 1994–95*, S. 72–73 (wie Anm. 1).

ersetzte, entwarfen Muir und O'Neill die technische Ausstattung der Studios. Innerhalb der Umstrukturierungen nahmen die sich wandelnden Kommunikationsmöglichkeiten einen zentralen Stellenwert ein und waren mit einem für die Verteilung von Dateien und Softwareprogrammen genutzten Server, der auch Zugang zu den Bibliotheken und elektronischen Ressourcen gewährte, Teil des neuen medialen Ensembles.

Die offene Atelieratmosphäre der *paperless studios* war gleichsam Ausdruck einer auf Netzwerken basierenden und vom Austausch bestimmten Form des Entwerfens.[12] Nicht länger befanden sich die Computer in den abgeschlossenen CAD Laboren, sondern waren – sichtbar für alle – Teil einer Entwurfskultur, bevor Ende der 1990er Jahre alle Arbeitsplätze einen Computer besaßen und eine größere Vertrautheit mit dem Werkzeug erreicht war.

Zunächst kam den Studios im obersten Geschoss von Avery Hall jedoch eine Sonderstellung zu, die durch die vertikale Anordnung der Entwurfsstudios – die des dritten Jahrgangs befanden sich über jenen des ersten und zweiten Jahrgangs – noch gestärkt wurde.[13] Bedingt durch ihren besonderen Status und den exklusiven Zugang zu den Technologien entwickelte sich eine kultähnliche Atmosphäre um die Studios. Der Mythos, der sich, wie Reinhold Martin schreibt, um die *paperless studios* herausgebildet hatte, erschwerte es allerdings auch, jene Zusammenhänge, welche die Entwicklungen der Computertechnologien bedingten, zu begreifen.[14]

Eine eigene Entwurfssprache, sowie Bezüge auf Modelle der Kybernetik, Biologie und Philosophie kennzeichneten die methodologischen Ansätze der Studios. Modelle anderer Disziplinen, die zeitliche Veränderungen und offene Prozesse erfassen, wurden in den Architekturdiskurs und das kritische Hinterfragen bestehender Entwurfstechniken einbezogen. Zum Zeitpunkt der Einführung des Computers im Entwurfsstudio stützten sich Architekten insbesondere auf Theorien des Poststrukturalismus. Das Werk von Gilles Deleuze und Félix Guattari bildete oftmals einen Leitfaden für Entwürfe, die sich mit der Konzeption des Raums und mit Prozessen architektonischer Formfindung befassten.[15]

Die spektakulären Bilder erzeugten, als sie den Mainstream erreichten, auch jenes homogene Bild, das mit den digitalen Entwurfsansätzen an Columbias Architekturfakultät verbunden war.[19]

studios of the time, was now replaced by offering generous horizontal working surfaces. In the scope of these restructuring efforts, the shifting possibilities for communication took on a strong significance and became a part of this new media ensemble. But in addition to facilitating a new spatial paradigm for studio working, a server enabled the distribution of documents and software programs, while also providing access to library materials and other electronic resources.

The construction of a well-serviced workspace, as well as the open atelier atmosphere of the paperless studio, was also an expression of a design form that was based on and informed by collaboration and exchange.[12] Computers were no longer only to be found in self-contained CAD laboratories. They had now infiltrated the curriculum and become part of a design culture. This was a particularly innovative approach given that it was not until the late 1990s that all student workspaces featured a computer, thus enabling a stronger level of familiarity with digital design tools.

Accordingly, the studio on the top floor of Avery Hall enjoyed a special status, which was further strengthened by the vertical arrangement of studio space in the building: third-year students were situated on the floor above their counterparts from the first and second years.[13] Due to the studios' unique status and exclusive access to technologies, a cult-like atmosphere developed. As Reinhold Martin has noted, a myth evolved that was centered on the paperless studio, thus placing it above critique. This special status essentially negated attempts to contextualize the digital techniques regarding contemporary technological changes in society.[14]

The methodological approach of the studios was distinguished by a unique design language. Furthermore, architects were inspired by analytical frameworks from cybernetics, biology, and philosophy. Models from these disciplines embrace temporal change and open processes and were duly integrated into the architectural discourse, thus challenging existing design techniques. At the time that computers were introduced into the design studio, architects were especially drawn to post-structuralist theory. The work of Gilles Deleuze and Félix Guattari frequently inspired designs that explored the conception of space as well as new processes for generating architectural form.[15]

---

12 Vgl. Allen: „Avery 700-Level", S. 9 (wie Anm. 8).

13 Vgl. Reinhold Martin: „Is Digital Culture Secular? On Books by Mario Carpo and Antoine Picon", in: *Harvard Design Magazine* 35 (2012), S. 60–65, hier S. 60–63.

14 Ebd., S. 62f.

15 Über die Theorie einer Non-Standard Architektur, die weniger die Gestaltung allgemeiner Züge, sondern vielmehr die Bestimmung variabler Aspekte eines Objekts in den Vordergrund stellte und in ihrer philosophischen Definition auf Gilles Deleuze und Bernard Caches Theorie des Objektiles zurück ging vgl. Mario Carpo: „Tempest in a Teapot", in: *Log* 6 (2005), S. 99–106.
Die digitalen Entwurfstheorien, die sich auf Gilles Deleuze bezogen, wendeten sich formal von der Architektur des Dekonstruktivismus, der als ihr Vorbote gelten kann, ab und plädierten für „glatte" Architekturmodelle, die Widersprüchliches integrierten. Vgl. dazu die Beiträge in Greg Lynn (Hg.): *Architectural Design. Folding in Architecture*, Chichester 1993. Die politischen Aspekte, die Deleuze und Guattari in Bezug auf die technologischen Entwicklungen, die die Gesellschaft verändern, thematisieren, blieben in den computerbasierten Ansätzen weitgehend unberücksichtigt.

12 Allen, "Avery 700-Level," p. 9 (see note 8).

13 Reinhold Martin, "Is Digital Culture Secular?: On Books by Mario Carpo and Antoine Picon," *Harvard Design Magazine* 35 (2012), pp. 60–65, esp. pp. 60–63.

14 Ibid., pp 62–63.

15 On the theory of a non-standard architecture that focused less on the design of general features than on the determination of the variable aspects of an object while, in its philosophical definition, making reference to Gilles Deleuze and Bernard Cache's theory of the objectile, see Mario Carpo, "Tempest in a Teapot," *Log* 6 (2005), pp. 99–106.
In terms of form, the digital design theories, which made reference to Deleuze moved away from an architecture of deconstruction, which can be considered its precursor, and argued for "smooth" architectural models that integrated contradictory elements. On this, see the essays in Greg

During the fall of 1994, Greg Lynn, Scott Marble, and Hani Rashid taught the computer studios, followed by Stan Allen, Keller Easterling, and Bernard Tschumi. The software used at the time was still in development. Because of this, and due to a lack of technical knowledge by the faculty, there was a tendency in the studios toward using the technology in a less formalized manner. Tschumi describes the situation as pre-digital: "Everyone was exploring the media, with their own sensibility [and] culture."[16] As such, the implementation of computers was initially determined by those techniques that had anticipated the computer's potential. The techniques ranged from multimedia collages that opened up sensory realms of experience to time-based geometric form experiments, in addition to approaches that investigated physical space in relation to information space. The studio culture was characterized by a lively exchange among faculty and students, with the latter often possessing more extensive knowledge of computer technology.[17] Studio critics were also involved in the design of new conceptual methods through facilitating exhibitions, competitions, and published texts which furthered the discourse on the use of new technologies.[18]

Conceptual tasks and designs were published annually in *Abstract*, the architecture department's journal. The publication of student work, which featured impressive cinemagraphic images and renderings, thus also became known to numerous architectural firms. When these spectacular images reached mainstream audiences, they gave rise to that homogeneous image associated with the digital design approaches at Columbia's architecture department.[19] This caused the heterogeneity of the paperless studios, which is the focus of the following reflections, to slip into the background.

Dynamic Processes of Form Generation. In the early 1990s, Greg Lynn had already developed theories where he considered the role of the computer as a form-generating tool.[20]

1994 unterrichteten Greg Lynn, Scott Marble und Hani Rashid die Computer-Studios, gefolgt von Stan Allen, Keller Easterling und Bernard Tschumi. Die damals verwendete Software, die noch in den Kinderschuhen steckte, sowie ein geringes Erfahrungswissen im Umgang mit der Software trugen dazu bei, dass die Lehrenden mit den Computertechnologien improvisierten. Tschumi beschreibt die Situation als prädigital: „Während die Lehrenden mit den neuen Medien experimentierten, wurden sie von ihrer eigenen Wahrnehmungskultur geleitet."[16] So war die Handhabung der Computer zunächst von jenen Techniken bestimmt, die die Möglichkeiten des Computers antizipiert hatten. Die Praktiken reichten von multimedialen Collagen, die sinnliche Erfahrungsräume eröffneten, über zeitbasierte geometrische Formexperimente zu Ansätzen, die den elektronischen Raum des Informationsaustausches in seiner Bedeutung für den physischen Raum untersuchten. Die *studio culture* war von einem regen Austausch zwischen den Lehrenden und den Studierenden geprägt, die oftmals über ein umfassenderes Wissen über die Computertechnologien verfügten.[17] Auch partizipierten Lehrende – über die Studios hinaus – an der Gestaltung neuer Entwurfspraktiken und hielten in Ausstellungen, Wettbewerben und publizierten Texten die Diskussionen um die Verwendung neuer Technologien im Modus der Verhandlung.[18]

Aufgabenstellungen und Entwürfe wurden jährlich in *Abstract*, der Zeitung der Architekturfakultät, publiziert. Und so zirkulierten die Abbildungen der Entwürfe, deren filmische Qualität beeindruckte, auch in den Architekturbüros. Die spektakulären Bilder erzeugten, als sie den Mainstream erreichten, auch jenes homogene Bild, das mit den digitalen Entwurfsansätzen an Columbias Architekturfakultät verbunden war.[19] Es ließ die Heterogenität der *paperless studios*, um die es im Folgenden gehen soll, in den Hintergrund treten.

Dynamische Prozesse der Formfindung. Greg Lynn hatte bereits Anfang der 1990er Jahre Theorien entwickelt, in denen er die Rolle des Computers als formgenerierendes Werkzeug erfasste.[20] Sein Interesse galt, wie er in seinem Aufsatz „Complex Variations" schreibt, dem Erforschen von Methoden, mit denen Geometrien von Strukturen, welche sich nicht auf eine ideale Form oder Typologie reduzieren lassen, erfasst werden konnten.[21] Die Einführung des Computers bot die Möglichkeit, Raum nicht als soliden Körper, sondern über die Verformung von Oberflächen her zu begreifen.

Lynn, ed., *Architectural Design: Folding in Architecture*, 63 (1993). The political aspects that Deleuze and Guattari have thematized in relation to technological developments that change society remained mostly unconsidered in the computer-based approaches.

16 Bernard Tschumi in conversation with the author, New York, April 2013.

17 Tschumi introduced the position of the "digital assistant." Students with exceptional computer skills found themselves in the position of teaching their instructors, who in turn transferred the knowledge about digital technology acquired in the studios to their own architectural practice. On this, see Ned Cramer and Anne Guiney, "The Computer School: In Only Six Years Columbia University's Grand Experiment in Digital Design Has Launched a Movement," *Architecture* 89, no. 9 (2000), p. 94.

18 Sulan Kolatan, William McDonald, Karl Chu, and Jesse Reiser were among the faculty at Columbia University exploring digital design techniques. Projects realized in their architectural firms were published in *Assemblage*. See "Computer Animism: Two Designs for the Cardiff Bay Opera House," *Assemblage* 26 (1995), pp. 8–37.

19 See Cramer and Guiney, "The Computer School," pp. 94–98 (see note 17).

20 See Greg Lynn, "Architectural Curvilinearity: The Folded, the Pliant, and the Supple," in Lynn, *Folding in Architecture*, pp. 8–15 (see note 15).

16 Gespräch der Autorin mit Bernard Tschumi, New York April 2013. Im Original: „Everyone was exploring the media, with their own sensibility culture."

17 Tschumi führte die Position des „digital assistant" ein: Studenten, die sich durch ihr Computerwissen auszeichneten, fanden sich in der Situation, in der sie ihre Lehrer unterrichteten, die wiederum das in den Studios erlernte Wissen über die digitalen Technologien in ihre eigene Architekturpraxis überführten. Vgl. dazu Ned Cramer/Anne Guiney: „The Computer School. In Only Six Years Columbia University's Grand Experiment in Digital Design Has Launched a Movement", in: *Architecture* 89, 9 (2000), S. 94.

18 Zu den Lehrenden, die an der Columbia University die Bedeutung digitaler Technologien für den Entwurf untersuchten, gehörten u.a. auch Sulan Kolatan, William McDonald, Karl Chu und Jesse Reiser. Projekte, welche die Lehrenden in ihren Büros realisierten, wurden in *Assemblage* veröffentlicht. Vgl. „Computer Animism. Two Designs for the Cardiff Bay Opera House", in: *Assemblage* 26 (1995), S. 8–37.

19 Vgl. Cramer/Guiney: „The Computer School", S. 94–98 (wie Anm. 17).

20 Vgl. Greg Lynn: „Architectural Curvilinearity. The Folded, the Pliant, and the Supple", in: ders. (Hg.) *Architectural Design. Folding in Architecture*, 63 (1993), S. 8–15.

21 Vgl. Greg Lynn: „Complex Variations", in: *Newsline* (1994), S. 5.

Das Potenzial der Softwarewerkzeuge und ihre Fähigkeit, ein verändertes Verständnis von Architektur und ihren Organisationsformen zu bewirken, wurde dann auch in Lynns erstem *paperless studio* mit dem Titel „The Topological Organization of Free Particles. Parking Garage Studio" zum Thema. Mit der Aufgabenstellung griff Lynn das Vorhaben von Metropark New Jersey auf, ein Parkhaus für eine an einem logistischen Knotenpunkt liegende Park and Ride-Anlage entlang der Bahnlinie Boston–Washington DC zu errichten. Die Funktionen des Terminals, Verkehrsflüsse und die zu erwartenden fluktuierenden Bewegungen von Nutzern bildeten die Grundlagen der zu entwerfenden Konstruktion.[22] In dem Animationsprogramm konnten die bedeutsamen Parameter des Entwurfs durch einzelne Elemente, zum Beispiel Partikel, die sich am Ort in unterschiedlichen Geschwindigkeiten und Dichten bewegten, dargestellt und die Verbindungen und Überschneidungen von Bewegungsflüssen/Partikeln erfasst werden. Die geometrischen Verformungen in den Computersimulationen resultierten aus der wechselseitigen Einwirkung der Kräfteflüsse, während die hervorgebrachte Ästhetik die Wahrnehmung auf die Oberflächenqualitäten richtete.

Lynns Überlegungen zur Formfindung waren unter anderem von Theorien des britischen Genetikers William Bateson inspiriert. Lynn griff die Ausführungen von Bateson auf, um gegen die Vorstellung der Symmetrie als idealem übergeordnetem Organisationsprinzip zu argumentieren. An die Stelle eines stabilen Systems trat die Auffassung, dass Form aus einem wechselseitigen Wirkungsverhältnis innerer und äußerer Bedingungen hervorgeht.[23] Auch das Werk des Biologen und Mathematikers D'Arcy Wentworth Thompson, *On Growth and Form,* wird in diesem Zusammenhang von Lynn erwähnt. Dabei ist es das von Thompson entwickelte Prinzip, durch einfache geometrische Operationen Formen verwandter Arten ineinander zu überführen, das auf die Techniken des Morphings in den 3D-Modellierungen hindeutet.[24] Das Verständnis einer sich permanent verändernden Form spiegelte sich auch in den zeitbasierten Untersuchungen der Entwürfe wider. Mithilfe der Modellierungswerkzeuge konnten algorithmische Methoden der Formgenerierung entworfen und variable Morphologien berechnet werden. Aus den Mensch-Maschine Interaktionen in Lynns Studio lässt sich zunächst ableiten, dass Überlegungen zur architektonischen Formfindung und die Handhabung der Software sich wechselseitig leiten.

> An die Stelle eines stabilen Systems trat die Auffassung, dass Form aus einem wechselseitigen Wirkungsverhältnis innerer und äußerer Bedingungen hervorgeht.[23]

Mediale Interfaces. Zusammen mit Lise Anne Couture hatte Hani Rashid bereits Anfang der 1990er Jahre interaktive Architekturen entwickelt, die

As noted in his essay "Complex Variations," Lynn was interested in conducting research on methods which could identify the geometries of structures that cannot be reduced to an ideal form or typology.[21] The introduction of computers presented an opportunity to understand space not as solid body but rather as defined by the plasticity of surfaces.

The potential of software tools and their ability to achieve a modified understanding of architecture and its organizational forms was thematized in Lynn's first paperless studio titled *The Topological Organization of Free Particles: Parking Garage Studio.* In following this conceptual task, Lynn focused on Metropark's plan to build a parking structure for a New Jersey park-and-ride facility situated at a logistical hub along the railway line between Boston and Washington, DC. The basics of the construction were aligned to the functions related to the terminal, the traffic flow, and the expected fluctuating movement of users.[22] The animation program allowed the relevant design parameters to be presented using individual elements. For instance, particles in motion at different speeds and densities on site were recorded regarding their interactions of movement. The geometric distortions in the computer simulation resulted from the reciprocal impact of forces, while the aesthetics were directed toward the perception of surface qualities.

Lynn's reflections on form generation were inspired by the theories of British geneticist William Bateson. Lynn invoked Bateson's findings in arguing against the idea of symmetry as an ideal, overriding principle of organization. In lieu of a stable system, the concept was fielded that form arises from a symbiotic relationship between interior and exterior conditions.[23] In this context, Lynn also cited the work of biologist and mathematician D'Arcy Wentworth Thompson published as *On Growth and Form.* Here, Thompson developed the principle that similar types of forms are transferred into one another through simple geometric operations, with this then alluding to the technique of morphing in 3-D modeling.[24] An understanding of constantly shifting forms was also reflected by the time-based studies of the designs. Thanks to modeling tools, algorithmic methods of form generation could be drafted and variable morphologies calculated. It can be deduced from the human-machine interaction in Lynn's studio that deliberation on architectural form generation and the handling of software reciprocally influence each other.

Media Interfaces. In the early 1990s, Hani Rashid, together with Lise Anne Couture, had already developed inter-

22 Vgl. *Abstract 1994–95*, S. 66 (wie Anm. 1).

23 Vgl. Greg Lynn: „The Renewed Novelty of Symmetry", in: ders.: *Folds, Bodies & Blobs. Collected Essays*, Brüssel 1998, S. 63–77, hier S. 64.

24 Vgl. Greg Lynn: „Multiplicitous and Inorganic Bodies", in: *Assemblage* No. 19 (1992), S. 32–49.

21 See Greg Lynn, "Complex Variations," *Newsline* (1994), p. 5.

22 See Hanrahan, *Abstract 1994–95*, p. 66 (see note 1).

23 See Greg Lynn, "The Renewed Novelty of Symmetry," in *Folds, Bodies & Blobs: Collected Essays* (Brussels, 1998), pp. 63–77, esp. p. 64.

24 See Greg Lynn, "Multiplicitous and Inorganic Bodies," *Assemblage* 19 (1992), pp. 32–49.

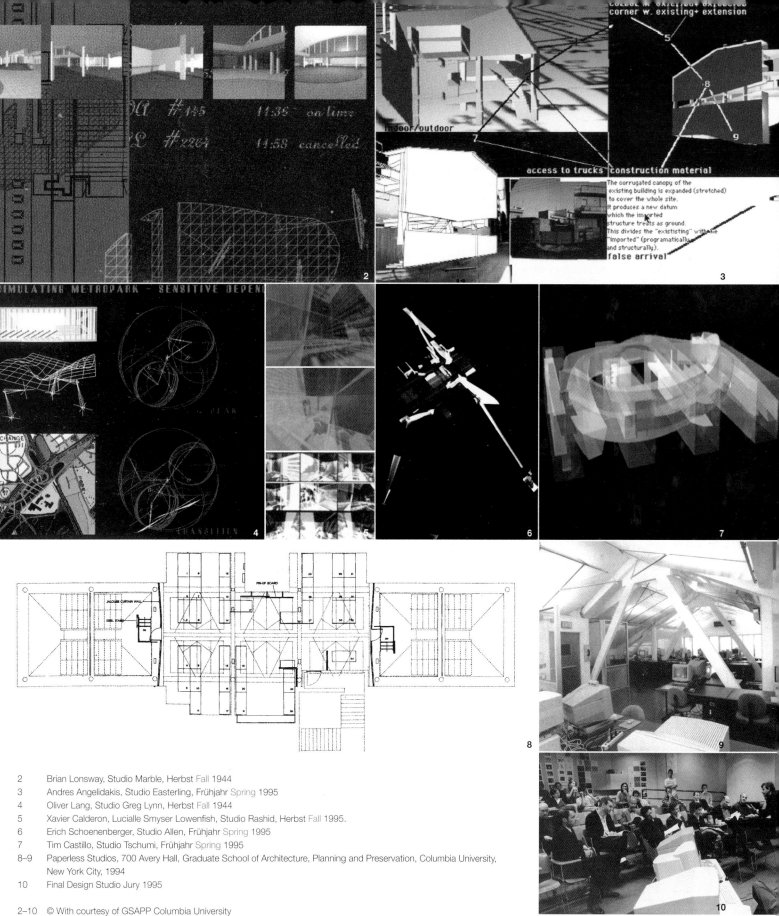

2   Brian Lonsway, Studio Marble, Herbst Fall 1944

3   Andres Angelidakis, Studio Easterling, Frühjahr Spring 1995

4   Oliver Lang, Studio Greg Lynn, Herbst Fall 1944

5   Xavier Calderon, Lucialle Smyser Lowenfish, Studio Rashid, Herbst Fall 1995.

6   Erich Schoenenberger, Studio Allen, Frühjahr Spring 1995

7   Tim Castillo, Studio Tschumi, Frühjahr Spring 1995

8–9   Paperless Studios, 700 Avery Hall, Graduate School of Architecture, Planning and Preservation, Columbia University, New York City, 1994

10   Final Design Studio Jury 1995

sich mit der Dominanz der Medien auseinandersetzten. Die Herausgeber von *Assemblage* betonten, dass die Oberflächen der von Couture und Rashid entworfenen Architekturen virtuellen Effekten materiellen Ausdruck verliehen und programmatische Veränderungen bewirken konnten.[25] Kennzeichnend für Rashids Ansatz ist, dass der Umgang mit dem Computer – angeregt durch räumliche Situationen des Films und der Medienkunst – an der Verschränkung von konkret physisch-räumlichen Konfigurationen und imaginären Vorstellungswelten ausgerichtet war. Das Interesse seines *paperless studio*: *Media City. Architecture at the Interval* galt den Möglichkeiten digitaler Technologien, Phänomene des Raumes zu entdecken und ihnen eine Plastizität zu verleihen.[26] Die Bilder des Films, Fernsehens und Internets wurden in ihrer Bedeutung für unser Denken und Kommunizieren, sowie für die durch Kommunikationstechnologien hervorgebrachten Ökonomien und Gemeinschaften untersucht. Dabei ist es gerade die durch die Zirkulation von Bildern erzeugte Räumlichkeit, die, so Rashid, die Architektur herausfordere.[27] Analysen von Filmen und digitaler Kunst lenkten den Fokus auf das Potenzial von Licht und Sound, Räume hervorzubringen. Die Erkenntnisse, die aus den Analysen gewonnen wurden, mündeten in eine Form der Architektur und Stadtplanung – einen Medienurbanismus, der die sinnliche Wahrnehmung zu erweitern suchte. Umgesetzt in raumgreifenden Installationen bewirkten die Computerentwürfe in der Überschneidung von Computerscreens, Projektionen und physisch gebauten Netzstrukturen ein Durchdringen von haptischen, visuellen und auditiven Erfahrungen. So konnte das Merkmal des Computers – verschiedene Medien zu synchronisieren und mit der Aufnahme, Übertragung und Verarbeitung von Informationen zu operieren – körperlich erfahren werden.

Diese Arbeiten stehen im Gegensatz zu den Entkörperlichungstendenzen, die oftmals mit dem Digitalen verbunden waren. Das Studio erforschte vielmehr, inwieweit die Technologien die Tätigkeit der Sinne stärken und erweitern könnten. Während die Betonung von Bewegung und Verzerrung die Aufmerksamkeit auf die operativen Qualitäten der digitalen Bilder lenkte, spielten die zeiträumlichen Bildanordnungsverfahren mit der Desorientierung der Betrachter und forderten sie zu Interaktionen auf.

1998 entwickelten Couture und Rashid einen Virtual Trading Floor für die New Yorker Börse. Ein virtuelles interaktives 3D-Modell des Börsenparketts erlaubte es, durch den Informationsraum der Börse zu navigieren und in ihm zu agieren. Das sich ständig verändernde Interface entsprach dem realen Layout der Börse und spiegelte deren Abläufe, die auf der Eingabe der Daten des NYSE beruhten, in 3D-Graphen wider. Während die Arbeiten des *paperless studio* den Computer eingesetzt hatten, um Grenzen der Raumerfahrung durch Irritationen zu testen, regten die Farben und dynamischen Formen des Interface zu einem intuitiven Navigieren durch den Datenraum an.

Informationsflüsse, Animation und Fabrikation. Mit der Frage, was die mit den Computertechnologien verbundenen Informationsflüsse für die

active architectural projects that examined the dominance of media. The editors of *Assemblage* emphasized that the surfaces of the architecture designed by Couture and Rashid could lend a sense of material expression to virtual effects and also facilitate programmatic changes.[25] It is characteristic for Rashid's approach that the use of computers—inspired by spatial situations in cinematic contexts and the media arts—was oriented to the interweaving of concrete physical-spatial configurations and imaginary mindscapes. His paperless studio *Media City: Architecture at the Interval* was devoted to the possibility of discovering the phenomena of space through digital technologies and imbuing it with a certain plasticity.[26] The pictures found in film and television and on the Internet were examined as to their importance for our thinking, as well as for the economies and collectives spawned by communication technologies. According to Rashid, it is precisely this spatiality embodied through the circulation of images that presents a challenge to architecture.[27] Analyses of films and digital art focused on the potential of light and sound in generating space. The insights gained from these analyses were joined in a form of urban planning: a media urbanism that sought to expand sensory perception. Realized as space-consuming installations—constellations of computer screens, projections, and physically constructed network structures—the computer designs fostered an infusion of haptic, visual, and auditory experiences. This allowed for the physical experience of the distinguishing character of the computer as one that synchronizes different media and processes of information.

These works contrast with the tendency toward disembodiment that were frequently associated with digital contexts. To a greater degree, the studio researched the extent to which technologies might enhance and expand sensory agency. While an emphasis on movement and distortion directed attention to the operative qualities of digital images, the spatiotemporal processes of arranging images engaged the viewers through disorientations.

In 1998, Couture and Rashid developed a virtual trading floor for the New York Stock Exchange. A virtual, interactive 3-D model of the stock-exchange trading floor made it possible to navigate and operate within the exchange's information space. The constantly changing interface mirrored the real layout of the exchange and used 3-D diagrams to reflect procedures based on the entry of NYSE data. While the pursuits of this paperless studio had implemented computers to probe

25   Vgl. Hani Rashid/Lise Anne Couture (Hg.): „Analog Space to Digital Field. Asymptote Seven Projects", in: *Assemblage* 21 (1993) S. 24–43, hier S. 26.

26   Zur Aufgabenstellung Rashids Studios siehe: *Abstract 1994–95*, S. 68 (wie Anm. 1).

27   Vgl. Hani Rashid: „Notes on Architecture", in: *Newsline* (1993), S. 2 und ders.: „Asymptote. The Architecture of Convergence", in: *Newsline* (1999), S. 2.

25   Hani Rashid and Lise Anne Couture, eds., "Analog Space to Digital Field: Asymptote Seven Projects," *Assemblage* 21 (1993), pp. 24–43, esp. p. 26.

26   On the conceptual focus of Rashid's studio, see *Abstract 1994–95*, p. 68 (see note 1).

27   See Hani Rashid, "Notes on Architecture," *Newsline* (1993), p. 2, and Hani Rashid, "Asymptote: The Architecture of Convergence," *Newsline* (1999), p. 2.

the boundaries of spatial experience by way of irritations, the colors and dynamic forms of the interface encouraged intuitive navigation through the data-space.

Information Flows, Animation, and Fabrication. The question as to what the information flows associated with computer technology might mean for architectural practice—especially its fabrication—was investigated by architect Scott Marble. Important in this context were the infrastructural conditions, as well as processes and practices of representation, which made the design negotiable through the transfer of information. His paperless studio *JFK Access* concentrated on the flows of movement and information running synchronously at John F. Kennedy International Airport.[28] The analyses focused on airport logistics and were initially carried out using 3-D computer models. The workflow of personnel, the paths taken by passengers, and the mechanisms of information and communication technologies were translated into graphic form. Furthermore, insight was gained about the complex temporalities to which passenger transportation and flows of information are subject. An overview of the site was achieved through 3-D mapping. However, in contrast to Lynn's project, animation was not implemented to generate form; instead, movement in the model served as a means for localizing design locations. In this particular case, acts of targeted intervention at junctions of information flow led to a change in the spatial constellation of the airport and to a reconfiguration of the already existing networks with their boundaries, distances, and paths. Switching between different modes of representation also made it possible to assemble divergent views of the site in order to produce new contexts.

By structuring the design through the sequence of work stages—measurement, analysis, and intervention—the attention was shifted from the object to the transformation of information. With such an emphasis on data flow, moments of upheaval came into play. It is in these moments of shifting direction that one decides which aspects of the design should be followed up on, and which tools should be used. Questions arise here that are related to the mechanisms of the software tools and, moreover, as to how one might sidestep the inherent logic of software when necessary. Marble's interest in the computer as the medium for designing organizational steps and communication processes greatly influenced his future research interests.[29]

Praxis der Architektur – insbesondere deren Fabrikation – bedeuten können, beschäftigte sich der Architekt Scott Marble. Bedeutsam waren in diesem Zusammenhang die infrastrukturellen Bedingungen, sowie die Visualisierungsprozesse und -praktiken, die den Entwurf über die Weitergabe von Informationen verhandelbar machten. Sein *paperless studio*: *JFK Access* beschäftigte sich mit den synchron verlaufenden Bewegungs- und Informationsflüssen am J.F. Kennedy Airport.[28] Die Analysen, die sich der Flughafenlogistik zuwandten, erfolgten zunächst an dreidimensionalen Computermodellen. Damit wurden die Arbeitsabläufe des Personals, die Wege der Passagiere, sowie die Mechanismen der Informations- und Kommunikationstechnologien übersetzt und anschaulich gemacht. Ferner konnten Einsichten über die komplexen Zeitlichkeiten, denen der Personentransport und die Informationsflüsse unterstehen, gewonnen werden. Die Wahrnehmung des Ortes erfolgte hier über Kartierungen im 3D-Modell. Animationen wurden nicht, wie bei Lynn, zur Formgenerierung eingesetzt, sondern die Bewegung durch das Modell diente als Mittel, um Orte des Entwurfs zu lokalisieren. In diesem Fall führte ein gezieltes Intervenieren an Schnittstellen der Informationsflüsse zu einer Veränderung der räumlichen

> Umgesetzt in raumgreifenden Installationen bewirkten die Computerentwürfe in der Überschneidung von Computerscreens, Projektionen und physisch gebauten Netzstrukturen ein Durchdringen von haptischen, visuellen und auditiven Erfahrungen.

Konstellation des Flughafens und zu einer neuen Konfiguration der bereits vorhandenen Netzwerke mit ihren Grenzen, Distanzen und Wegen. Das Wechseln zwischen verschiedenen Modi der Darstellung erlaubte es auch, unterschiedlichste Sichten auf den Ort zu montieren, um neue Zusammenhänge herzustellen.

Mit der Strukturierung des Entwurfs durch die Folge der Arbeitsschritte: Aufmaß, Analyse und Intervention, verschob sich die Aufmerksamkeit vom Objekt auf die Transformation von Informationen. Die Übersetzung von Daten, die den Entwurfsprozess wesentlich bestimmt, bringt auch Momente des Umbruchs ins Spiel. In den Momenten des Richtungswechsels werden Entscheidungen über die Weiterbearbeitung des Entwurfs, sowie die Auswahl der Software gefällt. Hier stellen sich Fragen nach den Mechanismen der Softwarewerkzeuge und ferner, wie die inhärente Logik der Software gegebenenfalls umgangen werden kann. Der Computer als das Medium, durch das sich Organisationsabläufe und Kommunikationsprozesse des Entwurfs planen lassen, ist ein Aspekt, der Marbles Interesse an weiteren Entwicklungen der Computertechnologie bestimmen sollte.[29]

28   On the conceptual focus of Scott Marble's design studio, see *Abstract 1994–95*, p. 67 (see note 1).

29   On the current development of computer applications for design at Columbia University, see The Columbia Building Intelligence Project (CBIP), http://c-bip.org/about (accessed November 2013).

28   Zur Aufgabenstellung des Entwurfsstudios von Scott Marble siehe: *Abstract 1994–95*, S. 67 (wie Anm. 1).

29   Über die aktuellen Entwicklungen von Computeranwendungen im Entwurf an der Columbia University siehe: The Columbia Building Intelligence Project (CBIP) http://c-bip.org/about (Stand: 01. November 2013).

Architektonische Form und Infrastruktur. Keller Easterling hatte in ihrem Buchprojekt *American Town Plans. A Comparative Time Line* (1993)[30] Computertechnologien eingesetzt, um Einblicke in die Entwicklung der US-amerikanischen Städte und Vorstädte zu gewinnen. Der übergreifende Blick auf die Geschichte und das versammelte Material geben Auskunft über die Mechanismen, die die Strukturierung der Landschaft und Planung der Städte prägen. Karten, Transportnetze, Haustypen, sowie Gesetzentwürfe legen die Prinzipien der Stadt- und Landschaftsplanung dar, die oft unsichtbar blieben, jedoch wesentlich für die Zersiedelung der amerikanischen Landschaft waren. Keller Easterlings Studio: *Interference. Webs of Sites* beschäftigte sich mit Organisationsstrukturen und ihrer Übersetzung in architektonische Räume, sowie mit Ansätzen des *Network Thinking*. Der Ort des Projekts befand sich an der Westseite Manhattans – im Umfeld der Gleisanlagen von Caemmerer West Side Yards – einer Gegend, in der sich Infrastrukturen dicht überlagern: Schienen, Highways, Tunnel und Überführungen, sowie Kabel- und Leitungsnetze. Die Analysen jener Strukturen, die Orte erschließen und Informationen zirkulieren lassen, rückten die mit den Netzwerken in Verbindung stehenden Ökonomien und ihren Austausch in den Fokus der Entwurfsprozesse.[31] Die Herausforderung der Aufgabenstellung bestand zunächst darin, die räumlichen Konsequenzen von materiellen und immateriellen Informationsflüssen zu erfassen. In diesem Fall erhielten die Transportnetze von Personen und Objekten die gleiche Aufmerksamkeit wie die der Daten. Des Weiteren sollten die durch Kartierungen sichtbar gewordenen Verläufe der Infrastrukturen, die oftmals auch im Widerspruch zueinander standen, so verbunden werden, dass sich neue Nachbarschaften entwickeln konnten. Die entworfenen Szenarien brachten physische und digitale, formale und informale Datenflüsse in Verbindung. Mit den Interventionen sollten weniger vorhersehbare Ergebnisse erzeugt, als vielmehr Möglichkeiten eröffnet werden.

Das Studio setzte die digitalen Technologien jedoch nicht nur ein, um Relationen von Hard- und Software zu erforschen, sondern wendete die Vernetzung auch auf die im Studio entwickelten Projekte an. Relationen und Abhängigkeiten der Projekte untereinander konnten so erprobt und die Entwicklungen der *paperless studios* über eine veränderte Studiopraxis reflektiert werden. Der Ansatz des Studios unterschied sich von jenen Computeranwendungen, die an den geometrischen Darstellungen der Morphologien

> Die Analysen jener Strukturen, die Orte erschließen und Informationen zirkulieren lassen, rückten die mit den Netzwerken in Verbindung stehenden Ökonomien und ihren Austausch in den Fokus der Entwurfsprozesse.[31]

Architectural Form and Infrastructure. In her book project *American Town Plans: A Comparative Time Line* (1993),[30] Keller Easterling used computer technology to gain insight into the development of cities and suburbs in the United States. A comprehensive view of history and the material collected provide information about mechanisms that impact the structuring of landscape and the planning of cities. Maps, transportation networks, housing types, and proposed legislation expose the principles of urban and landscape planning which often remain hidden, despite having been instrumental in saddling the American landscape with urban sprawl. Keller Easterling's paperless studio *Interference: Webs of Sites* took up organizational structures and their translation into architectural spaces and also touched on "networking thinking" approaches. The project was situated at Manhattan's West Side near the John D. Caemmerer West Side Yard—an area where infrastructures densely overlap: railway tracks, highways, tunnels and overpasses, as well as cable systems and supply networks. The analysis of those structures that make sites accessible and allow information to circulate placed the design focus on the network-associated economies and their exchange.[31] The conceptual task initially presented a challenge in developing an understanding of the spatial consequences of material and immaterial flows of information. In this case, the networks for transporting people and objects shared equal weight with data networks. Moreover, the infrastructural paths, which had been made visible through the process of mapping and could also be seen to frequently conflict with one another, thus giving rise to new proximities. The drafted scenarios brought together flows of physical and digital data of both a formal and informal nature. These interventions were meant to facilitate opportunities rather than simply generate foreseeable results.

Yet the studio did not only implement digital technology to research relations between hardware and software; it also applied networking to the projects developed in the studio. This made it possible to test relations and dependencies among the projects and to reflect on the evolution of the paperless studio through an altered studio practice. The approach taken by this studio differed from those computer applications that were interested in geometric representations of morphologies and in the forms resulting from algorithms. Network architecture was determined by efforts to understand the dynamic environment in which architecture participates. Architecture was viewed as an "active form," as a spatially operating system that shapes society.[32] Gregory Bateson's deliberations on networks, which

---

30   Keller Easterling: *American Town Plans. A Comparative Time Line*, New York 1993. Das Buch war als Mixed Media Format mit einer Hypercard entwickelt worden.

31   *Abstract 1994–95*, S. 70 (wie Anm. 1).

30   Keller Easterling, *American Town Plans: A Comparative Time Line* (New York, 1993). The book was developed with a hypercard as a mixed-media format.

31   See *Abstract 1994–95*, p. 70 (see note 1).

32   Keller Easterling, "Network Differentials," unpublished paper. Many thanks to Keller Easterling, who made this text available to me.

he put to paper in *Mind and Nature: A Necessary Unity*, were of central importance since he called for heterogeneity and a multiple use of concepts and models from various disciplines. Especially characteristic for this design studio was the fact that the computer-aided organizational processes were not limited to the computer itself but were rather conceived as elements of built space.

Iterative, Serial, and Abstract Operations. Stan Allen also developed his idea of "field conditions" in the context of the paperless studio. According to Allen, his idea of conceptualizing the city as a field of smallest-possible, self-resembling parts that react to outside influences was inspired by developments found in the paperless studio.[33] Allen was less interested in the compositions themselves than in systemic changes, which he more closely researched in his paperless studio *Field Condition: Purchase*. The aim here was to draft proposals for restructuring the State University of New York campus, striving for a new interplay between existing buildings by altering individual parts.[34] The topic "field conditions" directed attention to an architectural practice that, instead of setting out to develop a master plan, attempted to initiate an evolving process of spatial change by making minimal modifications. The analyses used in the studio tried to capture the complex relations of the site with a view to subsequently developing tactics for reacting to the formal, social, and programmatic circumstances on site. These design processes detracted attention from the object to rather focus on a field composed of specific individual elements. In bringing together the individual elements, the students employed intervals, repetition, extensions, and seriality. Taking the place of separating lines were connections established through surfaces.

Allen was opposed to the use of computer-based visualizations, such as renderings that aspired to portray an object as realistically as possible. He argued that one should benefit from the computational qualities of computers and operate according to the principle of translating individual elements (bits) into many different kinds of representations. In this way, the abstract system of rules could tentatively stabilize things while simultaneously remaining open. Transferred to the architectural and urban context, the iterative and recursive practices motivated the approach taken by the *field conditions*.

Notations and Knowledge Forms. Bernard Tschumi was interested in the dependencies between the representational

und an den aus einem Algorithmus resultierenden Formen interessiert waren. Die *Network Architecture* war davon bestimmt, die dynamische Umwelt, an der Architektur partizipiert zu verstehen. Architektur wurde als „active form", als räumlich operierendes System verstanden, das gesellschaftliche Ordnungen formt.[32] Bezüge auf Gregory Batesons Überlegungen, die er in *Mind and Nature. A Necessary Unity* zu Netzwerken formulierte, waren insofern von zentraler Bedeutung, als sie Heterogenität und eine multiple Anwendung von Begriffen und Modellen verschiedener Disziplinen forderten. Besonders auffällig für das Entwurfsstudio war, dass die rechnergestützten Organisationsprozesse nicht auf den Computer beschränkt, sondern als Bestandteile des gebauten Raumes begriffen wurden.

Iterative, serielle und abstrakte Operationen. Auch Stan Allen entwickelte sein Konzept der „field conditions" im Kontext der *paperless studios*. Die Stadt als ein Feld kleinster sich selbst ähnlicher Teile zu denken, die auf Einflüsse von außen reagieren, war, so Allen, von den Entwicklungen in den *paperless studios* geprägt.[33] Es waren weniger die Kompositionen als die Veränderungen von Systemen, für die sich Allen interessierte und in seinem *paperless studio*: *Field Condition*. *Purchase* näher erforschte. Dabei sollten Vorschläge für die Umstrukturierung des Campus' der State University von New York entwickelt und ein neues Zusammenspiel der existierenden Gebäude durch die Veränderung einzelner Teile bewirkt werden.[34] Das Thema *field conditions* lenkte die Aufmerksamkeit auf eine architektonische Praxis, die nicht auf die Entwicklung eines Masterplans abzielte, sondern versuchte, durch minimale Veränderungen einen sich entfaltenden Prozess räumlicher Veränderungen zu initiieren. Die im Studio angewendeten Analysen versuchten, die komplexen Zusammenhänge des Ortes zu erfassen, um anschließend Taktiken zu entwickeln, mit denen auf die formalen, sozialen und programmatischen Gegebenheiten des Ortes reagiert werden konnte. Diese Entwurfsprozesse lenken die Aufmerksamkeit weg von dem Objekt hin zu einem Feld, das sich aus einzelnen spezifischen Elementen zusammensetzt. Für das Zusammenführen der einzelnen Elemente operierten die Studenten mit Intervallen, Wiederholungen, Erweiterungen und Serialität. An die Stelle trennender Linien traten durch Oberflächen hergestellte Verbindungen.

Allen wandte sich gegen die Verwendung von Computervisualisierungen, wie etwa *Renderings*, die eine möglichst reale Darstellung eines Objektes anstrebten. Er plädierte dafür, die rechnerischen Qualitäten des Computers fruchtbar zu machen und mit dem Prinzip zu operieren, einzelne Elemente (Bits) in unterschiedlichste Darstellungen überführen zu können. Dabei konnte das abstrakte System der Regeln Dinge provisorisch stabilisieren und gleichzeitig offen bleiben. Auf den architektonischen und urbanen Kontext übertragen begründeten die iterativen und rekursiven Vorgehensweisen den Ansatz der *field conditions*.

33   Stan Allen writes: "This early exposure to computation led me to an idea of the city as a field of forces, and the aggregation of small, self-similar parts to create local difference while maintaining overall coherence." See Stan Allen in *Field Conditions Revisited*, ed. Giancarlo Valle (New York, 2010), n.p. Many thanks to Stan Allen, who made this text available to me.

34   On the conceptual focus of Stan Allen's paperless studio, see *Abstract 1994–95*, p. 69 (see note 1).

32   Keller Easterling: „Network Differentials", unpublished paper. Mit Dank an Keller Easterling, die mir den Text zur Verfügung stellte.

33   Stan Allen schreibt: „This early exposure to computation led me to an idea of the city as a field of forces, and the aggregation of small, self-similar parts to create local difference while maintaining overall coherence" Stan Allen in: Giancarlo Valle (Hg.): *Field Conditions Revisited*, New York 2010. o. Sz. Mit Dank an Stan Allen, der mir den Text zur Verfügung stellte.

34   Zur Aufgabenstellung von Stan Allens *paperless studio* siehe: *Abstract 1994–95*, S. 69 (wie Anm. 1).

NEWSLINE

AVERY ARCHITECTURAL AND FINE ARTS LIBRARY

COLUMBIA UNIVERSITY AVERY HALL NEW YORK NEW YORK 10027

COLUMBIA
ARCHITECTURE
PLANNING
PRESERVATION

SUMMER/SEPT/OCT '94

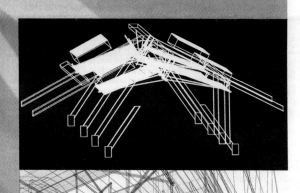

Stan Allen, assistant professor of architecture, designed the new Avery 700-Level computing studio. *(Top inset)* roof structure with diffusers; *(above inset)* perspective; *(background)* detail.

THIS ISSUE:

11

forms/notations of architecture and reasoning about architecture. In his own practice, Tschumi had turned to film and had developed forms of architectural representation that lent expression to aspects of both time and movement. His notations placed event, space, and movement into a potentiality field of relations.[35] The question and challenge presented by the computer as a medium, according to Tschumi, entailed whether it was possible to use computers to develop conceptual approaches in architecture. His paperless studio *Hard/Soft: Chelsea Piers Passing* initially hypothesized that architecture represents a connection between real and virtual realms, and that it is comprised of material (hardware) and immaterial (software) facets. Moreover, he postulated that computer modeling would bring forth a new form of architecture and that buildings might serve as catalysts for urban development. After a ten-day exercise in testing digital technology and gaining familiarity with the digital design environment, it was time to develop an event for Chelsea Piers in New York City. The students worked with transfer processes (anti-events served as virtual counterparts to the events) in order to research the reciprocal relationships between space and event by invoking a change of representations.[36] The objective was to comprehend architecture as animated and temporally influenced, as well as to activate the urban context through strategically implemented choreographies. The use of animation software was informed by film-editing techniques and was decisive in facilitating conceptual considerations of the designs.

Knowledge Practice and Interaction. The overview of the paperless studios detailed here has examined how the studios, though challenged by the technological developments of the time, nevertheless sought to engage design concepts and techniques via the capabilities of the modern computer. But what was actually crucial in the use of computers in the design process was not actually a pronounced technical knowledge, but rather an intuitive approach based on design-related experience—which in turn gave rise to unique modes of representation.

Indeed, digital technology was applied in different ways in the respective paperless studios, and—depending on the conceptualization—their agency changed in the design itself. While commonalities could be initially found in the studios' preoccupation with information flows, temporalities, and spatial dynamics, the approaches seen in the paperless studio

Notationen und Wissensformen. Bernard Tschumi interessierte sich für die Abhängigkeiten zwischen den Repräsentationsformen/Notationen der Architektur und dem Denken über die Architektur.

In seiner eigenen Praxis hatte sich Tschumi dem Film zugewandt und Formen der architektonischen Darstellung entwickelt, die Aspekte der Zeit und der Bewegung zum Ausdruck brachten. Seine Notationen setzten Programm, Raum und Bewegung (*Event, Space, Movement*) in ein Möglichkeitsfeld von Relationen.[35] Die Frage und Herausforderung, die sich für Tschumi durch das Medium Computer ergab, war jene, ob sich mit dem Computer konzeptionelle Ansätze der Architektur entwickeln ließen. Sein Studio *Hard/Soft. Chelsea Piers Passing* ging zunächst von den Hypothesen aus, dass Architektur eine Verbindung von Realem und Virtuellem darstellt, sich aus Materiellem (Hardware) und Immateriellem (Software) zusammensetzt. Ferner stellte er die These auf, dass Computermodellierungen eine neue Form der Architektur hervorbringen würden und Gebäude als Katalysatoren für städtische Entwicklungen dienen könnten. Nach einer zehntägigen Übung, in der digitale Technologien getestet und eine Vertrautheit mit der digitalen Entwurfsumgebung erlangt worden war, ging es darum,

> Die Frage und Herausforderung, die sich für Tschumi durch das Medium Computer ergab, war jene, ob sich mit dem Computer konzeptionelle Ansätze der Architektur entwickeln ließen.

ein Programm für die Chelsea Piers, NY zu entwickeln. Die Studenten arbeiteten mit Umkehrverfahren (Antiprogramme bildeten virtuelle Gegenstücke zu den Programmen), um durch den Wechsel von Darstellungen die reziproken Verhältnisse von Raum und Programm zu erforschen.[36] Ziel war es, Architektur als bewegt und zeitbasiert zu begreifen und durch strategisch eingesetzte Choreografien den Kontext der Stadt zu aktivieren. Entscheidend für die computerbasierten Operationen, die der Kommunikation der konzeptionellen Überlegungen dienten, war, dass Montagetechniken des Films den Umgang mit der Animationssoftware anregten.

Wissenspraktiken und Interaktionen. Die hier beschriebenen Ansätze der *paperless studios* charakterisiert, dass sie – herausgefordert von den technologischen Entwicklungen – Konzepte und Techniken des Entwerfens entwickelten, die mit Eigenschaften des Computers operierten. Weniger ein ausgeprägtes technisches Wissen, sondern vielmehr ein intuitives Vorgehen, das auf gestalterischen Erfahrungen beruht, entschied über die Anwendungen des Computers im Entwurf, die wiederum eigene Darstellungsweisen hervorbrachten.

35   As a reference for his reflections on a new conceptualization of architecture, Bernard Tschumi cites the representations developed in the project Manhattan Transcripts. See Tschumi's lecture "Modes of Notation" held on July 12, 2013 at the Toolkit 2013 workshop, Canadian Centre for Architecture, available online at http://www.youtube.com/watch?v=PE9LHXEsB4A (accessed November 2013).

36   See *Abstract 1994–95*, p. 71 (see note 1).

35   Bernard Tschumi führt als Referenz für seine Überlegungen zu einer neuen Konzeptualisierung der Architektur die im Projekt „Manhattan Transcripts" entwickelten Darstellungen an. Vgl. Bernard Tschumis Vortrag „Modes of Notation" am 12. Juli 2013 im Rahmen des Workshops Toolkit 2013 am Canadian Centre for Architecture. Online unter: http://www.youtube.com/watch?v=PE9LHXEsB4A (Stand: 01. November 2013).

36   Vgl. *Abstract 1994–95*, S. 71 (wie Anm. 1).

So traten die digitalen Technologien in den *paperless studios* jeweils anders in Erscheinung und wechselten – je nach Konzeptualisierung – ihren Akteurstatus im Entwurf. Die Ansätze der *paperless studios*, deren Gemeinsamkeit zunächst in der Beschäftigung mit Informationsflüssen, Zeitlichkeiten und räumlichen Dynamiken lag, können – auch wenn sich formale und konzeptionelle Überschneidungen feststellen lassen – in jene unterschieden werden, die a) mit den Computeranwendungen Räumlichkeiten/Interfaces entwickelten, in denen sich Digitales und Analoges verschränkte und die eine Erweiterung unserer Sinne durch digitale Technologien anstrebten, b) die Möglichkeiten der Formgenerierung erforschten und sich bei der Konzeption des architektonischen Körpers von biologischen Modellen inspirieren ließen und c) die den Fokus auf Kommunikationstechnologien und Netzwerke legten, die Räumlichkeiten strukturierten und hervorbrachten.[37] Während einerseits die Möglichkeiten der Interaktion durch den Computer – der die Wahrnehmung lenkt – geprägt waren, so bestimmten andererseits die Zielsetzungen der Studios die Rolle des Computers im Entwurf.

Bezeichnenderweise ermöglichten digitale Technologien gerade dann architektonische Erfahrungen, wenn sie nicht als eigenständige Funktionssysteme begriffen, sondern vielmehr in Gestaltungsprozesse eingebunden

> Bezogen auf den Einsatz digitaler Technologien ist von Bedeutung, dass nicht alle Entwurfsschritte codiert werden können und nicht determinierte, intuitive Anteile oftmals gestalterische Möglichkeiten eröffnen, die mit technologischem Fortschritt Kontingenzen schaffen.

waren und mit ihrer Handhabung ein spekulatives Vorgehen einherging. Es überrascht daher, dass gerade jene Ansätze, die für offene Systeme plädierten, über eine Ästhetik bekannt wurden, die auf geometrischen Formen beruht. Ebenfalls überraschend ist, dass die Verschränkung von digitalen und analogen Verfahren, auf der die frühen Ansätze basierten, in den oftmals ideologisch geführten Diskussionen in den Hintergrund trat. Wie Keller Easterling meint, stellten sich gerade die Ansätze als problematisch heraus, die in ihren Theorien die Koexistenz verschiedener Auffassungen verneinten und implizierten, dass die digitale die analoge Welt ersetzten würde. Auch waren jene Entwürfe wenig überzeugend, die sich durch eine technische Expertise zu legitimieren versuchten und durch die Werkzeuge dazu verleitet wurden, ihre Prozesse als pseudowissenschaftlich zu erklären oder die algorithmischen Operationen einsetzten, um eine Zwangsläufigkeit des Entwurfsprozesses zu suggerieren.[38]

can be segmented into three groups (though they may overlap at times when it comes to form and conception). Firstly, there were studios that used computer applications to develop spatialities/interfaces, where digital and analogue aspects became interwoven. Secondly, other studios researched the possibilities of geometric form generation and were inspired by biological models in conceptualizing architectural bodies. Thirdly, studios focused on communication technologies and networks that generated and structured space, thus facillitating changes between human and non-human actors.[37] Thus while opportunities for interaction were dependent on computers (which channel perception), at the same time the objectives of the studios similarly guided the agency of computers in the design process.

Tellingly, digital technologies facilitated architectural experience especially when conceived not as an autonomous functional system but rather as an integral part of the design process, especially when its use went hand in hand with an exploratory approach. Therefore it is surprising that those approaches especially advocating open systems became known for an aesthetics founded on geometric forms. It is also surprising that the interweaving of digital methods and analogue ones on which these approaches were based tended to be set aside in ideologically focused discussions. As Keller Easterling has noted, it is precisely those approaches that were problematic because they denied the coexistence of different views in their theories and inferred that the digital world would replace the analogue one. Also the less-convincing designs were those that tried to legitimize themselves through technical expertise and, based on these tools, were tempted to explain their processes in a pseudo-scientific way or to implement algorithmic operations to suggest inevitability in the design process.[38]

This already points to the problematic nature of all computer-driven design processes that invoke optimization strategies and effectivity in their reasoning without taking the history and effects of computer-based visualization techniques into consideration. Moreover, the question arises as to what extent models from other disciplines are capable of attaining relevance for processes of design, and also what significance they enjoy in relation to human–machine interaction.

Several general questions arise in this context, for example: Can architecture develop its own theory through practice? In relation to the use of digital technology, it is significant that not all design steps can be codified, and indeed intuitive areas

37   Der jüngst veranstaltete Workshop Toolkit 2013 am Canadian Centre for Architecture beschäftigte sich mit digital basieren Entwurfsprozessen und legte einen Fokus auf die *paperless studios*. Online unter: http://www.cca.qc.ca/en/study-centre/2162-toolkit-2013 (Stand: 01. November 2013).

38   Gespräch der Autorin mit Keller Easterling, New York, April 2013.

37   The most recent Toolkit 2013 workshop at the Canadian Centre for Architecture was concerned with digitally based design processes and focused on the paperless studios. See http://www.cca.qc.ca/en/study-centre/2162-toolkit-2013 (accessed November 2013).

38   Keller Easterling in conversation with the author, New York, April 2013.

frequently give way to design innovation by creating contingencies through technological progress. It is thus in the spatial setting of the university in which new strategies and opportunities arise for digital innovation. In 1994, when the studios were created, Muir and O'Neill were already planning future spatial changes, including "rendering farms" and workshops for providing a wide range of digitally controlled model-building techniques, which were to be integrated into the university's media ensemble over the long term.[39]

With the expansion of global networks and computer-based design and fabrication methods (BIM models, robot technology, etc.), technical infrastructure increasingly gained relevance for the communication and discourse of architectural practice. So while the spatial relationships and production conditions of architecture are constantly being refashioned, the architecture school as site of knowledge generation is once again being called upon to think beyond the margins of a medium and to situate the effects of advancing technology in a conceptual design context.

My thanks go to Reinhold Martin for his time and input. I would also like to thank Bernard Tschumi, Stan Allen, Keller Easterling, Greg Lynn, Scott Marble, and Hani Rashid for offering insight into the design practices of the paperless studios. I am grateful to Ed Keller, who generously made materials on the paperless studio available to me, and to Marta Caldeira for numerous insights. The project in which this paper arose is funded by the German Research Foundation (DFG).

Translation Dawn Michelle d'Atri

Damit wird bereits auf die Problematik jener computerbasierter Entwurfsprozesse verwiesen, die mit Optimierungsstrategien und Effektivität argumentieren, ohne dabei die Geschichte und Wirkung computerbasierter Visualisierungstechniken zu berücksichtigen. Auch wird die Frage aufgeworfen, inwieweit Modelle anderer Disziplinen für Prozesse des Entwerfens Relevanz gewinnen können und welche Bedeutung sie in Bezug auf die Mensch-Maschine Interaktionen erfahren.

In diesem Kontext stellen sich allgemeine Fragen, zum Beispiel, ob die Architektur eine eigene Theorie aus der Praxis heraus entwickeln kann und worin die spezifischen Möglichkeiten der Architektur liegen, in einem gesellschaftlichen Kontext zu agieren. Bezogen auf den Einsatz digitaler Technologien ist von Bedeutung, dass nicht alle Entwurfsschritte codiert werden können und nicht determinierte, intuitive Anteile oftmals gestalterische Möglichkeiten eröffnen, die mit technologischem Fortschritt Kontingenzen schaffen. In diesem Zusammenhang sei abschließend noch einmal auf die Räumlichkeiten der Universität, sowie auf die Zirkulation von Informationen hingewiesen. Bereits 1994, als die Studios eingerichtet wurden, planten Muir und O'Neill zukünftige räumliche Veränderungen: *rendering farms*, sowie Werkstätten, die unterschiedlichste digital gesteuerte Modellbautechniken anbieten, sollten langfristig gesehen in das mediale Ensemble der Schule integriert werden.[39]

Mit dem Ausbau von globalen Netzwerken und computerbasierten Entwurfs- und Fabrikationsmethoden (BIM Modellen, Roboter Techniken etc.) gewinnen technische Infrastrukturen zunehmend an Relevanz für die Kommunikations- und Diskussionsformen der Architekturpraxis. Während sich also die räumlichen Beziehungen und Produktionsbedingungen von Architektur verändern, ist die Architekturschule als Ort der Wissensgenerierung einmal mehr gefragt, Interaktionsformen zu entwickeln, die es ermöglichen, über die Grenzen eines Mediums hinaus zu denken und die Effekte der voranschreitenden Technologien in einen konzeptionellen Kontext des Entwerfens zu stellen.

Mein Dank gilt Reinhold Martin für seine Zeit und Anregungen. Ebenso danken möchte ich Bernard Tschumi, Stan Allen, Keller Easterling, Greg Lynn, Scott Marble und Hani Rashid für Einblicke in die Entwurfspraktiken der paperless studios. Gedankt sei außerdem Ed Keller, der mir großzügig Material über die paperless studios zur Verfügung stellte und Marta Caldeira für zahlreiche Hinweise. Das Projekt, aus dessen Zusammenhang dieser Text hervorgegangen ist, wird von der Deutschen Forschungsgemeinschaft (DFG) finanziert.

39   See Muir and O'Neill, "The Paperless Studio," p. 11 (see note 11).

39   Vgl. Eden Muir/Rory O'Neill: S. 11 (wie Anm. 11).

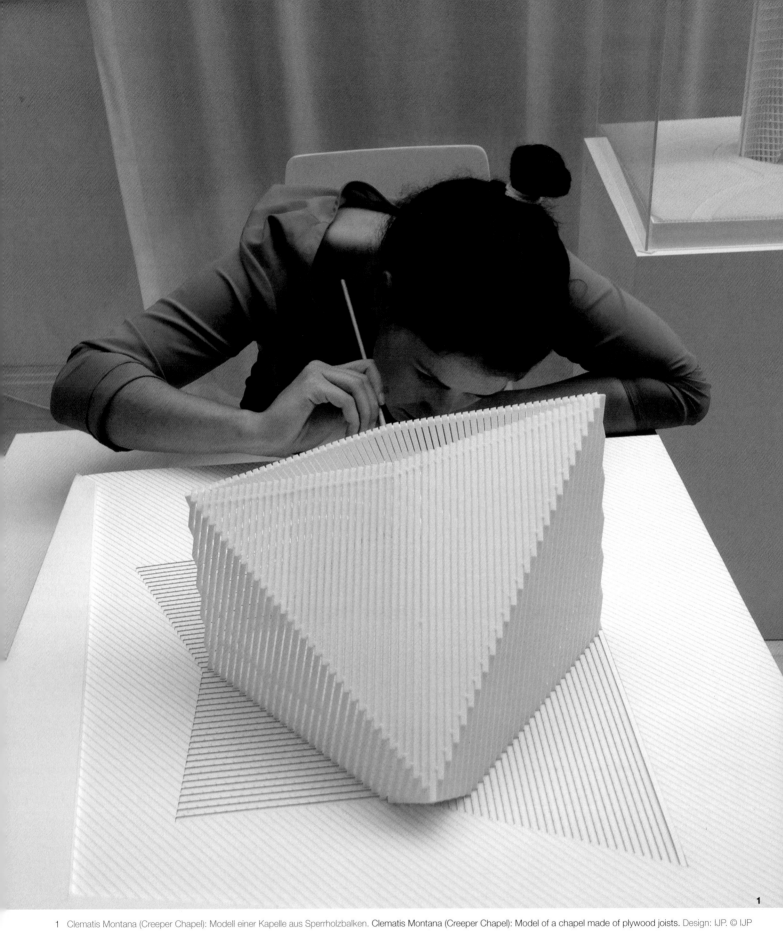

1 Clematis Montana (Creeper Chapel): Modell einer Kapelle aus Sperrholzbalken. **Clematis Montana (Creeper Chapel): Model of a chapel made of plywood joists.** Design: IJP. © IJP

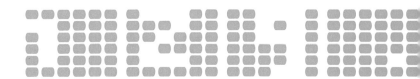

God Spare Me Intuition

(and I'll Take Care of the Machine Myself)

"As a factor in design, intuition is founded on a long process of cultivating awareness of unique and non-intentional qualities, and it ensures that things and phenomena can be quickly and precisely apprehended."[1]

Gott verschone mich mit Intuition (und um die Maschine kümmere ich mich selbst). „Als Entwurfsfaktor beruht [die Intuition] auf einem langen Prozess der Aufmerksamkeitsschulung für das Ungewöhnliche und Nicht-Intentionale; sie sorgt dafür, dass Dinge und Phänomene schnell und präzise erfasst werden können."[1]

GEORGE L. LEGENDRE

Back in the early nineties, a nutty professor sent us out to survey one of these old tenement houses in central Paris. The plan was to draw the otherwise invisible nuts and bolts uncovered by a team of builders/renovators stripping its decrepit floors and walls. Health and safety laid low on the agenda of that friendly crew, and most of them spoke only Arabic or Portuguese anyway; as a result, we got free rein to stand on the edge of gutted stairwells and dangle from crumbling stairs (it was quite fun). Since that was a while ago, I do not remember what grade we got, but I do remember a sharp argument with the (otherwise encouraging) instructor over how the original timber joists should be drawn. The man took objection to my using a ruler on the grounds that a three-hundred-year-old piece of wood is never straight. He was right, but beside the point. I was not trying to depict any joist in particular but a bunch of them together. This bunch, or *array* in technical speak, gave the structure the uniquely serial character which remains (for me anyway) to this day the main difference between modern and pre-modern architecture: old buildings were made of 100,000 pieces; new ones are made of no more than (say) 50, cast in a bewildering continuum of concrete and nowhere near as fun to survey (we also had been offered—and declined—the option to survey a 1960s office building). My reading of this traditional building structure was *machinic*, and I needed a mechanical way of communicating it. I was ready for Microstation[2] to be invented. And sure enough, the software hit the market a few months later.

Plainly put, the relevant question here is: Where does this first step come from? My position on that is that we should never trust intuition to deliver it by itself, whatever that means.

The world has moved on dramatically since the days of the plastic ruler and so have the problems (and opportunities) brought forward by the mechanization of the design process. The excellent topic of this issue of GAM, "Intuition and the Machine," is in constant need of critical and practical re-appraisal. As someone with a lifelong interest in parametric mathematics, I would like to address the question of intuition and the machine with regards to a narrow (but essential) part of our daily activity, i.e., the formulation of design concepts and ideas. I will deliberately restrict the discussion to the very first step of the design process, to what Beaux-Arts theorists called the *parti*[3] and present-day practitioners refer to as *concept* or *scheme design*—which is also the main priority in design schools worldwide. Plainly put, the relevant question here is: Where does this first step come from? My position on that is that we should *never* trust intuition to deliver it *by itself*, whatever that means.

Seinerzeit in den frühen Neunzigern ließ uns ein verschrobener Professor eines dieser alten Mietshäuser im Zentrum von Paris aufnehmen. Wir sollten die sonst unsichtbaren Schrauben und Muttern zeichnen, die ein Trupp von Bauarbeitern beim Abreißen der abgewohnten Wände und Böden freigelegt hatte. Gesundheit und Sicherheit waren bei der freundlichen Crew nicht gerade groß geschrieben, und die meisten sprachen ohnehin nur arabisch oder portugiesisch, sodass wir ungehindert am Rand entkernter Treppenhäuser stehen und uns von bröckelnden Stufen baumeln lassen konnten (es machte ziemlichen Spaß). Da das inzwischen eine Weile her ist, weiß ich nicht mehr, wie wir benotet wurden, aber ich erinnere mich noch an einen heftigen Streit mit dem sonst anregenden Professor über die richtige Art, die ursprünglichen Holzbalken zu zeichnen. Der Mann hatte Einwände dagegen, dass ich dazu ein Lineal verwendete, weil ein dreihundert Jahre altes Stück Holz nie gerade sei. Er hatte Recht, doch das war nicht der Punkt. Ich versuchte gar nicht, einen bestimmten Balken zu zeichnen, sondern gleich eine ganze Reihe davon. Diese Reihe oder – um es technisch auszudrücken – dieses *Array* gab dem Gebäude den einmaligen seriellen Charakter, der (für mich wenigstens) bis heute den Hauptunterschied zwischen moderner und vormoderner Architektur ausmacht: alte Gebäude wurden aus 100.000 Teilen erbaut; bei neuen sind es nicht mehr als (sagen wir mal) 50, gegossen als ein verwirrendes Betonkontinuum und lange nicht so lustig Aufzunehmen (wir hätten auch die Möglichkeit gehabt, ein Bürogebäude aus den 1960er Jahren aufzunehmen, lehnten aber ab). Meine Auffassung von der alten Gebäudestruktur war eine *maschinische*, und ich brauchte ein technisches Mittel, um das zu kommunizieren. Ich war bereit für die Erfindung von Microstation.[2] Und natürlich kam die Software dann wenige Monate später auf den Markt.

Die Welt hat sich seit den Tagen des Plastiklineals dramatisch weiterentwickelt, und mit ihr auch die Probleme (und Möglichkeiten), die die Mechanisierung des Entwurfsprozesses mit sich gebracht hat. Das ausgezeichnete Thema dieser Ausgabe von GAM „Intuition and the Machine" bedarf einer ständigen kritischen und praktischen Neubewertung. Als jemand, der sich sein Leben lang für parametrische Mathematik interessierte, möchte ich diese Frage in Hinblick auf einen engen (aber wesentlichen) Bereich unserer täglichen Arbeit erörtern: die Formulierung von Entwurfskonzepten und -ideen. Ich beschränke mich bewusst auf diesen ersten Schritt des Planungsprozesses: das, was die Beaux-Arts-Theoretiker als *parti*[3] bezeichneten

---

1   "Call for Papers: Intuition & the Machine," in *GAM* 9 (2012), p. 265.

2   Microstation is a CAD Production Software developed for the architecture, engineering, construction and operation of infrastructure types such as utility systems, roads, bridges, buildings or communication networks.

3   Literally, the French term *parti* translates to "departure point." In architectural discourse it refers to the underlying scheme of a design.

1   „Call for Papers: Intuition & the Machine", in: *GAM* 9 (2012), S. 265.

2   Microstation ist a CAD-Software für Architektur, Bautechnik, Konstruktion und Verwaltung von Infrastrukturen wie Versorgungssystemen, Straßen, Brücken, Gebäuden und Kommunikationsnetzwerken.

3   Der französische Ausdruck *parti* heißt wörtlich „Ausgangspunkt". Im Architekturdiskurs meint er die grundlegende Entwurfsidee.

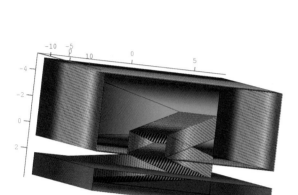

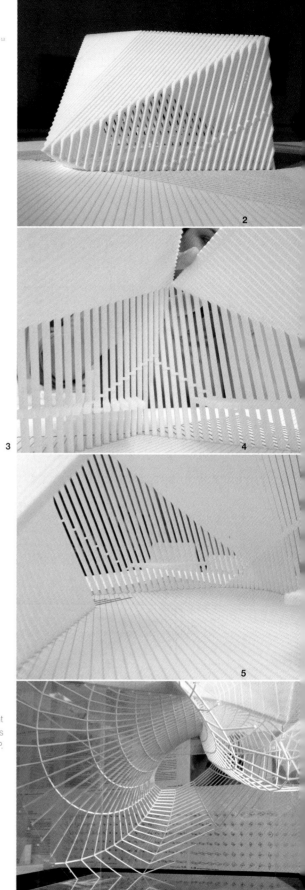

```
_SURFACE THREADS        M := 4        N := 200        scale1 := 3.5    scale2 := 10    sc_plan_i1 := 1.7·√2/2    _copyright George L. Legendre Mark Lewis IJP 2006-12

_BULK DIMENSIONS        WIDTH := 0    (unused)        HEIGHT := 10     A := 2π         sc_plan_i2 := 1.7·√2/2

_RANGES                 last_m := M                   last_n := N                      sc_plan_j1 := 3·√2/2

                        m := 0,1.. last_m             n := 0,1.. last_n    a := π/4    sc_plan_j2 := 1

_GENERAL VARIABLES      V_FREQ := 1   U_FREQ := 1              BRANCHES := 2

                        B := V_FREQ·π    C := 4U_FREQ·π       D1 := BRANCHES·π    D2 := 2π

                        b := 2/2·π       C := 1π/1            d1 := π/1           d2 := π/4
```

(in_formation1, in_formation2, in_formation3)

2   Clematis Montana (Creeper Chapel). Eine Kapelle aus Sperrholzbalken. Geplant für eine Situation mit ständiger Sonneneinstrahlung, bieten die Wände eine rhythmische Abschirmung des direkten Sonnenlichts – und Aussicht in die Umgebung. Mathematische Idee: Das Beschneiden und die „Begradigung" einer Kugel trägt dazu bei, das langweilige Erscheinungsbild des berühmten „Blob" zu überwinden (wenn einem das wichtig ist). Design von IJP.
Clematis Montana (Creeper Chapel). An outdoor chapel made of plywood joists. Designed for a sustained exposure to the sun, its walls provide a rhythmical screening of direct sunlight—and surrounding views. Mathematical idea: cropping a sphere and "straightening" it out helps jettison (if you care about such things) the tired look-and-feel of the famous blob. Design by IJP. © IJP

3   ARCSINE_COIL_EVERTED: (Partiell) Mathematische Formulierung (Partial) Mathematical formulation. Mathematik von **Mathematics by** George L. Legendre und **and** Mark Lewis mit **with** Arthur Liu, Nick Croft, Billy Quattlebaum (in Farbe **in color**). Die Formel liefert den Quellcode für das Everted Museum. **This formula provides the source code for the Everted Museum.** © IJP

4–5   Clematis Montana (Creeper Chapel): Innenansicht **Interior View.** Design von **by** IJP. © IJP

6   F01B (2009). Nahansicht des unteren Teils. Das Modell ist mit einem durchsichtigen Material umhüllt. **Close-up view of bottom half. The model is encased in a translucent.** © IJP und **and** John Pickering. Foto **photo:** Stefano Graziani

LEGENDRE 1. GEORGE

linearised Periodic Coil

_ranges $n1 := 0, 1 .. \ 360$ $m1 := 0, 1 .. \ 4$

_equations

$$iT(u,v) := \left[\left(\cos\left(2 \cdot u + \frac{\pi}{4}\right) \cdot \frac{3}{2} + 6 \, asin\left(\cos\left(\frac{v}{1} + \frac{\pi}{2}\right)\right)\right) \cdot 45\right]$$

$$jT(u,v) := \left(\sin\left(2 \cdot u + \frac{\pi}{4}\right) \cdot \frac{3}{2} + 2 \, asin\left(\cos\left(5v + \pi\right)\right)\right) \cdot 45$$

$$sh(u,v) := asin\left(\cos\left(6.5v + \pi\right)\right) \cdot \left(\frac{840}{3}\right)$$

$$iThread_{m1, n1} := iT\left(\frac{m1}{4}\pi, \frac{n1}{360}\pi\right) \qquad jThread_{m1, n1} := jT\left(\frac{m1}{4}\pi, \frac{n1}{360}\pi\right) \qquad shape_{m1, n1} := sh\left(\frac{m1}{4} \cdot \pi, \frac{n1}{360} \cdot \pi\right)$$

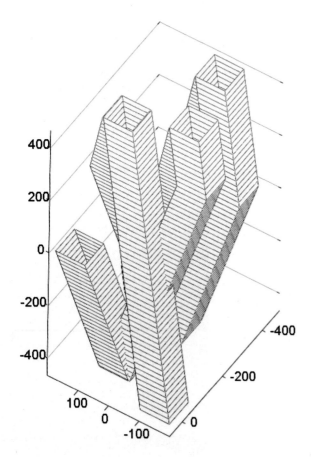

(jThread, iThread, shape)

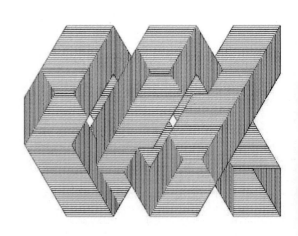

(jThread, iThread, shape)

7   ARCSINE_COIL_HINGING: (Partiell) Mathematische Formulierung. (Partial) Mathematical formulation. Mathematik von Mathematics by George L. Legendre und and Mark Lewis. Die Formel liefert den Quellcode für den Hinging Tower. This formula provides the source code for the Hinging Tower. © IJP

und was bei heutigen Architekten *Konzeptentwurf* oder *Entwurfsplanung* heißt – und in Hochschulen für Gestaltung weltweit den Ausbildungsschwerpunkt bildet. Einfach ausgedrückt geht es hier um die Frage: Woher kommt dieser erste Schritt? Meine Position in dieser Frage ist, dass wir diesbezüglich *nie* darauf vertrauen sollten, dass die Intuition das *schon irgendwie* erledigt, wie immer das aussehen mag.

Intuition hängt im Maschinenzeitalter eng mit der Frage der *Gestaltungsmacht* zusammen, d.h. der Frage nach der Urheberschaft eines Entwurfs, danach, wer den Entwurfsprozess steuert, einmal vorausgesetzt, dass das überhaupt jemand tut, was ja zunehmend in Abrede gestellt wird. Unser üblicher Umgang mit Gestaltungsmacht ist zumeist *nicht* produktiv. An den Ausbildungsstätten führen wir gewöhnlich einen latent schwelenden Kulturkampf gegen Studierende, werfen ihnen vor, zu viel Entscheidungsmacht an Algorithmen und Skripte abzugeben, ein Konflikt, der dann meist in altbekannten Jurystatements wie „Also bitte, das ist doch bloß designt!" oder „Wann drücken Sie eigentlich den Stopp-Knopf?" zum Ausdruck kommt. Der Konflikt ist leider völlig fehl am Platz: Nach fünfzehn Jahren breit unterstützten Experimentierens im Fach Entwerfen ist der algorithmische Ansatz heute weder neu noch subversiv; außerdem ist das Argument gegen das Abgeben der Gestaltungsmacht im Prinzip schwach: wir geben sie ohnehin kaum einmal ab. Ob wir es nun genau voraussagen können oder nicht, in den meisten Fällen liefert die Eingabe von Variablen in einen Algorithmus ein vorbestimmtes Ergebnis. So gesehen ist die Verwendung von Algorithmen gleichermaßen deterministisch wie jede andere Form der Entwurfsraumexploration. Was in dieser speziellen Auseinandersetzung fehlt, ist das Wissen und oft auch das Vokabular für eine genauere Erkundung eben dieser Form des Determinismus – im Gegensatz zu anderen, uns vertrauteren und geläufigeren Formen.

Indessen wird die Frage, *wie* (oder selbst *ob*) ein Projekt im 21. Jahrhundert noch *komponiert* werden kann, kaum je diskutiert.[4] Eine vereinfachte Version dieser wichtigen Fragestellung könnte folgendermaßen lauten: Ist es in Ordnung etwas zu *erfinden* (d.h. zu *designen*) oder sollte ich mich eher im Hintergrund halten und die innere Logik des jeweiligen Projekts (wie sie durch Bauland, Raumprogramm, Umstände, Algorithmen, Philosophie oder dergleichen vorgegeben ist) ihren Lauf ins noch Ungedachte nehmen lassen? Das „Fördern" oder „Unterbinden" der Gestaltungsabsicht, wie es Peter Eisenman in den Neunzigern ausdrückte,[5] ist ein wesentliches theoretisches

In the age of the machine, intuition in design depends on the notion of *design authority*, i.e., the question of who is the author of the design, who is in charge of the design process, assuming that someone is in charge—especially when numerous claims are made to the contrary. By and large, our habitual take on design authority is *not* productive. In schools we typically wage a low-burning culture war against students claiming to delegate too much authority to the use of algorithms and scripts, a conflict expressed through well-worn jury questions like "Come on, it's just designed, isn't it?" and especially, "When do you press the STOP button?" Sadly, this conflict is misguided: after 15 years of experimentation conducted with the broad support of the design faculty, the algorithmic approach is neither novel nor subversive; moreover, the argument against delegating authority *in principle* is weak: we hardly ever relinquish authority anyway. Regardless of whether we can precisely anticipate it, most of the time the input of variables into an algorithm will yield a fixed outcome: in this sense, the use of algorithms will be as deterministic as any form of design exploration. What is lacking in this particular conversation is the knowledge, and often even the vocabulary, to interrogate *this* form of determinism as opposed to the other, more familiar forms we are accustomed to.

Meanwhile, the question of how (and even whether) in the twenty-first century a project may be *composed*, is hardly ever discussed.[4] A simplified version of this seminal line of questioning would go like this: is it OK for me to *make something up* (i.e., *design* it), or should I place myself in the background instead and let the intrinsic logics surrounding the project (as dictated by site, program, circumstances, algorithms, philosophy, whatever) run their course into unthought-of territories? "Motivating" or "demotivating" design intent, as Peter Eisenman put it in the early nineties,[5] is an important theoretical problem in which intuition will play a key role.[6] Sorting out the question of how (and whether) to "demotivate" design intent is the central challenge to the emergence of new architectural concepts; it is also a prerequisite for innovation—the other main theme of this paper.

To produce new architectural diagrams (the so-called *concept designs* or *ideas*), intuition and the machine will have to work hand-in hand. *They*

> Regardless of whether we can precisely anticipate it, most of the time the input of variables into an algorithm will yield a fixed outcome: in this sense the use of algorithms will be as deterministic as any form of design exploration.

4   Eine Ausnahme ist Jacques Lucans bewundernswertes Buch *Composition, Non-Composition: Architecture and Theory in the Nineteenth and Twentieth Centuries*, Lausanne 2012.

5   Entwickelt wurde diese Position Ende 1993 in einem undokumentierten Theorieseminar, das als Ergänzung zum Entwurfsseminar „Serlio and the Uses of History" an der Harvard Graduate School of Design angeboten wurde.

4   As an exception serves Jacques Lucan's admirable book *Composition, Non-Composition: Architecture and Theory in the Nineteenth and Twentieth Centuries* (Lausanne, 2012).

5   This position was elaborated on in an undocumented theory seminar supplementing the graduate design studio 'Serlio and the Uses of History,' at the Harvard Graduate School of Design in late 1993.

6   I deal with this question systematically in my own graduate design studios at Harvard, and sometimes I deal with it in practice too.

will also have to keep one another in check. This is not about advocating blindly the pursuit of originality, nor the virtue of being innovative no matter what (*innovation* is not an end in itself). The point is simply that if we want to innovate, or stake a claim to innovation, we must approach it *rationally*. Intuition by itself will not cut it because, left to our own devices, we tend to do the same things over and over again. When it comes to willing something new into being, we will, more often than not, take the same first steps. After a decade spent exploring instrumental issues in school and practice on a global stage, I have only anecdotal evidence to offer, but most of it directly corroborates the conventional Warholian wisdom that we *all want to be the same*.

From 1999 to 2004, for example, some of the work in the Diploma school of the London based Architectural Association School of Architecture was so predominantly uniform as to be indistinguishable from a social science experiment (with spontaneous premises) on how we choose to bind our own free will.[7] Why would anyone, in the only institution worldwide where teachers are invited to run their own little schools inside the big one, end up doing exactly the same thing as the others? For some time I thought it had something to do with the constant flow of online communications. We do look at each other's work, and spending too much time looking at what others are doing will invariably take its toll. Lately, I have come to think that the causes may run deeper. Could it be simply that creativity is also subject to the shortcuts and prejudices (the so-called "bias" and "heuristics") that behavioral psychology has observed, empirically, in human nature at large?[8] Psychology posits that these shortcuts and prejudices loom large in our mental life by preventing us from being *systematically rational*. It stipulates that there is no point trying to fight them off, that finding a workaround is the only way forward. As we cannot reason our way out of this mess, the workaround is not a matter of good philosophy, but an applied task, a matter of brute tactics. Applying the workaround requires a stringent conscious effort on our part; demotivating the design intent, as Eisenman put it, can be very hard work indeed. This is where intuition steps aside, and lo and behold, the machine steps in.

Using as a starting point scripting, programming, or in this case, parametric equations, calculus, algebra, and other forms of "automatic writing," offers the following methodological benefits: an arbitrary point of departure;

> Could it be simply that creativity is also subject to the shortcuts and prejudices (the so-called "bias" and "heuristics") that behavioral psychology has observed, empirically, in human nature at large?[8]

Problem, beim dem die Intuition eine Schlüsselrolle spielt.[6] Die Klärung der Frage, wie (und ob) die Gestaltungsabsicht zu „unterbinden" ist, ist eine wichtige Bedingung für die Entstehung neuer Architekturkonzepte; es ist auch eine Voraussetzung für Innovation – das zweite Hauptthema dieses Artikels.

Zum Hervorbringen neuer Architekturzeichnungen (sogenannter *Concept Designs* oder *Ideen*) müssen Intuition und Maschine Hand in Hand arbeiten. *Sie müssen sich aber auch gegenseitig in Schach halten.* Es geht hier nicht darum, blind für das Streben nach Originalität oder Innovation um jeden Preis einzutreten (*Innovation* ist kein Selbstzweck), sondern lediglich darum, dass wir, wenn wir innovativ sein wollen oder Anspruch auf Innovation erheben, das Ganze *rational* angehen müssen. Intuition allein wird dazu nicht reichen, weil wir, auf die eigenen Mittel zurückgeworfen, dazu neigen, immer wieder dasselbe zu tun. Wenn wir gefordert sind, etwas Neues zu schaffen, unternehmen wir in aller Regel immer wieder die gleichen ersten Schritte. Als jemand, der sich seit einem Jahrzehnt auf einer internationalen Bühne mit Werkzeugfragen in Lehre und Praxis beschäftigt, kann ich zwar nur individuelle Beispiele anführen, aber die meisten davon bestätigen direkt die allgemein akzeptierte Warhol'sche Meinung, dass wir *alle gleich sein wollen*.

Von 1999 bis 2004 war zum Beispiel ein Teil der Arbeit in der Diploma School der AA in London von einer derartigen Gleichförmigkeit, dass sie praktisch ununterscheidbar war von einem sozialwissenschaftlichen Experiment (mit spontanen Prämissen) über die Bereitschaft zur Zügelung unseres freien Willens.[7] Wie kommt es, dass jemand in der weltweit einzigen Institution, in der die Lehrenden ihre eigene kleine Schule innerhalb der großen betreiben können, am Ende genau dasselbe macht wie die anderen? Eine Weile glaubte ich, es hätte mit dem unablässigen Strom der Online-Kommunikation zu tun. Wir sehen uns gegenseitig unsere Arbeiten an, und wenn man sich zu lange damit aufhält, was die anderen tun, muss das einfach irgendwann Folgen haben. In letzter Zeit bin ich zur Ansicht gekommen, dass die Ursachen tiefer gehen dürften. Unterliegt die Kreativität einfach nur denselben Verkürzungen und Vorurteilen (den sogenannten „Neigungen" und „Heuristiken"), die nach dem empirischen Befund der Verhaltenspsychologie in der menschlichen Natur überhaupt liegt?[8] Der Psychologie zufolge

7 My pseudo-statistical sample does not include the graduate school's Design Research Lab, where uniformity was systematically *coerced*. Unlike the AA Diploma School, this ten year-long program was actually *structured* as an experiment, which went to great lengths to demonstrate that if you require everyone to do the same, the result will be (mostly) uniform.

8 See Nicholas Nassim Taleb, *The Black Swan: The Impact of the Highly Improbable* (New York, 2010) as well as his other titles.

6 Ich beschäftige mich mit dieser Frage systematisch in meinen eigenen Entwurfsseminaren an der Harvard Graduate School, und gelegentlich auch in der Praxis.

7 Meine pseudostatistischen Beispiele beinhalten nicht das Design Research Lab der Graduate School, wo Uniformität systematisch *erzwungen* wurde. Anders als die AA Diploma School war dieses zehn Jahre laufende Programm tatsächlich als Experiment angelegt, das mit einigem Aufwand demonstrierte, dass wenn man von allen verlangt, dasselbe zu tun, die Ergebnisse (weitgehend) gleichartig sein werden.

8 Vgl. Nicholas Nassim Taleb, *Der schwarze Schwan: Die Macht höchst unwahrscheinlicher Ereignisse*, Übers. Ingrid Proß-Gill, München: Hanser Wirtschaft 2008, aber auch seine anderen Titel.

spielen diese Verkürzungen und Vorurteile eine enorme Rolle für unser Geistesleben, weil sie uns daran hindern, *systematisch rational* zu sein, und sie sagt klipp und klar, dass es keinen Sinn habe, sie zu bekämpfen, sondern dass eine Umgehung des Problems die einzige Möglichkeit ist weiterzukommen. Da wir diesem Schlamassel nicht mit Vernunft entrinnen können, ist die Umgehungslösung auch keine Frage guter Philosophie, sondern eine praktische Aufgabe, eine rein taktische Angelegenheit. Die Anwendung der Umgehungslösung erfordert von uns eine stringente, bewusste Anstrengung, denn die Gestaltungsabsicht zu blockieren, wie es Eisenman ausdrückte, kann wirklich harte Arbeit sein. Und an dieser Stelle tritt die Intuition zur Seite und die Maschine tritt auf den Plan.

Das Ausgehen von Skripten und Programmen oder in diesem Fall parametrischen Gleichungen, Kalkülen, Algebra und anderen Formen „automatischen Schreibens" besitzt folgende methodischen Vorteile: einen beliebigen Ausgangspunkt, eine abstrakte Funktionalität mit praktischen und theoretischen Herausforderungen, die denen des traditionelle Architekturdiskurses gleichen, und einen unendlichen „Lösungsraum" (auch als *schwarzes Loch* der parametrischen Variation bekannt, etwas, das Kopfzerbrechen bereitet). So nähert man sich der Architektur qua Analogie, und das ist gut, weil sie uns davor bewahrt, direkte und automatische Vorannahmen zu tätigen.

Man braucht sich zum Beispiel keine Gedanken über das Aussehen der Dinge zu machen; oder darüber, wie sie aussehen sollen. Es genügt, darauf zu achten, was sie tatsächlich tun. Unser Ausgangspunkt, einige ausgewählte Formeln oder *Keimzellen*, wie ich sie von nun an nennen will, gibt uns intuitive Raumeigenschaften wie die durchgehende Hülle (man denke: *Wände*), Interiorität (man denke: *Raum*), Überlappung (man denke: *Schnittpunkt* oder *Labyrinth*) oder punktuelle Abstützung (man denke: *Säule* oder *Hypostyl*). Diese diagrammatischen Bedingungen für die Produktion von Raum gehen konventionellen Fragen architektonischer Gestaltung voraus, stehen also weiter vorne in der Nahrungskette der Konzepte und Ideen. Sie tragen schillernde (und gesetzlich geschützte) Namen wie Asymptotic Box©, Arcsine Coil© oder Implicit Field© (die Namensgebung ist ein integraler Bestandteil des Spiels). Einige Keimzellen sind sehr gegenständlich, das heißt, sie gleichen Gebäuden, andere weniger. Der Grad ihrer Gegenständlichkeit und/oder intuitiven Verwendbarkeit bestimmt ihre Brauchbarkeit als Entwurfsinstrumente. Der Vergleich zwischen der Asymptotic Box© und dem Arcsine Coil© ist diesbezüglich bezeichnend.

Die Asymptotic Box© ist eine implizit dreidimensionale Fläche. Der besondere Charakter dieser Form besteht im hohen Exponentialfaktor ihrer dritten nachfolgenden Funktion, wodurch der parabolische Umriss der Fläche *nahezu* orthogonal wird. Es handelt sich also um keine Schachtel, sondern um eine „Beinahe-Schachtel" – die größtmögliche Annäherung daran durch die kontinuierliche Verformung einer glatten periodischen

an abstract functionality that offers practical and theoretical challenges *analogous* to the challenges of a traditional architectural discourse; and an infinite "solution" space (also known as the *black hole* of parametric variation, a source of headache). Working in this way, we approach architecture by analogy, and the analogy is good because it frees us from making direct and automatic assumptions.

We don't have to worry, for instance, about what things look like; or what they are supposed to look like; it is enough to focus on what they actually do. Our point of departure, a few selected formulas—or *seeds* as I will refer to them from now on, present us with intuitive spatial properties, such as continuous enclosure (think *walls*), interiority (think *room*), overlap (think *crossing* or *maze*), or point-support (think *column* or *hypostyle hall*). These diagrammatic preconditions for making space predate conventional questions of architectural design and hence come first in the food chain of concepts and ideas. They have colorful (and trademarked) monikers such as the Asymptotic Box©, the Arcsine Coil©, or the Implicit Field© (naming them is an integral part of the game). Some seeds are very figurative, i.e., they look like buildings, others less so. The degree to which they are figurative and/or intuitive to use determines their viability as design diagrams. In this sense, the comparison between the Asymptotic Box© and the Arcsine Coil© is very telling.

The Asymptotic Box© is an implicit three-dimensional surface. The special character of this form lies

> This seed has a great potential to produce complex interiors. Its rectangular envelope depends on a fine combination of variables, without which it will revert instantly to less regular configurations.

in the high exponential factor of its third antecedent function, which "devolves" the parabolic outline of the surface into a *nearly* orthogonal state. This isn't a box, only a "near box"—the closest equivalent obtained by the continuous deformation of a smooth periodic surface: hence the term *Asymptotic*, whereby the form tends towards orthogonality, without reaching it. As a bonus, its texture may be freely redefined by the application of embedded "deflected fields," which produce a layered tectonic arrangement with structural and aesthetic properties. The Asymptotic Box© is predictable, easy to imagine, and intuitive to work with. From Mies van der Rohe to Diener & Diener, the Asymptotic Box© is the mother of all boxes, of which there are quite a few.

At the other end of the spectrum, the Arcsine Coil© produces a continuously coiling ribbon privy to all possible planimetric and sectional adjustments. This seed has a great potential to produce complex interiors. Its rectangular envelope depends on a fine combination of variables, without which it will revert instantly to less regular configurations. The Arcsine Coil© is as potent in terms of *ground* as it is in terms of *figure*: the interstitial spaces between branches are as figurative and important as the branches themselves. Critically, this seed offers a complete antithesis to the latent compositional drive secreted in the piecemeal Asymptotic Box©. Here, the simultaneous

Working with the Arcsine Coil©,
on the other hand, offers little
more than the awareness of
continuous self-intersection, which,
in conjunction with other technically
difficult requirements such as
the need to maintain a regular
envelope, steers the mind away
from elementary spatial forms.

Fläche. Darum auch der Ausdruck *asymptotisch* – die Form nähert sich der Orthogonalität an, ohne sie zu erreichen. Zusätzlich lässt sich die Textur durch die Anwendung eingebetteter „Ablenkfelder", die ein geschichtetes tektonisches Arrangement mit strukturellen und ästhetischen Eigenschaften erzeugen, frei redefinieren. Die Asymptotic Box© ist vorhersehbar, leicht verständlich und intuitiv verwendbar. Sie ist die Mutter aller Schachteln, die von Mies van der Rohe bis Diener & Diener nicht gerade selten vorkommt.

Am anderen Ende des Spektrums erzeugt die Arcsine Coil© ein zu einer fortlaufenden Spule geformtes Band, das allen möglichen plani- und stereometrischen Manipulationen unterzogen werden kann. Diese Keimzelle besitzt großes Potenzial für die Erstellung komplexer Innenräume. Seine rechtwinkelige Hülle beruht auf einer ausgeklügelten Kombination von Variablen, ohne die er sofort in weniger regelmäßige Konfigurationen zurückfiele. Die Arcsine Coil© ist in Bezug auf *Grund* und *Figur* gleichermaßen mächtig: Die Räume zwischen den Strängen sind genauso figürlich und wichtig wie die Stränge selbst. Entscheidend ist aber, dass diese Keimzelle eine komplette Antithese zum latenten Kompositionsdrang darstellt, der von der einzelnen Asymptotic Box© ausgeht. Bei ihm löst die gleichzeitige Anwendung der Periodizität in allen drei Dimensionen ein unvorhersehbares gefühlsmäßiges Verhalten aus, das sich für ein „planendes" Vorgehen überhaupt nicht eignet; die Arcsine Coil© ist eine überaus sprunghafte Keimzelle. Auch wenn spätere Mutationen wohlgegliederte, potenziell auf eine „Hüllbox" beschränkte Verzweigungs- und Überlappungsmuster hervorbringen, bleibt diese Keimzelle ein erratisches Mittel der Raumgestaltung, das auf der Suche nach einem selbstbewussten Meister ist. In diesem Sinn übertrumpft es die Intuition fast bei jedem Schritt.

Bei beiden Keimzellen ist es erforderlich viel herumzuprobieren, um zu sinnvollen Ergebnissen zu gelangen. Wie alle algorithmischen Prozesse liefern sie in kürzester Zeit eine Fülle von Möglichkeiten, die dann irgendwie reduziert werden müssen. Der verbreitete Glaube, dass die (scheinbare) Beliebigkeit, die das Auflisten 1.000 verschiedener Zustände ein- und derselben Formel suggeriert, wegen der vermeintlichen „Offenheit" und „Differenziertheit" irgendwie wünschenswert sei, ist hier nicht angebracht. Für eine gelungene Anwendung parametrischer Modulation ist es notwendig, diese Vielfalt auf eine Handvoll Fälle zu reduzieren, wobei wir hier – intuitiv – zwei Dinge auf einmal bewerkstelligen müssen: das komplexe Verhalten periodischer Funktionen verstehen, um deren Resultat zu kontrollieren – und entscheiden, welche formelhafte Keimzelle Potenzial als Architektur besitzt. Die erste Aufgabe ist rein technisch. Wir erledigen sie *induktiv* (vom Ergebnis ausgehend und von ihm auf die Prämissen schließend) und ganz allein mithilfe von Intuition. Es ist festzuhalten, dass dabei – anders als bei einem wirklichen mathematischen Problem –

keine Notwendigkeit zu *deduktivem Denken* (dem Gegenteil der Induktion) besteht, weil wir kein Problem zu *lösen*, sondern eines zu *schaffen* versuchen. Der Unterschied zwischen Deduktion und Induktion erklärt auch, weshalb diese ungewöhnliche Methode so erfolgreich bei Entwurfsvorschlägen war und weshalb die eigentliche Arbeit mit wenigen Ausnahmen von absoluten Anfängern ausgeführt wurde.

Die zweite Aufgabe ist weniger rund. Wenn es darum geht zu entscheiden, welche Keimzelle architektonische Siegerqualitäten besitzt, kann die intuitive Natur und die damit einhergehende Ikonizität der jeweiligen Keimzelle (wie sie *aussieht* oder woran sie uns *erinnert*) genauso ein Segen wie ein Fluch sein. Da Ikonizität unsere Fantasie einzuschränken scheint, habe ich die Erfahrung gemacht, dass intuitive und ikonische Keimzellen wie die Asymptotic Box©, oder das Implicit Field© eine wesentlich kürzere Lebenszeit besitzen. Es ist fast unmöglich, in ihnen etwas anderes als eine Schachtel zu *sehen* und darum neigen oder *taugen* sie auch weniger dazu, sich zu etwas Komplexerem weiterzuentwickeln. Die Arcsine Coil© dagegen gibt wenig mehr als die Idee einer kontinuierlichen Selbstüberschneidung vor, die zusammen mit andern technisch anspruchsvollen Erfordernissen wie der Notwendigkeit eine reguläre Hülle aufrechtzuerhalten, das Denken von räumlichen Elementarformen wegführt. Es ist daher logisch, dass diese eine Formel bei ausreichend Zeit für die entsprechenden modulatorischen und dimensionalen Anpassungen zwei Ergebnisse zeitigt, die so einzigartig und unterschiedlich sind wie der *Hinging Tower*[9] und das *Everted Museum*.[10] Bei ersterem erfüllt die Komposition der periodischen Spule und des linearen Bandlaufs eine zentrale Funktionsanforderung, nämlich die gemeinsame Nutzung von Versorgungsfunktionen durch die Verbindung der Stränge. Die gemeinsame Nutzung von Versorgungsfunktionen ist eine Grundanforderung in der Hochhausplanung, wo die Versorgung stets kontinuierlich (wenn auch nicht immer vertikal) stattfindet. Die Keimzelle ermöglicht die Vereinigung verschiedener Stränge: ein Funktionsdiagramm, das 2002 von FOA für die „Bundle Towers" erfunden und seither unzählige Male repliziert wurde (im Gegensatz zu ihrem architektonische Vorläufer erzeugt die Arcsine Coil© die Vielfalt nicht durch die Aggregation unabhängiger Einheiten, sondern in einem Zug). Das *Everted Museum* beruht auf der Intuition, dass die Spule einen Teil ihrer selbst wie ein gigantisches Gedärm verdauen wird (*everted* heißt *umgestülpt*), um einen differenzierten Innenraum zu schaffen, der zwei Voraussetzungen erfüllt: er bildet eine durchgehende Schleife und

deployment on periodicity in all three dimensions produces an unpredictable and touchy-feely behavior totally unsuitable for "planning" moves; the Arcsine Coil© is a *very* jumpy seed. While subsequent mutations produce highly articulate patterns of branching and overlapping, potentially constrained to a dimensional "bounding box," this seed remains an erratic spatial device in search of a confident master. In this sense, it will trump intuition at almost every step.

Both seeds require a fair amount of trial and error to yield useful properties. Like all algorithmic processes, they yield a huge array of possibilities in a very short time, which must somehow be pared down. The widespread belief that the (apparent) randomness suggested by collating 1,000 alternate states of the same formula is somehow desirable because of the alleged "openness" and "differentiation," does not apply here. A successful application of parametric modulation requires us to funnel that multiplicity into a handful of instances only, using intuition to simultaneously achieve two things: work out the complex behavior of periodic functions to control their outcome—and decide which seed has potential as architecture. The first task is purely technical. We carry it out by *inference*, or *induction* (starting from a result and working our way back to its premises) and purely by intuition. It is important to note that, unlike an actual mathematical problem, there is no need at all for *deductive reasoning* (the opposite of induction), because we are not trying to *solve* a problem but to *create* one. The crucial difference between *deducing* and *inferring* explains why this unusual methodology has been so successful as a design proposition, and why the grunt work has been carried out, give or take a few exceptions, by absolute beginners.

The second task is less well-rounded. When it comes to selecting which seed may become a winner in the stakes of building, the intuitive nature and concomitant iconicity of that seed (what it *looks like* or *reminds us of*) can be a boon—or a curse. Because iconicity tends to pre-empt our imagination, I have found that intuitive and iconic seeds like the Asymptotic Box©, or the Implicit Field© have far shorter shelf lives. It is almost impossible to *see* them as anything other than a box, and hence they are less prone, or *fit*, to evolve into something richer. Working with the Arcsine Coil©, on the other hand, offers little more than the awareness of continuous self-intersection, which, in conjunction with other technically difficult requirements such as the need to maintain a regular envelope, steers the mind away from elementary spatial forms. It is therefore logical that given sufficient time to come up with the appropriate modulatory and dimensional adjustments, this one formula should yield two outcomes as unique *and* different from each other as the *Hinging Tower*[9] and the *Everted Museum*[10]. In the former, the composition of periodic coiling and linear thread distribution solves a key functional requirement, i.e., sharing core services though connecting branches. Sharing services is a key functional requirement of high-rise design, where services are always continuous (if not always vertical). The seed enables separate branches to come together as one, a functional diagram invented

9   Rising Masses II: Tall Cultivars for a Fast-Sprouting Type. Harvard Graduate School of Design, Advanced graduate Option Studio 3404. Mathematics by George L. Legendre, Ana Flor, Rodia Valladares.

10   Real and Imaginary Variables: Art Spaces I Option Studio GSD 1316. Mathematics by George L. Legendre, Arthur Liu, Nick Croft, Billy Quattlebaum.

9   Rising Masses II Tall Cultivars for a Fast-Sprouting Type. Harvard Graduate School of Design, Advanced graduate Option Studio 3404. Mathematics by George L. Legendre, Ana Flor, Rodia Valladares.

10   Real and Imaginary Variables: Art Spaces I Option Studio GSD 1316. Mathematics by George L. Legendre, Arthur Liu, Nick Croft, Billy Quattlebaum.

by FOA's "bundle towers" in 2002 and endlessly replicated since (unlike its architectural predecessor, the Arcsine Coil© does not produce multiplicity by aggregating independent units; it does so with a single stroke). The *Everted Museum*, on the other hand, is based on the intuition that the coil will digest part of itself like a giant intestine (*everted* means *turned inside out*) to produce a differentiated interior that satisfies two premises: it forms a continuous loop, and each space is nested inside the next, like a set of Russian dolls—which, in this case, comprises only *one* doll. The loop and figure-ground reversal capture the organization of the archetypal museum space very well, with its central requirement of circulation (museums are organized around a path or paths) and the need that every served space be matched by a commensurate amount of serving space (curators refer to this dichotomy as "front-of-house" versus "back-of-house"). Typically invisible to the visitor, the staggering ratio of front-of-house to back-of-house is a hallmark of the modern gallery, and this formulation of the Arcsine Coil© interprets it rather well.

Working in this manner engages intuition in different ways. The main point is that we will not depend on the convenience—and transparency—of off-the-shelf modeling software. More than efficiency or technique, mathematics is ultimately about another level of authority. When it comes to solving problems and creating new things, working with mathematical concepts and equations rather than with the standard modeling software disseminated by the industry, implies a direct recourse to generative symbols and marks.

Writing forms and processes in this manner is slower and requires another kind of authorial mindset. Modeling software being generally built by "chunking," or consolidating lower-level steps into higher-level ones—like a pyramidal structure—to work with commercial software is to work at the top of the pyramid, where the interaction is intuitive but the decisions have already been made. To write equations, on the other hand, is to work, if not at the bottom of the pyramid, at least pretty down low, where most of the room lies but little if anything is predefined. Hence to design with mathematics is not to design free of software, a futile if not wholly impossible claim in an age where software is the only idiom available: to work with mathematics is to work without interface, and the difference matters: like any channel of communication, the interface conveys as much as it fashions the message itself, further limiting our authority as designers. This is why I am not interested in the speed, fluency, and ease of use commonly enjoyed at the top of the pyramid. As the relative uniformity of digital architecture on the global stage suggests, these ever-increasing conveniences offer less and less resistance to intuition, and hence are hardly fit for purpose in the scales of evolutionary differentiation. *Only a calibrated struggle with instrumental opacity will nurture intuition while keeping it in check*, eventually taking us into the unthought-of territory of invention. The benefit of "relinquishing" intuition and delegating it to the machine through scripting, programing, parametric

jeder Raum befindet sich innerhalb des nächsten wie bei einer Matrjoschka – nur dass sie in diesem Fall lediglich *eine* Puppe enthält. Die Schleife und die Figur-Grund-Umkehrung entsprechen der Organisation des archetypischen Museumsraums mit seinen Hauptanforderungen der Zirkulation (Museen sind um einen oder mehrere Wege herum organisiert) und einer ausreichenden Menge an Versorgungsraum für jeden zu versorgenden Raum. Kuratoren sprechen in diesem Zusammenhang meist von „Back of House" (Funktionstrakt) und „Front of House" (Ausstellungstrakt). Das extrem ungleiche Verhältnis von Back-of House- und Front-of-House-Bereichen, das für Besucher meist unsichtbar bleibt, ist ein Kennzeichen des modernen Museums und diese Ausformulierung der Arcsine Coil© interpretiert das recht gut.

Diese Art des Arbeitens greift in mehrfacher Hinsicht auf Intuition zurück. Der springende Punkt ist, dass wir nicht von der leichten Bedienbarkeit – und Transparenz – kommerzieller Modelling-Software abhängig sein werden. Mathematik hat letztlich weniger mit Effizienz oder Technik als mit einer anderen Entscheidungsebene zu tun. Sich zur Lösung von Problemen oder zur Schaffung von Neuem mathematischer Konzepte und Gleichungen statt kommerzieller Modelling-Software zu bedienen, bedeutet, direkt auf generative Symbole und Zeichen zuzugreifen. Ein derartiges Schreiben von Formen und Prozessen ist langsamer und erfordert ein anderes Denken in Bezug auf Autorschaft. Kommerzielle Modelling-Software kommt meist durch die Verknüpfung von Codepaketen oder die Zusammenführung von niedrigeren zu höheren Schritten zustande, weist also eine Art Pyramidenstruktur auf. Folglich heißt auch, damit zu arbeiten, an der Spitze der Pyramide zu arbeiten, wo die Interaktion intuitiv ist, aber die Entscheidungen bereits getroffen wurden. Dagegen agiert man mit dem Schreiben von Gleichungen, wenn schon nicht am Fuß der Pyramide, so doch ziemlich weit unten, dort wo der Großteil des Raums liegt und noch wenig oder überhaupt nichts festgelegt ist. Allerdings heißt das nicht, ohne Software zu arbeiten – was ein zweckloses, wenn nicht unmögliches Unterfangen wäre in einer Zeit, in der Software die einzig verfügbare Sprache ist. Mit Mathematik zu entwerfen heißt, ohne Interface zu arbeiten, und das ist ein Unterschied, der ins Gewicht fällt: Wie jeder Kommunikationskanal überträgt nämlich das Interface die Nachricht nicht nur, sondern formt sie auch und beschneidet damit unsere Gestaltungsmacht als Entwerfer. Deshalb bin ich auch nicht an Geschwindigkeit, Flüssigkeit und leichter Bedienbarkeit interessiert, wie sie meist an der Spitze der Pyramide geschätzt wird. Wie die relative Gleichförmigkeit digitaler Architektur auf der internationalen Bühne zeigt, setzt die wachsende Nutzerfreundlichkeit der Intuition immer weniger Widerstand entgegen und ist daher in Bereichen wie der evolutionären Differenzierung wohl kaum „zweckdienlich". *Nur ein kalibrierter Kampf mit der Opazität des Instruments wird die Intuition* zugleich *fördern und in Schach halten* und uns schließlich ins Ungedachte der Erfindung führen. Der Verzicht auf Intuition und deren Delegation an die Maschine durch das Erstellen von Skripten, Programmen, parametrischen Gleichungen, Kalkülen und anderen Formen automatischen Schreibens ist einfach gute rationale Methodik. Paradoxerweise ist es auch eine Methode, die uns hilft, die tief sitzenden Verkürzungen und Vorurteile zu umgehen, die die ersten Schritte des Entdeckungsprozesses behindern, so ähnlich (vielleicht) wie die freie Assoziation in der klassischen Psychoanalyse die Kontrolle des Bewusstseins außer Kraft setzt und einen gewissen Zugang zur sonst unzugänglichen Black Box des Unbewussten eröffnet. Das hat nichts mehr mit Computern zu tun. Und in diesem engen aber wesentlichen Sinn hat ein wohltemperierter algorithmischer Ansatz vielleicht mehr mit einem „handgemachten" surrealistischen Gesellschaftsspiel wie dem *Cadavre exquis*[11] gemein als mit anderen digitalen Innovationen.

Übersetzung Wilfried Prantner

equations, calculus, or any other form of automatic writing, is simply good, rational methodology. Perversely, it is also a workaround which helps us circumvent the ingrained shortcuts and prejudices that mar the first steps of the discovery process, in the same way (perhaps) that verbal free-associating will break the hold of consciousness in classic psychoanalytic theory and provide some access into the otherwise black box of the subconscious. This is not about computers anymore. And in this narrow but essential sense, a well-tempered algorithmic approach may have more in common with a "manual" early twentieth-century Surrealist parlor game like the *Rotating Corpse*,[11] than with other digital innovations.

---

11 Eine Methode zur gemeinsamen Erstellung eines Textes oder Bildes, ohne dass eine Person – sprich: ein Autor – a priori die Kontrolle darüber besitzt. Die Mitwirkenden tragen nacheinander zur Komposition bei, indem sie entweder einer festgelegten Regel wie z.B. einem Satzschema folgen oder nur den Schluss des vom Vorgänger Beigetragenen zu sehen bekommen. Vgl. Wikipedia http://de.wikipedia.org/wiki/Cadavre_Exquis

11 A method by which a collection of words or images is collectively assembled (with no *a priori* control exerted by any one individual: note by the author). Each collaborator adds to a composition in sequence, either by following a rule as in "The green duck sweetly sang the dreadful dirge" or by being allowed to see only the end of what the previous person contributed. Available online at: http://en.wikipedia.org/wiki/Exquisite_corpse

1 „Handswriting", Maki Gallery, Tokio Tokyo 1982, Foto photo: Keisuke Oki © STELARC

Between Machine and Intuition, Thresholds and Hybridizations

For the first time in the history of homo sapiens, the machine rivals us in that which is our own: not only our intelligence, but also our intuition. Since the beginning of modern times we have known and marveled at the miracles that automats performed—small miracles, limited to the simplest of movements, or gestures, or words—that we observed with amusement as long as they were far from being able to imitate the simplest of animal movements, to say nothing of man himself.

Zwischen Maschine und Intuition, Schwellen und Hybridbildungen. Zum ersten Mal in seiner Geschichte sieht der Homo sapiens sich darin zur Maschine in Konkurrenz gestellt, was ihm eigen ist: nicht allein seine Intelligenz, sondern auch seine Intuition. Seit Anbeginn der Moderne kennt man die Wunderwerke der Automaten und hat sie oft gepriesen – wobei das Wunderbare gerade einmal so weit reichte, sich fortzubewegen, ein paar Gebärden auszuführen oder Wörter von sich zu geben. Man durfte ihnen mit Belustigung zusehen, solange sie nicht einmal die am wenigsten komplexen Verhaltensformen von Tieren nachahmen konnten – vom Menschen ganz zu schweigen.

CHRIS YOUNÈS

It's another world today: one where computers are essential to our most sophisticated activities. There is a considerable difference between classical technology, which was about the invention and use of machines, and information technology. In the first case, there was a diptych: that of the human mind and the material world. The conceiving and building of a machine was all that Plato needed to prove the triumph of the mind over matter. With computer science, technology has advanced to the point that it is starting to match the most specific of human characteristics—our understanding, our sensitivity and our intuition.

The question of the intelligent machine that confronts us today is not unrelated to one that philosophers have struggled to answer for centuries, particularly since classical times. The problem is twofold: it concerns both the object and the subject of knowledge. The first can be summarized as: how do we know what we know? And the second as: how does a lifeless machine manage to organize itself and to perceive? Both questions are combined in the case of the information-processing machine designed eventually to think for itself, to perceive and even to use intuition. Some of them perform in such a way that they seem like intelligent and sensitive beings. Of course we know that they're only machines, made up of arrangements of lifeless parts … and confirm it to be so when we turn off the power. But how can a being dependent on electrical power learn to perceive, to think and—as in the case of robots—to act independently?

We don't approach these questions as specialists of so-called artificial intelligence. We would rather describe certain historical milestones in "thinking" that should help convey something of the philosophical perspective. First of all, as soon as one thinks of the modern machine, the philosophy of "mechanism" comes to mind. We'll limit ourselves here to describing a crucial point that is the basis of this theory: The power required by a system of objects articulated in accordance with a plan or a genetic schema such that the movement of one piece causes the movement of others and little by little of the whole. Any system articulated in this way is capable of movement as soon as it is connected to a source of energy. Descartes observed this in the simple machines of his era and applied the model to the idea of living matter in his theory of the "animal-machine."

In fact, machine and animal-machine merged in the mind of the philosopher in so far as the automaton can be seen as a simplified animal. This view implied rejection of Aristotle's notion of the animal as autonomous. Aristotle believed that the living animal was independent of any external stimulation and so self-reliant. Descartes, on the other hand, viewed the animal as a complex automaton requiring the unlimited understanding of God and distinguished from the machine in the same way that our own limited awareness distinguishes us from the unlimited awareness of God. Nevertheless, confrontation and analogy between the living and the artificial led to new perspectives on both: the study of the machine led to improved physiological understanding and of the animal to fantastic advancements in technology. The birth of the sensitive machine was actually evoked by Descartes in *Discours de la methode*, in his description of a machine that, when touched in a certain part, could cry out that it hurt! The hypothesis defended by Descartes that was to take on its full importance at the beginning of the 20th century, was that the whole is more than the sum of its parts—depending on the precise arrangement of parts or what he termed

Ganz anders aber verhält es sich heute, da Computerprogramme in allen hoch entwickelten Arbeitsvorgängen unverzichtbar geworden sind. Es besteht ein beachtlicher Unterschied zwischen der klassischen Technik, in der es um Erfindung und Nutzung der Maschinen geht, und den informatischen Techniken. Im ersten Fall hatte man es mit einer Dichotomie zu tun: Geist und Materie. Konzeption und Konstruktion der Maschine sprachen erstaunlich klar zugunsten Platons. In der Tat obsiegte hier der Geist über die Materie. Mit der Informatik indes erreicht die Technik den Menschen auf der Stufe, die ihn am spezifischsten ausmacht, nämlich auf den Gebieten des Intelligiblen, des Sensiblen und des Intuitiven.

Aber die Frage, die solche Maschinen aufwerfen, ist nicht ganz unähnlich derjenigen, mit der Philosophen und Gelehrte sich seit Jahrhunderten und vor allem seit dem klassischen Zeitalter auseinandergesetzt haben. Das Problem ist ein zweifaches: Es betrifft sowohl das Subjekt als auch das Objekt der Erkenntnis. Ersteres lässt sich so zusammenfassen: Wie erkennt man, was man erkennt? Zweiteres lautet: Wie gelangt eine leblose Maschine dazu, sich zu organisieren und zu fühlen? Die beiden Fragen treffen im Falle der informatischen Maschine zusammen, soll diese doch am Ende gerade „fühlen", „denken", ja „Intuitionen entwickeln". Einige verhalten sich so, dass sie den Eindruck vermitteln, man habe ein intelligentes und empfindendes Wesen vor sich. Und doch sind wir überzeugt, dass es sich selbstverständlich um einen Apparat handelt, um ein gefügtes Zusammenspiel jeweils lebloser Teile. Wovon wir uns Gewissheit verschaffen, wenn wir die Stromzufuhr abstellen. Wie kommt ein Wesen ohne eigenen Antrieb dazu, von sich aus zu fühlen, zu denken und – im Falle der Roboter – zu handeln?

Wir nähern uns dieser Frage nicht aus der Warte der Fachleute der sogenannten künstlichen Intelligenz. Vielmehr möchten wir auf einige historische Anhaltspunkte hinweisen, die diese Frage relativieren. Zunächst einmal kommt einem, sobald man an eine moderne Maschine denkt, eine ganze philosophische Strömung in den Sinn, die in der Geschichte des neuzeitlichen Denkens unter dem Namen Mechanizismus bekannt ist. Wir begnügen uns hier damit, an einen entscheidenden Punkt zu erinnern, auf dem dieses Denken beruht, nämlich die Kraft, die ein System von Objekten erfordert, die gemäß einem genetischen Plan oder Schema gegliedert sind, dergestalt dass die Bewegung eines Teils andere Teile und dann nach und nach das Gesamtgefüge in Bewegung setzt. Jedes derart gegliederte System ist fähig, Bewegung zu erzeugen und sich selbst zu bewegen, sobald es an eine Energiequelle angeschlossen ist. Descartes sah dies in den einfachen Automaten seiner Zeit veranschaulicht. Dieses Modell wandte er auf die Konzeption des Lebendigen an, indem er eine Lehre vorlegte, die als Theorie von den Tier-Maschinen bezeichnet wird.

In Wirklichkeit greifen die beiden Modelle im Denken des Philosophen ineinander, insofern der Automat als ein vereinfachtes Tier erschien, das das aristotelische Postulat implizierte – und zugleich entkräftete –, das Tier sei ein selbstbewegendes Wesen, das heißt von jeder äußeren Bewegursache unabhängig, denn es besitze in sich eine solche Ursache. Umgekehrt wird das Tier als ein komplexer und die Unendlichkeit des göttlichen Verstandes erfordernder Automat vorgestellt, wobei der Unterschied zwischen Automat und Tier dem Unterschied zwischen unserem endlichen Verstand und dem unendlichen Verstand Gottes entspricht. Die Begegnung und Analogie zwischen künstlichem Automaten und Lebewesen eröffnete indes für beide sehr fruchtbare Perspektiven. Während die Maschine zur Untersuchung der Physiologie führte, bot das Lebendige seinerseits fantastische Aussichten für die Technologie. In einer berühmten Passage der *Abhandlung über die Methode* beschwört Descartes das Bild einer Maschine herauf, die, wenn man sie an einer bestimmten Stelle berührte, schrie, man tue ihr weh. Hier entstand bereits die Idee der empfindenden Maschine. Die von Descartes verfochtene These, die sich am Anfang des 20. Jahrhunderts zur vollen Bedeutung entfalten wird, besagt, dass das Ganze mehr sei als die Summe seiner Teile. Dabei betonte Descartes den Aspekt, den er „Anordnung der Organe" nannte. Streng mechanisch verstanden, bedeutet dies: Sobald in einem System einander entsprechende Elemente richtig aufeinander abgestimmt sind und eine Energiequelle vorhanden ist (die Triebfeder beim Automaten), zeitigt das System sofort eine erstaunliche Wirkung, die in keinem seiner Teile steckte, nämlich die Dynamik des Gesamtgefüges oder die Erledigung allerlei vorab berechneter oder erdachter Arbeiten. Eben dies gilt jedoch auch für die lebenden Systeme oder Organismen, deren jedes dem gleichen mechanischen Schema gehorcht oder darauf zurückgeführt werden kann, so dass man dem Tier keine Seele mehr zuschreiben muss.

Leibniz wird vor dieser gewagten Analogie zurückschrecken. Wiewohl er das Prinzip des Mechanismus aufrecht erhält, versucht er das Wesen des Tieres komplexer zu fassen, indem er es um finalistische und vitalistische Elemente ergänzt. Er entwickelt die bereits bei Descartes gegebene Idee, dass der Unterschied zwischen Maschine und Tier nicht nur zwischen dem Einfachen und dem Komplexen liege, sondern auch zwischen dem Endlichen und dem Unendlichen. Das Tier ist eine Maschine, deren jedes Teil selber eine Maschine ist, die unendlich viele weitere Maschinen umfasst, deren jede ebenso viele enthält, und so bis ins Unendliche. Das aber heißt, dass sie „eine wahrhaft unendliche Anzahl von Organen"[1] hat, eine *Maschine von Maschinen* ist. Im Gegenzug öffnet sich die künstliche Maschine bereits für das unendlich Kleine. So erscheint das

the "disposition of organs." From a strictly mechanical point of view, according to Descartes, a system of elements correctly arranged and supplied with energy (or connected to a power source) could produce an astonishing effect not contained in anyone of its individual parts: such as the dynamics of the whole, or any other work calculated or conceived in advance. The hypothesis is equally valid for any living system, or organism, made up of parts that obey a mechanical plan—or can be reduced to one—such that the idea of the animal soul becomes redundant.

Leibniz backed away from this audacious analogy. Whilst maintaining the principles of mechanism, he tried to frame the theory of the animal in a more complex fashion by extending it with the notions of finalism and vitalism. He developed the idea, already present in Descartes work, that something more than complexity distinguishes the animal from the simple machine, something more akin to comparing the finite with the infinite. The animal, according to Leibniz, is a machine comprised of an infinite number of parts that are themselves machines comprised of parts comprised of machines …

But how can a being dependent on electrical power learn to perceive, to think and—as in the case of robots—to act independently?

and so on, indefinitely. Comprised of a "truly infinite number of parts,"[1] the animal is a *machine of machines*. On the other hand, the artificial machine already tends towards the infinitely small. Thus the theory of particle physics appears as both a possibility and an impossibility, which is why Leibniz excluded it, reinstating "finalism" at the heart of "mechanism," acknowledging the impossibility that the human mind imagine, let alone create, a machine to match the animal. The gap between man and machine was immeasurable, but this didn't hinder the possibility of extraordinary development for the artificial machine—in the sense of integrating the infinitely small.

This line of thought led to another: one that Leibniz summarized as *small perceptions* and is in reality linked to the indivisible substance, or element, the *monad*. For Leibniz, reality is a phenomenon that results from the action of and relationship between monads, a relationship that consists of *representation* and *expression*. All monads express and represent all other monads. In every organized, or composite substance, argued Leibniz, all units of simple substance, or monads, perceive one another, unconsciously, until a series of perceptions raises interaction to a level of consciousness. A continued series of small perceptions results in perception everywhere, even in seemingly inert bodies. In Leibniz's world, there is life, soul and consciousness everywhere—in infinitesimally small quantities. "Nature is full of life."[2] And an artificial machine, because it is composed of monads, is a perceiving being. Or would be, if it were not for the fact that the machine

1   Gottfried Wilhelm Leibniz: *Neues System der Natur und der Gemeinschaft der Substanzen, wie der Vereinigung zwischen Körper und Seele* (1695), in: *Philosophische Werke. Zweiter Band*, Leipzig 1906, S. 264.

1   G.W. Leibniz, *Nouveaux essais sur l'entendement humain* [1765] (Paris, 1993). (Trans. S. M.)
2   G.W. Leibniz, *Principes de la nature et de la grâce* [1714] (Paris, 1954), p. 27. (Trans. S. M.)

And an artificial machine, because it is composed of monads, is a perceiving being. Or would be, if it were not for the fact that the machine is not a composition of substances, but rather an *agregatum* that, having neither a soul nor its equivalent, is not capable of integrating (in the mathematical sense) small perceptions to a level of consciousness. Nevertheless, if the machine can produce a result, it is because each of the monads within it possesses an active energy that combines with that of all the others to transform the whole body of potential energy into kinetic energy—movement.

Programm der Teilchenphysik als Möglichkeit wie auch als Herausforderung. Deshalb schließt Leibniz sie von vornherein aus, indem er im Kern des Mechanismus selbst den Finalismus rehabilitiert, insofern es dem menschlichen Verstand unmöglich ist, eine dem Tier entsprechende Maschine zu ersinnen oder gar zu bauen. Der Abstand zwischen den beiden bleibt unermesslich, was aber der Möglichkeit einer regen Entwicklung der künstlichen Maschine im Sinne der Integration des unendlich Kleinen nicht im Wege steht.

Dieser Gedankengang kreuzt sich mit einem weiteren, den Leibniz unter der Rubrik „kleine Wahrnehmungen" zusammenfasst und der mit der unteilbaren Substanz, bzw. dem Element, der Monade verbunden ist. Für ihn ist die Wirklichkeit nur ein Phänomen, das aus der Tätigkeit der Monaden und ihrem Verhältnis untereinander erwächst, ein Verhältnis, das in „Darstellung" und „Ausdruck" besteht. Alle Monaden stellen also einander dar und drücken einander aus. In einem organisierten Körper, der eine „zusammengesetzte Substanz" ist, nehmen die einfachen Substanzen oder Monaden sich untereinander wahr, aber diese Wahrnehmung bleibt unmerklich und unbewusst, solange sie nicht einen Grad erreicht hat, der sie auf die Ebene des Bewusstseins hebt. Dass die Abstufung der Wahrnehmungen kontinuierlich verläuft, bewirkt, dass es überall Wahrnehmung gibt, selbst in den Körpern, die uns leblos erscheinen. Überall in Leibnizens Welt ist Leben, überall Seele und Bewusstsein, auch wenn sie infinitesimal sind. „In der Natur ist alles erfüllt."[2] Die künstliche Maschine ist, da sie sich aus Monaden zusammensetzt, ein fühlendes Wesen. Nur dass die Maschine, da sie keine „zusammengesetzte Substanz" ist, sondern ein *aggregatum*, und weder eine Seele noch etwas Seelenähnliches hat, nicht imstande ist, diese kleinen Wahrnehmungen auf der Ebene des Bewusstseins (im mathematischen Sinn des Wortes) zu integrieren. Wenn die Maschine gleichwohl eine Wirkung hervorbringen kann, so deshalb, weil jede der sie bildenden Monaden mit einer Tatkraft begabt ist, so dass alle diese Kräfte zusammenkommen, um den ganzen Körper von der potenziellen zur kinetischen Energie zu befördern.

Das Schema vom Ganzen und von der Summe seiner Teile findet sich immer wieder, wobei mal das erstere der zweiteren überlegen ist, mal das Ganze etwas anderes ist als die Summe seiner Teile. Descartes begriff das Ganze, das heißt die Maschine, als eine mechanische Realität, die in Abhängigkeit von der „Anordnung" ihrer Teile und von der Energieeinspeisung agiert. Leibniz begreift es als eine zugleich stoffliche und geistige Realität, wobei jede Monade, aus der es besteht, zugleich eine (ursprüngliche) Materie und eine Entelechie oder Form ist. Es ist ein ideelles, aber auch materielles Wesen. Dennoch bewirkt die

is not a composition of substances, but rather an *agregatum* that, having neither a soul nor its equivalent, is not capable of integrating (in the mathematical sense) small perceptions to a level of consciousness. Nevertheless, if the machine can produce a result, it is because each of the monads within it possesses an active energy that combines with that of all the others to transform the whole body of potential energy into kinetic energy—movement.

The schema of the whole and its parts is recurrent, in so far as thc former is seen as superior to the latter or the whole as different from the sum of the parts. Descartes saw the whole, the machine, as a mechanical reality that acts in function of the arrangement of its parts and a source of power. Leibniz saw the machine as both a physical and spiritual entity, comprised of monads that were at the same time both simple matter and higher form (entelechy) that when brought together could lead to an entity capable of self-action. Leibniz didn't reject the metaphor of the machine, but found the notion of mechanism, fundamental to modern science, wanting when applied to natural phenomena and in particular living ones. For Leibniz, a synthesis of mechanism, vitalism and even animism was necessary to explain life and reflect the various aspects of nature. His philosophy recognized simultaneous possibilities, rather than alternatives.

The question of intuition itself, manifested in a flash of light, rather than as a product of conscious thought, is linked, according to Bergson, to a "vital impetus," or life force (*élan vital*). Does intuition represent a final threshold not only between human and other natural machines, but also between man and the man-made machine? For Bergson, the sciences missed the point: physics failed to explain movement and biology failed to explain life. One could say that physics, the science of movement, began by reducing *motion* to a succession of cinematic "stills". And that biology, the science of life, began by reducing the workings of life to those of a machine in order to understand them. These concepts await redefinitions that relieve them from their abstract natures and bring them closer to their supposed objects that so far remain untouched, awaiting an authentic and new approach. Indeed, understanding them means setting aside concepts in favor of a new way of knowing. Such insight is what Bergson called intuition. To understand his idea of intuition, we should acknowledge the opposition Bergson set up between the two accepted models of knowing, the two approaches to the real: the sciences and the arts. For Bergson, the artist is compelled to create by a life force, or flow of energy and consciousness, that is fundamental, but not unique to man. This same compulsion, or "spiritual energy" animates all living matter and innovates, creating the new, constantly.

This irresistible energy appears in animals in the form of instinct—a force of great strength that destroys or overturns whatever gets in its way. Man, however, has devoted time and energy to controlling his instincts, adapting and channeling them into more socially acceptable forms. Little by little, rational thought has overcome instinctive action, condemning it and our passions to submission, replacing them with reason and self-control. Social conventions have thus driven mankind to restrict itself in favor of stability. Bergson wanted to return singularity, spontaneity and our lost passions to us, recognizing our natural instincts as part of our essential being, fundamental to the understanding of what we are and also, therefore, to the understanding of our place in the natural world—such a model meant

---

2   Gottfried Wilhelm Leibniz, *Die Vernunftprinzipien der Natur und der Gnade* (1711), in: *Philosophische Werke. Zweiter Band*, a.a.O., S. 424.

removing the long-established gulf between man and the rest of the living world. The re-establishing of connections between man and lesser-advanced forms of life led Bergson to seek similarities between man and other types of beings; he thus sought to acknowledge that plants were not only living, but conscious.

For Bergson, consciousness is the power of decision and the corollary of any "spontaneous" act that results from deliberate choice. Thus "consciousness, originally emanating from all that lives, slumbers wherever there is no spontaneous movement, and intensifies whenever life impels towards free action."[3] Proof of the phenomenon can be found in the learning of craftsmanship: at first we pay attention to every specific act, but gradually, as time goes by our conscious self withdraws to be replaced by automatic gestures. For Bergson, the types of consciousness linked to life-ensuring behavior appeared to lack only in inert matter characterized by "inertia, geometry, necessity."[4] Life, on the other hand, is spontaneous movement, unpredictable and free. Living matter, constantly mutable, offers uncertainty in an otherwise inert but certain world. All living matter, it seemed to Bergson, was able to respond to its environment through modes of both retention and anticipation that enabled it to react to changing conditions over long periods of time. Therefore, he stated, "in right if not in fact consciousness is coextensive with life."[5] From a certain point of view, consciousness and materiality could be viewed as "antagonistic"—if one is freedom, then the other is necessity. Except that life reconciles them in a *modus vivendi* where life is "freedom interleaved with necessity that it turns to its advantage."[6] Life seeps into the cracks of physical matter, installing itself wherever there is room, enlarging them over time, as life is energy. Thus plants accumulate energy by absorbing that of sunlight and releasing it subsequently. Life indeed is this dual phenomenon of accumulation and release of energy; a phenomenon forced to exploit material such that even living material is passive in so far as it serves as accumulator and transmitter of energy. Life is defined by its ability to contract a long history of inert material into an instant and conversely, to instantaneously release energy stored up over ages.

Despite their opposition, matter and consciousness are thus always related to each other; neither can be explained by itself. In the evolution of life on earth, Bergson saw "consciousness traversing matter" to remain stifled in the plant and trapped in animals, bursting out only in humans. The theory of evolution describes how all life forms have adapted to environmental conditions to ensure survival of the species and that even the most elemental forms of life appear as terminal points at which life could have stopped definitively. Why would evolution favor more and more specialized forms that are at the same time increasingly daring and dangerous? Certainly because of what Bergson calls the *élan vital*, an "impulsion" or inner push, a sort of "immense stream of consciousness" that has somehow

3   Henri Bergson, *L'énergie spirituelle* (Paris, 1919), pp. 57–58. (Trans. S. M.)

4   Ibid.

5   Ibid.

148   6   Ibid.

Zusammenfügung dieser Einheiten, dass es der Selbsttätigkeit fähig wird. Leibniz weist die Maschinenmetapher nicht zurück, befindet aber, dass der Mechanismus – eine wesentliche Errungenschaft der modernen Wissenschaft – nicht ausreicht, wenn es darum geht, den natürlichen Phänomenen und insbesondere denjenigen, denen das Leben gemeinsam ist, Rechnung zu tragen. Eine Synthese aus Mechanizismus, Vitalismus und sogar Animismus ist notwendig, weil die Natur so beschaffen ist, dass sie diese verschiedenen Aspekte mit sich bringt. So hat Leibniz seine Philosophie als kompossible Welten entwickelt.

Die Frage der Intuition, die kein Produkt des Vernunftdenkens ist, sondern sich in einem Geistesblitz als leuchtende Evidenz manifestiert, ist nach Auffassung Bergsons mit dem *élan vital* (in etwa: Lebensschwung) verbunden. Bildet sie eine letzte Schwelle nicht nur zwischen den menschlichen Maschinen und den natürlichen Maschinen, sondern auch zwischen dem Menschen und der Maschine selbst? Für Bergson haben die Wissenschaften ihren Gegenstand verfehlt: Die Physik hat die Bewegung verfehlt, die Biologie hat das Leben verfehlt. Die Physik, welche die Wissenschaft von der Bewegung ist, beginnt in der Tat damit, diese wie im Kino auf eine Abfolge von Zuständen zu reduzieren. Die Biologie, Wissenschaft des Lebendigen, hat damit begonnen, dieses auf eine Maschine zu reduzieren, um es erkennen zu können. Hier sind also Begriffe neu zu bestimmen oder zu bearbeiten, um ihre abstrakten Aspekte auszuräumen und sie ihren Gegenständen anzunähern, die sozusagen unberührt geblieben sind und eines authentischen und neuen Herangehens harren. Es gilt, den Schleier der Begriffe zu lüften, um auf einem anderen Wege zu den Dingen selbst zu gelangen. Dieser Weg ist das, was Bergson die Intuition nennt. Um sie zu verstehen, muss man den von ihm aufgestellten Gegensatz zwischen den beiden Modellen des Wissens, den beiden Zugängen zum Realen, als da sind die Wissenschaft und die Kunst, in Betracht nehmen. Bergson ist der Auffassung, dass der Künstler eine dem Menschen wesentliche Kraft zur vollen Verwirklichung führt, eine Kraft, die ihm im Übrigen nicht alleine eignet, da sie sich auch auf die anderen Lebewesen erstreckt: Die Rede ist vom Fluss oder Lebensschwung und vom Bewusstsein. Diese Lebenskraft, dieses Bewegungsprinzip, diese „spirituelle Energie", welche die Materie beseelt und durchdringt, ist innovativ, das heißt, sie erschafft Neues in jedem Augenblick.

Diese Kraft erscheint beim Tier deutlich in Gestalt der unwiderstehlichen Energie, die der Instinkt darstellt; eine Energie, die nur ihren eigenen Schub anerkennt. Sie zerstört und stürzt alles, was sie womöglich aufhalten oder stören könnte. Hingegen versucht der Mensch seit langem, diesen Schwung zu begrenzen, ihn zu kanalisieren und seiner Lebenswelt anzupassen durch eine berechnende Intelligenz, die stets nach einem Kompromiss zwischen einer solchen Kraft und den gesellschaftlichen Anforderungen sucht. Nach und nach hat das rationale Denken die schöpferische Energie erstickt, indem sie den Instinkt und die Leidenschaften verurteilte und dazu aufrief, diese zu beherrschen. Somit hat das Gewicht der Normen und Konventionen den Menschen dazu geführt, sich zugunsten der Stabilität gegen sich selber zu stemmen. Für Bergson kommt es darauf an, ihm diese Singularität, diese Spontaneität, diese mit Füßen getretene und verpönte Lebenskraft zurückzugeben, aber auch, diese Dimension als Modell für die wahre Realität des Menschen und der Dinge zu nehmen, als Modell dafür, was es wahrhaft zu erkennen gilt. Dafür ist aber die erste Bedingung, die seit langem errichtete Kluft zwischen dem Menschen und den sonstigen Lebewesen aufzuheben. Die Kontinuität zwischen dem Gipfel des Lebens und seiner Grundlage wieder herzustellen, heißt, die Ähnlichkeit zwischen dem Menschen und den bescheidensten Wesen wiederzufinden. Daher sieht Bergson sich veranlasst, der Pflanze nicht nur ein Leben, sondern auch ein Bewusstsein zuzuerkennen.

Tatsächlich ist für ihn das Bewusstsein die Kraft, sich zu entschließen; es ist die logische Folge jeder „spontanen Handlung", weil jede derartige Handlung Überlegung und Wahl benötigt. Daraus ergibt sich, dass „das Bewusstsein, ursprünglich allem Lebenden immanent, dort einschläft, wo es keine spontane Bewegung mehr gibt, und sich erhebt, wenn das Leben zur freien Tätigkeit drängt."[3] Die Gegenprobe für dieses Phänomen liefert der handwerkliche Lernprozess. Anfangs achtet man auf jeden Schritt, den man tut, mit fortschreitendem Lernen aber zieht das Bewusstsein sich aus diesem Vorgang zurück und die Automatismen stellen sich ein. Das mit jedem neuen Verhalten, das heißt mit der die Zukunft eines Lebewesens betreffenden Wahl verbundene Bewusstsein scheint nur der leblosen Materie abzugehen: „Die Materie ist Leblosigkeit, Geometrie, Notwendigkeit."[4] Dagegen ist das Leben spontane, unvorhersehbare, freie Bewegung. Das Lebendige, das in jedem Augenblick wählt und schöpft, erzeugt Unbestimmtheit in einer leblosen Welt, in der alles bestimmt ist. Es bewahrt die Vergangenheit und greift der Zukunft vor, und zwar in einer „Dauer" oder vielmehr in mehreren Dauern, in denen sich Retention und Protension vermischen. Deshalb ist „das Bewusstsein von Rechts wegen, wenn nicht gar tatsächlich dem Leben koextensiv."[5] Bewusstsein und Materie sind unter einem bestimmten Gesichtspunkt „antagonistische" Realitäten: Ist das eine Freiheit, so ist das andere Notwendigkeit. Aber das Leben söhnt sie miteinander aus, indem es einen *modus vivendi* einrichtet. Denn das Leben ist „die Freiheit, die sich in die Notwendigkeit einschaltet und sie zu ihren Gunsten wendet."[6] Es dringt in die Risse

Proof of the phenomenon can be found in the learning of craftsmanship: at first we pay attention to every specific act, but gradually, as time goes by our conscious self withdraws to be replaced by automatic gestures. For Bergson, the types of consciousness linked to life-ensuring behavior appeared to lack only in inert matter characterized by "inertia, geometry, necessity."[4]

3 Henri Bergson: *L'énergie spirituelle*, Paris 1919, S. 57–58. (Übers. S.B.)

4 Ebd., S. 62. (Übers. S.B.)

5 Ebd.

6 Ebd.

managed to travel through physical matter and forge two different and in some ways opposite paths: leading to either the instinct of insects or the intelligence of man.

Bergson clarified his thoughts in his letters to Deleuze; in one letter he writes: "The intuition of which I speak is first and foremost one of continuity, and the passage of time has prescribed a method."[7] In another "I was particularly affected by the passages you dedicated to *Creative Evolution*. Just as matter is a result of creative impulsion, rather than its contradiction, intelligence is a pause in intuition, rather than an opposite trend: between the two there is an essential affinity."[8] In the third letter, Bergson stresses the importance that he and Deleuze both attach to the multiplicity of connections: "The idea of the 'rhizome' seems exactly right for explaining the type of heterogeneous and qualitative multiplicities that characterize evolving reality."[9] The "body without organs" imagined by Deleuze and Guattari was nothing more than a new machinal form of subjectivity and multiplicity of arrangements or rhizome: the body as a desiring machine. In their view, man is a machine of desires, a creative machine sustained in a state of interdependence with other machines: "An organ-machine plugged into an energy-source machine of constant flows and interruptions."[10]

In the contemporary world, a hybrid composite of human and non-human actors[11] linked through sophisticated socio-technological networks, it has become impossible to differentiate between the two, or to isolate either one.

In the contemporary world, a hybrid composite of human and non-human actors[11] linked through sophisticated socio-technological networks, it has become impossible to differentiate between the two, or to isolate either one.

One of these days the combination of technological and scientific progress will probably result in the fabrication of a substance that resembles living matter, without knowing how to imprint, or reproduce the "vital force" that is life itself. On the other hand, the association of man with more and more sophisticated digital machines, in a new mix that is much more than the sum of its parts, will doubtless open up new possibilities for human intuition; and perhaps, with the advent of the cyborg[12], in a cyberworld, a new type of life force.

Translation from the French version by Sophia Meeres

der Materie ein, dort, wo es eine „Elastizität" gibt, lässt sich darin nieder, und mit der Zeit vergrößert, entfaltet es die Risse, denn es ist Energie. So speichert die Pflanze Energie, indem sie die der Sonne aufnimmt, die sie anschließend freisetzt. Das Leben ist dieses doppelte Phänomen von Energiespeicherung und -freisetzung. Dazu ist es gezwungen, die Materie zu nutzen, so dass lebendige Materie insofern leblose Materie ist, als sie in einen Energiespeicher und -spender verwandelt wurde. Das Leben definiert sich durch diese Fähigkeit, eine lange Geschichte der leblosen Materie in einem Augenblick zusammenzuziehen und, umgekehrt, eine lange Zeit gespeicherte Energie augenblicks freizusetzen.

Trotz ihrer Gegensätzlichkeit bleiben Materie und Bewusstsein daher aneinander gebunden. Weder die eine noch die andere erklären sich durch sich selbst. Man muss in der Entwicklung des Lebens auf der Erde „eine Durchwanderung der Materie durch das Bewusstsein" sehen, das bei der Pflanze unterdrückt und beim Tier „eingesperrt" bleibt und nur beim Menschen hervorbricht. Die Evolutionstheorie hat gezeigt, wie gut jede Lebensform an ihre Bedingungen angepasst ist, so dass eine jede, von der elementarsten an, ein Schlusspunkt zu sein scheint, an dem das Leben hätte endgültig Halt machen können. Warum also hat die Evolution sich zu immer komplizierteren und immer riskanteren und gefährlichen Formen hin fortgesetzt? Sicher aufgrund der Existenz eines Schwungs, eines „inneren Schubs", einer Art „unermesslichen Bewusstseinsstroms", der die Materie und deren Widerstände durchlaufen haben muss, um sich zwei unterschiedliche und in manchen Hinsichten gegensätzliche Wege zu bahnen: der Instinkt der Insekten und die Intelligenz des Menschen.

In seinen Briefen an Deleuze erteilt Bergson überaus aufschlussreiche Auskünfte. Im ersten Schreiben präzisiert er: „Die Intuition, von der ich spreche, ist vor allem eine Intuition der Dauer, und die Dauer schreibt eine Methode vor."[7] Oder: „Besonders empfänglich war ich für die Passagen, die Sie der *Schöpferischen Entwicklung* widmen. Ganz wie die Materie eher ein Niederschlag des schöpferischen Schwunges ist als dessen aktive Negierung, ist die Intelligenz eher eine Ausdehnung der Intuition als eine gegensätzliche Tendenz: Das heißt, es gibt zwischen ihnen eine Wesensverwandtschaft."[8] Im dritten Brief unterstreicht er die Bedeutung, die er, wie Deleuze, der Mannigfaltigkeit der Verknüpfungen zuerkennt: „Das Bild des ‚Rhizoms' erscheint mir ganz und gar geeignet, den Typus heterogener und qualitativer Mannigfaltigkeit spürbar zu ma-

7   Henri Bergson, "Trois lettres 'inédites' de Henri Bergson à Gilles Deleuze," *Critique* 64, 732 (2008), pp. 398–409. (Trans. S. M.)

8   Ibid.

9   Ibid.

10   Gilles Deleuze and Félix Guattari, *L'anti-Œdipe. Capitalisme et schizophrénie* (Paris, 1972), p. 7. (Trans. S. M.)

11   See Bruno Latour, *Nous n'avons jamais été Modernes. Essai d'anthropologie symétrique* (Paris, 1991).

12   See Antoine Picon, *La ville-territoire des cyborgs* (Besançon, 1998).

7   Henri Bergson: „Trois lettres ‚inédites' de Henri Bergson à Gilles Deleuze," *Critique* 64, 732 (2008), S. 398–409. (Übers. S.B.)

8   Ebd.

chen, die der Textur einer werdenden Realität zukommt."[9] Der „organlose" Körper bei Deleuze und Guattari ist übrigens nur eine neue maschinenhafte Form von Subjektivität und von Mannigfaltigkeit der Anfügungen oder Rhizome. In dieser Auffassung wird der Mensch als eine begehrende und produzierende Maschine gesehen, die in einer Struktur wechselseitiger Abhängigkeiten zu anderen Maschinen einbegriffen ist: „Eine Organmaschine für eine Energiemaschine, fortwährend Ströme und Einschnitte."[10]

Da die heutige Welt zu einer hybriden Zusammensetzung aus menschlichen und nicht-menschlichen Akteuren geworden ist[11], die durch hoch entwickelte soziotechnische Netze miteinander verknüpft sind, ist es nicht länger möglich, diese Akteure voneinander zu trennen oder zu isolieren. Man darf annehmen, dass der vereinte Fortschritt von Technik und Wissenschaft eines Tages zur Herstellung einer Materie führen wird, die der lebendigen Materie ähnelt; jedoch wird man ihr jene Bewegung oder jenen »Schwung« nicht einprägen können, der das Leben selbst ist und die Reproduktion und Evolution der lebendigen Formen bewirkt. Die Assoziierung des Menschen mit immer komplexeren und sensibleren digitalen Maschinen dagegen, die eine neue Gesamtheit bildet, die etwas anderes ist als die Summe ihrer Teile, eröffnet der menschlichen Intuition neue Möglichkeiten; vielleicht sogar, mit dem Cyborg[12] und in einer Cyberwelt, einen neuen *élan vital*.

Aus dem Französischen von Stefan Barmann

9   Ebd.

10   Gilles Deleuze/Félix Guattari: *Anti-Ödipus. Kapitalismus und Schizophrenie I*, Übers. Bernd Schwibs, Frankfurt/M. 1977, S. 7.

11   Vgl. Bruno Latour: *Wir sind nie modern gewesen. Versuch einer symmetrischen Anthropologie*, Frankfurt/M. 2008.

12   Vgl. Antoine Picon: *La ville-territoire des cyborgs*, Besançon 1998.

1   Ludger Hovestadt

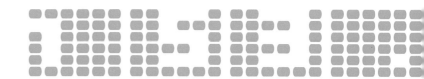

„Einfachheit ist für Anfänger"

Ludger Hovestadt (LH) im Gespräch mit Urs Hirschberg (GAM))
"Simplicity is for Beginners" Ludger Hovestadt (LH)
in Conversation with Urs Hirschberg (GAM)

Ludger Hovestadt ist seit Juli 2000 ordentlicher Professor für Architektur und CAAD an der ETH Zürich.[1] Unter dem Motto „Applied Virtuality" beschäftigt er sich gegenwärtig intensiv mit den theoretischen Grundlagen seines Faches und schaut dabei weit über dessen Grenzen hinaus, insbesondere in die Philosophie und in die Mathematik.

Ludger Hovestadt has served as professor of architecture and Computer Aided Architectural Design (CAAD) at the Swiss Federal Institute of Technology (ETH) since July 2000.[1] Following the motto "applied virtuality," he has devoted himself to studying the theoretical foundations of his field whilst simultaneously searching far beyond its boundaries, especially to the subjects of philosophy and mathematics.

LUDGER HOVESTADT

Ludger Hovestadt studierte Architektur an der RWTH Aachen und der HfG Wien, Meisterklasse Prof. Holzbauer. Nach seinem Diplom 1987 arbeitete er als wissenschaftlicher Mitarbeiter und Assistent bei Prof. Haller und Prof. Kohler an der Technischen Universität Karlsruhe (D), wo er 1994 promovierte. 2009 hat er mit Jenseits des Rasters ein viel beachtetes Buch herausgegeben, in welchem er die ersten zehn Jahre seiner Tätigkeit an der ETH zusammenfasst.[2] Seither hat Ludger Hovestadt einen in diesem Buch bereits angekündigten Schwenk in Richtung Theorie vollzogen: Die Bücher der „Applied Virtuality" Serie, die er zusammen mit der Philosophin und Medienwissenschaftlerin Vera Bühlmann dazu publiziert hat (*Printed Physics* [2012], *Sheaves* [2013], *EigenArchitecture* [2014]) sind durchaus sperrig: provokante Thesen werden mit Argumenten aus unterschiedlichsten Wissensgebieten untermauert. Hovestadt mutet seinen Lesern gewaltige Sprünge zu und räumt dabei auch selbst ein, dass das Ganze noch etwas Provisorisches besitzt. Er nennt die Texte selbst „ungeduldig", „skizzenhaft, schnell und etwas verschlungen" und empfiehlt, dass man sie in der Art eines Sudoku lesen möge, indem man mit einzelnen Ankerpunkten beginnt. Wenn man an die Grenzen eines Fachgebiets vorstoßen will, dann kann man nicht erwarten, dass dort alles leicht verständlich ist: „Einfachheit ist für Anfänger."[3]

Das folgende Gespräch diskutiert Hovestadts jüngste Publikation, *EigenArchitecture: Cultivating the Generic. A Mathematically Inspired Pathway for Architects*. Zum Zeitpunkt des Interviews war das Buch noch nicht erschienen und lag nur als Druckfahne vor. In der ersten Frage sind, sozusagen als Einleitung und als Kontext für den Leser, ein paar kurze Passagen aus diesem Buch wiedergegeben.

GAM: In der Einleitung zu EigenArchitecture *schreibst Du:* „Architektur und Informationstechnologie sind sich ähnlich. Sie sind beide nicht disziplinär, betreffen alle Bereiche unseres Lebens und beide sind sie eine Kunst des Fügens. Die eine Kunst 2500 Jahre alt und ehrwürdig, die andere Kunst gerade einmal 50 Jahre alt und ungeduldig. […] Computer scheinen so universell zu sein wie die Architektur, zumindest solange, wie sie als abstrakte Maschinen angesehen werden. Wenn sie jedoch, unter einem ungenauen Begriff von Abstraktion, nur als – wenn auch schnelle – einfache Maschinen angesehen werden, werden sie beängstigend. Die Schönheit der Computer liegt darin, dass sie nicht einfach Maschinen sind. Sie sind abstrakte Maschinen. Als Architekten, als Meister der Architektonik, d.h. der Kunst des Fügens von Dingen, wollen wir deshalb fragen: Wie sind diese neuen Dinge, diese Computer, beschaffen? Wie sprechen sie zueinander? Wie sprechen sie zu uns?"[4]

Es gibt also schon gleich zu Anfang die These einer Partnerschaft zwischen Architektur und Informationstechnologie, zwischen Mensch und Maschine, die in einen Dialog treten. So ähnlich hat das ja auch schon Nicholas Negroponte in seinem Buch The Architecture Machine *postuliert. Negroponte*

Ludger Hovestadt studied architecture at RWTH Aachen University and at the University of Applied Arts Vienna in the master class of Prof. Holzbauer. After earning his degree in 1987, he worked as a research associate and academic assistant for Prof. Haller and Prof. Kohler at the Karlsruhe Institute of Technology, where he received his doctorate in 1994. In 2009 he released a widely acknowledged book *Beyond the Grid*, which summarized the first ten years of his activity at ETH.[2] Since then, Hovestadt has gone through a shift announced in that book: towards theory. The "Applied Virtuality Series" books subsequently written in collaboration with philosopher and media theoretician Vera Bühlmann—*Printed Physics* (2012), *Sheaves* (2013), and *EigenArchitecture* (2014)—are challenging indeed: provocative theses substantiated by arguments from a broad range of disciplines. Hovestadt wants his readers to navigate the same great leaps that he does, admitting that the whole endeavor is somewhat experimental. He calls the texts "impatient," "fast, sketchy and a bit intricate," suggesting that readers take something of a Sudoku approach in perusing them, starting with whichever anchor points they choose. Indeed, those who wish to push the borders of a discipline cannot expect to find everything easily comprehensible: "Simplicity is for beginners."[3]

Hovestadt's most recent publication, *EigenArchitecture: Cultivating the Generic – A Mathematically Inspired Pathway for Architects*, is discussed in the following pages which are the record of a conversation. At the time the book had not yet been published and was only available as galley proofs. To give some context for the reader, the first question here contains two excerpts from this upcoming publication.

GAM: In the introduction to EigenArchitecture, *you write:* "Architecture and information technology are two species similar in kind, neither of them being in the least disciplinal: both affect everything, both are arts of gathering things. The one, 2500 years old and dignified, and the other, just 50 years of age and impatient. … Computers seem to be as universal as architecture, at least so long as they are thought of as abstract machines. But if, due to an improper notion of abstraction, they are perceived as mere—albeit fast—machines, they are frightening. [T]he beauty of computers lies precisely in their being not just machines. They are abstract machines. As architects, as masters of architectonics, i.e., the art of putting things together, we therefore ask: What then are these new things,

1   Die Fotostrecke auf den Seiten 88–97 dieser GAM-Ausgabe zeigt ein kürzlich an seinem Lehrstuhl entstandenes Projekt.

2   Vgl. dazu die Rezension „Cremige Diagramme" von Urs Hirschberg in *GAM.07 – Zero Landscape: Unfolding Active Agencies of Landscape*. Wien/New York 2011, S. 326–328.

3   Ludger Hovestadt/Vera Bühlmann (Hg.): *EigenArchitecture*, Wien 2014, S. 12.

4   Ludger Hovestadt/Vera Bühlmann (Hg.): *EigenArchitecture*, Wien 2014, Auszüge aus der Einleitung. Übers. von Ludger Hovestadt.

1   The photosection on pages 88 to 97 of this GAM issue shows a recent project by Hovestadt's group.

2   See the review "Creamy Diagrams" by Urs Hirschberg in *GAM.07 – Zero Landscape: Unfolding Active Agencies of Landscape* (Vienna and New York, 2011), pp. 326–328.

3   Ludger Hovestadt and Vera Bühlmann, *EigenArchitecture* (Vienna, 2014), p. 12.

these computers, like? How are they talking to one another? How are they talking to us?"[4]

So from the start you write about a partnership between architecture and information technology, and about the dialogue between man and machine. Nicholas Negroponte took a similar stance in his book The Architecture Machine, *but he is one of the first to be criticized in your retelling of the developments of the past fifty years. On this we read:* "To us architects, it may seem of interest to confront two contrasting attitudes taken vis-à-vis these developments. On the one side there is, e.g., Negroponte's *The Architecture Machine: Toward a More Human Environment* (1973), especially the experiment SEEK, a cybernetic habitat for gerbils, arranged and controlled by a robot through simple feedback loops. That set-up's architectural elements are simple blocks, their configuration controlled by simple rules, executed by the robot. The architecture is controlled as both to form and structure, internally and externally. This, we call a tyrannic set-up, with no escape. And the gerbils, indeed, died soon of stress, and needed frequent replacement."[5]

Most people in our field consider Negroponte's book as an important milestone. Yet you cite it as an example of a tyrannical and restrictive setup that limits and stultifies not only the gerbils. Contrasting examples that you subsequently use to counter Negroponte include the Bauhaus tenets of Itten and construction toys like Lego *and* Lectron *which are not restrictive.*

The topic of "necessity" versus "contingency" (or non-negotiable versus the negotiable) comes up repeatedly in the book, and you go on to criticize cybernetics and a whole ensemble of CAAD pioneers. But let's go back to Negroponte. It doesn't seem quite fair to write off his entire book because of the gerbil project, would you please explain what you feel is so wrong about Negroponte's experiment? Why the polemic tone?

LH: Well, to start with—in my view too, Negroponte's really is an important book. It significantly impacted the way I did research and was formative for my career. From a Continental European context, I was fascinated by these cybernetic ideas from across the Atlantic, by computers, and also by Negroponte's book. However, after ten years of research according to this paradigm I realized that we couldn't use it to solve the types of systemic problems that we face. I conducted research in Karlsruhe under Prof. Fritz Haller and worked with Ulrich Flemming to earn my doctorate. In those days we placed particular emphasis on shape grammar technology as pioneered by George Stiny. After some time had passed and I was working on more current theoretical issues, I came to realize that Stiny with his shape grammar was geometrizing algebra, that

gehört dann aber gleich zu den ersten, die Du in Deiner Nacherzählung der Entwicklung der letzten fünfzig Jahre heftig kritisierst. Wir lesen da: „Für uns Architekten mag es interessant sein, zwei verschiedene Haltungen diesen Entwicklungen gegenüber zu unterscheiden. Auf der einen Seite ist da z.B. Negropontes The Architecture Machine: Toward a More Human Environment (1973), und besonders das Experiment SEEK, ein kybernetisches Habitat für Wüstenrennmäuse, das durch eine Roboter mit simplen Feedbackloops aufgebaut und kontrolliert wird. Die Architektur besteht aus einfachen Blöcken, deren Konfiguration von ebenso einfachen Regeln bestimmt ist, die von einem Roboter ausgeführt werden. Das Habitat ist daher sowohl in Form als auch in Struktur, d.h. intern wie auch extern, kontrolliert. Das würden wir ein tyrannisches Setup nennen, denn es gibt keinen Ausweg aus dieser Kontrolle. Und die Mäuse starben tatsächlich sehr schnell an Stress und mussten häufig ersetzt werden."[5]

Von den meisten in unserem Fach wird dieses Buch von Negroponte als wichtiger Meilenstein gesehen. Du verwendest es als Beispiel für ein tyrannisches Setup, welches unsere Möglichkeiten einschränkt, uns verdummt. Die positiven Gegenbeispiele, die Du danach im Kontrast dazu anführst, sind die Bauhauslehre von Itten, oder Konstruktionsspielzeuge wie Lego *oder* Lectron, *welche eben nicht einschränken.*

Das Thema wird immer wieder aufgegriffen, du kritisierst die Kybernetik und eine ganze Reihe von Pionieren des Computer Aided Architectural Design. Aber bleiben wir erst mal bei Negroponte. Einmal abgesehen davon, dass es mir nicht ganz fair erscheint, das ganze Buch mit diesem Projekt mit den Wüstenmäusen gleichzusetzen, kannst Du erklären, was aus Deiner Sicht an Negropontes Experiment so verkehrt ist und vielleicht auch, wo der polemische Ton herkommt?

LH: Also zunächst einmal: auch für mich ist das ein bedeutendes Buch. Es war wichtig für die Art, wie ich Forschung gemacht habe, für meinen Werdegang. Aus einem kontinental-europäischen Kontext war ich fasziniert von diesen Angeboten der Kybernetik, von den Computern und eben auch von diesem Buch von Negroponte. Meine persönliche Erfahrung damit ist, dass ich 10 Jahre lang Forschung gemacht habe in diesem Paradigma, aber festgestellt habe, dass wir das, was wir an systematischen Problemen behandeln wollten, damit nicht lösen konnten. Ich habe an der Professur von Fritz Haller in Karlsruhe geforscht und mit Ulrich Flemming promoviert. Wir haben bei unseren Entwicklungen vor allem auf die Technologie der Shape Grammars gesetzt, welche besonders George Stiny geprägt hat. Mit etwas zeitlichem Abstand und durch die aktuelle theoretische Arbeit habe ich feststellen müssen, dass Stiny mit seinen Shape Grammars die Algebra geome-

> Aus einem kontinental-europäischen Kontext war ich fasziniert von diesen Angeboten der Kybernetik, von den Computern und eben auch von diesem Buch von Negroponte.

4   Ludger Hovestadt and Vera Bühlmann, *EigenArchitecture* (Vienna, 2014), excerpts from the introduction, pp. 3–5.

5   Ibid., p. 10.

5   Ebd., S. 10. Übers. von Ludger Hovestadt.

trisiert, sprich anschaulich macht und deswegen eine Lösung für nicht anschauliche Probleme verunmöglicht. Deswegen bin ich da etwas ärgerlich.

GAM: Kannst Du das etwas genauer erklären?

LH: Man kann mit Shape Grammars zum Beispiel ohne Schwierigkeiten isolierte Systeme wie Grundrisslayouts, Fassaden oder statische Konstruktionen generieren. Wir haben unsere Forschung aber mit gebäudetechnischen Systemen gemacht und hatten damit ein anders gelagertes Problem, denn die technischen Systeme konkurrieren um den Raum. Und jedes technische System hat einen anderen Raumbegriff – anders als die Gebäudekonstruktionen. Die Zuordnung ist nicht klar. Eine Shape Grammar à la Stiny braucht dagegen einen exklusiven Raumbegriff für alle und kann darin verhandeln. Das wäre nicht weiter schlimm, denn es zeigt nur, dass die Algorithmen von Stiny mit dem koordinierten Layout von technischen Systemen in Gebäuden nicht zurecht kommen können. Das Interessante ist nun aber, dass Stiny unverhohlen vom Mathematiker Hilbert (1899) eins-zu-eins und unreferenziert die veranschaulichenden Bilder für dessen zugrundeliegende Algebra übernommen hat und gezielt die Algebra selbst unterschlägt. Und heute stellt sich für mich heraus, dass sich mit der originalen Algebra von Hilbert unser Layoutproblem der technischen Systeme lösen lässt, was mit den trivialisierenden geometrischen Algorithmen von Stiny nicht geht.

GAM: Das heißt, inzwischen ist das Problem …

LH: … gelöst und zwar mit der Theorie von 1899, die mir Stiny 1972 verstellt hat. Das finde ich abenteuerlich!

GAM: Weiß das Stiny?

LH: *(lacht)* Das weiß ich nicht. Das Interessante ist, dass die technischen Gebäudesysteme in der gleichen Zeit entstanden sind wie die symbolische Algebra, deren Zusammenfassung Hilbert Ende des letzten Jahrhunderts moderierte, dass man faktisch mit Informationstechnologie diese Mathematik verfügbar macht, konzeptionell aber einen Rückschritt in die geometrische Anschaulichkeit macht. Deswegen kann man das, was in der zweiten Hälfte des 19. Jahrhunderts als Fragestellungen und Aufgaben gestellt worden ist, was man mathematisch präzise beschreiben konnte, einfach nicht mehr lösen. In der gesamten Literatur zu Computer Aided Design oder Modelling gibt es diesen Diskurs nicht. Das finde ich erstaunlich und es ärgert mich auch.

GAM: Du hättest das aber selber auch bei Hilbert nachlesen können, oder?

LH: Das habe ich ja am Ende. Aber durch die Vehemenz des Auftretens der Kybernetik, durch diese aggressive Ignoranz war mir das lange Zeit verbaut. Natürlich auch durch die Vehemenz der Infantilisierungen in *The Architecture Machine*. Wenn ich das heute genau lese, besonders das Ex-

> Wie konnte ich als junger Forscher darauf reinfallen, dass das irgendetwas mit einer Verbesserung von Mensch-Maschinen-Interaktionen, mit Architektur und so weiter zu tun haben kann, wenn diese Mäuse vor Stress immer sterben.

is, rendering it intuitive—which makes it impossible to find with it solutions for problems that are not intuitive. This irritated me.

GAM: Could you perhaps explain this in a little more detail?

LH: Shape grammars can easily be used to generate isolated systems like floor-plan layouts, façades, or static constructions. However, our research involved technical services (Heating, Ventilation, air conditioning, etc.), so the logic of the problems is different, as these technical elements compete with one another for space. And each one has a different concept of space—thus differing from building construction. The allocation of space is not clear. By contrast, shape grammar à la Stiny requires one exclusive spatial concept for all elements and can negotiate only within this realm. This alone would not be problematic, for it simply shows that Stiny's algorithms cannot aptly address the coordinated layout of technical services in buildings. What is of greater interest, however, is that Stiny adopted, without referencing them, images which mathematician David Hilbert (1899) had produced in order to explain the algebra that Stiny, by using the same images to illustrate a particular geometry, insolently suppresses. Recently I discovered that Hilbert's original algebra can solve our technical-systems layout problems, while Stiny's trivializing geometric algorithms cannot.

GAM: So this means that the problem has been …

LH: … solved! With a theory from 1899, which Stiny dissimulated from me in 1972. To me this is quite adventurous!

GAM: Is Stiny aware of this?

LH: *(laughs)* I'm not actually sure. It is interesting to note that technical services in buildings emerged during the same period as did symbolic algebra, which was summarized by Hilbert in the late 1800s. So, while information technology actually made this abstract form of math useful and widely available, conceptually it made a step backward (in the name of simplicity) into a notion of intuitivity with which we were familiar from before the rise of this math. Due to this, we find ourselves in a situation today where questions and problems fielded since the second half of the nineteenth century, in the form of exact mathematical formulations, appear to us as impossible to solve. This entire discussion is virtually nonexistent in literature on computer-aided design or modeling. I find it astonishing, and it frustrates me as well.

GAM: But couldn't you have read about it yourself in Hilbert's works?

LH: In the end I did just that. But due to the vehemence of the cybernetic discourse, and its aggressive ignorance, investigations in this direction were blocked for a long time—of course also due to the infantilization found in *The Architecture Machine*. When reading this again closely today, especially the experiment with the gerbils, I think to myself: How could I as a young researcher have believed that this experiment might have anything to do with improving human-machine interactions, with architecture, and so forth? Of course, the stress-induced deaths of these gerbils is not explicitly mentioned in the book, but it would have been worth at least a footnote, if you ask me.

GAM: But in his book, which was well received and widely read, wasn't Negroponte more concerned with something completely different? He had the pioneering idea of a computer that could be of assistance in the design process, as a partner. He took this idea and presented it to the world, thus inspiring, among other things, people like you who became interested in the topic.

LH: Sure, it is a masterful book. But it expresses the imperial gesture of its time: it takes new technology and uses it to conquer a discipline by trivializing this technology. What kind of architectural machine is that? What does it mean when someone designs a building-block world in an isolated cage and then even goes on to mechanize the interplay of blocks? This is in no way related to my conception of machines creating infrastructure for free use. Rather, it is the vision of a great "world machine."

GAM: You can interpret it this way, but didn't Negreponte intend something entirely different?
LH: No.

GAM: But isn't it a machine that enters into a dialogue—in this case, with a gerbil?
LH: No, most definitely not. It is a global Cartesian system that uses a few select rules to determine the surrounding environment. This means that there is no way out, which implies a tyrannical concept of the machine. In my book I compare this to the playthings which figured in the way I learnt about the world: Lego or Lectron. To me, these are open systems. They are easy to erect, but there is no prescribed way to use them. The poor gerbils, in turn, didn't have a chance, because both the elementary components and the environment were controlled by a narrow, logical Cartesian system.

GAM: In the case of Negroponte, the open system is signified by the thoughts that he triggers in his readers.
LH: True, but only for those standing on the outside tyrannizing the gerbils! In my mind, this is a strange concept of technology. And I also find it astounding that it took me fifteen years to realize it—although I never really felt drawn to those experiments. Ultimately it was through my criticisms of shape

periment mit den Wüstenmäusen, dann denke ich mir: Wie konnte ich als junger Forscher darauf reinfallen, dass das irgendetwas mit einer Verbesserung von Mensch-Maschinen-Interaktionen, mit Architektur und so weiter zu tun haben kann, wenn diese Mäuse vor Stress immer sterben. Allerdings wird das ja im Buch auch nicht erwähnt. Wenigstens eine Fußnote hätte das wert sein sollen, finde ich.

GAM: Ging es Negroponte mit diesem Buch, das sehr intensiv rezipiert wurde, nicht um etwas ganz anderes? Er hat die Idee von einem Computer, der mir im Entwurfsprozess assistieren kann, der mir ein Partner sein kann, das hat er in die Welt getragen und damit unter anderem dazu beigetragen, dass Leute wie Du sich für dieses Thema interessiert haben.
LH: Na klar, es ist ein meisterhaftes Buch. Aber es hat die imperiale Geste seiner Zeit: er nimmt die neue Technologie und erobert damit eine Disziplin durch Trivialisierung der Technologie. Was ist denn das für eine Architekturmaschine? Was heißt denn das, dass man in einem abgeschlossenen Käfig eine Welt aus Bauklötzen entwirft und auch noch das Zusammenspiel der Bauklötze mechanisiert? Mit meinem Verständnis von Maschinen als Infrastruktur für den freien Gebrauch hat das nichts zu tun. Das ist die Vorstellung einer großen Weltmaschine.

GAM: So kann man das lesen, aber ist das nicht ganz anders gemeint?
LH: Nein.

GAM: Ist das nicht eine Maschine, die in einen Dialog tritt – in diesem Fall mit einer Maus?
LH: Nein, definitiv nicht. Es ist ein globales, kartesisches System, welches mit wenigen Regeln bestimmt, was die Umwelt ist. Das heißt, es gibt keinen Ausweg, und das ist ein Maschinenbegriff, der tyrannisch ist. Im Buch vergleiche ich das mit den Spielsachen, mit denen ich sozialisiert wurde: Lego oder Lektron. Das sind in meinem Sinne offene Systeme. Sie sind einfach im Aufbau, aber sie sagen überhaupt nicht, was man damit tun soll. Diese armen Gerbils haben dagegen keine Chance, weil sowohl die elementaren Teile als auch die Umgebung in einem engen, logischen, kartesischen System kontrolliert werden.

GAM: Das, was bei Negroponte das offene System ist, sind die Gedanken, die er damit anstößt.
LH: Ja aber nur für den Außenstehenden, der diese Mäuse tyrannisiert! Das ist ein Technologiebegriff, der für mich seltsam ist. Für mich ist auch erstaunlich, dass ich 15 Jahre gebraucht habe, um das zu verstehen. Ich fand diese Experimente nie wirklich interessant. Schließlich bin ich über meine Kritik an den Shape Grammars darauf gekommen. Denn mit ihnen verhält es sich genauso: Auch mit ihnen hat man einzelne geometrische Elemente und gleichzeitig logische Regeln, denen das räumliche Spiel dieser Elemente folgt. Es ist die gleiche, kompakte, tyrannische Vorstellung von dem, was Design ist, wie bei der Architectural Machine von Negroponte.

GAM: Shape Grammars sind doch in Analogie zur Grammatik in der Sprache entwickelt worden: Sie geben keine Inhalte vor, sie sind im Grunde genommen wertfrei. Wie man sie dann verwendet, ist absolut offen.

2–4 Eine Self Organizing Map (SOM) ist ein von Teuvo Kohonen entwickeltes Modell eines künstlichen neuronalen Netzes. Eine SOM wird verwendet, um die Grundrisse der Zürcher Innenstadt so anzuordnen, dass ähnliche Grundrisse nebeneinander liegen. A Self Organizing Map (SOM) is a model of an artificial neural network developed by Teuvo Kohonen. An SOM is used to rearrange the plots of the inner city of Zurich so that similar plots are close to each other. © Benjamin Dillenburger/Architektur und and CAAD, ETH Zürich

grammars that I came to discover it. For shape grammars function in exactly the same way: there are individual geometric elements and, at the same time, logical rules that dictate the spatial interplay of the elements. It is the same compact, tyrannical conception of design as seen in the architectural machine of Negroponte.

GAM: But shape grammars were developed in analogy to grammar in language: they do not specify any content and are basically value free. Their potential use is completely open.

LH: That's right, as long as the rules are followed, everything is open. Which doesn't really mean anything, except that it is logical.

GAM: But your complaint is about not being able to solve certain problems with shape grammars.

LH: Indeed! Most interesting questions cannot be solved with pure logics. Nothing that is interesting can be solved this way. The same applies to the theories of Noam Chomsky and the linguistic turn. That is why I am so impatient when it comes to structuralism, or even poststructuralism: precisely the most interesting issues cannot be addressed by these theories. Self-contained logic in no way helps explain how something new emerges—when the elements are geometric, as it were, and the combination or structure of elements, meaning the topology of elements, is logical. So you're confronted with a tyrannical setup and no backdoor. It is a closed game whose combinations can be played out on the computer. Now you can get excited, or feel contented, that there are actually so many possible combinations that the computer could not cope with them anyway. But this would not change the fact that there is nothing new about the setup and that it cannot explain why interesting things are happening.

GAM: Let's speak about the term "intuition": it is quite frequently used in the context of Anschaulichkeit[6]. *In your book, you criticize the tendency to render things intuitive—you disagree with it. Why?*

LH: The concept of *Anschaulichkeit* is indeed difficult. We like to use it such that we don't need to explain in words what we mean. But whether something is clear to us has a lot to do with habit. After we have seen something a hundred times, it seems completely natural and we no longer question it. The same applies to instruments and machines. We can see how they function. In this sense, we may rely upon our visual understanding. However, in the case of electricity and information tech-

6   *Anschaulichkeit* is a German term that is difficult to translate, meaning the quality of being "easy to comprehend visually." When the term "anschaulich" is used in the German original it is usually translated as "visual" or "intuitively comprehensible."

LH: Ja genau, solange man den Regeln folgt, ist alles offen. Was aber nichts heißt, außer dass es logisch ist.

GAM: Dein Vorwurf ist aber, dass man gewisse Sachen damit nicht lösen kann.

LH: Ja, die meisten Fragestellungen lassen sich logisch nicht lösen. Alles was interessant ist, kann man damit nicht lösen. Das ist auch mit den Theorien von Noam Chomsky und dem Linguistic Turn so. Deswegen bin ich auch so ungeduldig mit dem Strukturalismus oder selbst dem Poststrukturalismus: genau die interessanten Fragestellungen lassen sich so nicht adressieren. Es lässt sich in einer abgeschlossenen Logik auf keine Weise erklären, wie etwas Neues entsteht. Wenn die Elemente sozusagen geometrisch sind und die Kombination oder die Struktur der Elemente, also die Topologie der Elemente, logisch ist. Damit erhältst Du direkt dieses tyrannische Setup ohne Ausweg. Es ist ein geschlossenes Spiel, das man kombinatorisch am Computer durchspielen kann. Jetzt kann man sich darüber ereifern oder sich damit beruhigen, dass es ja so viele Kombinationsmöglichkeiten gibt, dass der Computer damit ohnehin nicht fertig wird. Das ändert allerdings nichts daran, dass es in diesem Setup nichts Neues gibt und auch nicht erklärt werden kann, warum Interessantes passiert.

> Es lässt sich in einer abgeschlossenen Logik auf keine Weise erklären, wie etwas Neues entsteht.

GAM: Kommen wir zum Begriff der „Intuition": Dieser steht recht häufig in einem Zusammenhang mit der Anschaulichkeit. In Deinem Text gibt es viele Angriffe auf die Tendenz, Dinge anschaulich zu machen – das scheint Dir verkehrt zu sein. Warum?

LH: Der Begriff der Anschaulichkeit ist tatsächlich schwierig. Wir benutzen Anschaulichkeit gerne, um nicht viele Worte machen zu müssen. Deshalb hat anschaulich werden viel mit Gewohnheiten zu tun. Man findet etwas vollkommen natürlich, wenn man es hundertmal gesehen hat und stellt keine Fragen mehr. Bei Instrumenten und Maschinen ist das auch so. Man kann sehen, wie sie funktionieren. Darauf können wir uns mit unserer Anschauung verlassen. Bei dem elektrischen Strom und der Informationstechnologie ist das allerdings anders: Wir können nur sehen, dass sie funktionieren, nicht jedoch, wie sie funktionieren. Da sagt jeder mit der Sicherheit der Gewohnheit: Ist doch klar! Wenn ich den Knopf hier drücke, geht dort das Licht an. Aber zwischen dem Knopf und der Lampe bewegt sich nichts. Das ist überhaupt nicht anschaulich. Ich bekomme sogar einen elektrischen Schlag, wenn ich das offene Kabel anfasse. Das ist aus Sicht der mechanischen Anschaulichkeit reine Hexerei. Aber dennoch sagt jeder: „Ist doch vollkommen klar, wie das mit dem Strom funktioniert!" Wie ein Mobiltelefon funktioniert, ist auch nicht anschaulich, überhaupt nicht.

GAM: Aber wir haben trotzdem Arten und Weisen gefunden, das anschaulich zu machen.

LH: Nein, ich würde sagen, wir haben uns daran gewöhnt, darüber hinwegzusehen, dass es nicht anschaulich ist.

159

GAM: Aber beim Mobiltelefon ist es doch erstaunlich, wie das gelungen ist, diese Funktionen so verständlich zu machen: Obwohl das Gerät wahnsinnig kompliziert ist, kann es jeder bedienen. Ist das nicht anschaulich?

LH: Nein, es ist leicht zu bedienen, aber es ist nicht anschaulich. Anschaulich ist zum Beispiel das zeichnerische Verfahren zur Lösung von statischen Problemen, das Karl Culmann Mitte des 19. Jh. entwickelt hat und das wir heute noch alle als Architekten lernen. In der Anschauung versucht man mit einer Serie funktionaler Transformationen Probleme zu adressieren. Ein System funktioniert genau dann, wenn wir mit geometrischen Linien die Bewegungen der einzelnen Elemente nachzeichnen können. Das ist es, was ich streng genommen als anschaulich bezeichnen würde. Und in diesem Spiel der Anschauung kann ein Ding nicht erst ein Apfel und dann plötzlich eine Birne sein. Das wäre ein Klassifikationsfehler. Man kann dagegen aus dem Apfel Apfelmus machen, wenn man bestimmte Prozesse durchläuft. Man könnte ihn auch anmalen, oder maskieren. Aber die Dinge können nicht unmittelbar etwas anderes sein. Diese Kontinuität der Dinge, würde ich sagen, ist konstituierend für die Welt der Anschauung.

GAM: Aber das ist ja genau das, was die Informationstechnologie unterläuft.

LH: Ja. Allerdings wollen wir das nicht gerne wahrhaben. Deswegen versuchen wir immer die prinzipiell nicht-anschaulichen Phänomene der Informationstechnik mit einfachen Diagrammen zu veranschaulichen, um zu implizieren: „So ist es und nicht anders!" Man macht das so wie bei der „Sendung mit der Maus", die eindrücklich erklärt, wie zum Beispiel eine Stecknadel hergestellt wird. Da sieht man den Ablauf Schritt für Schritt, eine Maschine nach der anderen, und schließlich weiß man, wie das mit der Stecknadel funktioniert und es war anschaulich. Jetzt wird in der Informationstechnik zum Beispiel mit dem Programm Grasshopper genau dasselbe Spiel vorgeführt: sehr anschaulich und Schritt für Schritt. Mit dem Effekt, dass es Anfänger nutzen können und sofort „verstehen", weil sie nichts lernen müssen, weil sie Computer als die gewohnten Maschinen vorgestellt bekommen. Nun sind aber Computer keine Maschinen. Sie sind viel mächtiger als Maschinen und die Nutzer bleiben dumm.

GAM: Aber ist das so verkehrt, wenn man sagt: „Auf einer elementarsten Ebene besteht Informationstechnologie aus dem Verknüpfen von Werten und Operationen?"

LH: Das ist ja nicht anschaulich.

GAM: Aber Grasshopper macht es durch diese Boxen und Symbole anschaulich.

> Ein System funktioniert genau dann, wenn wir mit geometrischen Linien die Bewegungen der einzelnen Elemente nachzeichnen können. Das ist es, was ich streng genommen als anschaulich bezeichnen würde.

nology, this is different: we can only see that they function, but not how they function. Here the assurance of habit would cause anyone to say: "It's obvious that when I activate this switch here, the lamp over there goes on!" But no movement is registered between the switch and the lamp. What I see doesn't explain the phenomenon at all. If I touch an open cable, I will even experience an electrical shock. From the perspective of a mechanical, visual understanding, this is pure sorcery. But still, most would say: "It's totally obvious that electricity works that way!" The way a mobile phone works is not intuitively comprehensible either, not in the least.

GAM: But we have still found ways to make it intuitively comprehensible.

LH: No, I don't agree. I think we have become accustomed to overlooking that it is not intuitively comprehensible.

GAM: But with mobile telephones, it is pretty amazing how all of these functions have been made so easy to understand: although the device is incredibly complicated, anyone is capable of operating it. Isn't this intuitively comprehensible?

LH: No. It is intuitive to operate, but that doesn't make it intuitively comprehensible. An example of something intuitively comprehensible would be the drawing technique used to solve static problems developed by Karl Culmann in the mid-nineteenth century, which is still being taught to all of us architects today. When dealing with intuitive comprehension, we set out to address problems with a series of functional transformations. A system works precisely in that moment where we can trace the movements of individual elements with geometric lines. Strictly speaking, this is what I would call intuitive comprehensible. And in this game of intuitivity, something cannot first be an apple and then suddenly a pear. That would be a classification mistake. By contrast, you can make applesauce from the apple if certain processes are carried out. You could also paint it or disguise it. But things cannot actually become something else. I would say that this continuity of things is constitutive for the world of explanations that feel intuitive for us today.

GAM: But this is exactly what information technology undermines.

LH: Indeed. However, we don't really want to acknowledge it. This is why we use simple diagrams in an attempt to illustrate those information-technology phenomena that are principally non-intuitive in order to imply: "It's this way and no other!" This takes an approach like that of the children's television classic "Die Sendung mit der Maus" (The Program with the Mouse), where processes are explained in detail, such as how a stickpin is produced. You see the process step by step, one machine after another, and in the end you understand how a stickpin is made—and it was intuitively comprehensible. Now, let's say the program Grasshopper is used to present a similar process in the context of information technology: very visual and step by step. With the effect of beginners being able to use it and immediately "understand" what is going on since they don't have to learn anything, since computers have been introduced to them as being like the machines they are familiar with in these "intuitive" terms. But computers are not machines in that sense. They are much more powerful than those machines and the users remain ignorant.

GAM: But is it so wrong to say that on the most elementary level, information technology is made up of links between values and operations?

LH: There is nothing intuitively comprehensible about that.

GAM: But Grasshopper makes it visual with its boxes and symbols.

LH: Grasshopper uses transformations. You have boxes, which are objects. Then you have certain parameters or attributes, and these attributes are linked via arrows. Like this, the boxes can be transformed. You take a value and it is then linked—using a certain arithmetic, that is, a kind of transformation, which we call a function—with another value that has been assigned to a different object. If I then proceed to elevate a value, the other one changes, too: it becomes smaller or twice as large, and so on. This is mechanics. The problem is that we simply don't understand that this involves not mechanical processes with material objects but abstract operations on symbolized objects. Seen through the mechanical eyes of the material world, these operations can perform acts of magic! They simply go "ta-da"—no need to link anything.

GAM: So you consider Grasshopper to be a problematic tool, because it keeps the users in a state of ignorance. Yet can't we view this from an alternative perspective? By saying that the Grasshopper interface makes this relative complexity manageable in dealing with many different values and their effect on a geometric form—in a way that previous tools did not? Could it be that your polemic is incorrectly applied here? The program is actually trying to make it as easy as possible for as many people as possible to start programming.

LH: Using Grasshopper puts people on a fast track to becoming mechanics. This is a useful quality because it precisely mirrors the mechanical conception of the world that is depicted there. This is problematic when you consider that information technology is much more powerful than the mindset of the kind of non-symbolical mechanics to which Grasshopper users are being accustomed. This means that we are in danger of getting into great, uncontrolled mischief, because it is impossible to arrive at an understanding of what the computer

LH: Grasshopper verwendet Transformationen. Man hat Boxen, das sind Objekte, dann hat man bestimmte Parameter oder Attribute und diese Attribute werden über diese Pfeile, diese Boxen transformiert. Man nimmt einen Wert an und dieser wird dann über eine bestimmte Arithmetik also irgendeine Transformation, die wir Funktion nennen, verknüpft mit einem anderen Wert, der einem anderen Objekt zugewiesen wird. Wenn ich dann im Anschluss einen Wert höher mache, so verändert sich der andere: er wird kleiner oder doppelt so groß und so weiter. Das ist Mechanik. Das Problem ist, dass man dann eben nicht versteht, dass es ja nicht um mechanische Prozesse mit Objekten geht, sondern um die abstrakteren Operationen mit Symbolen. Diese Operationen können mechanisch zaubern! Die machen einfach „wupp", ohne dass man etwas verknüpft.

GAM: Du betrachtest Grasshopper also als ein problematisches Tool, weil es den User dumm hält. Kann man das nicht auch umgekehrt sehen, dass das Grasshopper Interface diese relative Komplexität vom Umgehen mit sehr vielen Werten und deren Auswirkung auf eine geometrische Form handhabbar macht, wie Werkzeuge davor noch nicht? Ist da nicht eigentlich Deine Polemik falsch angesetzt? Das Programm versucht ja, den Einstieg ins Programmieren möglichst vielen möglichst leicht zugänglich zu machen.

LH: Mit Grasshopper kann man sehr schnell Mechaniker werden. Dafür ist es auch gut, weil es exakt das mechanische Weltbild ist, das damit abgebildet wird. Das Problematische daran ist, dass die Informationstechnologie viel mächtiger ist als die Denkweise der Mechanik, die einem nahegelegt wird. Das heißt, man läuft Gefahr, großen, unkontrollierten Unfug zu machen, weil man keine Vorstellung davon bekommt, was der Computer eigentlich ist. Und der Schritt, wenn man einmal an dieser Stelle diesen unmittelbaren vermeintlichen Erfolg hat, dann ein anderes Denken zu kultivieren, der ist groß. Das Problem ist, dass man mit Grasshopper in keinster Weise zu verstehen lernt, was Computerdenken ist. Man lernt schnell, Maschinen zu bauen. Dass das anschaulich ist, dass das alten Vorstellungen von Intuition entspricht, ist vollkommen klar. Man macht es ja exakt so, wie man das gewohnt ist, mit jeder Mechanik.

GAM: Und was vergibt man sich?

LH: Man vergibt sich den Zugang zum zeitgemäßen Denken. Deswegen bin ich auch so polemisch. Es ist nicht nur so, dass das andere ein bisschen komplizierter ist, oder ein bisschen weniger anschaulich, es ist einfach ein anderes Denken. Die erforderliche Algebra ist einfach eine andere kulturelle Fertigkeit. Sehr leicht zu verstehen, wenn man es gewohnt ist, weil man es gelernt hat. Was Google zum Beispiel macht, kann man nicht mechanisch erklären. Das ist ja das absolut Faszinierende an Google, dass sie sich tatsächlich keine funktionale, anschauliche Vorstellung von dem machen, was sie indexieren und Google gerade deswegen funktioniert. Firmen dagegen, die sich Gedanken darüber machen, was sie informationstechnisch „abbilden" haben zunehmend Probleme. Yahoo, z.B., oder Microsoft. So kann man mit der Geschwindigkeit der Entwicklung unmöglich Schritt halten. Google macht diesen konzeptionellen Fehler präzise nicht. Die Mathematik dazu hat Markow 1913 formuliert. Die aus unserer Sicht für die Informationstechnologie zentralen mathematischen Theorien von De Morgan,

Boole, Dedekind, Riemann und dann über Markow zu Google: Das sind alles „Nicht-Anschaulichkeiten".

GAM: Ist die „Nicht-Anschaulichkeit" diesen Theorien inhärent, oder ist es noch nicht gelungen, sie anschaulich zu machen?

LH: Die Anschaulichkeit ist faktisch nicht mehr da. Alle Geschäftsmodelle, die heute funktionieren, alles was im Moment technologisch, in der Forschung und auch politisch von zunehmendem Interesse ist, ist einfach alles nicht mehr anschaulich. Technologisch und ökonomisch ist die Anschaulichkeit definitiv seit der „Internet-Bubble" im Jahr 2000 nicht mehr dominant. Seitdem gibt es soziale Medien und die Finanzierung ist in diese Technologien geflossen – das war ein definitiver technologischer Shift aus der Anschaulichkeit heraus. Mit dem PC und mit Microsoft waren die Dinge noch anschaulich, da war klar: die Applikation Word ersetzt eine Schreibmaschine, und so weiter. Das war eine inhaltliche Imitation mechanischer Prozesse. Das alles ist nicht mehr primär.

Natürlich nützt es nichts, auf der Abstraktion der Algebra zu bleiben. Das tun ja auch die sozialen Medien oder die Smartphones nicht. Dieses Operieren im Abstrakten muss sichtbar und attraktiv gemacht werden. Aber das, wenn man so will, mechanische Handwerk ist jetzt nachgelagert. Die Konsistenz dieser neuen Artefakte ist nicht mehr anschaulich. Dass man dann für einen konkreten Fall aus dieser „nicht-anschaulichen" algebraischen Indexstruktur, aus dieser symbolischen Struktur dann für einen konkreten Fall eine konkrete Anschaulichkeit als Antwort erzeugt ist ja vollkommen klar. Aber wenn dann eine andere Frage gestellt wird, erhält man eine andere Anschaulichkeit. Diese Anschaulichkeiten, die da gerendert werden, haben keine anschauliche Konsistenz im kartesischen Sinn. Es ist nicht möglich vom einen auf das andere zu schließen – es gibt keinen Transfer. Es existiert keine Maschinerie zwischen dem einen Artefakt und dem anderen.

GAM: Was bewirkt diese Situation für die Intuition?

LH: Die verschiebt sich. Der Begriff der Intuition grenzt sich ja immer gegen das ab, was offensichtlich gegeben ist oder explizit ist. Wenn ich also im „Maschinischen" bin, ist die Intuition das, wie ich mit Maschinen umgehe, damit ich schließlich das tun kann, was die Maschinen nicht können. Um das wirklich meisterhaft zu machen, muss ich als Ingenieur sehr viele Dinge geschickt kombinieren. Damit mir das gelingt, brauche ich Intuition. Das wird dann gefeiert – das sind die Genies, die großen Erfinder oder die Künstler in dieser Zeit. Dieses Geschick, funktionale Balancen aufzuspüren, lernten wir in den aufkommenden pädagogischen Systemen wie z.B. den Spielgaben von Fröbel. Ich glaube, das ist ein Begriff von Intuition, dem wir heute nachtrauern.

GAM: Wie wird der Begriff der Intuition jetzt durch die Informationstechnologie transformiert?

LH: Ich würde sagen, dass man auch beim Codieren, also im Kombinieren von Elementen auf einer symbolischen, algebraischen Ebene so etwas wie Intuition finden kann. Aber es ist etwas ganz anderes als bei Fröbel. Bei Fröbel ging es darum, Balancen der Natürlichkeit, der Farben, der Kräfte und so weiter zu erfühlen. Das heißt, die Intuition war quasi nach Innen gerichtet. Beim Codieren ist es allerdings so, dass man nichts hat als die

actually is. And once someone has reached the point of experiencing the immediate success purported by Grasshopper, it is difficult to take a step toward cultivating a different way of thinking. The problem is that when using Grasshopper we certainly cannot learn to understand how to think and reason with computers. It is easy to learn how to build machines. And it goes without saying that this is easily comprehensible, that it corresponds to the old notions of intuition. We do it exactly as we are used to doing with any kind of non-symbolical mechanics.

GAM: And what do we forfeit here?

LH: We forfeit access to a manner of thinking that is appropriate to our times. This is also why I am so polemic. Not only is the other a bit more complicated, or a bit less intuitive; it is an altogether different way of thinking, plain and simple. The algebra required is basically a different cultural skill. Very easy to understand if you are familiar with it, because it was taught to you. What Google does, for example, cannot be explained with mechanics. That is what is so absolutely fascinating about Google: they do not actually think in a functional, intuitively comprehensible manner about what they index, and it is precisely because of this that Google is successful. By contrast, companies that focus on what it is their information-technology represents, what their data means, are increasingly encountering problems. Yahoo or Microsoft, for example. It is impossible to keep pace with the speed of development in this way. Google expressly avoids making this conceptual mistake. In 1913 Andrey Markov formulated the related mathematics. The central mathematical theories which, in our view, are pivotal to information technology, those of Boole, Dedekind, Riemann, and then by way of Markov to Google—all of them challenge our accustomed notion of intuitivity.

GAM: Is it an inherent quality of these theories that no adequate visual representations of them have been found, or has just no one yet been able to visualize them?

LH: This possibilty to intuitively understand what they are about is de facto no longer there. All business models that are successful today—everything that is presently of growing interest in technology, in research, and in politics—is simply no longer intuitively comprehensible. In terms of technology and economics, an understanding of "Anschaulichkeit" as we are accustomed to has definitively lost significance since the "Internet bubble" in the year 2000. Since then social media have been on the rise and funding has flowed into these technologies, which was definitely a technological shift away. With the PC and Microsoft, things were still understandable in our inherited and accustomed manner; it was clear that the application Word replaced the typewriter, and so forth. It was a content-related imitation of mechanical processes. But none of this is of primary focus today.

Of course it doesn't make sense to remain on the abstraction level of algebra. Neither social media nor smartphones do so. Such operating in abstract realms must be rendered visible and attractive. But, as it were, the mechanical craftsmanship required for this step is now secondary. The consistency of these new artifacts is no longer in what is intuitively graspable of them. It goes without saying that for a concrete case of application, we need to make sense of these non-intuitive algebraic index structures by producing one of the many possible concrete visual representation its abstract symbols allow for. But when a different question is asked, a different visual representation may be given. Being rendered, the visual representations are devoid of consistency in a Cartesian sense. It is not possible to make inferences from one artifact to the next—there's no immediate transfer between them. No machinery exists between one artifact and another.

GAM: What impact does this situation have on the notion of intuition?

LH: It has shifted. The term intuition always serves, initially, to establish a contrast to those things that are self-evident or explicit. So when I am getting accustomed to "the world of machines," intuition signifies how I must deal with machines, so that I may ultimately achieve what machines cannot. In order to do this in a truly masterful way, I must cleverly combine many things in my role as engineer. To succeed in this, I need to interiorize how machines are dealt with. Retrospectively, this is then celebrated—these are the geniuses, the great inventors, or the artists of our time. Today, we have all learned the skills of divining functional balances that the pioneers in the "world of machines" were so good at through the emerging pedagogical systems, for example, the *Spielgaben* (toy gifts) by Fröbel. It seems to me that this is a concept of intuition that we are actually mourning today.

GAM: How has this concept of intuition been transformed in recent times through information technology?

LH: I would say that something like intuition can also be found in coding, that is in combining elements on a symbolic, algebraic level. But this is totally different than the case of Fröbel. Friedrich Fröbel was concerned with sensing balances of nature, color, forces, et cetera. This means that intuition was pretty much focused toward the inside. With codification, however, we only have the symbolic elements, so intuition would be associated with the way I expose myself to the outside. I am more of a player/actor than an inventor. It's in this inversion that we would have to search for intuition, today, similar to the cultural constellation in the Renaissance.

GAM: Certain phenomena have really only been made accessible to our senses through the computer. We can equip our

symbolischen Elemente, und Intuition wäre dann an die Art und Weise gekoppelt, wie ich mich nach Außen exponiere. Ich bin eher Akteur/Schauspieler als Erfinder. In dieser Inversion müsste man heute nach der Intuition suchen. Verwandt der kulturellen Konstellation in der Renaissance.

GAM: Gewisse Phänomene sind ja überhaupt erst durch den Computer der Anschauung zugänglich gemacht worden. Wir können unsere Umwelt mit Sensoren bestücken und dadurch Sachen messen und visualisieren, die wir sonst gar nicht sehen würden. Auf diese Weise können wir auch für neue Phänomene Intuition entwickeln.

LH: Ja, das ist ja genau der Fröbel-Ansatz: die neuen Dinge über das Balancieren vertraut machen. Diese pädagogische Entwicklung geht doch einher mit z.B. dem Röntgenapparat, mit dem man auf einmal durch die Leute durchgucken konnte. Das gleiche mit der Mikroskopie, der Fotografie und so weiter. Es ist ja mit jeder Technologie so, dass man die Möglichkeiten dessen, was man wahrnehmen kann, erweitert.

> Die Indexsysteme, die uns die Algebra liefert, die sind ja alle „nicht-spezifisch" … Man kann sie gar nicht analysieren, respektive in Balancen bringen! Das ist so wie bei den Quanten: sobald ich das Quantum messe, ist es tot, weil ich dann in das probabilistische Gefüge eingreife.

GAM: Genau. Die digitalen Medien sind aber nicht nur in der Lage, Dinge sichtbar zu machen, die wir irgendwo gemessen haben, sondern auch solche, die wir uns nur ausdenken. Parametric Design ist ein neues Entwurfswerkzeug, das uns Dinge entwickeln lässt, für die wir nicht diese durch das Spielen mit Fröbel-Bauklötzen angelegte Intuition besitzen. Die Frage ist jetzt: Können wir auch auf diese generativen Methoden unsere Intuition anwenden?

LH: Also man hätte das ja gerne. Dann wäre die technische Welt ja so schön einfach. Dann würde man die nach innen trainierte Intuition direkt nach außen stülpen. Das wäre genau die vorhin angeprangerte Tyrannei. Nein, wir brauchen eine neue Intuition nach außen. Und sie wird sich nicht in den verinnerlichten Balancen der Prozessdynamiken orientieren, sondern in der Probabilistik der Quantenphänomene. Die Indexsysteme, die uns die Algebra liefert, die sind ja alle „nicht-spezifisch" … Man kann sie gar nicht analysieren, respektive in Balancen bringen! Das ist so wie bei den Quanten: sobald ich das Quantum messe, ist es tot, weil ich dann in das probabilistische Gefüge eingreife. Bei Google ist das auch so. Ich kann ja nicht einfach nur gucken, was da ist. Sobald ich eine Frage stelle, habe ich eingegriffen. Dann ist das Ding da, genauso wie ich gefragt habe. Das heißt, die Herausforderung wird sein, ‚modellieren' zu lernen vor jedem Modell, beziehungsweise zu akzeptieren, dass Dinge in einem kontinuierlichen Fluss sind.

GAM: Aber genau für Dinge, die in einem kontinuierlichen Fluss sind, ist ja die Intuition das, was uns naturgegeben ist, um damit umzugehen.

LH: Ich würde aus den beschriebenen Gründen bezweifeln, erstens, dass Intuition naturgegeben ist und zweitens, dass unser heutiger Begriff von Intuition in der Lage ist, mit diesem Fluss umzugehen. Wir sind schlichtweg überfordert. Wir müssen diese Dinge quasi auf Quanten-Level im Fluss halten können und ab und an nachsehen, was man da hat: sich vergewissern, wie diese Indexstrukturen sind und damit leben, dass man das gar nicht genau zu wissen braucht, weil wir sowieso überversorgt sind mit diesen Informationen. Das ist genau das, was wir jetzt kultivieren. Die jungen Leute machen das so.

GAM: Nehmen wir an, dass sich eine neue Form von Intuition in Bezug auf Phänomene wie Google, etc. herausbildet, welche die jetzige Generation als Kulturtechnik implizit lernt. Du hast das jetzt als etwas Positives dargestellt, oder? Gleichzeitig liefert man sich ja auch damit aus, in diesem Fall an Google. Findest Du es nicht problematisch, dass wir von Google konditioniert werden in der Art und Weise, wie wir Informationen suchen?

LH: Ich bin nicht pessimistisch an der Stelle. Es könnte ein Machtproblem sein, aber eigentlich nicht. Google steht nicht so stabil da wie ein Unternehmen, das dezidiert Software oder sogar Maschinen verkauft. Wenn Google sich schlecht benimmt, geht das sehr schnell. Sehr viel schneller als wir das noch von Microsoft oder Nokia kennen. Es gibt viele, viele andere Firmen, die nur einen Klick entfernt sind und darauf warten, schnell viele Kunden zu bekommen.

> Das heißt, Du hast z.B. einen Satz von Modellen, oder besser noch Fragmente von Modellen, und je nachdem welche Frage Du stellst, werden diese Modelle neu geclustert. Und Du kannst nicht wirklich vorhersagen, was da passiert.

GAM: Am Ende von EigenArchitecture *kommst Du auf sogenannte „Self-Organizing Maps" (SOMs) zu sprechen. Du nennst sie die fortschrittlichsten und vielversprechendsten Algorithmen. Kannst Du kurz erklären, was es damit auf sich hat?*

LH: Das ist der einzige Algorithmus, den ich zur Zeit kenne – obwohl auch er in der Literatur nur anschaulich erklärt wird – bei dem man ohne Anschaulichkeit operieren und modellieren kann. Das heißt, Du hast z.B. einen Satz von Modellen, oder besser noch Fragmente von Modellen, und je nachdem welche Frage Du stellst, werden diese Modelle neu geclustert. Und Du kannst nicht wirklich vorhersagen, was da passiert. SOMs sind wohl auch eine Verallgemeinerung von dem, was Google macht. Während Google mit spezifischen Parametern für die Berechnung der Nachbarschaften agiert, braucht man bei SOMs diese Parameter nicht einmal zu spezifizieren. Das ist jedenfalls unsere Hypothese. Du steckst einfach Dinge rein und dann hilft dir der Algorithmus für den nächsten Schritt weiter. Man muss seine architektonischen Entwürfe in ein Kontinuum setzten, man muss einfach permanent Fragen stellen, dann kommt man weiter.

GAM: Was sind die Fragestellungen, die damit anders und besser gelöst werden können als mit, sagen wir einmal, Grasshopper?

environment with sensors so as to measure and visualize aspects of it that would otherwise be undetectable for us. In this way we can gradually develop an intuition for new phenomena.

LH: Yes, this is exactly the approach taken by Fröbel: familiarizing oneself with new things through an act of balancing. This pedagogical development of course goes hand in hand with, for example, the X-ray machine, which all of a sudden made it possible to look through people. The same applies to the microscope, to photography, and so forth. Any given technology will expand the potentialities of perception.

GAM: Exactly. But digital media are capable of making visible not only the things that we have measured somewhere, but also those that we conceptualize. Parametric design is a new design tool that allows us to develop things for which we do not possess an intuition of the kind facilitated by playing with Fröbel building blocks. So the question now arises: Can we also apply our conventional intuition to these generative methods?

LH: At first glance, that seems desirable. Then the technical world would be so nice and easy. Then we would directly invert the inward-trained intuition outward. But that would tie into the tyranny denounced above. No, we need a new intuition that is trained outward. And it will not be oriented to the internalized balances of processual dynamics, but rather to the probabilism of quantum phenomena. The index systems that algebra provides to us are really all "non-specific" … They are impossible to analyze, much less to bring into balance! It's similar to the quanta: as soon as I measure a quantum, it is dead, because I have infringed on its probabilistic texture. It's the same way with Google. I can't just look to see what's there. As soon as I ask a question, I have intervened: the thing appears, just as I had requested. This means that the challenge will lie in learning to "model" before any model, or rather, in accepting that things are constantly in flux.

GAM: But intuition is an inherent way to deal with things that are constantly in flux.

LH: For reasons already mentioned, I would cast doubt on whether, first, intuition is inherently-given and, second, today's conception of intuition is in a position to deal with this flux. We are downright overwhelmed. We basically have to keep these things in flux on a quantum level and then keep an eye on what we are dealing with: checking out how the index structures work and learning to live with the fact that on a non-structural level, we really don't need to know all the details because we are already oversaturated with information. This is what we are cultivating nowadays. The young generation already takes this approach.

GAM: Let's assume that a new form of intuition evolves in relation to phenomena like Google, et cetera, which the present

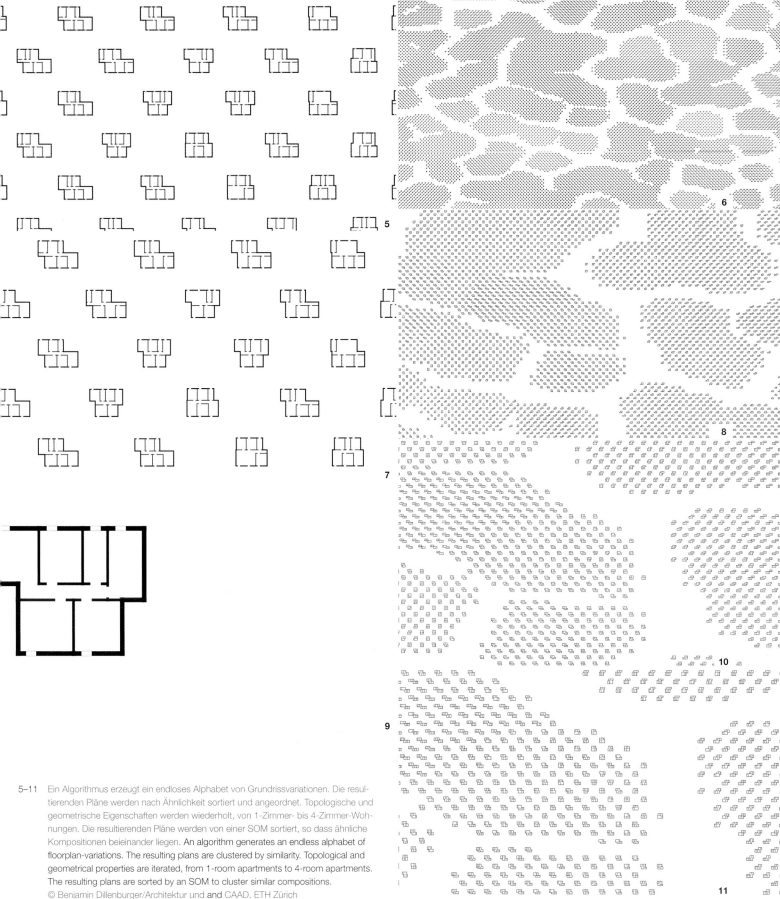

5–11 Ein Algorithmus erzeugt ein endloses Alphabet von Grundrissvariationen. Die resultierenden Pläne werden nach Ähnlichkeit sortiert und angeordnet. Topologische und geometrische Eigenschaften werden wiederholt, von 1-Zimmer- bis 4-Zimmer-Wohnungen. Die resultierenden Pläne werden von einer SOM sortiert, so dass ähnliche Kompositionen beieinander liegen. An algorithm generates an endless alphabet of floorplan-variations. The resulting plans are clustered by similarity. Topological and geometrical properties are iterated, from 1-room apartments to 4-room apartments. The resulting plans are sorted by an SOM to cluster similar compositions.

LH: Du kannst deine Entwürfe wirklich offen halten. Du musst nicht vorher den Raum der Möglichkeiten spezifizieren. Du kannst dich differenzierter und jenseits der Raster (ob sie etwas transformiert sind oder nicht, ist eigentlich egal) bewegen. Du kannst die Übersicht behalten, ohne dich mit Rastern oder Regeln absichern zu müssen und kommst gerade deshalb „weiter" als jede Optimierung. Was jetzt Benjamin Dillenburger zum Beispiel macht (Abb. 2–11). Du hast 5.000 oder besser noch 5 Millionen verschiedene Grundrisse, und Du kannst dennoch die Übersicht behalten und davon lernen. Das heißt, Du fängst an, etwas zu zeichnen, und kriegst dann die Clusterung dieser Grundrisse entsprechend deiner aktuellen Zeichnung und zwar so, dass das, was Du zeichnest, ein Cluster ist, und dann die anderen sechs (oder zwölf, das kannst du einstellen) Cluster von Grundrissen, jeweils die maximale gegenseitige Differenz zu sich haben und zu der Zeichnung, die du gerade machst. Bei Photoshop kennst Du das vielleicht: Du hast da ein Bild und verschiedene Farbvarianten darum herum – so kannst Du das entsprechend mit den Modellen machen. Das Interessante ist, die Modelle werden vollkommen hybrid sein. Du hast endlos viele Parameter, keine spezifische Ordnung. Du packst da alle Grundrisse rein, hast dann beliebig viele Parameter und die Cluster folgen dann nicht spezifischen Parametern, sondern können als Neuerfindungen von Parametern, als neue Begriffe gelesen werden. Das heißt, Du zeichnest etwas, und dann bietet Dir das System sechs neue Erfindungen für den nächsten Schritt für deinen Entwurf an.

GAM: Etwa so, wie man aus Texten automatisch „Wordmaps" mit den wichtigsten Wörtern generieren kann?

LH: Ja, wobei die Wordmaps ja auf einer einfachen Zählung basieren. Eine SOM kannst Du z.B. mit 5.000 kleinen Figuren füttern. Lass sie Dir für ein Experiment in Form, Farbe, Größe zufällig generieren. Jedes Pixel der SOM ist in diesem einfachen Experiment eine dieser Figuren. Jetzt setzt Du eine bestimmte Figur – die an der Du gerade arbeitest – in den Mittelpunkt der Map. Dann wird sich die ganze Map bezüglich dieses Mittelpunktes so in eine bestimmte Anzahl von Clustern sortieren, dass diese Cluster nach innen so homogen wie möglich sind, aber zu einander in einem maximalen Kontrast stehen. Und diese Cluster, das kann man sehr deutlich sehen, organisieren sich weder an der Größe, noch an der Farbe, oder der Anzahl der Kanten, es ist nichts von dem …

GAM: … was man erwarten würde?

LH: Ja, es sind immer spezifische Kombinationen aus allen verfügbaren Parametern, die die Eigenart der Cluster bilden. Das heißt, was dann angeboten wird, sind sechs neue Konzepte, die aus dem gesamten Erfahrungshorizont angeboten werden relativ zu dem, was Du gerade als Konzept formulierst.

GAM: Wenn man jetzt mit solchen Tools arbeitet und beim Entwerfen diese 5.000 Grundrisse auf Abruf im Hintergrund hat, die einem kontextbezogen angeboten werden, als Alternativen oder als Orientierung – entwickelt man dann eine neue Form von Intuition für Grundrissgestaltung?

LH: Ja, das kann man erwarten. Und diese Art, sich im Unbekannten zu bewegen ist gar nicht so fremd, wie man meinen möchte. Wenn wir z.B.

generation implicitly acquires as a cultural technique. You just characterized that as something positive, didn't you? At the same time, you are surrendering yourself, in this case, to Google. Don't you find it problematic that we are conditioned by Google in the way we search for information?

LH: When it comes to this issue, I am not pessimistic. Though it could potentially present a power issue, it actually doesn't. Google doesn't enjoy the stable position of companies that explicitly sell software or even machines. If Google displays poor conduct, the decline will be quick. Much quicker even than we saw happen with Microsoft or Nokia. There are many, many other companies that are but a click away and that are just waiting to acquire many customers very quickly.

GAM: At the end of EigenArchitecture *you bring up the topic of Self-Organizing Maps (SOMs). You call them the most advanced and promising algorithms. Could you briefly explain what you mean by this?*

LH: This is the only algorithm that I am presently familiar with—though it, too, is only explained in a manner that corresponds to our old notion of intuition in literature—where we can actually work and model without making the presumptions that are necessary to maintain such a sense of intuitivity. This means that you for instance have a set of models or, even better, fragments of models; depending on the questions you ask, the models become newly clustered. And you cannot really tell in advance what is going to happen. SOMs basically reflect a generalization of the Google approach. While Google works with specific parameters for calculating neighborhoods, in the case of SOMs it is not even necessary to specify such parameters. This is our hypothesis, at any rate. You simply put things in and then the algorithm helps you get to the next step. We have to position our architectural designs in a continuum; we just have to continually ask questions, and then we will make progress.

GAM: Which questions can be better solved this way than, let's say, with Grasshopper?

LH: You can really keep your designs open. You don't need to specify the space of potentiality ahead of time. You can operate in a more differentiated manner and beyond the grids (whether they are somewhat transformed or not really doesn't matter). You can maintain an overview without having to use grids or rules to secure your position, and for precisely this reason you can go "further" than any optimization. This is actually what Benjamin Dillenburger is doing (see figs. 2–11): you have five thousand or, even better, five million different floor plans, but you can still keep track of them and learn from them. This means that you start drafting and are then shown the clustering of these floor plans in accordance with your current drawing. So that which you are drafting is one cluster, and then there are six (or twelve, since this is a configurable setting) other clusters of floor plans that each display the maximal reciprocal margin to each other and to the drawing that you are currently working on. Perhaps you are familiar with this from Photoshop: you have an image and some color variants off to the side. And this is how it works with the models as well. The interesting thing is that the models will be totally hybrid. You have an endless number of parameters and no specific regime. You include all the floor plans, which gives you any number of parameters; and then the clusters build out according to non-specified parameters. You can read each cluster as reinvention its own parametrization, and in that sense, as emergent new "concepts". In other words: you draw something, and then the system offers you six new creations for the next step in your design process.

GAM: Similar to using texts to automatically generate "wordmaps" with the most important words?

LH: Yes, although wordmaps are actually based on a simple count. You can feed five thousand little figures to an SOM, for example—have them randomly generated for an experiment in form, color, size. Each pixel of the SOM is one of these figures in this simple experiment. Now you place a certain figure—the one you are currently working on—at the center of the map. Based on this center point, the entire map will be sorted into a certain number of clusters, with the clusters being as homogenous as possible toward the inside while contrasting with each other to a maximum. And these clusters—this is very apparent—are not organized according to size or color or number of edges. It is nothing like …

GAM: …one might expect?

LH: Correct. The unique nature of the clusters always results from specific combinations of all available parameters. This means that six new concepts are presented, which are offered from the entire horizon of experience in relation to the concepts you are currently drafting.

GAM: When we start working with such tools and during the design process have these five thousand floor plans on call in the background, offered according to context as alternatives or as orientation—do we develop a new form of intuition for floor-plan design?

LH: Yes, this is to be expected. And this way of navigating uncharted waters is not as foreign as one might think. For example, when taking a week-long excursion with students, even just five years ago we had to distribute maps, schedules, and what not. Today this is no longer necessary. All the students need is GPS access, a smartphone, and they must make sure to have a SIM card that functions locally for Internet access—we can organize everything from there. This type of navigation

mit Studierenden eine Woche auf eine Exkursion fahren, dann war das noch vor fünf Jahren so, dass man allen Leuten Karten, Zeitplan etc. verteilen musste. Das braucht man heute alles nicht mehr. Die müssen einfach alle ein GPS, ein Smartphone haben, die müssen sehen, dass sie an dem Ort eine Simkarte haben, für den Zugang zum Internet und ab da organisieren wir uns. Diese Art von Navigation (Smartphone, GPS, usw.) ist das neue Entwerfen. Du brauchst es nicht mehr auf einer Karte vorher zu verzeichnen, Du bewegst Dich in den Dingen, die passieren. Du bist viel schneller, viel anpassungsfähiger. Und Du weißt nicht warum. Es gibt auch gar keine Referenz mehr. Du bist tatsächlich viel schneller als das Optimum.

GAM: (lacht) Das wäre ein sehr schöner Schlusssatz.
LH: Das ist jedenfalls das, was wir uns versprechen. Du bist schneller, weil Du nicht mehr wissen willst, warum.

GAM: Nicht wissen warum: damit sind wir dann auch wieder in der Nähe der Intuition, oder?
LH: Das ist die neue Intuition. Aber die ist ganz anders gelagert als das, was wir so naturalisieren als geniale Intuition. Die Intuition heute ist eher so etwas wie eine Abstraktion vom Handwerk. Das Handwerk ist explizit. Die Intuition ist implizit. Mit dem Handwerk erzeugt man immer ein Ding. Von Genies erwartet man dagegen eher, dass sie nichts tun. Sie können einfach nur genial sein. Einem Handwerker verzeiht man dagegen nicht, wenn er nicht gut arbeitet und die Dinge nicht richtig macht. Deswegen hat das, was ich jetzt unter dieser neuen Intuition verstehen würde, viel mit Handwerk zu tun. Man muss schon gut navigieren können, sonst säuft man ab in den vielen Daten, verirrt sich und so weiter.

GAM: Wie weit muss man auch selber Hand anlegen können, um quasi eben der mündige Nutzer zu sein?
LH: Die Algorithmen braucht man nicht selbst zu programmieren. Aber man sollte auf der neuen Abstraktionsebene denken und sich bewegen lernen. Was im Übrigen nur für uns Alte kompliziert ist. Meine Kinder machen das ganz intuitiv. Wir beklagen uns noch über die vielen falschen Informationen im Internet – das interessiert die überhaupt nicht. Für die ist vollkommen klar, dass sie sich nicht verlassen können auf das, was da steht. Es ist eine altmodische Vorstellung, dass irgendwo eine Referenz ist, auf die man sich beziehen kann, wie in einem Lexikon zum Beispiel. So sehe ich das mit meinen Kindern, die jetzt auch schon über 20 sind …

> Das Handwerk ist explizit. Die Intuition ist implizit. Mit dem Handwerk erzeugt man immer ein Ding. Von Genies erwartet man dagegen eher, dass sie nichts tun. Sie können einfach nur genial sein. Einem Handwerker verzeiht man dagegen nicht, wenn er nicht gut arbeitet und die Dinge nicht richtig macht.

GAM: Die wissen, dass man sich auf nichts verlassen kann …

LH: Nicht ganz. Sie verlassen sich zwar nicht auf externe Referenzen, aber auf irgendetwas müssen sie sich ja verlassen. Bei ihnen ist es die prinzipielle Operationalität. Sie brauchen einfach permanent das Internet und ihr Smartphone. Sie wissen, dass wenn diese Verfügbarkeit da ist, dass man schon zurechtkommt, wenn man navigieren kann. Dass man schneller zurechtkommt, als wenn man versuchen würde zu verstehen, was da wirklich steht. Natürlich ist es interessant, wie z.B. Google funktioniert, aber um es zu gebrauchen, muss ich die Algorithmen nicht verstehen. Man muss ja auch nicht die Mechanik eines Autos verstehen, damit man fahren kann. Das ist nicht das Problem. Wichtiger sind die Denkweisen. Ich bin sehr sicher, dass die Denkweise der jungen Generation heute adäquat zu dieser Welt ist und sie die richtige Intuition haben.

GAM: Autos gibt es ja jetzt schon einige Jahre und auch zum Autofahren entwickelt man eine spezifische Intuition. Google gibt es jetzt gerade mal fünfzehn Jahre oder so und es hat sich in der Zeit ständig gewandelt. Ist jetzt das, wofür wir unsere Intuition entwickeln, etwas Instabiles?

LH: Angst vor der Instabilität entsteht nur dann, wenn die Begriffe, mit denen man operiert, nicht abstrakt genug sind. Wenn etwas zu schnell geht, ist man nicht abstrakt genug. Wenn etwas zu divers ist, muss man abstrakter denken und dann wird es wieder stabil. Die Prozesse, von denen wir da jetzt reden ändern sich vielleicht in 100 Jahren. Auch der Computer wird sich in absehbarer Zeit nicht ändern.

> Natürlich ist es interessant, wie z.B. Google funktioniert, aber um es zu gebrauchen, muss ich die Algorithmen nicht verstehen. Man muss ja auch nicht die Mechanik eines Autos verstehen, damit man fahren kann.

GAM: Das Prinzipielle am Computer hat schon Konrad Zuse verstanden, aber was jetzt dazu gekommen ist, ist diese unglaubliche Geschwindigkeitssteigerung, die alle möglichen qualitativen Änderungen ermöglicht …

LH: Immer darauf zu stieren, dass die Computer immer schneller werden ist Quatsch! Im Gegenteil: Sie sind immer zu langsam! Das ist auch sehr konstant, Computer sind eigentlich konstant zu langsam.

GAM: Aber dass sie schon schneller geworden sind, das interessiert dich doch auch, im Hinblick darauf, dass man schon sagen kann, was man dann in fünf Jahren damit machen kann.

LH: Ja, aber alle Prognosen sind ja falsch. Das ist ja das Fantastische an der ganzen Geschichte. Die sagen immer nur, alles geht schneller, aber die sind nur richtig in der Prognose, dass die Computer schneller werden. Die sind immer falsch in der Prognose, was man damit machen wird. Und das interessiert uns doch! Das Interessante ist: man weiß nicht, was man machen will, aber man weiß, dass man nicht weiß, was man damit machen will. Das ist eine gute Nachricht für Architekten und für deren Intuition.

(smartphone, GPS, etc.) reflects the new design. You no longer need to first draw a map, for you move based on the things that happen. You are much quicker, much more adaptable. And you don't know why. There is no longer a particular point of reference. You are in fact much quicker than any optimum.

GAM: (laughs) That would be a great concluding sentence.

LH: At any rate, that is what we tell ourselves. You are quicker because you no longer want to know why.

GAM: Not knowing why—this once again brings us close to intuition, doesn't it?

LH: This is the new intuition. But it is of a different character than that which we naturalize as ingenious intuition. Today, intuition is something more like an abstraction of craftsmanship. Craftsmanship is explicit. Intuition is implicit. Craftsmanship is used to generate something. Geniuses are rather expected to do nothing. They can simply be ingenious. Yet it is not permitted for a craftsman to not work well or not do things right. This is why what we call "new intuition" is closely associated with craftsmanship. You have to be able to aptly navigate the waters, otherwise you will drown or get lost in the wealth of data.

GAM: To what extent must we be able to understand or customize these tools in order be competent users?

LH: It is not necessary to program the algorithms oneself. But you should be capable of thinking and willing to learn to move on the new level of abstraction. Which, by the way, is only complicated for us old ones. My children already do this completely intuitively. While we're still complaining about all of the inaccurate information on the Internet, they don't even care. To them, it's totally obvious that no one can trust what they read there. It is an old-fashioned idea that somewhere there has to be a reference to which we can point, such as a dictionary. I've noticed this in watching my children, who are now over twenty …

GAM: They are aware that we can't rely on anything …

LH: Not really. They may not rely on external references, but they must be able to rely on something. For them, this means a state of being principally operational. They need to be permanently connected to the Internet and their smartphone. They know that if this accessibility is ensured, then they will find their way if they have developed their ability to navigate—that they can manage better if they don't try to understand what is actually going on with the schemata available from another technical reality. Of course it would be interesting to know how Google works, as an example—but to build out an intuition for it (not an understanding of it), it is not necessary to understand the algorithms. You don't need to understand the mechanics of a car to be able to drive it. So that's not the problem. The mindset is more important here. I'm very convinced that the mindset of today's younger generation is suitable to this world and that they are developing the right intuition.

GAM: Cars have of course been around for quite a few years now, and we have developed a specific intuition for driving them. Google has only been here for about fifteen years or so, and during that time it has been subject to constant change. Are the things to which our intuition is becoming attuned actually instable?

LH: Fear of instability arises only if the concepts with which we operate are not abstract enough. If something is going too fast, then we are not abstract enough. If something is too diverse, then we must think more abstractly and it will stabilize again. The processes we are discussing here will change maybe every hundred years. Even the computer will not really be changing in the foreseeable future.

GAM: The basic principles of the computer were already comprehended by Konrad Zuse, but the new aspects, this unbelievable increase in speed, which makes so many different qualitative changes possible …

LH: This continual focus on how computers keep accelerating in speed is nonsense! It is quite the opposite: they are always too slow! This is also a constant: computers are in fact always too slow.

GAM: But the fact that they have become faster, this must interest you as well, considering that we can anticipate now what we will be able to do with them in five years.

LH: That's true, but all of the prognoses are wrong. That is what is so amazing about the whole thing. People are always saying that everything is getting faster, but they are only right in predicting that computers will get faster. They are always wrong in predicting what we will be able to do with them. And this would be of interest to us! The fascinating part is: we don't know what we want to do, but we do know that we don't know what we want to use them for. This is good news for architects and their intuition. And one thing is for sure: computers will be too slow. What more could you want? It's something stable to be relied on! (*laughs*)

Translation Dawn Michelle d'Atri

Und man weiß auf jeden Fall, dass Computer zu langsam sein werden. Was willst Du mehr, ist doch sehr stabil?! (*lacht*)

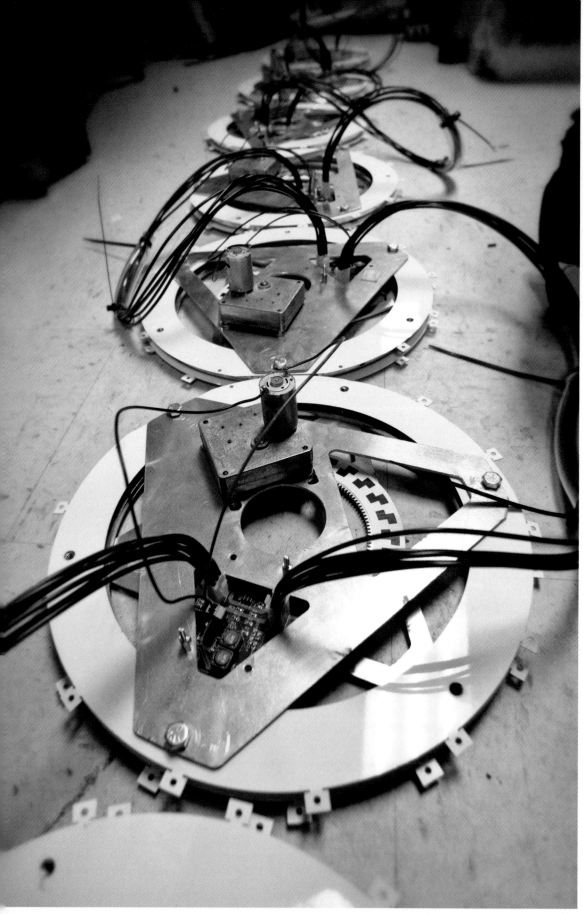

Decibot, 2009 © Skylar Tibbits mit dem with the Center for Bits and Atoms, MIT

Decibot, 2009 © Skylar Tibbits **mit dem** with the Center for Bits and Atoms, MIT

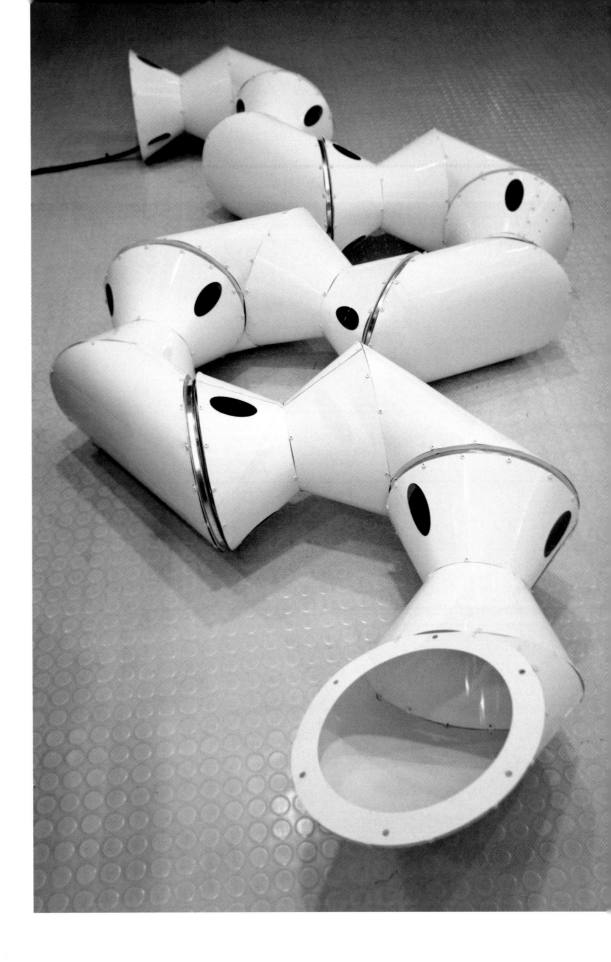

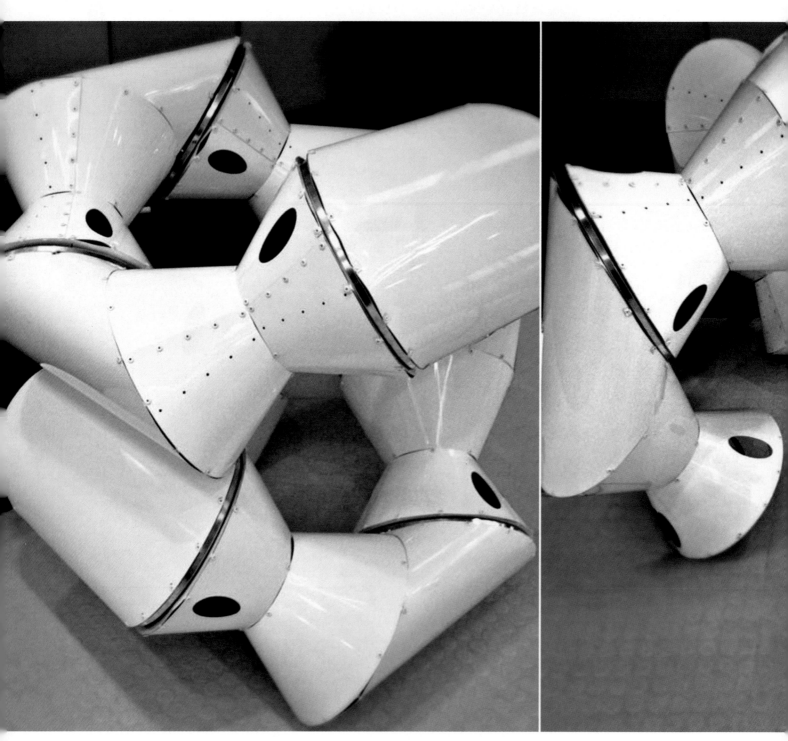

Decibot, 2009 © Skylar Tibbits **mit dem** with the Center for Bits and Atoms, MIT

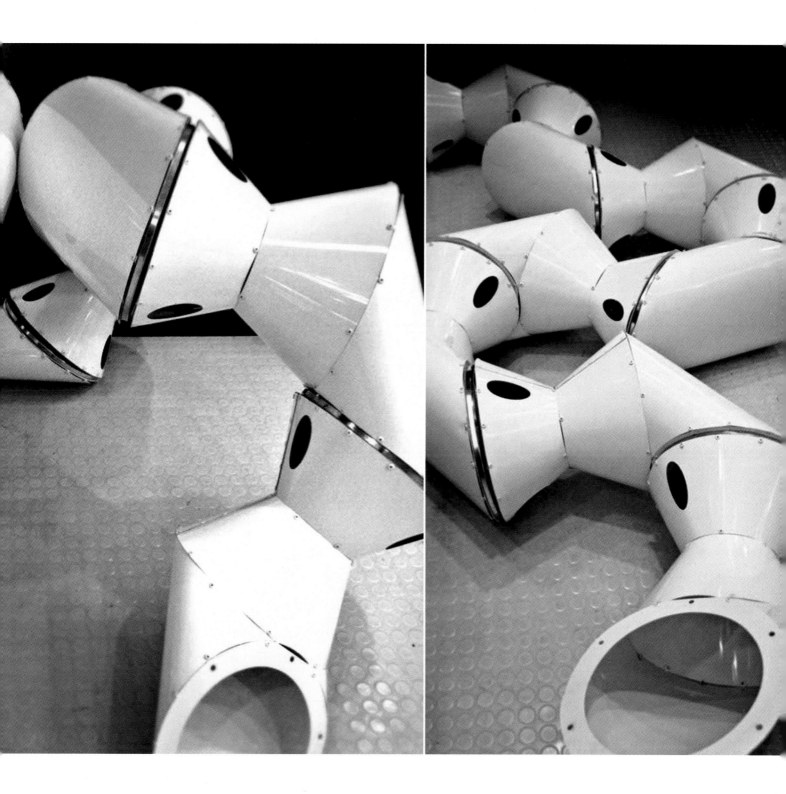

Decibot, 2009 © Skylar Tibbits mit dem with the Center for Bits and Atoms, MIT

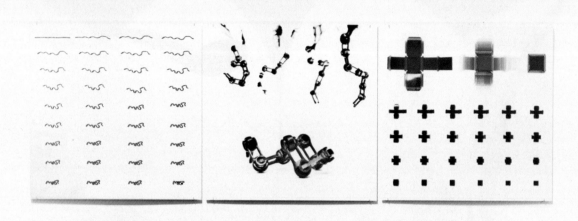

Fluid Crystalization, 2013 © Self-Assembly Lab, MIT

Fluid Crystalization, 2013 © Self-Assembly Lab, MIT

Interactions
& Mutations

1 FABRICATE 2011, London, Installation „Stratifications": Ein auf dem Roboter angebrachter Scanner liefert dem System die Feedbackinformation. A scanner mounted on the robot provides information feedback to the system. © Gramazio & Kohler, Architecture and Digital Fabrication, ETH Zurich

Digital-Material Feedback

Extending Intuition into the Production Process
Digital-materielles Feedback.
Zur Ausdehnung der Intuition auf den Produktionsprozess

Architectural thinking interweaves two contrasting and complementing cognitive processes: one analytical, anticipatory, restrictive, which attempts to exert control over matter and form, and one intuitive, creative, and speculative, which goes beyond established rational thresholds.

Architektonisches Denken verbindet zwei gegensätzliche und komplementäre kognitive Prozesse: der eine ist analytisch, antizipatorisch, restriktiv, der Versuch, Kontrolle über Materie und Form auszuüben; der andere intuitiv, kreativ, spekulativ, der Versuch, etablierte rationale Grenzen zu sprengen.

FELIX RASPALL

Both methods play important roles during the architect's workflow, traditionally divided into two well-defined phases: first, design (the intellectual work), then production (the material realization). It is the design phase that concentrates the creative process, as designers progressively formalize all material, formal, conceptual intentions into a well-defined and complete project. A variety of intuitive and rational methods drive the process. Early in the design process, the design problem is ill-defined and intuition heuristically searches for solutions, but as the project crystallizes, rational thinking takes the lead.

During the production phase, planning prevails, as fabricators unfold the precise instructions contained in the project. The materialization process is highly deterministic and relies on the standardization of materials and assembly processes, as well as strict contractual obligations. Changes during this phase are laborious and expensive and are therefore avoided; the designer's intuition has little room to operate.

How does materiality enter the design process when material decisions happen before—and do not coexist with—actual production? How does intuitive thinking embrace material problems and proposes creative solutions while detached from real matter? Material feedback is, in a broad sense, information from materials and assembly processes that steers the creative process and determines formal, spatial, and conceptual decisions. Traditionally, this information comes from previous experience and education of designers and consultants, disconnected from the specific material problem on hand. In this framework, designers with strong material research resort to mockups and prototypes in order to obtain ad-hoc empirical information during the design process.

Recent advances in digital technologies are opening new opportunities to bring materiality into the designer's immediacy. The research efforts in this area can be grouped into three approaches, according to how materiality enters the design process. The first two approaches are experimental; nevertheless they fit into the established architectural workflow, and have been adopted by practicing architects and theorized by critics.[1] The third approach is an emerging field of research which, building on the accomplishments of the first two approaches, questions the deterministic nature of fabrication by extending feedback and decision-making into the production stage. The aim of this article is to scrutinize the possibilities of digital technologies and feedback systems to foster material intuition during the design and fabrication process. It briefly presents the first and second approach and discusses the characteristics, potentials, and implications of the third approach in greater detail.

> The materialization process is highly deterministic and relies on the standardization of materials and assembly processes, as well as strict contractual obligations.

In der Arbeit von Architekten, die sich gewöhnlich in zwei klar voneinander abgegrenzte Phasen aufteilt – den Entwurf (die geistige Arbeit) und die Produktion (die materielle Umsetzung) – spielen beide Prozesse eine wichtige Rolle. Der kreative Prozess findet hauptsächlich in der Entwurfsphase statt, in der alle materiellen, formalen und konzeptuellen Vorstellungen nach und nach zu einem wohldefinierten Projekt geformt werden. Vorangetrieben wird der Prozess durch eine Reihe intuitiver und rationaler Methoden. Anfangs ist das Gestaltungsproblem nur vage definiert und die Suche nach Lösungen vor allem intuitionsgesteuert; hat das Projekt Gestalt gewonnen, übernimmt das rationale Denken die Führung.

In der Produktionsphase, wenn die den Bau Ausführenden die im Projekt implizierten genauen Anweisungen herausarbeiten, steht die Planung im Vordergrund. Der Materialisierungsprozess ist in hohem Maße determiniert; er hängt von standardisierten Materialien und Fertigungsprozessen ab und muss sich an strenge vertragliche Vereinbarungen halten. Änderungen sind in dieser Phase arbeitsaufwändig und kostspielig und werden daher vermieden; für die Intuition des Gestalters bleibt wenig Spielraum.

Wie fließt die Materialität in den Entwurfsprozess ein, wenn die Materialentscheidungen vor und nicht im Wechselspiel mit der tatsächlichen Produktion fallen? Wie kann sich das kreative Denken Materialproblemen widmen und kreative Lösungen dafür vorschlagen, wenn es losgelöst vom eigentlichen Material stattfindet? Materialfeedback meint im weitesten Sinn Informationen über Materialien und Fertigungsverfahren, die den kreativen Prozess steuern und formale, räumliche und konzeptuelle Entscheidungen beeinflussen. Traditionellerweise verdanken sich diese Informationen der früheren Erfahrung und Ausbildung der entwerfenden Architekten und Bauberater, haben also keinen direkten Bezug zum jeweiligen Materialproblem. In diesem System greifen Gestalter mit großem Materialinteresse auf Modelle und Prototypen zurück, um ad hoc an empirische Informationen zu gelangen.

Jüngste Entwicklungen in der Digitaltechnik eröffnen nun neue Möglichkeiten, um Materialaspekte in den unmittelbaren Erfahrungsbereich des Gestalters zu bringen. Die einschlägigen Forschungsbemühungen lassen sich grob in drei Ansätze unterteilen: Die ersten beiden sind zwar experimenteller Art, lassen sich aber dennoch mit den üblichen architektonischen Arbeitsabläufen vereinbaren und wurden sowohl von praktizierenden Architekten verwendet als auch eingehend theoretisch begründet.[1] Beim dritten Ansatz handelt es sich um ein

---

1   Several publications theorize and analyze case studies of the first and second approaches. Relevant volumes include: Rivka Oxmans special issue of *Architectural Design* (80,4, 2010), entitled *The New Structuralism: Design, Engineering, and Architectural Technologies*, provides background and case studies of the first approach. Lisa Iwamoto, *Digital Fabrications: Architectural and Material Techniques* (New York, 2009) compiles several projects that fit the second approach.

1   Beispiele für die ersten beiden Ansätze wurden in mehreren Publikationen analysiert und theroretisch erörtert. Rivka Oxmans Sonderausgabe von Architectural Design (80, 4, 2010) mit dem Titel *The New Structuralism: Design, Engineering, and Architectural Technologies* liefert Hintergrundinformationen und Fallbeispiele für den ersten Ansatz; Lisa Iwamotos *Digital Fabrications: Architectural and Material Techniques*, New York 2009, versammelt mehrere Projekte, die für den zweiten Ansatz stehen.

im Entstehen begriffenes Forschungsgebiet, das, aufbauend auf die Errungenschaften der ersten beiden Ansätze, den deterministischen Charakter der Bauausführung infrage stellt und Feedback und Entscheidungsfindung in die Produktionsphase hinein ausdehnt. Ziel dieses Artikels ist es, die Möglichkeiten digitaler Technologien und Feedbacksysteme zur Steigerung der intuitiven Materialhandhabung im Gestaltungs- und Bauprozess zu sondieren. Dazu werden zunächst die ersten beiden Ansätze kurz vorgestellt und dann ausführlicher auf die Merkmale, Potenziale und Implikationen des dritten eingegangen.

Der erste Ansatz: Spezialisierte Bauberater. Eine Reihe von Beratungsbüros und Expertenteams innerhalb von Ingenieur- und Architekturbüros spezialisieren sich auf die Verbesserung des Informationsaustausches zwischen Gestaltern und Produzenten in der frühen Entwurfsphase. Einige der führenden Akteure auf diesem Gebiet sind das p.art (Parametric Applied Research Team) von AKT II, das AGU (Advanced Geometry Unit) von Ove Arup, designtoproduction und Evolute.

Die Tätigkeit dieser Beraterfirmen oder -gruppen unterscheidet sich von jener konventioneller Ingenieurbüros dadurch, dass sie nicht auf die Lieferung fertiger Lösungen beschränkt ist. Vielmehr besteht ein wesentlicher Teil ihrer Arbeit in der projektspezifischen Anpassung von Entwurfswerkzeugen und im Einbetten von Materialien und Fertigungsprozessen in die Modellierungsplattformen. So können die Gestalter in maßgeschneiderten digitalen Umgebungen auch ohne direkten Kontakt mit Materialien und Fertigungsprozessen intuitiv Materiallösungen erkunden. In diesen Umgebungen fließt der simulierte Materialwiderstand in den Modellierungsprozess ein und verwandelt damit geometrische Entwurfsinstrumente in Instrumente der Materialexploration.

Der zweite Ansatz: Direkte Materialexperimente. Der zweite Ansatz wird von Gestaltern verfolgt, die sich direkt mit materiellen Produktionsprozessen auseinandersetzen. Mehrere, meist kleinere, experimentell orientierte und massiv mit digitalen Technologien arbeitende Büros erobern sich die Fabrikation als Domäne. Beispielhaft für diesen Ansatz sind etwa die Arbeiten und Forschungen von Lisa Iwamoto, Achim Menges oder MOS, um nur einige zu nennen.

Ziele und Werkzeuge sind im Allgemeinen ähnlich wie beim ersten Ansatz, nur sind hier Entwurf, Programmierung und Erzeugung in kleineren Teams konzentriert, wodurch sich eine flexiblere informelle Struktur ergibt. Begünstigt wird das durch den leichteren Zugang zu Fabrikationsstätten und verbesserte Interfaces, die die Programmierung und Steuerung der Produktionsmittel auf ein für den Gestalter brauchbares Niveau bringt. Neuere Forschungen zum Einsatz von Robotik in der Gestaltung gehen ähnlich vor, um Kontrolle über neue Materialien und Verfahren zu gewinnen. Meist in einem akademischen

The First Approach: Specialized Consultants. A number of specialized consultancy offices, as well as expert groups within engineering and architectural offices focus on strengthening information exchange between designers and producers during the early design phase. Some of its most renowned actors include p.art (Parametric Applied Research Team) of AKT II, Ove Arup's AGU (Advanced Geometry Unit), designtoproduction, and Evolute, among others.

The work of these consultants differs from conventional engineering practices in that their activity is not limited to the delivery of fixed solutions. Rather, an essential part of their work is the ongoing customization of tools for designers, embedding material and fabrication constraints into modeling platforms. Although designers are not in direct contact with materials and fabrication processes, they can intuitively discover material solutions within tailored digital environments. Through these environments the simulated friction from materiality provides feedback during the modeling process; converting previously geometric tools into instruments for material exploration.

The Second Approach: Direct Material Experimentation. A second approach is followed by designers who actively engage in material production processes. Several practices, typically of smaller scale, experimental, and significantly involved with digital technologies, reclaim fabrication as their domain. The work and research of Lisa Iwamoto, Achim Menges, MOS, to name only a few, are exemplary of this approach.

Goals and tools are generally shared with the first approach; however, design, programming, and fabrication are concentrated in a smaller team, creating a more flexible and informal structure. This is facilitated by the increased accessibility to fabrication shops and improved interfaces that bring programming and operation of the production means to a non-expert level suitable for designers. Recent research on robotics for design follows the same line, intended to gain control over new materials and processes. Either working in relationship with academic environments or in relationship with fabrication labs, immediate contact with production processes enables intuitive, fertile material experimentation.

The Third Approach: Material Feedback and Adaptable Production Processes. The first and second approach explore new ways to support material feedback during the design process; however, the production phase remains a deterministic process in which precise instructions are followed to accomplish predefined outputs.

The third approach groups a set of experimental efforts that aims at extending feedback into the production phase. Material feedback is not information that aids the development of more complex designs, but information that steers production itself. Consequently, the deterministic nature of conventional construction is challenged, opening a window of opportunities for alternative non-deterministic processes in which intuition can actively engage fabrication.

The third approach is supported by two technological developments which lie at the core of approaches one and two: first, parametric models which are able to update their configuration when parameters change and second, digital workflows that automate the operation of CNC machines

2–3   Professur für Architektur und Digitale Fabrikation, ETH Zürich: Installation „Stratifications", London, 2011 (2) Eine vordefinierte Grundfläche gibt eine allgemeine Form vor, (3) doch die Bewegungen sind vor allem darauf abgestimmt, die große Höhenvarianz der Bauelemente auszugleichen. Chair of Architecture and Digital Fabrication, ETH Zurich: installation "Stratifications," 2011 (2) A predetermined footprint guides the overall form; (3) however, the motion is fine tuned to accommodate the large variations in brick heights. © Gramazio & Kohler, Architecture and Digital Fabrication, ETH Zurich

4–6   Professur für Architektur und Digitale Fabrikation, ETH Zürich: „Die endlose Wand", 2011 (4) Eine auf dem Boden eingezeichnete Linie gibt die Grundfläche der Wand vor. (5) Aufgrund dieser Information wird der Bauprozess errechnet und ausgeführt. (6) Der Roboterarm ist mit einer 3D-Kamera ausgestattet, die es ermöglicht, die Linie auf den Boden zu lesen. Chair of Architecture and Digital Fabrication, ETH Zurich: "The Endless Wall," 2011 (4) A line drawn on the floor determines the footprint of the wall. (5) With this information the construction sequence is calculated and executed. (6) The robotic arm includes a three-dimensional camera that allows to read the line on the floor. © Gramazio & Kohler, Architecture and Digital Fabrication, ETH Zurich

Umfeld oder in Verbindung mit FabLabs finden hier in unmittelbarem Kontakt mit Produktionsprozessen intuitive und fruchtbare Materialexperimente statt.

Der dritte Ansatz: Materialfeedback und adaptierbare Produktionsprozesse. Die ersten beiden Ansätze beschreiten zwar neue Wege zur Integration von Materialaspekten in den Entwurfsprozess, doch die Produktionsphase selbst bleibt deterministisch, ein Vorgang, bei dem genaue Instruktionen befolgt werden, um ein vorher definiertes Ziel zu erreichen.

Der dritte Ansatz umfasst eine Reihe von experimentellen Versuchen, das Materialfeedback auf die Produktionsphase auszuweiten. Materialfeedback meint hier nicht Informationen, die die Entwicklung komplexerer Entwürfe ermöglichen, sondern Informationen, die die Produktion selbst steuern. Damit wird der deterministische Charakter herkömmlichen Bauens infrage gestellt und ein Fenster für Möglichkeiten geöffnet, alternative, nicht-deterministische Verfahren zu entwickeln, bei denen der Intuition eine aktive Rolle in der Fabrikation zukommt.

Begünstigt wird dieser Ansatz durch zwei technologische Entwicklungen, die auch schon den ersten beiden Ansätzen zugrunde liegen: erstens, parametrischen Modellierungsverfahren, die in der Lage sind, die Konfiguration zu aktualisieren, wenn sich die Parameter ändern, und zweitens digitalen Arbeitsabläufen, die die automatische Bedienung von CNC-Maschinen direkt vom parametrischen Modell erlauben. Verbindet man diese miteinander, führt das zu flexiblen digitalen Modellen, in denen sich Veränderungen der Parameter automatisch auf das jeweilige Projekt und die Produktion auswirken.

In der herkömmlichen Architektur wie auch in den ersten beiden Ansätzen sind Änderungen in der Produktionsphase kostspielig und mühsam und daher unerwünscht. Beim dritten Ansatz werden mithilfe digitaler Technologien Produktionssysteme entwickelt, die die Fähigkeit besitzen, sich in der Bauphase anzupassen. Um diese Flexibilität zu erreichen, benötigen digitale Arbeitsprozesse zwei zusätzliche Funktionen: eine, die das Einspeisen von Informationen während des Fabrikationsprozesses ermöglicht (über entsprechende Eingabevorrichtungen) und eine, die darüber entscheidet, wie auf diese Informationen reagiert werden soll. Eingabevorrichtungen sind u.a. Benutzerinterfaces und Sensoren, die die Information aus der physischen Umgebung entnehmen. Digitale Modelle, Eingabegeräte und CNC-Maschinen werden dann so programmiert, dass sie auf Änderungen in Echtzeit reagieren können.

Die Möglichkeiten solcher adaptiver Systeme werden derzeit in einer Reihe akademischer Forschungsprojekte und wegweisender industrieller Anwendungen – und zwar sowohl in der Architektur als auch in anderen Bereichen – erkundet. Die akademische Forschung geht vor allem in zwei Richtungen: einerseits erforscht sie die Mensch-Maschine-Interaktion wie Nutzer bestimmte Entscheidungen in den Produktionsprozess einzubeziehen.

directly from parametric models. In combination they generate flexible digital models, in which changes in parameters renew project and production immediately.

In conventional architecture, as well as in approaches one and two, adjustments during the production process are costly, effortful, and therefore not desirable. The third approach uses digital technologies to develop production systems with the capacity to adjust during the construction phase. In order to gain this flexibility, digital workflows require the incorporation of two additional features: a feature to introduce information during the fabrication process (via input devices), and another one that decides how to react to that information. Input devices include user interfaces and sensors that read information from the physical environment. Digital models, input devices, and computer numerically controlled (CNC) machines are then programmed to react to changes in real-time.

The possibilities of these adaptable systems are currently explored by a set of academic initiatives and pioneering industrial processes, outside and within architecture. Academic research orients towards two main directions: On the one hand, human-machine interaction explores how users can introduce specific decisions during the production process. In this way, human instructions,

> The system calculates the assembly of a wall using a curve drawn on the floor as input for the wall's footprint.

including intuitive responses, guide fabrication. On the other hand, autonomous fabrication workflows research production systems which can adjust to changing material information. The behavior of these systems cannot be described as intuitive; however, as algorithms controlling these systems are executed in time and changing environments, they can lead to emergent behaviors that exceed a deterministic logic.

For almost a decade, the Chair of Architecture and Digital Fabrication at the Swiss Federal Institute of Technology in Zurich (ETH) has developed several projects related with robotic brick piling and the challenges of on-site robotics. A specific research project, exhibited at the "Scientifica 2011," proposes a production system without a predetermined output, which requires human instructions on the site to complete the project (figs. 4–6).[2] The system calculates the assembly of a wall using a curve drawn on the floor as input for the wall's footprint. A three-dimensional camera mounted on a robotic arm recognizes the curve; this information is used to compute the motions which are executed by the robot. Once the wall is finished, the system waits for an extension of the line to be drawn in order to resume the execution. In this project, a specific aspect of the design—the wall's footprint—is decided during construction; the gestural nature of the input invites intuition to shape production directly.

2   See Volker Helm, Selen Ercan, Fabio Gramazio and Matthias Kohler, "In-Situ Robotic Construction: Extending the Digital Fabrication Chain in Architecture," in *Proceedings of the 32nd Annual Conference of the Association for Computer Aided Design in Architecture – (ACADIA)* (San Francisco, 2012), pp. 169–176.

As the system is operating, it shows some "emergent" properties: unplanned changes introduced by a human user, such as rotating or moving a brick in the pile, triggers changes in subsequent construction automatically. This reactive behavior represents a non-standard mode of collaboration between human actions and machine reaction.

bringen können; damit wird die Fabrikation durch menschliche Anweisungen, also auch intuitive Reaktionen steuerbar. Andererseits testen autonome Fabrikationsabläufe, also von Produktionssystemen, die sich an neue Materialinformationen anpassen können. Das Verhalten solcher Systeme kann zwar nicht als intuitiv beschrieben werden, aber da die sie steuernden Algorithmen in der Zeit und in wechselnden Umgebungen abgearbeitet werden, können sie zu emergenten Verhaltensweisen führen, die über die deterministische Logik hinausgehen.

Seit fast einem Jahrzehnt werden an der Professur für Architektur und Digitale Fabrikation an der ETH Zürich verschiedene Forschungsprojekte durchgeführt, die sich mit robotischem Ziegellegen und den Anforderungen des Robotikeinsatzes vor Ort beschäftigen. Eines dieser Forschungsprojekte, das bei der „Scientifica 2011" gezeigt wurde, schlägt ein Produktionssystem ohne vorgegebenen Output vor, das zur Ausführung der Arbeit menschlicher Anweisungen vor Ort bedarf (Abb. 4–6).[2] Das System errechnet den Aufbau einer Wand aus einer auf dem Boden eingezeichneten Kurvenlinie. Eine auf dem Roboterarm angebrachte 3D-Kamera erfasst die Kurve und errechnet aus dieser Information die vom Roboter auszuführenden Bewegungen. Ist die Wand fertig, wartet das System auf eine Verlängerung der Linie, um die Tätigkeit fortzusetzen. Bei diesem Projekt wird ein bestimmter Gestaltungsaspekt – die Grundfläche der Wand – erst während des Bauens festgelegt; der gestische Charakter des Inputs ermöglicht die direkte intuitive Gestaltung der Produktion.

„Interlacing" ist ein von Kathrin Dörfler und Romana Rust an den Technischen Universitäten von Graz und Wien entwickeltes Projekt (Abb. 7–9).[3] Wie im vorher geschilderten Fall wird hier der menschliche Input als Teil des Produktionsprozesses erforscht. Ein User „füttert" einen Roboter willkürlich und ohne feste Reihenfolge mit Stäben unterschiedlicher Länge. Mithilfe von maschinellem Sehen erkennt das System den Materialinput und bestimmt die Zielposition, indem es eine Auswahl zwischen möglichen stabilen Positionen im System trifft. Auf der Grundlage der gespeicherten Daten über den bereits bestehenden Stapel werden statistische Berechnungen angestellt und die entsprechende Bewegung ausgeführt; dann wartet das System auf die Zufuhr eines neuen Stabs. Das System versucht nicht, eine vorgegebene Konfiguration des Sta-

2   Vgl. Volker Helm/Selen Ercan/Fabio Gramazio/Matthias Kohler: „In-Situ Robotic Construction: Extending the Digital Fabrication Chain in Architecture", in: *Proceedings of the 32nd Annual Conference of the Association for Computer Aided Design in Architecture – (ACADIA)* 2012, San Francisco 2012, S. 169–176.

3   Vgl. Kathrin Dörfler/Florian Rist/Romana Rust: „Interlacing: An Experimental Approach to Integrating Digital and Physical Design Methods", in: *RobArch 2012: Robotic Fabrication in Architecture, Art and Design* (2013), S. 82–91. Vgl. dazu den Beitrag von Dörfler, Rist, Rust mit dem Titel: „Moderation der Unschärfe. Experimente zur Verschränkung physischer und digitaler Formfindungsprozesse" in der vorliegenden GAM Ausgabe.

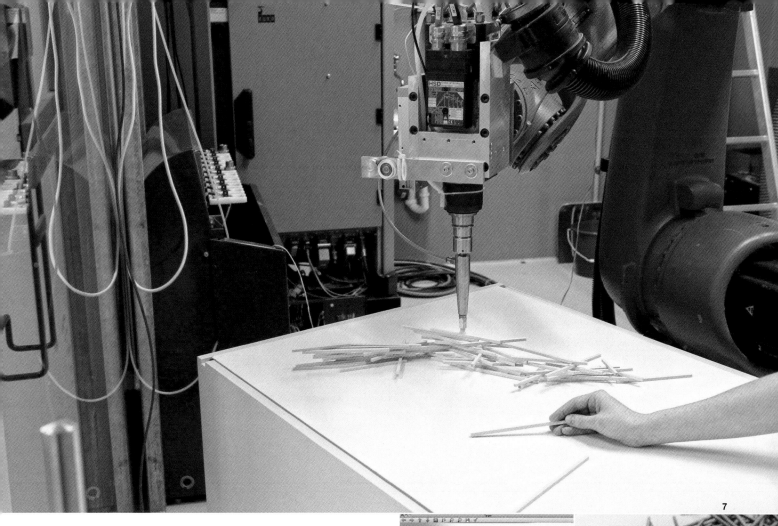

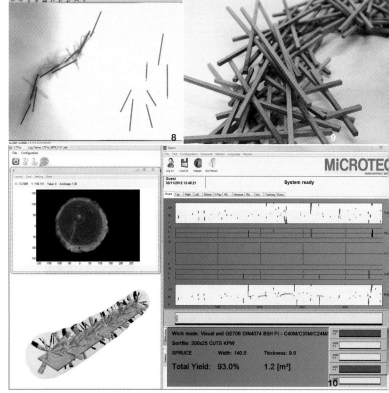

7–9   Interlacing, 2012: (7) Das System wird mit einem Stab gefüttert, (8) der vom
System erkannt, (9) und an einer stabilen Position des Stapels platziert wird. Die
endgültige Konfiguration ist das Ergebnis einer Abfolge von Aktionen, die nicht
im Voraus festgelegt sind. Interlacing, 2012: (7) A stick is fed to the system,
(8) recognized by the system and (9) located in a stable position in the pile.
The final configuration is the result of an accumulation of actions, not predetermined in advance. © Kathrin Dörfler, Florian Rist und and Romana Rust

10   Industrielle Anwendungen: 3D-Scanning in der Holzindustrie von Microtec
Industrial applications: 3D scanning in the sawmill industry by Microtec
Screenshot © Microtec srl

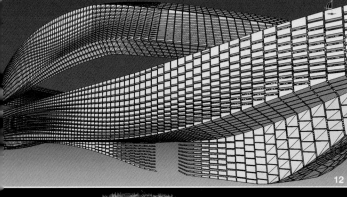

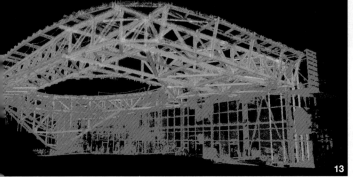

11–13 Barclays Center, Brooklyn, New York, 2012. (12) Das ursprüngliche parametrische Modell errechnet die einmalige Geometrie eines jeden Verkleidungselements. (13) Nach Fertigstellung der Tragwerkskonstruktion wurde diese dreidimensional erfasst und zur Aktualisierung des ursprünglichen Modells herangezogen. (11) Mithilfe dieses iterativen Prozesses konnte das Verkleidungssystem ohne ein festes digitales Modell fertiggestellt werden. Barclays Center, Brooklyn, New York: (12) The original parametric model calculates the unique geometry of each cladding panel. (13) Once the supporting structure was completed, it was 3D scanned and used to update the original model. (11) This iterative process allowed the completion of the cladding system without a fixed digital model © SHoP Construction

pels zu erstellen, sondern die Endform ist das Ergebnis einfacher, ad hoc getroffener Entscheidungen. In diesem Fall tragen sowohl menschliche Entscheidungen (über die Art des Materials) als auch die Berechnung der Maschine (über dessen Verwendung) zum Endergebnis bei.

„Stratifications", ein weiteres Projekt der bereits erwähnten Professur an der ETH-Zürich erforscht Prozesse zum Erkennen und Einbeziehen unvorhersehbarer Variationen, die beim Mauerbau aufgrund der Größenunterschiede der Bausteine in Echtzeit verarbeitet werden müssen (Abb. 1–3).[4] Das System folgt einer vorgegebenen Reihenfolge von zu positionierenden Holzelementen, wobei aber jeder Schritt aufgrund von Informationen über die vom Roboter vorher gebaute Wand und mithilfe eines Linescaners kalibriert wird. Das bei der Fabricate-Konferenz 2011 in London vorgestellte Projekt war in der Lage, Elemente mit stark differierenden Höhen anzuordnen, eine Aufgabe, die mit vorausdefinierten Anweisungen nicht zu bewältigen wäre. Das System legt gewisse „emergente" Eigenschaften an den Tag: Von einem menschlichen Bediener eingebrachte ungeplante Änderungen wie das Verdrehen oder Versetzen eines Elements ruft automatisch Änderungen in der nachfolgenden Anordnung hervor. Dieses reaktive Verhalten läuft auf eine nicht genormte Zusammenarbeit zwischen menschlicher Aktion und Maschinenreaktion hinaus.

Manche Industriezweige nutzen materiell-digitales Feedback zur Systematisierung schwieriger Automatisierungsaufgaben. Das gilt vor allem für Industriezweige, die mit variablen Materialien und komplexen Materialoperationen arbeiten. Die holz- und fleischverarbeitende Industrie verwendet eine Reihe von sensor- und computertechnischen Mitteln, um die Verarbeitung ihrer organischen Materialien zu optimieren. Technisch avancierte Sägewerke können mit schneller dreidimensionaler Tomografie jeden Stamm erfassen, der in das Werk gebracht wird. Mithilfe dieser Information lassen sich Astknoten und Wuchsunregelmäßigkeiten im Inneren des Stammes erkennen und der Schnitt so anpassen, dass eine qualitative und quantitative Verbesserung des Ergebnisses erreicht wird (Abb. 10). Ähnlich macht sich auch die fleischverarbeitende Industrie das Materialfeedback zunutze: Jeder in die Verarbeitung gelangende Tierkörper wird dreidimensional gescannt, um die optimale Abfolge der Schnitte festzulegen. In manchen Fällen kann das mehrere Male geschehen, um die Schnitte immer wieder neu anzupassen.

In der Bauindustrie befindet man sich beim Einsatz von Feedbackmechanismen noch im Experimentierstadium. Ein wegweisendes Verfahren wurde von SHoP Architects und SHoP Construction für das Barclays Center in Brooklyn, NY, entwickelt (Abb. 11–13). Die Außenhaut der Arena ist eine Frei-

"Interlacing" is a project developed by Kathrin Dörfler and Romana Rust for their master thesis jointly at the Graz University of Technology and Vienna University of Technology (figs. 7–9).[3] Like the previous case, it investigates human input as part of the operation of the production process. A user "feeds" the robot with sticks of variable length at will, without any pre-established sequence. Using computer vision, the system recognizes the material input and determines the target position by selecting from a range of possible stable locations in the pile. Statics calculations are performed using memory of the existing pile. The motion is then executed and the system waits for a new stick to pile. The system does not aim at accomplishing a predefined pile configuration; rather, the final form is the result of simple, instantaneous decisions. In this case, both human choice (what material to use) and machine calculation (how to use it) contributes to the final outcome.

"Stratifications," a project that aggregates timber elements, developed by the same group at the ETH studies processes that recognize and react to unpredictable variations that brick piling needs to accommodate in real life due to the dimensional differences of bricks (figs. 1–3).[4] The system follows a predetermined sequence of bricks to place, but each action is calibrated using information from the wall that the robot previously built using a line scanner sensor. The project, demonstrated during the Fabricate 2011 conference in London, was capable of handling the accumulation of bricks of significantly different heights, a task impossible to achieve with the usual pre-defined, fixed instructions. As the system is operating, it shows some "emergent" properties: unplanned changes introduced by a human user, such as rotating or moving a brick in the pile, triggers changes in subsequent construction automatically. This reactive behavior represents a non-standard mode of collaboration between human actions and machine reaction.

> The system does not aim at accomplishing a predefined pile configuration; rather, the final form is the result of simple, instantaneous decisions.

Some industrial processes take advantage of material-digital feedback as a means to systematize difficult automation problems, in particular industries that deal with variable material sources and complex material operations. The sawmilling industry and the meat processing industry use a variety of sensing and computing mechanisms to optimize the processing of materials from organic sources. Advanced sawmills can implement fast three-dimensional tomography scanning for each log that enters the mill. This information is used to detect knots and irregularities inside the log and customize the cutting process aiming to improve the quality and quantity of the output (fig. 10). In an analogous way, the meat processing industry

3   Kathrin Dörfler, Florian Rist, and Romana Rust, "Interlacing: An Experimental Approach to Integrating Digital and Physical Design Methods," in *RobArch 2012: Robotic Fabrication in Architecture, Art and Design* (2013), pp. 82–91. See also their contribution in this GAM issue entitled "Moderation of Vagueness: Experiments on the Interconnection between Physical and Digital Processes of Form Generation."

4   Vgl. Helm et al., „In-situ Robotic Construction" (wie Anm. 2).

4   See Helm et al., "In-situ Robotic Construction" (see note 2).

also incorporates material feedback: each carcass entering the production line is three-dimensionally scanned to compute the optimal slicing sequence. In some cases, meat can be scanned several times in order to iteratively adjust the cuts.

In the construction industry, the use of feedback mechanisms is still experimental. A pioneering case was successfully developed and implemented by SHoP Architects and SHoP Construction for the Barclays Center in Brooklyn, NY (figs. 11–13). The skin of the arena is a freeform surface cladded in folded weathering steel panels. Because deformations in the structure—particularly those at the large cantilever over the access square—were impossible to estimate with enough precision, the cladding panels could not be completed in advance. In order to tackle this assembly challenge, an alternative method was conceived. After the structure was completed, it was scanned several times using point-cloud survey. Each time this information was used to update the original parametric model, which automatically modified the fixation for each panel to fit the existing structure on the site.

These industrial examples use material feedback to increase efficiency and feasibility. Although they do not aim for creativity during production, they represent real-life working systems in which material processes are designed to change and constitute an adaptive approach to manufacturing that designers are starting to appropriate.

The innovations inherent in the three approaches enable real-time material feedback and support more intuitive ways to explore materiality during the design process and into the material production.

Material Feedback: An Outlook. In conventional workflows, architects make almost all material decisions during the design phase, i.e, before construction; creative work is therefore detached from the immediacy of material processes. The innovations inherent in the three approaches enable real-time material feedback and support more intuitive ways to explore materiality during the design process and into the material production.

The first two approaches, already part of the architectural domain, enrich the creative process by fostering material explorations during the design phase. Using customized design tools that simulate production constraints and interface with production machines, designers have access to materiality during the creative process. In this way, intuition is not limited to static information from previous experiences and professional knowledge, but is stimulated by the real-time response in three-dimensional models.

The third approach, which is still in an early and experimental phase, extends the capacity for creative, intuitive responses into the production stage. Its implications are multiple and potentially significant, because it questions the basic structure of the discipline: architects are no longer designers of well-defined projects but designers of flexible production processes through which they can make decisions or program behaviors that steer the production process. However, the benefits of this increased flexibility are mirrored by the challenges of increased uncertainty. The depar-

formfläche, die mit gekanteten rostenden Stahlplatten verkleidet ist. Da die Strukturverformungen – vor allem in der gewaltigen Auskragung über dem Eingangsplatz – nicht mit ausreichender Genauigkeit im Voraus abschätzbar waren, konnten die Verkleidungsplatten nicht vorproduziert werden. Zur Bewältigung dieses Problems wurde eine alternative Methode erdacht. Nachdem der Rohbau fertiggestellt war, wurde er mehrere Male als Punktwolke gescannt. Mithilfe dieser Information wurde das ursprüngliche parametrische Modell bei jedem Durchgang aktualisiert, wodurch die Befestigungspunkte jeder einzelnen Platte automatisch an die real existierende Struktur angeglichen wurden.

In diesen Beispielen aus der Industrie dient das Materialfeedback zur Verbesserung von Effizienz und Machbarkeit. Auch wenn es dabei nicht um Kreativität im Produktionsprozess geht, so handelt es sich doch um real eingesetzte Systeme, in denen materielle Prozesse so gestaltet werden, dass sie sich verändern und auf einen adaptiven Ansatz in der Produktion hinauslaufen, den Gestalter sich zunehmend zu eigen machen.

Materialfeedback: Ein Ausblick. Im herkömmlichen architektonischen Arbeitsprozess fallen fast alle Materialentscheidungen in der Entwurfsphase, d.h. vor dem eigentlichen Bau; die kreative Arbeit findet getrennt von Materialien und Fertigungsverfahren statt. Das Innovative der drei erwähnten Ansätze besteht darin, dass sie ein unmittelbares Feedback durch das Material ermöglichen und damit intuitivere Formen der Materialerkundung im Gestaltungsprozess und bis hinein in den Produktionsprozess fördern.

Die beiden ersten bereits in die architektonische Praxis eingedrungenen Ansätze bereichern den Gestaltungsprozess, indem sie das Ausloten von materiellen Aspekten schon in der Entwurfsphase gestatten. Maßgeschneiderte Entwurfswerkzeuge, die Produktionsbeschränkungen simulieren und direkt an Fertigungsmaschinen anschließen, bieten Gestaltern schon im Entwurfsprozess Zugang zur Materialität. Damit ist die Intuition nicht auf statische Informationen aus früheren Erfahrungen und Fachkenntnissen beschränkt, sondern wird durch Echtzeit-Reaktionen in dreidimensionalen Modellen stimuliert.

Der dritte Ansatz, der sich noch in einem frühen Experimentalstadium befindet, erweitert die Möglichkeit zu kreativen und intuitiven Reaktionen bis in den Produktionsprozess hinein. Er hat vielfältige und potenziell weitreichende Folgen, weil er die Grundstruktur des ganzen Fachs infrage stellt: Mit ihm sind Architekten nicht mehr Gestalter fest umrissener Projekte sondern flexibler Produktionsprozesse; er ermöglicht es ihnen, Entscheidungen zu treffen und Verhaltensweisen zu programmieren, die die Produktionsabläufe steuern. Den Vorteilen dieser erhöhten Flexibilität stehen allerdings die Schwierigkeiten der größeren Unbestimmtheit gegenüber. Der Verzicht auf eine genaue Vorherbestimmung des Ergebnisses wirft eine Fülle von Problemen auf, die von der Kostenschätzung über die Ästhetik bis zu Haftungsangelegenheiten reichen.

Die Implementierung des Materialfeedbacks erfordert erhebliche digitaltechnologische Kenntnisse und Vorarbeiten. Anstelle von Gebäude müssen Architekten nun Produktionsprozesse entwerfen, wobei die Flexibilität des Systems vor Baubeginn konzipiert und programmiert werden muss. Damit wird Raum für spontane, intuitive Entscheidungen während der gesamten Entwurfs- und Produktionsphase geschaffen.

Verlangen die ersten beiden Ansätze die Programmierung flexibler parametrischer Modelle, die bestimmte Materialinformationen verarbeiten, was ein gutes Verständnis der Produktionsmethoden voraussetzt, so geht der dritte Ansatz einen Schritt weiter: Er umfasst die Definition sämtlicher Aspekte, über die erst während der Bauausführung entschieden wird, dazu die Informationen, die diese Entscheidungen beeinflussen, sowie die Programmierung der Algorithmen, die sie errechnen.

Eine Reihe von Applikationen werden gegenwärtig entwickelt. Sie reichen von direkten menschlichen Anweisungen während des Produktionsprozesses, z.B. beim „The Endless Wall"- oder beim Interlacing-Projekt, über den Umgang mit unregelmäßigen Materialien in der Holz- und Lebensmittelindustrie bis zur Steuerung unscharfer Montageprozesse beim „Stratifications"-Projekt und beim Barclays Center.

In den Unwägbarkeiten einer sich immer schneller verändernden Welt, in denen die Architektur operiert, ist die Intuition ein effizientes Mittel der Lösungssuche. Materialfeedback verbessert die Möglichkeiten von Gestaltern zum intuitiven Umgang mit Materialien und Fertigungsprozessen, indem es die für spontane Entscheidungen notwendige Echtzeitinformation liefert. Wann und inwieweit diese Methoden für die Architektur wirklich nutzbar werden, bleibt abzuwarten.

Projekt Stratification (2011): Gramazio & Kohler, Architektur und Digitale Fabrikation, ETH Zürich. Team: Andrea Kondziela, Volker Helm, Ralph Bärtschi, Dominik Weber. © Gramazio & Kohler, Architektur und Digitale Fabrikation, ETH Zürich. Quelle: http://dfab.arch.ethz.ch/web/e/forschung/206.html (Stand: 02.09.2013)

Projekt "The Endless Wall" (2011): Gramazio & Kohler, Architektur und Digitale Fabrikation, ETH Zürich. Team: Andrea Kondziela, Volker Helm, Ralph Bärtschi, Ryan Luke Johns, Dominik Weber. © Gramazio & Kohler, Architektur und Digitale Fabrikation, ETH Zürich. Quelle: http://dfab.arch.ethz.ch/web/e/forschung/216.html (Stand: 02.09.2013)

Übersetzung Wilfried Prantner

ture of a precise anticipation of the output poses a myriad of practical questions, from cost estimation to aesthetics and liabilities.

The implementation of material feedback demands substantial upfront work and proficiency in digital technologies. Instead of designing buildings, architects are required to design production processes; and the flexibility of the system needs to be conceived and programmed before construction. In this way, designers secure space for spontaneous, intuitive decisions throughout design and production.

While the first and second approaches require the programming of flexible parametric models that compute specific material information, which involves a close understanding of production methods, the third approach goes a step forward: it comprises the definition of all the aspects that will be left open to decision during construction, the information that will trigger these decisions and the programming of algorithms that will compute them.

A set of applications is already starting to emerge, from direct human instructions during fabrication, e.g. "The Endless Wall" or "Interlacing," to the use of irregular materials, e.g., the sawmill or meat processing industries, and the control of imprecise assembly processes, e.g., Stratifications and the Barclays Center.

As architects operate within the uncertainties of a world of increasing velocity of change, intuition is an effective tool to look for solutions. Material feedback improves the ways in which designers apply intuition when working with materials and assembly processes, because it provides realtime information crucial for spontaneous decisions. When and at which scale these methods will represent a real utility for architecture still remains to be explored.

Project Stratification (2011): Gramazio & Kohler, Architecture and Digital Fabrication, ETH Zurich. Team: Andrea Kondziela, Volker Helm, Ralph Bärtschi, Dominik Weber. © Gramazio & Kohler, Architecture and Digital Fabrication, ETH Zurich. Source: http://dfab.arch.ethz.ch/web/e/forschung/206.html (accessed September 2, 2013)

Project "The Endless Wall" (2011): Gramazio & Kohler, Architecture and Digital Fabrication, ETH Zurich. Team: Andrea Kondziela, Volker Helm, Ralph Bärtschi, Ryan Luke Johns, Dominik Weber. © Gramazio & Kohler, Architecture and Digital Fabrication, ETH Zurich. Source: http://dfab.arch.ethz.ch/web/e/forschung/216.html (accessed September 2, 2013)

1 Ergebnis des Prozesses: Stapel aus Holzstäben, Wien, 2012 **The result of the process: A stack of wooden sticks, Vienna, 2012** © Florian Rist

Moderation der Unschärfe

Experimente zur Verschränkung
physischer und digitaler Formfindungsprozesse
Moderation of Vagueness: Experiments on the Interconnection
between Physical and Digital Processes of Form Generation

Die physische Welt, die uns umgibt, besteht aus kontinuierlichen, komplexen dynamischen Prozessen. Sie befindet sich in stetiger Veränderung und Transformation. Unser Bild dieser Prozesse bleibt, ob ihrer inneren Bestimmtheit, inhärent ungenau und unscharf, unabhängig davon, wie genau wir sie auch zu erfassen suchen. Die digitale Welt hingegen, deren Elemente diskret und statisch sind, ist schon per Definition frei von Unschärfe.

The physical world that surrounds us is made up of continuous and complex dynamic processes. It is immersed in constant change and transformation. Our picture of these processes remains, regardless of its inner determinacy, inherently imprecise and vague—no matter how faithfully we strive to record them. In contrast, the digital world with its discrete and static elements is per definition already free of vagueness.

KATHRIN DÖRFLER · ROMANA RUST · FLORIAN RIST

Die im Folgenden dargestellte Auseinandersetzung beschreibt Methoden zur Verschränkung von physischen und digitalen Wirklichkeiten anhand verschiedener systematischer Experimente. Sie dienen der Untersuchung der Fragestellung, ob die Einbindung der materiellen Umwelt mit ihrer Unschärfe und Unbestimmtheit in digital gesteuerte Regelkreise mittels Feedbackschleifen das Potenzial besitzt, neuartige Formfindungsprozesse im Architekturentwurf zu ermöglichen. Die gezeigten Konzepte arbeiten bewusst mit und nicht gegen diese Unschärfe, versuchen sie nicht zu eliminieren, sondern zu moderieren.

Feedbackschleifen zwischen digitalen und physischen Domains.

Entgegen einer Entmaterialisierung der Architektur im Informationszeitalter ist der gegenwärtige Diskurs geprägt von Bestrebungen, digitale Architektur auf verschiedenen Wegen zu re-materialisieren.[1] Daraus ergibt sich, dass beispielsweise Eigenschaften physischer Prozesse wie Beschaffenheit und Verhalten von Materialien oder Montage- und Fertigungstechniken in digitale Modelle integriert werden[2] und die Projekte, der digitalen Prozesskette folgend, mithilfe von CAD/CAM Technologien realisiert bzw. materialisiert werden. Diese digitalen Modelle basieren auf einem abstrakten Modell der Wirklichkeit, und können neben Informationen über Form und Geometrie auch verschiedenartige Verhältnisse und Organisationsstrukturen abbilden.

Häufig wird versucht, relevante Aspekte der materiellen Welt in einem virtuellen Modell zu implementieren, sowie Designaufgaben für Berechnungen zu quantifizieren und zu operationalisieren, um effiziente und optimierte Formen zu generieren. Unter der Annahme, dass man Probleme ganzheitlich erfassen könnte, würden sich Lösungen in einer solchen objektivierten Situation allein aus einer Designaufgabe ableiten lassen und wären nicht mehr von dem/der Gestalter/in abhängig. Das ist in der Realität nicht der Fall: zu Designlösungen führt immer eine Kombination aus rationalen sowie intuitiven Strategien.[3]

Zudem sind Prozesse in der physischen Welt nicht beliebig genau reproduzierbar, und es ist unmöglich, komplexe physikalische Prozesse im Digitalen realistisch zu simulieren. Jedes auf einer Simulation basierende Experiment ist verzerrt durch die fehlenden Eigenschaften, die nicht implementiert sind, die jedoch für die Herausbildung von emergenten Phänomenen möglicherweise essentiell sein könnten.[4] Umgekehrt wiederum ist es mit

> Die gezeigten Konzepte arbeiten bewusst mit und nicht gegen diese Unschärfe, versuchen sie nicht zu eliminieren, sondern zu moderieren.

The analysis presented in the following lines describes methods for interconnecting physical and digital realities based on various systematic experiments. They serve to investigate the explorative question of whether the integration of the material environment, with its vagueness and indeterminacy, into digitally driven control systems through feedback loops offers the potential to facilitate innovative processes of form generation in the context of architectural design. The concepts examined here purposefully work with this vagueness instead of against it; they try to moderate instead of eliminate it.

Feedback Loops between Digital and Physical Domains.

Contrary to a dematerialization of architecture in the information age, current discourse is distinguished by endeavors to rematerialize digital architecture through different approaches.[1] This for instance results in properties related to physical processes—such as the nature and properties of materials or assembly and production technology—being integrated into digital models,[2] or in projects being realized or materialized with the aid of CAD/CAM technology, fully in line with the digital process chain. These digital models are based on an abstract model of reality and, besides information about form and geometry, can also picture different kinds of relationships and organizational structures.

Attempts are frequently made at implementing relevant aspects of the material world in a virtual model, as well as quantifying and operationalizing design tasks when making calculations in order to generate efficient and optimized forms. If operating under the assumption that it is possible to view a problem in its entirety, then solutions would evolve from a design task itself in such an objectified situation and would no longer be dependent on the designer. Yet in reality this is not the case: design solutions always result from a combination of both rational and intuitive strategies.[3]

What is more, processes in the physical world cannot be precisely reproduced at will, and it is impossible to realistically simulate complex physical processes using digital means. Each experiment based on a simulation is skewed by missing properties that have not been implemented, but which may well be essential in allowing emergent phenomena to take form.[4] Conversely, it is not possible to use objects from the

1   Vgl. Fabio Gramazio/Matthias Kohler: *Digital Materiality in Architecture*, Baden 2008.

2   Vgl. Georg Vrachliotis: „On Conceptual Histories of Architecture and Digital Culture", in: Tomas Valena/ Tom Avermaete/Georg Vrachliotis (Hg.): *Structuralism Reloaded*, Stuttgart 2011, S. 256–268.

3   Vgl. Reinhard König: „Generative Planning Methods from a Structuralist Perspective", in: Valena/Avermaete/ Vrachliotis (Hg.): *Structuralism Reloaded*, S. 275–280 (wie Anm. 2).

4   Vgl. Daniel Bisig/Rolf Pfeifer: „Understanding by Design", in: *Explorations in Architecture. Teaching, Design, Research*, Basel/Boston/Berlin 2008, S. 124–133.

1   See Fabio Gramazio and Matthias Kohler, *Digital Materiality in Architecture* (Baden, 2008).

2   See Georg Vrachliotis, "On Conceptual Histories of Architecture and Digital Culture," in *Structuralism Reloaded*, ed. Tomas Valena, Tom Avermaete, and Georg Vrachliotis (Stuttgart, 2011), pp. 256–68.

3   See Reinhard König, "Generative Planning Methods from a Structuralist Perspective," in Valena et al., *Structuralism Reloaded*, pp. 275–80 (see note 2).

4   See Daniel Bisig and Rolf Pfeifer, "Understanding by Design," in *Explorations in Architecture: Teaching, Design, Research* (Basel, Boston, and Berlin, 2008), pp. 124–33.

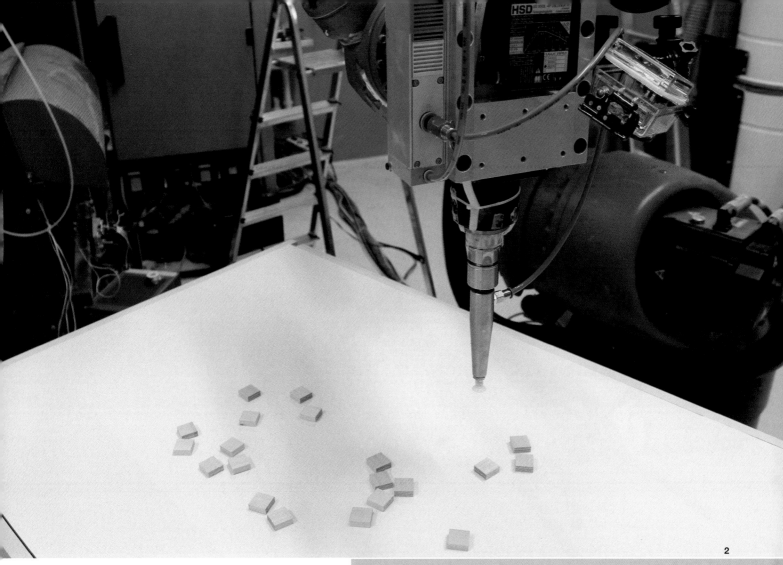

2

2–4 Verschränkung eines physischen und digitalen Modells: Physische Eigenschaften (Anzahl, Position, Orientierung) der Holzquader werden aus einem aktuellen Zustand mittels optischem Tracking extrahiert. Diese sind Informationsgrundlage für das digitale Modell, in welchem die Holzquader zusätzlich virtuelle Partikel mit einer Masse repräsentieren, die einander anziehen. Aus einem aktuellen Frame wird eine Zustandsänderung berechnet (Änderung der Position eines einzelnen Holzquaders), und durch einen Aktuator, in diesem Fall ein Industrieroboter, wird der Quader versetzt. Nach mehreren Iterationsschritten bilden sich Cluster von Holzquadern, wobei das Bilden solcher Strukturen kein expliziter Teil des Algorithmus ist. Das fortwährende Erfassen des aktuellen Zustandes mittels Sensoren erlaubt auch ein intuitives Eingreifen des Menschen, z.B. ein Verschieben oder Wegnehmen von Quadern mit der Hand. Interconnection between a physical and a digital model: the physical properties (number, position, orientation) of the wooden blocks were assessed based on a current state by means of optical tracking. This provided basic information for the digital model in which the wooden blocks additionally used mass to represent virtual particles that reciprocally attract one another. Taking a current frame, a change in state was calculated (positional change of a single wooden block); using an actuator, in this case an industrial robot, the block was relocated. After several iterative steps, clusters of wooden blocks formed, although the creation of such structures was not explicitly part of the algorithm. The continuous tracking of the current state via sensors also allowed humans to intuitively intervene, for instance by displacing or removing blocks by hand.
© Foto photo: Kathrin Dörfler

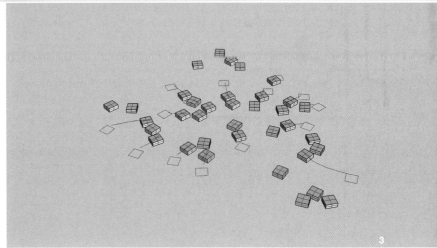

3

4

5

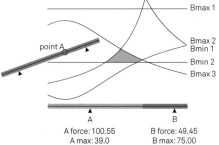

point A

Bmax 1
Bmax 2
Bmin 1
Bmin 2
Bmax 3

A   B
A force: 100.55   B force: 49.45
A max: 39.0   B max: 75.00

6

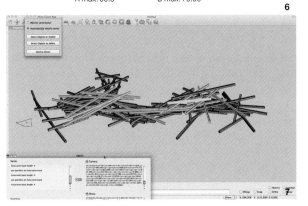

5–7 Operationale und nicht-operationale Probleme: Die Aufgabe, einen Stapel aus Holzstäbchen unterschiedlicher Länge zu bauen, erscheint im ersten Augenblick trivial. Je höher der Stapel wird, desto schwieriger wird es jedoch, das Gleichgewicht aufrecht zu erhalten, vor allem, wenn man den Stapel nicht auf eine einfache, leicht verständliche Struktur limitiert. Deshalb wurde in diesem Experiment das Stabilitätsproblem rationalisiert, und ein Stapel-Algorithmus implementiert, der die Stabilität ohne weitere Einschränkungen in der Formgebung gewährleistet. Es existiert keine explizite formale Definition im Voraus, was den Entstehungsprozess der Struktur zu spontanen formalen und intuitiven Entscheidungen hin öffnet. Anstatt genaue Positionen von Stäben vorweg zu definieren, können vom/von der Gestalter/in Richtungen und Impulse vorgegeben werden (über die Startkonfiguration in erster Ebene, hingelegte Stäbe, Länge der Stäbe, etc.). Die einzelnen Elemente werden dann in Folge vom Aktuator an den ermittelten Positionen, abhängig von den Stabilitätsberechnungen, platziert. Dies setzt, genauso wie im ersten erwähnten Experiment, eine fortwährende Kohärenz des digitalen Modells und der physischen Struktur voraus. Operational and non-operational problems: the task of building a stack of wooden sticks of different lengths may seem trivial at first glance. Yet the higher the stack becomes, the more difficult it is to maintain balance, especially if the stack is not limited to a simple, easily comprehensible structure. For this reason, the stability problem was rationalized in this experiment, and a stacking algorithm was implemented that ensures stability without restricting form generation in any way. There was no explicit formal definition ahead of time that would have opened the structural design process up to spontaneous form-related and intuitive decisions. Instead of specifying process positions for the sticks in advance, the designers were able to predefine directions and impulses (regarding the initial configuration at the first level, placement of sticks, length of sticks, etc.). The individual elements were then placed by the actuator in the determined positions, contingent on the stability calculations. Just like in the first experiment, this presupposed an ongoing coherence of the digital model and the physical structure. © Foto photo: Romana Rust

purely material world to represent semantic relations and information which extend beyond their inherent physical properties. This observation has led to a quest for hybrid systems that are digital and physical at the same time, that is, discrete and continuous—an undertaking that has now replaced previous efforts dedicated to the utter abstraction of physical reality.

Feedback loops between digital and physical domains and the direct intertwining thereof open up new possibilities for channeling flows of mass, energy, and information in a coherent way (see cyber-physical systems[5]), with physical processes being monitored and controlled in the process. The data extracted in this way can flow into digital processes and algorithms. By the same token, information in digital form can be transferred into physical space through actuators. When both realms are interconnected, physical objects become carriers of digital information and simultaneously serve as an information source for their virtual counterpart (figs. 2–4). In the context of form-generating strategies, this entwinement concurrently lays the foundations for an integration of operational, algorithmic, and non-operational, intuitive design methods.

Implementation of a Design Tool. First, various experimental setups were developed to comprehend emergent behavior in combination with operationalizable and non-operationalizable methods. This was then used to investigate the synthesis of digital logic and the physical performance of different material and material systems. The studies and experiments thus conducted out may be considered exemplary and are presented as indicators for a broader research field that is introduced through this topic.

As a requirement for carrying out the experiments, a system was designed and implemented that enables ongoing communication and data exchange between the sensors and actuators in a network. This allows computer-operated machines, as actuators and conveyers of digitally existing information, to be interactively controlled as part of an open process and utilized as a design-tool component. During such ongoing (design) processes, there is the physical environment with objects or structural elements, but also a correlating digital model that is continually synchronized and reconciled through feedback loops.

Tools and Intuition. Each tool that is implemented changes and modifies our bodies' interaction with the environment based on its particular operation mode, and consequently our thought-based perception as well.[6] This also applies to digital

Objekten der reinen materiellen Welt nicht möglich, semantische Relationen oder Informationen zu repräsentieren, die über ihre inhärenten physikalischen Eigenschaften hinausgehen. Die aus dieser Beobachtung resultierende Suche nach hybriden Systemen, die gleichzeitig digital und physisch, also diskret und kontinuierlich sind, ersetzt die vorangegangenen Bemühungen der vollkommenen Abstraktion der physischen Wirklichkeit.

Feedbackschleifen zwischen digitalen und physischen Domains und deren direkte Verflechtung eröffnen neue Möglichkeiten, Ströme von Masse, Energie und Information auf kohärente Weise zu leiten (vgl. Cyber-Physical-Systems[5]): Dabei werden physikalische Prozesse von Sensoren beobachtet und kontrolliert. Daraus extrahierte Daten können in digitale Prozesse und Algorithmen einfließen. Umgekehrt dazu kann digital vorhandene Information mittels Aktuatoren in den physischen Raum übertragen werden. Sind beide Welten miteinander verschränkt, werden physische Objekte Träger von digitaler Information und dienen gleichzeitig als Informationsquelle für ihr virtuelles Pendant (Abb. 2–4). Im Zusammenhang mit Formfindungsstrategien schafft diese Verflechtung zugleich die Voraussetzung für eine Integration von operationalen, algorithmischen und nicht-operationalen, intuitiven Entwurfsmethoden.

> Feedbackschleifen zwischen digitalen und physischen Domains und deren direkte Verflechtung eröffnen neue Möglichkeiten, Ströme von Masse, Energie und Information auf kohärente Weise zu leiten.

Implementierung eines Gestaltungswerkzeugs. Zu Beginn wurden verschiedene Versuchsaufbauten entwickelt, um emergentes Verhalten in Kombination von operationalisierbaren und nicht-operationalisierbaren Methoden zu verstehen. Anhand dieser wurde weitergehend die Synthese von digitaler Logik und dem physikalischen Verhalten verschiedener Materialien und Materialsysteme untersucht. Die durchgeführten Studien und Experimente sind exemplarisch und werden als Indikatoren für ein größeres Forschungsfeld aufgeführt, das durch dieses Thema eröffnet wird.

Als Voraussetzung für die Durchführung der Experimente wurde ein System entworfen und implementiert, welches eine fortlaufende Kommunikation und Datenaustausch zwischen Sensoren und Aktuatoren in einem Netzwerk ermöglicht. Computergesteuerte Maschinen als Aktuatoren und als Vermittler digital vorhandener Information können damit interaktiv in einem offenen Prozess gesteuert und als Bestandteil eines Gestaltungswerkzeuges verwendet werden. Während eines solchen laufenden (Gestaltungs-) Prozesses gibt es einerseits die physische Umgebung mit Objekten bzw. Bauelementen, sowie ein dazu korrelierendes, digitales Modell. Diese beiden stehen in einem wechselseitigen Verhältnis miteinander und werden über Feedbackschleifen kontinuierlich synchronisiert und aufeinander abgestimmt.

5   See Lui Sha, Sathish Gopalakrishnan, Xue Liu, and Qixin Wang, "Cyber-Physical Systems: A New Frontier," in *Machine Learning in Cyber Trust: Security, Privacy, and Reliability*, ed. Philip S. Yu and Jeffrey J. P. Tsai (New York, 2009), pp. 3–13.

6   See Shaun Gallagher, *How the Body Shapes the Mind* (Oxford, 2006).

5   Vgl. Lui Sha/Sathish Gopalakrishnan/Xue Liu/Qixin Wang: „Cyber-Physical Systems: A New Frontier", in: Philip S. Yu, Jeffrey J. P. Tsai (Hg.): *Machine Learning in Cyber Trust. Security, Privacy, and Reliability*, New York 2009, S. 3–13.

Werkzeuge und Intuition. Jedes Werkzeug, das wir benutzen, verändert und modifiziert die Interaktion unseres Körpers mit der Umwelt aufgrund seiner speziellen Handhabung, und infolgedessen auch die Wahrnehmung unseres Denkens.[6] Dies trifft auch auf digitale Werkzeuge zu,[7] wenn man das Handwerk als Verbindung zwischen Handwerker/innen und dem von ihnen gewählten Medium versteht. In einem Zusammenspiel aus (fachlicher) Kompetenz und Improvisation bearbeiten und überarbeiten Handwerker/innen ihr Medium in einem fortlaufenden Feedbackprozess, und aus diesem heraus können rationale, wie auch intuitive Entscheidungen getroffen werden. Dieser Prozess bzw. diese „Bewegung" ist laut Henri Bergson Voraussetzung für intuitives Handeln: „Für die Intuition ist Veränderung das Wesentliche. [...] Sie erfasst eine Aufeinanderfolge, die keine Nebeneinanderstellung ist, ein Wachstum von innen her, die ununterbrochene Verlängerung der Vergangenheit in eine Gegenwart hinein, die ihrerseits in die Zukunft eingreift."[8]

Die im Rahmen der Experimente untersuchte Integration von digitalen und regel-basierten Entwurfswerkzeugen in den physischen Raum erlaubt ein intuitives Hantieren mit Materialien und Bauelementen, die als Erweiterung Bestandteil und Informationsquelle eines digitalen Modells sind. Umgekehrt dazu ist die gleichzeitige Manipulation dieser Materialien mit computergesteuerten Aktuatoren die wechselseitige Übersetzung digitaler Information. In der Verwendung dieses Systems als Entwurfswerkzeug können operationale Aufgaben im Gestaltungsprozess automatisiert und auf die Maschine übertragen werden, während Raum gelassen wird für die Einbindung menschlicher Intelligenz und Intuition, zum Lösen von nicht-operationalen Problemen.[9] Im Unterschied zu herkömmlichen Vorgehensweisen, bei denen der Materialisierungsprozess entkoppelt und meist am Ende der digitalen Entwurfskette angesiedelt ist, sind hier die Übergänge fließend und die Grenzen unbestimmt (Abb. 5–7).

Wenn der Mensch am Entstehungsprozess der Gestalt mitwirkt und in direkter Interaktion mit dem System und seiner physischen Struktur steht, kann dieser gleichsam als Aktuator oder Sensor betrachtet werden, beziehungsweise als eine komplexe Kombination daraus. Objekt und Subjekt werden enthierarchisiert und gleichgestellt, während der Fokus auf dem

> Wenn der Mensch am Entstehungsprozess der Gestalt mitwirkt und in direkter Interaktion mit dem System und seiner physischen Struktur steht, kann dieser gleichsam als Aktuator oder Sensor betrachtet werden, beziehungsweise als eine komplexe Kombination daraus.

tools[7] if we understand artisanship to be a nexus between the artisans and their chosen medium. Through interplay of (specialized) expertise and improvisation, artisans practice and adapt their medium in an ongoing feedback-based process, which serves as a basis for making both rational and intuitive decisions. According to Henri Bergson, this process or "movement" presupposes intuitive action: "For intuition the essential is change … it grasps a succession which is not juxtaposition, a growth from within, the uninterrupted prolongation of the past into a present which is already blending into the future."[8]

The integration of digital and rule-based design tools into physical space allows for an intuitive handling of materials and structural elements that serve as beneficial components and information sources for a digital model. Conversely, the concomitant manipulation of these materials on the part of computer-controlled actuators represents a reciprocal translation of digital information. When using this system as a design tool, operational tasks can be automated as part of the design process and transferred to the machine, while still making room for the integration of human intelligence and intuition in order to solve non-operational problems.[9] In contrast to conventional approaches in which the materialization process is decoupled and usually situated at the end of the digital design chain, here the transitions are fluent and the boundaries indeterminate (figs. 5–7).

When human individuals contribute to the process of creating a form, thus directly interacting with the system and its physical structure, they can actually be viewed as actuators or sensors, or as a complex combination of the two. Object and subject become de-hierarchized and equated, while the focus is placed on engendering interfaces and facilitating feedback loops (between human and machine or between machines).

If we draw an analogy between the design processes described in the experiments (figs. 2–4 and 5–7) and the relationship between artisans and their medium, then the otherwise interacting designer initially takes on the role of the observer. Through one's own action and reaction to the system, the designer as observer can recognize certain causal coherencies and learn how to handle them in the process. It is only over time, with practice, that a contemplative mechanism evolves, whereby the designer becomes immersed in the movement. This ludic dialogue between human and machine thrives on moments of surprise and on a touch of unpredictability; it involves a kind of deceleration that results from the duration of the physical experience.

6   Vgl. Shaun Gallagher: *How the Body Shapes the Mind*, Oxford 2006.

7   Vgl. Malcolm McCullough: *Abstracting Craft: The Practiced Digital Hand*, Cambridge, MA 1996.

8   Henri Bergson: *Denken und schöpferisches Werden*, Hamburg 1993, S. 46.

9   Vgl. König: „Generative Planning Methods" (wie Anm. 3).

7   See Malcolm McCullough, *Abstracting Craft: The Practiced Digital Hand* (Cambridge, MA, 1996).

8   See Henri Bergson, *The Creative Mind: An Introduction to Metaphysics*, trans. Mabelle L. Andison (1946; repr., Mineola, NY, 2007), pp. 20 and 22.

9   See König, "Generative Planning Methods" (see note 3).

8

8–10 Adaptive, nicht-lineare Prozesse in der automatisierten Fabrikation: Installation im k/haus, Wien, Ausstellung „Zeichnen, Zeichnen", 2013. Die Installation besteht aus einem Seilroboter mit drei Achsen, der durch Auf- und Abrollen der Seile einen Effektor über einer Plattform bewegen kann. Dieser ist mit einer Spule zum Abwickeln eines Fadens und einem optischen Sensor ausgestattet. Das Beispiel zeigt das Entfalten einer Gestalt in einer integrierten digitalen und physischen Umwelt, innerhalb einer geschlossenen Feedback-Schleife zwischen Sensor und Aktuator: Das Verhalten des abgewickelten Fadens, auf welche Art und wo genau dieser auf die Oberfläche fällt, ist nicht vorherbestimmbar. Aus diesem Grund wird an der Stelle, wo der Faden auf die Plattform auftrifft, der Helligkeitswert sensorisch erfasst und gespeichert, welcher die Berechnung neuer Positionen des Roboters beeinflusst. Die leere Fläche zu Beginn entspricht dem leeren digitalen Speicher. Über die Zeit hinterlässt der Faden Spuren in der physischen Umwelt, und die Fläche füllt sich. Die Maschine kann die Spuren an den verschiedenen Positionen, die sie abfährt, wahrnehmen, und füllt den digitalen Speicher. Aus den kleinen Bewegungen kann ein Gesamtbild generiert werden. Die entstehende Struktur ist nicht prädeterminiert, sondern ergibt sich aus der Wechselwirkung einfacher Regeln eines Algorithmus und dem Reagieren auf lokale Geschehnisse und dem Feedback. Das Auftreten von Mustern, die man als emergente Phänomene bezeichnen kann, ist die Konsequenz des sich selbst regulierenden Systems und des Zusammenspiels seiner Elemente und deren nichtlinearer Verstärkung. Diese Vorgänge passieren in der Installation für das menschliche Zeitempfinden äußerst langsam und Veränderungen sind nur über einen längeren Zeitraum ersichtlich. Adaptive, nonlinear process in automated production: installation at k/haus, Vienna, as part of the exhibition "Zeichnen, Zeichnen," 2013. The installation was comprised of a cable robot with three axes that could move an effector across a platform by rolling back and forth. The device was equipped with a bobbin for winding thread and an optical sensor. This example shows the unfolding of a figure in an integrated digital and physical environment, within a closed feedback loop between sensor and actuator: the behavior of the unwound thread (where precisely this surface ended up and in which way) could not be predetermined. For this reason, the brightness value was sensorially captured and recorded in the place where the thread intersected with the platform, which in turn influenced the calculation of new robot positions. The empty surface at the beginning reflected the empty digital memory. Over time, the thread left behind traces in the physical environment, and the surface began to fill up. The machine was capable of perceiving the traces left in the different positions along which it moved, and it filled the digital memory, allowing an overall picture to be generated from the small movements. The evolving structure was not predetermined, but rather the result of interaction between simple algorithmic rules and the reaction to local proceedings and the feedback provided. The occurrence of patterns that may be called emergent phenomena was the consequence of the self-regulating system and the interplay among its elements and their nonlinear reinforcement. In the installation these processes took place extremely slowly, from a human sense of time perspective, and were only evident over an extended period of time. © Foto photo: Florian Rist

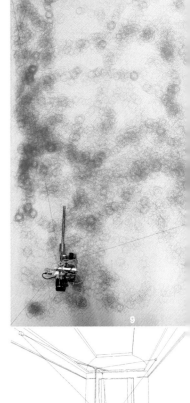

9

10

Erzeugen von Schnittstellen und dem Ermöglichen von Feedback-Schleifen (zwischen Mensch und Maschine oder zwischen Maschinen) liegt.

Betrachtet man die in den Experimenten (Abb. 2–4 und 5–7) beschriebenen Gestaltungsprozesse in Analogie zu der Beziehung der Handwerker mit ihrem Medium, so befinden sich die interagierenden Gestalter zunächst in der Rolle der Beobachter, die durch eigene Aktionen und Reaktionen des Systems gewisse kausale Zusammenhänge erkennen und dadurch dessen Handhabung erlernen können. Erst mit der Dauer, der Übung, entsteht eine Art kontemplativer Vorgang, ein sich Hineinversetzen in die Bewegung. Dieser spielerische Dialog zwischen Mensch und Maschine lebt vom Moment der Überraschung und einer partiellen Unvorhersehbarkeit, er geht einher mit einer Art von Entschleunigung, die eine Folge der Dauer von physischen Geschehnissen ist.

Synchronisation von Aktuatoren und Sensoren. Zeitlichkeit im physischen Sinn bedeutet Wandlung und Übergang von einem Zustand in den nächsten. In einer physischen Welt mit kontinuierlichen räumlich-zeitlichen Abfolgen können einzelne Zustände nicht wiederhergestellt werden. Zudem sind Vorgänge, wenn man sie auf einer makroskopischen Ebene betrachtet, nicht beliebig wiederholbar. In der digitalen Welt wiederum hat Zeitlichkeit eine vollkommen andere Bedeutung. Hier sind Vorgänge exakt reproduzierbar und können in verschiedene Richtungen, vorwärts wie rückwärts, laufen.

Sobald digitale Berechnungsverfahren einen Bezug zur physischen Welt haben, besitzen Daten immer auch einen zeitlichen und räumlichen Kontext. Neben den Größen, die Messungen und Aktionen beschreiben, muss auch ihre Chronologie verarbeitet werden. Das bedeutet einerseits, dass physikalische Vorgänge mit hinreichender zeitlicher Auflösung (Frequenz) erfasst werden müssen, um den Vorgang rekonstruieren zu können. Zum anderen müssen die Datenerfassung, die Kommunikation zwischen den Knoten im Netzwerk[10] als auch die Bewegung der Aktuatoren synchronisiert und hinreichend schnell erfolgen. Dabei bestimmen die Geschwindigkeiten der physikalischen Vorgänge und die Anforderungen an die Interaktivität des Systems die notwendige maximale Zykluszeit (Abb. 8–10).

Werden auf diese Weise, wie in den Experimenten beschrieben, Formen und Strukturen erzeugt, so zeigt sich ein essenzieller Unterschied zur reinen virtuellen Generierung von Formen: Sie werden allmählich, in graduellen Schritten aufgebaut und eventuell auch abgebaut, Vorgänge können nur hintereinander passieren und sind gezwungen, einer bestimmten Reihung zu folgen.

> Zeitlichkeit im physischen Sinn bedeutet Wandlung und Übergang von einem Zustand in den nächsten.

Unscharfe Materialsysteme in automatisierten Fabrikationsprozessen. Betrachtet man die beschriebenen Experimente außerhalb eines reinen

Synchronization of Actuators and Sensors. Temporality in a physical sense signifies transformation and transition from one state to another. In a physical world of continual spatiotemporal sequences, certain states cannot be reestablished. Moreover, when viewed at a macroscopic level, processes cannot be repeated at will. Yet in the digital world, temporality takes on completely different meaning. Here, processes are precisely reproducible and can run in different directions, both forward and backward.

As soon as digital calculation methods are associated with the physical world, the data always also possesses a temporal and a spatial context. Besides the factors that describe measurements and actions, the related chronology must also be processed. On the one hand, this means that physical processes must be captured with sufficient temporal resolution (frequency) in order for each process to be conceivably reconstructed. On the other, data acquisition, communication between the network hubs,[10] and the movement of the actuators must all be synchronized and take place quickly enough. Here the various speeds of physical processes and the demands made on the interactivity of the system serve to determine the necessary maximum cycle time (figs. 8–10).

If forms and structures are generated in this way, as demonstrated in the experiments, then an essential difference becomes apparent as compared to the pure virtual generation of forms. These forms are slowly constructed through gradual steps and sometimes also deconstructed; the processes can only be carried out one after another, and they are compelled to follow a certain sequence.

Vague Material Systems in Automated Production Processes. If we view the experiments described here outside of a straightforward design process, then several aspects related to digital production processes in general can be observed and assessed.

The integration of physical processes using digital information processing can lead to a simplification of algorithms: by foregoing any attempts at implementing all material-related properties in a digital model, the acts of measuring and sampling—that is, the direct inclusion of physical properties—make a digital simulation obsolete.

To date, the utilization of detailed, granular, asymmetrical, or soft materials in automated production processes has seen very limited application.[11] The reason for this lies not only in

10 See Sha et al., "Cyber-Physical Systems" (see note 5).

11 See Carola Dierichs and Achim Menges, "Natural Aggregation Processes as Models for Architectural Material Systems," in *Proceedings of the Design and Nature Conference* (Pisa and Southampton, 2010), pp. 17–27. Fabio Gramazio and Matthias Kohler, *Procedural Landscapes*, ETH Zürich, 2010, available online at http://dfab.arch.ethz.ch/web/e/lehre/208.html and http://dfab.arch.ethz.ch/web/e/lehre/211.html (accessed August 2013).

10 Vgl. Sha et al.: „Cyber-Physical Systems" (wie Anm. 5).

the complex behavior of such materials, which cannot be accurately predicted or simulated, but in the fact that, in many cases, conventional joining technology is not practicable. Many of these materials react in potentially emergent ways and are thus difficult to analyze, for local and global properties are mutually dependent.

The approaches detailed here present an opportunity to employ these materials in a controlled manner in an open and adaptive production process using iterative methods. Such feedback-based methods display properties similar to those found in natural emergent systems, such as robustness and the ability to correct mistakes.

A contribution to the current interdisciplinary discourse on cyber-physical systems is made by our exploration of the unpredictability, indeterminacy, and vagueness of the material environment—the complex macroscopic behavior of certain materials and material systems—as embedded in digitally driven control systems and our investigation of their reciprocal interaction. The conceptual approaches seamlessly blend into many branches of research and science where direct regulatory approaches and global control mechanisms are replaced by local, dynamic, networked approaches that exercise self-organization and emergence.

Acknowledgments: The implementation of this system would not have been possible without the open source projects freely accessible online and the aid of various developers. We are also grateful to the participating universities and institutes for their support: Institute of Architecture and Media, Graz University of Technology, and Institute of Art and Design, Vienna University of Technology.

Translation Dawn Michelle d'Atri

Gestaltungsprozesses, kann man mehrere Aspekte beobachten und extrahieren, die digitale Fabrikationsprozesse im Allgemeinen betreffen:

Die Integration physischer Prozesse mit digitaler Informationsverarbeitung kann zu einer Vereinfachung von Algorithmen führen: Indem man nicht alle Eigenschaften von Materialien in ein digitales Modell zu implementieren versucht, wird mit dem Messen und Abtasten, also der direkten Einbindung physikalischer Eigenschaften, eine digitale Simulation obsolet.

Bislang war die Verwendung von kleinteiligen, körnigen, ungleichförmigen oder weichen Materialien in automatisierten Fabrikationsprozessen sehr beschränkt.[11] Der Grund hierfür liegt nicht nur in deren komplexem Verhalten, welches sich nicht exakt voraussagen oder simulieren lässt, sondern auch darin, dass bisherige traditionelle Fügetechniken in vielen Fällen nicht anwendbar sind. Viele dieser Materialien verhalten sich potenziell emergent und lassen sich schwer analysieren, da lokale und globale Eigenschaften einander gegenseitig bedingen.

Die dargestellten Ansätze zeigen eine Möglichkeit, diese Materialien in einem offenen und adaptiven Fabrikationsprozess über iterative Verfahren kontrolliert zu verwenden. Diese auf Feedback basierenden Methoden weisen Eigenschaften wie Robustheit und die Fähigkeit zur Fehlerkorrektur auf, wie sie auch bei natürlichen emergenten Systemen beobachtet werden können.

Die Auseinandersetzung mit der Unvorhersehbarkeit, Unbestimmtheit und Unschärfe der materiellen Umwelt – das komplexe makroskopische Verhalten von bestimmten Materialien und Materialsystemen – eingebunden in digital gesteuerte Regelkreise und deren gegenseitige Wechselwirkung, versteht sich auch als Beitrag zum aktuellen interdisziplinären Diskurs über Cyber-Physical-Systems. Die Denkansätze fügen sich nahtlos in vielen Forschungs- und Wissenschaftszweigen ein, in denen direkte Regelungsansätze und globale Kontrollmechanismen ersetzt werden durch lokale dynamische, vernetzte Ansätze, die die Selbstorganisation und Emergenz nutzen.

Anerkennung: Die Implementierung des Systems wäre ohne über das Internet verfügbare Open Source Projekte und der Unterstützung durch Entwickler/innen nicht möglich gewesen. Wir danken außerdem den beteiligten Hochschulen und Instituten für ihre Unterstützung: Institut für Architektur und Medien, TU Graz, Institut für Kunst und Gestaltung, TU Wien.

11 Vgl. Carola Dierichs/Achim Menges: „Natural Aggregation Processes as Models for Architectural Material Systems", in: *Proceedings of the Design and Nature Conference*, Pisa/Southampton 2010, S. 17–27. Fabio Gramazio/Matthias Kohler: *Procedural Landscapes*, ETH Zürich 2010, online unter: http://dfab.arch.ethz.ch/web/e/lehre/208.html und http://dfab.arch.ethz.ch/web/e/lehre/211.html (Stand: 19.08.2013).

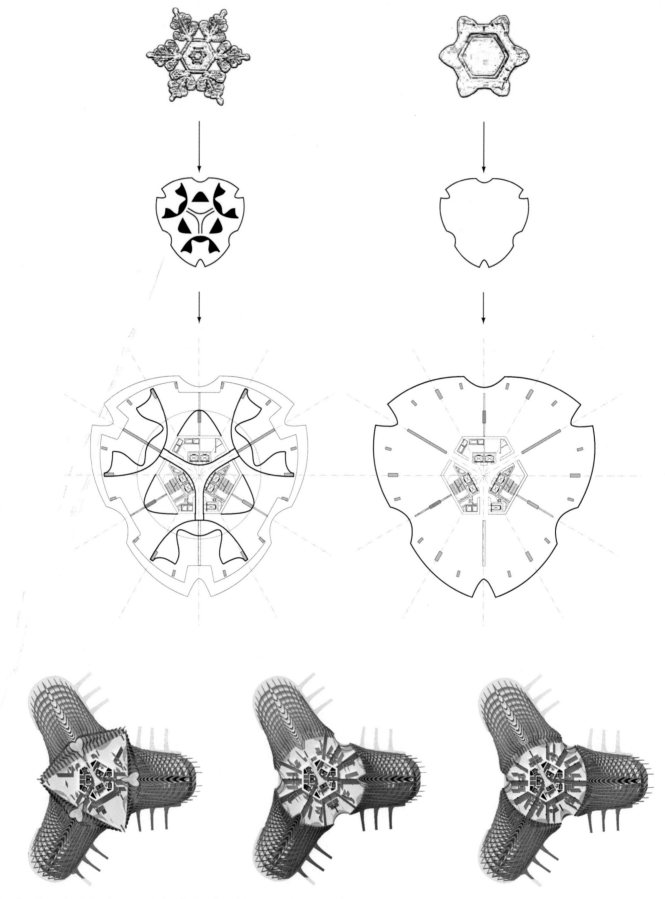

1 Snowflake Tower. Inspiration der geometrischen Struktur Snowflake geometry inspiration. © LAVA (Laboratory for Visionary Architecture, Berlin, Stuttgart, Sydney)

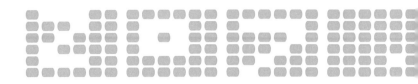

Parametrische Adaption. Eine Evolution des Entwurfsprozesses

Der englische Architekturtheoretiker und -historiker Robin Evans hat in seinem Buch *The Projective Cast*[1] dargelegt, dass Architektur traditionell unlösbar mit Geometrie verbunden und ein Entwurf von den zur Verfügung stehenden Darstellungstechniken abhängig ist. Für ihn wurde die historische Entwicklung der Architektur vor allem durch die Möglichkeiten der Projektionszeichnungen geprägt.

Parametric Adaption: An Evolution of the Design Process. In his book *The Projective Cast*,[1] the English architecture theorist and historian Robin Evans asserted that, traditionally, architecture is inextricably linked to geometry and that a design is dependent on the available techniques of representation. In his eyes, the historical development of architecture was predominately influenced by the possibilities inherent to projection drawing.

TOBIAS WALLISSER

Der Zusammenhang zwischen der Wiedergabe und der Konzeption von architektonischen Entwürfen ist nach Evans daran erkennbar, dass alle architektonischen Aktivitäten (Entwerfen, Bauen und Überprüfen) mittels einer „projektiven Transaktion" stattfinden. Dies gilt für alle nacheinander folgenden Zwischenschritte gleichermaßen, vom Aufskizzieren der inneren Vorstellung über die Präsentation des Projekts mittels einer Perspektivdarstellung an den Bauherrn bis zur Ausführung mittels orthografischer Pläne. Entwerfen ist „Handeln aus der Distanz",[2] schließt Evans, beschränkt durch die zur Verfügung stehenden Übersetzungsmöglichkeiten der verwendeten Darstellungstechniken. Digitale Techniken bieten nun auf jeder der von Robin Evans beschriebenen Ebenen – Darstellung und Konzeption, Präsentation und Realisierung – neue konzeptionelle Möglichkeiten.

Bei der Computerdarstellung eines Entwurfs werden geometrische Elemente durch variable Attribute definiert, die Parameter heißen. Eine sogenannte parametrische Software erlaubt die Darstellung und Erstellung von Variationen parametrisch definierter Elemente und ermöglicht dem Entwerfer dadurch direkte Eingriffsmöglichkeiten und Kontrolle. Bei diesen assoziativen Geometriemodellen werden Objekte als parametrische Geometrien definiert, die direkt vom Prozess ihres Entstehens abhängig sind; es wird somit nicht nur die Form definiert, sondern darüber hinaus auch Veränderungsmöglichkeiten. Das Arbeiten mit diesen Programmen erfordert ein anderes Verständnis von Zusammenhängen und Abhängigkeiten als untrennbare Eigenschaften jeder Form. Der Entwerfer kann wieder intuitiv, unmittelbar an einem dreidimensionalen Objekt arbeiten und dies sogar gleichzeitig von außen und von innen betrachten.

Ein weiterer Schritt sind regelbasierte Systeme, bei denen der Entwerfer zuerst den Prozess entwirft und dann anfängt, Varianten innerhalb eines Regelwerks zu optimieren und zu selektieren. Ein eindrucksvolles Beispiel ist die Arbeit von Mark Burry an der Rekonstruktion und Weiterentwicklung der Geometrie der von Gaudí in Barcelona errichteten und bis heute unvollendeten Kirche Sagrada Família[3]. Auch wenn der Entwurf selbst lange vor der Erfindung des Computers konzipiert wurde, ist er ein Beispiel für parametrisches Entwerfen. Er ist gekennzeichnet durch eine systematische Herangehensweise an die Schaffung von Formen und bietet einen guten Ausgangspunkt, um den Nutzen des Computers bei Entwurf und Konstruktion zu analysieren. Da die meisten der Originalmodelle von Gaudí zerstört waren, wurde mittels „Reverse Engineering" versucht, die ursprüngliche Logik nachzuvollziehen und die eingescannten Fragmente der Gipsmodelle zu ergänzen. Dem Entwurf liegt ein Codex für reichhaltige Formgenerierung zugrunde, der eine wiederholbare, innerhalb von Regeln veränderbare, präzise Beschreibung der Geometrie erzeugt. Viele

According to Evans, the correlation between the conception and the rendering of architectural design is identifiable in that architectural activity (designing, building, and reviewing) takes place by way of a "projective transaction." This equally applies to all successive interim stages, from sketching one's own ideas to presenting the project to the client using perspectival representation, or to the project's execution based on orthographic plans. Evans concludes that "design is action at a distance,"[2] limited by the available possibilities for transferring the representational techniques used. Digital technology is now offering new conceptual opportunities on each of the levels described by Robin Evans: representation and conception, presentation and realization.

In a computer-enabled design environment, geometric elements are defined by variable attributes called parameters. So-called "parametric software" makes it possible to depict and create variations of parametrically defined elements, which in turn provides the designer with direct ways of intervening and with control. In the case of these associative geometric models, objects are defined as parametric geometries that are immediately dependent on the process of their creation. Therefore, it is not only form that is being defined, but rather possibilities for change as well. Working with these programs requires a different understanding of contexts and dependencies as inseparable properties of each form. The designer can then once again work with a three-dimensional object intuitively and directly, even observing it from the outside and the inside simultaneously.

A further step entails rule-based systems where the designer first outlines the process and then starts selecting and optimizing variants within a body of rules. An impressive example is Mark Burry's work on the reconstruction and further development of the geometry of the Sagrada Família church in Barcelona, erected by Gaudí and still unfinished today.[3] Even if the design itself was drafted well prior to the invention of the computer, it is an example of parametric design. Characterized by a systematic approach to generating form, it offers a fitting starting point for analyzing the use of computers in design and structural work. Since most of Gaudí's original models were destroyed, reverse engineering was used to trace the original

1   Robin Evans: *The Projective Cast. Architecture and Its Three Geometries*, Cambridge, MA 1995, siehe auch die Auszüge aus Evans *The Projective Cast* in deutscher Übersetzung in *Arch+* 137 ("Die Anfänge moderner Raumkonzeptionen") in: *Arch+* 137 (1997), S. 18–23.

2   Robin Evans: „Durch Papier sehen", Übers. von Gerrit Jackson, in: Christoph Hoffmann/Barbara Wittmann (Hg.): *Wissen im Entwurf*, Bd. 4, Zürich 2011, S. 157–193, hier S. 185.

3   Antoni Gaudí i Cornet (*1852 in Reus; †1926 in Barcelona), katalanischer Architekt und herausragender Vertreter des Modernisme Català. Mark Burry: „Gaudí Unseen", Vortrag Staatliche Akademie der Bildenden Künste Stuttgart, 2007 und Mark Burry/Jane Burry: „Gaudí and CAD", in: *The Effects of CAD on Building Form and Design Quality*, ITcon 11 (2006), S. 437–446, online unter: http://itcon.org/2006/32 (Stand: 04. November 2013).

1   Robin Evans, *The Projective Cast: Architecture and Its Three Geometries* (Cambridge, MA, 1995). See also the excerpts from Robert Evans, *The Projective Cast*, in German translation in *Arch+* 137: Robin Evans, "Die Anfänge moderner Raumkonzeptionen," *Arch+* 137 (1997), pp. 18–23.

2   Robin Evans, "Seeing Through Paper," in *The Projective Cast*, p. 363 (see note 1).

3   Antoni Gaudí i Cornet (born 1852 in Reus, died 1926 in Barcelona), Catalan architect and outstanding representative of Modernisme Català. Mark Burry, "Gaudí Unseen," lecture at the Stuttgart State Academy of Art and Design, 2007, and Mark Burry and Jane Burry, "Gaudí and CAD," *The Effects of CAD on Building Form and Design Quality*, ITcon 11 (2006), pp. 437–46, available online at http://itcon.org/2006/32 (accessed November 2013).

logic and to complete the scanned fragments of the plaster models. The design is based on a codex for extensive form generation, which produces an iterable and precise geometrical description that is alterable within rule-based systems. Many of the elements employed by Gaudí are geometrically ruled surfaces, being subject to a production process that was part of the form development. Rules require very few resources to be built, and their easily developable nature makes it possible for reinforced bars in particular to be placed on double-curved surfaces. Here, complexity and diversity of form arise through the superimposition of simple elements.

The advantage of integrating computer-based techniques in design—as may be reasoned here—rests in the creation of continuity and flowing geometries, for one, but also in the maximization of local differentiation. Quantitative and qualitative differences within a coherent overall system arise through the interplay between human and machine. If we understand the mechanism of design as a process, then we might illustrate the difference between conventional and computer-based design techniques by contrasting two games, Chess and Go. While in Chess the form of each figure displays its potential and its value, in the game Go all tokens are equal to begin with. Their meaning accrues solely from their potential, from their position in relation to one's own tokens or to those of the opponent.[4]

The question remains as to which medium or which strategies designers should work with—and which software should be used when and to what end? A similar issue has always emerged when building models: the medium defines the form-related possibilities in part, regardless whether the object is fashioned from cardboard or plaster. Here the selection of material already becomes part of creative expression. However, the possibilities presented by digital technology are far greater and not limited to certain aspects as is the case in model building. In the future it will be advantageous for architects to possess the ability to process both material and geometric properties at the same time while employing the available computer-based techniques. Such skills allow architects to more proficiently control the implementation of their designs, to heighten the chance of realization, and thus to assume responsibility and retain control of the process. At present there is much discussion about whether this signifies the emergence of a new professional field, namely, that of the digitally working architect or the programming "digital creator."[5] The latter designation was coined by architect Sarah Benton in her dissertation in order to define and describe the role of architects who have

Elemente bei Gaudí sind geometrische Regelflächen; ihr Herstellungsprozess war Teil der Formentwicklung, denn Regelflächen sind mit wenigen Hilfsmitteln baubar, ihre einfache Abwickelbarkeit erlaubt es, gerade Bewehrungsstäbe in doppelt gekrümmten Flächen anzuordnen. Komplexität und Formenvielfalt entstehen hier durch Überlagerung einfacher Elemente.

Die Vorteile computerbasierter Techniken im Entwurf bestehen – so lässt sich hier schlussfolgern – zum einen in der Schaffung von Kontinuität und fließenden Geometrien, zum anderen in der Maximierung lokaler Differenzierung. Quantitative und qualitative Unterschiede innerhalb eines kohärenten Gesamtsystems entstehen im Zusammenspiel von Mensch und Maschine. Versteht man den Vorgang des Entwurfs als Prozess, könnte man den Unterschied zwischen den herkömmlichen und den computerbasierten Entwurfstechniken vielleicht mit dem Unterschied zwischen den beiden Spielen Schach und Go illustrieren. Während beim Schachspiel die Form jeder Figur ihr Potenzial und ihren Wert anzeigt, sind beim Go alle Spielsteine zunächst gleichwertig. Ihre Bedeutung entsteht allein aus ihrem Potenzial, aus ihrer Position in Beziehung zu den eigenen und den gegnerischen Spielsteinen.[4]

Es bleibt die Frage, mit welchem Medium oder welcher Strategie man als Entwerfer arbeitet, welche Software man zu welchem Zeitpunkt und wofür benutzt? Eine ähnliche Fragestellung hat sich schon immer beim Modellbau ergeben. Ob man ein Objekt mit Pappe oder Gips entwickelt: das Medium definiert die formalen Möglichkeiten zu einem Teil. Hier wird die Wahl des Materials bereits Teil der gestalterischen Aussage. Allerdings sind die Möglichkeiten digitaler Techniken viel weitgehender und nicht auf einzelne Aspekte beschränkt, wie das beim Modellbau der Fall ist. Zukünftig wird es von Vorteil sein, wenn Architekten die Fähigkeit der simultanen Bearbeitung materieller und geometrischer Eigenschaften unter Verwendung der zur Verfügung stehenden computerbasierten Techniken besitzen. Denn dadurch werden sie in der Lage sein, die Umsetzung ihrer Entwürfe besser zu steuern, die Realisierungschancen zu vergrößern und somit Verantwortung und Kontrolle im Prozess zu behalten. Es wird derzeit viel darüber diskutiert, ob dafür ein neues Berufsfeld entsteht: jenes des digital arbeitenden Architekten oder des programmierenden „digital creators".[5] Diese Bezeichnung wurde von der Architektin Sarah Benton in ihrer Dissertation definiert, um die Rolle eines Architekten, der sich im Umgang mit digitalen Techniken und deren Anwendungsmöglichkeiten für den architektonischen

> Versteht man den Vorgang des Entwurfs als Prozess, könnte man den Unterschied zwischen den herkömmlichen und den computerbasierten Entwurfstechniken vielleicht mit dem Unterschied zwischen den beiden Spielen Schach und Go illustrieren.

4   Jesse Reiser and Nanako Umemoto, *Atlas of Novel Tectonics* (New York, 2006).

5   Sarah Benton, "The Architectural Designer and Their Digital Media" (diss. Royal Melbourne Institute of Technology, 2008).

4   Jesse Reiser/Nanako Umemoto: *Atlas of Novel Tectonics*, New York 2006.

5   Sarah Benton: *The Architectural Designer and Their Digital Media*, Diss. Royal Melbourne Institute of Technology 2008.

Entwurf spezialisiert hat, zu beschreiben. Um an dieser Schnittstelle arbeiten zu können, braucht man sowohl technische Erfahrung als Architekt als auch digitales Know-how. Die Rolle des „Digital Creators" ist es, ausschließlich am Computer im Zusammenspiel mit anderen im Team zu entwerfen, für gestalterische Ideen oder technische Zusammenhänge die entsprechenden digitalen Techniken zu finden und parametrische Modelle dafür zu definieren. Da dies oft die Kapazitäten einzelner Personen übersteigt, arbeiten in größeren Büros ganze Teams in diesem Bereich. Während Frank Gehry gleich eine eigene Abteilung unterhält, die zunächst Softwaretools für das Büro entwickelte und heute vertreibt, gibt es z.B. bei Herzog & de Meuron in Basel die „Advanced Geometry Unit",[6] die neben der parametrischen Optimierung zum Zwecke der Baubarkeit immer öfter bereits von Anfang an Gebäudestrukturen aufgrund programmatischer, konstruktiver oder anderer Abhängigkeiten programmiert und Entwurfsvarianten untersucht. Ein Teil der Rolle des Entwerfers wird in diesem Prozess auf das Feld der Interaktion zwischen Mensch und Maschine übertragen.

Aus meiner eigenen Erfahrung als Architekt kenne ich unterschiedliche Entwicklungsstufen des Arbeitens mit dem Computer in den letzten 15 Jahren. Bei der Arbeit am neuen Bahnhof von Arnheim, genannt „Arnhem Centraal", von UNStudio[7] (seit 1997 im Bau) haben wir den Fokus auf die Entwicklung räumlicher Kontinuität durch die Transformation von gekrümmten Flächen gelegt. Dabei wurde Software aus der Animationsindustrie verwendet, die ein anderes Verständnis von Flächen als Resultat von Bewegung im Raum ermöglichte. Im Entwurf haben wir uns von konzeptionellen mathematischen Ideen leiten lassen und diese dann intuitiv räumlich weiterentwickelt. Umsetzungsmöglichkeiten oder Aspekte der Realisierung spielten erst nach der Entwurfsphase eine wichtige Rolle. Die hierdurch entstehende Trennung zwischen Entwurf und Ausführungsplanung ist vergleichbar mit der Realisierung des Guggenheim Museums in Bilbao von Frank Gehry, bei dem der Entwurf weitestgehend ohne Computer entstand, die Ausführung aber als erstes Projekt mit durchgängiger Planung mit Software aus der Automobil- oder Flugzeugindustrie.[8]

> Ein Teil der Rolle des Entwerfers wird in diesem Prozess auf das Feld der Interaktion zwischen Mensch und Maschine übertragen.

specialized in dealing with digitial technology and its applicability to architectural design. Working at this intersection requires both technical experience as an architect and digital know-how. The role of the digital creator is to do design work solely on the computer in collaboration with others in the team, to find the right digital technology for creative ideas or technical contexts, and to define the related parametric models. Since this often exceeds the capacity of the individual involved, larger architectural firms have whole teams working on this area. Frank Gehry, for instance, maintains an entire department that first developed software tools for the firm and today markets them, while Herzog & de Meuron in Basel has an "advanced geometry unit,"[6] which, besides parametric optimization for the purpose of determining suitability for building, from the outset programs building structures based on programmatic, structural, or other dependencies with increased regularity and also explores design variants. Part of the designer role is transferred to the field of human-machine interaction during this process.

Based on my own experience as an architect, I am familiar with the various developmental stages of working with the computer during the last fifteen years. While working on the new railway station in Arnhem by UNStudio,[7] which is called Arnhem Centraal and has been under construction since 1997, we have placed focus on the development of spatial continuity by transforming curved surfaces. Here software from the animation industry was used since it facilitates a different understanding of surfaces as a result of movement in space. In the design we allowed ourselves to be guided by conceptual mathematical ideas and then cultivated them in an intuitively spatial manner. Feasibility or aspects or realization did not play an important role until after the designing phase had been concluded. The resultant separation of design and implementation planning is comparable to the realization of Frank Gehry's Guggenheim Museum in Bilbao where computers were left out of the design process to a great extent, but later the execution was carried out as the first project to continuously use software from the automobile or aeronautical industry.[8]

6 Die Advanced Geometry Unit, Herzog DeMeuron wird von Kai Strehlke geleitet. Zu den Aufgaben gehörte die parametrische Optimierung für die Umsetzung der Fassade der neuen Messe in Basel und die Entwicklung der Geometrie des Fussballstadions in Bordeaux.

7 UNStudio, gegründet 1988 in Amsterdam von Ben van Berkel und Caroline Bos, gehört zu den Pionieren beim Einsatz von Computerprogrammen im Entwurf. Tobias Wallisser war von 1997 bis 2007 als Creative Director für die Entwicklung und Implementierung digitaler Entwurfsansätze zuständig. Das Projekt Arnhem Centraal entstand in der Zusammenarbeit mit Cecil Balmond. Große Teile des Projekts sind ausgeführt, die doppelt gekrümmte Dachkonstruktion der zentralen Transferhalle ist derzeit im Bau. Online unter: www.arnhemcentraal.nu (Stand: November 2013).

8 Gehry Technologies entwickelte die speziell auf die Bedürfnisse von Architekten angepasste Software. CATIA Digital Project ist eine Suite leistungsfähiger 3D Building Information Modeling (BIM)-Anwendungen, erstellt von Gehry Technologies mithilfe von Dassault Systèmes CATIA V5 als zentraler Modellierplattform. Online unter: http://www.3ds.com/de/products/catia/portfolio/digital-project/ (Stand: November 2013).

6 The advanced geometry unit at Herzog & de Meuron is headed by Kai Strehlke. Its tasks include parametric optimization for façade implementation at the new trade fair facility in Basel and geometric development of the soccer stadium in Bordeaux.

7 UNStudio, founded 1988 in Amsterdam by Ben van Berkel and Caroline Bos, counts among the pioneering firms to use computer programs in the design process. Tobias Wallisser was creative director from 1997 to 2007 and responsible for the development and implementation of digital design approaches. The project Arnhem Centraal was created in cooperation with Cecil Balmond. Large portions of the project have already been executed; the double-curved roof construction of the central transfer hall is still under construction. See www.arnhemcentraal.nu (accessed November 2013).

8 Gehry Technologies has developed a software program that is specially attuned to the needs of architects. CATIA Digital Project is a suite of high-performance 3-D building information modeling (BIM) applications, created by Gehry Technologies with the assistance of Dassault Systèmes CATIA V5 as key modeling platform. see http://www.3ds.com/de/products/catia/portfolio/digital-project/ (accessed November 2013).

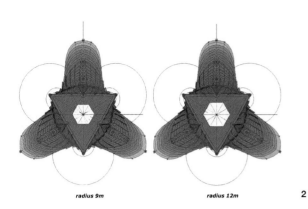

radius 9m   *radius 12m*   **2**

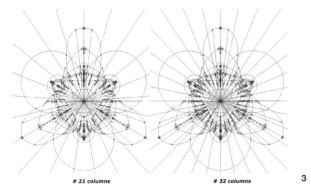

 # 21 columns   *# 32 columns*   **3**

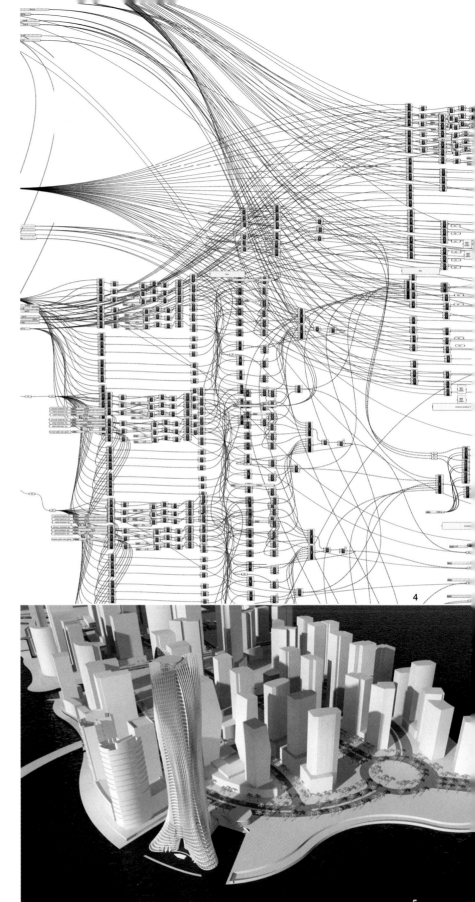

4

5

2–5 Snowflake Tower
- (2) Parametrische Studien für den Aufzugskern.
  Parametric studies for core radius and shape.
- (3) Snowflake Tower. Studien zur Organisation der Stützen.
  Parametric studies for placement of columns.
- (4) Grasshopper-Dokument des Projekts, parametrischer Aufbau.
  Grasshopper file of the project, parametric setup.
- (5) Urbaner Kontext auf Reem Island, Abu Dhabi, Visualisierung,
  parametrischer Aufbau. Urban context on Reem Island,
  Abu Dhabi, rendering, parametric setup.

© LAVA (Laboratory for Visionary Architecture, Berlin, Stuttgart, Sydney)

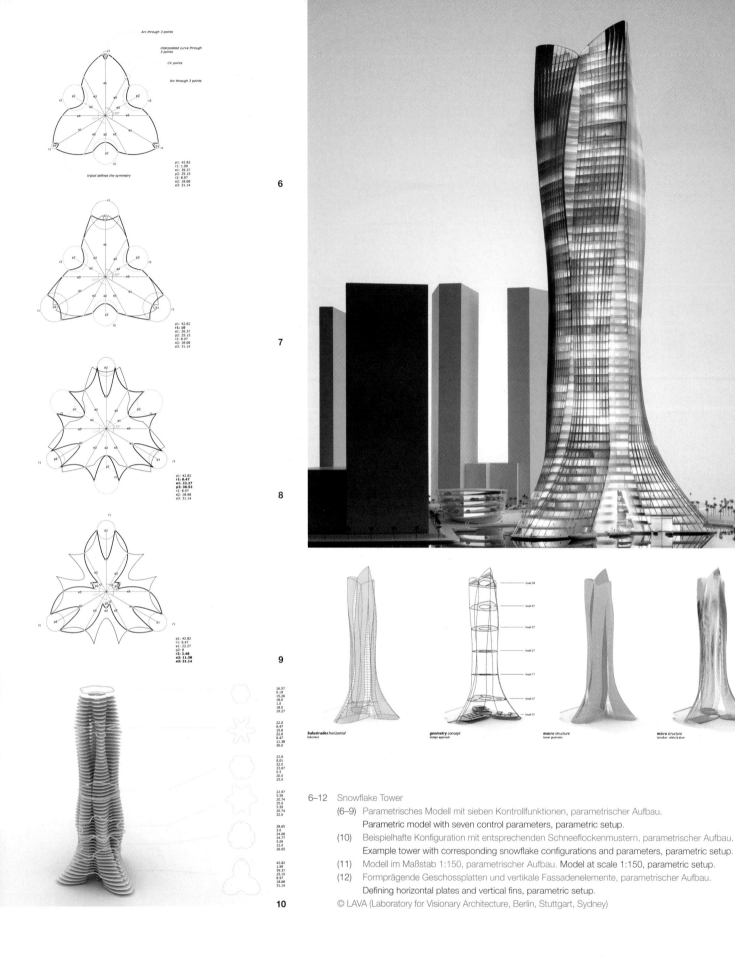

6

p1: 42.82
r1: 1.99
e1: 39.37
p2: 25.15
r2: 8.97
e2: 18.68
e3: 31.14

Arc through 3 points

interpolated curve through 3 points

CV points

Arc through 3 points

tripod defines the symmetry

7

p1: 42.82
r1: 10
e1: 39.37
p2: 25.15
r2: 8.97
e2: 18.68
e3: 31.14

8

p1: 42.82
r1: 6.47
e1: 22.27
p2: 36.52
r2: 8.97
e2: 18.68
e3: 31.14

9

p1: 42.82
r1: 6.47
e1: 22.27
p2: 8
r2: 2.48
e2: 11.38
e3: 31.14

10

16.57
0.19
15.26
18.0
1.0
18.0
19.27

22.0
6.47
15.0
22.0
6.47
11.38
30.0

22.0
0.01
22.0
23.67
0.5
20.0
25.0

22.97
5.59
20.74
25.0
5.59
20.74
32.0

28.65
3.0
24.08
24.77
5.09
22.0
26.65

42.82
6.47
39.37
25.15
8.97
18.68
31.14

balustrades horizontal
balconies

geometry concept
design approach

macro structure
tower geometry

micro structure
lamellas - white & silver

level 58

level 47

level 37

level 27

level 17

level 07

level 01

12

6–12 Snowflake Tower

(6–9) Parametrisches Modell mit sieben Kontrollfunktionen, parametrischer Aufbau.
Parametric model with seven control parameters, parametric setup.

(10) Beispielhafte Konfiguration mit entsprechenden Schneeflockenmustern, parametrischer Aufbau.
Example tower with corresponding snowflake configurations and parameters, parametric setup.

(11) Modell im Maßstab 1:150, parametrischer Aufbau. Model at scale 1:150, parametric setup.

(12) Formprägende Geschossplatten und vertikale Fassadenelemente, parametrischer Aufbau.
Defining horizontal plates and vertical fins, parametric setup.

© LAVA (Laboratory for Visionary Architecture, Berlin, Stuttgart, Sydney)

At the Mercedes-Benz Museum (UNStudio, 2001–06) such a separation was avoided. The design's complexity resulted from an overlapping of individual themes and geometries. The influence of technical parameters was already explored during the design process in cooperation with Arnold Walz from designtoproduction. However, it was carried out separately for certain systems (concrete shell construction, façade). Nevertheless, both the design-motivated changes and the technically necessary ones could be processed in a three-dimensional model. Back then, the difficulty still lay in seamlessly integrating the other planners in this process.[9]

The Snowflake Tower (figs. 1–12). In designing the Snowflake Tower (LAVA, 2008), we took the parametric approach even further. The objective was to produce, in addition to a parametric deformation of specific elements, housing types with distinct qualities within an overall system. A sports marketing company had developed a concept for marketing luxury apartments on an artificial island near Abu Dhabi using the name of a famous racecar driver. This provided several points of departure for the client, such as a desire to achieve high recognition value, to foster an aura of dynamism and luxury, and to implement innovative technical solutions. At the same time, it was important to remain open to a potential need to flexibly address the demands of the housing market.

Arising from this conceptual task in the design process was the question of how feasible it would be to combine a special, recognizable silhouette with maximal flexibility in terms of floor-plan size and type. Following a flash of mathematical inspiration, we decided on the snowflake as a metaphor for viewing the relationship between contour length (façade) and area (apartment size) as a control element for the development of different apartment types. We introduced the design approach of the snowflake as key recognition feature in such a way that these different housing qualities can be regulated through the geometric dependencies of floor plan and sectional figures. The vertical linking of various contour lines fostered a strongly parameterized design tool for volume studies of the Snowflake Tower.

If the silhouette is altered, it is not only the overall form that adapts; particular floor-plan characteristics also change in accordance with the defined dependencies. Shapes take form analogous to the fractal geometry of the snowflake, depending on the length of the contour, which tend to appear either planar or jagged. In this case, designing the design tool was a decisive part of the process, similar to the process of recursion, in which the definition of the explorative question already represents an

Beim Mercedes-Benz Museum (UNStudio, 2001–2006) wurde diese Trennung vermieden. Die Komplexität entstand aus der Überlagerung einzelner Themen und Geometrien. Der Einfluss von technischen Parametern wurde bereits im Entwurfsprozess in Zusammenarbeit mit Arnold Walz von designtoproduction untersucht. Dies erfolgte jedoch noch für verschiedene Systeme (Betonrohbau, Fassade) getrennt. Trotzdem konnten sowohl gestalterisch motivierte als auch technisch notwendige Veränderungen in einem dreidimensionalen Modell bearbeitet werden. Die Schwierigkeit bestand damals jedoch noch in der nahtlosen Einbindung der anderen Planer in diesen Prozess.[9]

Der Snowflake Tower (Abb. 1–12). Beim Entwurf des Snowflake Tower (LAVA, 2008), haben wir die parametrischen Ansätze weiterentwickelt. Ziel war es, neben einer parametrischen Deformation einzelner Elemente Wohnungstypen mit unterschiedlichen Qualitäten innerhalb eines Gesamtsystems zu erzeugen. Eine Firma aus dem Sportmarketing hatte ein Konzept entwickelt, Luxus-Wohnungen auf einer vor Abu Dhabi künstlich angelegten Insel mithilfe des Namens eines Rennfahrers zu vermarkten. Daraus entstanden als Ausgangspunkte für den Bauherrn der Wunsch nach einem hohen Wiedererkennungswert, einer dynamisch-luxuriösen Ausstrahlung und dem Einsatz von innovativen technischen Lösungen. Gleichzeitig sollte die Möglichkeit gegeben sein, um flexibel auf Anforderungen des Wohnungsmarktes eingehen zu können.

Aus dieser Aufgabenstellung stellte sich für den Entwurf die Frage nach der Möglichkeit, eine besondere, wiedererkennbare Silhouette einerseits, aber maximale Flexibilität für Grundrissgrößen und Typen andererseits miteinander zu kombinieren. Wir entschieden uns einer mathematischen Inspiration folgend für die Schneeflocke als Metapher für die Betrachtung des Verhältnisses von Umrisslänge (= Fassade) und Fläche (Wohnungsgrößen) als Steuerungselement für die Entwicklung unterschiedlicher Wohnungstypen. Wir haben den Entwurfsansatz der Silhouette als Hauptmerkmal des Wiedererkennungswertes so eingesetzt, dass diese unterschiedliche Qualitäten für die Wohnungen durch geometrische Abhängigkeiten von Grundriss und Schnittfigur steuern kann. Durch eine vertikale Verknüpfung unterschiedlicher Umrisslinien entstand ein vollständig parametrisiertes Entwurfswerkzeug für Volumenstudien des Snowflake Towers.

> Wir haben den Entwurfsansatz der Silhouette als Hauptmerkmal des Wiedererkennungswertes so eingesetzt, dass diese unterschiedliche Qualitäten für die Wohnungen durch geometrische Abhängigkeiten von Grundriss und Schnittfigur steuern kann.

9 On the design and realization of the Mercedes-Benz Museum in Stuttgart, see also Ben van Berkel, Caroline Bos, Thomas Thiemeyer, and Hugo Daiber, *Buy Me a Mercedes-Benz: Das Buch zum Museum* (Barcelona, 2006).

9 Zum Entwurf und der Realisierung des Mercedes-Benz Museums in Stuttgart siehe auch Ben van Berkel/Caroline Bos/Thomas Thiemeyer/Hugo Daiber: *Buy Me a Mercedes-Benz: Das Buch zum Museum*, Barcelona 2006.

Wird die Silhouette verändert, passt sich nicht nur die Gesamtform an, sondern es verändern sich auch besondere Merkmale des Grundrisses gemäß der definierten Abhängigkeiten. Analog zur fraktalen Geometrie der Schneeflocken entstehen je nach Länge des Umrisses Gebilde, die eher flächig oder eher zerklüftet wirken. Der Entwurf des Entwurfswerkzeugs war hierbei ein entscheidender Teil des Prozesses, vergleichbar mit dem Prozess der Rekursion, bei dem die Definition der Fragestellung bereits einen wichtigen Teil der Beantwortung darstellt. Die Schneeflocke stellt hierbei nicht nur eine Metapher dar, sondern besitzt bereits ein inhärentes mathematisch-geometrisches Prinzip, das es erlaubt, auf spielerische Weise einen funktionellen Beitrag zur Formfindung des Hochhauses zu leisten. Ausgehend von der parametrischen Definition einer zweidimensionalen Grundrisskonfiguration haben wir zunächst einzelne Ebenen mit unterschiedlichen Verhältnissen von Umrisslinie und Innenräumen konzipiert.

Je nach Lage im Gebäude standen unterschiedliche Parameter im Vordergrund:

- Die Anordnung von Wharf Apartments mit direktem Zugang vom Wasser in die unteren Geschosse machen diese zu hochwertigen Ebenen. Das klassische Problem des Hochhauses, die geringe Attraktivität der unteren Ebenen kann damit aufgehoben werden.
- Die kompakte Form in der Mitte schafft durch eine geringe Fassadenfläche eine günstige Konfiguration für kleinere Wohnungen.
- Große Sky Apartments im oberen Bereich haben wenig Kontaktfläche zu den Nachbarn und damit Villen-Qualität.
  Als Parameter für die Entwurfsbearbeitung wurden gewählt:
- Die Gesamtlänge des Umfangs (der Fassade),
- die Anordnung eines innenliegenden Balkonbereichs (Loggia) und
- die Fassadenlänge der Wohnung.
  Durch die Verknüpfung unterschiedlicher Grundrisskombinationen in der Vertikalen entstand das Volumen des Turms. Dabei haben wir eine einfache Freiformkurve zur Definition der Transformation zwischen den entwurflich festgelegten Geschossebenen als Leitlinie für eine kontinuierliche Transformation gewählt. Die einfache Veränderung weniger Punkte erlaubt es so, der gestalterischen Intuition folgend simultan die Silhouette, die Grundrissflächen und das gesamte Volumen zu kontrollieren. Eine Unterscheidung in Makro-Parameter (mit globaler Veränderung der Geometrie) und Mikro-Parameter (nur lokale Anpassungen) ermöglicht die Begrenzung der Auswirkungen von Änderungen bzw. einen nicht reziproken Zusammenhang von Veränderungen.

Die Hierarchisierung der Einflussmöglichkeiten der Parameter ist ein wichtiger Teil des Entwurfs eines parametrischen Werkzeugs. Nicht-reziproke Zusammenhänge stellen bereits wichtige Weichen für die gestalterischen Möglichkeiten. Die Definition von Abhängigkeiten und die Reihenfolge ihrer Auswahl sind Festlegungen des Entwerfers und als solche immer

important part of the answer. Here the snowflake moves beyond metaphor status since it already holds an inherently mathematical-geometric princple, which allows it to make a function-related contribution to the high-rise's form generation in a playful manner. Based on the parametric definition of a two-dimensional floor-plan configuration, we started out by drafting individual levels using various contour-line and interior-space relations.

Different parameters were important depending on the respective location within the building:

- The placement of the Wharf Apartments on the lower levels, with direct access to the waterfront, makes them premium floors. The classic problem found in high-rises of lower levels being less attractive could thus be counteracted.
- The compact form of the middle section, with its low façade surface area, facilitates a favorable configuration for smaller apartments.
- The large Sky Apartments in the upper section have minimal contact area with the neighboring units and thus offer villa quality.
  The following parameters were selected for the design development:
- The overall length of the periphery (of the façade)
- The configuration of a recessed balcony area (loggia)
- The façade length of the apartment
  The volume of the tower was created by linking the different floor-plan combinations vertically. As a guiding principle for continual transformation, we selected a simple free-form curve here to define the transition between the floor levels specified in the design. Following design-related intuition, it becomes possible to simultaneously control the silhouette, the floor-plan surfaces, and the entire building volume by simply changing several points. Differentiating between macro parameters (with a universal shift in geometry) and micro parameters (only local adjustments) allows the ramifications of changes to be contained, that is, it facilitates a nonreciprocal context of changes.

The hierarchization of the parameters' scope of influence is a significant part of designing a parametric tool. Nonreciprocal contexts already set an important course for design opportunities. The definition of dependencies and the sequence of their selection are determinations made by the designer and, as such, should be repeatedly scrutinized during the process. Here it is interesting to note that a definition of basic, rule-based dependencies also allows unexpected threshold values and speculative configurations to be examined. These "mistakes," or solutions outside the envisaged solution framework, can cultivate design innovation and new qualitative approaches that may involve a reprogramming of dependencies.

Although there was no height limit associated with the plot, maximum utilization of the floor-space ratio was required, so this became a determining criterion in choosing the final configuration. The parametric overall model allowed different configurations to be tested while simultaneously considering aesthetic, functional, and technical criteria:

- The total useful floor area and the volume of the building
- The shape of the silhouette in connection with the maximally allowed structural overhang
- The differing size within an apartment type (the allowed deviation was set at 10 percent by the client)
- Optimization of load deflection
- Optimization of shading elements (penetration/energy input)

The development of a parametric machine for the project facilitated the quick examination of a multitude of variants in the design phase. This allowed the surveying of design alternatives to be visually assessed, which promotes an intuitive approach; at the same time, numerical values for technical factors and usability aspects could be considered on the spot. Thanks to being able to simultaneously observe positions both outside the building (silhouette, locality) and in interior space (views outward, impression of the façade from the inside), it was possible to take different criteria into consideration as compared to using a physical model. With the associative geometric model developed in this way, modification requests on the part of the client could be addressed to a certain degree.

During the initial phase of this project, we spent a significant amount of time honing the definition of dependencies and translating this into a design tool, which ultimately proved beneficial. Therefore, by implementing a radial axis system despite the façade differing on each level, we succeeded in creating a great amount of freedom for arranging the dividing walls of the apartments in order to maintain variability for the ratio of apartments. At the same time, it proved vital that a design concept be established, in addition to a functional machine, that can inspiringly serve as a guiding principle for the intuitive operation of the machine.

HFT Voxel Box (figs. 13–18). In our project designed for the technical university in Stuttgart, Hochschule für Technik (HFT), the interaction between machine and design-related specifications is even more clearly discerned. We decided to participate in the competition to design a new building for the architecture faculty at the HFT Stuttgart because we saw an opportunity to make a contribution, together with the structural engineers Bollinger + Grohmann,[10] to the correlation between the processes of design and development—closely aligned to Winston Churchill's aphorism, "We shape our buildings, and

wieder im Prozess zu hinterfragen. Interessant ist hierbei, dass die Definition einfacher regelbasierter Abhängigkeiten auch die Untersuchung von Grenzwerten und spekulativen Konfigurationen erlaubt, die nicht geplant waren. Aus diesen „Fehlern", also Lösungen außerhalb des vorgesehenen Lösungsrahmens, können gestalterische Innovation und qualitative neue Ansätze entstehen, die eine Umprogrammierung der Abhängigkeiten nach sich ziehen können.

Da für das Grundstück kein Höhenlimit gegeben war, jedoch eine maximale Ausnutzung mittels GFZ als Vorgabe bestand, wurde dies zum bestimmenden Kriterium bei der Auswahl der finalen Konfiguration. Das parametrische Gesamtmodell erlaubte den Test unterschiedlicher Konfigurationen bei gleichzeitiger Betrachtung ästhetischer, funktionaler und technischer Kriterien:

- Die Gesamtnutzfläche und das Volumen des Gebäudes,
- die Ausprägung der Silhouette im Zusammenhang mit der maximalen konstruktiven Auskragung,
- die Unterschiedlichkeit der Größe innerhalb eines Wohnungstyps (die zulässige Abweichung wurde vom Bauherrn mit max. 10% festgelegt),
- eine Optimierung der Lastabtragung und
- die Optimierung der Verschattungselemente (Durchsicht/Energieeintrag).

Durch die Entwicklung einer parametrischen Maschine für das Projekt wurde die schnelle Untersuchung einer Vielzahl von Varianten in der Entwurfsphase möglich. Die Überprüfung von Entwurfsalternativen konnte visuell bewertet werden, was ein intuitives Vorgehen fördert, gleichzeitig konnten sofort Zahlenwerte für technische Faktoren und Aspekte der Nutzbarkeit berücksichtigt werden. Durch das simultane Betrachten von Standpunkten sowohl außerhalb des Gebäudes (Silhouette, Ortsbezug) als auch im Innenraum (Aussicht, Wirkung der Fassade von innen) konnten im Unterschied zu physischen Modell unterschiedliche Maßstäbe berücksichtigt werden. Mit dem so entwickelten assoziativen Geometriemodell ließen sich Änderungswünsche des Bauherrn innerhalb gewisser Grenzen berücksichtigen.

Wir haben bei diesem Projekt in der Anfangsphase viel Zeit auf die Definition der Abhängigkeiten und die Umsetzung in einem Entwurfswerkzeug verwendet, was sich am Ende ausgezahlt hat. So gelang es, mittels eines radialen Achsensystems trotz der in jedem Geschoss unterschiedlichen Fassade eine große Freiheit für die Anordnung der Wohnungstrennwände zu schaffen, um Variabilität für den Wohnungsschlüssel zu behalten. Gleichzeitig hat es sich als unerlässlich erwiesen, neben einer funktionalen Maschine ein gestalterisches Konzept festzulegen, das aufgrund seiner Inspiration als Leitlinie für die intuitive Bedienung der Maschine dient.

HFT Voxel Box (Abb. 13–18). Bei unserem Projekt für die Hochschule für Technik (HFT) in Stuttgart ist das Zusammenspiel von Maschine und gestalterischen Festlegungen noch deutlicher abzulesen.

Wir hatten uns entschlossen, am Wettbewerb für ein neues Gebäude der Architekturfakultät der HFT in Stuttgart teilzunehmen, da wir darin die Gelegenheit sahen, zusammen mit den Tragwerksplanern Bollinger + Grohmann[10]

10 Klaus Bollinger, Manfred Grohmann, and Oliver Tessmann, "Structured Becoming: Evolutionary Processes in Design Engineering," *AD* 80 (2005), pp. 34–39.

10 Klaus Bollinger/Manfred Grohmann/Oliver Tessmann: „Structured Becoming: Evolutionary Processes in Design Engineering", *AD*, 80 (2005), S. 34–39.

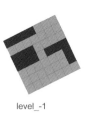
level_-1

level_00

level_01

level_02

level_03

level_04

level_05

level_06

Dach

14

15

16

13–16 HfT VOxEL, Erweiterungsbau für die Hochschule für Technik in Stuttgart; Wettbewerbsbeitrag 2009
Extension for the Hochschule für Technik in Stuttgart, Competition entry 2009.

(13) Straßenperspektive Street view.

(14) Binärkarte zur Festlegung der Bereiche mit Möglichkeiten zur Anordnung von Schottwänden für jedes Geschoss. The binary maps indicating structurally dense and open areas for each floor.

(15) Das Arbeitsmodell der finalen Konfiguration zeigt die punktweise Überlappung der tragenden Scheiben. Card board model of final configuration showing the overlapping points of structure.

(16) Dreidimensionale „Schwammstruktur" auf Basis einer 4 m-Matrix. Three dimensional structural "sponge" system based on a 4 m matrix. © LAVA und and Bollinger + Grohmann

© LAVA (Laboratory for Visionary Architecture, Berlin, Stuttgart, Sydney)

afterwards our buildings shape us."[11] Where could this context be more pivotal than in the form of a building which, for its part, serves to further architectural education? If the goal in educating architects involves acquiring a sensitivity to dealing with material and space, a proficiency in creating spaces, an understanding of functional, social, economic, and technical relationships, as well as their complete integration within the system as a whole, then the building that houses the architecture faculty is certainly called upon to make an important contribution. It should activate all of the senses, arouse curiosity, and use spatial experience to convey the architectural potentialities of space creation. We see this as a chance to redefine the nexus among framing structure, space, and space allocation. Our design defines the new architecture faculty building as a three-dimensional space continuum with diverse options for utilization and easy changeability, reflecting the questions of our time—energy-related sustainability, adaptability, robustness—and also as communication platform and research laboratory. Besides freedom in creating the floor plan, there is the possibility of flexibility in usage applied to various interrelated platforms. Instead of reducing all rooms to the smallest possible denominator, that is, to an axial grid underlying the building, we newly categorized and evaluated space allocation using the parameter "spatial structure." This entailed dividing the entire system into the categories of "dense" rooms (e.g., office space and ancillary rooms) and "open" rooms (e.g., lecture halls and presentation areas). We selected a three-dimensional grid measuring 4 × 4 × 4 meters, a so-called "voxel." Space allocation was mixed and arranged as building volume, distributed across six levels, with each level comprised of a grid of 8 × 8 voxels. The "program elements" were not considered boxes but were rather dismantled into four-meter grids through the placement of load-bearing shear walls, which enhances usage flexibility. Not only the conversion of seminar space into smaller rooms was possible, but also the interconnection of office space and ancillary rooms. An atrium opening up above all levels joined these areas together and spread diagonally across the most important ones, situated in the fourth and sixth stories as intermediate lobbies offering a view of the city. All areas encompassed by the atrium were designated as "voids."

On the basis of this grid, an evolutionary algorithm was used to find a three-dimensional, load-bearing system that defined the differently scaled room areas in terms of various utilizations, such as seminar rooms, small lecture halls, and offices. Evolutionary algorithms generated and manipulated elements that served as genotypes for diverse structures. The

einen Beitrag zum Zusammenhang von Gestaltung und Entstehungsprozess leisten zu können, und zwar ganz im Sinne von Winston Churchills Aphorismus: „Zuerst formen wir unsere Gebäude … Danach formen unsere Gebäude uns."[11] Wo wäre dieser Zusammenhang zentraler als bei einem Gebäude, das wiederum der Architekturausbildung dient? Wenn das Ziel der Ausbildung zum Architekten das Erlernen einer Sensibilität im Umgang mit Material und Raum, die Befähigung zum Schaffen von Räumen, das Verständnis funktionaler, sozialer, wirtschaftlicher und technischer Zusammenhänge und ihre vollständige Eingliederung in ein Gesamtsystem darstellt, muss das Gebäude der Fakultät einen wichtigen Beitrag leisten. Es soll alle Sinne ansprechen, Neugier wecken und durch das Raumerlebnis die architektonischen Möglichkeiten der Raumbildung vermitteln. Wir sehen darin die Chance einer neuen Definition der Zusammenhänge von Tragwerk, Raum und Raumprogramm. Unser Entwurf definiert den Neubau der Architekturfakultät als dreidimensionales Raumkontinuum mit vielfältigen Nutzungsangeboten und einfacher Veränderbarkeit als Ausdruck der Fragen unserer Zeit – energetische Nachhaltigkeit, Anpassungsfähigkeit, Robustheit – als Kommunikationsplattform und Forschungslabor. Neben der Freiheit im Grundriss entsteht die Möglichkeit der

Statt alle Räume auf einen kleinsten gemeinsamen Nenner, also ein dem Gebäude zugrundeliegendes Achsraster zu reduzieren, haben wir das Raumprogramm mit dem Parameter „Raumstruktur" neu kategorisiert und bewertet.

Nutzungsflexibilität auf verschiedenen, miteinander verbundenen Plattformen. Statt alle Räume auf einen kleinsten gemeinsamen Nenner, also ein dem Gebäude zugrundeliegendes Achsraster zu reduzieren, haben wir das Raumprogramm mit dem Parameter „Raumstruktur" neu kategorisiert und bewertet. Dabei wurde das gesamte Programm in die Kategorien „dichte" Räume wie Büroflächen und Nebenräume und „offene" Räume, also z.B. Hörsäle und Präsentationsbereiche differenziert. Wir haben als gemeinsamen Nenner ein dreidimensionales Raster von 4 × 4 × 4 m definiert, einen „Voxel". Das Raumprogramm wird gemischt auf sechs Ebenen verteilt in einem Gebäudevolumen angeordnet, wobei jede Ebene aus einem Raster von 8 × 8 Voxeln besteht. Die „Programmelemente" werden nicht als Boxen gesehen, sondern durch die Anordnung von tragenden Wandscheiben im 4-m-Raster aufgelöst, wodurch Nutzungsflexibilität entsteht. Nicht nur die Konversion der Seminarräume in kleinere Räume ist möglich, sondern auch das Zusammenschalten von Büro- und Nebenräumen. Ein über alle Geschosse offenes Atrium verbindet diese Bereiche und erstreckt sich diagonal zwischen den wichtigsten dieser Bereiche, die als Zwischenfoyers im dritten

11 Winston Churchill, speech to the House of Commons, October 2, 1943, in *Never Give In!: The Best of Winston Churchill's Speeches* (New York, 2003), p. 385.

11 „We shape our buildings, and afterwards our buildings shape us." Winston Churchill: Speech to the House of Commons (October 2, 1943), in: *Never Give In!: The Best of Winston Churchill's Speeches*, New York 2003. S. 385.

und sechsten Stock mit Sicht zur Stadt angeordnet sind. Die von ihm betroffenen Bereiche werden als Lufträume gekennzeichnet.

Auf Basis dieses Rasters wird mittels eines evolutionären Algorithmus' nach einem räumlichen Tragsystem gesucht, das unterschiedlich große Raumbereiche für die verschiedenen Nutzungen wie Seminarräume, kleine Hörsäle und Büros definiert. Evolutionäre Algorithmen generieren und manipulieren Elemente, die als Genotypen für unterschiedliche Strukturen dienen. Der Genotyp dient als Ausgangsdatensatz für parametrische Strukturmodelle, die Phänotypen werden. Diese werden nach und nach analysiert und ausgewertet, wobei die Kriterien nicht nur aus konstruktiven, sondern auch aus architektonischen Randbedingungen kommen. Das Ziel dieser Untersuchungen ist nicht eine monothematische Optimierung, sondern das Ausbalancieren verschiedener Anforderungen. Das architektonische und konstruktive Konzept der Schaffung eines nicht-hierarchischen Gebäudes wird übertragen in ein konstruktives System, in dem Bodenelemente und Wandscheiben als räumliche Matrix entsprechend funktionaler und konstruktiver Erfordernisse angeordnet werden. Die Gebäudestruktur kann als „kantiger Schwamm", als räumlich dreidimensional entwickelte Struktur mit verschiedener Porosität verstanden werden.

Das konstruktive System wurde mittels eines evolutionären Prozesses entwickelt, basierend auf einer Unterscheidung der Zellen in zwei Kategorien:
- „offene" Zellen frei von jeder Konstruktion (für Lufträume),
- „dichte" Zellen mit der Möglichkeit der Anordnung tragender Wände entlang der Seiten.

Auf Basis dieser Unterscheidung (dargestellt mittels einer digitalen Maske für jede Ebene) wurde jede Zelle mit einem konstruktiven Modul ohne oder mit einem bzw. zwei Schottwänden besiedelt, so dass ein differenziertes Gesamtsystem entstehen konnte. Zunächst wurden 50 mit Zufallsgenerator erstellte Konfigurationen untersucht. Dafür wurden folgende Kriterien zur Bewertung benutzt:
- Biegemomente in den Böden basierend auf Eigenlast,
- Momente in den Wandscheiben bei horizontaler Belastung,
- Anordnung der Wandscheiben.

Anschließend wurden die aufgrund dieser Bedingungen jeweils besten Varianten ausgewählt, um weitere Ableger zu erzeugen. Diese Nachfolgegenerationen basierend auf erfolgreichen Lösungen wurden weiter miteinander kombiniert, bis nach ca. 200 Generationen ein System entstand, das sowohl die unterschiedlichen architektonisch-räumlichen Kriterien als auch die tragwerkstechnischen Notwendigkeiten erfüllen kann.

> Das architektonische und konstruktive Konzept der Schaffung eines nicht-hierarchischen Gebäudes wird übertragen in ein konstruktives System, in dem Bodenelemente und Wandscheiben als räumliche Matrix entsprechend funktionaler und konstruktiver Erfordernisse angeordnet werden.

genotype in turn served as an initial data set for parametric structural models that became phenotypes. The latter were then analyzed and evaluated, whereby the criteria originated from both structural and architectural framework conditions. The objective of these investigations lay not only in monothematic optimization, but also in the counterbalancing of different requirements. The architectural and structural concept of creating a nonhierarchical building was transferred to a structural system in which floor slabs and shear walls proliferated into a three-dimensional matrix according to functional and structural requirements. The building construction can be conceived as a "square-edged sponge," as a spatially developed, three-dimensional structure of varying porosity.

The structural system was developed through an evolutionary process based on a division of the cells into two categories:
- "open" cells that are free of any structure (for voids)
- "dense" cells that are capable of having load-bearing walls placed along the edges

On the basis of this differentiation (represented using a digital mask for every level), each grid cell was subsequently populated with a structural module consisting of one or two shear walls, or none at all, in order to produce a differentiated overall system. Initially, fifty random configurations were generated and analyzed, and the following three evaluation criteria were used:
- Bending moments in the floor slabs under dead load
- Moments in the shear walls under horizontal loads
- Placement of shear walls

Based on these conditions, the best respective configurations were then selected for creating further offspring. These successor generations founded on successful solutions continued to be intercombined until, after two hundred generations, the process yielded a system which adapted to divergent three-dimensional architectural criteria while at the same time effectively addressing structural necessities.

The structures of varying density reciprocally interacted with their utilization—each depending on the openness and proximity to the communication areas. As an advancement of the supporting grid, the shear walls with their differing orientation facilitated flexibility in the third dimension; the layering of larger and smaller span lengths thus became possible. The building would be able to do without a load-bearing core, for reinforcement was achieved through the positioning of the shear walls. Only now did space allocation allow for detailed structural mapping, since based on the initial hypothesis all usage types should be possible on each floor, but not in every place. Therefore, an unprecedented building type was created that possesses a highly specific load-bearing system while simultaneously still offering usage flexibility.

Admittedly, we did manually reposition several shear walls, for instance in order to improve lighting. Here we achieved

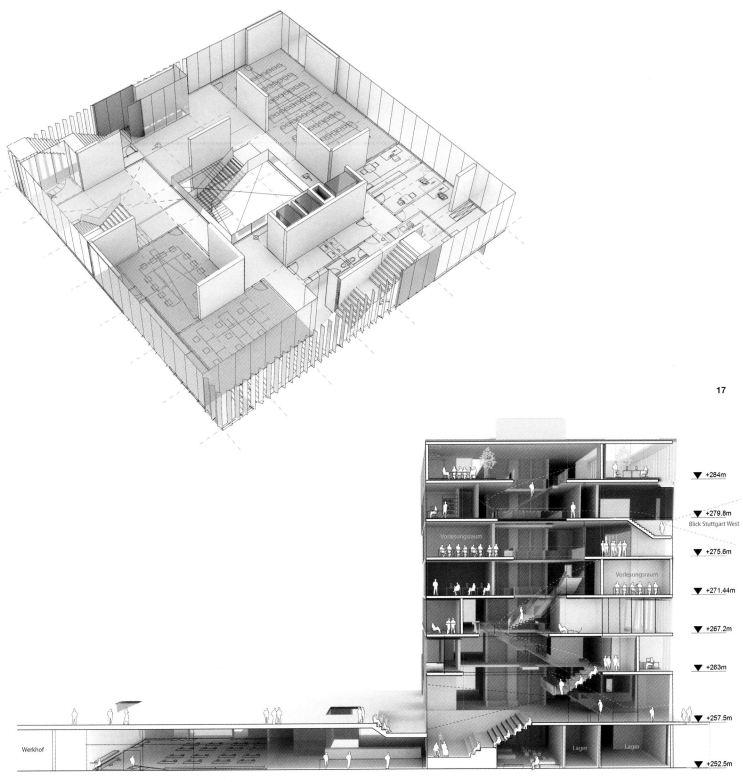

17

18

17–18 HfT VOxEL, Erweiterungsbau für die Hochschule für Technik in Stuttgart; Wettbewerbsbeitrag 2009
Extension for the Hochschule für Technik in Stuttgart, Competition entry 2009.

(17)   Grundriss, Ebene 4 Floor-plan, level 4.

(18)   Perspektivschnitt Section.

© LAVA (Laboratory for Visionary Architecture, Berlin, Stuttgart, Sydney)

Die unterschiedlich dichten Strukturen stehen in Wechselwirkung mit der Nutzung – je nach Offenheit und Nähe zu den Kommunikationsbereichen. Als Weiterentwicklung des Stützenrasters erlauben die unterschiedlich orientierten Wandscheiben Flexibilität in der dritten Dimension, die Schichtung großer und kleiner Spannweiten wird möglich. Das Gebäude benötigt keinen tragenden Kern, die Aussteifung erfolgt über die Positionierung der Wandscheiben. Erst jetzt erfolgt die detaillierte Zuordnung des Raumprogramms in die Struktur, da aufgrund der Ausgangshypothese jede Nutzungsart in jedem Geschoss möglich sein soll, aber nicht an jedem Ort. Somit ist ein neuartiger Gebäudetyp entstanden, der einerseits ein hochgradig spezielles Tragsystem besitzt, gleichzeitig jedoch Nutzungsflexibilität bietet.

Zugegebenermaßen haben wir ein paar wenige Tragschotten noch von Hand umplatziert, um zum Beispiel die Belichtung zu verbessern. Während wir hier einerseits eine multi-funktionale Optimierung mittels Algorithmen an den Computer abgegeben haben, haben wir andererseits klare Vorgaben entworfen. Bevor wir eine solche Maschine sinnvoll einsetzen konnten, mussten wir gemeinsam mit den Ingenieuren die Randbedingungen festlegen und dabei bereits gestalterische Vorgaben wie die Kubatur, das zugrundeliegende Achssystem und die Anordnung der Lufträume festlegen. Erst auf dieser Basis wurde das parametrische Modell konzipiert. Die Zusammenarbeit zwischen Architekt und Ingenieur wurde hier durch die gemeinsame Arbeit am dreidimensionalen Modell und einen iterativen Prozess geprägt, in dem wir viele Faktoren, wie die Konfiguration der Lufträume aber sogar auch die Größe des Achsrasters im Laufe des Prozesses anpassen konnten.

> Der Einsatz von digitalen Entwurfstechniken erlaubt schnelleres Feedback und führt zu zirkulären Prozessen, bei denen unterschiedliche Extreme ausgelotet und die Abhängigkeiten entsprechend überarbeitet werden können.

Fazit. Entwurfsprozesse waren nie linear. Der Einsatz von digitalen Entwurfstechniken erlaubt schnelleres Feedback und führt zu zirkulären Prozessen, bei denen unterschiedliche Extreme ausgelotet und die Abhängigkeiten entsprechend überarbeitet werden können. Der große Mehrwert der Definition von mathematischen Beziehungen zwischen einzelnen Elementen besteht darin, dass statt einer eindimensionale Optimierung in Hinsicht auf einen Einzelaspekt ein interaktives Abwägen unterschiedlicher Anforderungen beinahe in Echtzeit möglich wird und dem entwerfenden Architekten visuelle Informationen als Basis der Entscheidungsfindung bietet. Somit bleibt der Entwerfer und seine Intuition entscheidend, denn mittels der Verknüpfungen erlaubt der Computer auch Möglichkeiten, die aus gestalterischen Gründen kaum akzeptabel sind. Es handelt sich also keineswegs um eine technische, mathematisch-geometrische „Optimierung" gemäß der vorhandenen Parameter, dafür sind die Möglichkeiten zu zahlreich und die Zielsetzung zu offen.

multifunctional optimization on the computer using algorithms, but we also drafted clear specifications. Before such a machine could be sensibly installed, we had to work with engineers to set the framework conditions and, in the process, already determine design-related specifications like cubature, basic axis system, and placement of voids. Not until this foundation was laid could the parametric model be designed. The cooperation between architects and engineers was influenced by collaborative work on the three-dimensional model and by an iterative process, which allowed us to adapt many factors in the process, such as the confirmation of voids and even the size of the axial grid.

Conclusion. Design processes have never been linear. The implementation of digital design technology allows for quicker feedback and gives rise to circular processes through which different extremes are explored and dependencies can be adjusted accordingly. The greatest added value that comes from defining mathematical relations between individual elements is clearly the fact that, instead of one-dimensional optimization applied to a single aspect, it becomes possible to interactively gauge various requirements almost in real time, which provides the designing architect with visual information on which to base his or her decision making. As such, the intuition of designers remains vital because links allow the computer to work in ways that are hardly acceptable from a design perspective. So in no way does this involve a technical, mathematical-geometric "optimization" pursuant to existing parameters—the possibilities are too numerous and the purpose too open for that to be the case.

The application of rule-based or associative models alone does not occasion the creation of better architecture. Instead, the parametric system serves to visually survey intuitive design proposals simultaneously and to quantitatively assess them in terms of characteristic values. Even without the HFT design having been realized, we have learned a great deal from its conception, not only about the balance between rational control mechanisms and the speculative development of dependencies, but also about the development of project-dependent design tools, their flexibility, and their limitations.

Although the potential for new qualities in design is owed to complex calculations and rules, in the end something that moves beyond a comprehensible rationalization of the process should ultimately be created—or, as Louis Kahn has phrased it, "a building must begin with the unmeasurable, must go through measurable means when it is being designed and in the end must be unmeasurable."[12] The human intuition of the

12 Louis Isidore Kahn, "Form and Design," in *Louis I. Kahn*, ed. Vincent Scully (New York, 1962), pp. 114–21, esp. p. 149. Lois Isidore Kahn (born 1901 in Kuressaare on Saaremaa Island, Estonia, died 1974 in New York) was an American architect, urban planner, and university professor.

designer will continue to assume an important role in the creation of architecture, at least in the conceptualization of—predominately digital—tools.

Project Participants Snowflake Tower: LAVA: Chris Bosse, Tobias Wallisser, Alexander Rieck, Gilles Retsin, Sebastian Schott, Stephan Albrecht, Jarrod Lamshed, Kim Ngoc, Erik Escalante, Esan Rahmani, Anh-Dao Trinh, Mi Jin Chun, Pascal Tures. Partners: Wenzel + Wenzel Architekten: Reinhold Blersch, Angelika Babucke, Markus Major, Marion Schmelzle, Svetlana Bogoslovova, Tobias Knappe.

Project Participants HfT LAVA: Tobias Wallisser, Alexander Rieck, Chris Bosse mit Achim Kaufer, Dominyka Mineikyte, Gilles Retsin. Partners: Supporting Framework: Bollinger + Grohmann; Air Conditioning Technology: Transsolar Climate Engineering.

Translation Dawn Michelle d'Atri

Die Anwendung regelbasierter oder assoziativer Modelle alleine erzeugt keine bessere Architektur. Das parametrische System dient vielmehr dazu, intuitive Entwurfsvorschläge simultan optisch und quantitativ in Bezug auf Kennwerte zu überprüfen. Auch wenn die HFT nicht gebaut worden ist, haben wir aus der Konzeption nicht nur vieles über die Balance von rationalen Kontrollmechanismen und dem spekulativen Entwickeln von Abhängigkeiten gelernt, sondern auch über das Entwickeln von projektabhängigen Entwurfswerkzeugen, ihre Flexibilität und ihre Grenzen.

Denn obwohl das Potenzial für neue Entwurfsqualitäten komplexen Berechnungen und Regeln zu verdanken ist, am Ende muss immer etwas entstehen, was über die nachvollziehbare Rationalisierung des Prozesses hinausgeht, oder wie Louis Kahn formuliert hat: „Ein großartiges Gebäude muss mit dem nicht Messbaren beginnen, muss durch messbare Prozesse gehen und muss am Ende nicht messbar sein."[12] Die menschliche Intuition des Entwerfers wird zumindest für die Konzeption der – überwiegend digitalen – Werkzeuge weiterhin bei der Entwicklung von Architektur eine wichtige Rolle spielen.

Projektmitarbeiter Snowflake Tower: LAVA: Chris Bosse, Tobias Wallisser, Alexander Rieck, Gilles Retsin, Sebastian Schott, Stephan Albrecht, Jarrod Lamshed, Kim Ngoc, Erik Escalante, Esan Rahmani, Anh-Dao Trinh, Mi Jin Chun, Pascal Tures. Partner: Wenzel + Wenzel Architekten: Reinhold Blersch, Angelika Babucke, Markus Major, Marion Schmelzle, Svetlana Bogoslovova, Tobias Knappe.

Projektmitarbeiter HfT: LAVA: Tobias Wallisser, Alexander Rieck, Chris Bosse mit Achim Kaufer, Dominyka Mineikyte, Gilles Retsin. Partner: Tragwerk: Bollinger + Grohmann; Klimatechnik: Transsolar Klima Engineering.

12 „A building must begin with the unmeasurable, must go through measurable means when it is being designed and in the end must be unmeasurable." Louis Isidore Kahn: „Form and Design" in Vincent Scully (Hg.): *Louis I. Kahn*, New York 1962. S. 114–121, hier S. 149. Lois Isidore Kahn (*1901 in Kuressaare auf der Insel Saaremaa, Estland; †1974 in New York) war ein US-amerikanischer Architekt, Stadtplaner und Hochschullehrer.

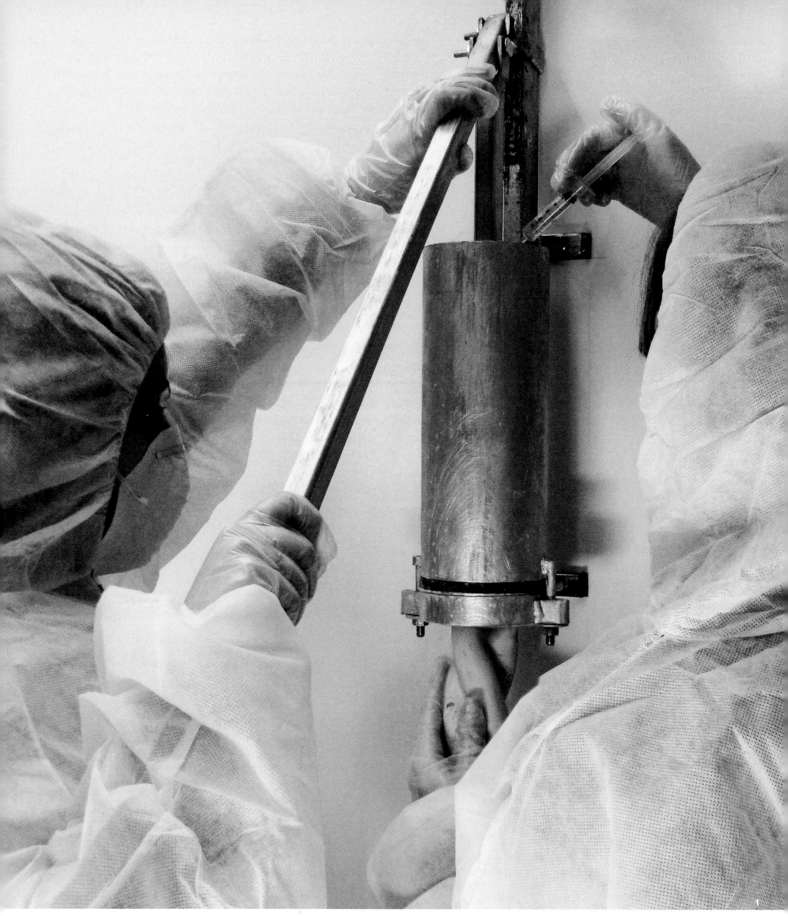

1 Biozement-Weberei: Entwicklung eines viskosen, klebenden, sekretierbaren Baustoffs zur Errichtung morphologisch komplexer Bauwerke. Bio-cement weaving: Development of a viscous and adherent secretable material so as to produce a morphologically complex structure. © New-Territories

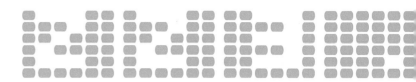

An Architecture
des Humeurs

"An Architecture *des Humeurs*,"[1] a research project initiated in 2010 by New-Territories/R&Sie(n), seeks to create a kind of alphabet book of apparatuses, of knowledge strategies, to drift from the psycho-methodology of collecting "desires" to the mathematics that interpret them as relationships, or rather set-belonging situations.

„An Architecture *des Humeurs*",[1] ein seit 2010 laufendes Forschungsprojekt von New-Territories/R&Sie(n), versucht eine Art Abecedarium einschlägiger Apparate und Wissensstrategien zu erstellen, um von der Psychomethodik des „Wünsche"-Sammelns zu einer Mathematik zu gelangen, die diese „Wünsche" als Beziehungen oder genauer als zu einer Vielheit gehörige Situationen interpretiert.

FRANÇOIS ROCHE

The project shifts from psycho-chemistry to the logic of aggregation, from the physio-morphological computation of the multitude to C++ operators for structural optimization as an artifact of a logic of discovery, from bio-knit physicality for the operation of a nonlinear geometry to a robotic process and behavior, and from biochemical research to robotic design and G-code algorithms for automated manufacture. An architecture *des humeurs* is based on the potential which contemporary sciences offer to reread the human corporalities via their physiology and their chemical balance. The term "humors" is used here in Hippocrates' sense, namely as a concept brought up to date by today's possibilities for detecting body chemistry. The assumption of an architecture *des humeurs* attempts to make palpable and prehensible through technologies the emotional transactions of the "body animal," i.e., the body headless, the chemistry of the body, informing us of its adaptation, its sympathy and empathy, in the face of specific situations or environments. In the following, two approaches will be introduced which serve as the main apparatuses for the architectural assemblages on transactional and structuring protocols: The first involves data collection on the chemical body, while the second is designed to generate an urban structure.

> The term "humors" is used here in Hippocrates' sense, namely as a concept brought up to date by today's possibilities for detecting body chemistry.

Until now, the collection of information involved in the protocol of the residential unit has been exclusively based on visible and reductive data (e.g., surface area, number of rooms, access mode and party walls). Instead, this experiment presents the opportunity to interrogate an obscure area that could be called "the emission of desires" through the capture of physiological signals based on neurobiological secretions. During a seven minutes interview, the participants (or future tenants) are put into a psychological state during which a machine collects their chemical data, hence generating information about the relationship between bodies and space, and especially about the social relationship of bodies, both inside a single housing unit and in terms of the osmosis of vicinity. Hence it is the future purchasers, who function as inputs to generate a diversity of habitable morphologies as well as the relationships between them. The signal collection station makes it possible to perceive individual variations and how these changes in emotional state affect the resulting geometries and influence the morphological protocol at the "living together" level. The physiological test, which works like an emotion detector, implements a chemistry of the humors which helps, for example, to map the visitor's future dwelling area. Specifically, the focus

Das Projekt reicht von der Psychochemie bis zur Logik der Aggregation, von physiomorphologischen Mannigfaltigkeitsberechnungen bis zu C++ Operatoren für deren Strukturoptimierung als Artefakte einer Logik des Entdeckens, von der Physikalität von Biogeweben für die Handhabung einer nonlinearen Geometrie bis zu robotischen Prozessen und Verhaltensweisen und von biochemischer Forschung bis zum Roboterdesign und zu G-Code-Algorithmen für automatisierte Fabrikation. Eine Architektur der *Humore* („Körpersäfte") nutzt das Potenzial, das die zeitgenössische Wissenschaft bietet, um menschliche Befindlichkeiten physiologisch und chemisch neu zu lesen. Der Begriff „Humor" wird im hippokratischen Sinn verwendet, aktualisiert durch die neuesten Methoden zur Analyse der Körperchemie. Eine Humoralarchitektur versucht, mit technischen Mitteln die emotionalen Transaktionen des animalischen, d.h. azephalen Körpers fassbar zu machen, um etwas über seine Anpassung an, sowie Sympathie und Empathie für bestimmte Situationen oder Umgebungen zu erfahren. In der Folge werden zwei Bausteine vorgestellt, die als Hauptapparate für die Schaffung architektonischer Gefüge nach Transaktions- und Strukturprotokollen dienen: Beim ersten geht es um die Sammlung der chemischen Körperdaten, beim zweiten um die Generierung einer urbanen Struktur.

Bis heute geht es bei Planungsgesprächen für eine Wohneinheit einzig und allein um die Erhebung sicht- und reduzierbarer Daten (z.B. Grundfläche, Raumanzahl, Zugangssituation, Kommunwände etc.). Demgegenüber bietet dieses Experiment die Möglichkeit, durch die Erfassung physiologischer Signale in Form neurobiologischer Körperabsonderungen einen dunklen Bereich zu erforschen, der vielleicht als „Wunschemission" zu bezeichnen ist. In einem siebenminütigen Interview werden die Teilnehmer (bzw. künftigen Bewohner) in einen psychischen Zustand versetzt, währenddessen eine Maschine ihre chemischen Daten erfasst, um daraus Informationen für die Beziehung zwischen Körper und Raum, insbesondere die sozialen Beziehungen der Körper sowohl innerhalb der Wohneinheit als auch in Bezug auf die Osmose mit der Umgebung zu gewinnen. Die künftigen Käufer fungieren also als Input für die Generierung einer Vielfalt habitabler Formen sowie deren Beziehungen untereinander.

Die Station zur Erfassung der Körpersignale ermöglicht es, individuelle Variationen zu erkennen und zu schauen, wie sich die unterschiedlichen Schwankungen der emotionalen Zustände

---

1   *Humeurs* derives from the Latin word *umor* meaning "liquid" and from the Greek word *thumos* denoting the passions. In the context of medicine it stands for a fluid contained in an organism. This fluid can be real, like blood, lymph, and bile, or supposedly real or even hypothetical, like black bile. In the field of psychology it refers to the original thymic state governing the emotions and affect. Also the four temperaments are linked to the four *humeurs* (Hippocrates, 479–377 B.C.E.). Each humor corresponds to an element: phlegm corresponds to water (phlegmatic), blood corresponds to air (sanguine), yellow bile corresponds to fire (choleric), black bile corresponds to the earth (melancholic, but also tense).

1   *Humeurs* geht (wie das deutsche Wort Humor, A.d.Ü.) auf lateinisch *umor* – „Flüssigkeit" – und altgriechisch *thymos* – „Lebenskraft", „Leidenschaft" – zurück. In der Medizin steht das Wort für die Körpersäfte. Dabei kann es sich ebenso um reale Säfte wie Blut, Lymphflüssigkeit und Galle handeln, wie auch um vermeintlich reale oder hypothetische, z.B. schwarze Galle. In der Psychologie steht der Begriff für den grundlegenden thymischen Zustand, der Emotionen und Affekte steuert. Auch die vier Temperamente hängen mit den vier Körpersäften (Humoren) zusammen (Hippokrates, 479–377 v.u.Z.). Jeder davon entspricht einem Element: Schleim dem Wasser (phlegmatisch), Blut der Luft (sanguinisch), gelbe Galle dem Feuer (cholerisch) und schwarze Galle der Erde (melancholisch, aber auch angespannt).

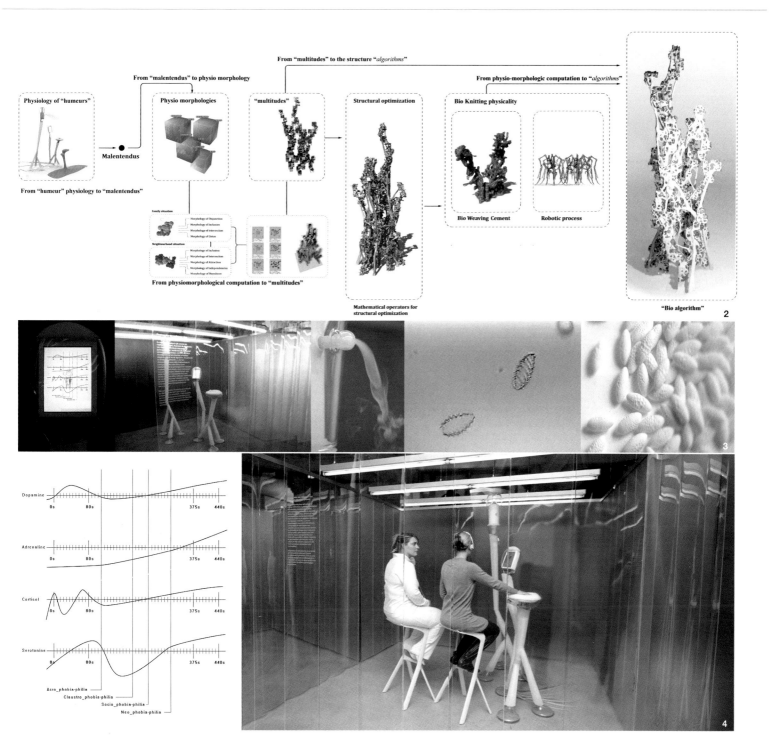

2   Dieses Diagramm zeigt die verschiedenen Stufen des Forschungsprozesses von der Gewinnung der physiologischen Daten zu den psychomorphologischen Analysen, den Aggregations-
protokollen, der Strukturoptimierung, den biochemischen Verfahren und den robotischen Prozessen. Diagram showing the development of the information collected from physiology to
a step by step research consisting of psycho-morphological analyses, protocols of aggregation, structural optimization, bio chemistry extrusion and robotic process. © New-Territories

3–4   Die physiologische Teststation, in der die Bio-Interviews geführt werden. Der physiologische Test fungiert mit der Messung des geistigen und körperlichen (Un-)Gleichgewichts
während eines 7-minütigen Interviews als eine biologische Bestandsaufnahme. Ein Emotionssensor erfasst die biochemischen Sekretionen (hauptsächlich Moleküle wie Dopamin,
Adrenalin, Serotonin und Cortisol), die die atavistischen Reaktionen der jeweiligen Person anzeigen (ihren Grad an Lust oder Abscheu, Anziehung oder Desinteresse), um daraus
eine Kartografie unausgesprochener Wünsche zu erstellen, die sich auf die Kluft, das *malentendu* zwischen zwei Formen der Sprache, Biopsychismus und freiem Willen, stützt.
Während des Tests wird eine Art Nebel aus Nanopartikeln versprüht. The physiological testing station where the bio-interviews are conducted. The physiological test works as a
bio scan, setting a baseline by measuring mind and bodily (de-)equilibrium over a 7 minutes interview. An emotions sensor collects the bio-chemical reactions (mainly molecules
such as dopamine, adrenaline, serotonin and hydrocortisone) that indicate the atavism reaction of the subject (degree of pleasure or repulsion, attraction or absence of interest) to
approach the cartography of unformulated desire, re-questioning the gap, the *malentendu* between two types of language, bio-psychism, and free-will. During the test a kind of
vapor (nanoparticles) is released. © New-Territories

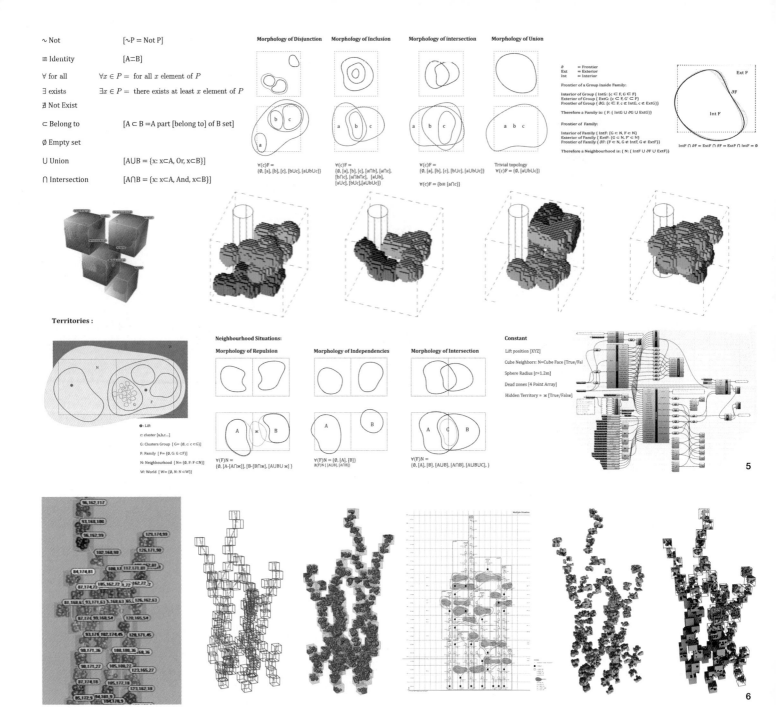

5–6 Physio- und Aggregationsmorphologien. Die *malentendus* (widersprüchlichen Wünsche) der Zugehörigkeit werden mit mathematischen Hilfsmitteln aus der Mengenlehre (Inklusion, Überschneidung, Differenz etc.) in eine Kartografie des Bewusstseins übersetzt (Anziehung, Ausschluss, Berührung, Abstoßung, Indifferenz), um die „Distanzen" zwischen den Individuen (zwischen ihnen und ihrer näheren Umgebung) zu ermitteln. Anfangs besteht jede Wohneinheit aus einem Kubus von 12 Metern Seitenlänge. Die Besiedlung dieses abstrakten Raums geschieht über die Ermittlung oder Aushandlung der Distanz zwischen Clustern (Familienmitgliedern)/der Distanz zu den Erschließungswegen (Lift – Notausgang)/der Distanz zu den Außengrenzen (Fassaden)/der Distanz zur Nachbarschaft, ein Verweben der Beziehungen zwischen Phobien/Phylien aus dem *malentendus*-Bericht.

Physio and aggregative morphologies. Mathematical tools to translate the initial *malentendus* (contradictory desires) of belonging relationship with set theory tools (inclusion, intersection, difference, etc.) to extract a cartography of the mind (attraction, exclusion, touching, repulsion, indifference, etc.) as a negotiation of: "distances" between the human beings (from themselves to near environment). Each initial habitable volume is composed by a cube of 12 meter. The colonization of this void is resolved by negotiation on; distance between clusters (family members)/distance to distribution (lift-escape)/distance to the limits (facades)/distance to neighborhood, interlacing relationship between phobia/phylia from *malentendus* report. © New-Territories

auf die jeweiligen Geometrien auswirken und das Morphologieprotokoll auf der Ebene des „Zusammenlebens" beeinflussen. Der als eine Art Emotionsdetektor fungierende physiologische Test setzt also die Humoralchemie dazu ein, den künftigen Wohnbereich der getesteten Personen zu entwerfen. Konkret geht es bei dieser experimentellen Biostation darum, mithilfe von Nanotechnologie[2] die physiologischen Daten sämtlicher künftiger Bewohner zu erfassen, um aus den so erschlossenen „Stimmungen" – einer (post)modernen Übersetzung der hippokratischen Humoralpathologie – die Grundzüge einer sich permanent wandelnden, von unserem Unbewussten modellierten (und modulierten) Architektur zu erarbeiten.

Die Studie befasst sich mit dem unklaren Bereich der Seele, der sich zwischen Begehren und Bedürfnis auftut. Die Grundarbeit besteht in einer Reinterpretation der *malentendus*,[3] die sich schon aus der Erscheinungsweise dieser beiden Formen menschlichen Verlangens ergeben: derer, die aufgrund der sprachlichen Mitteilbarkeit ihrer Vorlieben offen zutage liegen, und derer, die – vielleicht beunruhigender, aber ebenso wirksam – unter der Oberfläche gären. Aufgrund der Letzteren können wir den Körper als eine Wunschmaschine begreifen, die mit ihrer eigenen Chemie ausgestattet ist: Dopamin, Cortisol, Melatonin, Adrenalin und andere vom Körper produzierten Moleküle, die dem durch sie hervorgerufenen Bewusstseinszustand unbemerkt vorausgehen. So wird die Produktion von Architektur durch eine andere Realität, eine andere Komplexität modifiziert, eine, die in den Täuschungsmechanismus der Sprache einbricht, um seine widersprüchlichen Signale oder *malentendus* mitsamt den vom azephalen Körper aufgezeichneten Daten räumlich umzusetzen. Eine Station zum Erfassen dieser Signale ermöglicht die Wahrnehmung dieser chemischen Variationen und der Schwankungen des Gemütszustands, so dass sie sich auf die entstehenden Geometrien und das Konstruktionsprotokoll auswirken. Es kommt einem Eingriff in die Logik der Dinge gleich, wenn sich die Sprache so mit den Tiefenschichten des Körpers auseinandersetzen muss.

Die Erhebung der Humoralzustände erfolgt auf der Basis von Interviews, die den Konflikt, ja das schizophrene Verhältnis zwischen den Wünschen, dem (biochemisch und neurobiologisch) Abgesonderten und dem über das Interface der Sprache Ausgedrückten sichtbar machen. Die während des Inter-

here is on using nanotechnology[2] through an experimental bio-station to capture physiological data from all future tenants to prepare and model, by means of these "moods"—a (post)modern translation of Hippocrates' four humors—the foundations of an architecture in permanent mutation, modeled (and modulated) by our unconscious.

The study is concerned with the confused region of the psyche that lies between pleasure/desire and need/want. The groundwork comes from a rereading of the *malentendus*[3] inherent in the very expression of two forms of human desires: Those that traverse public space through the ability to express a choice by means of language, i.e., on the surface of things, and those that are beneath the surface, being perhaps more disturbing but equally valid. By means of the latter we can appraise the body as a desiring machine with its own chemistry: dopamine, hydrocortisone, melatonin, adrenaline and other molecules secreted by the body itself that are imperceptibly anterior to the consciousness these substances generate. Thus, the making of architecture is inflected by another reality, another complexity, breaking and entering into language's mechanism of dissimulation in order to physically construct its contradictory signals or *malentendus*, including the data that the acephalous body collects. A station for collecting these signals makes it possible to perceive these chemical variations and capture the changes in emotional state, so that they affect the geometries emitted and influence the construction protocol. This means staging a break-in to the logic of things when language has to negotiate with the depths of the body.

The collection of humors is organized on the basis of interviews that make visible the conflict and even schizophrenic qualities of desire, between those secreted (biochemically and neurobiologically) and those expressed through the interface of languages. During the physiological test the corporal chemical reactions, i.e., molecules like dopamine, adrenalin, serotonin and hydrocortisone, generate information about a participants animal reactions, i.e., degree of pleasure or repulsion, curiosity, or disinterest. The aim of the protocol is to generate a reactive emphasis of phobia-phylia inputs and to record, using the emitter-sensor-detector feature, the biochemical evolution of the "mind" and read this data as relationship outputs comprising psycho-perturbation and psycho-stuttering as a result of attractor-repulsor emotional contingencies.

> The study is concerned with the confused region of the psyche that lies between pleasure/desire and need/want.

---

2   Mithilfe von einatembaren Nanorezeptoren lässt sich der chemische Zustand des Körpers quasi „erschnüffeln". Diese Nanorezeptoren konzentrieren sich wie Pollen in den Bronchien und heften sich an die Blutgefäße an. So wird es ihnen möglich, Spuren des vom Hämoglobin transportierten Stresshormons Cortisol zu entdecken. Sobald sie damit in Berührung kommen, löst sich die Phospholipidmembran der Nanopartikel auf, und sie geben verschiedene Moleküle, u.a. gasförmiges Formaldehyd (H_2CO) ab. Diese im Atemtrakt abgewiesenen Moleküle werden mittels Cavity-ring-down-Spektroskopie (CRDS) aufgespürt. Dabei handelt es sich um eine mit Laserlicht einer bestimmten Frequenz arbeitende optische Analysemethode, mit der man die Dichte der in der Luft befindlichen Moleküle messen kann. Die Wellenlänge zum Aufspüren von Formaldehyd beträgt rund 350 Nanometer.

3   Das französische Wort *malentendu* impliziert sowohl ein akustisches wie ein begriffliches Missverständnis und ist in diesem Sinne schwer übertragbar.

2   Nano receptors can be inhaled, making it possible to "sniff" the chemical state of the human body. Like pollens, they are concentrated in the bronchia and attach themselves to the blood vessels. This location makes it possible for them to detect traces of stress hormones (hydrocortisone) carried by the haemoglobin. As soon as they come into contact with this substance, the phospholipidic membrane of the NP (nanoparticles) dissolves and releases several molecules, including formaldehyde (H_2CO) in a gaseous state. The molecules rejected by the respiratory tract are detected using cavity ring-down spectroscopy (CRDS). This is a method of optical analysis using laser beams programmed to a particular frequency, making it possible to measure the density of airborne molecules. The wavelength used for the detection of formaldehyde is around 350 nanometers.

3   *Malentendu* is a French word the denotation of which is navigating between mishearing and misunderstanding and which lacks an accurate translation in English.

Mathematical concepts borrowed from set theory are used as a strategic relational tool to extract from these multiple misunderstandings, a morphological potential (attraction, exclusion, touching, repulsion, indifference) as a negotiation of the "distances" between humans and humans, humans and limits, humans and access that constitute these collective aggregates. As a branch of mathematics, set theory was founded by the German mathematician Georg Cantor in the late 19th century. Its aim is to define the concepts of sets and belonging (union, inclusion, intersection and disjunction). Set theory can be used to describe the structure of each situation as a kind of collective, defining the relationships between the parts and the whole, while taking into consideration that the latter is not reducible to the sum of its part (or even the ensemble of relationships between the parts). Mathematical formulas become the matrix for the relational structure on which an inhabitable space is based, defining all the properties of a given situation in relational modes: both the relationships between the elements themselves (residential areas) and those between these elements and the ensemble or ensembles. It describes morphologies characterized by their dimensions and position in the system and, above all, by the negotiations of distance they carry out with the other parts and as multiple artifacts, produce relational protocols, relational relationships and relational aesthetics: protocols of attraction, repulsion, contiguity, dependence, sharing, indifference, exclusion.

These relational modes are simultaneously elaborated within the residential cell and on its periphery in relation to the neighboring colonies. The multiplicity of possible physio-morphological layouts based on mathematical formulations offers a variety of habitable patterns in terms of the transfer of the self to the other, and to others as well. The data obtained from the physiological interview by means of nanoparticles concerns the following issues: familial socialization (distance and relationship between residential areas within a single unit), neighborhood socialization (distance and relationship between residential units), modes of relations to externalities (biotope, light, air, environment), and also seeing, being seen, and hiding, modes of relating to access (receiving and/or escaping, even self-exclusion) and the nature of the interstices (from closely spaced to panoptic).

In contrast to the standard-model formatting of habitats, this mathematical tool offers contingencies that produce the potential to negotiate with the ambiguities of one's own humors (tempers) and desires. It enables the mixing of contradictory compulsions (appearances) and even some *malentendus*: "I'd like that but at the same time/maybe/not/and the opposite." These *malentendus* are directly influenced by the pathologies generated by collective living, oscillating between phobia and philia (claustrophobia/philia, agoraphobia/philia, xenophobia/philia, acrophobia/philia, noctophobia/philia, sociophobia/philia, neo-phobia/philia).

> The multiplicity of possible physio-morphological layouts based on mathematical formulations offers a variety of habitable patterns in terms of the transfer of the self to the other, and to others as well.

views auftretenden chemischen Körperreaktionen (erkennbar z.B. an den vorhin erwähnen Molekülen) werden gemessen und vermitteln Informationen über den Grad an Lust oder Abscheu, Neugierde oder Desinteresse, die die jeweilige Person aufweist. Ziel des Protokolls ist es, eine Reaktion auf Phobie- bzw. Phylie-Inputs zu generieren und mithilfe der Sender-Sensor-Detektor-Vorrichtung die biochemische Entwicklung des „Bewusstseins" aufzuzeichnen – Daten, die dann als beziehungsrelevanter Output gelesen werden können, der etwas über die psychische Beunruhigung oder Verstörung durch die jeweils Lust oder Abscheu erregenden emotionalen Kontingenzen sagt.

Mathematische Operationen aus der Mengenlehre (Zugehörigkeit, Inklusion, Überschneidung, Differenz, etc.) dienen als strategisches Mittel, um aus diesen vielfältigen Missverständnissen morphologisches Potenzial (Anziehung, Ausschluss, Berührung, Abstoßung, Indifferenz) zu ziehen, mit ihnen die „Distanzen" zwischen den Menschen (aber auch zwischen Menschen und Grenzen, Menschen und Zugängen) zu ermitteln, die dann diese kollektiven Aggregate bilden sollen. Die Mengenlehre ist ein im 19. Jahrhundert von Georg Cantor begründeter Zweig der Mathematik. Ihr Ziel ist es, Mengenbegriffe und Zugehörigkeiten zu definieren, mit deren Hilfe man die Struktur jeder Situation als eine Art Kollektiv beschreiben und die Beziehungen zwischen den Teilen und dem Ganzen bestimmen kann, unter Beachtung des Umstands, dass Letzteres nicht auf die Summe seiner Teile (oder auch nur die Menge der Beziehungen zwischen den Teilen) reduzierbar ist. So werden mathematische Formeln zur Matrix für die relationale Struktur, auf der bewohnbarer Raum beruht, indem sie sämtliche Eigenschaften einer Situation relational definieren: als Relationen zwischen den Elementen (Wohnbereichen) selbst und als solche zwischen den Elementen und dem Ensemble (oder mehreren davon). Die Struktur bildet Morphologien, die durch ihre Dimensionen und ihre Position im System, vor allem aber durch die Distanz charakterisiert sind, die sie mit den anderen Teilen und als vielfältige Artefakte aushandeln. Dabei entstehen relationale Protokolle, relationale Beziehungen und eine relationale Ästhetik: Protokolle der Anziehung, Abstoßung, Kontiguität, Abhängigkeit, Gemeinsamkeit, Indifferenz, Exklusion.

Diese relationalen Modi werden gleichzeitig in der einzelnen Wohnzelle und an ihrer Grenze zu den Nachbarkolonien entwickelt. Die Vielfalt möglicher physiomorphologischer Anordnungen auf der Grundlage mathematischer Formulierungen eröffnet eine breite Palette bewohnbarer Muster im Sinn der Übertragung des Selbst an den oder die anderen. Die beim physiologischen Interview mithilfe der Nanopartikel erhobenen Daten berühren folgende Aspekte: Familiensozialisation (Abstand und Relationen zwischen den verschiedenen Bereichen innerhalb der Wohneinheit), Nachbarschaftssozialisation (Abstand und Relationen zwischen den Wohneinheiten), Art der Relation zur Außenwelt (Biotop, Licht, Luft, Umwelt), aber auch

Shape Optimization

We are looking for a domain ω minimizing a functional J, called "objective function", chosen to take into account the constraints imposed to the shape. For example find the most rigid object that can be done with a given amount of a given elastic material.

$$\min_{(\omega \text{ admissible shapes})} J(\omega)$$

$u : \omega \to \mathbb{R}^3$ displacement field solution of

$$\begin{cases}
-\mathrm{div}(Ae(u)) &= f \quad \text{in } \omega \\
u &= 0 \quad \text{on } \Gamma_D \\
Ae(u) \cdot n &= g \quad \text{on } \Gamma_N \\
e(u) &= \tfrac{1}{2}(\nabla u + \nabla u^T) \\
\sigma &= Ae(u) \quad \text{Hooke's law of the material}
\end{cases}$$

Example of objective function: $J(\omega) = \int_\omega Ae(u) \cdot e(u)\, dx = \int_\omega fu\, dx + \int_{\Gamma_N} g.n\, ds$.

Shape representation using level set:

$\Omega \subset \mathbb{R}^3$ is given, containing all the admissible shapes.

$\psi : \Omega \to \mathbb{R}$ level set function characterizing the shape:

$$\begin{aligned}
\omega &= \{x \in \Omega,\ \psi(x) < 0\} \\
\partial\omega &= \{x \in \Omega,\ \psi(x) = 0\} \\
D \setminus \overline{\omega} &= \{x \in \Omega,\ \psi(x) > 0\}
\end{aligned}$$

Changing the shape $\omega \Leftrightarrow$ transport ψ through the Hamilton Jacobi equation:

$$\frac{\partial\psi}{\partial t} + V|\nabla\psi| = 0$$

where $V(x)$ is computed using the shape derivative $\frac{\partial J}{\partial\omega}$.
In the above example.

$$\frac{\partial J}{\partial\omega}(\omega) \cdot \theta = -\int_{\partial\omega} (Ae(u) \cdot e(u))\, \theta \cdot n\, ds \quad \text{and} \quad V(x) = Ae(u) \cdot e(u)(x) \quad \forall x \in \partial\omega.$$

———————————— formules :

$$\begin{cases}
\dfrac{\partial\psi}{\partial t} + V|\nabla\psi| = 0 \\[2mm]
\dfrac{\partial J}{\partial\omega}(\omega) \cdot \theta = -\displaystyle\int_{\partial\omega} (Ae(u) \cdot e(u))\, \theta \cdot n\, ds \ \longrightarrow \ V(x) = Ae(u) \cdot e(u)(x) \quad \forall x \in \partial\omega.
\end{cases}$$

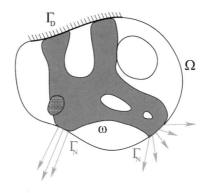
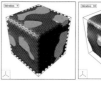

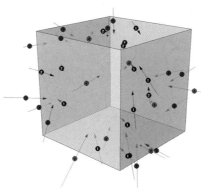
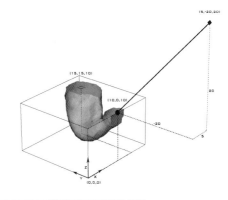

7 3D-Druck von Ergebnissen einer früheren Berechnung. 3D print of outputs from a previous calculation. © New-Territories

8 Strukturoptimierungsstrategien und -verfahren. Mathematische Prozesse zur Erzielung einer inkrementellen und rekursiven Optimierung (exolokal, lokal und hyperlokal). Sie berechnen und gestalten zugleich die tragenden Strukturelemente für die Physiomorphologien. Die Formen entstehen ausschließlich durch Iterationen, die die Morphologien durch die physische und strukturelle Verfestigung der Zwischenräume verbinden, so dass sie sich sowohl einzeln (lokale Kalkulation) als auch als Cluster (exolokale Kalkulation) gegenseitig stützen. Die Berechnungen beruhen auf exakten Eingaben (Grenzen und Eigenschaften der verwendeten Materialien, Ausgangsbedingungen, Eigengewicht und Kräfteableitung, Stärke und Vektorisierung der Kräfte, etc.). Structural optimization strategies and procedures. Mathematical process meant to obtain incremental and recursive optimization (exo-local, local, and hyper-local). It simultaneously calculates and designs the structural elements supporting the physio-morphologies. The shapes are made only through successive iterations that join the morphologies by physically and structurally coagulating the space between them, so that they can support each other both individually (local calculations) and as clusters (exo-local calculation). The calculation meets precise inputs (constraints and characteristics of the building material, initial state, dead load and transfer of forces, intensity and vectorization of these forces, etc.). © New-Territories

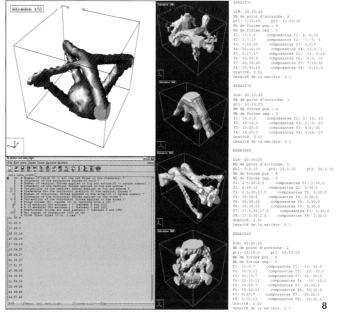

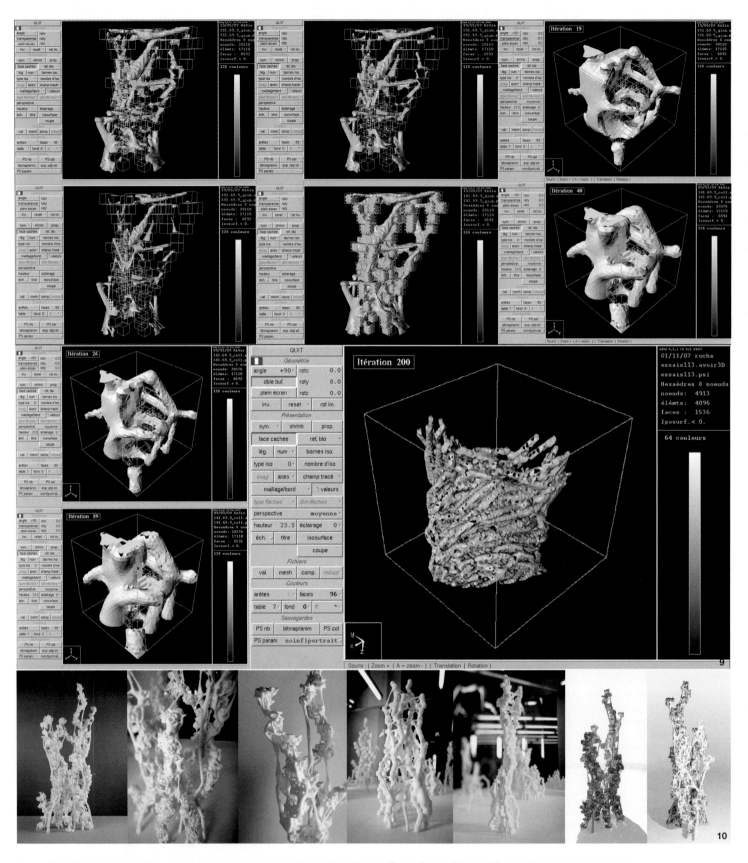

9 Screen Shot des Kalküls (C++ Linux) der exolokalen, lokalen und hyperlokalen Situation. Screen Shot on Calculus (C++ Linux) showing exo-local, local, hyper-local situation. © New-Territories

10 3D-Druck der Strukturoptimierungsergebnisse. 3D print of structural optimization outputs. © New-Territories

Dinge wie Sehen und Gesehenwerden, Abtauchen, Zugänglichkeit (offen und/oder eskapistisch bis zum Selbstausschluss) sowie die Natur der Zwischenräume (von eng bis panoptisch).

Im Gegensatz zur üblichen Planung von Lebensräumen lässt dieses mathematische Modell Kontingenzen zu, die das Potenzial besitzen, mit den Unwägbarkeiten der eigenen Stimmungslagen und Wünsche umzugehen. Es ermöglicht die Verbindung widerstreitender Zwänge (Erscheinungen) und sogar einiger *malentendus*: „Ich möchte das haben, aber zugleich/vielleicht/nicht/und das Gegenteil." Diese *malentendus* sind direkt von Pathologien beeinflusst, die durch das Zusammenleben zustande kommen und zwischen Ab- und Zuneigung changieren (Klaustrophobie/philie, Agoraphobie/philie, Xenophobie/philie, Acrophobie/philie, Noctophobie/philie, Soziophobie/philie, Neophobia/philie).

Der zweite Baustein besteht aus computergestützten, mathematischen und maschinischen Verfahren, die nach bestimmten Protokollen eine urbane Struktur aus unwahrscheinlichen, aufeinanderfolgenden Unbestimmtheiten, Ansammlungen und Anordnungen generiert, die die Verbindung zwischen Individuum und Kollektiv reartikulieren sollen. Die Anordnung der morphologisch erzeugten[4] Wohneinheiten und Strukturverzweigungen, die das soziale Leben tragen, wird dabei a posteriori und nicht a priori geplant und entwickelt. Diese Elemente werden mit Optimierungsprotokollen errechnet, die zugleich inkrementell und rekursiv sind und deren Hauptergebnis in der damit einhergehenden Physikalität und Morphologie einer Architektur besteht.

Der von François Jouve entwickelte „Algorithmus" ist eine mathematische Umsetzung der „empirischen" Optimierungsmethode, bei der Formen aus Beschränkungen geschaffen werden und nicht umgekehrt.[5] Der Strukturoptimierungsalgorithmus unterscheidet sich von direkten Berechnungsmethoden wie der Berechnung des Tragwerks eines Gebäudes nach dessen Planung. Im Gegensatz zu diesen lässt er die architektonische Form aus den Trajektorien der Kraftübertragung hervorgehen – und zwar zugleich mit ihrer Berechnung. Der Algorithmus basiert u.a. auf zwei mathematischen Strategien, wovon die erste auf die von Forschungen des französischen Mathematikers Jacques

The other approach is comprised of computational, mathematical, and machinist procedures designed to generate an urban structure following certain protocols of improbable and uncertain successive indeterminations, aggregations, and layouts to rearticulate the link between the individual and the collective. The layout of the morphological[4] residential units and the structural trajectories that support social life are conceived and developed here *a posteriori* and not as an *a priori*. These structures are calculated following simultaneously incremental and recursive structural optimization protocols whose principle result is the concurrently generated physicality and morphology of an architecture.

The "algorithm" developed by François Jouve is a mathematical calculation for "empirically" seeking optimization by creating forms out of constraints and not vice-versa.[5] The structural optimization algorithm differs from directly calculated structural methods such as calculating the load-bearing structure of a building after it has been designed. In contrast, the algorithm allows the architectural form to emerge from the trajectories of the transmission of forces simultaneously with the calculation that generates them. The algorithm is based on (among other things) two mathematical strategies, one taken from the derivative initiated by the research of the French mathematician Jacques Hadamard[6] and the other from the protocol of the representation of complex shapes by Cartesian meshing through level set.[7] Through the use of these computational, mathematical, and mechanization procedures, the urban structure engenders successive, improbable, and uncertain aggregations that constantly rearticulate the relationship between the individual and the collective.

Animist, vitalist, and machinist: the architecture of humors rearticulates the need to confront the unknown in a contradictory manner by means of

> The structural optimization algorithm differs from directly calculated structural methods such as calculating the load-bearing structure of a building after it has been designed.

---

4 Diese Morphologien werden als Matrix einer Kombinatorik für die Mischung und Verknüpfung der vielfältigen Beziehungen aufgefasst. Die Mengen werden ausgehend von den Elementen gebildet, und die Elemente ergeben die Mengen. Auf dieser Ebene haben die Elemente einer Menge keine anderen Merkmale als die Beziehungen, in denen sie zueinander und zum System stehen. Daher werden sie einfach als Variablen bezeichnet: a, b, c, usw. Operationen wie Zugehörigkeit, Vereinigung, Inklusion, Überschneidung, Disjunktion beschreiben Morphologien, welche die Distanzen wiedergeben und auf Protokolle wie Ausschluss, Anziehung, Berührung, Abstoßung, Abhängigkeit, Gemeinsamkeit, Indifferenz usw. referieren. Ehe die Morphologie einer Wohneinheit auf einen Funktionstyp reduziert wird, wird sie als Austauschbereich ausgearbeitet. Mathematische Formeln sind ein Hilfsmittel für die Entwicklung von Kombinationen und können eine relationale Struktur generieren, die dann als Grundlage für einen Wohnraum verwendet wird.

5 Vgl. das Formoptimierungskonzept (C++ unter Linux, entwickelt von François Jouve).

4 These morphologies are considered as the matrix of a "combinatory," blending and stitching their multiple relationships. Sets are constructed based on these elements, and these elements produce sets. At this point the elements of a set have no characteristics other than the relationships between them and between them and the system. Consequently, they are designated simply as variables: a, b, c, etc. Operations such as belonging, union, inclusion, intersection, and disjunction describe morphologies that negotiate the distances between each other and indicate the protocols of exclusion, attraction, touching, repulsion, dependence, sharing, indifference and so on. Before the morphology of a residence unit is reduced to a functional typology, it is first worked out as an area of exchanges. Mathematical formulas are an aid to the development of combinations and can generate a relational structure on which a residence space is based.

5 See the concept of shape optimization (C++ on Linux, developed by François Jouve).

6 This strategy serves to modify a shape by successive infinitesimal steps, to improve the criteria we want to optimize, as a permanent variation of boundaries.

7 To understand locally what could be the line of the highest or lowest resulting point, if we project the local incremental iterative calculus onto a 2-D diagram, to extract the X,Y position in the space as data to be reinjected into the next step of the calculation.

computational and mathematical assessments for bottom-up aggregative[8] empirical assemblage. The architecture of *des humeurs* is also a tool that will give rise to "multitudes" and their palpitation and heterogeneity, the premises of a relational organization protocol. The research project is organized around the following levels:

1. From the Physiology of Humors to *Malentendus*. The humors collection is organized on the basis of interviews that make visible the conflict and even schizophrenia of desires, between those secreted (via biochemical and neurobiological processes) and those expressed through the interface of language (via free will). Mathematical tools taken from set theory are used so that the "misunderstandings" produce a morphological potential as a negotiation of "distances" between the human beings who are to constitute these collective aggregates.

2. *Malentendus*. This level treats conflicts as an operational mode, allowing architecture to become their transactional vector. "I'd love to but at the same time/and maybe/not/and the contrary." These misunderstandings are directly influenced by the pathologies of collective living: Claustro (phobia-philia)/Agora (phobia-philia)/Xeno (phobia-philia)/Acro (phobia-philia)/Nocto (phobia-philia)/Socio (phobia-philia)/Neo (phobia-philia).

3. From the Misunderstanding of Humors to Physio-Morphological Computation. These relational modes are simultaneously elaborated within the residential cell and on its periphery in relation to the neighbors. The multiplicity of possible physio-morphological layouts based on mathematical formulations offers a variety of habitable patterns in terms of the transfer of the self to the other and to others. This is an informational area, a so called "Temporary Autonomous Zone," allowing future purchasers to have access to a morphological combinatorics with multiple permutations produced jointly by the expression of their avowed desires and their indiscrete biochemical secretions. The volume of an entity-unit is 12 × 12 × 12 meters. This is the basis on which our calculations and hypotheses have been made.

These relational modes are simultaneously elaborated within the residential cell and on its periphery in relation to the neighbors.

---

8   An assemblage … like a multiplicity that contains many heterogeneous ends and establishes links, relationships of different kinds. The only thing holding the assemblage together is co-functioning, or in other words symbiosis, "sympathy" in the original sense. What matters are not filiations but alliances and alloys, not inheritance and descent but contagion and epidemics. "An assemblage comprises two segments, one of content and the other of expression. On the one hand it is a mechanical assemblage of bodies, of actions and passions, an intermingling of bodies reacting to one another, on the other hand it is a collective assemblage of enunciation, of acts and statements, of incorporeal transformations attributed to bodies. Then on a vertical axis, the assemblage has both territorial sides, or reterritorialized sides, which stabilize it, and cutting edges of deterritorialization, which carry it away." Gilles Deleuze and Felix Guattari, *A Thousand Plateaus: Capitalism and Schizophrenia*, trans. Brian Massumi (London, 2011), p. 88.

Hadamard[6] angestoßene und nach ihm benannte Hadamar-Ableitung, die zweite auf das Protokoll der Darstellung komplexer Formen mit dem kartesischen Gitter nach der Level-Set-Methode zurückgeht.[7] Mittels dieser computergestützten, mathematischen und maschinischen Verfahren bringt die urbane Struktur sukzessive, unwahrscheinliche und unbestimmte Ansammlungen hervor, in der sich die Beziehung zwischen Individuum und Kollektiv fortwährend reartikuliert.

Animistisch, vitalistisch, maschinisch: die Humoralarchitektur reartikuliert die Notwendigkeit der Konfrontation mit dem Unbekannten auf paradoxe Weise mithilfe computergestützter, mathematischer Berechnungen für ein sich von unten nach oben entwickelndes aggregatives empirisches Gefüge.[8] Die Humoralarchitektur ist auch ein Mittel, das „Vielheiten" mit ihrem aufgeregten Geflatter und ihrer Heterogenität hervorbringt, Voraussetzung für ein relationales Organisationsprotokoll. Das Forschungsprojekt verteilt sich auf die folgenden Ebenen:

1. Von der Humoralphysiologie zu den *malentendus*. Auf der Grundlage von Interviews werden Humoralzustände erhoben, die den Konflikt, bzw. das schizophrene Verhältnis zwischen den Wünschen, dem (biochemisch und neurobiologisch) Abgesonderten und dem über das Interface der Sprache Ausgedrückten (dem freien Willen), sichtbar machen. Mithilfe mathematischer Operatoren aus der Mengenlehre wird aus diesen „Missverständnissen" morphologisches Potenzial gezogen, indem sie die Ermittlung der „Distanzen" zwischen den Menschen verhandeln, aus denen sich die kollektiven Aggregate bilden sollen.

2. *Malentendus*. Diese Ebene behandelt Konflikte als Operationsmodus, wodurch die Architektur zu ihrem Transaktionsvektor werden kann: „Ich möchte das haben, aber zugleich/vielleicht/nicht/und das Gegenteil." Diese *malentendus* sind direkt von den Pathologien des Zusammenlebens beeinflusst: Klaustrophobie/

---

6   Diese Strategie dient dazu, eine Form durch eine Abfolge von Infinitesimalschritten zu modifizieren, um die zu optimierenden Kriterien als permanente Variation von Grenzen zu verbessern.

7   Ein lokales Verständnis dessen, wie die Linie des höchsten und tiefsten resultierenden Punktes aussehen könnte, wenn wir die lokale inkrementelle Iterativrechnung auf ein 2D-Diagramm projizieren, und die Ermittlung der X, Y Position im Raum, um sie als Daten in den nächsten Berechnungsschritt einzusetzen.

8   Ein Gefüge ist laut Deleuze eine Mannigfaltigkeit, die sich aus vielen heterogenen Teilen zusammensetzt und unterschiedliche Verbindungen, Beziehungen zwischen ihnen herstellt. Was ein Gefüge zusammenhält, ist einzig und allein sein Miteinanderfunktionieren, seine Symbiose, „Sympathie" im ursprünglichen Sinn des Wortes. Was zählt, sind nicht Verwandtschaftsbande, sondern Allianzen, Legierungen, nicht Vererbung und Abstammung, sondern Ansteckung und Epidemien. „Ein Gefüge [enthält] zwei Segmente, ein Inhaltssegment und ein Ausdruckssegment. Einerseits ist es ein Maschinengefüge von Körpern, Aktionen und Passionen, eine Mischung von Körpern, die aufeinander reagieren; andererseits ist es ein kollektives Äußerungsgefüge, ein Gefüge von Handlungen und Aussagen, von körperlosen Transformationen, die zu den Körpern hinzukommen. Und auf einer vertikal ausgerichteten Achse hat das Gefüge einerseits reterritorialisierte oder *territoriale* Seiten, die es stabilisieren, und andererseits *Deterritorialisierungspunkte*, die es fortreißen." Gilles Deleuze und Felix Guattari, *Tausend Plateaus: Kapitalismus und Schizophrenie*, Übers. Gabriele Ricke und Ronald Voullié, Berlin 1992, S. 124.

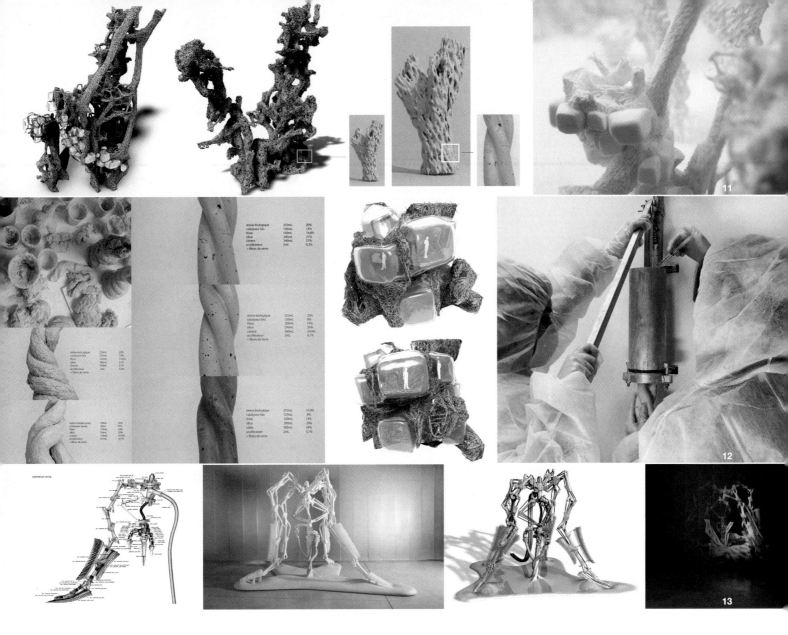

11 Nichtlineare Gewebeextrusion. Entwicklung eines Bauverfahrens, das durch Methoden der Sekretion, Extrusion und Agglutination in der Lage ist, mit komplexen, abweichenden Geometrien umzugehen. Non-linear knitting extrusion. Development of a construction processes that can deal with complex, non-standard geometries through an agenda of secretion, extrusion, and agglutination. © New-Territories

12 Biozement-Weberei (Materialwissen). Entwicklung eines viskosen, klebenden, sekretierbaren Baustoffs zur Errichtung morphologisch komplexer Bauwerke. Es handelt sich um einen Biozement, eine Mischung aus Zement und einem von der Agro-Polymer-Industrie entwickelten Naturharz, das die Steuerung der Parameter Viskosität, Flüssigkeitsgrad und Polymerisation erlaubt und damit die chemische und physikalische Verfestigung gleich nach der Sekretion ermöglicht. Bio-cement weaving (material expertise). Development of a viscous and adherent secretable material so as to produce a morphologically complex structure. This is a bio-cement component, a mix of cement and bio-resin developed by the agricultural polymers industry that makes it possible to control the parameters of viscosity, liquidity, and polymerization, thus producing chemical and physical agglutination at the time of secretion. © New-Territories

13 Robotischer Prozess, Verhalten und Gestaltung. Entwicklung einer Sekretions- und Webmaschine, die mithilfe von Press- und Sinterverfahren (Eins-zu-Eins-3D-Druck) eine vertikale Struktur erzeugen kann. Sie verwendet dazu ein hybrides Rohmaterial (einen Bio-Plastik-Zement), das sich chemisch zu einer räumlichen Umsetzung der computer-generierten Trajektorien verbindet. Diese Baukalligrafie funktioniert wie eine maschinische Stereotomie aus einem fortlaufenden geometrischen Muster, das nach einem repetitiven Protokoll entsteht. Robotic process, behavior, and design. Development of a secretion and weaving machine that can generate a vertical structure by means of extrusion and sintering (full-scale print) using a hybrid raw (a bio-plastic-cement) that chemically agglomerates to physically constitute the computational trajectories. This structural calligraphy works like a machinist stereotomy comprised of successive geometrics according to a strategy based on a repetitive protocol. © New-Territories

4. From Physio-Morphological Computation to the Multitude. A multitude of aggregations of physio-morphological layouts is organized according to parameters of chronological positioning and variable distances between the entities (collective, tribal, human clusters or conversely singleton units). This includes public layouts and micro-places.

5. Mathematical Operators for Structural Optimization. As indicated above, these operators are mathematical processes whose purpose is to achieve an incremental and recursive optimization (ex-local, local, and hyperlocal) that simultaneously calculates and designs support structures for the physio-morphologies. Forms are fabricated only by successive iterations that link, by physically and structurally coagulating, the interstices between morphologies so that they support each other. The calculations satisfy precise inputs (constraints and characteristics of the materials used, initial conditions, dead load and transfer of forces, intensity as well as the vectorization of these forces, etc.).

6. The "Algorithm(s)". Basically, this is the name of a physio-morphological residence unit. More precisely put, it is a name that characterizes a structural aesthetics thought as a geometry resulting posterior to the morphological fabrication of residential areas. The point is to emancipate architecture from the conceptual logic that takes structuration as the starting point, and instead allow the emergence of a physical matrix that can react to the multiplicity of morphologies and the ambiguity of the desires of future purchasers. Thus, this open-source mechanism can replace the determinist and predictable topology of collective habitats.

> This structural calligraphy works like a machinist stereotomy comprised of successive geometrics according to a strategy based on a repetitive protocol.

7. From the "Algorithm(s)" to Bio-Knit Physicality. The development of a construction protocol that can deal with complex, non-standard geometries through a process of secretion, extrusion, and agglutination frees the construction procedure from the usual frameworks that are incompatible with a geometry constituted by a series of anomalies and singularities.

8. Toolings/The Robotic Process. The robotic process refers to the development of a secretion and weaving machine that can generate a vertical structure by means of extrusion and sintering (full-size 3D printing) using a hybrid raw material (a bioplastic-cement) that chemically agglomerates to physically constitute the computational trajectories. This structural calligraphy works like a machinist stereotomy comprised of successive geometrics according to a strategy based on a repetitive protocol. This machine is both additive and formative. It is called Viab02.

9. Tooling/Bio-cement Weaving (Material Expertise). The study also involves the development of a viscous and adherent secretable material so

philie, Agoraphobie/philie, Xenophobie/philie, Acrophobie/philie, Noctophobie/philie, Soziophobie/philie, Neophobia/philie.

3. Vom humoralen Missverständnis zur physiomorphologischen Berechnung. Diese relationalen Modi werden gleichzeitig in der einzelnen Wohnzelle und an ihrer Grenze zur Nachbarschaft entwickelt. Die Vielfalt möglicher physiomorphologischer Anordnungen auf der Grundlage mathematischer Formulierungen eröffnet eine breite Palette bewohnbarer Muster im Sinn der Übertragung des Selbst an den oder die anderen. Dabei handelt es sich um einen informationellen Bereich, eine sogenannte „Temporäre Autonome Zone", die künftigen Wohnungskäufern Zugang zu einer morphologischen Kombinatorik verschaffen, deren vielfältige Permutationen sich aus dem gemeinsamen Ausdruck ihrer erklärten Wünsche und ihrer indiskreten biochemischen Absonderungen ergeben. Das Volumen einer Einheit beträgt 12 × 12 × 12 Meter. Auf dieser Grundlage haben wir unsere Berechnungen durchgeführt und unsere Hypothesen aufgestellt.

4. Von der physiomorphologischen Berechnung zur Vielheit. Nach Parametern chronologischer Positionierung und variabler Distanzen zwischen den Einheiten wird eine Vielheit an Aggregationen physiomorphologischer Anordnungen organisiert (kollektive, gruppen-, personenbezogene Cluster oder Einzeleinheiten). Dazu gehören auch öffentliche Räume und Mikroplätze.

5. Mathematische Operatoren der Strukturoptimierung. Wie bereits erwähnt handelt es sich bei diesen Operatoren um mathematische Prozesse, deren Ziel eine inkrementelle und rekursive Optimierung (exolokal, lokal und hyperlokal) ist, die tragende Strukturen für die Physiomorphologien gleichzeitig berechnet und entwirft. Die Formen werden ausschließlich durch fortlaufende Iterationen erzeugt, die die Zwischenräume zwischen den Morphologien durch physische und strukturelle Verfestigungen verbindet, so dass sie sich gegenseitig stützen. Die Berechnungen beruhen auf exakten Eingaben (Grenzen und Eigenschaften der verwendeten Materialien, Ausgangsbedingungen, Eigengewicht und Kräfteableitung, Stärke und Vektorisierung der Kräfte, etc.)

6. Der „Algorithmus". Im Grunde ist das der Name einer physiomorphologischen Wohneinheit. Genauer gesagt charakterisiert er eine strukturelle Ästhetik, die als eine Geometrie gedacht wird, die *nach* der morphologischen Fabrikation der Wohneinheiten entsteht. Es geht hier darum, die Architektur von der konzeptuellen Logik zu befreien, die die Strukturierung als Ausgangspunkt nimmt, und stattdessen die Entstehung einer physischen Matrix zu ermöglichen, die auf die Vielfalt der Morphologien und die Ambiguität der Wünsche der künftigen Käufer einzugehen vermag. So kann dieser Open-Source-Mechanismus die deterministische und vorhersehbare Typologie kollektiver Lebensräume ersetzen.

7. Vom „Algorithmus" zur Physikalität von Biogeweben. Die Entwicklung eines Konstruktionsprotokolls, das durch Prozesse der Sekretion, der Extrusion und der Agglutination mit komplexen, abweichenden Geometrien umzugehen vermag, befreit den Bauprozess von den üblichen Skeletten, die mit einer aus Anomalien und Singularitäten gebildeten Geometrie nicht vereinbar sind.

8. Fertigungsmittel/Robotischer Prozess. Hiermit ist die Entwicklung einer Sekretions- und Webmaschine gemeint, die mithilfe von Press- und Sinterverfahren (Eins-zu-Eins-3D-Druck) eine vertikale Struktur erzeugen kann. Sie verwendet dazu ein hybrides Rohmaterial (einen Bio-Plastik-Zement), das sich chemisch zu einer räumlichen Umsetzung der computergenerierten Trajektorien verbindet. Diese kalligrafische Struktur funktioniert wie eine maschinelle Stereotomie aus einem fortlaufenden geometrischen Muster, das nach einem repetitiven Protokoll entsteht. Die Maschine ist gleichermaßen additiv wie formativ. Sie heißt Viab02.

9. Fertigungsmittel/Biozement-Weberei (Materialwissen). Der Forschungsprozess umfasst auch die Entwicklung eines viskosen, klebenden, sekretierbaren Baustoffs zur Errichtung dieses morphologisch komplexen Bauwerks.[9] Es handelt sich um einen Biozement, eine Mischung aus Zement und einem von der Agro-Polymer-Industrie entwickelten Naturharz, das die Steuerung der Parameter Viskosität, Flüssigkeitsgrad und Polymerisation erlaubt und damit die chemische und physikalische Verfestigung gleich nach der Sekretion ermöglicht. Die mechanischen Fähigkeiten des Materials werden sichtbar gemacht (Verhinderung von Brüchen durch Zug, Druck, Schub usw.). Das Material emittiert wenig CO_2.

Am Forschungsprojekt beteiligt sind der Mathematiker François Jouve, der für die Ausarbeitung der dynamischen Strukturentwicklungsstrategien verantwortlich ist; der Architekt und Robotikdesigner Stephan Henrich, der zusammen mit Winston Hampel, Natanael Elfassy und mit Unterstützung von Marc Fornes an der evolutionären Programmierung arbeitet; und Gaetan Robillard und Fréderic Mauclere, die, ausgehend von einem Nanotechnologie-Szenario von R&Sie(n) und Berdaguer & Pejus die physiologische Datensammelstation entwickeln.

Übersetzung Wilfried Prantner

9   Das Material und die Verfahrensweisen gleichen denen des Contour-Crafting-Verfahrens, das wir mit dem Labor von Behrokh Khoshnevis an der USC für das Projekt „I've heard about" entwickelt haben.

as to produce this morphologically complex structure.[9] This is a bio-cement component, a mix of cement and bio-resin developed by the agricultural polymers industry that makes it possible to control the parameters of viscosity, liquidity, and polymerization and thus produce chemical and physical agglutination at the time of secretion. The mechanical expertise of this material is made visible (constraints of rupture induced by traction, compression and shearing, etc.). This material emits low CO_2.

This research is being carried out with François Jouve, the mathematician in charge of working out dynamic structural strategies; with the architect and robotics designer Stephan Henrich, with Winston Hampel, Natanael Elfassy on the computational development, including the help of Marc Fornes; and Gaetan Robillard and Fréderic Mauclere on the physiological data collection station, following a nano-technologies scenario by R&Sie(n) and Berdaguer & Pejus.

9   The material and the procedures used are similar to the contour-crafting developed with the Behrokh Khoshnevis Lab at USC for the "I've heard about" project.

1

1   Erstellung einer Flächenstruktur durch Umfliegen bereits montierter Teile. **Assembly of surface structure by flying around already constructed members.** © Gramazio & Kohler, ETH Zürich

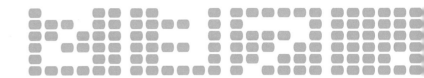

Designing Behavior

Materializing Architecture with Flying Machines

The digital design space (in which architecture is represented) and the physical building space (in which it is materialized) are converging. Traditionally, architects used technical drawings to translate design information into a set of building instructions. Craftsmen then interpreted and evaluated these drawings in order to link the conceptual design to its material realization.[1]

Die Gestaltung von maschinellem Verhalten. Architekturmaterialisierung mit Flugmaschinen. Der digitale Entwurfsraum (in dem Architektur dargestellt wird) und der physische Bauraum (in dem sie sich materialisiert) konvergieren immer mehr. Bisher übersetzten Architekten die Gestaltungsinformation üblicherweise mittels technischer Zeichnungen in eine Reihe von Handlungsanweisungen. Die Handwerker interpretierten und bewerteten die Zeichnungen, um den konzeptionellen Entwurf materiell umzusetzen.[1]

AMMAR MIRJAN · JAN WILLMANN · FABIO GRAMAZIO · MATTHIAS KOHLER

However, the mainstream adoption of digital design tools and the increasingly commonplace practice of transferring production from mechanically operated machines to computer-controlled robots calls into question the relationship between the designer and the artifact.[2] Digital design information can be directly linked with the process of making, and the skills of the designer are now explicitly coupled with the performance of the artifact.

Yet while in 2012 *The Economist* argued that digital fabrication was about to create a "third industrial revolution,"[3] the machines that would enable this "revolution" have already existed for half a century. The CNC-machine was developed in the 1950s, six-axis industrial robots have been on the market since the early 1970s, and 3D printers have become a useful tool since the early 1980s.[4] Computer-aided manufacturing was predominantly regarded as an advanced instrument of production rather than a programmable design tool. Today, through availability (off-the-shelf technology) and accessibility (control interfaces), these tools have entered the everyday domain of architects.[5]

Recent improvements in sensing, computation, and control, however, have led to the development of machines with capabilities that are profoundly different from those of conventional mechanical devices, and today's machines are both smarter than their predecessors (they can adapt their behavior to their environment and learn from their own actions) and more versatile. Flying robots are an excellent embodiment of these developments, as they enable aerial materialization and open up three-dimensional space to architecture in entirely new ways.[6]

From Speculation to Reality. The narratives of the flying house (for example in the tale of the *Santa Casa di Loreto*)[7] and the aerial city (for example in the book *Gulliver's Travels*)[8] have been used in art and literature for centuries. Flight, construction, and machines were first linked together in Leonardo da Vinci's experiments with human-powered mechanical flight in the 15th century.[9] It was in the context of 1920 post-revolutionary Soviet Constructivism that the visionary concept of using flying machines in architecture found prominent expressions (fig. 2). Vladimir Tatlin's "Letatlin" or Georgii Krutikov's "The City of the Future" serve as prominent examples here. In the same decade, Buckminster Fuller presented a scheme for a lightweight housing tower that could be transported with an airship to various

---

1 See Tobias Bonwetsch, Fabio Gramazio and Matthias Kohler, "Digitales Handwerk," *GAM 06* (2010): pp. 172–179.

2 See Nick Callicott, *Computer-Aided Manufacture in Architecture: The Pursuit of Novelty* (Oxford, 2000), pp. 79–97.

3 Paul Markillie, "The Third Industrial Revolution," *The Economist*, April 21, 2012.

4 See Callicott, *Computer-Aided Manufacture in Architecture* (see note 2), pp. 45–53.

5 See Tobias Bonwetsch, Fabio Gramazio and Matthias Kohler, "Towards a Bespoke Building Process," in *Manufacturing the Bespoke*, ed. Bob Sheil (Chichester, 2012), pp. 78–87.

6 See Jan Willmann et al., "Aerial Robotic Construction: Towards a New Field of Architectural Research," *International Journal of Architectural Computing* 10,3 (2012), pp. 439–460.

7 According to a legend, the *Santa Casa di Loreto*, the house in which the Virgin Mary grew up, was aerially transported by angels from Nazareth to Loreto, Italy, from 1291 to 1294, where it is now situated in the *Basilica della Santa Casa*. See Italo Tanoni, "Le culte marial de la Sainte Maison de Lorette et son evolution," in *Social Compass* 10 (1986), pp. 107–139.

8 See Jonathan Swift, *Travels into Several Remote Nations of the World. In Four Parts. By Lemuel Gulliver, First a Surgeon, and then a Captain of several Ships* better known as *Gulliver's Travels* (London, 1726).

9 See Aurélien Vernant, "Towards Aerial Architectures," in *Flight Assembled Architecture*, ed. Fabio Gramazio, Matthias Kohler and Raffaello D'Andrea (Orléans, 2013), pp. 152–163.

Doch die breite Verwendung digitaler Entwurfswerkzeuge und die zunehmende Verschiebung der Produktion von mechanisch bedienten Maschinen hin zu computergesteuerten Robotern stellt die bisherige Beziehung zwischen Entwerfer und Artefakt infrage.[2] Digitale Entwurfsinformationen können direkt mit dem Produktionsprozess verknüpft werden, und die Fähigkeiten des Entwerfers sind damit explizit an die Ausführung des Artefakts gekoppelt.

Die digitale Fabrikation, schrieb der *Economist* 2012, sei im Begriff, eine „dritte industrielle Revolution" auszulösen,[3] doch die Maschinen, die diese „Revolution" möglich machen sollen, gibt es bereits seit einem halben Jahrhundert. Die CNC-Maschine wurde in den 1950er Jahren entwickelt, sechsachsige Industrieroboter sind seit den frühen 1970ern auf dem Markt und 3D-Drucker avancierten in den frühen 1980ern zu einem brauchbaren Werkzeug.[4] Allerdings galten computergestützte Fertigungstechniken in erster Linie als fortschrittliche Produktionsmittel und nicht als programmierbare Gestaltungswerkzeuge. Heute sind diese Werkzeuge durch ihre allgemeine Verfügbarkeit (serienmäßig hergestellte Technologie) und Zugänglichkeit (benutzerfreundliche digitale Steuerung) in den architektonischen Alltag eingedrungen.[5]

Neueste Errungenschaften auf dem Gebiet der Sensor-, Computer- und Steuerungstechnik haben jedoch auch zur Entwicklung von Maschinen geführt, deren Fähigkeiten sich fundamental von denen konventioneller, rein mechanischer Maschinen unterscheiden; heutige Maschinen sind sowohl intelligenter (sie können ihr Verhalten an ihre Umgebung anpassen und aus dem eigenen Handeln lernen) als auch vielseitiger als ihre Vorläufer. Flugroboter verkörpern diese Entwicklung par excellence; sie ermöglichen der Architektur eine Materialisierung im freien Luftraum und eine völlig neue Erschließung dreidimensionaler Räumlichkeit.[6]

Von der Spekulation zur Realität. Erzählungen von fliegenden Häusern (z.B. die Legende der *Santa Casa di Loreto*)[7]

---

1 Vgl. Tobias Bonwetsch/Fabio Gramazio/Matthias Kohler: „Digitales Handwerk", in: *GAM* 06 (2010), S. 172–179.

2 Vgl. Nick Callicott: *Computer-Aided Manufacture in Architecture: The Pursuit of Novelty*, Oxford 2000, S. 79–97.

3 Paul Markillie: „The Third Industrial Revolution", in: *The Economist*, 21.04.2012.

4 Vgl. Callicott: *Computer-Aided Manufacture in Architecture*, S. 45–53 (wie Anm. 2).

5 Vgl. Tobias Bonwetsch/Fabio Gramazio/Matthias Kohler: „Towards a Bespoke Building Process", in: Bob Sheil (Hg.), *Manufacturing the Bespoke*, Chichester 2012, S. 78–87.

6 Vgl. Jan Willmann et al.: „Aerial Robotic Construction: Towards a New Field of Architectural Research", in: *International Journal of Architectural Computing* 10,3 (2012), S. 439–460.

7 Der Legende zufolge wurde die *Santa Casa di Loreto*, das Elternhaus der Jungfrau Maria, zwischen 1291 und 1294 durch Engel von Nazareth ins italienische Loreto getragen, wo es heute in der *Basilica della Santa Casa* steht. Vgl. Italo Tanoni: „Le culte marial de la Sainte Maison de Lorette et son evolution", in: *Social Compass* 10 (1986), S. 107–139.

und schwebenden Städten (z.B. in *Gullivers Reisen*)[8] sind in Kunst und Literatur seit vielen Jahrhunderten in Umlauf. Mit Konstruktion und Maschinen verbunden wurde das Fliegen erstmals im 15. Jahrhundert bei Leonardo da Vincis Versuchen mit mechanischen, durch menschliche Muskelkraft betriebenen Fluggeräten.[9] Die visionäre Idee der Verwendung von Flugmaschinen in der Architektur fand dann im sowjetischen Konstruktivismus der 1920er Jahre – etwa in Wladimir Tatlins „Lctatlin" oder Georgij Krutikovs „Zukunftsstadt" – einen prominenten Ausdruck (Abb. 2). Im selben Jahrzehnt präsentierte auch Buckminster Fuller seinen Plan für einen leichten Wohnturm, der sich per Luftschiff an verschiedene Orte transportieren ließ.[10] Und in der Zeit nach dem Zweiten Weltkrieg (speziell in den 1960er Jahren) waren zahlreiche Architekturprojekte durch technologiebasierte, utopische Konzepte gekennzeichnet, in denen Fluggeräte wie Ballone, Luftschiffe und Hubschrauber eine Rolle spielten. All diese frühen Flugmaschinen standen für eine neue Fortschrittsideologie, die Luftraum, Schwerelosigkeit und Mobilität als neue Paradigmen sah, die zu einer sinnlicheren und verhaltensbezogenen Architekturerfahrung führen sollte.[11]

In der konkreten Bauausführung kommen Flugmaschinen seit den 1950er Jahren zum Einsatz. So werden zum Beispiel Hubschrauber eingesetzt, um Baumaterial an abgelegene Baustellen ohne Straßenanbindung zu bringen oder im Fernleitungsbau Strommasten an die vorgesehenen Orte zu hieven und die Kabel zwischen ihnen zu spannen. Allerdings ist das manuelle Manövrieren der Flugmaschinen auf der Baustelle eine höchst diffizile und gefährliche Angelegenheit und so werden sie lediglich in Situationen eingesetzt, in denen traditionelle Baumethoden nicht infrage kommen. Insofern besteht eine erhebliche Diskrepanz zwischen der architektonischen Spekulation des Bauens aus der Luft und ihrer praktischen Umsetzung. Flugroboter könnten diese Kluft überwinden und der Architektur den Luftraum erschließen, indem sie Architekten ein Werkzeug in die Hand geben, mit dem sie das Entwerfen (mit seinen räumlichen, funktionalen und ästhetischen Eigenschaften) direkt mit dem Bauen (mit seinen physischen Qualitäten und maschinellen Beschränkungen) verbinden können.[12]

Digitale Fabrikation mit Flugrobotern. Flugmaschinen sind grundsätzlich in der Lage, Bauaufgaben auszuführen, die nicht den Beschränkungen digital-kontrollierten Produktions-

locations.[10] In the era after the Second World War (and particularly during the 1960s), many architectural projects were characterized by technology-based, utopian concepts that incorporated aerial machines such as balloons, airships and helicopters. These early flying machines came to symbolize a new ideology of progress, which saw airspace, weightlessness, and mobility as the new parameters leading to a more sensual and behavioral architectural experience.[11]

In building construction, aerial machines have been used on construction sites since the 1950s. Helicopters, for example, are commonly used to lift and transport building material to remote locations with no access to streets, and in high-line construction, they can be used as aerial cranes to carry power poles to designated locations or string cables between masts. However, the mechanical maneuvering of aerial machines in construction is challenging and dangerous, and, at present, manually-operated aerial machines are used solely in situations where no traditional construction method can be applied. As such, there is a deficit between the architectural speculation of aerial construction and its practical realization. Yet flying robots could bridge this gap by providing architects a tool to link the act of design (with its spatial, functional, and aesthetic attributes) to the act of making (with its physical qualities and machinic constraints), opening up airspace to architecture.[12]

Digital Fabrication with Flying Robots. Flying machines can perform construction tasks that are not limited by the same constraints as ground-based machines. First of all, the vehicle is physically decoupled from its working space. In contrast, conventional robotic arms and CNC-machines have constrained working areas that limit their use in architecture to small artifacts or building components. The large working range of a flying robot, however, allows it to reach points in space not otherwise accessible by computer-controlled construction machines, and enables its use at the full architectural scale. Secondly, digital control enables the vehicles to cooperate during assembly tasks. While traditional stationary robots tend to block each other's operational range when working cooperatively and are therefore usually constrained to repetitive assembly-line tasks, flying robots can interact with and maneuver around each other in three-dimensional space and can be used for cooperative tasks in a more flexible manner. Their ability to interact enables flying machines to collectively aggregate structures that could not be sequenced by an individual machine. And finally, the flying robot can fly through and around existing objects while performing fabrication maneuvers. These distinctive attributes differentiate aerial robots

> And finally, the flying robot can fly through and around existing objects while performing fabrication maneuvers.

8   Vgl. Jonathan Swift: *Travels into Several Remote Nations of the World. In Four Parts. By Lemuel Gulliver, First a Surgeon, and then a Captain of several Ships,* besser bekannt als *Gulliver's Travels,* London 1726.

9   Vgl. Aurélien Vernant: „Towards Aerial Architectures", in: Fabio Gramazio, Matthias Kohler und Raffaello D'Andrea (Hg.), *Flight Assembled Architecture,* Orléans 2013, S. 152–163.

10   Vgl. Buckminster R. Fuller: *4D Time Lock,* Chicago 1928.

11   Vgl. Jeannot Simmen et al.: *Schwerelos. Der Traum vom Fliegen in der Kunst der Moderne,* Stuttgart 1991.

12   Vgl. Matthias Kohler: „Aerial Architecture", in: *Log* 25 (2012), S. 23–30.

10   See Buckminster R. Fuller, *4D Time Lock* (Chicago, 1928).

11   See Jeannot Simmen et al., *Schwerelos: Der Traum vom Fliegen in der Kunst der Moderne* (Stuttgart, 1991).

12   See Matthias Kohler, "Aerial Architecture," *Log* 25 (2012), pp. 23–30.

from all other construction machines and allow them to materialize structures that could not be built with other fabrication methods.

Architectural Experimentation. By assembling a six-meter tall tower out of 1,500 foam elements, the first flight assembled architecture installation at the FRAC centre in Orléans, France, (figs. 3 and 5) demonstrated the ability of aerial robots to autonomously erect a differentiated structure.[13] The exhibition featured a live robotic build-up, performed by four flying quadrotor helicopters, or "quadrocopters," and displayed cooperative architectural assembly procedures. The flying vehicles attracted the attention of the exhibition's visitors who often cheered and applauded when the quadrocopters successfully positioned a building element in the structure, as if the robots would appreciate human encouragement. The visitors experienced the movements and the behaviors of the machines as intuitive and natural. The dynamic motions of the vehicles were in fact the result of a sophisticated algorithmic control system. Flying machines are inherently unstable. Sensors provide the vehicles with information from the environment. Yet, it is the algorithms that make sense of the information and provide awareness to the machines. Conventionally, mechanical machines operate according to deterministic rules as for example in the industrial production of identical parts. In contrast, algorithms can be designed to be adaptive, generative or to incorporate machine learning. As such, they enable the user of the system to intervene in the architectural design and fabrication process.

> Conventionally, mechanical machines operate according to deterministic rules as for example in the industrial production of identical parts.

The experimental case studies presented here are the first results of the subsequent research project "Aerial Constructions" and explore the unique capacity of flying vehicles in architecture. The experiments are performed in the "Flying Machine Arena," a $10 \times 10 \times 10$ meter indoor testbed for aerial robotic research at ETH Zurich.[14] The space is protected by nets and padding and is equipped with a motion capture system that provides vehicle position and attitude measurements. This information is sent to a PC, which runs algorithms and control strategies and sends commands to the vehicles in order to guide them in the three dimensional space.[15] The testbed experiments are usually done by using quadrocopters: in the past decade, these have emerged as the unmanned aerial vehicle (UAV) of choice for researchers. Their mechanical design is less complex than that of other types of helicopters, and they are relatively safe thanks to their four separate, smaller propellers, which store less kinetic energy than a comparable conventional helicopter's main rotor. The outward mounting and independent control of the four propellers offers considerable advantages in

maschinen unterliegen. Zunächst einmal sind Flugroboter nicht physisch an ihren Einsatzort gebunden. Im Gegensatz zu ihnen besitzen konventionelle Roboterarme und CNC-Maschinen einen begrenzten Arbeitsraum, was ihre Einsatzmöglichkeit in der Architektur auf die Herstellung kleiner Artefakte oder Einzelkomponenten beschränkt. Mit seinem großen Arbeitsraum erreicht ein Flugroboter dagegen all diejenige Punkte im Raum, die für computergesteuerte Baumaschinen bisher unzugänglich waren, so dass er für die volle Maßstäblichkeit der Architektur eingesetzt werden kann. Zweitens können digital gesteuerte Flugroboter bei Bauaufgaben kooperieren. Während sich ortsgebundene Roboter bei der Zusammenarbeit meist gegenseitig behindern und daher gewöhnlich auf repetitive Arbeiten beschränkt sind, können Flugroboter im dreidimensionalen Raum frei interagieren und einander umfliegen, sodass sie sich leichter für kooperative Tätigkeiten einsetzen lassen. Aufgrund dieses Interaktionsvermögens können Flugmaschinen gemeinsam Bauten fertigen, die einzelne Maschinen allein nicht zustande brächten. Und nicht zuletzt können Flugroboter bei ihren Manövern zwischen bereits gebauten Objekten hindurch oder um sie herum fliegen. Mit genau diesen Eigenschaften, durch die sie sich von allen anderen Baumaschinen unterscheiden, können sie Bauwerke realisieren, die mit anderen Fabrikationsmethoden unrealisierbar wären.

Experimentelle Architektur. Mit dem Bau eines sechs Meter hohen Turms aus 1.500 Schaumstoffelementen wurde am FRAC in Orléans (Abb. 3 und 5) erstmalig eine Architekturinstallation gezeigt, bei welcher Flugroboter selbständig ein differenziertes, architektonisches Objekt errichteten.[13] Die Ausstellung bestand aus dem in Echtzeit durchgeführten robotischen Aufbau des Turms durch vier Quadrocopter und führte kooperative architektonische Bauverfahren vor. Die Fluggeräte erregten damit große Aufmerksamkeit bei den Besuchern, die immer dann jubelten und applaudierten, wenn ein Baustein erfolgreich platziert wurde, so, als würden Roboter tatsächlich Wert auf menschlichen Zuspruch legen. Offenbar erlebten die Besucher das Verhalten der Maschinen als etwas Intuitives, gar Natürliches. Tatsächlich aber waren die dynamischen Bewegungen der Fluggeräte das Ergebnis eines komplexen algorithmischen Steuerungssystems. Die im Grunde instabilen Luftfahrzeuge werden von Sensoren mit Umgebungsinformationen versorgt, doch erst die Algorithmen erlauben es, diese zu verarbeiten und die Maschinen gewissermaßen mit einer eigenen „Wahrnehmung" auszustatten. Mechanische Maschinen operieren – wie etwa in der industriellen Verarbeitung identischer Bauteile – nach deterministischen Regeln. Algorithmen dagegen können so angelegt werden, dass sie anpassungs- und lernfähig sind. Damit geben

13   See Fabio Gramazio, Matthias Kohler and Raffaello D'Andrea, *Flight Assembled Architecture* (Orléans, 2013).

14   See Raffaello D'Andrea, accessible online: www.flyingmachinearena.org

15   See Sergei Lupashin et al., "The Flying Machine Arena as of 2010" (paper presented at the IEEE International Conference on Robotics and Automation, Shanghai, May 9–13, 2011).

13   Vgl. Fabio Gramazio/Matthias Kohler/Raffaello D'Andrea: *Flight Assembled Architecture*, Orléans 2013.

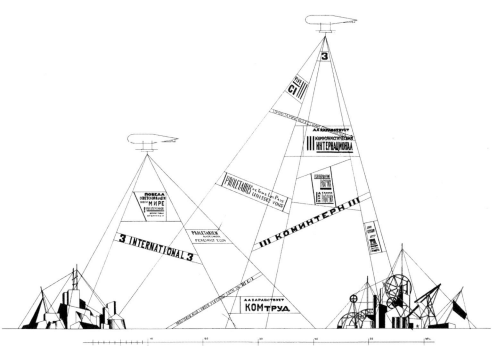

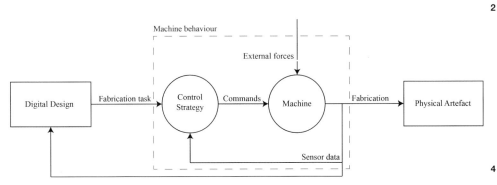

2 Ljubow Popowa und Alexander Vesnin, „Entwurf für ein theatrales Massenspektakel zu Ehren der Dritten Internationale" (Moskau, 1921). Liubov Popov and Alexander Vesnin, "Design for a theatricalized mass maneuver in honor of the Third International" (Moscow, 1921).

3 Installation „Flight Assembled Architecture" am FRAC in Orléans, 2011–2012. © Gramazio & Kohler und Raffaello D'Andrea in Kooperation mit der ETH Zürich. Flight Assembled Architecture installation at FRAC Centre Orléans, 2011–2012. © Gramazio & Kohler and Raffaello D'Andrea in cooperation with ETH Zürich. Foto photo: François Lauginie

4 Der digitale Entwurf bildet das Interface zum robotischen System, das das physische Artefakt erstellt. Die Sensordaten ermöglichen zum einen die Adaption des digitalen Entwurfs an das tatsächlich Gebaute, zum andern die Adaption der Maschine. Die Steuerungsstrategie, eine Sammlung aus verschiedenen Komponenten (Steueralgorithmen) wandelt die Fabrikationsaufgabe in eine Flugbahn um und sendet Befehle an das Gefährt, die sein Verhalten definieren. Diese Komponenten können für verschiedene Bauaufgaben maßgeschneidert werden, zum Beispiel um die Flugrichtung der Maschine bei der Anbringung eines Seils festzulegen oder dessen Spannung zu variieren. Andere sind mehr generischer Natur, betreffen z.B. die Drehzahl der Propeller oder die Einschätzung der Flughöhe. The digital design is the interface to the robotic system materializing the physical artifact. Sensor information allow on the one hand the adaptation of the digital design to what is actually being built and on the other hand the adaptation of the machine. The control strategy, a collection of different components (control algorithms) transforms the fabrication task into a trajectory and sends commands to the vehicle, defining its behavior. These components can be specifically designed for certain construction tasks, for example to adjust the heading of the vehicle when deploying a rope or to vary the tension of the cable. Others are more generic, for example to take care of the spinning the propellers or to estimate the vehicle attitude. © Gramazio & Kohler, ETH Zürich

5 Ausstellungsbesucher beim Betrachten des robotischen Montageprozesses. Exhibition visitors watching the robotic build-up. © Gramazio & Kohler und and Raffaello D'Andrea in Kooperation mit der ETH Zürich

6

7

6 Lufttransport einer Kohlenfaserröhre für die Montage dreidimensionaler Strukturen aus diskreten Elementen. Quadrocopter können sich in einer quasi-statischen Position nicht
um ihre x- oder y-Achse drehen: Ein Wechsel des Rotations-
winkels führt zu einer Beschleunigung. Die Methode löst das
Problem mit einer erdgebundenen Ladestation, in der die Fluggeräte vorausgerichtete Bauelemente aufnehmen. Mit einem
leichten Jamming-Greifer kann die Maschine Elemente in unterschiedlichen Winkeln aufnehmen, damit an das vorgegebene Ziel fliegen und sie dort ablegen. Aerial transportation of
a carbon tube for the spatial assembly of three-dimensional
structures with discrete elements. Quadrocopters cannot
rotate around their x and y axes in a quasi-static position:
changing the rotation angles of the vehicle results in acceler-
ation. The method proposes a pick-up station on the ground
where the vehicles grasp pre-oriented building elements. A
lightweight jamming gripper allows the machines to grip elements at variable angles, fly with them to a target point and
release them in space. © Gramazio & Kohler, ETH Zürich

7 Errichtung einer Hängekonstruktion zwischen zwei auseinan-
derliegenden Stützen. Erection of a tensile link between two
distant structural supports. © Gramazio & Kohler, ETH Zürich

sie dem Architekten die Möglichkeit, in den architektonischen Entwurf und den Fabrikationsprozess einzugreifen.

Mit den hier vorgestellten Fallbeispielen werden erste Ergebnisse des Forschungsprojekts *Aerial Construction* aufgezeigt. Dieses untersucht die Möglichkeiten von Flugrobotern in der Architektur. Durchgeführt werden die Experimente in der „Flying Machine Arena", einem 10 × 10 × 10 Meter großen Indoor-Labor für Flugrobotikforschung an der ETH Zürich.[14] Das Labor ist durch Netze und Polsterungen geschützt und mit einem Bewegungserfassungssystem ausgestattet, das die Lage und Neigung der Fluggeräte in Echtzeit erfasst. Diese Informationen werden an eine Steuerungseinheit mit entsprechenden Algorithmen und Steuerungsprogrammen geschickt, welche die Maschinen im dreidimensionalen Raum leitet.[15] Die Versuche werden in der Regel mit Quadrocoptern durchgeführt, die sich im Verlauf des letzten Jahrzehnts in der Forschung als bevorzugte computergesteuerte Fluggeräte herauskristallisiert haben. Der Aufbau solcher unbemannten Luftfahrzeuge oder UAVs (Unmanned Aerial Vehicle) ist weniger komplex als der anderer Fluggeräte und dank ihrer vier separaten, kleineren Propeller, die weniger kinetische Energie als der vergleichbare Hauptrotor eines Hubschraubers speichern, sind sie relativ sicher. Die äußere Positionierung und unabhängige Steuerung der vier Propeller bringt zudem deutliche Vorteile für die Manövrierbarkeit. Mit den neuesten Fortschritten in der Bauweise – u.a. leichteren Bauteilen und einem verbesserten Propellerdesign – hat sich die Tragkraft und die Geschicklichkeit der Maschinen erhöht. Heute stellen Quadrocopter einen guten Kompromiss zwischen Nutzlastkapazität, Beweglichkeit und Robustheit dar.[16]

In der digitalen Fabrikation vergrößern solche Flugroboter den Arbeitsraum und machen damit neue, mit ortsfesten Maschinen nicht realisierbare Bautechniken möglich. Umgekehrt erfordert das Bauen mit Flugmaschinen sowohl die Entwicklung adäquater Methoden zur physischen Interaktion mit der Umwelt als auch die Erforschung von neuen Materialsystemen und in der Luft anwendbaren Fertigungsverfahren. Flugroboter sind wie Industrieroboter generische Maschinen, die je nach Transport- und Bearbeitungsform mit verschiedenen Werkzeugen bestückt werden können. Allerdings spielt bei Flugrobotern das Gewicht eine entscheidende Rolle. Flugmaschinen haben eine begrenzte Nutzlastkapazität und die Last hat erhebliche Auswirkungen auf die Manövrierbarkeit. Das hat zur Folge, dass die Baumaterialien (ebenso wie sämtliche an die Maschinen angebrachten Werkzeuge) sehr leicht sein müssen und das Konstruktionssystem so geartet sein muss, dass Material effi-

terms of maneuverability. The recent progress made in vehicle design such as the introduction of lighter components and improved propeller design has allowed the machines to achieve higher lift capabilities and greater autonomy. Today, quadrocopters offer an excellent compromise between payload capabilities, agility, and robustness.[16]

Aerial robots enlarge the design space for digital fabrication in architecture and offer new construction techniques that would not be possible with machines fixed to a physical location. Research in construction with flying machines requires both the development of adequate methods for hover-capable UAVs to physically interact with the environment and also the investigation of material systems and new constructive processes that are robotically transportable and configurable at heights. Similar to industrial robots, aerial robots are generic and can be equipped with different tools to transport and manipulate material in different ways, but a key factor in their ability to do so is weight. The payload capacities of flying machines are limited, and their maneuverability is greatly influenced by the load. This demands that building materials (as well as any tool or gripper attached to the machine) be lightweight and that the constructive system makes use of the material in an efficient way. The material quantity of an aggregated artifact must therefore be low in comparison to its building volume. This relation between weight and strength, as well as the aerodynamic aspects of the elements, require investigation into lightweight construction systems such as tensile structures and space frame structures (fig. 6).

Figures 1, 7 and 8 show the first results in using flying robots to build tensile structures. The vehicles are equipped with a cable dispenser and a roller on which the tension elements are wound up. The friction of the roller can be adjusted, thus influencing the tension of the cable during its deployment. Figure 7 shows the construction of a linear suspension structure by spanning a horizontal link between two support points independently of the conditions on the ground. By winding the tensile element around existing structural members, it can be used to form connections between them. Using the "capstan" equation,[17] the loading force can be calculated in order to dimension the strength of the knot (fig. 9). It can be specified whether it is a gliding connection or a fix node with a large holding force. Because of its exponential nature, it takes only a few rotations around an object to prevent the unreeving of the cable and to generate a knot.[18] In the experiment, the distance between the support points is five meters. However, the construction technique is easily scalable, allowing the establishment of structural links between supports that are much further apart (assuming the lifting capacities of the machine allow it).

> By winding the tensile element around existing structural members, it can be used to form connections between them.

14   Vgl. Raffaello D'Andrea, online unter: www.flyingmachinearena.org

15   Vgl. Sergei Lupashin et al.: „The Flying Machine Arena as of 2010" (Vortrag auf der Internationalen IEEE-Konferenz über Robotics und Automation in Shanghai Shanghai, 9.–13. Mai 2011).

16   Vgl. Markus Hehn/Raffaello D'Andrea: „A Flying Inverted Pendulum" (Vortrag auf der Internationalen IEEE-Konferenz über Robotics und Automation in Shanghai, 9.–13. Mai 2011).

16   See Markus Hehn and Raffaello D'Andrea, "A flying inverted pendulum" (paper presented at the IEEE International Conference on Robotics and Automation, Shanghai, May 9–13, 2011).

17   The capstan equation is a formula relating the forces acting on a rope wound around a cylinder. A small holding force (applied tension by the vehicle) exerted on one side of the cylinder, can carry a much larger loading force on the other side.

Figure 1 shows the construction of a surface structure created by interlacing two linear structures. The trajectory of the machine resembles a continual re-drawing of a figure 9 in space. When erecting such a structure, the sequencing is crucial (fig. 10). Rather than constructing it layer by layer, the vehicle flies through and around already constructed members while performing the fabrication maneuver. Figure 8 shows a multi-vehicle cooperation of two UAVs, establishing a tensile node at a defined position in the three dimensional design space. The free positioning of a knot in space is a maneuver that cannot be accomplished by a single vehicle and shows the materialization potential of multiple interacting flying robots.

The Design of Robotic Behavior. An aerial robot is dependent on information about its environment. The feedback systems that bring these machines to life must couple the physical presence of the device with its digital environment in real time. The vehicles' awareness of their spatial situation can also be utilized when interacting with material. Conventionally, fabrication data is first generated from a digital design and is then handed over to a machine as a work instruction. The capacities of sensory data question this linear and deterministic manufacturing process. Production information from the physical building space can be fed back and managed in the digital design environment, offering a circular relationship between design and fabrication. Rather than executing pre-computed instructions, this approach allows the orchestration of dynamic manufacturing decision based on discrepancies between physical reality and digital model, and the assignment of specific behaviors or skills (a control strategy) to the machines (fig. 4).

> An aerial robot is dependent on information about its environment. The feedback systems that bring these machines to life must couple the physical presence of the device with its digital environment in real time.

For the erection of tensile structures, a behavior was developed to guarantee the smooth deployment of cables. The vehicle dynamically adjusts its heading along the cable direction when encircling a structural member (fig. 7). The forces acting on the quadrocopter are estimated. This information is processed by control algorithms, which modify the vehicle trajectory accordingly.[19] This method also allows for the adjustment of the force applied to the cable and thus varying its tension.

An adaptable computational design using such operating rules not only defines the spatial flight along coordinates but also specifies the spatio-temporal performance of material action. Fabrication information need no longer be stiff or stated as formal expression. Instead, it can reflect the

zient genutzt wird, d.h. die Materialmenge im Vergleich zum Bauvolumen klein bleibt. Dieses Kraft-Masse-Verhältnis, aber auch die aerodynamischen Aspekte der Bauelemente, machen es erforderlich, vor allem mit Leichtbausystemen wie Seilnetzen und Raumfachwerken zu experimentieren (Abb. 6).

Die Abbildungen 1, 7 und 8 zeigen die ersten Ergebnisse der Errichtung von Seilnetzen mithilfe von Flugrobotern. Die Maschinen sind mit Trommeln ausgestattet, auf die die Seile bzw. Zugelemente aufgerollt sind. Der Reibungswiderstand der Trommel ist einstellbar, so dass sich die Seilspannung bei der Montage verändern lässt. Abbildung 7 zeigt die Errichtung einer Seilkonstruktion zwischen zwei Stützen, wobei die Verbindung unabhängig von der Bodenbeschaffenheit hergestellt werden kann. Um Verbindungen herzustellen, wird das Zugelement um bestehende Teile der Konstruktion gewickelt. Mithilfe der Euler-Eytelwein-Formel[17] lässt sich die Zugkraft für die Dimensionierung des Knotens ermitteln (Abb. 9). Es kann festgelegt werden, ob es eine gleitende Verbindung oder eine feste Verbindung mit hoher Haltekraft sein soll. Wegen des exponentiellen Charakters der Formel bedarf es nur einiger weniger Windungen um ein Objekt, um ein Nachgeben des Seils zu verhindern und einen Knoten zu bilden.[18] In unserem Experiment beträgt die Distanz zwischen den Stützen fünf Meter. Die Konstruktionstechnik ist leicht skalierbar und ermöglicht somit die Fabrikation struktureller Verbindungen zwischen Auflagepunkten, die wesentlich weiter voneinander entfernt sind (sofern das die Hubleistung der Maschine erlaubt).

Abbildung 1 zeigt die Erzeugung einer Oberflächenstruktur durch das Verweben zweier bereits fabrizierter Seilverbindungen. Die Flugbahn der Maschine gleicht einem ständigen Überschreiben der Zahl 9 im Raum. Bei der Herstellung eines solchen Gebildes spielt die Sequenzierung eine wesentliche Rolle (Abb. 10). Statt es Schicht um Schicht aufzubauen, fliegt das Fluggerät bei den Fabrikationsmanövern durch die bereits konstruierten Elemente hindurch und um sie herum. Abbildung 8 zeigt zwei miteinander kooperierende UAVs beim Fabrizieren eines Knotens an einer vorgegebenen Stelle im dreidimensionalen Raum. Die freie Positionierung eines Knotens im Raum ist ein Manöver, das von einem Gerät allein nicht ausgeführt werden kann. Dies deutet das enorme Potenzial miteinander interagierender Flugroboter an.

Das Gestalten von maschinellem Verhalten. Ein Flugroboter ist von seinen Umgebungsinformationen abhängig. Die Feedbacksysteme, die diesen Maschinen quasi „Leben" einhauchen, müssen deren physische Bewegung in Echtzeit an

---

18 See Clifford W. Ashley, *The Ashley Book of Knots* (London, 1944).

19 See Federico Augugliaro et al., "Building Tensile Structures with Flying Machines," (paper presented at the IEEE/RSJ International Conference on Intelligent Robots and Systems, Tokyo, November 3–8, 2013).

17 Die Euler-Eytelwein-Formel beschreibt die Kräfte, die auf ein um einen Zylinder gewickeltes Seil wirken. Eine geringe, auf der einen Seite des Zylinders angewandte haltende Kraft (vom Fluggerät geübter Zug) kann eine viel größere ziehende Kraft auf der anderen Seite halten.

18 Vgl. Clifford W. Ashley: *The Ashley Book of Knots*, London 1944.

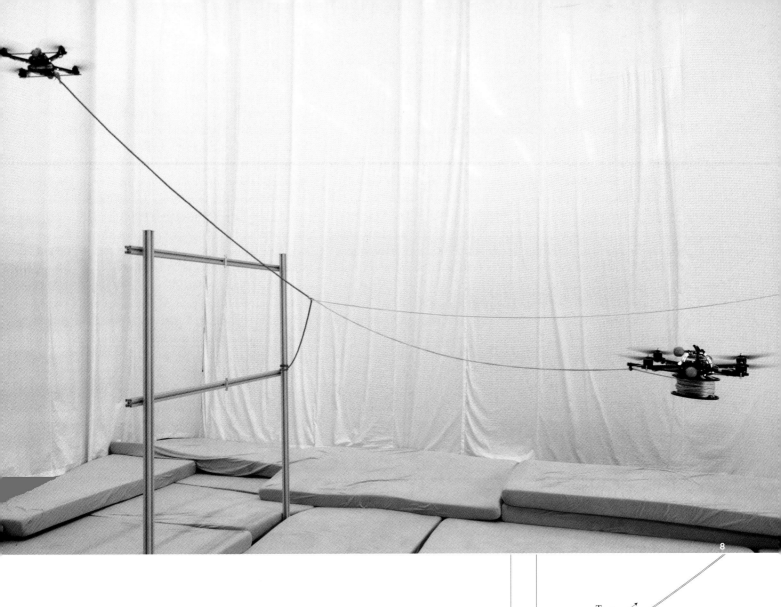

8

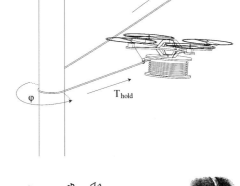

9

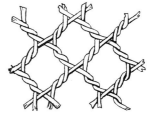 

10

8   Bildung eines Knotens im Raum durch Kooperation mehrerer Maschinen. **Building of a knot in space by multi-vehicle cooperation.** © Gramazio & Kohler, ETH Zürich

9   In Abhängigkeit vom Reibungskoeffizienten (µ) und den Windungen um das Objekt (φ, angegeben in Radianten), lässt sich die ziehende Kraft (T_{load}) aus der haltenden Kraft (T_{hold}) errechnen. Eine kleine Haltekraft auf der einen Seite kann eine wesentliche größere ziehende Kraft auf der anderen halten. Depending on the coefficient of friction (µ) and the amount of turns around the object (angle in radians φ), the loading force (T_{load}) can be calculated from the holding force (T_{hold}). A small holding force on one side can carry a much larger loading force on the other side.

10   Gottfried Semper, „Die textile Kunst für sich betrachtet und in Beziehung zur Baukunst" (Frankfurt/M, 1860). Die Gewebestruktur links könnte von einem Flugroboter dadurch erzeugt werden, dass er zuerst die sich kreuzenden Diagonalen erzeugt, bevor er sich an das Geflecht macht. Die Herstellung der Zopfstruktur auf der rechten Seite dagegen ist nicht von einer einzigen Maschine zu bewerkstelligen. Dafür müssten vier Flugmaschinen ein koordiniertes, kooperatives Manöver fliegen. The woven structure on the left could be constructed by an aerial robot by first erecting the crossing diagonals before intertwining into an assembly. The erection of the braid on the right however, cannot be sequenced by a single vehicle. To construct it, four flying machines would have to coordinate the maneuver in a cooperative manner.

generative process of making, and enable designers to intervene in this process. The methodology envisions architectural materialization as a negotiation between digital design and physical artifact. The architect becomes a designer of materialistic machine behaviors.

A New Way of Materializing Architecture. With this premise, the exploration of flying machines paves the way for new conditions in digitally fabricated architectures. It represents the next logical step of robotic fabrication and directly connects to previous experimentation.[20] Similarly to the industrial robot, the flying robot is an off-the-shelf product that is available on the commercial market and, similarly to the industrial robot, the quadrocopter has a strong generic nature; it can be variously adapted and applied for dealing with different design and fabrication situations. (Flying) robots are a suitable tool to converse between designing and materializing architecture. The algorithmic design of robotic fabrication processes enables the explicit intervention of humans in the production processes. The digital conceptualization of the physical act of making links the machinic with the intuitive.

According to Mario Carpo, the division between the intellectual act of design and the material act of production that has existed since the Renaissance dissolves, changing the way architecture is intellectually conceived, programmed, and designed.[21] In analogy to Carpo's thesis one can argue that, conversely, programming (flying) robots can be interpreted as a horizontal form of integrating design and materialization. The result is an added architectural value through the interactive connection of the human and the machine, who are not equal but rather "equivalent" partners.

> Similarly to the industrial robot, the flying robot is an off-the-shelf product that is available on the commercial market and, similarly to the industrial robot, the quadrocopter has a strong generic nature; it can be variously adapted and applied for dealing with different design and fabrication situations.

As such, the quadrocopter represents a device that can radically expand the present capacities of digital fabrication technologies and facilitate instead architectural experimentation that excludes neither the possibility of constructive concretization nor a possible built reality of the future. It is not a pure technological vision that stands in the foreground: above all, it is a matter of pointing out, comprehending, and implementing an architectural process with all its spatial, aesthetic, and

ihre digitale Umwelt koppeln. Die „Wahrnehmung", die die Maschinen von ihrer Lage im Raum haben, lässt sich auch für die Interaktion mit dem Material nutzen: Herkömmlicherweise werden die Fabrikationsdaten zuerst aus einem digitalen Plan extrahiert und dann als Arbeitsanweisung an eine Maschine weitergegeben. Mit den Möglichkeiten solcher Feedbacksysteme wird dieser lineare, deterministische Fabrikationsprozess infrage gestellt. Die Produktionsinformation aus dem physischen Bauraum kann wieder in die digitale Entwurfsumgebung zurückgeführt und dort verarbeitet werden, so dass eine Wechselbeziehung zwischen Entwurf und Fabrikation stattfindet. Statt der bloßen Ausführung zuvor errechneter Anweisungen ermöglicht dieser Ansatz eine „Orchestrierung" dynamischer Produktionsentscheidungen, die auf Diskrepanzen zwischen physischer Realität und digitalem Modell sowie der Zuteilung bestimmter robotischer Verhaltensweisen oder Fähigkeiten (einer bestimmten Steuerungsstrategie) basiert (Abb. 4).

Für die Errichtung von Seilnetzen wurde beispielsweise ein Verhalten entwickelt, das für eine laufruhige Montage der Seile sorgt. Das Fluggerät passt seine Flugbahn dynamisch in Seilrichtung an, wenn es ein Strukturelement umwickelt (Abb. 7). Die auf den Quadrocopter wirkenden Kräfte werden geschätzt. Diese Information wird dann von Steueralgorithmen verarbeitet und die Flugbahn entsprechend modifiziert.[19] Diese Methode ermöglicht auch die Anpassung der auf das Seil angewandten Kraft und damit die Variation der Seilspannung.

Ein mit solchen Regeln arbeitendes, adaptierbares computergestütztes Design definiert nicht nur die Bewegung im Raum entlang gewisser Koordinaten, sondern legt auch den raumzeitlichen Ablauf der materiellen Tätigkeiten fest. Die Fabrikationsinformation muss nicht starr als formalisierter Ausdruck niedergelegt werden, sondern kann einen generativen Fabrikationsprozess beschreiben und dem Entwerfer erlauben, direkt in ihn einzugreifen. Die Methode läuft mithin auf eine Materialisierung von Architektur hinaus, die als „dynamischer" Verhandlungsprozess zwischen digitalem Entwurf und physischem Artefakt stattfindet. Der Architekt wird zum Gestalter materieller Verhaltensweisen von Maschinen.

Eine neue Form architektonischer Materialisierung. So gesehen bahnt die Erforschung von Flugrobotern den Weg zu radikal neuen Bedingungen für die digitale Fabrikation von Architektur. Es ist der nächste logische Schritt robotischer Fabrikation und schließt direkt an bisherige Experimente und Prozesse an.[20] Wie der Industrieroboter, so ist auch der Flugroboter ein Serienprodukt und ein generisches Werkzeug, das für den Umgang mit unterschiedlichen Entwurfs- und Produktionssitua-

---

20 See www.dfab.arch.ethz.ch

21 See Mario Carpo, "Revolutions: Some New Technologies in Search of an Author," *Log* 15 (2009), pp. 49–54.

19 Vgl. Federico Augugliaro et al.: „Building Tensile Structures with Flying Machines", (Vortrag auf der internationalen IEEE/RSJ-Konferenz über „Intelligent Robots and Systems" in Tokyo, 3.–8. November 2013).

20 Siehe www.dfab.arch.ethz.ch

tionen adaptiert werden kann. In der Tat, (Flug-)Roboter sind ein authentisches Vermittlungsinstrument zwischen architektonischem Entwurf und materieller Ausführung. Die algorithmische Form des robotischen Fabrikationsprozesses ermöglicht den expliziten Eingriff des Menschen in den (maschinellen) Produktionsprozess. Die digitale Konzeptualisierung der physischen Bautätigkeit verbindet das Maschinische mit dem Intuitiven.

Im digitalen Zeitalter ist Mario Carpo zufolge die seit der Renaissance bestehende Trennung zwischen dem geistigen Gestaltungsakt und dem materiellen Produktionsakt in Auflösung begriffen und verändert die Art, wie Architektur konzipiert, programmiert und gestaltet wird.[21] In Analogie zu Carpos These könnte man das Programmieren von (Flug-)Robotern als eine solche Integration von Entwurf und Materialisierung auffassen. Das Ergebnis ist die interaktive Verbindung von Mensch und Maschine, die zwar nicht gleichwertige, aber einander ergänzende Partner sind.

Somit stellt der Quadrocopter ein Mittel dar, dass die gegenwärtigen Möglichkeiten digitaler Fabrikationstechniken vielfach erweitern und eine Form architektonischen Experimentierens in Gang setzen könnte, das weder die Möglichkeit konstruktiver Konkretisierung noch eine mögliche künftige Baurealität ausschließt. Dabei steht nicht eine rein technologische Vision in Vordergrund. Es geht vor allem auch darum, einen architektonischen Prozess – mit all seinen räumlichen, ästhetischen und funktionalen Konsequenzen – aufzuzeigen, zu verstehen und umzusetzen. In dieser Hinsicht eröffnet das Entwerfen und Bauen von Architektur mit Flugmaschinen eine ganz spezifische materielle Praxis und steckt ein neues Forschungsgebiet in diesem zweiten digitalen Zeitalter der Architektur ab.

Danksagung: Die Verbindung von Architektur und Flugrobotik verlangt Kompetenzen, die teils außerhalb des Fachbereichs Architektur liegen. Die hier dargestellte Forschung beruht auf einem interdisziplinären Forschungsprojekt der Professur für Architektur und Digitale Fabrikation (Institut für Technologie in der Architektur, ITA) und der Forschungsgruppe von Prof. Raffaello D'Andrea (Institute for Dynamic Systems and Control, IDSC) an der ETH Zürich. Projektmitarbeiter am IDSC ist Federico Augugliaro. Die Arbeit stützt sich auf die Beiträge zahlreicher früherer Mitarbeiter der Flying Machine Arena und der Professur für Architektur und Digitale Fabrikation. Ein spezieller Dank gebührt Hallie Siegel für die redaktionelle englische Überarbeitung dieses Artikels. Die Forschung wird unterstützt von der Hartmann Mueller-Stiftung: ETH Research Grant ETH-30 12-1.

Übersetzung Wilfried Prantner

functional consequences. Thereby, designing and constructing architecture with flying machines opens up a distinct material practice and characterizes a novel field of research in this second age of digital architecture.

Acknowledgements: The integration of architecture and aerial robotics requires competence outside the discipline of architecture. This research is thus based on an ongoing interdisciplinary project between the Chair of Architecture and Digital Fabrication (Institute for Technology in Architecture, ITA) and the Institute for Dynamic Systems and Control (IDSC) of Prof. Dr. Raffaello D'Andrea at ETH Zurich. Project collaborator at the IDSC is Federico Augugliaro. The work is supported by and builds upon prior contributions by numerous collaborators of the Flying Machine Arena project and the Chair of Architecture and Digital Fabrication. An extra thanks goes to Hallie Siegel for her efforts on the editorial revision of this article. The research is supported by the Hartmann Mueller-Fonds on ETH Research Grant ETH-30 12-1.

21 Vgl. Mario Carpo: „Revolutions: Some New Technologies in Search of an Author", in: *Log* 15 (2009), S. 49–54.

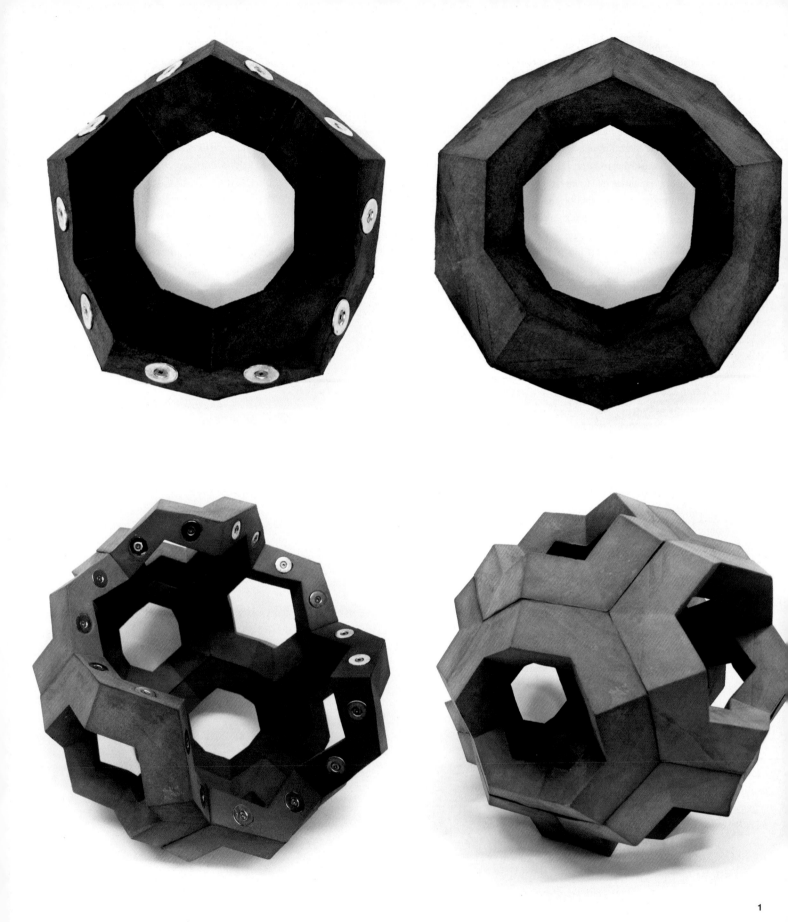

1 *Self-Assembly Line*, Composite, 2012. © Skylar Tibbits, Arthur Olson und and Seed Media Group.

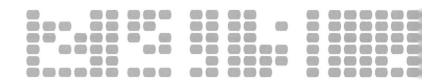

"Surprise is almost everything in design!"

Skylar Tibbits (ST) in Conversation with Urs Hirschberg (GAM)

„Überraschung ist beim Entwerfen fast alles!" Skylar Tibbits (ST) im Gespräch mit Urs Hirschberg (GAM)

Skylar Tibbits is a trained Architect and Computer Scientist whose research focuses on developing self-assembly and programmable material technologies for industrial applications in our built environment. Currently a faculty member in MIT's Department of Architecture, he is the director of the MIT Self-Assembly Lab and the founder and principal of the multidisciplinary architecture, art and design practice, SJET LLC.

Skylar Tibbits ist gelernter Architekt und Computerwissenschaftler, der vorwiegend zur Entwicklung selbstassemblierender und programmierbarer Materialtechnologien für Industrieanwendungen in der gebauten Umwelt forscht. Er lehrt im Fachbereich Architektur am MIT, leitet das MIT Self-Assembly-Lab und ist Gründer und Leiter der multidisziplinären Architektur-, Kunst- und Designpraxis SJET LLC.

SKYLAR TIBBITS

Started in 2007 as a platform for experimental computation and design, SJET has grown into a research-based practice crossing disciplines from architecture, design, sculpture, fabrication, computer science, toys to robotics.

Skylar Tibbits has a Professional Bachelor of Architecture degree and minor in experimental computation from Philadelphia University. Continuing his education at MIT, he received a Masters of Science in Design + Computation and a Master of Science in Computer Science. He was recently awarded a TED2012 Senior Fellowship, a TED2011 Fellowship and has been named a Revolutionary Mind in SEED Magazine's 2008 Design Issue. He has exhibited work at a number of venues around the world including the Guggenheim Museum NY and the Beijing Biennale. He has been published in numerous articles and built large-scale installations around the world. This interview with him was conducted via Skype.

GAM: It is a unique thing you introduced to the design world. Would you talk a bit about how you got started with the idea of self-assembly?

ST: I have a background in architecture. I started going to MIT right about the time when a lot of people were pushing software tools and starting to write their own code, and generative art and design was flourishing. At the exact same time digital fabrication was coming onto the scene and every school around the world was trying to buy at least laser cutters, CNC routers, 3D printers, that kind of thing … So this was the time when code was starting to influence how we could design and how we could make. At MIT I really wanted to study computer science and I did two different masters there, one in design computation and one in computer science. But at the same time I was collaborating a lot with Marc Fornes and we were doing large scale installations around the world. They were generative design installations using digital fabrication.

My interest in self-assembly came from the Programmable Matter research field. I was working with Neil Gershenfeld, the Director of the MIT Center for Bits and Atoms. He had a DARPA (Defense Advanced Research Projects Agency) grant called "Programmable Matter." It's the vision that if we can program matter we can program it to change shape and properties and be whatever we wanted it to be, kind of fluidly: software becomes hardware. And vice versa. It basically inspired me to think that there maybe was another opportunity or a third stage to this computer revolution. Computation can influence what design is, computation can influence our fabrication tools, but it can also influence the way we assemble things and the way we make things after fabrication. So then this became my full-fledged focus: I wanted to find ways to program things to change shape and build themselves. I started out working on robotics, really large-scale reconfigurable robots with Neil's group. (*See projects Macrobot, figs. 2–4, and Decibot, pp. 170–177.*) Since then I've tried to go more and more passive, to find ways to re-configure how strands and sheets can re-configure into different shapes, using just external energy, geometry, material properties. And then I started collaborating with Arthur Olson, who is a molecular biologist. That got me into pure self-assembly, which is a bit different than programmable materials and different than reconfiguration. Self-assembly is really about individual parts that are completely autonomous, that come together on their own. Art Olson and I have now built a number of different installations, looking at self-assembly at different scales, with different numbers of components.

Die 2007 initiierte Plattform für experimentelles Computing und Design hat sich mittlerweile zu einer forschungsbasierten Praxis entwickelt, die Disziplinen von der Architektur, vom Design und von der Bildhauerei über die Fabrikationstechnik und Computerwissenschaft bis hin zur Spielzeugtechnik und Robotik vereint.

Skylar Tibbits studierte zunächst Architektur mit Nebenfach Experimental Computing an der Philadelphia University, bevor er ans MIT ging, wo er einen Master of Science in Design + Computation und ein Master of Science in Computerwissenschaft erwarb. Die Design-Ausgabe der Zeitschrift SEED zählte ihn 2008 zu den Revolutionary Minds, 2011 wurde er TED Fellow und 2012 TED Senior Fellow. Er hat weltweit großformatige Installationen realisiert, an Orten wie dem Guggenheim Museum New York oder der Beijing Biennale ausgestellt und umfassend in Zeitungen, Fachjournalen und Büchern publiziert. Das folgende Interview wurde per Skype geführt.

GAM: Du hast in die Welt des Designs etwas ganz Einzigartiges eingeführt. Kannst Du ein wenig darüber erzählen, wie Du auf die Idee der Selbstassemblierung (engl. self-assembly) gekommen bist?

ST: Ich komme von der Architektur. Ans MIT ging ich zu einer Zeit, als gerade eine Menge Leute anfingen, die Entwicklung von Software-Tools voranzutreiben und ihren eigenen Code zu schreiben, und als generative Kunst und generatives Design ihre Blüte erlebten. Zur selben Zeit kam auch die digitale Fabrikation auf, und jede Uni auf der Welt versuchte, zumindest Lasercutter, CNC-Fräsen, 3D-Drucker und dergleichen anzuschaffen … Es war also die Zeit, als Code unsere Gestaltungs- und Produktionsmöglichkeiten zu beeinflussen begann. Am MIT wollte ich eigentlich Computerwissenschaft studieren und am Ende absolvierte ich dort zwei Masterstudien: eines in Design Computation und eines in Computerwissenschaft. Gleichzeitig arbeitete ich viel mit Marc Fornes zusammen und realisierte mit ihm großformatige Installationen in aller Welt. Es waren mit digitalen Fabrikationsmitteln hergestellte generative Designinstallationen.

Mein Interesse an der Selbstassemblierung entwickelte sich aus dem Bereich „Programmierbare Materie" heraus. Ich arbeitete mit Neil Gershenfeld, dem Leiter des MIT Center for Bits and Atoms zusammen. Er hatte eine Förderung von der DARPA (Defense Advanced Research Projects Agency) für „Programmierbare Materie" erhalten. Die Idee dabei ist: Wenn es uns gelingt, Materie zu programmieren, dann können wir ihre Form und Eigenschaften verändern und sie – quasi fließend – zu allem machen, was wir wollen: Software wird Hardware – und umgekehrt. Das hat mich auf den Gedanken gebracht, dass es vielleicht eine weitere Möglichkeit oder eine dritte Stufe dieser Computerrevolution geben könnte. Wenn Rechenprozesse die Gestaltung und Fabrikation beeinflussen können, warum sollten sie dann nicht auch beeinflussen, wie wir Dinge zusammenbauen, was wir nach ihrer Fabrikation daraus machen? So wurde das zu meinem eigenständigen Forschungsgebiet: Ich wollte Möglichkeiten finden, die Dinge so zu programmieren, dass sie von selbst die Form verändern, sich selbst bauen. Zunächst arbeitete ich mit Robotik, richtig großen rekonfigurierbaren Robotern gemeinsam mit der Gruppe von Neil (vgl. die Projekte Macrobot, Abb. 2–4, und Decibot, S. 170–177). Seither habe ich versucht, immer passiver zu werden, Möglichkeiten zu finden, wie sich Stränge und Flächen – allein durch externe Energiezufuhr, Geometrie und Materialeigenschaften – zu verschiedenen Formen umwandeln können. Dann begann ich mit Arthur Olson, einem Molekularbiologen, zu arbeiten. So gelangte ich zur reinen Selbstassemblierung, die ein wenig anders funktioniert als programmierbare Materialien und die Rekonfiguration. Bei der Selbstassemblierung geht es eigentlich um völlig autonome Einzelelemente, die selbst zueinanderfinden. Art Olson und ich realisierten eine Reihe von Installationen, die in unterschiedlichen Maßstäben und mit unterschiedlich vielen Komponenten Selbstassemblierungsprozesse untersuchen (vgl. die Projekte Self-Assembly Line, Abb. 1 5–6, und Fluid Cristallization, Abb. 7–8). Ich komme also eigentlich von der Gestaltung her, sehe das Ganze als Informatik fürs Bauen.

GAM: *Es ist interessant, dass die Inspiration von der Forschung ausging. Zumal man beim Thema Selbstassemblierung an gewisse Science-Fiction-Filme wie* Transformers *denkt. Inspiriert Dich eigentlich auch diese Art von Populärkultur? Siehst Du darin etwas, das mit Deiner Arbeit zu tun hat?*

ST: Es hat mich sicher nicht dahin gebracht, wo ich jetzt stehe, aber ich denke schon, dass es einen Zusammenhang gibt. Der Replikator aus *Star Trek* wird ja allgemein als Inspirationsquelle für den Bereich programmierbare Materie angeführt. Selbst Neil Gershenfeld und die Programmmanager der DARPA sprechen davon als „ultimative Zielvorstellung“. *Transformers* und *Terminator* sind weitere Beispiele: Sie alle handeln davon, Dinge so zu programmieren, dass sie sich auflösen und wieder neu zusammensetzen. Die Inspiration geht aber nicht wirklich von den Filmen aus, ich suche in ihnen nicht nach Ideen, die mich weiterbringen. Aber selbstverständlich sehen wir alle die Verbindung, interessieren und begeistern uns dafür.

GAM: *Manche Künstliche-Intelligenz-Forscher sagen, HAL 9000, der berühmte Computer aus Kubricks* 2001: Odyssee im Weltraum, *habe ihnen irgendwie die Forschung verdorben, weil ihm alles, was sie in der Folge zu bieten hatten, so heillos unterlegen war, dass sie auf Jahrzehnte hinaus niemanden beeindrucken konnten. Es wurde vergessen, dass es lediglich ein Film war. Fürchtest Du nicht, dass etwas Ähnliches auch bei der Selbstassemblierung eintreten könnte? Dass Leute, die ständig realistisch wirkende Filme sehen, in denen*

(*See projects Self-Assembly Line, figs. 1, 5–6, and Fluid Cristallization, figs. 7–8.*) So I'm really coming from the design side, I see it as computation for construction.

GAM: *It's interesting that your inspiration came from research. After all, the self-assembly topic reminds one of certain Sci-Fi movies such as* Transformers. *Is this type of popular culture also something that inspires you? Do you see that it has something to do with your work?*

ST: It definitely didn't inspire me to get here, but I do think there is a connection. Everyone quotes the *Star Trek*-Replicator as the inspiration for programmable matter. Even Neil Gershenfeld and the DARPA program managers talk about the *Star Trek*-Replicator as the "ultimate vision." *Transformers* is another one, *Terminator* is another one: they're all about programming things to dissolve, deconstruct and then reassemble themselves. These films are not really an inspiration per se, I'm not looking at them to get ideas to move forward, but obviously we see the correlation, are interested and excited about it.

GAM: *In the field of Artificial Intelligence some researchers say that HAL 9000, the famous computer in Kubrick's* 2001: A Space Odyssey *somehow spoiled it for their research, because anything they came up with subsequently was so inferior to what HAL could do back in the 1960s, that for decades it was impossible to impress anyone. People simply forgot that this was only a movie. Do you fear that something like that could happen with self-assembly too? Do you think that when people keep watching realistic-looking movies with machines that are changing shape fluidly, within seconds, making all the problems you struggle with look trivial, that they might eventually be underwhelmed by your progress?*

ST: Not really, I think it's a benefit. We work on what we can do now, pushing ourselves and trying to do seemingly impossible tasks, understanding more about them. We're really in a research mentality—but everyone else is interested in what this means in 20 or 50 years' time. What is construction going to look like in the future? We are also curious about that, but it's really hard to paint the picture. In some ways, I think, popular culture and movies can help people connect the dots: "Ok, I know this is a movie, but I can kind of see where this could go." I'm not saying that that's exactly where we'll go, but it brings it down to where people can get it again. So in that way popular culture helps us, because it gives people an idea of what we're working on.

GAM: *So you are not worried about false expectations, about people getting impatient? — This leads me to the question about the impact of your*

> These films are not really an inspiration per se, I'm not looking at them to get ideas to move forward, but obviously we see the correlation, are interested and excited about it.

251

work. You've become a research celebrity: you're one of the TED senior fellows—hundreds of thousands of people watch your TED talks on the Internet. Your ideas are out there and people are fascinated by them. So the question is: Can you follow up with new developments? Can you keep step with the expectations that come from your earlier work? Much of what you do is quite remote from architectural applications at this point. What's your expectation, how soon can you fill that gap?

ST: That's a good point. There is lots of pressure. I don't feel the pressure on the architecture side necessarily, but generally there is an expectation to continually outdo yourself and to get bigger and more press, more importance and larger projects, larger budgets, that kind of stuff. That's how the game goes. We are up to the challenge, we keep developing and we hope that we'll do things more interesting each time. But the application side … I don't feel it as much. I defined the realm that we work in by starting a research lab at MIT, called the Self-Assembly Lab. It's a useful way of saying: "Ok, we do research—basic research and applied research." In applied research we work with industry partners. That allows us to find very specific, somewhat near-term applications and to implement them. They are not grandiose visions for totally changing the construction industry but small implementations that for us are nevertheless huge steps forward. Research becomes less abstract and more tangible. Sometimes the press and everyone gets super excited about our projects, but for us it's just really important to also get them out of academia.

> They are not grandiose visions for totally changing the construction industry but small implementations that for us are nevertheless huge steps forward. Research becomes less abstract and more tangible.

GAM: Let's suppose for a moment that self-assembly really catches on and becomes an established way of constructing things. After all, there are many cases to be made for it: saving material and manual labor, structures that can self-repair etc. So let's suppose that all this works. Will this technology then also influence the way we design? Or will architects just continue designing the way they do and let somebody else figure out how their design can be constructed in a self-assembly manner?

ST: I think for sure it's going to change the way we design. When you have materials that change properties you'll need to think about both what you design and how you design it in very different ways. That's one of the reasons why we have a strong partnership with Autodesk®, the design software company. They are specifically looking at the life sciences, because there is really big change in the nano-tech and synthetic biology-space and they are building design tools for that area. There are correlations with what design could mean for us. When we start thinking about materials as code, or as blueprints, and assembly processes not just as dumb cold things that we force together but as behaviors of materials that hold information, it will change how we design and what we design.

Maschinen in Sekundenschnelle fließend ihre Form ändern und so die Probleme, mit denen Du Dich herumschlägst, trivial erscheinen lassen, von Deinen Fortschritten irgendwann nicht mehr beeindruckt sind?

ST: Eigentlich nicht, ich halte das für einen Vorteil. Wir arbeiten an dem, was gerade möglich ist, nehmen uns aber viel vor und versuchen scheinbar unmögliche Aufgaben zu lösen, sie jedenfalls besser zu verstehen. Wir befinden uns in einem Forschungsmodus – aber alle anderen fragen sich, was daraus in 20 oder 30 Jahren werden könnte, wie das Bauen in Zukunft aussehen könnte. Wir interessieren uns zwar ebenfalls dafür, aber es ist wirklich schwer, das große Bild zu zeichnen. In gewisser Weise helfen uns Populärkultur und Film, die Teile zu einem Ganzen zu fügen: „Ja, ich weiß, das ist nur ein Film, aber ich verstehe, wohin das ungefähr gehen könnte." Ich sage nicht, dass es genau in diese Richtung gehen wird, aber es wird auf eine Ebene gebracht, wo es allgemein verständlich wird. Die Populärkultur hilft uns also, indem sie eine Vorstellung von dem schafft, woran wir arbeiten.

GAM: Du machst Dir demnach keine Sorgen wegen der falschen Erwartungen, die die Leute hegen, ihrer Ungeduld? – Das bringt mich zur Frage nach den konkreten Wirkungen Deiner Arbeit. Du bist ja eine Art Forscherberühmtheit geworden: Du bist TED Senior Fellow, und Hunderttausende sehen sich Deine TED-Vorträge im Internet an. Deine Ideen sind im Umlauf und faszinieren zahlreiche Menschen. Die Frage ist also: Kannst Du neue Entwicklungen nachlegen? Kannst Du Schritt halten mit den durch die früheren Arbeiten geweckten Erwartungen? Vieles von dem, was Du tust, ist ja momentan noch recht weit entfernt von einer architektonischen Anwendung. Was meinst Du, wie bald kannst Du diese Lücke füllen?

ST: Das ist ein gute Frage. Es herrscht ziemlich großer Druck, wenn auch nicht unbedingt von der Architekturseite. Aber ganz allgemein wird erwartet, dass man sich ständig überbietet, um mehr Presse zu bekommen, mehr Bedeutung zu gewinnen, größere Projekte und Budgets an Land zu ziehen und dergleichen. So läuft das Spiel nun mal. Wir sind der Herausforderung gewachsen, wir entwickeln immer weiter und hoffen, jedes Mal etwas Interessanteres zustandezubringen. Was die Sache mit der Anwendung betrifft … da empfinde ich den Druck nicht so stark. Ich habe unseren Arbeitsbereich mit der Gründung eines Forschungslabors am MIT, des Self-Assembly Labs, eingegrenzt. Das ist eine nützliche Art zu sagen: „Okay, wir betreiben eben Forschung – Grundlagenforschung und angewandte Forschung." In der angewandten Forschung arbeiten wir mit Partnern aus der Industrie zusammen. Das ermöglicht uns, nach ganz spezifischen, kürzerfristigen Anwendungen zu suchen und sie umzusetzen. Dabei handelt es sich um keine grandiosen Visionen für die völlige Umkrempelung der Bauindustrie, sondern kleine Anwendungen, die für uns aber große

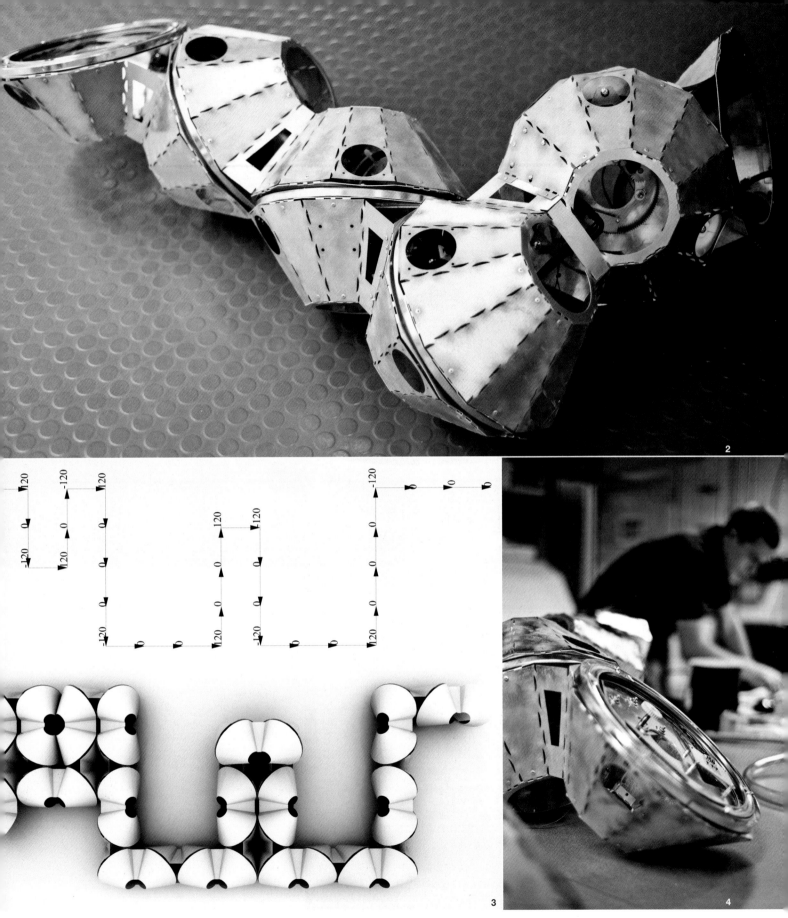

2–4 Macrobot, 2009 © Skylar Tibbits mit dem with the Center for Bits and Atoms, MIT.

5

6

5–6 *Self-Assembly Line*, 2012 © Skylar Tibbits, Arthur Olson und and Seed Media Group.

Fortschritte darstellen. So wird Forschung weniger abstrakt und direkter greifbar. Manchmal flippen Presse und Allgemeinheit bei unseren Projekten richtig aus, aber für uns ist es einfach nur wichtig, sie aus dem akademischen Raum hinauszubefördern.

GAM: Nehmen wir einmal an, dass die Selbstassemblierung richtig einschlägt und zu einer gängigen Art des Bauens wird. Schließlich spricht Einiges dafür: Einsparung von Material und Handarbeit, Strukturen, die sich selbst reparieren können usw. Nehmen wir also an, all das funktioniert. Wird diese Technologie auch unsere Entwurfsweise beeinflussen? Oder werden Architekten einfach fortfahren wie gehabt und es anderen überlassen, darüber nachzudenken, wie sich ihr Entwurf selbstassemblierend umsetzen lässt?

ST: Ich bin ganz sicher, dass es die Entwurfsweise verändern wird. Wenn man Materialien zur Verfügung hat, die ihre Eigenschaften verändern können, wird man sich sowohl über das, was man entwirft als auch darüber wie man es entwirft ganz neue Gedanken machen müssen. Darum sind wir auch eine enge Partnerschaft mit der Designsoftwarefirma Autodesk® eingegangen. Die interessiert sich besonders für die Life Sciences, weil in der Nanotechnologie und der synthetischen Biologie gerade große Umbrüche stattfinden und die Firma Entwurfswerkzeuge für diese Bereiche entwickelt. Das korreliert auch mit der potenziellen Bedeutung des Entwerfens. Wenn wir anfangen, Materialien als Codes, oder als Pläne und Assemblierungsprozesse zu sehen, wenn wir sie also nicht mehr bloß als stumme, kalte, gewaltsam zusammengefügte Dinge auffassen, sondern als mit Information angereicherte Materialien mit Verhaltensweisen, so wird das auch Auswirkungen auf unsere Entwurfsweise und die Art der Dinge haben, die wir entwerfen.

GAM: Du verwendest für Deine Arbeit den Begriff 4D-Druck – aber sprechen wir zunächst über den 3D-Druck, der in den letzten Jahren zum großen Schlager geworden ist. Es gibt ihn ja schon eine ganze Weile, aber nun wird er gerade zum Mainstream: Er ist in den Nachrichten, alle Welt hat davon gehört und spricht davon. Was hältst Du davon? Ist das bloß ein Hype oder ist da mehr dran?

ST: In unseren Augen ist es ein Hype. 3D-Drucker können durchaus von Nutzen sein, aber sie haben auch etliche Nachteile, und wahrscheinlich gibt es eine ganze Reihe anderer Maschinen, die das besser können, je nach Werkstück. Es gibt gewisse Dinge, die mit Spritzguss oder CNC-Fräsen billiger und leichter herzustellen wären, oder die man – je nachdem – aus Platten fertigen, mit Laser oder Wasserstrahl ausschneiden könnte. Der 3D-Druck ist ein leistungsfähiges Werkzeug, aber wir betrachten es nur als eines von vielen. Neil Gershenfeld vergleicht die Einführung des 3D-Druckers gern mit jener der Mikrowelle – die hat uns auch nicht davon abgehalten, den Herd weiterzubenutzen, sie ist lediglich ein zusätzliches Küchengerät. Also

GAM: You talk about 4D printing in your work—before we get to that, let's talk about 3D printing, which has become all the rage during the last couple of years. It's been around for some time, but right now it's moving into the mainstream: it's in the news, everybody knows about it, everybody talks about it. How do you see it? Is it just hype or is there more to it?

ST: We see it as hype. There are benefits to 3D printers but also many downsides and there is probably a number of other machines that could do better depending on each case. There are certain things that you could injection mold more cheaply and easily or you could CNC-mill or build it out of flat sheets, laser-cut or water-jet, whatever is appropriate. It is a powerful medium, but we see 3D printing as only one tool in a suite of tools. Neil Gershenfeld often says that the introduction of the 3D printer is like the introduction of the microwave—the microwave didn't stop you from using the stove, it's just another tool in the kitchen. So yeah, it's a really exciting machine but there are many other ones. I think they have huge potential, and, of course, everyone, no matter what industry, is looking at 3D printing in additive manufacturing. We still have to overcome certain challenges like bed size, printer speed, better materials—we think smarter materials not just stronger—but if we can really overcome all these challenges, I think there is a lot of opportunity.

One of the reasons why we came up with the 4D printing work was specifically to tackle smarter materials. It's basically 3D printing combined with smart materials. And smart materials are super exciting! There are a lot of benefits to using them,

> We were looking at how folding could be a strategy for making large things from machines with small bed sizes.

and they are present in a number of industries, but the problem is that they are still somewhat expensive and that you are limited to what's available on the shelf. You still can't customize how that smart material is made or how it's embedded and there is always an extra assembly step. So combining the two technologies means you can design the materials in any shape and any orientation and then print them so that they activate and transform into whatever you want.

GAM: We talked about the limits in size that these 3D printers nowadays still have. You have just won a prize at Ars Electronica with a project that demonstrates one way to go beyond this limit in size … In your definition, is that also 4D printing?

ST: No. For the Ars Electronica prize we weren't doing 4D printing at all. I worked with Formlabs and Marcelo Coelho. Form Labs have a new low cost high precision 3D printer. We were looking at how folding could be a strategy for making large things from machines with small bed sizes. The chandelier folds out to become much larger than the volume it was printed in. But the folding must be done manually. It doesn't happen autonomously as in 4D printing. *(See project 4D printing, figs. 9–11)* But of course you can see how those two could combine! I see a lot of potential for self-folding systems. For the moment we are using two different technologies.

Changing conventional notions
of how we can make things is
surprising, but that is really what
we are after. There are established
ways to build stuff at the human scale.
We want to shift the established way
of thinking and say: "Hey, there are
many other ways that we haven't
yet thought about," because they
may be at a different scale or
they may not be intuitive.

gut, es ist schon eine aufregende Maschine, aber es gibt auch viele andere. Ich denke, 3D-Drucker haben großes Potenzial, und natürlich sind sie in allen Industriezweigen interessant für die additive Fertigung. Wir haben noch immer gewisse Probleme zu lösen, zum Beispiel Bauraumgröße, Druckgeschwindigkeit, bessere – sprich intelligentere, nicht stärkere – Materialien, aber wenn wir das schaffen, denke ich, bieten sich eine Menge Möglichkeiten.

Einer der Gründe, weshalb wir mit dem 4D-Drucken angefangen haben, war speziell, um das Problem intelligenterer Materialien anzugehen. Im Grunde handelt es sich um 3D-Druck mit intelligenten Materialien. Und intelligente Materialien sind unheimlich spannend! Sie bringen eine Menge Vorteile und sie werden bereits in einer Reihe von Industriezweigen verwendet. Das Problem ist, dass sie immer noch ziemlich teuer sind, sodass man auf Standardware angewiesen ist. Man kann die Zusammensetzung oder Einbindung dieser intelligenten Materialien noch immer nicht an die eigenen Erfordernisse anpassen, sodass es immer eines zusätzlichen Assemblierungsschritts bedarf. Die Kombination der beiden Technologien bedeutet also, dass man den Materialien eine beliebige Form und Orientierung mitteilen und sie ausdrucken kann, worauf sie sich aktivieren und in die gewünschte Form verwandeln.

GAM: Wir haben vorhin von den Größenbeschränkungen gesprochen, die 3D-Drucker immer noch aufweisen. Du hast bei der Ars Electronica soeben einen Preis für ein Projekt erhalten, das eine Möglichkeit aufzeigt, dieses Größenlimit zu überwinden. Handelt es sie dabei nach Deiner Definition auch um 4D-Druck?

ST: Nein. Für die Ars Electronica, das war überhaupt kein 4D-Druck. Ich arbeitete mit Formlabs und Marcelo Coelho zusammen. Formlabs hat einen neuen billigen, hochpräzisen 3D-Drucker entwickelt. Wir haben untersucht, inwiefern Faltung eine mögliche Strategie zur Herstellung großer Dinge in Geräten mit kleinen Bauräumen sein könnte. Der Lüster lässt sich z.B. auf eine Größe ausfalten, die die seines Bauraums bei weitem übersteigt. Allerdings muss die Faltung hier manuell erfolgen. Sie geschieht nicht automatisch wie im 4D-Druck *(vgl. das Projekt 4D Printing, Abb. 9–11)*. Aber man sieht natürlich, wie die beiden ineinandergreifen könnten! Ich sehe viel Potenzial für selbstfaltende Systeme. Derzeit verwenden wir zwei verschiedene Technologien. Unser 4D-Druck wurde mit Connex Multimaterial-3D-Druckern in Kooperation mit Stratasys® durchgeführt. Wir arbeiten wirklich eng mit der Firma zusammen. Das tun wir übrigens mit einer Reihe ganz unterschiedlicher Akteure aus der Industrie.

GAM: Kommen wir nun zur Frage der Intuition: Das Bestechende an Deinen Selbstassemblierungsprojekten ist, dass wir das so noch nicht gesehen haben. Die Selbstassemblierung ist uns zwar vertraut, aber nur in lebenden Organismen. Jede Pflanze kann das. Diesen Vergleich bringst Du auch häufig in Deinen Vorträgen: Zellteilung ist Selbstassemblierung par excellence. Dennoch siehst Du Dich nicht als Bioniker. Du willst die Natur nicht imitieren. Du entwirfst einfach Dinge, die in der Lage sind, sich selbständig zusammenzusetzen. Einige Deiner Projekte sind absolut verblüffend. Ihre wesentliche Eigenschaft scheint zu sein, dass sie der Intuition widersprechen.*

ST: Das ist eines unserer Ziele: Möglichkeiten zur Erzeugung physischer Konstrukte und Systeme zu finden, die auf nicht-intuitiven Phänomenen beruhen. Die Änderung herkömmlicher Vorstellungen davon, wie man etwas macht, überrascht, aber genau das streben wir an. Für Dinge im menschlichen Maßstab haben sich bestimmte Herstellungsmethoden etabliert. Diese etablierten Denkweisen wollen wir verrücken und sagen: „Hey, es gibt unzählige andere Möglichkeiten, an die noch keiner gedacht hat" – weil sie einer anderen Größenordnung angehören oder der Intuition widersprechen. Wir finden sie, wie Du richtig sagst, meist in der Welt der Chemie und Biologie – vor allem in lebenden Systemen. Aber ich möchte noch einmal betonen, dass wir nicht biomimetisch arbeiten. Die Zusammenarbeit mit Art Olson habe ich bereits erwähnt – wir arbeiten auch mit einigen anderen Biologen und Chemikern zusammen und sind zweifellos sehr fasziniert von dem, was sich in der Biologie abspielt. Aber wir wissen auch, dass es noch viele andere Arten der Selbstassemblierung gibt. Ein herausragendes Beispiel ist das Kristallwachstum, und das ist nun bestimmt kein lebendes System. Man könnte aber auch die Bewegungen von Tieren oder Menschen, wechselnde Wetterlagen, Verkehrsstaus, Magnetik und Astronomie heranziehen … es finden sich auch jenseits der Nano- und Mikroebene der Biologie zahlreiche derartige Phänomene. Sie existieren in auch in anderen Maßstäben, weisen Anzeichen kollektiver Intelligenz auf und sind eindeutig physikalischer Natur. Wir wollen sie anzapfen und für industrielle Prozesse nutzbar machen. Faszinierend ist, dass sie nicht intuitiv sind. Hat man sie aber einmal erkannt und begriffen, wie und warum sie funktionieren, werden sie intuitiv verständlich und damit auch nützlich.

GAM: Hast Du eine Intuition dafür entwickelt?

ST: Ja, sicher. Es ist eigenartig, aber sobald das passiert, ist die Überraschung weg. Und man vergisst, wie es war, überrascht zu werden. Bei jedem Projekt gibt es dieses Überraschungsmoment, aber es verflüchtigt sich sehr rasch – und so finde ich es manchmal schwierig, es festzuhalten und anderen zu zeigen. Man ist dann eigentlich überrascht, dass andere überrascht sind! Man entwickelt einfach so schnell ein intuitives Gefühl für die Assemblierung und auch dafür, wie viel Energiezufuhr das System benötigt. Es ist wirklich interessant! Nehmen wir zum Beispiel die Selbstassemblierung der Biomoleküle in den Glaskolben (*vgl. das TED-Projekt Bio-Molecular Self-*

Our 4D printing was done with the Connex multi-material line 3D printers in collaboration with Stratasys®. We have a really strong collaboration with them. We try to collaborate with a number of different industrial players in tackling some of these problems.

GAM: Let's move on to the question of intuition: Your self-assembly projects are intriguing because they are unlike anything we've ever seen. We are already familiar with self-assembly, but only in living organisms. Any plant can do it. In fact, this is a comparison which you often use in your talks: Cell-division is self-assembly par excellence. At the same time, you don't see yourself as a bionic designer. You don't want to mimic nature. You just design things that are able to autonomously self-assemble. It's difficult to wrap one's head around some of your projects. Their very essence seems to be that they're counter-intuitive.

ST: That's one of our interests: to find ways to build physical devices and systems that are based on non-intuitive phenomena. Changing conventional notions of how we can make things is surprising, but that is really what we are after. There are established ways to build stuff at the human scale. We want to shift the established way of thinking and say: "Hey, there are many other ways that we haven't yet thought about," because they may be at a different scale or they may not be intuitive. You are right that this happens very often in the chemical and biological world, mostly in living systems. But I want to emphasize that our work is not biomimetic. I already mentioned our work with Art Olson—we also work with some other biologists and chemists and we are certainly fascinated about what's happening in biology. But we know that there are many other examples of self-assembly. Crystal growing is a great example, which is certainly not part of a living system. But you could also look at the movement of animals, or people, changing patterns in the weather, traffic jams, magnetics, astronomy, … many phenomena that exist outside the nano- or micro-scales of biology. These kinds of phenomena exist at many other scales, they have collective intelligence properties and they are definitely physical. We want to be able to tap into them and use them for industrial processes. The fascination is that they are not intuitive. But once you recognize them and you figure out why and how they work, they become intuitive and then they become useful.

GAM: Have you developed an intuition for them?

ST: Yeah, certainly. It's funny because once it happens it loses the surprise. And you forget what it was like to have that surprise anymore. With every project there is this moment of surprise but then very quickly you lose it—and so sometimes I find it hard to hold on to and show other people. You're actually surprised that other people are surprised! Because you quickly build an intuition for assembling and you also build an intuition for how much energy is needed in the system. It's really interesting! For example, take the bio-molecular self-assembly flasks. *(See project TED "Bio-Molecular Self-Assembly Kit," figs. 12–13)* I'm really good at assembling them because I know just the right amount of energy it needs to get it right. But when someone new comes up they are not so sure, they have to do a huge search, you know shaking it hard, shaking it soft, going back to hard—they are trying to find the right balance. And so you build up an intuition for what it needs in order to assemble, about how strong it needs to be, how many interactions, how many parts … that kind of stuff. It's kind of funny to build an intuition about a non-intuitive process.

GAM: It's interesting to know that even though it's self-assembly there is still an element of dexterity involved in bringing it on, that experience in making still matters. One reason why your work is so interesting is that the challenge of the traditional assembly-part is so often underestimated. Many architecture schools are experimenting with digital fabrication, building pavilion-sized non-standard structures of dissimilar parts for example. But although the pieces are produced by computer-controlled machines, in the end, somebody always needs to put them together and that's often a major undertaking. The details are tested and the pieces fit together all right, but as soon as there are hundreds or thousands of them and they're all different, sorting them and putting them where they need to go opens up a whole order of logistical challenges. There seems to be a scale issue that people tend to overlook. Is there a danger that you also underestimate such a scale issue? That you say you now have a feeling for how long it takes to shake all the pieces into place, but that as soon as there are vastly more pieces in play, the whole question of assembly becomes a major issue again?

ST: I think the assembly part is the elephant in the room in terms of architecture schools or at least for some of the projects that are happening there. They do these beautiful installations, but people don't talk about how many days, weeks, months they have spent, how many bolts, rivets, panels, unique parts had to be put together. Basically, how much manual labor, how many free interns it took. No one really wants to talk about that part. I am guilty of it many times and in my past work as well. That's why self-assembly became interesting for me. When I got to MIT I saw the opportunity and it was: Wait! There's a whole other world of how things come together. And it fits perfectly in line with the idea of computation for design. Why do we use computation in design and fabrication and then forget about it afterwards when it comes to putting things together? So that really became the goal. And the question of scaling up: I think there are two ways to scale up, obviously. One way is large parts and the other way is many parts.

> We can definitely do self-assembly at the scale of consumer products. But the questions of how many and how quickly and how efficiently, that's where our challenges are. There is a different set of metrics.

GAM: Yes, but in your case it probably would be both, right?

ST: Yes, we are interested in both, but they could be separated. I give you an example of many parts: If you go to the manufacturing sector and you want to do consumer products, they might not be that large, in fact, we are already at that scale. We can definitely do self-assembly at the scale of consumer products. But the questions of how many and how quickly and how efficiently, that's where our challenges are. There is a different set of metrics. If you look at how we are manufacturing things right now there is

Assembly Kit, Abb. 12–13). Ich bin richtig gut darin, sie zusammenzuschütteln, weil ich genau die richtige Energiemenge kenne, die dafür nötig ist. Wenn man es dagegen zum ersten Mal versucht, fehlt diese Sicherheit, man muss lange herumprobieren – heftig schütteln, leicht schütteln, dann wieder heftig usw. –, um die richtige Balance zu finden. So entwickelt man allmählich ein intuitives Gefühl dafür, was zum Assemblieren nötig ist, wie stark die Energie sein muss, wie vieler Interaktionen es bedarf, wie vieler Teile, usw. Es ist irgendwie seltsam, dass man eine Intuition für einen nicht-intuitiven Prozess entwickelt.

GAM: Das ist interessant, dass auch mit der Selbstassemblierung noch ein Element der Geschicklichkeit einhergeht, dass Erfahrung auch hier eine Rolle spielt. Deine Arbeit ist unter anderem auch deshalb so interessant, weil der Anteil der traditionellen Assemblierung oft unterschätzt wird. Viele Architekturinstitute experimentieren mit digitaler Fabrikation und errichten etwa pavillongroße, nicht-standardisierte Bauwerke aus ungleichen Teilen. Aber auch wenn die Teile von computergesteuerten Maschinen erzeugt werden, so müssen sie letztlich doch von jemandem zusammengebaut werden, und das ist oft ein ziemliches Unternehmen. Die Details sind zwar alle vorher getestet worden, und die Stücke passen auch gut zusammen, aber wenn es dann um Hunderte oder Tausende davon geht und jedes anders ist, stellt ihre Sortierung und richtige Positionierung eine enorme logistische Herausforderung dar. Es scheint hier ein Skalierungsproblem zu geben, das gerne übersehen wird. Besteht die Gefahr, dass es dieses Problem auch bei der Selbstassemblierung gibt? Du sagst, Du hast nun ein Gefühl dafür, wie lange es dauert, alle Teile zusammenzuschütteln, aber wird nicht die ganze Frage der Assemblierung erneut zum Problem, sobald erheblich mehr Teile im Spiel sind?

ST: Ich denke, die Frage der Assemblierung ist das Riesenthema, das immer verschwiegen wird in den Architekturschulen oder wenigstens in einigen ihrer Projekte. Die machen da diese wunderbaren Installationen, sprechen aber nicht darüber, wie viele Tage, Wochen, Monate dafür aufgewendet, wie viele Bolzen, Nieten, Platten, und eigens gefertigte Elemente dafür verbaut werden mussten, kurzum, wie viel Handarbeit und kostenlose Praktikantenarbeit da eingeflossen ist. Das wird stillschweigend übergangen. Auch ich mache mich dessen oft schuldig, auch schon in früheren Arbeiten. Eben deshalb wurde die Selbstassemblierung interessant für mich. Als ich ans MIT kam, erkannte ich die Gelegenheit und sagte mir: „Moment mal, es gibt doch eine Welt, in der die Dinge ganz anders zusammenkommen." Und die verbindet sich perfekt mit der Entwurfsinformatik. Warum entwerfen und fabrizieren wir mithilfe von Computern und vergessen darauf, wenn es um das Zusammensetzen der Teile geht? So wurde das zum eigentlichen Ziel. Aber auch die Frage der Größensteigerung – die offensichtlich in zwei

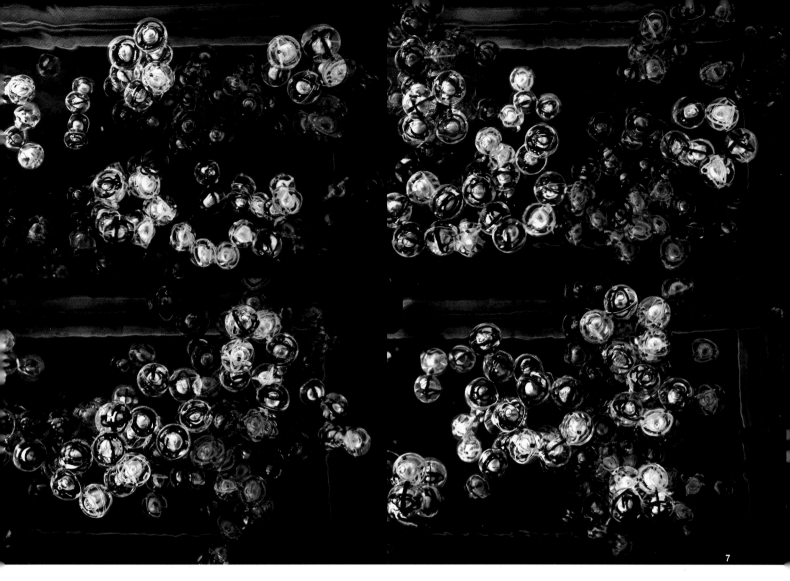

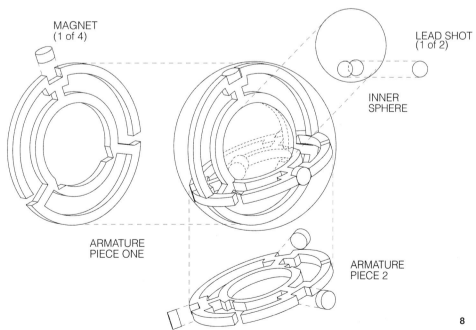

MAGNET
(1 of 4)

LEAD SHOT
(1 of 2)

INNER
SPHERE

ARMATURE
PIECE ONE

ARMATURE
PIECE 2

7–8   *Fluid Crystalization*, 2013 © Self-Assembly
Lab, MIT

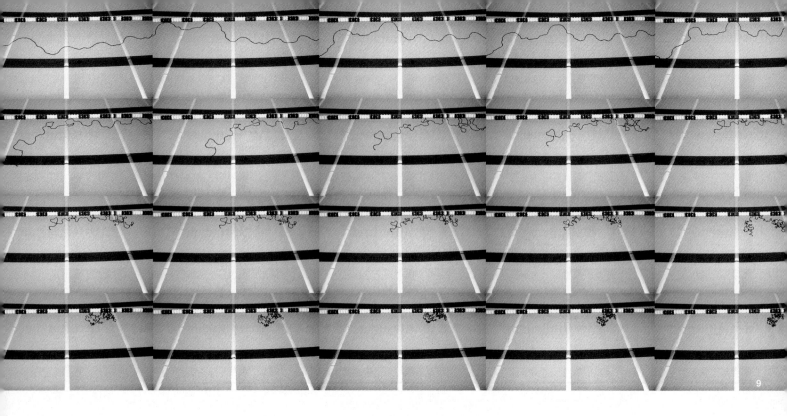

9

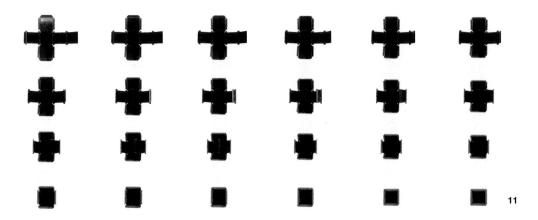

10

11

Richtungen gehen kann: in Richtung größerer Teile und in Richtung einer großen Menge von Teilen.

GAM: In Deinem Fall aber wahrscheinlich in beide Richtungen, oder?

ST: Ja, wir interessieren uns für beide, aber man kann sie trennen. Ich gebe Dir ein Beispiel für eine große Menge von Teilen: Geht man etwa in den Produktionssektor und möchte Konsumartikel erzeugen, so müssen die gar nicht so groß sein. Eigentlich operieren wir bereits in dieser Größenordnung, wir sind definitiv bereits zur Selbstassemblierung von Konsumartikeln fähig. Die Frage ist nur, in welcher Menge, wie schnell und wie effizient. Hier liegen die Herausforderungen. Dabei geht es um vollkommen andere Maßstäbe. Betrachtet man unsere heutige Produktionsweise, so bedarf sie der Zufuhr einer bestimmten Energiemenge. Bei Industrierobotern, die irgendwelche Konsumgüter, Autos oder dergleichen zusammenbauen, aber auch bei Fertigungsstraßen mit menschlichen Arbeitskräften, steht die zugeführte Energie in einem linearen Verhältnis zur Anzahl der produzierten Teile. Bei der Selbstassemblierung ist es der Energie egal, wie viele Teile sich in dem System befinden. Man braucht es nicht stärker zu schütteln, wenn sich mehr oder weniger Teile darin befinden.

GAM: Bist Du Dir da sicher?

ST: Selbstverständlich. Der Energie ist das egal. Stell Dir eine sich drehende Trommel vor *(vgl. das TED-Projekt „Bio-Molecular Self-Assembly Kit", Abb. 12–13)*. Wenn man zwei Teile hineinwirft, werden die sich genauso zusammenfügen wie wenn es 20 wären. Die Trommel weiß nicht, und schert sich nicht darum, ob es sich um zwei oder 20 Teile handelt. Die Variable ist die Zeit – die lässt sich nicht steuern. Sie wird stochastisch. Die Teile können sich in Stunden, Tagen oder sonst wann zusammensetzen. Wir suchen gerade nach Möglichkeiten, die Teile rascher in den niedrigeren Zustand zu befördern. Sie in behagliche Zustände zu befördern, darum geht es eigentlich. Das führt zu einer anderen Auffassung von Effizienz. Man kann auch ganz ungeordnete Energiequellen verwenden, anstelle von Kraftstoffen, Strom und dergleichen. Man kann derartige Quellen anzapfen und es scheint mir durchaus zweckmäßig, solche Möglichkeiten zu verfolgen, wenn es um das Assemblieren einer größeren Menge geht.

Die andere Möglichkeit der Größensteigerung ist viel schwieriger zu bewerkstelligen. Ich denke, sie ist möglich, wird aber sicher länger dauern und wesentlich mehr Arbeit und Ressourcen erfordern. Einige meinen, die Selbstassemblierung funktioniere nur, weil sie im kleinen Maßstab nicht gegen die Schwerkraft ankämpfen muss, aber ich halte das für falsch. Wir verfügen im großmaßstäblichen Bereich über gewaltige Energiequellen! Die Schwerkraft selbst ist eine solche Quelle, wenn wir sie nicht als etwas Negatives sehen. Sie ist eine positive,

a certain input of energy. So if you look at industrial robots that build products or cars or whatever, or even human assembly lines, there is a certain input of energy and a linear relationship with how many parts you produce. In self-assembly the energy doesn't care how many parts are in the system. You don't have to shake it any more if there are more parts or fewer parts.

GAM: Are you sure about that?

ST: Yes, definitely. The energy doesn't care. Think about a spinning chamber. *(See project TED Bio-Molecular Self-Assembly Kit, figs. 12–13)* If you throw two parts in the chamber they'll assemble, if you throw 20 parts in the chamber, the chamber doesn't know and doesn't care whether there are two parts or 20 parts. The variable is time—you can't control the time. Time becomes stochastic. It may assemble in seconds, or it may assemble in hours, days, whatever. So we are trying to find ways to guide the parts into the lower state more quickly—guiding them into comfortable states: that's the real challenge. It leads to a different mentality about what efficiency means. You can use noisy energy sources instead of fuel and electrical current and all that kind of stuff. You can use those sources, and I think it's totally feasible to explore those options when we talk about assembling many parts.

The other option of scaling up is much more challenging. I think it's feasible but it'll definitely take more time and a lot more work and resources. People say self-assembly works because it doesn't fight gravity at small scales, but I think that's wrong because we have huge energy sources at large scales! Gravity is a huge source and if we don't think about it as a negative source, it's a positive, it's huge. Think about wave energy, think about wind energy, or avalanches, earth quakes. There are massive energy forces that we could use to build large scale structures, but we normally think of them as destructive forces. We need to switch that. You know it's going to be hard, we probably need to be working with a crane, with massive machines, perhaps in extreme environments: working in space, deep oceans and those kinds of places. So it's definitely challenging! I don't think it's going to replace our existing methods of construction anytime soon, but there may be ways to assemble things in more extreme scenarios that we can't use today.

GAM: One topic that you also bring up in this context is the notion of self-repair, meaning that structures are not only able to self-assemble but to adapt to their environment.

ST: We already have a few ways to do that, I'm sure there are many more. It's a big topic right now in the material sciences, a lot of people researching at much smaller scales. We see our work as macro-scale material science. We don't really invent new materials, but we invent new ways that dumb materials can come together to make smarter ones—based on geometry, on

> Gravity is a huge source and if we don't think about it as a negative source, it's a positive, it's huge. Think about wave energy, think about wind energy, or avalanches, earth quakes.

You can use 4D printing to manufacture products in this laminated manner. You print the tube, you puncture it, the secondary layer is activated, it swells and closes up the hole. That's a really simple method and I think there are many other potentials. We haven't implemented any of this in any kind of real-world applications yet, but it's one of our interests and something we are looking at.

gewaltige Kraft. Denken Sie auch an Wellenenergie, Windenergie, Lawinen, Erdbeben. Es gibt enorme Kräfte, die wir dazu heranziehen könnten, großmaßstäbliche Strukturen zu errichten, doch sehen wir sie gewöhnlich als destruktiv an. Das müssen wir ändern. Das wird sicherlich schwer, wir werden mit Kränen, riesigen Maschinen, unter extremen Umweltbedingungen arbeiten müssen: im Weltall, in der Tiefsee usw. Also definitiv eine Herausforderung! Ich glaube nicht, dass das unsere gegenwärtigen Konstruktionsmethoden bald ersetzen wird, aber es gibt vielleicht Möglichkeiten, in extremeren, heute noch unzugänglichen Umgebungen zu fertigen.

GAM: Etwas, das Du in diesem Zusammenhang ebenfalls ins Spiel bringst, ist die Idee der Selbstreparatur, das heißt, dass sich die Dinge nicht nur selbst zusammensetzen, sondern auch an die Umwelt anpassen können.

ST: Wir verfügen bereits über einige Möglichkeiten, das zu erreichen, aber ich bin mir sicher, dass da noch mehr drin ist. Es ist gerade ein großes Thema in den Materialwissenschaften, wo eine Menge Leute in einem wesentlich kleineren Maßstab forschen. Wir betrachten unsere Arbeit als Makro-Materialwissenschaft. Wir erfinden eigentlich keinen neuen Materialien, aber wir erfinden neue Wege, wie sich dumme Materialien zu intelligenteren verbinden können – auf der Grundlage ihrer Geometrie, Kombinierfähigkeit und Energieumsetzung. Eine Möglichkeit der Reparatur ist ganz einfach die Lamination. Nehmen wir zum Beispiel einen Fahrradschlauch: Wenn in ihm ein Loch entsteht, aktiviert das eine zweite Schicht, die anschwillt und das Loch verstopft. Man kann solche laminierten Produkte mithilfe von 4D-Druck erzeugen. Wenn man in ein auf diese Weise gedrucktes Rohr dann ein Loch sticht, so wird die zweite Schicht aktiviert, sie schwillt an und flickt das Loch. Das ist wirklich eine einfache Methode, aber ich bin sicher, dass da noch viel mehr Potenzial besteht. Wir haben noch nichts von all dem in einer Realweltanwendung umgesetzt, aber das ist eines unserer Ziele, etwas, woran wir arbeiten.

GAM: Du sprichst vom Einpflanzen von „Intelligenz" in ein reales Bauteil. So wie Du es eben beschrieben hast: Wird eine zweite Schicht stimuliert, versteht diese, dass sie anschwellen und das Rohr flicken soll. Wie sieht hier Deine grundsätzliche Vorgangsweise aus? Nutzt Du einfach nur die natürlichen Materialeigenschaften oder verwendest Du auch Chips oder Motoren oder sonst etwas, das in dem Objekt eine vordefinierte Abfolge von Instruktionen ablaufen lässt, quasi als würde es sich sagen: „Ich muss nun das und das tun, um mich zu reparieren." Wie geht dieses Intelligenz-Einpflanzen vor sich?

ST: Ich überlege, wie ich Materialien aufgrund ihrer Eigenschaften, ihrer Geometrie, ihrer Kombinierbarkeit und ihrer Reaktionen auf Energiezufuhr intelligenter machen kann.

12–13 *Bio-Molecular Self-Assembly*,
TED Global 2012. © Skylar Tibbits,
Arthur Olson und and Autodesk Inc.

how you combine them, how they respond to energy. So, one way to do repair is simply through lamination. For example: you have a tube, and if you puncture that tube, it activates a secondary layer that swells and fixes the puncture. You can use 4D printing to manufacture products in this laminated manner. You print the tube, you puncture it, the secondary layer is activated, it swells and closes up the hole. That's a really simple method and I think there are many other potentials. We haven't implemented any of this in any kind of real-world applications yet, but it's one of our interests and something we are looking at.

GAM: You talk about "intelligence" being imbedded in an actual individual part. Just like you just described: when the second layer is stimulated it understands that it has to swell and therefore fix the tube. What's your general approach to do this? Are you simply exploiting a natural material property or do you also deploy chips or engines or something in the object that is triggered and reacts by running through a predefined set of instructions, rather like saying to itself: "Okay now I have to go through this process in order to fix myself." How is this embedding of intelligence done?

ST: I think about how to make materials smarter based on their material properties, geometry shape, how they combine and respond to energy.

GAM: So there are no built-in chips or anything?

ST: Definitely not! We are trying to find passive solutions that minimize or eliminate motors, electromechanical devices, sensors, electronics, all of that. We want to go back to using fundamentally cheap, simple materials that can be combined in elegant ways to allow some new kind of intelligence. If they can carry code, they can have actuation, they can sense things, they can respond. They can have that "intelligence," although I don't think about it as intelligence necessarily. But more like code, logic, response, those kinds of things, reconfiguration … And it's totally feasible! It goes back to smart materials. If you look at the work in that area, a lot of people will argue that you can embed a code or that you can embed some type of decision making in smart materials. So the difference is we are doing that with "un-smart" materials. We're just making smart materials in different ways. You could look at DNA as a great example of a material that carries a code and can replicate and pass on information without electronics.

GAM: What about the user interface? Do you think the question of user interface in the built environment will become a major issue as a consequence of smart materials being deployed? Do you see that happening?

ST: For sure. If we have the capability to program physical matter then the question becomes: "What is the interface and how can we actually design and interact with those things?" Again that's why we are working with Autodesk® in seeking new design tools and pushing the boundaries of what's possible. We need design tools that are physical and digital and communication between both. But what is the tangible interface? And how do you interact with it? We've tried to play around with that a bit: are users simply adding energy? Or are users also adding design intent? Are users adding more parts? What is the users' will in that process? That's also something we're interested in.

GAM: Also keine eingebauten Chips oder dergleichen?

ST: Sicher nicht! Wir suchen nach passiven Lösungen, die den Einsatz von Motoren, elektromechanischen Mitteln, Sensoren, Elektronik usw. minimieren oder ganz ausschalten. Wir wollen zurück zur Verwendung billiger, einfacher Materialien, die sich auf elegante Weise kombinieren lassen, so dass eine neue Art von Intelligenz entsteht. Wenn sie Träger von Code sein können, dann können sie auch Dinge in Ganz setzen, erfassen, auf sie reagieren. Sie können diese Art von „Intelligenz" aufweisen, auch wenn ich das nicht unbedingt als Intelligenz im eigentlichen Sinne sehe. Es hat eher etwas mit Code, Logik, Ansprechbarkeit, Rekonfiguration zu tun … Und es ist absolut realisierbar! Es kommt aus dem Bereich „Intelligente Werkstoffe". In dem Gebiet hört man von vielen Leuten, man könne Werkstoffen einen Code oder irgendeine Art von Entscheidungsfindung einpflanzen. Der Unterschied ist, dass wir das mit „unintelligenten" Materialien versuchen. Wir machen intelligente Materialien lediglich auf andere Weise. Ein großartiges Beispiel für ein Material, das einen Code befördert, sich replizieren und ohne Elektronik Information weitergeben kann, ist die DNA.

GAM: Und was ist mit dem User Interface? Wird die Frage nach dem User Interface in der gebauten Umwelt nicht zu einem großen Thema werden, wenn man mit intelligenten Materialien arbeitet? Siehst Du das kommen?

ST: Absolut. Wenn wir die Fähigkeit erlangen, Materie zu programmieren, taucht unweigerlich die Frage auf: „Was ist das Interface und wie können wir das alles tatsächlich gestalten und mit ihm interagieren?" Auch deshalb arbeiten wir mit Autodesk® zusammen, um neue Entwurfswerkzeuge zu entwickeln und die Grenzen des Möglichen zu erweitern. Wir benötigen Entwurfsmittel, die gleichzeitig physisch und digital sind und zwischen beidem kommunizieren können. Aber wie sieht dieses Tangible User Interface aus? Wie interagiert man damit? Wir haben versucht, damit ein wenig Herumzuspielen: Fügen Nutzer lediglich Energie hinzu? Oder auch Gestaltungsabsichten? Fügen sie weitere Teile hinzu? Was ist der Nutzerwille bei diesem Vorgang? Auch das sind Dinge, die uns interessieren.

GAM: Die Frage nach dem User Interface führt wieder schön auf das Thema Intuition zurück. Möchtest Du dazu noch etwas anmerken, das wir bisher nicht berührt haben?

ST: Nein, die zwei wesentlichsten Aspekte haben wir, glaube ich, erwähnt. Es gibt eine Intuition, die ich und mein Team entwickeln, weil wir tagtäglich mit diesen Prozessen Umgang haben. Damit können wir gewissenmaßen erraten, welcher Zutaten es zur Selbstassemblierung bedarf. Und dieses intuitive Vermögen haben wir ausgebaut und sind gut darin geworden. Aber zugleich interessiert uns auch noch eine andere Art von Intuition, nämlich die Entwicklung handhabbarer Modelle zur Beschreibung nicht-intuitiver Prozesse. Es ist wirklich aufregend, bahnbrechende intuitive Momente zu erleben, das sind Heureka-Momente. Es tut sich eine gänzlich neue Welt auf, wenn man plötzlich erkennt: „Halt, warum funktioniert das, das ist nun wirklich überraschend!" Und dann geht's sofort los: „Wahnsinn, jetzt kann ich das für X, Y und Z verwenden." Das sind die Augenblicke, die man eigentlich anstrebt.

GAM: Aus der Sicht des Nutzers kann Überraschung natürlich ein zweifelhafter Segen sein. Um noch einmal auf Transformers *zurückzukommen: Wenn Dinge plötzlich ihre Form verändern, kann das ganz schön unheimlich sein. Es kann zum Beispiel zu Missverständnissen zwischen Dir und Deinem intelligenten Tisch führen, wenn der Tisch plötzlich zusammenklappt, während Du etwas darauf ablegen willst. In einer Welt selbstassemblierender intelligenter Objekte könnten wir derartige Überraschungen erleben.*

ST: Wir betrachten Materialien quasi als Entwurfswerkzeuge. Überraschung ist beim Entwerfen fast alles, vor allem wenn man kollaborativ arbeitet: Man möchte, dass einem die Person, mit der man arbeitet, etwas vorlegt, das einen überrascht, weil man es sonst ja längst selbst hätte machen können! Ähnlich sehen wir auch die Arbeit mit diesen Materialien als Kollaboration: Ich möchte, dass sie mir etwas anbieten, das ich nie erwartet hätte und auf das ich selbst nicht gekommen wäre. Kurzum: In dieser Zusammenarbeit machen die Materialien etwas, das ich nicht mache, und ich mache etwas, das sie nicht machen. Und mit Energiezufuhr entsteht wieder etwas anderes, und bei Maschineneinsatz noch einmal. Es handelt sich also um das Zusammenwirken vieler Akteure, so dass das Überraschungspotenzial riesig ist. Auch wenn man intelligente Objekte als rein funktional konzipiert, wenn sie auf eine bestimmte Weise reagieren sollen, kann man seine Überraschungen erleben. Sagen wir, man entwirft ein Gebäude, dass bei einer bestimmten Art von Energiezufuhr elastisch wird. Das könnte durchaus überraschend sein! Wenn man aber einmal weiß, was passiert, ist das nicht mehr der Fall. Verstehst Du, was ich meine? Überraschung ist also immer möglich, aber ich betrachte sie eher als Teil des Entwurfsprozesses.

Übersetzung Wilfried Prantner

GAM: The question of user interface links nicely back to the topic of intuition. Is there anything to add about human intuition that you haven't touched upon yet?

ST: No, I think we mentioned the two main aspects. There is an intuition that I build or my team builds because we work with these processes everyday. Therefore, we can kind of guess what we need in terms of the right ingredients for assembly and we have started to build this intuition and started to get good at it. But the other type of intuition that we are interested in, is in building tangible models to describe non-intuitive processes. Experiencing moments of ground-breaking intuition is really exciting, they are moments of discovery. It opens up a whole new world when you realize something is like "Wait, why does that work, that's so surprising!" and then it's like "Wow, now I can use this for X, Y and Z." Those are the moments we do really try to find.

GAM: Of course from a user's perspective surprise can be a mixed blessing. If we go back to Transformers *again: when things suddenly change shape, that can be scary. Simple misunderstandings, let's say between you and your smart table, which folds up when you're trying to place something on it. In a world of self-assembling smart objects we might be in for such surprises.*

ST: We see materials as design tools in a way. Surprise is almost everything in design, especially if there's an aspect of collaboration: you want the person you collaborate with to bring something to the table that surprises you because otherwise you could have already done it yourself! In the same way we see working with these materials as a collaboration—I want them to offer things that I would have never expected or that I couldn't have known. In other words, in our collaboration the materials do something that I don't do and then I do something that they don't do. And energy provides something else, and machines provide something else too, you know. So it's a collaboration of many actors and therefore the potential for surprise is huge. But if you think about smart objects as purely functional, you want them to respond and act in certain predefined ways, you'll also get surprising things. Let's say you design a building that responds to a certain type of energy and becomes flexible. That could be surprising! But once you know what it does, it's not surprising anymore when it does it. You know what I mean? So surprise is always possible, but I like to think of it more as part of the design process.

> Experiencing moments of ground-breaking intuition is really exciting, they are moments of discovery.

Edith Ackermann hat im Fach Entwicklungspsychologie an der Universität Genf promoviert und ist heute Visiting Scientist an der MIT School of Architecture sowie Senior Research Associate an der Harvard Graduate School of Design in Cambridge, MA. Zuvor hat sie als Associate Professor für Media Arts and Sciences am MIT Media Laboratory, als Senior Research Scientist am MERL (Mitsubishi Electric Research Lab, Cambridge, MA) und als Scientific Collaborator am Centre International d'Epistémologie Génétique in Genf unter der Leitung von Jean Piaget gearbeitet. Gegenwärtig ist sie an folgenden Institutionen forschend und beratend tätig: the Responsive Environments Group an der Harvard Graduate School of Design, der Personal Robots Group am MIT Media Lab, der LEGO Group und weiteren Organisationen und Institutionen, die sich mit dem Zusammenhang von Spiel, Imagination und kindlicher Kreativität in Lernprozessen beschäftigen.

Nathalie Bredella ist wissenschaftliche Mitarbeiterin am Institut für Geschichte und Theorie der Gestaltung der Universität der Künste Berlin (UdK), wo sie im Rahmen eines eigenen DFG-Projekts zum Thema „Architektur und neue Medien" forscht. Nach ihrem Studium der Architektur an der Technischen Universität Berlin und der Cooper Union New York wurde sie 2008 mit einer Arbeit über Film und Architektur promoviert. Sie war Research Fellow im Rahmen des Programms „Werkzeuge des Entwerfens" am Internationalen Kolleg für Kulturtechnikforschung und Medienphilosophie (IKKM) der Bauhaus-Universität Weimar. Zu ihren jüngsten Publikationen zählen: „Modelle des Entwerfens. Zur Bedeutung digitaler Werkzeuge im Entwurfsprozess von Frank O. Gehry" und *Infrastrukturen des Urbanen*, herausgegeben gemeinsam mit Chris Dähne bei transcript 2013.

Mario Carpo ist Vincent Scully Visiting Professor of Architectural History an der Yale School of Architecture und seit 1993 Associate Professor an der École d'Architecture de Paris-La Villette. Nach seinem Studium (Architektur und Geschichte) in Italien war er als wissenschaftlicher Mitarbeiter an der Universität Genf tätig. Mario Carpos Forschung ist an der Schnittstelle von Architekturtheorie, Kulturgeschichte und Medien- bzw. Informationstechnologie angesiedelt. Sein preisgekröntes Buch *Architecture in the Age of Printing* (MIT Press, 2001) wurde in zahlreiche Sprachen übersetzt. Zu seinen jüngsten Publikationen zählen *The Alphabeth and the Algorithm* (MIT Press, 2011) und *The Digital Turn in Architecture, 1992–2012* (Wiley, 2012). Außerdem hat er wissenschaftliche Beiträge in *Log, The Journal of the Society of Architectural Historians, Grey Room, L'Architecture d'aujourd'hui, Arquitectura Viva, AD, Perspecta, Harvard Design Magazine, Domus* und *Arch+* veröffentlicht.

Kristof Crolla ist Architekt und lehrt an der Chinese University of Hong Kong, School of Architecture (CUHK) im Bereich Computational Design. Zuvor unterrichtete er an der Architectural Association School of Architecture, London (AA) und arbeitete viele Jahre als leitender Architekt für Zaha Hadid Architects. Nach seinem Abschluss an der Ghent University mit „Magna Cum Laude" ging er 2005 nach London, wo er am AA Master Program Design Research Laboratory teilnahm. Seine Studentenarbeit (gemeinsam mit „Sugar Inc.") wurde 2006 auf der Architekturbiennale in Venedig ausgestellt. Seitdem war er als Kritiker, Lektor und Lehrbeauftragter an verschie-

Edith Ackermann holds a Doctorate in Developmental Psychology from the University of Geneva and is currently a Visiting Scientist at the MIT School of Architecture and a Senior Research Associate at the Harvard Graduate School of Design in Cambridge, MA, USA. Previously an Associate Professor at the MIT Media Laboratory, and Senior Research Scientist at MERL—Mitsubushi Electric Research Laboratory, Cambridge, MA—Edith Ackermann also worked as a Scientific Collaborator at the Centre International d'Epistémologie Génétique in Geneva, under the direction of Jean Piaget. Current appointments and collaborations include: the Responsive Environments Group at the Harvard Graduate School of Design, the Personal Robots group at the MIT Media Lab and the LEGO Group—as well as other organizations and institutions interested in the relations between play, imagination, and creativity in human learning.

Nathalie Bredella is Assistant Professor at the Institute for the History and Theory of Design at the Universität der Künste Berlin (UdK), where she works on a DFG-funded project on architecture and new media. After her studies at the Technische Universität Berlin and the Cooper Union, New York, she received her PhD in architectural theory in 2008 with a doctoral thesis on architecture and film. She was a research fellow at the IKKM (Internationales Kolleg für Kulturtechnikforschung und Medienphilosophie) of the Bauhaus-Universität Weimar. Her most recent publications include: "Modelle des Entwerfens. Zur Bedeutung digitaler Werkzeuge im Entwurfsprozess von Frank O. Gehry" and *Infrastrukturen des Urbanen*, co-edited with Chris Dähne, which was published with transcript in 2013.

Mario Carpo is Vincent Scully Visiting Professor of Architectural History at Yale School of Architecture and since 1993 serves as Associate Professor at the École d'Architecture de Paris-La Villette. After studying architecture and history in Italy, Mario Carpo was an Assistant Professor at the University of Geneva in Switzerland. Mr. Carpo's research and publications focus on the relationship among architectural theory, cultural history, and the history of media and information technology. His award-winning book *Architecture in the Age of Printing* (MIT Press, 2001) has been translated into several languages. His most recent books are *The Alphabet and the Algorithm* (MIT Press, 2011) and *The Digital Turn in Architecture, 1992-2012* (Wiley, 2012). Mario Carpo's recent essays and articles have been published in *Log, The Journal of the Society of Architectural Historians, Grey Room, L'Architecture d'aujourd'hui, Arquitectura Viva, AD, Perspecta, Harvard Design Magazine, Domus*, and *Arch+*.

Kristof Crolla is a licensed architect and works as an Assistant Professor in Computational Design at the Chinese University of Hong Kong, School of Architecture (CUHK). He taught at the Architectural Association School of Architecture, London (AA) and worked for many years as Lead Architect for Zaha

Hadid Architects. After graduating Magna Cum Laude at Ghent University and practicing in Belgium, he moved to London in 2005 and attended the AA's master program Design Research Laboratory, from where his student work with team "Sugar Inc." was exhibited at the 2006 Venice Architecture Biennale. He has been invited as a jury critic, lecturer and tutor in numerous institutions in Europe, Asia, Chile and South Africa and moved to Hong Kong in 2010 where he currently teaches and runs his architectural practice Laboratory for Explorative Architecture & Design Ltd. (LEAD).

Kathrin Dörfler is a PhD candidate at the Chair of Architecture and Digital Fabrication (Prof. Fabio Gramazio, Prof. Matthias Kohler) at the ETH Zurich. She studied Architecture at the TU Graz and TU Vienna, and Digital Arts at the University of Applied Arts Vienna. Her thesis "Integration of Digital and Physical Design Methods" was developed in cooperation with Romana Rust and was awarded at the GAD Awards '12 in Graz and the archdiploma13 in Vienna. In her research she focuses on the study of adaptive and flexible fabrication processes in changing and dynamic environments, as well as with difficult to control material systems.

Martin Emmerer is an architect and the co-founder of the architecture collective Hope of Glory. The new southern wing of the caste museum in Linz can be named one of his most important realized projects. He has also taught at Graz University of Technology for several years. His focus on drafting was always attended by a strong interest in computer science and a long-standing autodidactic engagement in programming, which led him to the development of architecture-specific software tools. Since 2011 he has been working on his doctoral thesis entitled *Architektur Routine(n): Solving the Hardworking Draftsman Problem* (HDP).

Fabio Gramazio is Professor for Architecture and Digital Fabrication at the Department of Architecture at ETH Zurich. In 2000 he founded the architecture practice Gramazio & Kohler, which has realized numerous award-winning projects. Opening also the world's first architectural robotic laboratory at ETH Zurich in 2005, Gramazio & Kohler's research has been formative in the field of digital architecture, setting precedence and de facto creating a new research field merging advanced architectural design and additive fabrication processes through the customized use of industrial robots. This ranges from 1:1 building prototypes such as the robotically fabricated Gantenbein Vineyard Facade (2006) and live installations such as Flight Assembled Architecture (2011) to robotic fabrication at a large scale. His most recent publications include *Digital Materiality in Architecture* (2008), the *Architectural Design* (AD) issue "Made by Robots" (2014) and *The Robotic Touch – How Robots Change Architecture* (2014).

Sean Hanna is a reader in Space and Adaptive Architectures at UCL, director of the Bartlett Graduate School's MSc/MRes

denen Institutionen in Europa, Asien, Südamerika und Südafrika tätig. Seit 2010 lebt er in Hong Kong, wo er lehrt und sein Büro „Laboratory for Explorative Architecture & Design Ltd." (LEAD) betreibt.

Kathrin Dörfler ist Doktorandin an der Professur für Architektur und digitale Fabrikation (Prof. Fabio Gramazio und Prof. Matthias Kohler) der ETH Zürich. Nach ihrem Architekturstudium an der TU Graz, TU Wien und der Universität für angewandte Kunst in Wien hat sie ihr Studium 2012 mit ihrer Arbeit *Nach vor und zurück – Verschränkung physischer und digitaler Gestaltungsprozesse* beendet. Die Diplomarbeit wurde gemeinsam mit Romana Rust angefertigt und mit dem GAD Award 12 in Graz als auch mit dem archdiploma13 in Wien ausgezeichnet. In ihrer Forschung beschäftigt sich Kathrin Dörfler mit der Analyse von adaptiven und flexiblen Fabrikationsprozessen in wechselhaften und dynamischen Umgebungen, sowie mit schwer kontrollierbaren Materialsystemen.

Martin Emmerer ist Architekt und Mitbegründer des Architekturkollektivs Hope of Glory. Zu seinen wichtigsten realisierten Bauwerken zählt unter anderem der Südflügel des Schlossmuseums Linz. Neben seiner Architekturpraxis unterrichtete Martin Emmerer mehrere Jahre an der Technischen Universität Graz. Sein Fokus auf die entwerferischen Tätigkeiten wurde stets von einem starken Interesse für die Informatik und die langjährige autodidaktische Beschäftigung mit der Computerprogrammierung begleitet. Dies führte ihn auch zur Entwicklung architekturspezifischer Softwaretools. Seit 2011 schreibt er an seiner Dissertation mit dem Titel *Architektur Routine(n). Solving the Hardworking Draftsman Problem* (HDP).

Fabio Gramazio ist Professor für Architektur und Digitale Fabrikation am Departement Architektur der ETH Zürich. 2000 hat er das Architekturbüro Gramazio & Kohler zusammen mit Matthias Kohler gegründet. Seitdem realisierten sie eine Reihe von preisgekrönten Bauwerken. In ihrer Forschung bauten Gramazio & Kohler bereits 2005 das erste Roboterlabor für die Herstellung nicht-standardisierter Bauelemente an der ETH Zürich auf und eröffneten damit ein vollkommen neues Forschungsgebiet in der Architektur. Die Arbeit mit dem Roboter reicht von 1:1-Bauprojekten wie der durch einen Roboter erstellten Fassade des Weinguts Gantenbein (2006) über Ausstellungsinstallationen wie Flight Assembled Architecture (2011) zum digitalen Entwurf robotergebauter großmaßstäblicher Gebäudetypologien. Zu seinen jüngsten Publikationen zählen *Digital Material in Archi-*

tecture (2008), die *Architectural Design* (AD) Ausgabe *Made by Robots* (2014) sowie *The Robotic Touch – How Robots Change Architecture* (2014).

Sean Hanna lehrt im Fachbereich Space and Adaptive Architectures an der UCL und ist der Leiter der MSc/MRes Studienprogramme für Adaptive Architecture and Computation an der Bartlett Graduate School. Zudem ist er der akademische Leiter des UCL Doctoral Training Center für den Zweig Virtual Environments, Imaging and Visualization. Seine aktuelle Forschung setzt sich vorwiegend mit der Entwicklung von computergestützten Methoden für komplexe Entwurfsprozesse im gebauten Raum auseinander. Darunter fallen auch vergleichende Raumentwürfe und deren Wahrnehmung über Maschinen, sowie der Einsatz von maschinellem Lernen und Optimierungstechniken für den Entwurf und die Realisierung von gebauten Strukturen. Zu seinen aktuellen Veröffentlichungen zählen: „The inverted genotype and its implications for the flexibility of architectural models" in *The Journal of Space Syntax* (2011) und „Thinking machines and adaptive architecture" in *Space* (2012).

Michael Hansmeyer und **Benjamin Dillenburger** lehren und forschen am Lehrstuhl für CAAD der ETH Zürich, wo sie sich mit computergestützten Entwurfs- und Fertigungsprozessen in der Architektur auseinandersetzen. Zu ihren aktuellen Projekten zählt „Digital Grotesque" – eine im 3D-Druckverfahren produzierte Grotte aus künstlichem Sandstein, die sie für die Ausstellung ArchiLab 2013 in Orléans entworfen haben.

Urs Hirschberg ist Professor für Darstellung der Architektur und Neue Medien an der Architekturfakultät der TU Graz. Er leitet das Institut für Architektur und Medien (IAM) der TU Graz seit dessen Gründung 2004. Seit 2013 ist er auch Leiter des TU Graz Field of Expertise „Sustainable Systems" und Vize-Dekan der Fakultät für Architektur, nachdem er zuvor neun Jahre lang Dekan war. Er hat an der ETH Zürich Architektur studiert und doktoriert. Bevor er an die TU Graz berufen wurde, war er wissenschaftlicher Assistent und Dozent am Lehrstuhl für Architektur und CAAD der ETH Zürich und danach Assistant Professor of Design Computing an der Harvard Graduate School of Design. In seiner Forschung beschäftigt er sich mit „Augmented Architecture" und der Frage, wie digitale Techniken die Entwurfs- und Produktionsbedingungen der Architektur verbessern, und wie neue Medien Teil unserer gebauten Umwelt werden können. Er ist Gründungsmitglied der Redaktion von GAM.

Ludger Hovestadt ist Architekt und Informatiker und seit 2000 Professor für Computer Aided Architectural Design an der ETH Zürich. Er arbeitet an der Grenze der Berechenbarkeit und versucht komplexe Informationstechnologien in der Architektur verfügbar zu machen. Er ist Gründer mehrerer Firmen in den Bereichen „digitale Fabrikation", „intelligente Gebäudetechnik" und zuletzt der Digitalisierung unserer Stromnetze. Seit 2009 hat sich sein Schwerpunkt von der Anwendbarkeit zur Grundlagenforschung zum Verhältnis von Architektur und Information verschoben. Seine wichtigsten Publikationen sind: *Jenseits des Rasters – Architektur und Informationstechnologie* (2009), *Printed Physics – Metalithicum Series Vol. 1* (2012), *SHEAVES – When Things Are Whatever Can Be The Case* (2013) und *EigenArchitecture. Computability as Literacy* (2014).

programmes in Adaptive Architecture and Computation, and academic director of UCL's Doctoral Training Center in Virtual Environments, Imaging and Visualisation. His current research focuses primarily on developing computational methods for dealing with complexity in design and the built environment, including the comparative modelling of space and its perception by machines, and the use of machine learning and optimisation techniques for the design and fabrication of structures. Publications include "The inverted genotype and its implications for the flexibility of architectural models" in *The Journal of Space Syntax* (2011), and "Thinking machines and adaptive architecture" in *Space* (2012).

Michael Hansmeyer and **Benjamin Dillenburger** are based in the CAAD group at the Swiss Federal Institute of Technology's architecture department in Zürich. Their research focus is on computational design and fabrication methods for architecture. One recent project is "Digital Grotesque," a full-scale 3D-printed grotto that was presented at the 2013 ArchiLab exhibition in Orléans.

Urs Hirschberg serves as Professor for the Representation of Architecture and New Media at Graz University of Technology. He is the founding Director of the Institute of Architecture and Media (IAM) and Vice-Dean of the Architecture Faculty. Having served as Dean of his Faculty for nine years, in 2013 he was appointed Director of the TU Graz Field of Expertise "Sustainable Systems." He holds a Diploma in Architecture and a Doctorate from ETH Zurich. Before joining TU Graz he served as Research Assistant and Lecturer at the Chair of Architecture, CAAD at ETH Zurich and as Assistant Professor of Design Computing at the Harvard Graduate School of Design. His research interests concern the notion of "augmented architecture" and the ways in which the use of new media can enhance architectural design and production and augment our built environment. He is a founding editor of GAM.

Ludger Hovestadt is an architect and computer scientist and since 2000 Professor for Computer Aided Architectural Design at the ETH Zürich. He is working at the borderline of calculability and brings complex information technology into disposal for architecture. He is the founder of several companies in the fields of digital fabrication, smart buildings and the digitalization of our energy grids. Since 2009 his focus of research has shifted towards basic research on architecture and information. His most important publications are: *Beyond the Grid – Architecture and Information Technology* (2009), *Printed Physics–Metalithicum Series Vol. 1* (2012), *SHEAVES: When Things Are Whatever Can Be The Case* (2013) and *EigenArchitecture: Computability as Literacy* (2014).

Matthias Kohler is Professor for Architecture and Digital Fabrication at the Department of Architecture at the ETH Zurich. In 2000 he founded the architecture practice Gramazio & Kohler, which has realized numerous award-winning projects. Opening also the world's first architectural robotic laboratory at ETH Zurich in 2005, Gramazio & Kohler's research has been formative in the field of digital architecture, setting precedence and de facto creating a new research field merging advanced architectural design and additive fabrication processes through the customized use of industrial robots. This ranges from 1:1 building prototypes such as the robotically fabricated Gantenbein Vineyard Facade (2006) and live installations such as Flight Assembled Architecture (2011) to robotic fabrication at a large scale. Since 2014 he leads the new National Centre of Competence in Research (NCCR) in Digital Fabrication supported by the Swiss National Science Foundation (SNSF). His most recent publications include *Digital Materiality in Architecture* (2008), the *Architectural Design* (AD) issue *Made by Robots* (2014) and *The Robotic Touch – How Robots Change Architecture* (2014).

George Legendre is the co-founder of IJP, a London-based practice exploring the natural intersection between space, mathematics, and computation, which he founded together with Lluis Viu Rebes and Marc Fouquet. He graduated from the Harvard Graduate School of Design in 1994 and served as Assistant Professor of Architecture there from 1995–2000. Prior to founding IJP in 2004, he was Visiting Professor at ETH Zurich (2000), Princeton University (2003–05), and the London AA School of Architecture (2002–08). A regularly published essayist, he has written *IJP: The Book of Surfaces*, as well as *Bodyline: The End of Our Meta-Mechanical Body*, and the main critical essay in *Mathematical Form: John Pickering and the Architecture of the Inversion Principle* (all AA Publications 2003-06). He has guest-edited a special issue of *AD* on the Mathematics of Space (2011). His latest research opus, *Pasta by Design*, was published in 2011 and translated into German the following year.

Ammar Mirjan is a PhD candidate at the Chair for Architecture and Digital Fabrication (Prof. Fabio Gramazio, Prof. Matthias Kohler) at the ETH Zurich. He has a background in automation engineering, received a B.A. degree in architecture from Bern University of Applied Sciences and a M.Arch. degree from the Bartlett School of Architecture, London. His research focuses on the relationship between designing and building with intelligent machines and, more specifically, on architectural fabrication processes with flying robots.

Felix Raspall is an architectural designer and researcher, working at the intersection of traditional building methods with digital design and fabrication. His current research focuses on applications of digital technologies as a means to expand the structural and formal limits of artisanal construction. Felix Raspall holds a professional degree in architecture from the University of Buenos Aires and a post-professional Master of Architecture from Yale University. He is currently a doctoral candidate at Harvard University where he is also project manager at the Design Robotic Group and member of the Energy Consortium. His research and design work has been published in several books and journals.

Matthias Kohler ist Professor für Architektur und Digitale Fabrikation am Departement Architektur der ETH Zürich. 2000 hat er das Architekturbüro Gramazio & Kohler, zusammen mit Fabio Gramazio gegründet. Seitdem realisierten sie eine Reihe von preisgekrönten Bauwerken. In ihrer Forschung bauten Gramazio & Kohler bereits 2005 das erste Roboterlabor für die Herstellung nicht-standardisierter Bauelemente an der ETH Zürich auf und eröffneten damit ein vollkommen neues Forschungsgebiet in der Architektur. Die Arbeit mit dem Roboter reicht von 1:1-Bauprojekten wie der durch einen Roboter erstellten Fassade des Weinguts Gantenbein (2006) über Ausstellungsinstallationen wie Flight Assembled Architecture (2011) zum digitalen Entwurf robotergebauter großmaßstäblicher Gebäudetypologien. Seit 2014 leitet er den neuen Nationalen Forschungsschwerpunkt (NFS) Digital Fabrication, welcher durch den Schweizerischen Nationalfonds (SNF) gefördert wird. Zu seinen jüngsten Publikationen zählen *Digital Material in Architecture* (2008), die *Architectural Design* (AD) Ausgabe *Made by Robots* (2014) sowie *The Robotic Touch – How Robots Change Architecture* (2014).

George Legendre hat gemeinsam mit Lluis Viu Rebes und Marc Fouquet das Londoner Büro IJP gegründet, das sich an der Schnittstelle von Raum, Mathematik und computerbasierten Entwurfsprozessen verortet. Nach seinem Abschluss an der Harvard Graduate School of Design 1994 war er an der gleichnamigen Institution von 1995–2000 als wissenschaftlicher Mitarbeiter für den Fachbereich Architektur tätig. Vor der Gründung von IJP im Jahre 2004 war er Gastprofessor an der ETH Zürich (2000), an der Princeton Universität (2003–2005) und an der London AA School of Architecture (2002–2008). Zu seinen zahlreichen Publikationen zählen: *IJP: The Book of Surfaces* und *Bodyline: The End of Our Meta-Mechanical Body*, sowie der Hauptbeitrag in *Mathematical Form: John Pickering and the Architecture of the Inversion Principle* (2003–2006). Er war außerdem Gastherausgeber einer Sonderausgabe von *AD* zum Thema Mathematics of Space (2011). Sein jüngstes Buch *Pasta by Design* ist 2011 erschienen und wurde ein Jahr später ins Deutsche übersetzt.

Ammar Mirjan ist Doktorand an der Professur für Architektur und Digitale Fabrikation (Prof. Fabio Gramazio und Prof. Matthias Kohler) an der ETH Zürich. Nach einer Ausbildung im Bereich der Automatisierungstechnik erhielt er einen Bachelor of Architecture von der Berner Fachhochschule und einen Master of Architecture von der Bartlett School of Architecture, London. Seine Forschungsarbeit behandelt die Wechselwirkung von Entwurf und Materialisierung, gekoppelt durch intelligente Maschinen. Im Speziellen befasst er sich mit architektonischen Konstruktionsprozessen mit Flugrobotern.

Felix Raspall ist Architekt und forscht an der Schnittstelle von traditionellen Baumethoden und digitalen Design- und Fertigungsprozessen. Seine aktuelle Forschung beschäftigt sich mit der Anwendung von digitalen Technologien und den Möglichkeiten, die handwerkliche Konstruktion in struktureller und formaler Hinsicht zu erweitern. Er hat an den Universitäten Buenos Aires und Yale Architektur studiert und ist gegenwärtig Doktorand an der Harvard Universität, wo er auch als Projektmanager der Design Robotic Group sowie als Mitglied des Energy Consortiums tätig ist. Seine Forschung hat er in zahlreichen Büchern und Journals veröffentlicht.

Florian Rist forscht und lehrt an der Technischen Universität Wien. Er studierte Mathematik und Architektur an der TU München und arbeitete als Architekt in Deutschland, unter anderem für Gerber Architekten in Dortmund. In seiner Forschung beschäftigt er sich mit Fragen der digitalen Fertigung und des algorithmischen Entwerfens in Architektur, Kunst und Gestaltung, besonders unter dem Gesichtspunkt der Integration digitaler und physischer Entwurfsmethoden. Zu seinen Publikationen zählen Aufsätze wie „Controlling Caustics" (*GPD*, 2013) und „Integrating Physical and Digital Design Methods" (Detail, 2012).

Francois Roche ist der Leiter von New-Territories (R&Sie(n)/[eIf/b∧t/c]). Er lebt hauptsächlich in Bangkok [eIf/b∧t/c], manchmal in Paris R&Sie(n) und im Herbst in NY, wo er an der GSAPP der Columbia University ein Forschungsstudio leitet. Durch diese unterschiedlichen Strukturen suchen seine architektonischen Arbeiten und Protokolle das Reale und/oder das Fiktionale zu artikulieren, indem sie Narration und physische Produktion ununterscheidbar machen sowie Szenarios entwerfen und Apparate entwickeln, um Situationen zu verändern. Francois Roche war Gastprofessor an folgenden Institutionen: der Bartlett School, London (2000), der Technischen Universität Wien (2001), der ESARQ Barcelona (2003/2004), der University of Pennsylvania in Philadelphia (2006, 2013), der Angewandten Wien (2008), der USC Los Angeles (2009) und seit 2006 an der GSAPP der Columbia University, New York, wo er eine Position als Research Professor innehat. Seine Arbeiten wurden international ausgestellt unter anderem an der Columbia Universität New York, der UCLA (Los Angeles), ICA (London), dem Mori Art Museum (Tokyo), dem Centre Pompidou (Paris), der Tate Modern (London) und auf zahlreichen Architekturbiennalen in Venedig zwischen 1990 und 2010. Im Jahr 2012 war er Gastherausgeber von *Log* 25, einer Ausgabe mit dem Titel „Reclaim Resi(lience)stance".

Romana Rust arbeitet seit 2013 als Doktorandin an der Professur für Architektur und Digitale Fabrikation (Prof. Fabio Gramazio und Prof. Matthias Kohler) an der ETH Zürich. Sie studierte Technische Mathematik und Architektur an der TU Graz und schloss ihr Architekturstudium mit der Diplomarbeit *Nach vor und zurück – Verschränkung physischer und digitaler Gestaltungsprozesse*, die sie in Kooperation mit Kathrin Dörfler entwickelte, im Jahr 2012 ab. Der Fokus ihrer Forschung liegt bei der Gestaltung und Untersuchung von interaktiven, auf Feedback basierenden Fabrikationsprozessen und der Entwicklung von geeigneten Tools für deren Anwendung im Architekturkontext.

Skylar Tibbits, der Leiter des MIT Self-Assembly-Labs, beschäftigt sich in seiner Forschung mit selbstassemblierenden und programmierbaren Materialtechnologien für Industrieanwendungen. 2013 wurde ihm der Architectural League Prize als auch der Next Idea Award der Ars Electronica verliehen. Neben seinen Vorträgen am MoMA und an der SEED Media Group's MIND08 wurden seine großräumigen Installationen bereits international ausgestellt, unter anderem im Guggenheim Museum, NY und der Beijing Biennale. Er ist der Gründer der multidisziplinären Architektur-, Kunst- und Designpraxis SJET LLC und lehrt im Fachbereich Architektur am MIT (Masters & Undergraduate Design Studios) und ist einer der Leiter von *How to Make (Almost) Anything*.

Florian Rist teaches at Vienna University of Technology, where he also conducts research. He studied mathematics and architecture at TU München (TUM) and practiced at Gerber Architekten in Dortmund. In his research he explores questions concerning digital production and algorithmic design in architecture, art and design, with a special emphasis on the integration of digital and physical design methods. His publications include the essays "Controlling Caustics" (*GPD*, 2013) and "Integrating Physical and Digital Design Methods" (*Detail*, 2012).

Francois Roche is the principal of New-Territories (R&Sie(n)/ [eIf/b∧t/c]). He is based mainly in BKK, [eIf/b∧t/c], sometimes in Paris, R&Sie(n), and at fall time in NY, with his studio of research at GSAPP, Columbia University. Through these different structures, his architectural works and protocols seek to articulate the real and/or fictional, confusing narration and physical production, writing scenarios and developing apparatuses to transform situations. Francois Roche was a guest professor at the Bartlett School in London in 2000, the Vienna TU in 2001, the Barcelona ESARQ in 2003/2004, the University of Pennsylvania in Philadelphia in 2006 and 2013, the Angewandte in Vienna in 2008, the USC Los Angeles in 2009 and holds the position of Research Professor since 2006 at GSAPP, Columbia University, New York. His architectural designs have been shown at, among other places, Columbia University (New York), UCLA (Los Angeles), ICA (London), Mori Art Museum (Tokyo), Centre Pompidou (Paris), Tate Modern (London) and at numerous Venice Architecture Biennales between 1990 and 2010. In 2012 he has been the guest editor of *Log* 25 holding the title "Reclaim Resi(lience)stance."

Romana Rust is a PhD candidate at the Chair for Architecture and Digital Fabrication (Prof. Fabio Gramazio and Prof. Matthias Kohler) at the ETH Zurich since 2013. She studied technical mathematics and architecture at Graz University of Technology, where she graduated in 2012. Her diploma thesis, which she co-authored with Kathrin Dörfler, is entitled *Nach vor und zurück – Verschränkung physischer und digitaler Gestaltungsprozesse*. Her research focuses on the design and analysis of interactive, feedback-based, fabrication processes and the development of suitable tools to be used in the context of architecture.

Skylar Tibbits the director of the Self-Assembly Lab at MIT, researches self-assembly and programmable material technologies for industrial applications in the built environment. He was recently awarded the Architectural League Prize (2013) and the Next Idea Award at Ars Electronica 2013. He has designed and built large-scale installations around the world and exhibited at the Guggenheim Museum, NY, the Beijing Biennale and lectured at MoMA and SEED Media Group's MIND08. He is also the founder of a multidisciplinary research-based practice, called SJET LLC. Skylar is a Research Scientist at MIT's Department of Architecture, teaching Masters and Undergraduate Design Studios and co-teaching *How to Make (Almost) Anything* at MIT's Media Lab.

Tobias Wallisser is Professor of Innovative Construction and Spatial Concepts and Vice-President at the State Academy of Fine Arts in Stuttgart. In 2007, he co-founded LAVA (Laboratory for Visionary Architecture), together with Chris Bosse and Alexander Rieck. LAVA serves as a think tank network. 45 architects works on projects in Europe, Saudi Arabia, China, and Australia. From 1997 to 2007, Tobias Wallisser was Creative Director at UNStudio in Amsterdam where he was responsible for many projects, including the Mercedes-Benz Museum in Stuttgart. He lectures at universities worldwide and has won numerous awards.

Makoto Sei Watanabe is an architect, founder of MAKOTO SEI WATANABE/ARCHITECTS' OFFICE, and professor at the Space-Generating Lab, Faculty of Urban Life Studies, Tokyo City University. Sensually, his work is characterized by a feeling of movement and tactile qualities that make the visitor want to touch it, while theoretically it is informed by a continuing investigation into verbalization of the act of design and its translation into computer programs. WEB FRAME (2000), created according to this new INDUCTION DESIGN/ALGOrithmic-Design methodology, was the world's first work of architecture to be generated by using a computer program to solve specified conditions. His work has received numerous awards, including The Prize of AIJ 2002 (Japan) and the ASLA Awards 1997 (USA). His books include *INDUCTION DESIGN* (2002/2004) and *ALGOrithmic Design EXecution and Logic"* (2012).

Jan Willmann is Senior Assistant at the Chair of Architecture and Digital Fabrication at ETH Zurich. He studied architecture in Liechtenstein, Oxford and Innsbruck where he received his PhD degree in 2010. Previously, from 2007 to 2010, he was a research assistant and lecturer at the Chair of Architectural Theory of Professor Ir. Bart Lootsma. His research focuses on digital architecture and its theoretical implications as a composed computational and material score. Among his latest publications are: *The Robotic Touch – How Robots Change Architecture* (2014) co-edited with Fabio Gramazio and Matthias Kohler.

Chris Younès holds a PhD in philosophy and serves as a professor at the École Nationale Supérieure d'Architecture de Paris La Villette and the École Spéciale d'Architecture. She is the chair of GERPHAU, a laboratory conducting research in "Architecture, Urban, Philosophy" and the PhilAU international network. Furthermore, she heads the "Architecture des Milieux" post-graduate program and is member of Europan's Scientific Committee. Her research interests are located at the intersection between aesthetics and ethics. Among her recent publications are *Le Territoire des Philosophes* (2009), *Espace et Lieux dans la pensée occidentale* (2012) and *Architecture et Perception* (2012).

Tobias Wallisser ist Professor für Innovative Bau- und Raumkonstruktionen sowie Prorektor an der Staatlichen Akademie der Bildenden Künste in Stuttgart. 2007 gründete er LAVA (Laboratory for Visionary Architecture) mit den Partnern Chris Bosse und Alexander Rieck. LAVA operiert als weltweites Netzwerk. Derzeit arbeiten 45 Architekten an Projekten in Europa, Saudi Arabien, China und Australien. Von 1997 bis 2007 war Tobias Wallisser als Creative Director bei UNStudio in Amsterdam für viele Projekte verantwortlich, darunter das Mercedes-Benz Museum in Stuttgart. Er hält weltweit Gastvorträge und hat zahlreiche Preise gewonnen.

Makoto Sei Watanabe ist Architekt und Gründer des Architekturbüros MAKOTO SEI WATANABE/ARCHITECTS' OFFICE. Außerdem ist er Professor am Space-Generating Lab der Fakultät für Urban Life Studies an der Tokyo City Universität. In seinen Arbeiten versucht er einerseits das Sinnliche festzuhalten, wie zum Beispiel das Gefühl der Bewegung oder taktile Eigenschaften einer Konstruktion, andererseits ist seine Arbeit von einem ständigen Versuch der Verbalisierung des Entwurfsaktes und seiner Übersetzung in Computerprogramme geprägt. WEB FRAME (2000) ist das Ergebnis seiner neuen INDUCTION DESIGN/ALGOrithmicDesign Methode, mit der er die weltweit erste computergenerierte architektonische Struktur entwarf, die sich speziellen Bedingungen anpasste. Ausgezeichnet wurde er mit dem Prize of AIJ 2002 und den ASLA Awards 1997. Er ist der Autor von INDUCTION DESIGN (2002/2004) und *ALGOrithmic Design EXecution and Logic"* (2012).

Jan Willmann ist Oberassistent an der Professur für Architektur und Digitale Fabrikation der ETH Zürich. Nach seinem Architekturstudium in Liechtenstein und Oxford arbeitete er von 2007–2010 als Universitätsassistent an der Universität Innsbruck am Lehrstuhl für Architekturtheorie von Prof. Ir. Bart Lootsma, wo er auch promovierte. Sein Forschungsschwerpunkt ist die historische und architekturtheoretische Auseinandersetzung mit dem digitalen Zeitalter in der Architektur, insbesondere die Verknüpfung von algorithmischen Entwurfs- und Materialisierungsprozessen. Seine neueste Veröffentlichung ist: *The Robotic Touch – How Robots Change Architecture* (2014), die erste Anthologie des Roboters in der Architektur, herausgegeben gemeinsam mit Fabio Gramazio und Matthias Kohler.

Chris Younès ist promovierte Philosophin und Professorin an der École Nationale Supérieure d'Architecture de Paris La Villette und der École Spéciale d'Architecture. Sie ist im Vorstand von GERPHAU, einem Forschungslabor, das sich mit dem Thema „Architektur, Stadt, Philosophie" beschäftigt und leitend in der internationalen Forschungsplattform PhilAU tätig. Des Weiteren ist sie die Leiterin des Graduiertenprogramms „Architecture des Milieux" und Mitglied des wissenschaftlichen Komitees von Europan. Ihre Forschungsinteressen liegen an der Schnittstelle zwischen Ästhetik und Ethik. Zu ihren aktuellsten Publikationen zählen *Le Territoire des Philosophes* (2009), *Espace et Lieux dans la pensée occidentale* (2012) und *Architecture et Perception* (2012).

Lernen von Splitterwerk?

Immer noch Lernen von Las Vegas.
Zur Autoikonographie und figurativen
Architektur der City of Entertainment (1)
Mark Blaschitz/Edith Hemmrich/
Katharina Köglberger
Wien, New York: Springer, 2013
Deutsch, 204 Seiten, 177 SW-Abbildungen,
broschiert
ISBN 978-3-99043-534-2
EUR 29,99

Unter dem Titel *Immer noch Lernen von Las Vegas* präsentieren Mark Blaschitz, Edith Hemmrich und Katharina Köglberger, Partner bzw. Mitarbeiterin des Grazer Büros Splitterwerk, die Ergebnisse einer vielfältigen Auseinandersetzung mit Las Vegas, der *City of Entertainment*. Im Mittelpunkt steht neben der tatsächlichen Stadt und ihrer konkreten Architektur vor allem auch die Neuinterpretation des 1968 von Robert Venturi, Denise Scott Brown und Steven Izenour durchgeführten Seminars an der Yale University und der daraus entstandenen berühmten Publikation *Learning from Las Vegas*, die 1972 erstmals veröffentlicht wurde.

Neuinterpretation ist dabei wörtlich zu nehmen, was schon die äußere Aufmachung des Buches verdeutlicht: Das 2013 bei Springer erschienene Werk bezieht sich in Layout und Covergestaltung direkt auf die deutschsprachige Erstveröffentlichung von *Learning from Las Vegas* im Jahr 1979 in der Reihe *Bauwelt Fundamente* des Vieweg-Verlags. In Bezug auf seine Entstehungsgeschichte gleicht *Immer noch Lernen von Las Vegas* ebenso seinem historischen Vorgänger. Genau wie exakt vierzig Jahre zuvor wurde Las Vegas 2008 im Rahmen eines Universitätsseminars – in diesem Fall an der Technischen Universität Graz – mit einer Gruppe Studierender besucht und analysiert. Diese Analyse bildet den ersten Teil der Publikation, während sich der zweite Teil den Projekten von Splitterwerk im Kontext der in Las Vegas gewonnenen Erkenntnisse widmet. Auch der Aufbau des Buches ist mit den beiden Hauptteilen also *Learning from Las Vegas* nachempfunden. Lediglich ein zusätzlicher zentraler Exkurs bricht die Symmetrie. Dieser Abschnitt wurde von Angelika Fitz und Klaus Stattmann verfasst und teilweise bereits in der *Bauwelt* 45/2009 veröffentlicht.

Inhaltlich korrelieren die beiden Hauptteile unterschiedlich mit ihren Pendants aus *Learning from Las Vegas*. Im ersten Teil – betitelt mit „Die dekorierte Ente oder Lernen von Las Vegas" – wird der Text des Vorbilds nach Möglichkeit beibehalten. Allein durch Streichungen, Ergänzungen und den Austausch von einzelnen Passagen, Phrasen oder stellenweise einzelnen Wörtern erfolgt eine inhaltliche Neuausrichtung bzw. Aktualisierung. Was die literarische Qualität betrifft, ist das Ergebnis der gewählten Strategie zwiespältig. Während die Möglichkeiten des Überschreibens, durch kleinste Ursachen größtmögliche Wirkungen zu erzielen, stellenweise virtuos ausgeschöpft werden, verursacht diese Methode stellenweise auch sperrige Passagen. Die Spuren der älteren Formulierungen und Satzkonstruktionen geraten mitunter zum Ballast.

Reviews

Learning from Splitterwerk?

Immer noch Lernen von Las Vegas:
Zur Autoikonographie und figurativen
Architektur der City of Entertainment (1)
Mark Blaschitz, Edith Hemmrich, and
Katharina Köglberger
Vienna and New York: Springer, 2013
German, 204 pages, 177 black-and-white
illustrations, Paperback
ISBN 978-3-99043-534-2
EUR 29.99

Under the title *Immer noch Lernen von Las Vegas* (Still Learning from Las Vegas), authors Mark Blaschitz, Edith Hemmrich, and Katharina Köglberger, who are partners or colleagues at the Splitterwerk firm in Graz, are presenting the results of their multifaceted study of Las Vegas, the "city of entertainment." Besides the city itself and its concrete architecture, the focus is first and foremost placed on a new interpretation of the Yale University seminar carried out by Robert Venturi, Denise Scott Brown, and Steven Izenour in 1968 and the famous publication that followed, *Learning from Las Vegas*, first released in 1972.

The phrase "new interpretation" is thus to be taken literally here, underscored by the external presentation of the book: both layout and cover design of this 2013 volume, published by Springer, directly reference the first German release of *Learning from Las Vegas* from the year 1979 as part of Vieweg-Verlag's series *Bauwelt Fundamente* (Building World Foundations). *Immer noch Lernen von Las Vegas* resembles its historical predecessor in regard to its genesis as well. In 2008, just as four decades before, to the very year, a university seminar on Las Vegas was held—this time at Graz University of Technology—and then the city was visited by a group of students for analysis. This study takes up the first section of the present publication, while the second section is dedicated to Splitterwerk projects in the context of the insight gained in Las Vegas. The organization of the book has likewise been adapted to mirror the two main sections of *Learning from Las Vegas*. Only a central excursus that has now been added disrupts the symmetry. This part was composed by Angelika Fitz and Klaus Stattmann and already published in part in the journal *Bauwelt* 45 (2009).

The two main parts also correspond to their counterparts from *Learning from Las Vegas* when it comes to content. In the first section—titled "Die dekorierte Ente oder Lernen von Las Vegas" (The Decorated Duck or Learning from Las Vegas)—the text of the 1972 book is maintained as closely as possible. The only content-related changes made to reframe or update the original material are achieved through deletions, additions, and the exchange of individual passages, phrases, or in certain cases individual words. In

Die Entwicklung der Argumente folgt zwangsweise *Learning from Las Vegas*, wobei die wesentlichen Begriffe und Konzepte durch ihre gegenwärtigen Entsprechungen ersetzt werden. Die Analyse der Stadt und ihrer Architektur zeigt, dass sich in den letzten Jahrzehnten entscheidende

Veränderungen in Bezug auf städtischen Maßstab und Gebäudetypologie vollzogen haben: War zur Zeit von *Learning from Las Vegas* die Ausrichtung auf den Autoverkehr wesentlich, so wird die heutige Stadt durch den Fußgängerverkehr geprägt. Die Casinos des *alten* Las Vegas, von Venturi/Scott Brown/Izenour als „dekorierte Schuppen" interpretiert, wurden in den letzten 40 Jahren durch Themenhotels ersetzt, bei Blaschitz/Hemmrich/Köglberger als „dekorierte Enten" bezeichnet.

Es ergeben sich folglich auch wesentliche Unterschiede in der Kontextualisierung und Bewertung der gemachten Beobachtungen. Waren für Venturi/Scott Brown/Izenour die Architekten der 1970er Jahre „auf das Räumliche hin erzogen"[1] und der reinen Form verpflichtet, als deren Gegenspieler sie das Symbolische propagieren, so erscheint vierzig Jahre später *Prozess* als zentraler Begriff, dessen Primat zugunsten des Figurativen zu brechen sei. Am Ende dieser Entwick-

1   Robert Venturi/Denise Scott Brown/Steven Izenour: *Lernen von Las Vegas. Zur Ikonographie und Architektursymbolik der Geschäftsstadt*, Braunschweig, Wiesbaden 1979, S. 16.

terms of literary quality, the chosen strategy leads to ambivalent results. While the possibility of using overwriting to achieve the greatest possible effects through the smallest means is masterly exploited in places, this method also gives rise to cumbersome passages. The traces of original formulations and sentence constructions sometimes become burdensome in the process.

The way the arguments evolve is forcibly aligned to *Learning from Las Vegas*, though the significant terms and concepts have been replaced by their present-day correlates. The analysis of the city and its architecture demonstrates the decisive changes that have come to pass in recent decades in regard to urban scale and building typology. For example, during the era of *Learning from Las Vegas*, a concentration on motor traffic was essential, while today the city is distinguished by pedestrian traffic. And the casinos of the *old* Las Vegas—interpreted as "decorated sheds" by Venturi/Scott Brown/Izenour—have been replaced by theme hotels in the last forty years, now deemed to be "decorated ducks" by

Blaschitz/Hemmrich/Köglberger.

It follows that there are also substantial differences in the contextualization and evaluation of the observations made. In the view of Venturi/Scott Brown/Izenour, the architects of the 1970s were "brought up on Space"[1] and were committed to pure form in opposition to the symbolism which they—Venturi/Soctt Brown/Izenour—propagated: forty years later the *process* emerges as the pivotal concept, the primacy of which must be broken in favor of the figurative. At the end of this development stands the "autoiconographic building as figure" (p. 37).

This concept presents the point of contact with the architecture of Splitterwerk, which is the nexus of the book's second main section. In contrast to *Learning from Las Vegas*, where an architectural theory of the ugly and the everyday is developed by example of architectural projects by the firm Venturi and Rauch, in *Immer noch Lernen von*

1   Robert Venturi, Denise Scott Brown, and Steven Izenour, *Learning from Las Vegas*, revised edition (1972; repr., Cambridge, MA, 2001), p. 7.

lung stehen „autoikonographische Gebäude als Figur" (S. 37).

Dieses Konzept bildet auch den Anknüpfungspunkt zur Architektur Splitterwerks, die im Fokus des zweiten Hauptteils des Buches steht. Anders als bei *Learning from Las Vegas*, wo anhand der Diskussion eigener Architekturprojekte von Venturi und Rauch eine Architekturtheorie des Hässlichen und Alltäglichen entwickelt wird, illustrieren hier die theoretischen Bezüge mehr das Œuvre Splitterwerks, das anhand zahlreicher Abbildungen präsentiert wird – selbstverständlich in *referenzierendem* Schwarz-Weiß gehalten. Der Text stellt ein fiktives Gespräch von Katharina Köglberger und Angela Fitz mit dem Grazer Büro dar, dessen Statements der Publikation *Splitterwerk. Whoop to the Duck! Es lebe die Ente!*[2] aus dem Jahr 2005 entnommen wurden. Besprochen werden wesentliche Konzepte Splitterwerks wie die *Multiinzidente Hülle* – ein neutraler Raum, der durch die Zuschaltung von Funktionen transformiert wird – und die Entwicklung einer *Figurativen Architektur*.

Der Schlüssel zu diesen Ansätzen liegt in der Neuinterpretation des Ornaments. Splitterwerk setzt in seinen Entwürfen dieses von der Moderne abgelehnte architektonische Element wieder ein, von der zweidimensionalen Gestaltung von Oberflächen bis hin zu dreidimensionalen Ornamenten des Stadtraums in Form von riesigen Figuren. Diese Figuren beziehen sich direkt auf das von Venturi/Scott Brown/Izenour formulierte Konzept der *Ente* – eines zeichenhaften Gebäudes – und stellen eine Weiterentwicklung dar, indem Splitterwerks *Enten* – eine Menagerie von Laubfröschen, Oktopussen, Fischen, Tigern etc. – ihre Zeichenhaftigkeit ablegen und somit zu *autoikonographischer* Architektur werden, die auch das gegenwärtige Las Vegas prägt.

Der Exkurs in der Mitte des Buches widmet sich dem 2009 eröffneten CityCenter, mit dem Las Vegas im Kontrast zu den Komplexen der Themenhotels ein neues urbanes Zentrum mit *authentischer* zeitgenössische Architektur bekommen sollte. Entstanden ist jedoch wiederum so etwas wie ein *Themenpark*, der Entwürfe von Stararchitekten wie Helmut Jahn, Norman Foster oder Daniel Libeskind sowie Skulpturen und Installation von Starkünstlern als Gesamtkunstwerk vermarktet. Architektur und Kunst dienen dabei vor allem auch dem *Branding*. Dazu passen auch die zahlreichen Flagshipstores diverser Luxusmarken, die in Las Vegas anzutreffen sind. Die Verfasser stellen insgesamt fest: „Las Vegas multipliziert und verdichtet nicht nur den Bilbaoeffekt, sondern auch die Logik des Flagshipstores […]" (S. 122).

Wie lässt sich diese aus drei so unterschiedlichen Abschnitten zusammengesetzte Publikation nun bewerten? Der erste Teil liefert sowohl eine kompakte Bestandsaufnahme der gegenwärtigen architektonischen Situation in Las Vegas als auch einen teilweise sehr aufschlussreichen aktuellen Kommentar zu Venturi/Scott Brown/Izenour. Über die Arbeiten Splitterwerks findet sich andernorts sicher Gehaltvolleres, einen guten ersten Einblick kann vorliegendes Buch jedoch geben. Bleibt noch der kurze zentrale Exkurs: Dieser erweist sich kurioserweise als die Passage, die vielleicht am meisten zu bieten hat. Hier werden die wohl interessantesten Fragen gestellt,

2   Mark Blaschitz u.a.: *Splitterwerk. Whoop to the Duck! Es lebe die Ente!*, Wien 2005.

3   Dieter Hoffmann-Axthelm: „Lernen von Las Vegas – hier in diesem Land" in: Robert Venturi/Denise Scott Brown/Steven Izenour: *Lernen von Las Vegas. Zur Ikonographie und Architektursymbolik der Geschäftsstadt*, Braunschweig, Wiesbaden 1979, S. 195.

Las Vegas the theoretical associations go beyond illustrating Splitterwerk's oeuvre, which is presented through numerous figures—in *referential* black-and-white, of course. The text represents a fictitious conversation conducted by Katharina Köglberger and Angela Fitz with the Graz firm, whose statements were culled from the 2005 publication *Splitterwerk: Whoop to the Duck! Es lebe die Ente!*[2] Here Splitterwerk's essential concepts are discussed, such as the *Multiinzidente Hülle* (Multi-Incident Shell)—a neutral space that is transformed through the activation of functions—and the development of a *figurative architecture*.

The key to these approaches lies in the new interpretation of the ornament. In its designs, Splitterwerk once again employs this architectural element that was spurned by modernism—from the two-dimensional drafting of surfaces to the three-dimensional ornamentation of urban space in the form of giant figures. These figures are a direct reference to the concept of the "duck" developed by Venturi/Scott Brown/Izenour, used to designate an emblematic building, and reflect a further development of the concept. Splitterwerk's "ducks"—a menagerie of tree frogs, octopuses, fish, tigers, etc.—cast off their symbolism to thereby become the *autoiconographic* architecture that distinguishes Las Vegas today.

The excursus in the middle of the book is devoted to the CityCenter, inaugurated in 2009, which was designed to give Las Vegas a new urban center featuring authentic contemporary architecture to contrast with the thematic hotel complexes. Yet what was created in its stead is something resembling a theme park, which—as a Gesamtkunstwerk—markets designs by *starchitects* like Helmut Jahn, Norman Foster, and Daniel Libeskind, as well as sculptures and installations by leading artists. Here, architecture and art predominantly serve the end of branding. Countless flagship stores of the diverse luxury brands to be found in Las Vegas fit right in here. In general, the authors ascertain that "Las Vegas multiplies and densifies not only the Bilbao effect, but also the logic of the flagship stores …" (p. 122).

How might we now assess this publication that is assembled from three markedly different parts? The first section offers both a compact survey of the current architectural situation in Las Vegas and up-to-date commentary on Venturi/Scott Brown/Izenour, which at times proves very illuminating. Though richer content on the work of Splitterwerk might be found elsewhere, the book reviewed here certainly offers a sound initial view. Now to the remaining brief central excursus: curiously enough, it turns out to be the passage that may well have the most to offer. It seems that the most interesting questions are posed here, though they remain unanswered for now. In summary, Dieter Hoffmann-Axthelm's statement in the epilogue of the German version of *Learning*

2   Mark Blaschitz et al., *Splitterwerk: Whoop to the Duck! Es lebe die Ente!* (Vienna, 2005).

3   Dieter Hoffmann-Axthelm, "Lernen von Las Vegas – hier in diesem Land," in Robert Venturi, Denise Scott Brown, and Steven Izenour, *Lernen von Las Vegas: Zur Ikonographie und Architektursymbolik der Geschäftsstadt* (Braunschweig and Wiesbaden, 1979), p. 195.

die jedoch vorerst unbeantwortet bleiben. Es gilt zusammenfassend also nach wie vor, was Dieter Hoffmann-Axthelm im Nachwort der deutschen Ausgabe von *Learning from Las Vegas* schreibt: „Der Versuch, von Las Vegas zu lernen, muss […] weitergehen."[3]

Stefan Fink

Kann Architektur Armut lindern? Ein besetztes Hochhaus als Wohnmodell für Mega-Cities

Torre David. Informal Vertical Communities (2)
Alfredo Brillembourg/Hubert Klumpner (Hg.)
Zürich: Lars Müller Publishers, 2013
Englisch, 416 Seiten, 406 Farbabbildungen,
Hardcover
ISBN 978-3-03778-298-9
EUR 45,00

Lange Zeit ist das soziale Leben und Wohnen in den städtischen Armutsvierteln – gemeinhin unter dem Oberbegriff *Slums* bekannt – als Diskussionsthema von unserer Gesellschaft und auch der Architektur gemieden worden. Über die Jahre sind diese Wohnviertel vor allem in den großen Metropolen der Schwellenländer zu riesigen Siedlungen angewachsen und erweisen sich als nahezu resistent gegenüber jeglichen Regulierungsmaßnahmen von außen. Heute leben Schätzungen zufolge etwa eine Milliarde Menschen weltweit in Slums oder sogenannten informellen Siedlungen. Und doch wissen wir noch immer relativ wenig darüber, wie das Leben der Menschen in den Armutsvierteln wirklich aussieht – wie etwa Infrastrukturen aufgebaut werden, gemeinschaftliche Einrichtungen entstehen oder das soziale Zusammenleben der Bewohner funktioniert. Vorurteile betreffend Elend, schlechte Hygiene und Kriminalität bestimmen unsere Vorstellung eines typischen Slums.

Gerade aus diesem Grund sind echte Einblicke in das Innenleben solcher informellen Gemeinschaften äußerst spannend und speziell für ArchitektInnen und StädteplanerInnen auch überaus lehrreich. Eine Tatsache, die den großen Reiz des vorliegenden Buches ausmacht, für das die Autoren Alfredo Brillembourg und Hubert Klumpner –

auch bekannt als Urban-Think Tank oder kurz U-TT – über ein Jahr lang intensiv die architektonische, räumliche und soziale Organisation eines von mittellosen Menschen besetzten Hochhauses inmitten von Caracas, dem sogenannten

---

from Las Vegas still applies today: "The attempt to learn from Las Vegas must … be continued."[3]

Stefan Fink (translation Dawn Michelle d'Atri)

Can Architecture Alleviate Poverty? An Occupied High-Rise as Housing Model for Megacities

Torre David: Informal Vertical Communities (2)
Alfredo Brillembourg and Hubert Klumpner (eds.)
Zurich: Lars Müller Publishers, 2013
English, 416 pages, 406 color illustrations,
hardcover
ISBN 978-3-03778-298-9
EUR 45.00

Social life and housing in poverty-stricken urban areas—generally known under the generic term "slums"—has long been a topic of discussion in our society, and also avoided in architectural circles. Over the years, these residential districts have grown into giant settlements, especially in the large metropolitan areas found in threshold countries, and they have proven to be almost completely resistant to any regulatory measures implemented from the outside. Today an estimated one billion people live in slums or so-called "informal communities" worldwide. Yet, we still remain relatively unaware of how life functions in these poverty areas—for instance, how infrastructures and community facilities are established or how social cohesion among inhabitants functions. Preconceptions about states of misery, poor hygiene, and criminality color our concept of a typical slum.

Precisely for this reason, true insight into the inner workings of such informal communities is highly fascinating and also exceedingly educational, especially for architects and urban planners. This fact is in part responsible for the strong appeal of the book under review here, *Torre David: Informal Vertical Communities*. The authors Alfredo Brillembourg and Hubert Klumpner—also known as the Urban-Think Tank or simply "U-TT"—spent over a year intensively studying the architectural, spatial, and social organization of a high-rise called Torre David, occupied by destitute individuals in Caracas, Venezuela. Their investigations were conducted not on a research basis at the Swiss Federal Institute of Technology in Zurich, but rather directly on site, at the heart of interaction and in collaboration with the residents.

The architectural history of Torre David alone would have been spectacular enough to fill a book: in 1990, during a period of economic upswing in Venezuela, the large-scale investor David Brillembourg (cousin of the architect Alfredo Brillembourg) arranged for the construction of a colossal high-rise in the capital city of Caracas which was to house the headquarters of a major bank, including an office complex and a hotel. In a state of near completion, the ambitious project met an abrupt end when Brillembourg passed away in 1993 and Venezuela was swept into financial crisis the following year. What remained is a building shell—almost finished but not quite ready for occupancy. Since the government is unable to fi-

Torre David, untersucht haben. Und zwar nicht von ihrer Forschungsbasis, der ETH Zürich, aus, sondern direkt vor Ort, inmitten des Geschehens und in Zusammenarbeit mit den BewohnerInnen.

Allein die Baugeschichte des *Torre David* wäre für ein Buch spektakulär genug: Der Großinvestor David Brillembourg (ein Cousin des Architekten Alfredo Brillembourg) veranlasst im Jahr 1990 im Zuge des wirtschaftlichen Aufschwungs Venezuelas in der Hauptstadt Caracas den Bau eines riesigen Hochhauses als Sitz einer Großbank inklusive Bürokomplex und Hotel. Beinahe fertiggestellt, kommt das ehrgeizige Projekt zu einem jähen Ende, als Brillembourg im Jahr 1993 verstirbt und im Folgejahr die Finanzkrise Venezuela voll erfasst. Was übrig bleibt ist ein Rohbau – so gut wie fertig, aber eben noch nicht bezugsfertig. Da sich in Folge auch die Regierung den Ausbau des Bauwerks nicht leisten kann, bleibt der 45 Stockwerke umfassende und knapp 200 Meter hohe Turm mitten in bester Lage leer und ungenutzt stehen.

Doch die gescheiterte Bauruine ist noch nicht das Ende der Geschichte des Torre David. Nach einem Dornröschenschlaf von über zehn Jahren wird das Gebäude im Jahr 2007 praktisch über Nacht von einigen Bewohnern aus den Armenvierteln auf der Flucht vor Überschwemmungen besetzt. Und hier beginnt die wirklich interessante Geschichte eigentlich erst. Innerhalb von kürzester Zeit suchen immer mehr Menschen auf der Suche nach besseren Lebensbedingungen Zuflucht im Hochhaus und bevölkern schrittweise die leerstehenden Etagen. Es entwickelt sich eine informelle vertikale Wohngemeinschaft, die heute ganze 3000 Bewohner umfasst. Unter der Leitung einer eigens gegründeten *Cooperative* bauen die Menschen mit geringsten Mitteln und viel Improvisationskunst ihren Turm zu einem funktionierenden Zuhause aus. So werden etwa neue Wege mittels Wanddurchbrüchen geschaffen und der fehlende Lift durch Brückenverbindungen zum angrenzenden Parkhaus inklusive Taxiservice in die oberen Stockwerke kompensiert. Über die 28 besetzten Etagen verteilen sich nicht nur Wohneinheiten – allesamt mit Strom und fließendem Wasser versorgt –, sondern auch öffentliche Einrichtungen wie Einkaufsläden, Friseursalons und Cafés. Im Erdgeschoß gibt es einen Basketballplatz, auf einer der oberen Dachterrassen ein Fitnessstudio – alles für die Gemeinschaft jederzeit frei zugänglich.

Diesen besonderen Einblick in die Geschichte und innere Struktur des Torre David bauen die Autoren geschickt über die vier Hauptkapitel des Buches auf, ohne dafür viele Worte zu benötigen. Die Basis bildet eine Abhandlung über die geschichtlichen und politischen Hintergründe des Bauwerks (Kapitel I: „Past", S. 70–130), welche den Kontext des Bauwerks klärt. Die Vermittlung der sozialen Organisation des Hochhauses (Kapitel II: „Present", S. 130–334) überlassen sie zum größten Teil den eindrucksvollen Fotografien von Iwan Baan, die den Blick von innen so richtig lebendig werden lassen. Über die Analyse hinausgehend entwickeln die Architekten gemeinsam mit den Bewohnern Zukunftsszenarien (Kapitel III: „Possibility", S. 334–360) für Torre David, welche die Wohnsituation nachhaltig verbessern sollen. Diese greifen – ganz der üblichen Vorgehensweise von U-TT folgend – nur minimal in den Ort ein, wie etwa der Vorschlag, den fehlenden Lift zu bauen oder Dachterrassen für Begrünung und Bewirtschaftung zu nutzen, und wären allesamt relativ kostengünstig und einfach realisierbar. Dennoch steht ihre Umsetzung infrage, wie auch die Autoren selbst kritisch anmerken, da erstens Investoren vonnöten wären und zweitens

nance the removal of the building, this perfectly situated tower, which rises two hundred meters high and boasts forty-five stories, has been left standing in a state of disuse.

Nonetheless, the story of Torre David does not end with this stranded, unfinished building. After deeply slumbering for over ten years, the building was occupied practically overnight in 2007, with a number of slum residents seeking shelter from flooding. And this is where the truly interesting story actually begins. Within a very short space of time, more and more people sought refuge in the high-rise, looking to improve their living conditions. The empty floors were populated in stages, and an informal, vertical housing community developed, which today comprises over three thousand inhabitants. Under the direction of a specially founded cooperative, people use minimal means and great improvisational skills to convert their tower into a well-functioning living environment. For example, new paths have been created by tearing down walls, and the missing elevators are offset by bridges built to the adjacent parking garage, which includes taxi service to the upper levels. Spread across the twenty-eight occupied floors are not only housing units—all supplied with electricity and running water—but also public facilities like retail stores, hair salons, and cafés. On the ground level there is a basketball court and on one of the upper roof terraces a fitness studio can be found—all freely accessible to the community at any time.

This in-depth look at the history and inner structure of Torre David is adeptly established by the authors through the four main chapters of the book, without excessive use words. The foundation is laid with discourse on the historical and political background of the building (Chapter I, "Past," pp. 70–130), which clarifies the context of the building. The social organization of the high-rise (Chapter II, "Present," pp. 130–334) is conveyed for the most part by the impressive photographs of Iwan Baan, which bring alive an inside view of the building. Moving beyond analysis, the architects developed future scenarios for Torre David together with the residents (Chapter III, "Possibility,"

pp. 334–60), with an aim to sustainably improve the housing situation. These scenarios only minimally intervene in the site—fully in line with the typical U-TT approach—and the suggestions, such as installing the absent elevator or using roof terraces for greening and cultivation, would all be relatively inexpensive and easy to implement. All the same, it is questionable as to whether they will actually be realized, as the authors themselves critically note. For one, it would be necessary to find willing investors, and secondly, the tight-knit community remains very skeptical about any intervention originating from the outside. It follows that the book closes not by mentioning the (im)possibilities for Torre David, but by once again elevating the topic to a more general level (Chapter IV, "Potential," pp. 360–84) where the informal community of the occupied high-rise is discussed as a referential example for developing potential solutions to address housing shortages in the megacities of threshold countries.

According to U-TT, this topic should be a top priority for architects and urban planners world-

die eingeschworene Gemeinschaft der Bewohner sehr skeptisch gegenüber allen Eingriffen von außen ist. So schließt das Buch auch nicht mit den (Un-)Möglichkeiten für Torre David, sondern hebt das Thema am Ende nochmal auf eine allgemeinere Ebene (Kapitel IV: „Potential", S. 360–384), welche die informelle Gemeinschaft des besetzten Hochhauses als ein Referenzbeispiel für mögliche Lösungen der Wohnungsnot in den Mega-Cities der Schwellenländer diskutiert.

Laut U-TT sollte dieses Thema eines der Hauptanliegen von ArchitektInnen und StädteplanerInnen weltweit sein, für das es soziale Verantwortung zu übernehmen gilt. Brillembourg und Klumpner selbst beschäftigen sich schon seit vielen Jahren mit Projekten in Wohngegenden, die von Armut und prekären Verhältnissen geprägt sind, und präsentieren ihre Erkenntnisse und Erfahrungen laufend in Publikationen und Vorträgen, mit dem Ziel, die Lebensverhältnisse sozial benachteiligter Schichten zu verbessern und allgemein zu politischer Veränderung und Demokratisierung beizutragen.

Mit der Veröffentlichung dieses Buches ist U-TT gewiss ein weiterer wichtiger Schritt in diese Richtung gelungen. Besonders, da das Buch

nicht nur inhaltlich, sondern auch grafisch eine gelungene Komposition darstellt. Fernab von Hochglanz führen Texte, Bilder, Grafiken und Pläne im gekonnten Wechsel zu einer lockeren Vermittlung des Inhalts. Die Gestaltung ist nicht nur ansprechend und innovativ (besonderes Highlight: die „grafische Novelle" von Andre Kitagawa zu Beginn des Buches, S. 52–80), sondern bleibt auch stets den Grundsätzen der Informationsvermittlung treu. Somit erfüllt das Buch für seine Hauptzielgruppe –ArchitektInnen und StädteplanerInnen – alle Bedingungen, um zur Pflichtlektüre zu werden.

Claudia Wrumnig

 ### Haltlose Architektur?

trans 22 – Haltung (3)
trans magazin Nr. 22, transRedaktion, ETH Zürich (Hg.)
Zürich: gta Verlag, 2013
Deutsch/Englisch/Französisch, 190 Seiten,
88 SW- und Farbabbildungen, broschiert

ISBN 978-3-85676-317-6
EUR 20,00

Stellen wir uns für einen Moment vor, wir befinden uns in einem Wohnzimmer im Prager Stadtteil Střešovice. Genauer gesagt in der Villa Müller, erbaut von einem gewissen Adolf Loos in den Jahren 1928 bis 1930. Hier findet man keinen einzigen Stuhl, der mit einem anderen in diesem Raum identisch ist. Sollten wir nun gebeten werden Platz zu nehmen, auf welchen Stuhl setzen wir uns? Keine leichte Entscheidung, stehen wir doch vor der Qual der Wahl. Selbstverständlich ist das in dieser Situation kein Zufall, sondern „one of Loos' fantastic intuitions", wie Francois Charbonnet in einem Interviewbeitrag der vorliegenden Publikation meint: „Everyone entering the room has to find his own seat and by doing so, one defines his position and his territory. […] Something similar takes place when defining your stance as an architect" (S. 128). Unterschiedliche Stühle verlangen uns eine entsprechende (Körper)Haltung ab. Ebenso verhält es sich in der Architektur. Oder sollte man besser sagen: So verhielt es sich?

Eben diese Frage diskutiert das halbjährlich erscheinende *trans magazin*, Fachmagazin der Archi-

wide as it is important that they assume responsibility for social issues. For many years now, Brillembourg and Klumpner have been personally involved with projects in residential areas that are subject to poverty and precarious conditions. The authors regularly present their findings and experiences in publications and lectures with the objective of improving the living conditions of socially disadvantaged groups and contributing to political change and democratization in general.

With the publication of this book, U-TT has doubtlessly succeeded in taking a further step in this direction, especially with its favorable composition, both in terms of content and graphics. A skillfully arranged assortment of texts, photographs, graphics, and blueprints that does without glossiness serves to convey the content with ease. The graphic design is not only appealing and innovative—a special highlight is the "graphic novella" by Andre Kitagawa near the front of the book, pp. 52–80—but also consistently faithful to the principles of communicating information. The publication thus fulfills all of the conditions

necessary to make it required reading material for its main target group: architects and urban planners.

Claudia Wrumnig
(translation Dawn Michelle d'Atri)

Stanceless Architecture?

trans 22 – Haltung (3)
trans magazin no. 22, transRedaktion,
ETH Zürich (ed.)
Zurich: gta Verlag, 2013
German/English/French, 190 pages,
88 b/w and color illustrations, paperback
ISBN 978-3-85676-317-6
EUR 20.00

Let's take a moment to imagine that we are in a living room in the Prague district of Střešovice, or more precisely, in the Villa Müller, built by a certain Adolf Loos between 1928 and 1930. Here we cannot find a single chair that is identical to another

in the room. If we were asked to be seated, which chair would we choose? Not an easy decision; we are faced with the agony of choice. Of course this is no coincidence here, but rather "one of Loos' fantastic intuitions," as Francois Charbonnet noted in an interview contribution to the publication under review here. "Everyone entering the room has to find his own seat and by doing so, one defines his position and his territory. … Something similar takes place when defining your stance as an architect" (p. 128). Different chairs require our (bodily) stance to conform to their respective shape. The same applies to architecture. Or should we perhaps rather say "the same applied"?

Precisely this question is discussed in the current issue of *trans magazin*, a specialist journal published biannually by the architecture department of the Swiss Federal Institute of Technology in Zurich (ETH Zürich). It investigates the topic of *stance* in present-day architectural discourse by juxtaposing various theories and approaches by international authors in the form of a collection of articles, interviews, and image contributions.

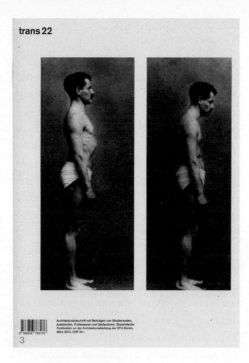

trans 22

tekturabteilung der ETH Zürich, in seiner aktuellen Ausgabe. Es behandelt das Thema *Haltung* im heutigen Architekturdiskurs, indem es in Form einer Sammlung von Artikeln, Interviews und Bildbeiträgen unterschiedliche Theorien und Ansätze internationaler Autoren gegenüberstellt.

Das Thema der *Haltung* blickt auf eine lange Tradition in der Architektur zurück und ist seit einigen Jahren, vor allem durch die Frage nach dem architektonischen Manifest als schriftlicher und besonders in den 1920er und 1960er Jahren beliebter Ausdruck einer klaren Position, wieder allgegenwärtig.

Das Interview mit dem Genfer Architekten François Charbonnet ist nur einer der vielen Diskussionsbeiträge und beschreibt den Kern der Problematik. Wie andere Autoren sieht Charbonnet die Ursache für die heute kaum vorhandene *Haltung* in der zunehmenden Orientierungslosigkeit und dem mangelnden Verantwortungsgefühl der Architekten (S. 130). Auch Philip Ursprungs Artikel *Architektur politisch machen?* stellt auf Basis einer kurzen Geschichte zum architektonischen Manifest die aktuelle Situation kritisch dar (S. 22) und hinterfragt so, wie auch Miroslav Šik und Lindsay Blair Howe, die *Haltung* nicht nur in der Architekturpraxis, sondern vor allem in der Lehre. Die verschiedenen Diskussionsstränge werden durch den inhaltlichen Aufbau der Publikation geschickt und kurzweilig miteinander verwoben. Dies geschieht besonders durch die abwechslungsreiche Gegenüberstellung verschiedener

Publikationsformen wie Interview, Artikel oder Fotoessay, aber auch fachübergreifender Sichtweisen. So wird *Haltung* auch nicht-architektonisch, z.B. rein physikalisch, betrachtet, wie im erhellenden Beitrag *We are all quantum made* der Physikerin Bonnie Qian (S. 82).

Interviews mit namenhaften Architekten verschiedener Generationen, wie Luigi Snozzi, Peter Zumthor und Jacques Herzog, stellen als subjektiv gezeichnete Bilder ein gutes Gegengewicht zu den wissenschaftlich-theoretischen Texten dar. Aus der Feder von Studierenden kommen einige kreative, künstlerisch-literarische Beiträge, welche durch ihre provokante Art zur Reflexion anregen. Ein hervorragendes Beispiel hierfür ist der Beitrag *Spending Days in Non-Topia*, der mit Hilfe tagebuchartiger Beschreibungen die aktuelle Situation als eine voller Leere und Haltlosigkeit beschreibt. Gestrandet auf einer Insel des Nicht-Raumes, wo alles verloren scheint (S. 105) und nur die eigene Vorstellungskraft den letzten Ausweg darstellt, kommt die Autorin zu dem Schluss: „Sitting on my armchair, staring at my Non-topia's endless horizon, I realize that I cannot reconstruct the world. What I should begin reconstructing is the (damaged) territory of my imaginary" (S. 107).

The topic of *stance* has enjoyed a long tradition in architecture. In more recent times it has once again become ubiquitous, especially due to the architectural manifesto as the written expression of a clear position, which was particularly favored between the 1920s and 1960s.

The interview with the Geneva-based architect François Charbonnet is but one of many discussion contributions and describes the heart of the problem issues. Like some of the other authors, Charbonnet locates the cause for today's strong lack of *stance* in an increasing disorientation and insufficient sense of responsibility on the part of architects (p. 130). Philip Ursprung's article "Architektur politisch machen?" (Making Architecture Political?) critically portrays the current situation by relating a brief story about the architectural manifesto (p. 22): He thus questions, as do Miroslav Šik and Lindsay Blair Howe, the role of *stance* not only in architectural practice but most especially in architectural instruction. The various discursive threads are adeptly and divertingly interwoven through the structure of content within the pub-

lication. This is notably achieved with the varied juxtaposition of different publication forms, such as interview, article, or photo essay, but also with the integration of interdisciplinary perspectives. Thus *stance* is also viewed as non-architectural, that is, as purely bodily connoted, such as in the eye-opening contribution "We are all quantum made" by physicist Bonnie Qian (p. 82).

Interviews with renowned architects of different generations, including Luigi Snozzi, Peter Zumthor, and Jacques Herzog, as subjectively sketched pictures, offer a fitting counterweight to the scholarly, theoretical texts. A number of creative, artistic/literary contributions are penned by students, prompting reflection with their provocative style. An outstanding example of this is the contribution "Spending Days in Non-Topia" featuring diary-like descriptions, which describes the present situation as characterized by utter vacuity and stancelessness. Stranded on the isle of nonspace, where everything seems lost (p. 105) and one's own imagination is the last resort, the author reaches this conclusion: "Sitting on my armchair,

staring at my Non-topia's endless horizon, I realize that I cannot reconstruct the world. What I should begin reconstructing is the (damaged) territory of my imaginary" (p. 107).

The fact that the question of *stance* is giving the architectural community such headaches is demonstrated not only by this controversial debate but also by previous research approaches to the topic. The latter have proven to be rare, and certain publications hardly warrant mention, for example, an issue of *ICON Magazine* dedicated to the theme of the manifesto while taking the superficial style of a glossy magazine, which under the title "50 Manifestos"[1] invited the same number of authors to reveal their "stance." While events like the *Manifesto Marathon*[2] and the GSAPP conference *What happened to the architectural mani-*

1   "50 Manifestos," *Icon Magazine* 50 (August 2007).

2   *Manifesto Marathon*, Serpentine Gallery, London, October 18–19, 2008.

Dass die Haltungsfrage der Architektenschaft Bauchschmerzen bereitet, zeigen nicht nur diese kontroverse Debatte, sondern auch die bisherigen Forschungsansätze zum Thema. Diese erweisen sich als rar: Kaum Erwähnung verdienen Publikationen wie z.B. eine Ausgabe des *ICON Magazine*, die sich ganz im Stil der Oberflächlichkeit eines Hochglanzmagazins dem Thema des Manifests widmet und unter dem Titel *50 Manifestoes*[1] ebenso viele Autoren einlädt, ihre „Haltung" preiszugeben. Veranstaltungen wie der *Manifesto Marathon*[2] und die GSAPP Konferenz *What happened to the architectural manifesto?*[3] bemühen sich um eine fundierte Auseinandersetzung, zeichnen sich jedoch eher durch ihren fragwürdigen Event-Charakter und fehlende Internationalität aus. Das Thema *Haltung* wird zunehmend und kontrovers diskutiert, jedoch leider bisher nicht in Form einer wissenschaftlich ernstzunehmenden Publikation angegangen. Vor allem fällt bei allen das Fehlen der studentischen Perspektive auf.

Natürlich vermag auch die nun vorliegende Publikation als Zeitschrift (noch) keine tiefgehende Forschung zu leisten, doch stellt sie, verglichen mit den bisherigen Veröffentlichungen, in vielerlei Hinsicht eine erfreuliche Ausnahme dar. Durch die gute Mischung aus verschiedenen Beiträgen, die sich nicht nur in Form und Ansatz unterscheiden, sondern auch durch Autoren unterschiedlichen Alters, Fachgebiets und Status, kann das Thema breiter und tiefgehender diskutiert werden. Es eröffnen sich verschiedene interessante Perspektiven, die interdisziplinär miteinander in einen Dialog treten. Ein zudem schlichtes, aber dennoch ansprechendes Layout wird der Sache gerecht, macht das Lesen leicht, kurzweilig und fokussiert die wichtigen inhaltlichen Aspekte. Der Leser wird so bei Laune gehalten und zum Mitdenken angeregt. Einziger Wehmutstropfen: Fast alle beteiligten Autoren kommen aus der Schweiz bzw. dem französischen Sprachraum oder stehen in einem Verhältnis zur ETH. Dies verursacht beim kritischen Leser möglicherweise ein leichtes Stirnrunzeln und so verwundert dann, obwohl laut Herausgeber international ausgerichtet, die durch die Zeitschrift vollzogene Ausgrenzung der nicht französisch-sprachigen Leserschaft auch nicht mehr.[4]

Der Tatsache, dass die interessante und abwechslungsreich strukturierte Publikation eine hervorragende Möglichkeit bietet, sich mit dem Thema der *Haltung* auseinanderzusetzen, tut dies jedoch keinen Abbruch. Letztlich bleibt es jedoch bei der in der Kurzinformation des Verlages bereits angekündigten *Momentaufnahme*. Die Frage der *Haltung* in der Architektur bleibt offen. Doch möglicherweise lässt uns die Publikation aufhorchen und vermag uns zu sensibilisieren. Vielleicht betrachten wir ja unsere eigene *Haltung* nun in einem inneren Spiegel, in einem größeren Zusammenhang? Denn die mangelnde *Haltung* ist nicht nur ein architektonisches, sondern ein globales Problem. Die aktuelle Weltpolitik eines reinen Pragmatismus, allgemein Neoliberalismus genannt, zeichnet sich durch eine ausschließlich auf wirtschaftlichen Profit fokussierte, opportunistische Struktur aus. Sie ist Ausdruck des Verzichts klarer Positionen zugunsten einer allseits geforderten Flexibilität. Dies spiegelt sich in der zeitgenössischen Architektur wider und zeigt sich

1. Icon Magazine No. 50: *50 Manifestoes*, London 2007.
2. Serpentine Gallery: *Manifesto Marathon*, London, 18.–19. Oktober 2008.
3. The Graduate School of Architecture, Planning and Preservation, Columbia University: *What happened to the architectural manifesto?*, New York, 18. November 2011.
4. Einige Texte sind auf Französisch abgedruckt – ohne (englische) Übersetzung.

festo?[3] have sought to pursue a substantiated investigation of the topic, they have been distinguished by a questionable event character and a lack of internationality. *Stance* as a theme has lately been increasingly discussed, often in a controversial manner, but it has not yet been tackled in the form of a serious scholarly publication. What is more, all previous approaches have been lacking a student perspective.

Obviously the publication we are reviewing, in its form as magazine, does not (yet) need to conduct in-depth research; however, it does represent a gratifying exception to previous publications, in many respects. The topic is more broadly and profoundly discussed here thanks to a favorable blend of contributions that differ not only in form and approach, but also in terms of authors from divergent age groups, specialty fields, and status. Various interesting perspectives open up and engage in reciprocal, interdisciplinary dialogue. Moreover, a sober yet appealing layout does justice to the theme, facilitates easy and enjoyable reading, while keeping the focus on important content-related aspects. As such, the publication caters to the reader and encourages us to actively think in the process. There is only one downside: almost all participating authors originate from Switzerland and other French-speaking areas or are directly involved with the ETH Zürich. This is likely to elicit a slight frown on the part of critical readers, and so it is not really astonishing that the magazine, despite the editors' claim to an international orientation, excludes the non-French-speaking audience throughout the publication.[4]

Certainly, this does not detract from the fact that this interesting and diversely structured publication offers an excellent opportunity to explore the topic of *stance*. Ultimately, it "dares to investigate," as is announced in the snippet provided by the publisher—yet the question of *stance* in architecture remains open. Perhaps the publication encourages us to listen attentively and sets out to sensitize us. Or maybe we are now gazing at our own *stance* in an inner mirror, in a broader context? Indeed, lack of *stance* is not only an architectural but also a global problem. The current weltpolitik of pure pragmatism, generally known as neoliberalism, is distinguished by an opportunistic structure that is solely focused on economic profit. It embodies a sacrificing of clear positions in favor of the flexibility demanded from all sides. This is reflected by contemporary architecture and is apparent in the soulless countenances of capitalist metropolises. The great utopias of the twentieth century are long gone. A scarcity of pioneering, venturesome projects rich in ideas appears to be undisputed. In the eyes of architectural theorist Ana Jeinić, however, this has arisen from the crisis of neoliberalism: "… another, much deeper and more concerning one: the crisis of (any) alternative project."[5] She discovers the potential to change

3. *What happened to the architectural manifesto?*, The Graduate School of Architecture, Planning and Preservation, Columbia University, New York, November 18, 2011.
4. Some texts are printed in French without providing (English) translations.
5. Ana Jeinić, "Neoliberalism and the Crisis of the Project … in Architecture and Beyond," in *Is There (Anti-)Neoliberal Architecture*, architektur + analyse vol. 3, ed. Ana Jeinić and Anselm Wagner (Berlin, 2013), p. 64.

in den seelenlosen Gesichtern kapitalistischer Großstädte. Die großen Utopien des 20. Jh. sind Vergangenheit. Der Mangel an ideenreichen, zukunftsweisenden und wagenden Projekten scheint unbestritten. Für die Architekturtheoretikerin Ana Jeinić folgt jedoch aus der Krise des Neoliberalismus „[…] another, much deeper and more concerning one: the crisis of (any) alternative project."[5] Hier sieht sie in der Architektur als „*the* discipline of the project (*Entwurf*)"[6] das Potenzial, diesen Status quo zu ändern. Ihrer Meinung nach könnte dies durch innovative Projekte, die einerseits konkrete Zukunftsvisionen entwerfen, andererseits aber stets der Veränderung und Transformation den nötigen Raum lassen, geschehen. Solche Projekte sind durch eine klare Positionierung in der Lage, dem System des Neoliberalismus eine ernstzunehmende Alternative gegenüberzustellen – und das nicht zuletzt durch das architektonische Manifest. Mit der Frage der *Haltung* schließt sich somit der Kreis wieder.

5 Jeinić, Ana: „Neoliberalism and the Crisis of the project … in Architecture and beyond", in: Ana Jeinić/ Anselm Wagner (Hg.): *Is There (Anti-) Neoliberal Architecture?*, architektur + analyse 3, Berlin 2013, S. 64.

6 Ebd., S. 67.

Und plötzlich befinden wir uns wieder in einem einfachen Wohnzimmer: Was suche ich mir für einen Stuhl? Nehme ich einen Le Corbusier? Vielleicht ziehe ich einen Eames vor? Oder baue ich mir gar meinen Eigenen? Letztlich ist das alles nicht von Bedeutung. Eine *Haltung* haben wir immer. Das Wichtigste und zugleich Schwierigste ist aber, sich dieser bewusst zu werden und zu ihr zu stehen – egal auf welchem „Stuhl" man sitzt! Eine klare *Haltung*, sei es in Form eines Manifests, eines Projekts oder einer Architektur, ist stets ein zur Diskussion gestellter Entwurf, eine „positiv formulierte These" (S. 188), die Kommunikation erzeugt, stets neu hinterfragt und geprüft werden will, und so die Position stärkt. „Die klare Haltung ist damit unabdingbare Grundlage jeder Form von Architektur überhaupt", wie Andreas Thuy in seinem Beitrag *Wir sind Architekten* richtig erkennt (S. 189). Eines sollte uns jedoch klar sein: Etwas zu diskutieren und zu fordern ist eine Sache, es tatsächlich zu tun eine ganz andere.

In diesem Sinne wirkt der Beitrag *Mit Haltung in Käfighaltung* von Manfred Wolff-Plottegg (S. 114ff.) bezogen auf die Frage der *Haltung* in der Architektur fast wie ein längst überfälliger Kommentar beißender Ironie: Sein Text, der sich am meisten von einer klaren *Haltung* distanziert, ist das einzige Manifest in der Publikation.

Florian Engelhardt

Nach der Bilbaoisierung

Kultur:Stadt/Culture:City (4)
Wilfried Wang (Hg.) für die Akademie der Künste, Berlin
Zürich: Lars Müller Publishers, 2013
Deutsch oder Englisch, 232 Seiten,
406 Abbildungen, Hardcover
ISBN 978-3-03778-336-8 (Deutsch)
ISBN 978-3-03778-335-1 (Englisch)
EUR 40,00

Nahezu jede Stadt, die etwas auf sich hält, hat eines. Und alle, die noch keines haben, hätten gerne eines. Ein extravagantes Museum oder Theater, am besten von einem *Star*-Architekten, das, so die Mär der letzten 20 Jahre, alle Probleme lösen könne. Ikonische Kulturbauten bewirken ohne Zwei-

---

this status quo in architecture "as *the* discipline of the project (*Entwurf*)."[6] In her opinion, this could transpire through innovative projects which, on the one hand, draft concrete visions of the future, but which, on the other, always allow the necessary space for change and transformation. Due to clear positioning, such projects are capable of providing a feasible alternative to the system of neoliberalism—not least through the architectural manifesto. With the question of *stance*, the circle thus comes to a close.

And suddenly we find ourselves back in a simple living room: What kind of chair should I select? One by Le Corbusier? Or would I prefer one by Eames? Or maybe I could even build my own? In the end, none of this matters. We will always have a *stance*. What is most important and, at the same time, most difficult is becoming aware of and standing up for this fact—regardless of the "chair" we're sitting in! A clear *stance*—be it in the form of a manifesto, a project, or archi-tecture—is always a draft that has been put up for discussion, a "positively phrased hypothesis" (p. 188) that gives rise to communication, that wants to be continually challenged and scrutinized, and that hence strengthens the position. "The clear stance is thus the inevitable foundation for absolutely every form of architecture" (p. 189), as Andreas Thuy correctly discerns in his contribution "Wir sind Architekten" (We Are Architects). But one thing should be clear to us: discussing and demanding something is one thing; actually doing it is something entirely different.

In this sense, the contribution "Mit Haltung in Käfighaltung" (With Stance in Cage Culture) by Manfred Wolff-Plottegg (pp. 114–15), related to the question of *stance* in architecture, almost seems to be a long-overdue commentary of caustic irony: his text, which distances itself from a clear *stance* most of all, is the only manifesto in the publication.

Florian Engelhardt
(translation Dawn Michelle d'Atri)

After Bilbaoization

Kultur:Stadt/Culture:City (4)
Wilfried Wang (ed.) for the Academy of Arts, Berlin
Zurich: Lars Müller Publishers, 2013
German or English, 232 pages,
406 illustrations, hardcover
ISBN 978-3-03778-336-8 (German)
ISBN 978-3-03778-335-1 (English)
EUR 40.00

Almost every city that takes pride in itself has one. And all cities that are not yet so lucky would like to have one. An extravagant museum or theater, preferably designed by a *starchitect*—an architectural structure to solve all problems, or so the myth of the last twenty years goes. Without doubt, iconic cultural buildings occasion changes in urban life, in public and social space, and engender signs that have a ripple effect beyond the city. Yet these structures are anything but uncontroversial; "flashy container[s] without much content" (p. 61) is what the architectural historian and critic William Curtis calls

fel Veränderungen des städtischen Lebens, des öffentlichen und sozialen Raums und schaffen Zeichen, die über die Stadt hinaus wirken. Aber sie sind alles andere als unumstritten; „auffällige Container ohne großen Inhalt" (S. 61) nennt sie etwa der Architekturhistoriker und -kritiker William Curtis. Das Buch *Kultur:Stadt* widmet sich – wie auch die gleichnamige, vom Architekten Matthias Sauerbruch konzipierte Ausstellung – der Frage, wie sich kulturelle Angebote und deren Manifestation als gebaute Stadt als Faktor urbaner Entwicklung äußern. Große Kulturbauten werden mit alternativen Kultur- und Kunstprojekten, mit „von unten" organisierten Initiativen konfrontiert. Der Fokus liegt dabei auf „Post-Bilbao-Strategien": verschiedenen Ansätzen der Integration von Kultureinrichtungen in be- oder entstehende soziale Strukturen.

Während in der Ausstellung die einzelnen Projekte im Vordergrund stehen, werden ihnen im vorliegenden Buch kontextualisierende Texte vorangestellt. Herausgeber Wilfried Wang, Autor zahlreicher Mono- und Topografien zur Architektur des 20. Jahrhunderts, versammelte, wie schon der thematisch verwandte, ebenfalls von der Berliner Akademie der Künste publizierte Band *Wiederkehr*

der Landschaft (2010, Hg. Donata Valentien), eine interdisziplinäre Runde an Autoren wie Ricky Burdett, Jochen Gerz, Michael Mönninger oder Richard Sennett, die sich kritisch verschiedenen Schwerpunkten widmen. Zwischen den rund ein Drittel des Buches einnehmenden Texten und den Projekten lassen sich immer wieder Querverbindungen herstellen, ein nicht-lineares Lesen macht hier durchaus Sinn. Die 37 Projekte, von ikonenhaften Bauten über teils unscheinbare Interventionen und Umdeutungen bis hin zu sozialen Kunstprojekten, sind gut aufgearbeitet und umfangreich illustriert. Positiv stechen Details wie die Angabe des Eintrittspreises in Kombination mit dem Durchschnittseinkommen der jeweiligen Region ins Auge. Schade ist hingegen, dass die sehenswerten, anlässlich der Ausstellung von jungen Filmemachern zu vielen der Projekte gedrehten Autorenfilme nicht verfügbar sind.

Mit der Ikone der ikonischen Gebäude, dem Guggenheim Museum in Bilbao (wenn es auch nicht der erste ins Ikonische überhöhte Kulturbau ist, diese Rolle kommt Jørn Utzons Opernhaus in Sydney zu), setzte Frank Gehry 1997 gezielt ein spektakuläres Zeichen, das die Transformation der Stadt symbolisieren sollte und sie erfolgreich auf

die kulturelle (und touristische) Weltkarte setzte. Der viel zitierte und kopierte Bilbao-Effekt wird in *Kultur:Stadt* zugleich nachgewiesen und entzaubert: Das Museum war nur ein Teil einer umfassenden und komplexen Stadterneuerung mit einem hohen Anteil an Infrastrukturmaßnahmen. Die heutige *Signature*-Architektur hingegen tendiert dazu, Stadt und Stadtplanung zu ersetzen.

---

them. The book *Culture:City* is dedicated—as is the eponymous exhibition conceptualized by Matthias Sauerbruch—to the question of how cultural policy and its manifestation as a built city comes to be expressed as a factor in urban development. Large cultural buildings are challenged by cultural and artistic projects, by initiatives organized "from the bottom up." Here the focus lies on "post-Bilbao strategies": various approaches to integrating cultural institutions into existing or developing social orders.

While the exhibition highlights individual projects, the accompanying publication places emphasis on contextualizing texts. The book's editor, Wilfried Wang, author of numerous monographs and topographies on architecture of the twentieth century, has brought together an interdisciplinary circle of authors, including Ricky Burdett, Jochen Gerz, Michael Mönninger, and Richard Sennett, who critically explore various main topics—similar to the thematically related volume *Return of Landscape* (2010, ed. Donata Valentien), also released by Berlin's Akademie der Künste. Amid the

texts and projects that take up roughly one third of the book, cross-connections are repeatedly established; a nonlinear reading experience certainly makes sense here. The thirty-seven projects—ranging from iconic buildings to partly nondescript interventions and reinterpretations or social art projects—are favorably treated and comprehensively illustrated. Eye-catching details like the mention of entrance fees in combination with the average income of the respective region make a positive impression. On the other hand, it is too bad that the "auteur films," specially created for the exhibition by young filmmakers on many of the projects, are not available in the book.

In 1997 Frank Gehry set a spectacular example in creating the icon of all iconic buildings, the Guggenheim Museum in Bilbao (although it wasn't the first excessively iconic cultural building made, which is a distinction that must go to Jørn Utzon's opera house in Sydney). The Bilbao museum was designed to symbolize the transformation of the city and successfully positioned it on the cultural (and tourist) world map. In *Culture:City*, the fre-

quently cited and copied "Bilbao effect" is substantiated and demystified in equal measure: the museum was only one part of a complex and extensive urban renewal project that included a large number of infrastructural measures. In contrast, the signature architecture of today tends to replace both city and urban planning.

Is culture only a pretense for "buildings in search of the limelights?" (p. 11). The global competition to draw tourists and prestige disrupts the actual tasks to be carried out in everyday cultural business. In the quest to build ever bigger icons that are more expensive and extravagant, small cultural institutions are inevitably marginalized, because the budget for programs, presentations, and local cultural practice is lacking. Arising in their stead are cultural giants which, to invoke the diction of neoliberalism, are "too big to fail."

The contributions found in *Culture:City*, many of which have already been published elsewhere, attempt to more or less closely approximate the term "culture," a word that has enjoyed inflationary use and has become increasingly vague. The

Ist Kultur nur mehr der Vorwand für „nach Aufmerksamkeit heischende Bauten?" (S. 11) Der globale Wettbewerb um Touristen und Prestige verzerrt die eigentlichen Aufgaben des kulturellen gesellschaftlichen Alltags. Im Streben, immer größere, teurere und extravagantere Ikonen zu bauen, werden kleinere Kultureinrichtungen marginalisiert, das Budget für Programm, Bespielung und lokale kulturelle Praxis fehlt. An deren Stelle entstehen Kulturriesen, die, in der Diktion des Neoliberalismus, *too big to fail* sind.

Unterschiedlich konsequent versuchen die teilweise schon andernorts publizierten Beiträge, sich dem inflationär verwendeten und schwammig gewordenen Begriff „Kultur" anzunähern und ihn in einer Welt zu positionieren, die sozialen nur allzu oft durch ökonomischen Wert ersetzt. Während ein Teil der Autoren die Gefahr der Ökonomisierung von Kultur beschwört, operieren andere mit Begriffen wie Kreativwirtschaft und Kulturindustrie, Standortfaktor und Umwegrentabilität. So entsteht eine Inkonsistenz, die sich nicht nur im thematischen Fokus der Texte, sondern auch in Argumentationsstil, Abstraktionsgrad und wissenschaftlicher Tiefe äußert.

Auch die unvermeidliche Gentrifizierung bleibt nicht unerwähnt, wobei die Kreativen und Kulturschaffenden gleichermaßen als Täter und Opfer identifiziert werden. Große Kultur-Neubauten verdrängen eben genauso Kultur „von unten", die rohe, uneindeutige und vor allem billige Räume in der Stadt braucht. Ein solcher sozialer Raum für Kunst ist das Inner-City Arts in einem der ärmsten Stadtteile von Los Angeles, das über 13 Jahre schrittweise einen geschützten Ort für Jugendliche etablieren konnte. Gänzlich von der baulichen Repräsentation losgelöst Projekte wie die Nachbarschaftsinitiative Detroit Soup oder das partizipative Kunstprojekt *2–3 Straßen* bilden den Kontrapunkt zu den marktwirksamen Ikonen. Sie sind deren genaues Gegenteil: prozesshaft und absolut unspektakulär. Im lesenswerten Konzept zu *2–3 Straßen* skizziert Jochen Gerz u.a. die (Rück-)Verwandlung des Kunstwerks in Nichtkunst und kreative Praxis.

Die *Branding*-Architektur hingegen „brennt nicht mehr heterotopische Löcher in die Textur der Stadt", meint Michael Mönninger, sondern „generiert Fremd-Orte mit exzessivem Objektcharakter" (S. 56). Er hält ihnen aber die „kritische Dekonstruktion der versteinerten Verhält-

nisse" zugute, die sich jedoch zu einem Architektur-*Branding* entwickelt hat, das „systemstabilisierend die Aufmerksamkeitsökonomie der Markenwerbung, Standortpolitik und Kulturindustrie" (S. 56) bedient. Nicht wenige jüngere Bibliotheksbauten bewegen sich indes erfolgreich im Spannungsfeld von „marktwirksamer Geste und dem Wunsch nach Authentizität" (S. 18) und werden zu Orten des Austauschs und zu einem Teil des öffentlichen Raums. Die durchaus ikonische Seattle Central Library (OMA) wurde für viele Obdachlose zum Ersatz für ein Zuhause und die Parque Bibliotheca España (Giancarlo Mazzanti) im kolumbianischen Medellín bietet den Bewohnern eines von Armut geprägten Arbeiterviertels Zugang zur Wissensgesellschaft und verleiht dem Quartier eine neue Identität. Der umstrittene Metropol Parasol von Jürgen Mayer H. nimmt weder in Maßstab, Material noch Form Bezug zur Altstadt von Sevilla, scheint aber die Anziehungskraft einer starken Form zu belegen: Er wurde zum Kristallisationspunkt sozialer Proteste und hat damit seine Berechtigung als politischer Raum gefunden.

Allein aufgrund der gut gewählten und präsentierten Projekte lohnt sich ein ausführlicher

---

contributions try to position it in a world where social value is all too often replaced by economic value. While some of the authors cite the dangers inherent to the economization of culture, others operate with concepts like creative business and cultural industry, location factor and detour profitability. This fosters an inconsistency that is expressed not only in the thematic focus of the text material, but also in terms of argumentational style, degree of abstraction, and scholarly depth.

The unavoidable gentrification is also mentioned, whereby culture-promoting and creative individuals are identified as both perpetrator and victim. New large-scale cultural buildings are indeed prone to suppress precisely this "bottom-up" culture that relies on unrefined, ambiguous, and most of all inexpensive urban space. Such a social venue for art is Inner-City Arts, situated in one of the poorest districts in Los Angeles. Over the course of thirteen years it has succeeded in establishing, step by step, a sheltered site for youth. Projects that are utterly detached from architectural representation, such as Detroit Soup neighborhood

initiative or the participative art project *2–3 Streets* in Germany's Ruhr region, form a counterpoint to those icons facilitating high market impact. They are in fact the exact opposite: in the concept paper on *2–3 Streets*, which is very worth reading, Jochen Gerz and others detail the conversion of the artwork (back) into non-art and creative practice.

The branding architecture, in turn, "no longer burns heterotopic holes in the fabric of the city" as Michael Mönninger notes. Rather, it "generates strange spaces of otherness" with „excessive object character" (p. 56). However, he grants them the "critical deconstruction of a fossilized society" that has developed into an architecture branding, which draws on the "attention economy of advertising, commerce, and the cultural industries" in a system-stabilizing way (ibid.). Meanwhile, quite a few more recent library buildings are posited in the ambivalent realm of "market-oriented gestures and a certain desire for authenticity" (p. 17) and are becoming places of exchange and thus a part of public space. The by all means iconic Seattle Central

Library (OMA) has become a surrogate home for many homeless, while the Parque Bibliotheca España (Giancarlo Mazzanti) in the Columbian city of Medellín offers the residents of an impoverished working neighborhood access to the knowledge society and imbues the urban quarter with a new identity. The controversial Metropol Parasol by Jürgen Mayer H. eschews any kind of reference to Sevilla's old town, be it in terms of scale, material, or form, yet it appears to confirm the appealing force of a strong form: the structure has turned into a crystallization point for social protest and has thus legitimately become political space.

Culture:City is well worth an elaborate perusal on the basis of the well-selected and—presented projects alone. The texts add a critical perpective to the neutral descriptive texts and generate a context that incidentally ends up being more broad than in-depth. Encompassing a wide spectrum, this book presents an introduction to the themes and problems related to iconic (cultural) architecture. It sketches the ways in which these structures ide-

Blick in *Kultur:Stadt*. Die Texte ergänzen die neutral gehaltenen Beschreibungen um eine kritische Perspektive und erzeugen einen Kontext, der allerdings mehr in die Breite als in die Tiefe führt. Das ein weites Spektrum aufspannende Buch stellt einen Einstieg in die Thematik und Problematik ikonischer (Kultur-)Bauten dar und skizziert, wie diese im Idealfall kulturelles Leben und Aktivitäten zur Entfaltung bringen – und wie sich andererseits Städte und Architekten im Wettbewerb um flüchtige mediale Aufmerksamkeit immer wieder zu Extravaganzen hinreißen lassen, die nur einen sehr überschaubaren Mehrwert für Stadt und Gesellschaft bergen.

Martin Grabner

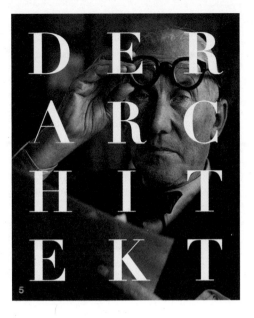

München: Prestel, 2012
Deutsch, 816 Seiten, 422 Farbabbildungen, 283 SW-Abbildungen, 2 Bände Hardcover im Schuber
ISBN: 978-3-7913-5276-3
EUR 98,00

Der Architekt: 4,5 Kilogramm, 816 Seiten – die fünf Jahrtausende durchmessende Geschichte die-

ses Berufs bis in die Gegenwart erfordert etwas an Gewicht. Die Publikation erschien als Katalog zur Abschiedsausstellung des langjährigen Leiters des Architekturmuseums der TU München in der Pinakothek der Moderne, Winfried Nerdinger. *Prachtband* ist angesichts dieses Materials untertrieben, es handelt sich um zwei Leinenbände im schmucken Schuber. Den Umschlag zieren einerseits ein Porträt des ägyptischen Baumeisters Bekenchon, in der Zeit Ramses II. (1279–1213 v. Chr.) verantwortlich für Tempelbauten in Karnak; andererseits ein Porträt Le Corbusiers von 1956, der, die charakteristische Brille auf die Stirn geschoben, den Betrachter mit versteinerter Miene anblickt, wohl um die respektgebietende Bedeutung dieses Berufs augenblicklich klarzumachen. Verstärkt wird dieses ernüchternde Berufsbild noch durch die großen weißen Lettern auf dem schwarzgrauen Hintergrund: DER ARCHITEKT. Es ist, diesen Bildern nach zu schließen, eine erhabene, dunkle, männliche Figur, dieser *Architekt*, der die Welt um uns baute und baut.

Ursprünglich als Lexikon mit mehreren tausend Einträgen geplant, wurde die Publikation in eine Aufsatzsammlung umkonzipiert, die vorliegend 45 Essays von verschiedenen AutorInnen

Architekt, vielseitig und übergewichtig, sucht ambitionierte LeserIn

Der Architekt. Geschichte und Gegenwart eines Berufsstandes (5)
Winfried Nerdinger (Hg.)

ally succeed in allowing cultural life and activity to unfold—and details how, in contrast, competing cities and architects that are grappling to attain any kind of transient media attention are wont to indulge in extravagant measures which offer only negligible added value to the respective city and to society at large.

Martin Grabner
(translation Dawn Michelle d'Atri)

Architect, Multifaceted and Overweight, Seeking Ambitious Readers

Der Architekt: Geschichte und Gegenwart eines Berufsstandes (5)
Winfried Nerdinger (ed.)
Munich: Prestel, 2012
German, 816 pages, 422 color illustrations,
283 black-and-white illustrations, 2 vols.,
hardcover in slipcase

ISBN: 978-3-7913-5276-3
EUR 98.00

Der Architekt: 4.5 kilograms, 816 pages—a history of a profession that spans five millennia and extends into the present necessitates a bit of weight. The book was published as a catalogue to accompany the final exhibition curated by Winfried Nerdinger, the longtime head of the Architekturmuseum der Technischen Universität München in Munich at the Pinakothek der Moderne. Considering this material, the term *luxury volume* is rather understated, for there are two linen-bound volumes sheathed in a decorative slipcase. Gracing the covers respectively are a portrait of the Egyptian master builder Bekenchon from the era of Ramesses II (1279–13 BC), who was responsible for building the Karnak temple complex, and a portrait of Le Corbusier from 1956, with the architect pushing his characteristic glasses up onto his forehead while staring at the beholder with a stony expression, probably meaning to instantly drive home the redoubtable meaning of his profession. This

sobering occupational image is further heightened by large, white capital letters against a black-gray background: DER ARCHITEKT. These impressions seem to imply that the architect who has built this world around us is a lofty, dark, male figure.

Originally conceived as a lexicon with several thousand entries, the publication was redesigned to embody a collection of essays that accommodates forty-five contributions by different authors on the history of the profession and also its current state, followed by a catalogue of the objects thematized in the exhibition and the usual lists of references, involved individuals, and illustrations. The texts, accompanied by large-format illustrations at times, encircle the profession of the architect in a geographical and historical tour through various centuries and cultural spheres, from Europe to Asia, Japan, India, to the Ottoman Empire and North America. The first volume explores the status of the architect in ancient Egypt, where the master builder commanded one of the highest positions, while in Greece the *architekton*, the "head carpenter," was closely tied to skilled trade. In Mesopo-

zur Geschichte und Gegenwart des Berufsstandes umfasst, gefolgt von einem Katalog der Objekte der Ausstellung und den üblichen Verzeichnissen zu Literatur, Personen und Abbildungen. Die Beiträge mit teils großformatigen Abbildungen umkreisen den Beruf des Architekten in einer geografischen und historischen Tour durch verschiedene Jahrhunderte und Kulturkreise von Europa bis Asien, Japan, Indien, ins Osmanische Reich und Nordamerika. Der erste Band untersucht den Status des Architekten im alten Ägypten, wo der Baumeister eine der höchsten Stellen repräsentierte, während in Griechenland der *architekton,* der „führende Zimmermann", eng an das Handwerk geknüpft war. In Mesopotamien übernehmen die Herrschenden selbst öffentlichkeitswirksam die Bauaufgaben, die Ausführenden bleiben ungenannt. Die dienenden Baumeister des Mittelalters ächzen einer abgebildeten Säulenfigur gleich unter der handwerklichen Last der Aufgabe, in der Renaissance wächst der Stolz der Profession bis zu den Architekten des 20. Jahrhunderts und der Gegenwart, deren Drang nach Prestige unermesslich scheint. Spezifische Themen wie Architektur als öffentliche Angelegenheit oder berufssoziologische Porträts werden angesprochen: der Architekt als Sozialingenieur, als Star, als Diener der Mächtigen.

Der zweite Band spiegelt das vielseitige und sich wandelnde Bild des Architekten; die Liste der vielen Gesichter der Zunft wird länger und länger: der Architekt als Konstrukteur, Künstler, Organisator, Beamter, visionärer Baukünstler, Dienstleister, Theoretiker, Lehrer. Auch Klischees, die immer auch ein bisschen Wahrheit beinhalten, tauchen auf: der Opportunist, der Eitle, der Schwarzgekleidete. Der Essay mit dem erheiternden Titel nach einem Zitat von Cedric Price, „It's not a house you need, it´s a divorce", beleuchtet das Konfliktpotenzial der Beziehung Bauherr und Architekt. Gleich zwei Texte widmen sich den Arbeitswerkzeugen für die Herstellung von Modell, Zeichnung, Plan und baulichen Details. Leider bleiben sie inhaltlich im Historischen und thematisieren die größte Veränderung der letzten Jahrzehnte nicht: jene weg vom Tuschestift zur Computermaus. Die Titel „Kunstakademien und Architektenausbildung" und „Der Architekt als Erzieher" fokussieren auf die Geschichte und Bedeutung der Ausbildung, die starren Systeme, das Dilemma der Trennung von Planung und Ausführung und die gegenwärtigen Möglichkeiten und Probleme an den Hochschulen, wo die ProfessorInnen, zugleich auch praktizierende ArchitektInnen, jeweils ihre eigene Entwurfsphilosophie als unhinterfragbar absichern. Lösungen für die Zukunft werden keine vorgeschlagen. Die folgenden Artikel präsentieren weitere Facetten des sich ständig wandelnden Berufsbildes: der Global Player, der Gartengestalter, der Stadtplaner, der Ingenieur.

Gewissermaßen als Quotenessay fungiert der Text „Aller Anfang sind wir – Wege von Architektinnen im 20. Jahrhundert", kaum überraschend mit Zaha Hadid am Titel der *L'Uomo Vogue* 2009 bebildert. Der inhaltlich sehr gut recherchierte Text erschreckt am Beginn mit Sätzen wie: „Nicht erst seit der Verleihung des Pritzker-Preises an Zaha Hadid 2004 haben Architektinnen – entgegen vieler Vorbehalte – gezeigt, dass sie Kreativität, Intellektualität und Praxis sehr wohl miteinander verbinden können. Längst haben Planerinnen unter Beweis gestellt, dass sie nicht nur begnadete Künstlerinnen und Entwerfernaturen sind, sondern es eben auch verstehen, ihren Job selbst zu machen." Solche Sätze im 21. Jahrhundert noch lesen zu müssen lässt nicht nur Feministinnen, sondern jeden aufgeklärten Menschen

tamia, rulers often publicly took on building projects themselves, with the individuals who executed the plans remaining unnamed. The servient master builders of the Middle Ages sighed like one of the depicted pillar figures under the burden of the craftsman's task, while starting in the Renaissance a pride in the profession grew and was to extend into the present day with the twentieth-century architects whose drive to attain prestige appears to know no bounds. Specific topics like architecture as a public affair or socioprofessional portraits are also touched upon: the architect as social engineer, as star, as servant of the powerful.

The second volume mirrors the versatile and changing picture of the architect, and the list of many faces in the guild becomes longer and longer: the architect as draftsman, artist, organizer, civil servant, visionary builder, service provider, theorist, and teacher. What is more, clichés make an appearance that contain a kernel of truth: architects who are opportunist, vain, dressed in black. The essay with the amusing title taken from a Cedric Price quote, "It's not a house you need, it's a divorce," highlights the conflict potential found in the relationship between building contractor and architect. Two texts deal with the topic of working tools for the production of model, drawing, plan, and architectural details. Unfortunately, the content of both remains tied to history and fails to thematically touch on the greatest change of the last few decades: the move from drawing ink to computer mouse. The contributions "Kunstakademien und Architektenausbildung" (Art Academies and Architectural Education) and "Der Architekt als Erzieher" (The Architect as Educator) focus on the history and meaning of education, fixed systems, the dilemma of separating planning from execution, and the current opportunities and problems at universities where professors are simultaneously practicing architects and thus tend to ensure that their own personal design philosophy remains undisputed. Indeed, future-oriented solutions are avoided. The articles that follow present further facets of this continually shifting occupation: the global player, the landscape designer, the urban planner, the engineer.

The text "Aller Anfang sind wir: Wege von Architektinnen im 20. Jahrhundert" (The First Step Starts with Us: Paths of Female Architects in the 20th Century) might be considered a "quota essay," as it were, and features a surprising photo of Zaha Hadid on the cover of *L'Uomo Vogue* in 2009. The exceedingly well-researched text frightens from the outset with sentences like this one: "It is not only since Zaha Hadid received the Pritzker Prize in 2004 that female architects have shown—despite many outside reservations—that creativity, intellectuality, and practice can indeed be combined. Female planners have long proven that they are not only highly gifted artists and designers, but that they certainly also know how to do their jobs." Still being faced with such sentences in the twenty-first century would make not only feminists but also any enlightened reader turn pale. Or is architecture as a profession perhaps to be considered especially behind the times with regard to equality that should be self-evident? The essay "Entlassen, vertrieben, eingesperrt, ermordert, im Widerstand" (Fired, Banished, Incarcerated, Mur-

erblassen. Oder ist vielleicht der ArchitektInnenberuf gerade hinsichtlich einer selbstverständlichen Gleichberechtigung besonders rückständig? Dass sich die Architektur und deren VertreterInnen nicht von gesellschaftlichen und politischen Strukturen trennen lässt, demonstriert auch der Artikel zu den ArchitektInnen in der NS-Zeit „Entlassen, vertrieben, eingesperrt, ermordet, im Widerstand".

Als äußerst lesenswert entpuppen sich die Essays zu den Ausflügen der Architekten in andere Erzählformen wie Musik, Film und Bühne; es scheint, dass der ephemere Charakter dieser Medien zu besonders mutigen Entwürfen anspornt. Einprägsam und vielleicht sogar noch heute Wunschfigur der ArchitekturabsolventInnen angesichts der Arbeitslosenrate in der Branche ist die Pose von Cary Grant im Film *The Fountainhead* von 1949: Der einsame, elegante, der Welt entrückte, unerreichbare Meister vor dem modernen Wolkenkratzer.

Die Essays der Publikation wirken durch die verschiedenen Schreibstile der AutorInnen unterschiedlich in Niveau, Struktur und Sichtweise, teilweise treffen sie nicht das Thema des Buches oder halten nicht, was ihr Titel verspricht. Die Gegenwart und Zukunft des ArchitektInnenberufs bleibt unterrepräsentiert: Wie planen angesichts der Arbeitslosigkeit, der inhaltsleeren Icon-Buildings, der grässlichen Star-Architekturen, der Baukrisenruinen, der delogierten Familien neben leerstehenden Wohnbauten in Bankenbesitz? Dennoch bietet das Buch ein abwechslungsreiches Lesevergnügen und ist ein üppiges Nachschlagewerk für alle, die noch ausreichend Platz in der Bibliothek haben. Trotz Fülle und Gewicht eignet es sich hervorragend als Geschenk für die lesenden VertreterInnen der besprochenen Zunft.

Margareth Otti

Architektur als Wissensspeicher

Architekturwissen. Grundlagentexte aus den Kulturwissenschaften
Susanne Hauser/Christa Kamleithner/Roland Meyer (Hg.)

Bd. 1: Zur Ästhetik des sozialen Raumes (6)
Bielefeld: transcript, 2011

Deutsch, 363 Seiten, Hardcover
ISBN 978-3-8376-1551-7
EUR 24,80

Bd. 2: Zur Logistik des sozialen Raumes
Bielefeld: transcript, 2013
Deutsch, 442 Seiten, Hardcover
ISBN 978-3-8376-1568-5
EUR 28,60

Die vorliegende zweibändige Anthologie von kulturwissenschaftlichen Grundlagentexten spiegelt nicht nur den erweiterten Architekturbegriff wider, der sich auf Objekte, Interventionen und vor allem ihre Funktion im sozialen Raum bezieht und diese explizit ausdrückt. Vielmehr erschaffen die ausgewählten Positionen ein Ordnungssystem, das nicht nur in Lehre und Forschung, sondern auch in der architektonischen Praxis eine differenzierte Orientierung bietet: Architektur als Zeichen, Artefakt, Dispositiv, Wissensspeicher und Gedächtnisort (S. 10). Die Texte ermöglichen damit umfassende Einblicke in die aktuellen Diskurse und ihre Bedeutung für Architekten und Stadtplaner, um die soziale Dimension des gebauten Raumes, die komplexen Verschränkun-

---

dered in the Name of Resistance) about architects during National Socialism demonstrates how architecture and its proponents cannot be liberated from the constraints of societal and political structures.

Especially worth reading are the essays about architects' forays into other narrative forms like music, film, and theater; it seems that the ephemeral character of these mediums serves to stimulate especially bold designs. Very memorable—and maybe even representing an idealized figure considering the high unemployment rate in the field—is the pose assumed by Cary Grant in the film *The Fountainhead* of 1949: the solitary, elegant architect detached from the real world, an unattainable master against the modern skyscraper.

The essays in this publication lack a sense of coherency due to the distinct writing styles of the authors, which makes them appear disparate in terms of niveau, structure, and perspective; at times the texts deviate quite strongly from the book's theme or do not deliver what their respective title promises. Also, the present and future of architecture as a profession remain inadequately represented: How should designs address our world today, considering the unemployment, the contentless iconic buildings, the dreadful star architectures, the real-estate-crisis ruins, the evicted families next to empty residential buildings owned by banks? Nonetheless, the book provides an enjoyable and diversified reading experience and is a voluminous reference book for anyone who has plenty of space in their library. Despite its plenitude and weight, the publication is perfectly suited as a gift for the well-read representatives of this particular guild.

Margareth Otti (translation Dawn Michelle d'Atri)

Architecture as Knowledge Reservoir

Architekturwissen: Grundlagentexte aus den Kulturwissenschaften
Susanne Hauser, Christa Kamleithner, and Roland Meyer (eds.)

Vol. 1: Zur Ästhetik des sozialen Raumes (6)
Bielefeld: transcript, 2011
German, 363 pages, hardcover
ISBN 978-3-8376-1551-7
EUR 24.80

Bd. 2: Zur Logistik des sozialen Raumes
Bielefeld: transcript, 2013
German, 442 pages, hardcover
ISBN 978-3-8376-1568-5
EUR 28.60

Architekturwissen (Architectural Knowledge), a two-volume anthology of fundamental texts from the cultural studies field, goes beyond simply reflecting and explicitly expressing an expanded concept of architecture that references objects and interventions, particularly their function in social space. In fact, the selected positions establish a system of order, which offers differentiated orientation, not only in the contexts of teaching and research, but also in architectural practice: architecture as sign, artifact, dispositif, knowledge

Susanne Hauser,
Christa Kamleithner,
Roland Meyer (Hg.)

Architekturwissen.
Grundlagentexte aus den
Kulturwissenschaften
Zur Ästhetik des
sozialen Raumes

Architekturen

[transcript]

6

gen, historischen Bedingungen und vielfältigen Entwicklungsmöglichkeiten für die Zukunft

besser zu verstehen. Ausgehend von einem funktionalen Verständnis der Moderne, das der Architektur eine rein formale, autonome Ästhetik zuerkennt, doch nur vorbestimmte Funktionen zulässt, wird hier ein sozialer Raum gedacht, der sich auf die soziologischen Theorien von Henri Lefebvre und Pierre Bourdieu bezieht.

Mit dem ersten Band *Zur Ästhetik des sozialen Raumes* wird auf unterschiedliche Sichtweisen eingegangen, die Architektur als Medium für Dinge und Prozesse wahrnehmbar und lesbar macht. Die Themen dieser Medienästhetik und ihrer Techniken gliedern sich in sechs Kapitel (1. Architektur und Kunst, 2. Techniken der Wahrnehmung, 3. Geschichte der Sinne, 4. Körper, Leib und Raum, 5. Lesbarkeit, 6. Praktiken und Situationen), in denen neben Texten zu Beginn oder Mitte des 20. Jahrhunderts von Adolf Loos, Theodor W. Adorno, Sigfried Giedion, Walter Benjamin, Georg Simmel, Maurice Merleau-Ponty, Marcel Mauss und Ervin Goffman vor allem auch Autoren aus den letzten beiden Jahrzehnten zu Wort kommen, wie Emily Thompson, Judith Butler, Mario Carpo und Gernot Böhme. Die Einleitungen zu den einzelnen Kapiteln zeichnen die ideengeschichtliche Entwicklung der angesprochenen

Thematik auf, ohne jedoch kanonisierend wirken zu wollen. Wesentlich in der Auswahl der Quellen über Wahrnehmungstheorien ist ihre Präsenz in der Architekturdebatte, die sie mit Impulsen und zentralen Thesen, Metaphern und relevanten Fragestellungen mitgestaltet haben.

Beispielsweise wird im sechsten Kapitel dem Körper selbst und seinen Handlungsmöglichkeiten im Raum nachgegangen. So etwa beschreibt Mauss in „Die Techniken des Körpers" (1934) anhand von ethnologischen Darstellungen die Schwimm- und Tauchtechnik als performative Handlung, wobei er den seinen Kopf über Wasser haltenden Brustschwimmer als eine Art Dampfschiff – einer primären Ikone der Moderne – interpretiert, die er der späteren Technik des *crawl* (Kraulens) diametral gegenüberstellt (S. 327f.). Er betont in diesem Beispiel die soziale Natur des *habitus*, ein Begriff der weit über erworbene Gewohnheit und Körpererziehung hinausweist und Techniken des Körpers bezeichnet, die eine *traditionelle*, *wirksame* Handlung vollziehen und sich so in die Individuen einschreiben.

Bei der feministischen Theoretikerin Butler werden in „Körper von Gewicht" (1993) die Entstehung und Festigung sozialer Identitäten zwar

reservoir, and place of memory (p. 10). The texts therefore provide comprehensive insight into current discourse and its significance for architects and urban planners, helping them to achieve a better understanding of the social dimension of built space, the complex interconnections, the historical conditions, and the diverse opportunities for future development. Presupposing a functional understanding of modernism, which assigns architecture merely formal, autonomous aesthetics while only permitting predetermined functions, here a social space is conceived on the basis of the sociological theories of Henri Lefebvre and Pierre Bourdieu.

The first volume, *Zur Ästhetik des sozialen Raumes* (On the Aesthetics of Social Space), addresses different perspectives that make architecture perceptible and readable as a medium for things and processes. The themes related to this media aesthetic and its techniques are organized into six chapters: 1. Architektur und Kunst (Architecture and Art), 2. Techniken der Wahrnehmung (Perception Techniques), 3. Geschichte der Sinne

(History of the Senses), 4. Körper, Leib und Raum (Body and Space), 5. Lesbarkeit (Readability), 6. Praktiken und Situationen (Practices and Situations). While the chapters present texts from the early or mid-twentieth century by the likes of Adolf Loos, Theodor W. Adorno, Sigfried Giedion, Walter Benjamin, Georg Simmel, Maurice Merleau-Ponty, Marcel Mauss, and Ervin Goffman, the focus primarily lies on the words of authors from the past two decades, such as Emily Thompson, Judith Butler, Mario Carpo, and Gernot Böhme. The introductions to the individual chapters trace the development of the history of ideas in the topics at hand, yet without any canonizing effects. An essential criterion in the selection of sources on perception theories is their presence in architectural discourse, which they have helped to shape through impulses, pivotal theories, metaphors, and relevant research questions.

For example, the sixth chapter thematically explores the body itself and its scopes for action in space. In "Die Techniken des Körpers"

(Techniques of the Body, 1934) Mauss describes swimming and diving techniques as a performative act by referring to ethnological accounts: he interprets the breaststroke swimmer, with the head above water, as a kind of steamboat—a central icon of modernism—and diametrically opposes it with the later technique of the crawl (pp. 327–28). With this example he emphasizes the social nature of the *habitus*, a concept that goes significantly beyond acquired habit and physical education but designates bodily techniques which carry out "effective traditional action" and thus become inscribed in the individuals.

Likewise, in "Körper von Gewicht" (Bodies that Matter, 1993) by feminist theorist Butler, the genesis and affirmation of social identities are described on the basis of a performative model of repetitions, yet this technique is understood to be closely connected to spatial design. Architecture is thus assigned a central role in the construction of meaning; it is interpreted as a "materialization" or "matrix" of relationships (p. 335), especially of gender roles.

ebenso mit einem performativen Modell von Wiederholungen beschrieben, doch wird diese Technik eng mit der räumlichen Gestaltung verbunden gesehen. Damit wird Architektur eine zentrale Rolle in der Konstruktion von Bedeutungen zugewiesen; sie wird als „Materialisierung" bzw. „Matrix" von Beziehungen (und vor allem geschlechtlichen Rollen) interpretiert (S. 335).

Als drittes Beispiel dieses Kapitels geht Goffman in „Ort und ortsbestimmtes Verhalten" (1959) nicht nur auf die Körpertechnik selbst, sondern auf die soziale Darstellung in Alltagssituationen ein, wobei er wie Butler den spezifischen Raum als primären Rahmen versteht. In seiner Analyse der verschiedenen „Szenen" unterscheidet er zwischen Vorderbühne und Hinterbühne, Darsteller und Publikum, Festivalisierung und Alltag, Authentischem und Inszenierung (S. 347f.). Entscheidend für das „Geheimnis des Schauspiels", das eine (einfache) Technik der Manipulation darstellt, ist die strikte räumliche Trennung der Bereiche mithilfe einer Zwischenwand, dem Bühnenbild, das sich für Goffman nicht nur im Theater sondern auch in Verkaufsräumen, Arbeitsstätten und Privathäusern findet.

Dieses letzte Kapitel im ersten Band leitet zur Organisation der mobilen Praktiken als zentrale Themenstellung im zweiten Teil *Zur Logistik des sozialen Raumes* über. Wiederum werden unterschiedliche Bedeutungsebenen im architektonischen „Gefüge" bzw. „Akteur-Netzwerk" in sechs Kapiteln vorgestellt (1. Orte und Identitäten, 2. Schwellen und Grenzen, 3. Anordnungen und Verteilungen, 4. Wege und Kanäle, 5. Märkte, Eigentum und Verwertung, 6. Handeln und Entwerfen). Als Texte finden sich Klassiker von Michel Foucault, Georg Simmel, Anthony Vidler, Mary Douglas, Beatriz Colomina, Rem Koolhaas, Gilles Deleuze/Félix Guattari oder Bruno Latour – während andere Autoren überraschen, wie beispielsweise der Ägyptologe Jan Assmann oder die Geografin Doreen Massey. Assmann untersucht in „Kollektives Gedächtnis und kulturelle Identität" (1988) die Unterschiede zwischen dem identitätskonkreten, kommunikativen Alltagsgedächtnis und dem alltagstranszendenten, kulturellen Gedächtnis, das mittels *Erinnerungsfiguren* signifikante vergangene Ereignisse lebendig hält – wie der jüdische Festkalender über Jahrtausende hinweg (S. 66). Doch Assmann betont, dass erst die normative Wertperspektive einer Gesellschaft die

identitätsstiftende Geschichte an Orten, Denkmälern oder Landmarken hervortreten lässt. Masseys Essay „Ein globales Ortsbewusstsein" (1991) hingegen definiert Orte als zeitliche Prozesse ohne exakte räumliche Grenzlinien, sodass der Charakter eines Ortes nicht durch eine bestimmte, kulturell historische Identität sondern vielmehr durch Konflikte und Widersprüche gekennzeichnet ist. So stellt sie dem Bedeutungsverlust von physischen Grenzen und Entfernungen ein progressives Ortsbewusstsein (*sense of place*) gegenüber, in dem sich die *Geometrie der Macht* ausdrückt (S. 88).

Die Kulturwissenschaftlerin Susanne Hauser, die zusammen mit ihren MitarbeiterInnen Christa Kamleithner und Roland Meyer die beiden Bände herausgegeben hat, ist Inhaberin einer Professur für Kunst- und Kulturgeschichte an der Universität der Künste Berlin und hat sich bereits mit dem 2009 gemeinsam mit Daniel Gethmann herausgegebenen Buch *Kulturtechnik Entwerfen: Praktiken, Konzepte und Medien in Architektur und Design Science* mit dieser Thematik beschäftigt.[1]

---

1   Susanne Hauser/Daniel Gethmann (Hg.): *Kulturtechnik Entwerfen. Praktiken, Konzepte und Medien in Architektur und Design Science*, Bielefeld 2009.

A third example from this chapter provides "Ort und ortsbestimmtes Verhalten" (Regions and Region Behavior, 1959), where Goffman explores not only the techniques of the body itself but also social presentation in everyday situations—and considers, like Butler, the specific space as primary framework. In an analysis of the various "scenes," Goffman differentiates between frontstage and backstage, performer and audience, festivalization and everyday life, the authentic and the staged (pp. 347–48). What is decisive for the "secrets of a show," which represents a (simple) technique of manipulation, is the strict spatial separation of domains using a partition: the stage set. For Goffman, this applies not only to theater, but also to salesrooms, workplaces, and private homes.

This last chapter of the first volume leads to the organization of mobile practices as a central issue in the second volume, *Zur Logistik des sozialen Raumes* (On the Logic of Social Space). Again, in six chapters the editors introduce into various planes of meaning in the architectural

"fabric" or "actor-network": 1. Orte und Identitäten (Places and Identities), 2. Schwellen und Grenzen (Thresholds and Boundaries), 3. Anordnungen und Verteilungen (Orders and Distributions), 4. Wege und Kanäle (Paths and Channels), 5. Märkte, Eigentum und Verwertung (Markets, Property, and Utilization), 6. Handeln und Entwerfen (Trading and Designing). There are classic texts by authors like Michel Foucault, Georg Simmel, Anthony Vidler, Mary Douglas, Beatriz Colomina, Rem Koolhaas, Gilles Deleuze and Félix Guattari, or Bruno Latour—while other contributors are more of a surprise, for instance the Egyptologist Jan Assmann or the geographer Doreen Massey. In "Kollektives Gedächtnis und kulturelle Identität" (Collective Memory and Cultural Identity, 1988), Assmann investigates the differences between communicative everyday memory related to concrete identity, on the one hand, and cultural memory that transcends everyday life, on the other. The latter keeps significant past events alive by way of *Erinnerungsfiguren* (memory figures)—such as the Jewish festival

calendar has done for centuries now (p. 66). However, Assmann emphasizes how it is a society's normative value perspective that will allow identity-establishing history to emerge at sites, memorials, and landmarks. Massey's essay "Ein globales Ortsbewusstsein" (A Global Sense of Place, 1991), in turn, defines places as temporal processes devoid of exact spatial boundaries. It follows that the character of a place is not distinguished by a specific cultural-historical identity, but to a greater degree by conflicts and contradictions. The author thus juxtaposes the loss of meaning related to physical boundaries and distances with a progressive sense of place, which is expressed through the "power geometry" (p. 88).

Susanne Hauser, a cultural scientist who edited the two volumes in collaboration with her colleagues Christa Kamleithner and Roland Meyer, is a professor of art history and cultural history at the Berlin University of the Arts. Together with Daniel Gethmann, she had previously explored related themes in the 2009 publication *Kulturtechnik Entwerfen: Praktiken, Konzepte und*

Auch in jenem Band werden die Entwurfspraxis, ihre historische Entwicklung und Visualisierungstechniken als Grundlage der architektonischen Zukunftsgestaltung analysiert.

Der umfassende Zugang der vorliegenden Anthologie zeigt interdisziplinäre Forschungsperspektiven auf, die in den letzten zwei Jahrzehnten Theorie und Geschichte der Kulturtechniken und Medien, die Geschichte der Sinne und des Körpers, das kulturelle Gedächtnis oder Konstruktionen von Identitäten geprägt haben. Dieser Foucaultsche Wissensbegriff bezieht sich neben den Erkenntnissen selbst vorrangig auf die verwendeten Diskurse und Praktiken der Erkenntnisproduktion, die im engen Zusammenhang mit Machtsstrukturen und strategischen Weltmodellen stehen.

Ingrid Böck

Sonne, Meer und Architektur zum Verkauf

Holidays after the Fall. Seaside Architecture and Urbanism in Bulgaria and Croatia (7)

Medien in Architektur und Design Science.[1] Here, too, design practice with its historical development and visualization techniques was analyzed as the basis of shaping the future through architecture.

The comprehensive approach taken by this anthology highlights interdisciplinary research perspectives which, over the past twenty years, have proven influential to the theory and history of cultural techniques and media, the history of the senses and the body, as well as cultural memory or the construction of identities. Besides the insight gained itself, this Foucauldian concept of knowledge primarily references the applied discourses and practices of knowledge production, which closely correlate with power structures and strategic world models.

Ingrid Böck (translation Dawn Michelle d'Atri)

1   Susanne Hauser and Daniel Gethmann, eds., *Kulturtechnik Entwerfen: Praktiken, Konzepte und Medien in Architektur und Design Science* (Bielefeld, 2009):

Michael Zinganel/Elke Bayer/Anke Hagemann (Hg.)
Berlin: Jovis, 2013
Englisch, 240 S., zahlreiche Farb- und SW-Pläne und -Abbildungen, broschiert
ISBN 978-3-86859-226-9
EUR 29,80

Holidays after the Fall betrachtet die Entwicklung der Freizeitarchitektur an den Meeresküsten Bulgariens und Kroatiens in der Periode der Durchdringung und letztendlich der Überwindung ideologischer Abgrenzungen zwischen Ost und West. Das Thema ist in Anbetracht der Wiederentdeckung dieser Küsten als Freizeitdestination und Investitionspotenzial von besonderer Aktualität. Die AutorInnen untersuchen Freizeitarchitektur im Kontext der politischen und ökonomischen Zusammenhänge, wobei sie schwerpunktmäßig den Wandel der Freizeitarchitektur nach der Wende und den Umgang mit den natürlichen Ressourcen behandeln.

Viele Ähnlichkeiten machen Bulgarien und Kroatien zu vergleichbaren Forschungsobjekten. In beiden sozialistischen Ländern stand zu Beginn der soziale Tourismus im Vordergrund. Die Effekte des internationalen Tourismus für die Moderni-

Sun, Sea, and Architecture For Sale

Holidays after the Fall: Seaside Architecture and Urbanism in Bulgaria and Croatia (7)
Michael Zinganel, Elke Bayer, and Anke Hagemann (eds:)
Berlin: Jovis, 2013
English, 240 pages, numerous color and black-and-white illustrations and maps, softcover
ISBN 978-3-86859-226-9
EUR 29.80

The book *Holidays after the Fall* takes a look at the development of leisure architecture along the seacoasts of Bulgaria and Croatia during the period when the ideological boundaries between East and West were being penetrated and ultimately overcome. This theme is particularly topical considering the rediscovery of these coasts as leisure destinations and investment potential. The authors investigate leisure architecture in the context of political and economic circumstances, with a focus

sierung, die Bereicherung des öffentlichen Raums und die Erweiterung der ästhetischen Leitbilder wurden bald erkannt und ein Freizeitkonzept, nach dem soziale und wirtschaftliche Aspekte Hand in Hand gehen, eingeleitet. Die Freizeitarchitektur bewahrte ihren Wert als Zeichen der Egalität, gewann aber auch als Symbol des Begehrens nach modernen Lebensstilen an Bedeutung. Sie ist in beiden Ländern Ausdruck einer kulturellen Ambition und Symbol der verspäteten Modernisierung. Beiden Planungskulturen waren die modernistische Überlappung von Architektur und Städtebau und ein respektvoller Umgang mit den Naturressourcen eigen.

Die AutorInnen verweisen auch auf Differenzen: In Bulgarien wurde mit kompakten Tourismuseinrichtungen dem Erhalt der Strände und Dünenlandschaften Tribut gezollt und somit ein wohltuender Kontrast zwischen Natur und Architektur erzeugt. Die Zentralisierung der Tourismuswirtschaft hat die konsequente Umsetzung dieses Leitbilds ermöglicht. Demgegenüber haben in Kroatien die Ausrichtung auf kleinere Freizeitanlagen, das weitaus größere Potenzial an Naturraum und nicht zuletzt das jugoslawische Modell der Selbstverwaltung und Dezentralisierung zu

placed on the changes seen in leisure architecture after 1989 and the treatment of natural resources.

Many similarities make Bulgaria and Croatia fitting subjects of comparative research. Social tourism was initially prioritized in both socialist countries. The effects of international tourism on modernization were soon recognized, as were the enhancement of public space and the expansion of general aesthetic guidelines. This led to the introduction of a leisure concept that embraced social and economic aspects in equal measure. Leisure architecture safeguarded its value as symbol of égalité, but it also took on significance as an emblem reflecting how coveted modern lifestyles were. In both countries, it was an expression of cultural ambition and a symbol of belated modernization. Distinctive for planning culture in each of these countries was the modernist imbrication of architecture and urban development, as well as a respectful approach to dealing with natural resources.

Yet the authors also make note of discrepancies. Bulgaria for instance paid tribute to the

Holidays after the fall

Seaside Architecture and Urbanism in Bulgaria and Croatia
Edited by Elke Beyer, Anke Hagemann and Michael Zinganel

einer Übereinstimmung von Natur und Architektur geführt. Unterschiedlich sind die Geschwindigkeiten der Privatisierung nach der Wende – dem investitionsfreundlichen Klima in Bulgarien steht eine zögerliche Haltung in Kroatien gegenüber.

Michael Zinganel und Elke Beyer setzen mit dem Kapitel über Küsten, Tourismus und die Produktion von Raum einen breiteren Kontext. Sie erörtern die Voraussetzungen für den modernen Massentourismus in der aufkommenden Wertschätzung der Erholung als soziales Recht und Mittel der Erziehung in der frühen UdSSR. Das Phänomen des sozialen Tourismus ist jedoch nicht ein Einzelerkennungsmerkmal für den staatlichen Sozialismus, sondern hat auch im faschistischen Italien, im nationalsozialistischen Deutschland, im Volksfront-Frankreich, aber auch in dem vom Fordismus beeinflussten Großbritannien das entsprechende Erbe hinterlassen. Der CIAM-Kongress in Paris 1937 wird als ein Meilenstein für die Intellektualisierung des Themas gewertet. Die vom Kongress vorgezeichneten Wege begleiten später die Internationalisierung und Ökonomisierung des Tourismus in Bulgarien und Kroatien. Die AutorInnen ziehen hierzu Parallelen zum Fordismus, dem wirtschaftlichen Nutzbarmachen von Freizeit und unentwickeltem Land.

Elke Beyer und Anke Hagemann untersuchen den Wandel der bulgarischen Schwarzmeerküste. Die ersten Freizeitarchitekturen folgten hier dem Konzept der sozialen Mischung mithilfe vielfältiger Organisationsformen. Mit dem Beginn der internationalen Vermarktung wurde die Küste zum baukünstlerischen Experimentierfeld und „Flaggschiff" der modernen bulgarischen Architektur, die das Land im internationalen Spitzenfeld etablierte. Seit den 1990ern vollzieht sich infolge der stürmischen Privatisierung und Deregulierung ein dramatischer Wandel, der mit fünf kontrastierenden Beispielen veranschaulicht wird. Abschließend gelingt es den Autorinnen anhand von zwei Fällen, auf die aufkommende kritische Haltung einer sich formenden Zivilgesellschaft sowie auf sich anbahnende Interferenzen zwischen Tourismus und Alltag aufmerksam zu machen.

Die Entwicklung der kroatischen Adriaküste von einem Ort für den sozialen Tourismus zum Paradies der Massenmarktkonsumenten schildert Michael Zinganel. Er erläutert die Mechanismen der Produktion von Raum für den internationalen Tourismus in der sozialistischen Phase und die Gründe für die zähflüssigen Reformen danach.

Die sozialistische Phase wird von Maroje Mrduljas in einem selbständigen Kapitel näher präzisiert. Er setzt den Akzent auf die Raumordnung, die sich den Ideen des CIAM verpflichtet fühlte und den Tourismus als integralen Bestandteil der sozioökonomischen Entwicklung betrachtete. Die geschilderte Kooperation mit der UNO

---

preservation of beaches and dune landscapes by building compact tourism facilities, thus engendering a beneficent contrast between nature and architecture. The centralization of the tourist industry facilitated the consistent realization of this guiding principle. In Croatia, by contrast, an orientation toward smaller leisure facilities—coupled with vastly higher potential in terms natural space and, not least, the Yugoslavian model of self-administration and decentralization—led to conformity between nature and architecture. Also different was the speed at which privatization progressed after the political shift: in Bulgaria an investment-friendly climate prevailed, as opposed to a more hesitant attitude in Croatia.

Michael Zinganel and Elke Beyer establish a broad context with their respective chapters on coasts, tourism, and the production of space. They reason that the foundations of modern mass tourism lie in the nascent appreciation of relaxation as both social right and educational medium in the early years of the Soviet Union. However, the phenomenon of social tourism as a distinguishing characteristic was not only found under state socialism—it also left behind a legacy in Italy under fascist rule, in Germany under National Socialism, in France under the popular front, and even in Great Britain under Fordism. The CIAM congress of 1937 in Paris is judged by the authors to be a milestone for the intellectualization of the topic. The paths predetermined at the congress were later to accompany the internationalization and economization of tourism in Bulgaria and Croatia. Here the authors draw parallels to Fordism and the profitable utilization of leisure time and undeveloped land.

Elke Beyer and Anke Hagemann explore the changes that evolved along the Bulgarian coast of the Black Sea. Here, the first examples of leisure architecture pursued the concept of social diversity with the aid of diverse organizational forms. With the advent of marketing on a global scale, the coast turned into a field of architectonic experimentation and a "flagship" of modern Bulgarian architecture, which the country established among the international ranks. Starting in the 1990s, as a result of stormy privatization and deregulation, a dramatic shift took place, which is illustrated through five contrasting examples. Citing two cases, Beyer and Hagemann conclude by successfully calling attention to the rising critical stance of a formative civil society and also to incipient interferences between tourism and everyday life.

The evolvement of the Adriatic seacoast in Croatia from a place for social tourism to a paradise for mass-market consumers is delineated by Michael Zinganel. He expounds on the mechanisms used in producing space for international tourism during the socialist phase and the reasons for the sluggish reforms later on.

The socialist phase is more closely rendered by Maroje Mrduljas in a separate chapter. He places emphasis on the spatial planning that was beholden to CIAM ideas, viewing tourism as an integral part of socioeconomic development. Mrduljas rules the cooperative relationship with the United Nations in creating a regional planning methodology, as portrayed here, to be a belated enterprise, **291**

zur Erstellung einer regionalen Planungsmethodologie wertet Mrduljas als verspätetes Vorhaben, dessen Effekt jedoch in einer detaillierten Inventur und Ressourcenanalyse sowie einer brauchbaren Methode liegt. Aufhorchen lässt die relativ früh aufkommende Kritik an den parasitären Strukturen des internationalen Tourismus vonseiten theoretischer Fachkreise. Der Autor schildert die kausalen Verbindungen zwischen dem jugoslawischen System der Dezentralisierung, Selbstverwaltung und halbherzigen Marktwirtschaft einerseits und der Freizeitarchitektur andererseits.

Der Balkan-Experte Norbert Niediek erläutert die Ursachen für die verzögerte Transformation der Freizeitarchitektur in Kroatien. Er identifiziert das jugoslawische Selbstverwaltungsmodell mit seiner ungeklärten Positionierung zwischen staatlich und privat zum Stolperstein für die Privatisierung. Dem adaptierten Treuhandmodell der ehemaligen DDR folgend, verläuft die Privatisierung der vormals „sozialen Unternehmen" über den zeitraubenden Zwischenschritt der Nationalisierung. Die Kriegsphase, die lokalen, mitunter auch nationalistischen Widerstände gegen Privatisierungen, die internationale Investoren abgeschreckt haben, und nicht zuletzt die

von den neuen Machthabern verfolgte undurchdringliche „200-Familien-Privatisierung" hat sich ebenfalls als Schwelle erwiesen. Die Überlegungen des Autors werden mit ausgewählten emblematischen Beispielen veranschaulicht.

Die AutorInnen des Sammelbandes kommen aus unterschiedlichen Fachrichtungen. In diesem Werk vereint sie das Thema der Freizeitarchitektur sowie vorangehende Arbeiten über Architektur und Städtebau in Osteuropa. *Holidays after the Fall* führt unterschiedliche Wissensrichtungen zusammen und trägt daher wesentlich zur Erkenntnis und Visualisierung von Aspekten der Freizeitarchitektur und den dahinterliegenden wirtschaftlichen und politischen Umständen bei. Das breite Spektrum an fundierten Beiträgen macht das Werk zu einer vielschichtigen Darstellung des Wandels an den Küsten Bulgariens und Kroatiens und gibt Impulse für den Abbau noch bestehender Asymmetrien im Informationsstand zwischen West und Ost. Schließlich bietet das Buch auch einen methodologischer Beitrag zur multi-disziplinären Herangehensweise an baukünstlerische Phänomene und nicht zuletzt eine Lektüre, die Neugier weckt.

Grigor Doytchinov

Wort-Bauten: Vom räumlichen Potenzial der Imagination

Zwischen Architektur und literarischer Imagination (8)
Andreas Beyer/Ralf Simon/Martino Stierli (Hg.)
München: Wilhelm Fink, 2013
Deutsch, 391 Seiten, zahlreiche Farb- und SW-Abbildungen, Hardcover
ISBN 978-3-7705-5514-7
EUR 56,00

Was passiert, wenn man Architektur durch die Linse der Literaturwissenschaften betrachtet? Wenn also Literatur, Imagination und Architektur eine Alliance eingehen? Diesen Fragen ist der von Andreas Beyer, Ralf Simon und Martino Stierli herausgegebene Sammelband *Zwischen Architektur und literarischer Imagination* gewidmet, der im Rahmen des Nationalen Forschungsschwerpunkts (NFS) Bildkritik eikones der Universität Basel im Anschluss an eine Tagung (2009) entstanden ist. Der Band stellt einen innovativen Anschluss an Winfried Nerdingers gewichtige Ausstellungspublikation *Architektur wie sie im*

---

the effects of which, however, rest in a detailed inventory and resource analysis, and also in a viable method. Worth noting is the criticism of the parasitic structures of international tourism that arose relatively early in circles of theory experts. The author touches on the causal relations between the Yugoslavian system of decentralization, self-administration, and half-hearted market economy, on the one hand, and leisure architecture, on the other.

The Balkan expert Norbert Niediek elucidates the causes of the delayed transformation of leisure architecture in Croatia. He identifies the Yugoslavian self-administration model, with its unclear positioning between state and private interests, as a stumbling block on the path to privatization. Following a fiduciary model adapted from the former German Democratic Republic, the privatization of the onetime "social enterprises" proceeded via the time-consuming intermediate stage of nationalization. Other barriers proved to be the wartime phase, the local (and sometimes nationalist) resistance against privati-

zation which scared away international investors, and, not least, the impervious "200-family privatization" lauded by the new authorities in power. The author's reflections are illustrated by select emblematic examples.

The authors of the edited volume originate from different specialty areas. In this book they are united by the theme of leisure architecture and by antecedent works about architecture and urban planning in Eastern Europe. *Holidays after the Fall* gathers together different types of expertise, thus substantially contributing to an understanding and visualization of aspects of leisure architecture and the underlying economic and political conditions. The broad spectrum of well-founded contributions turns the book into a multifaceted representation of the changes impacting the coasts of Bulgaria and Croatia, and it provides impetus for dismantling any still existing asymmetries in the level of information between the West and the East. Ultimately, the book offers a methodological contribution to the multidisciplinary approach to architectural phenomena—and

indeed also a reading experience that arouses curiosity.

Grigor Doytchinov
(translation Dawn Michelle d'Atri)

Word Constructions: On the Spatial Potential of Imagination

Zwischen Architektur und literarischer Imagination (8)
Andreas Beyer, Ralf Simon, and Martino Stierli (eds.)
Munich: Wilhelm Fink, 2013
German, 391 pages, numerous color and black-and-white illustrations, hardcover
ISBN 978-3-7705-5514-7
EUR 56.00

What happens when we view architecture through the lens of literary studies? When literature, imagination, and architecture enter into an alliance? The

Buche steht (2007) dar, indem er das semantische Beziehungsgeflecht zwischen Architektur und Literatur um die Dimension der Bildlichkeit erweitert. Obwohl die Beiträge unterschiedlichen disziplinären Logiken folgen, bedienen sich alle Texte des analytischen Tools der Bildkritik, das als *tertium comparationis* die Brücke zwischen Sprache und Architektur spannt. Auch wenn Architektur und Sprache denselben Strukturprinzipien folgen, wie Simon und Stierli in der Einleitung überzeugend darlegen, ist das Wechselverhältnis zwischen Sprache, Imagination und Gebautem dennoch äußerst komplex.

Diese Komplexität spiegelt sich in der disparaten Anordnung der Beiträge wider. Die Texte folgen zwar einer chronologischen Ordnung von der Gegenwart bis in die Neuzeit, aber gleichzeitig stellt sich die Frage, ob nicht eine Gliederung in thematische Abschnitte die Inhaltsorganisation kohärenter gestaltet hätte. Gestrafft wird die Komposition wiederum durch den in der Einleitung präzise formulierten Fokus auf Bildlichkeit, dem die Fallstudien auch strikt Folge leisten. Stellvertretend für die thematische Ausrichtung des Bandes werden im Folgenden Beiträge vorgestellt, die einerseits explizit auf die Wechselwirkungen

von Text, Bild, und Bauwerk verweisen, gleichzeitig aber auch die unterschiedlichen Ausdrucksformen dieses Zusammenspiels aufzeigen.

Der Großteil der Beiträge widmet sich architektonischen Motiven in literarischen Texten, in denen Bau- und Raumtypen mit spezifischen Bedeutungen belegt werden. So zum Beispiel der äußerst lesenswerte Beitrag von Heinz Brüggemann, der sich mit der literarischen und geschichtsphilosophischen Aufarbeitung der Pariser Passagen durch Walter Benjamins *Passagenwerk* (1927–40) und Louis Aragons *Le Paysan de Paris* (1926) auseinandersetzt. Aragons magischer Realismus und Benjamins Phantasmagorien lassen, so Brüggemann, den Architekturtypus der Passage zum „poetischen Visionsraum" (S. 205) werden. Brüggemann bedient sich der Benjaminschen Metapher der Passage als Hohlraum, in dem sich nicht nur die Geschichte konserviert, sondern auch die innere Isolation des vom Ennui zermürbten modernen Individuums physisch manifestiert.

Ebenso betrachtet Melanie Beschel eine Konstruktion im imaginativ-architekturalen Sinn, indem sie das poetologische Bild des Kegelbaus in Thomas Bernhards Roman *Korrektur* (1975) untersucht. Genauer gesagt bringt die Erzählung

den Prozess des architektonischen Entwerfens direkt mit der schriftlichen Aufarbeitung von Geschichte in Verbindung. Beschel argumentiert überzeugend, dass Bernhards Text auch linguistisch dem geometrischen Prinzip des Kegels folgt und damit die Form der Erzählung auch den In-

---

anthology *Zwischen Architektur und literarischer Imagination* (Between Architecture and Literary Imagination), edited by Andreas Beyer, Ralf Simon, and Martino Stierli, is devoted to answering these questions. The volume was created in the context of eikones, the National Center of Competence in Research (NCCR) Iconic Criticism at the University of Basel, after a 2009 conference. It innovatively follows up on Winfried Nerdinger's substantial exhibition publication *Architektur wie sie im Buche steht* (The Architecture of Fiction, 2007) by expanding the semantic relational fabric of architecture and literature to include the dimension of pictoriality. Although the contributions pursue different disciplinary logics, all texts draw on the analytical tool of iconic criticism, which as *tertium comparationis* spans a bridge between language and architecture. Although architecture and language adhere to the same structural principles, as Simon and Stierli convincingly assert in the preface, the reciprocal relationships among language, imagination, and built structures are actually exceedingly complex.

This complexity is mirrored in the distinct arrangement of the contributions. The texts are chronologically ordered from the present to the modern era, yet the question still arises as to whether an arrangement according to thematic sections would have lent more coherency to the organization of content. On the other hand, composition is streamlined through the preface's concisely phrased focus on pictoriality, to which the case studies are closely aligned. In the following, contributions will be introduced in a way that reflects the thematic orientation of the volume. The contributions explicitly point to the interactions between text, image, and architectural structure, while simultaneously calling attention to the different ways of expressing this interplay.

The vast majority of the contributions are dedicated to architectural motifs in literary texts, where types of construction and space are assigned specific meanings. This is apparent in the essay by Heinz Brüggemann, which is very worth reading with its literary and historico-philosophical work-up of the Parisian arcades by example of Walter

Benjamin's *Passagenwerk* (1927–40) and Louis Aragon's *Le Paysan de Paris* (1926). According to Brüggemann, Aragon's magical realism and Benjamin's phantasmagorias turn the arcade as architectural model into a "visionary poetic space" (p. 205). The author avails himself of the metaphor of the arcade as a cavity that not only serves to preserve history, but where the inner isolation of the ennui-plagued modern individual manifests in physical form.

Melanie Beschel likewise takes an imaginative-architectural approach to a construction when investigating the poetological image of the cone structure in Thomas Bernhard's novel *Korrektur* (Correction, 1975). More precisely, the narrative directly associates the process of architectural design with the act of processing history in writing. Beschel convincingly argues that Bernhard's text follows the geometric principle of the cone linguistically as well, with the narrative structure thus also reflecting the content or the main showplace. Regrettably, Beschel's interpretation of the conical symbolism turns out to be rather general, so

halt, bzw. den zentralen Schauplatz widerspiegelt. Leider fällt Beschels Interpretation der Symbolik des Kegels etwas allgemein aus und so bleibt es dem Leser bzw. der Leserin überlassen, diese auf eine spezifische Bedeutung zu beziehen.

Ralf Simon nähert sich dem Zusammenhang zwischen literarischem Text und Architektur über den Begriff des Weltbildes. Die Literaturwissenschaft gehört für Simon in den Bereich der Bildkritik, die den poetischen Text als ein „weltmodellierendes Gerüst" (S. 90) betrachtet und ihn in einem topologischen oder architektonischen Kontext verortet. Exemplarisch untersucht wird *Kosmas oder Vom Berge des Nordens* (1955), ein Kurzroman des Schriftstellers Arno Schmidt, in dem der Konflikt um ein christliches Weltmodell zum zentralen Thema wird. Schmidt, so die These Simons, bedient sich dabei aber bewusst keiner Metaphern, die räumliche Ordnung und die Orientierung des Menschen in der Welt ermöglichen, sondern sprachlicher Mittel, welche die Dekonstruktion von Dreidimensionalität (und damit das klassische Verständnis von Architektur) zugunsten der zweidimensionalen Fläche (des Textes) und schließlich zugunsten der Imagination selbst zum Ziel haben.

Die generische Vielschichtigkeit, in der sich das Thema des Bandes verortet, belegen auch die Beiträge von Martino Stierli und Matthias Noell. Ganz im Gegensatz zu Ralf Simon stellt Noell mit seinem Beitrag die Metapher als Gleichsetzungsinstrument wieder in den Mittelpunkt. Noell zeigt jene Beispiele in der Literatur-, Kunst- und Architekturgeschichte auf, in denen ein direkter Vergleich von Mensch und Architektur vollzogen wird. Besonders spannend sind seine Überlegungen zum Raum als autobiografischem Werk, die er mit einer Fotografie des Ateliers von Piet Mondrian oder dem gebauten Selbstportrait des Künstlers Jean-Pierre Raynaud exemplifiziert.

Für Stierli erschließt sich das Feld der literarischen Imagination über Rem Koolhaas' vielzitiertes Manifest *Delirious New York* (1978), das er als „Rekonstruktion eines imaginierten Manhattan" (S. 60) deutet. Stierli argumentiert außerdem, dass die urbane Ordnung von Manhattan in das Manifest selbst eingeschrieben sei. Genauso wie die Gebäude in Manhattans *grid* stünden die Textfragmente in *Delirious New York* als individuelle, heterogene Bausteine nebeneinander. Die Funktion des Architekten geht für Stierli damit über das bloße Entwerfen am Zeichenbrett

hinaus und gründet sich in der diskursiven Dimension, die jedem architektonischen Entwurf vorausgeht. Stierli bedient sich in seinem Aufsatz auch Koolhaas' Metapher des Architekten als Ghostwriter, der die Stadt intellektuell konzipiert und schreibend interpretiert.

Einen profunden Überblick darüber, wie sich Fiktionen als Architekturen in der Geschichte materialisiert haben, liefert der Beitrag von Winfried Nerdinger. „Vom Bauen imaginärer Architektur" gleicht einem wilden Streifzug durch verschiedene Länder, Epochen und Architekturtypen, und so diskutiert er das neogotische Herrenhaus Fonthill Abbey als architektonische Übersetzung des Romans *Vathek* (1782) von dessen Bauherren William Beckford oder beschreibt Tomaso Buzzis Adaption des Franziskanerklosters La Scarzuola, welche, laut Nerdinger, auf der literarischen Vorlage des Renaissanceromans *Hypnerotomachia Poliphili* (1499) beruht.

Insgesamt rückt der Band die imaginative Dimension von Architektur in den Vordergrund und belegt erneut, dass es sich als produktiv erweist, Architektur nicht ausschließlich als Gebrauchswerk, sondern vielmehr als eine Verkörperung des Geistigen, das heißt, des Raum entwerfenden Den-

---

it is up to the reader to ascertain which specific meaning is intended.

Ralf Simon focuses on the relationship between literary text and architecture by exploring the Weltbild concept. In Simon's eyes, literary studies is aligned to the domain of iconic criticism, which views the poetic text as a "world-modeling framework" (p. 90) and localizes it in a topological or architectural context. The short novel *Kosmas oder Vom Berge des Nordens* (Kosmas, or On the Mountains of the North, 1955) by the author Arno Schmidt is taken as an example here, with the conflict surrounding a Christian model of the world becoming a central theme. Simon asserts that Schmidt purposefully avoided using metaphors that would facilitate spatial order and human orientation within the world, relying instead on linguistic means that aim to deconstruct three-dimensionality (and thus the classical understanding of architecture) in favor of the two-dimensional plane (of text), and ultimately also in favor of imagination itself.

The generic multifacetedness in which the topic of the volume is localized is also underscored by the contributions by Martino Stierli and Matthias Noell. In strong contrast to Ralf Simon, the metaphor is once again placed center stage by Noell in its function as instrument of equalization. He cites examples from the history of literature, art, and architecture where a direct comparison between human and architecture is drawn. Especially fascinating are his reflections on space of an autobiographical nature, for which he cites as examples a photograph of Piet Mondrian's studio and the built self-portrait of the artist Jean-Pierre Raynaud.

The field of literary imagination is made accessible through Rem Koolhaas's oft-cited manifesto *Delirious New York* (1978), which Stierli in his contribution interprets to be the "reconstruction of an imaginary Manhattan" (p. 60). Furthermore, the author argues that the urban structure of Manhattan is inscribed into the manifesto itself. He views the text fragments in *Delirious New York* as individual, extremely heteroge-

nous building blocks set adjacently, comparable to the buildings in Manhattan's grid. The function of the architect is thus considered by the author to extend beyond the act of simply sitting at the drawing board; it is founded in the discursive dimension that predates each and every architectural design. In his essay, Stierli also invokes Koolhaas's metaphor of the architect as a ghostwriter who intellectually conceptualizes the city and puts his interpretations into writing.

Winfried Nerdinger's contribution offers a profound overview of how fictions have materialized as architectures over the course of history. "Vom Bauen imaginärer Architektur" (On Building Imaginary Architecture) equates to a wild foray through various countries, epochs, and types of architecture. As such, it discusses the neo-Gothic manor Fonthill Abbey as an architectural translation of the novel *Vathek* (1782) by its builder William Beckford or describes Tomaso Buzzi's adaptation of the Franciscan monastery La Scarzuola, which, according to

kens zu betrachten. Das Buch überzeugt durch den multidisziplinären Dialog und sein konsequentes Augenmerk auf sprachlich konstruierte Raumbilder. Gewünscht hätte man sich eine stärkere Positionierung des Bandes in der aktuellen Diskussion zum schreibenden Architekten oder Architekturkritiker, wie sie zum Beispiel gegenwärtig von Jane Rendell (in *Site-Writing: The Architecture of Art-Criticism*, 2010) oder Tom Spector und Rebecca Damron (in *How Architects Write*, 2013) geführt wird. Dass es auch für Architekten wieder an der Zeit ist, sich vom Einfluss der Zweidimensionalität architektonischer Reproduktionen zu befreien und stattdessen das „räumliche Potenzial der Imagination freizusetzen" (S. 16), haben die Herausgeber mit diesem Buch jedoch eindrucksvoll dargelegt.

Petra Eckhard

Fractals, not Linguistics

Archaeology of the Digital: Peter Eisenmann, Frank Gehry, Chuck Hoberman, Shoei Yoh (9)

Greg Lynn (Hg.)
Canadian Centre for Architecture, Montreal;
Berlin: Sternberg Press, 2013
Englisch, 396 Seiten, 279 Farb- und
18 SW-Abbildungen
ISBN 978-3-943365-80-1
EUR 29,00

Unter dem Titel *Archaeology of the Digital* hat Greg Lynn eine Ausstellung für das Canadian Centre for Architecture kuratiert. Das hier besprochene Buch ist der gleichnamige Katalog zu dieser Ausstellung. Schon die Typografie des Buchumschlags nimmt einen auf eine Zeitreise: Die unregelmäßig gepixelten Buchstaben signalisieren im Zeitalter der Retina-Displays das Abtauchen in die ferne Vergangenheit der späten Achtzigerjahre des letzten Jahrhunderts. „Today, it's time to start to write a history and a theory of digital technology", liest man in derselben grob-pixeligen Schrift auf der Buchrückseite. Die großspurige Ankündigung bereitet einen aber nicht wirklich angemessen vor auf das, was einen dann im Buch erwartet: ein äußerst lesenswertes, persönliches und informatives Kompendium, welches einem die Arbeit von vier sehr unterschiedlichen

Pionieren des Digitalen in der Architektur auf sympathisch unangestrengte Weise näherbringt.

In der Informationstechnologie schreitet die Entwicklung schneller voran als in anderen Bereichen. Es gibt hier das bekannte Mooresche Gesetz, demzufolge sich die Geschwindigkeit der Compu-

---

Nerdinger, is based on the literary model of the Renaissance novel *Hypnerotomachia Poliphili* (1499).

On the whole, the volume highlights the imaginative dimension of architecture and once again verifies how very productive it is to view architecture not solely in a utilization context, but rather as an embodiment of the intellectual sphere—of thought that charts space. The book is convincing thanks to its multidisciplinary dialogue and a consistent focus on linguistically constructed spatial imagery. Nonetheless, a stronger positioning of the publication in the current discourse on architects or architecture critics as authors is missing here, as for example has been recently provided by Jane Rendell (in *Site-Writing: The Architecture of Art-Criticism*, 2010) or Tom Spector and Rebecca Damron (in *How Architects Write*, 2013). In any case, the editors have impressively succeeded in demonstrating that the time has once again come for architects to liberate themselves from the influence of two-dimensional architectural reproduc-

tion and to instead "set free the spatial potential of the imagination" (p. 16).

Petra Eckhard (translation Dawn Michelle d'Atri)

Fractals, not Linguistics

Archaeology of the Digital: Peter Eisenmann, Frank Gehry, Chuck Hoberman, Shoei Yoh (9)

Greg Lynn (ed.)
Canadian Centre for Architecture, Montreal;
Berlin: Sternberg Press, 2013
English, 396 pages, 279 color illustrations and
18 black-and-white illustrations
ISBN 978-3-943365-80-1
EUR 29.00

In 2013, under the title *Archaeology of the Digital*, Greg Lynn curated an exhibition at the Canadian Centre for Architecture. The book discussed here is the catalogue that accompanies the exhibition. The typography of the book cover already takes

us on a journey through time: in our present age of the retina display, these irregularly pixelated letters signify a descent into the distant past—as far back as the late 1980s. "Today, it's time to start to write a history and a theory of digital technology"—these words, printed in the same coarsely pixelated font, mark the book's back cover. Yet this pretentious announcement does not quite prepare the reader for what awaits inside the book: a personal and informative compendium that is well worth reading and takes a pleasantly relaxed approach to familiarizing us with the work of four very different pioneers of the digital in architecture.

Development progresses much more swiftly in information technology than in other fields. According to the so-called "Moore's Law," the speed of computers doubles every one-and-a-half years. This exponential growth, which has been going on for forty-five years now, has taught us a new concept of time when it comes to all things digital: here five years are half an eternity, so we can hardly remember what was going on ten years ago. Viewed from this angle, it really is fitting to call a voyage

ter alle anderthalb Jahre verdoppelt – ein exponentielles Wachstum, welches seit nunmehr bereits 45 Jahren tatsächlich so stattfindet und uns im Bezug auf das Digitale einen anderen Zeitbegriff gelehrt hat: Hier sind fünf Jahre schon eine halbe Ewigkeit und an das, was vor zehn Jahren war, mag man sich kaum mehr erinnern. So gesehen ist es tatsächlich angemessen, die Entdeckungsreise in die Vergangenheit von vor gerade einmal 25 Jahren, die in Lynns Buch gemacht wird, als „Archäologie" zu bezeichnen. Zumal sich auch zeigt, dass das Digitale die Geschichtsforschung vor ganz neue Herausforderungen stellt: Die digitalen Daten aus jener Zeit sind zum größten Teil bereits verschwunden und mit ihnen die Programme und die Hardware, auf denen sie entwickelt wurden.

Es ist ein besonderes Verdienst von Lynns Ausstellung und Buch, dass so viele Artefakte aufgespürt und versammelt wurden, und dass diese durch Kommentare und Erläuterungen auch verständlich werden und zu sprechen beginnen. Dass dies gelingt, liegt freilich auch daran, dass die jeweiligen Autoren noch leben und Fehlendes aus ihrer Erinnerung ergänzen können. Nicht zuletzt Greg Lynn selbst, der mit den vier Protagonisten

und ihren Mitstreitern (es sind tatsächlich lauter Männer …) Interviews geführt hat, trägt mit seinen eigenen Erinnerungen dazu bei, dass dies gelingt. Er kennt die vier persönlich und hat bei Eisenman sogar im Büro gearbeitet, als dieser sich erstmals in digitale Gefilde vorwagte. Dass dieser persönliche Zugang in einem gewissen Widerspruch zum auf dem Umschlag angekündigten Anspruch einer Geschichtsschreibung steht, könnte man kritisieren, in Wirklichkeit ist es aber genau das Überzeugende an Lynns Projekt.

Die vier ausgewählten Protagonisten stehen jeweils für sehr unterschiedliche Zugänge zum Digitalen. Frank Gehry und Peter Eisenman waren beide bereits Stars, als sie begannen, den Computer in ihren Projekten einzusetzen. Gehry fing an, Software aus der Flugzeugindustrie zu verwenden, um seine extravaganten Formen präziser bauen zu können. Eisenman trat in einen Dialog mit dem Form Z-Entwickler Chris Yessios, weil er sich für die algorithmische Umsetzung seiner abstrakten Vokabulare und für Fraktale interessierte. Shoei Yoh ist ein japanischer Architekt, der schon Anfang der Neunzigerjahre aus performativen Kriterien entwickelte, unregelmäßige Raumfachwerke baute. Chuck Hoberman hat sich mit seinen transfor-

mierbaren Objekten – etwa der von ihm patentierten sogenannten Hoberman Sphere, die man als Miniatur in Museumsshops kaufen kann – einen Namen gemacht. Für ihn war der Computer ein Mittel, die Komplexität seiner Entwürfe in den Griff zu bekommen und die digitale Fabrikation diente ihm dazu, die für ihre Beweglichkeit notwendige Präzision in der Ausführung zu erreichen. Von den vier ausgewählten Pionieren ist er als gelernter Maschineningenieur nicht nur der einzige Nicht-Architekt, sondern auch der einzige, der selbst programmieren kann und seine eigenen digitalen Werkzeuge entwickelt hat.

Die Publikation ist in zwei separate, durch die Schutzhülle verbundene Teile gegliedert. Der erste Teil, „Field Notes" betitelt, enthält die Interviews mit den vier Protagonisten und den jeweiligen Mitarbeitern. Sie lesen sich angenehm unprätentiös. Frank Gehry etwa gibt unumwunden zu, dass er nach wie vor wenig Ahnung vom Computer hat und ihn (bis vor kurzem) nie selbst bedient hat. Er erzählt auch, dass er sich nur sehr schwer von dessen Potenzial überzeugen ließ. Zunächst war es der sterile, seelenlose „Look" der Computerrenderings, welcher Gehry abstieß. Was ihn dann aber überzeugte, war der handfeste öko-

of discovery into the past "archaeology"—one that lies only twenty-five years back, as undertaken by Lynn's book. This holds especially true considering that the digital has presented historical research with entirely new challenges: digital data from that period has disappeared for the most part, and with it also the programs and hardware used in developing it.

It is a special achievement of Lynn's exhibition and book that so many artifacts were tracked down and brought together, and that these items are described and commented in such a way that they begin to speak for themselves. This obviously relates to the fact that the protagonists are living and have used their personal recollections to help reconstruct lost information. It is not least Greg Lynn himself who aptly supplies his own memories in conducting his interviews with the four protagonists and their colleagues (an all male cast, by the way). Lynn is on personal terms with all four, and he even worked in Eisenman's firm back when the latter dared to first step into the digital realm. One might criticize that this personal approach

conflicts to a certain extent with the claim to historiography announced on the cover, but in reality it is precisely this facet of Lynn's project that proves convincing.

Each of the four protagonists selected stands for a very different point of access to the digital. Both Frank Gehry and Peter Eisenman were already famous when they began using computer technology in their projects. Gehry started out by using software from the aviation industry in order to be able to build his extravagant forms with higher precision. Eisenman entered into dialogue with the form·Z developer Chris Yessios, because he was interested in the algorithmic realization of his abstract vocabulary and in fractals. Shoei Yoh is a Japanese architect who in the early 1990s was already building enormous non-standard roof-trusses based on performative criteria. Chuck Hoberman made a name for himself with his transformable objects, for example the extraordinary Hoberman Sphere (patented) that can be purchased as a miniature in museum shops. To him, computers represented a means of getting to grips with

the complexity of his designs, and digital fabrication helped him achieve the precision necessary for their intricate mechanisms. Of the four selected pioneers, Hoberman as a trained mechanical engineer was the only non-architect, but he was also the only one capable of doing computer programming himself and thus developing his own digital tools.

The publication is cleverly presented as two books in one held together by the back cover. The first part, called "Field Notes," contains refreshingly down-to-earth interviews with the four protagonists and their respective colleagues. Frank Gehry, for example, frankly admits to still being more or less computer illiterate when it comes to design and to having only just recently operated one himself. He also notes how resistant he was to being convinced of its potential. At first, it was the sterile, soulless "look" of the computer renderings that Gehry found disagreeable. But he later came to be convinced by the substantial economic advantage to be gained by the use of CATIA software. In the interview, he cited the enormous re-

nomische Vorteil, der sich durch die Verwendung der Software CATIA erzielen ließ. Im Interview erwähnt er die enorme Kostenreduktion beim Guggenheim in Bilbao: „[...] eighteen percent under budget. After that there was really no turning back [...]" (S. 26). Bekanntlich hat er mit Gehry Technologies auch eine Firma gegründet, die zunächst die hauseigene Weiterentwicklung von CATIA für Architekten verkaufen wollte, sich inzwischen aber als Dienstleister für die Umsetzung komplexer Konstruktionen am Markt etabliert hat.

Im Interview mit Eisenman kann sich dieser gar nicht mehr daran erinnern, dass beim Biozentrum-Projekt in Frankfurt überhaupt ein Computer zum Einsatz kam. Der Rechner war tatsächlich nicht im Büro, sondern an der Ohio State University, wo Eisenman den Programmierer Chris Yessios kennengelernt hatte. Eisenman war fasziniert von den digitalen Möglichkeiten, die seiner Art zu denken sehr verwandt waren. Er verlangte von Yessios immer wieder neue Funktionen, wovon dieser bei der Entwicklung seiner Software, welche er später unter dem Namen Form Z auf den Markt brachte, profitierte. Beim Biozentrum-Projekt wollte Eisenman den Plan aus einem for-malen Spiel mit den vier Aminosäuren der DNS entwickeln. Der Plan durchlief dabei viele Iterationen aufgrund von Eisenmans immer wieder modifizierten Angaben. Von der OSU kamen per FedEx die geplotteten Pläne ins Büro, in dem Lynn von Hand zeichnete und versuchte, mit dem Computer Schritt zu halten. Lynn erklärt, dass Eisenman eigentlich der Computer gewesen sei und er, Lynn, der menschliche Plotter, der sich bemühte, seinen Job zu behalten, indem er zeichnete wie wild. Lynn sieht in Eisenman den Erfinder des Parametrismus. Dieser bedankt sich artig, aber er besteht darauf, dass er nichts dergleichen im Sinn hatte und einfach seinen Interessen folgte. Es hatte auch noch nichts mit seinen später an Derrida und anderen entwickelten linguistischen Theorien zu tun. „What we were looking at were fractals. That was Mandelbrot, not linguistics" (S. 49).

Im seitenstärkeren zweiten Teil, „Project Files", findet man die in der Ausstellung gezeigten Pläne und Modelle der in den Interviews besprochenen Projekte. Während weder Gehry noch Eisenman detailliert auf die handwerklichen Einzelheiten eingehen wollen (oder können), geben sowohl die Interviews mit ihren Mitarbeitern als auch die abgebildeten Artefakte ein sehr aufschluss-reiches und authentisches Bild. Es wird deutlich, wieviel improvisiert werden musste, wie beschränkt die Möglichkeiten verglichen mit heute waren, vor allem aber, dass hier nichts zufällig passierte, sondern dass die Beteiligten das Neuland mit erstaunlicher Zielstrebigkeit betraten.

Dieser Pioniergeist, der in den Aussagen der weniger prominenten Interviewpartner deutlicher zu spüren ist als bei den beiden Megastars, ist es, welcher das Buch lesenswert macht. Greg Lynn ist es gelungen, die Geschichte dieser Umbruchzeit zu erzählen und so anschaulich zu illustrieren, dass auch Dinge, die sonst nur Geeks interessieren, interessant werden. Der auf dem Umschlag angekündigten Geschichtsschreibung wird das Buch insofern gerecht, als die vier besonders prononcierten Positionen tatsächlich ein breites Spektrum abdecken und durch die Reduktion auf nur vier auch die Möglichkeit entsteht, sich die Dinge genauer anzusehen. Die Auswahl wirkt stimmig und authentisch, auch weil sie sehr persönlich ist: Sie ist gewissermaßen ein Spiegel der intellektuellen Biografie von Greg Lynn.

Urs Hirschberg

---

duction of cost in building the Guggenheim in Bilbao: "… eighteen percent under budget. After that there was really no turning back …" (p. 26). It is common knowledge that he founded a company, Gehry Technologies, which had initially wanted to sell a version of CATIA for architects that had been further developed in-house. The company has meanwhile become established as a service provider for the implementation of complex constructions in the marketplace.

In the interview with Eisenman, the architect notes that he cannot recall a computer having been used in the Biozentrum project in Frankfurt. The computer in question was not actually situated in his office but rather at Ohio State University (OSU), where Eisenman had met the programmer Chris Yessios. Eisenman was fascinated by the digital possibilities, which shared a close affinity with his way of thinking. He requested more and more new functions from Yessios, who in turn profited from the development of his software, which he later marketed under the name form·Z. In the Biozentrum project, Eisenman wanted to develop the architectural plan by playing with the form of the four DNA amino acids. The plan experienced much iteration due to the repeatedly modified requests issued by Eisenman. The plotted plans were sent by OSU via FedEx to Eisenman's office, where Lynn worked on the drafts by hand and tried to keep up with the computer. Lynn explains how Eisenmann himself was really the computer and how Lynn, the human plotter, was drawing like crazy in an effort to keep his job. Lynn views Eisenman as the inventor of parametricism. And though the latter courteously expresses his thanks, he insists that it was nothing of the sort, that he was merely pursuing his own interests. Eisenman also states that the work on the Biozentrum project had nothing to do with his later linguistic theories related to Derrida and others: "What we were looking at were fractals. That was Mandelbrot, not linguistics" (p. 49).

The longer second part, "Project Files," features plans and models of the projects discussed in the interviews, which were also shown in the exhibition. Although neither Gehry nor Eisenman wanted (or were able) to expound on technical details, the interviews with their colleagues as well as the depicted artifacts offer a very informative and authentic picture. It becomes clear how strong a role improvisation played, how limited the possibilities were compared to the present day and, most of all, how nothing here transpired by chance—indeed, all those involved stepped into virgin territory with remarkable determination.

It is this pioneering spirit—more strongly present in the statements of the less prominent interview partners than in those of the two megastars—that make this book so worth reading. Greg Lynn has succeeded in telling and vividly illustrating the story of this transitional period in such a way that things that might have otherwise interested the geeks only become fascinating. The book addresses the historiographical approach signalized on the cover in that the four highlighted positions certainly do cover a broad spectrum. By limiting the positions to only four, the author was able to examine issues more closely. The selection comes across as coherent and authentic, not least

Aus der Hecke geschossen

The Sniper's Log: Architectural Chronicles of Generation X (10)

Alejandro Zaera-Polo

Barcelona: ACTAR, 2012 (in Zusammenarbeit mit Princeton University School of Architecture)

Englisch, 592 Seiten, Fotografien und Illustrationen in Duoton, broschiert

ISBN 978-84-92861-22-4

EUR 34,00

Seien wir mal ehrlich, als Buchtitel ist *Architectural Chronicles of Generation X* eher sperrig und um den Aufbau des Buches besser zu repräsentieren, verwendet Alejandro Zaera-Polo den wesentlich eingängigeren Begriff *The Sniper's Log*. Die einfache, gleichwohl überzeugende Geste des Titels wie auch des Covers (weiße Schrift auf schwarzem Hintergrund) lassen einiges vermuten. Die Assoziation mit einem wachsamen, zielgerichteten und dynamischen Beobachter erweckt große Erwartungen – und wir werden nicht enttäuscht.

Zaera-Polo selbst beschreibt die Metapher des Scharfschützen als Protagonisten für eine Erkennt-

nistheorie der Gegenwart (S. 4). Der Scharfschütze zielt aus der Entfernung. Er bewahrt so den Überblick und eine kritische Distanz zum anvisierten Subjekt. Eine seiner wesentlichen Eigenschaften ist die moralische und politische Unbestimmtheit, die es ihm ermöglicht, der Gefahr der Konformität zu entgehen. Dementsprechend folgt das umfassende Werk, welches mehr als 20 Jahre von Zaera-Polos architektonischen Schriften beinhaltet, dem Format einer analytischen Berichterstattung in einem weiten und offenen Betrachtungsfeld. Jeder Eintrag steht für sich und ist dennoch ein Beitrag zum übergreifenden Konzept, Architekturtheorie und ihren Bezug zur Praxis neu zu denken.

Für diejenigen, die befürchten, dass diese Zusammenstellung auf 592 Seiten nur eine weitere aufgeblasene Architekt-wird-Autor-Sammlung von Daten und Bildern sei – keine Sorge, sie ist es nicht! Die eingehende Beobachtung des architektonischen Metiers und dessen vielseitiger Referenzen in Verbindung mit einem scharfsinnigen Schreibstil machen dieses Buch nicht nur zu einem informativen, sondern auch sehr unterhaltsamen literarischen Werk im Bereich der Architektur. Es setzt die Arbeiten einiger der bekann-

testen Global Player, die eigenen Arbeiten des Autors für FOA[1] und charakteristische Aspekte des Architekturdiskurses wie Typologie und Material in ihren wirtschaftlichen, sozialen, kulturellen und politischen Zusammenhang. Das Ergebnis ist eine Themensammlung mit unterschiedlichem Maßstab und Schreibstil, präsentiert in einer schnellen Abfolge, die überrascht, bisweilen irritiert, aber dabei einen ausgesprochen reichhaltigen Nährboden für architektonisches Denken und Handeln bietet. Das Buch beansprucht weder Ausgiebigkeit noch Vollständigkeit, obwohl der Begriff *Chronik* Gegenteiliges vermuten ließe. Es wurde nicht in einem Zug geschrieben und so sollte es auch nicht gelesen werden. Stattdessen enthüllt es allmählich die Blindflecken des architektonischen Spektrums, die eine weiterführende Betrachtung fordern. *The Sniper's Log* ist kein Manifest, sondern der Aufruf zu einer Diskussion, die nach Meinung des Autors zu einer architektonischen Identität der *Generation von Nomaden* beitragen kann.

1   Zaera-Polo gründete Foreign Office Architects im Jahr 1993 zusammen mit seiner Partnerin Farshid Moussavi. Das Büro wurde 2011 aufgelöst. Seit 2013 leitet er AZPML zusammen mit Maider Llaguno.

because it is very personal—almost a mirror of the intellectual biography of Greg Lynn.

Urs Hirschberg
(translation Dawn Michelle d'Atri)

Fired from Ambush

The Sniper's Log: Architectural Chronicles of Generation X (10)

Alejandro Zaera-Polo

Barcelona: ACTAR, 2012 (with the collaboration of Princeton University School of Architecture)

English, 592 pages, photographs and illustrations in duotone, paperback

ISBN 978-84-92861-22-4

EUR 34.00

Well, let's face it, as a book title *Architectural Chronicles of Generation X* is a bit of a mouthful and to better represent the composition of the book, Alejandro Zaera-Polo added the some-

what catchier phrase: *The Sniper's Log*. The simple, yet strong gesture of both the title and the cover (white font on black background) suggest greater things to come. The association with an alert, precise and dynamic observer raises high expectations—and we shall not be disappointed.

Zaera-Polo himself describes the metaphor of the sniper as a "protagonist for a contemporary epistemology of the now" (p. 4). The sniper takes aim from a distance, thus maintaining a broad overview and crucial independence from the subject he is targeting. Evading moral and political correctness is one of his essential attributes allowing him to avoid conformism. Consequently, the extensive volume, comprising more than 20 years of Zaera-Polo's architectural writings, follows the format of an analytical register with a rather broad and open framework. It allows each entry to stand for itself while contributing to the overall concept of reconfiguring the position of architectural theory and its relationship to practice.

For those of you who fear that this compilation on 592 pages might be yet another puffed up

architect-cum-author collection of data and images—rest assured, it's not! Providing a thorough observation of the architectural field and its varied points of reference in combination with a sharp-witted style of writing, make this book not only an informative but also very entertaining piece of architectural literature. It puts the work of some of the best known global players, the author's own projects at FOA[1] and general issues of the architectural spectrum, such as typology and material, into economic, social, cultural and political context. The result is a collection of subject-matters varying in scale and style, arranged in a fast-paced sequence that might seem surprising, even irritating at times, but which presents a remarkably rich breeding ground for architectural thought and practice. The book does not claim comprehensive-

1   In 1993, Zaera-Polo established Foreign Office Architects together with his partner Farshid Moussavi. The office was dissolved in 2011. As of 2013 he runs AZPML together with Maider Llaguno.

Daher verwirft das Protokoll auch jeglichen chronologischen Ablauf und ist stattdessen in vier Kapitel unterteilt, die den inhaltlichen Rahmen definieren: 1) Global Positioning Systems,

2) Breeding Sciences, 3) Nomad Practices, und 4) Material Politics. Die Texte sind so vielseitig wie Zaera-Polos Verbindungen zur Architektur im Laufe seiner Karriere. Sie reichen von Artikeln und Kritiken in Fachzeitschriften wie *El Croquis*, *Arch+* und *Log* bis zu Eröffnungsreden bei der Venedig Biennale und akademischen Aufsätzen während seiner Lehrtätigkeit in Yale, Berlage oder seit kurzem als Dekan in Princeton. Seine Schriften sind durchgängig von biografischen Elementen begleitet, die auf die eine oder andere Art das Leben des Autors und das Verfassen der Texte beeinflusst haben. Obwohl sie eine persönliche Auflistung darstellen, erleichtern sie es, seinen Gedanken zu folgen.

Abgesehen von der inhaltlichen Zuordnung unterscheidet Zaera-Polo auch nach acht Textgenres, wie z.B. theoretisch, anleitend und gesprochen, die durch unterschiedliche Layouts und Schriften hervorgehoben sind. Insgesamt spielt die grafische Darstellung für die Orientierung des Lesers beim Manövrieren durch das anspruchsvolle Werk eine große Rolle. Dennoch lassen sich die Layouts nicht leicht lesen, da sie beständig durch eine Vielzahl von Bildern im Duoton-Stil unterbrochen sind – kleinformatige Fotografien

und Illustrationen in gedämpften Farben, die nie direkt mit dem Text in Verbindung gebracht werden und deren Referenzen erst im Anhang des Buchs zu finden sind. Zaera-Polo fordert uns somit auf, Bilder nicht als Erläuterung des Texts zu verstehen, sondern als Mittel, ihn im Gesamtzusammenhang einzubetten. Bilder schaffen eine Stimmung. Sie lassen unseren Assoziationen freien Lauf. Tatsächlich stellen sie zumeist bekannte Personen und Ereignisse dar, die durch ihre Vertrautheit leicht verständlich sind.

Der Scharfschütze bewegt sich gewandt über das architektonische Feld. Obwohl er innerhalb weniger Augenblicke sein Ziel ändert, gibt er sich nie nur mit einem Kratzer an der Oberfläche zufrieden. Ein Ziel treffen, heißt es zu durchdringen. Somit ist das Ziel niemals nur das jeweilige Thema, sondern auch der/die Lesende selbst. Zaera-Polos Buch ist ein Gewehrfeuer von Konzepten, Vorschlägen und Gedankenfetzen, die unseren Verstand ins Visier nehmen mit dem einzigen Ziel, unsere „grauen Zellen" zu entzünden. Seine Texte jonglieren mit den grundlegenden Paarungen des Architekturdiskurses: Stabilität und Nomadentum, Kritik und Paradigma, Praxis und Theorie. Dies bestimmt die eigentliche Relevanz des

---

ness, let alone completeness, though the term *chronicles* might suggest otherwise. It was not written in one go, nor is it meant to be read as such. Instead, it slowly unravels the blind spots of architectural discourse which demand further reflection. *The Sniper's Log* is not a manifesto but a starting point for a debate, which, according to the author, could inform the architectural identity of the *nomad generation*.

Therefore, the log abandons chronological order and instead is structured in four chapters, which provide the contextual framework: 1) Global Positioning Systems, 2) Breeding Sciences, 3) Nomad Practices, and 4) Material Politics. The texts are as manifold as Zaera-Polo's engagement with architecture throughout his career ranging from essays and critiques published in periodicals like *El Croquis*, *Arch+* and *Log* to opening speeches at the Venice Biennale and academic proposals while teaching at Yale, Berlage, or most recently holding the position of dean at Princeton. His writings are continuously framed by biographic elements that have, in one way or another, been

influential in the author's life and the production of the text. Despite being a personal account, they allow us to relate to his train of thoughts.

Apart from the content-based allocation, Zaera-Polo also assigns the collection to eight different text genres, such as theoretical, instructive and conversational, visually accentuated by varying layouts and fonts. Overall, the graphic representation plays a major role in the reader's orientation when maneuvering through the ambitious volume. However, these layouts do not read easily as they are continuously broken up by a multitude of images in duotone style—small-sized photographs and illustrations in subtle colors, never directly linked to the text and only referenced in the credit section at the end of the book. Thus, Zaera-Polo requires us to change our way of understanding imagery not as an illustration of the text but rather as a means of grounding it in its wider context. Images are setting the mood. They let our associations run wild. Indeed, most of them depict well-known persons and events that read fluently due to their familiarity.

The sniper moves quickly across the architectural field. Though he changes his target in an instant, he never settles for a mere scratch on the surface. Hitting a target means penetrating it. As such, the target is never only the subject at hand, but also the reader himself or herself. Zaera-Polo's book is a gunfire of concepts, proposals, and shreds of thoughts taking accurate aim at our minds with the only purpose to ignite our 'grey matter.' His writings juggle the quintessential juxtapositions of architectural discourse: steadiness and nomadism, critique and paradigm, practice and theory. This constitutes the actual relevance of the book. According to Zaera-Polo, theory is a means of understanding one's surroundings and "bring[ing] order to the realms we operate within" (p. 3). As such, theory is a practice. Linking the production of architecture to the production of thought seems more promising than enforcing the concept of generation.

I am avoiding direct references to any one of the texts as no single entry can fully capture the significance of the completed log—with one **299**

Buches. Nach Zaera-Polo ist Theorie ein Mittel zum Verständnis der Umgebung und des Rahmens, in dem wir tätig sind (S. 3). Theorie ist somit Praxis. Die Produktion von Architektur eng mit der Produktion von Gedanken zu verbinden, scheint vielversprechender, als das Konzept der Generation zu bemühen.

Ich vermeide hier direkte Referenzen zu den einzelnen Texten, weil kein alleiniger Eintrag die Bedeutung des Gesamtprotokolls wiedergeben kann – mit einer Ausnahme: eine Bemerkung Zaera-Polos in der Mitte des Buches. In seinem Aufruf für Londons Olympische Spiele 2012 im Grunge-Stil, um besser die Identität der Gastgeberstadt zu reflektieren, notiert er: „Die erstaunlichste Schönheit ist niemals die, die wir erwarten, sondern die, die uns überrascht." (S. 364). Als abschließenden Kommentar zum vorliegenden Buch und als Betonung seiner konzeptuellen Stärke, die in den verschwommenen Konturen von Inspiration, Bildung und reinem Vergnügen zu finden ist, möchte ich diesen Satz umformulieren: Der fesselndste Gedanke ist der, der aus der Hecke geschossen kommt.

Uta Gelbke

Modernisierung als Übersetzung

Architecture in Translation. Germany, Turkey, and the Modern House (11)
Esra Akcan
Durham/London: Duke University Press, 2012
Englisch, 392 Seiten, SW-Abbildungen, broschiert
ISBN 978-0822353089
EUR 18,90

In den letzten Jahren steigt das Interesse an den Transformationsprozessen der europäischen Architekturmoderne in nicht-westlichen Ländern. Auch zur Türkei sind kürzlich Einzelstudien, etwa zu Ernst Egli, erschienen. Nach einigen Werkuntersuchungen von türkischer Seite in den 1980er Jahren hat Bernd Nicolai 1998 das Forschungsterrain der deutsch-türkischen Beziehungsgeschichte aus der Perspektive der – im Bereich der Architekturgeschichte erst sehr spät einsetzenden – Exilforschung eröffnet.[1] Mittlerweile ist auch die Postkolonialismus-Forschung, die sich von den Begriffen (zivilisiert/rückständig), Hierarchisierungen und Asymmetrien der kolonialen Kulturkritik und dem Mythos einer problemfreien Modernisierung und „Verwestlichung" distanziert, für die Architekturforschung interessant geworden.

Die Verschiebung des architekturhistorischen Standpunktes in einen postkolonialistischen Kontext steht auch im Zentrum der Forschungsinteressen von Esra Akcan, die an der Universität Istanbul Architektur studiert hat, an der Columbia University promoviert wurde und derzeit an der University of Illinois in Chicago Kunstgeschichte lehrt. In ihrem Buch *Architecture in Translation* untersucht sie die kulturellen Interaktionen und hybriden Artefakte, die in der „Kontaktzone" zwischen Deutschland und der Türkei von den 1920er bis in die 1950erJahre entstanden sind, und wählt dazu das Konzept der kulturellen Übersetzung.

Vor dem Hintergrund der postkolonialen Theorien nimmt Akcan ihren Ausgangspunkt in der Überzeugung, dass angesichts der bestehenden geo- und soziopolitischen Hierarchien Übersetzung nicht als neutrale Brücke zwischen Kulturen aufgefasst werden kann. In diesem Sinn wird die von der kemalistischen Elite forcierte

1 Bernd Nicolai, *Moderne und Exil. Deutschsprachige Architekten in der Türkei 1925–1955*, Berlin 1998.

---

exemption: a statement Zaera-Polo puts forward about half way through the book. In his plead for a Grunge-style London Olympics 2012, in order to better reflect the identity of its host city, Zaera-Polo notes: "The most astonishing beauty is never the one we expect, but the one that takes us by surprise" (p. 364). As a final comment on the book and to exemplify its conceptual strength nested in the blurred outlines of inspiration, education, and pure pleasure, I want to re-phrase this sentence: The most intriguing thought is the one fired from ambush.

Uta Gelbke (translation Uta Gelbke)

Modernization as Translation

Architecture in Translation: Germany, Turkey, and the Modern House (11)
Esra Akcan
Durham and London: Duke University Press, 2012
English, 392 pages, black-and-white illustrations, paperback
ISBN 978-0822353089
EUR 18.90

In recent years interest has been growing in the transformative processes of European architectural modernism on the part of non-Western countries. Lately, also studies focused on Turkey have appeared, for instance on Ernst Egli. After several thematic analyses were carried out on the Turkish end in the 1980s, Bernd Nicolai opened up the research terrain of German-Turkish relational history in 1998 in pursuing a perspective of exile studies, which did not become a part of the architectural history field until very late in the game.[1] Now also of interest in an architectural research context is the field of postcolonial studies, which distances itself from the terms, hierarchizations, and asymmetries of colonial cultural criticism and from the myth of a smooth modernization and "Westernization."

The shift of the architectural-historical stance to a postcolonial context is one of the main research interests of Esra Akcan, who studied architecture at the University of Istanbul, earned her doctorate at Columbia University, and currently teaches art history at the University of Illinois in Chicago. In her book *Architecture in Translation*, she explores the cultural interactions and hybrid artifacts that arose in the "contact zone" between Germany and Turkey over a time span from the 1920s to the 1950s. Here she pursues the concept of cultural translation.

Against the backdrop of postcolonial theory, Akcan finds her point of departure in the conviction that translation—despite the existing geo- and sociopolitical hierarchies—cannot be conceived as a neutral bridge between cultures. In this sense the modernization of the new Turkish nation-state, as forced by the Kemalist elite, is understood to be a translation where the transfer

1 Bernd Nicolai, *Moderne und Exil: Deutschsprachige Architekten in der Türkei 1925–1955* (Berlin, 1998).

Modernisierung des neuen türkischen National-
staates als Übersetzung verstanden, in der sich
die Übertragungsbewegungen von Architekten,
architektonischen Ideen, Bildern, Informationen
und Technologien keineswegs als reibungslos
und egalitär erweisen.

Nach der 1923 erfolgten Gründung der türkischen Republik wurde eine große Zahl hoch
qualifizierter und erfahrener deutschsprachiger
Experten aus dem Bereich Architektur und Stadtplanung in die Türkei berufen (ab 1933 als Exi-
lanten), um der neuen Hauptstadt Ankara und
anderen Städten einen ebenso modernen wie re-
präsentativen Stempel aufzudrücken (was zum
Teil als Fernbeziehung über jeweils übersetzte
Briefe verlief) und die Ausbildung türkischer Architekturstudenten zu übernehmen. Von den türkischen Architekten hatten einige in Deutschland
studiert oder kannten die deutschen Positionen
zumindest aus Zeitschriften und anderen Publikationen.

Esra Akcan beschränkt sich in ihrer Studie
auf das Thema des modernen Wohnhauses. Dadurch fällt einerseits der für den *nation-building*-
Prozess besonders aufschlussreiche Bau von Re-
gierungs- und Bildungsgebäuden (der bei früheren Studien zu den deutschsprachigen Architekten in der Türkei meist einen wichtigen Teil aus-
gemacht hat) weg, andererseits wird dadurch
aber erst die Untersuchung von Auffassungen
und Modellen der türkischen Architekten möglich, unter denen kaum einer mit öffentlichen
Aufträgen betraut wurde. Somit kann nicht nur
die Asymmetrie in der Vorstellung eines Kul-
turimports überwunden, sondern auch das Dilemma der türkischen Architekten „of being
modern without ‚being absorbed' or ‚colonized
by Europe'" (S. 133) betrachtet werden.

Im ersten Kapitel steht die Transformation
der historisch unbedeutenden Provinzstadt Ankara
zur modernen Hauptstadt der Türkei als „Modernisierung von oben" und „smooth translation"
im Zentrum. Akcan diskutiert die verschiedenen
Gartenstadtkonzepte und deren Bedeutungsände-
rungen im Übersetzungsprozess (von England
nach Deutschland und von Deutschland in die
Türkei) im Hinblick auf die Anlage von Wohn-
siedlungen innerhalb der Stadtplanungen des
Berliner Architekten Herrmann Jansen. Mit den
Bauten von Clemens Holzmeister und Ernst Egli
entstand das „neue Haus", das die Symbole des
mit den osmanischen Machthabern assoziierten

ESRA AKCAN

ARCHITECTURE
IN TRANSLATION   GERMANY,
                 TURKEY,
                 & THE
                 MODERN
                 HOUSE
11

orientalischen Lebens vergessen machen sollte
und einen höheren Sozialstatus bedeutete.

Das Dilemma der Glorifizierung der westlichen Kultur und des dadurch simultan hervorge-

---

movements of architects, architectural ideas, images, information, and technology may by no
means be considered fluent and egalitarian.

After the successful founding of the Turkish
Republic in 1923, a large number of highly quali-
fied and experienced native-German-speaking
experts from the field of architecture and urban
planning were called to Turkey (as expatriates
starting in 1933). The objective was to make a
modernist and representative mark on the new
capital city of Ankara and other cities (which
ensued in part through letters translated on both
ends) and also to assume responsibility for educating Turkish architecture students. Some of
the Turkish architects had studied in Germany
or were at least familiar with German positions
from journals and other publications.

Esra Akcan limited her study to the topic of
modern residential buildings. On the one hand,
this omitted the construction of the government
and education buildings that had taken on special significance in the nation-building process
(and which played an important role in earlier
studies conducted by architects from German-
speaking countries in Turkey). On the other hand,
this research approach allowed an investigation
of concepts and models developed by Turkish
architects that were so rarely developed under
public commissions. Therefore, it was possible
not only to overcome the asymmetry associated
with the idea of importing culture, but also to consider the Turkish architects' dilemma "of being
modern without 'being absorbed' or 'colonized
by Europe'" (p. 133).

The first chapter presents the transformation
of the historically insignificant provincial town
of Ankara into the modern capital of Turkey as
"top-down modernization" and deems it to have
been a "smooth translation." Akcan discusses
the various garden city concepts and changes in
meaning associated with the translation process
(from England to Germany, and from Germany
to Turkey) and cites the establishment of housing settlements that were part of urban-planning
measures by the Berlin architect Herrmann Jansen.
In the case of the structures built by Clemens

Holzmeister and Ernst Egli, a "new house" of
higher social status emerged that was intended to
move beyond the symbols of Oriental life associated with the Ottoman rulers.

According to Akcan, the dilemma related to
the glorification of Western culture and the related
simultaneously evoked feelings of fragility, inse-
curity, and inferiority manifested in a state of mel-
ancholy among the artists and intellectuals in
Istanbul, as is thematized in the following chapter. The wooden structures of the Ottoman period,
having been left to deteriorate, were now considered to be treasured vestiges of a lost civilization
and were accordingly drawn upon in the design
process, with the author citing buildings by the
architect Sedad Eldem.

In the third section, Akcan works with the
concept of the *subaltern*, with an orientation to
Antonio Gramsci and Gayatri Chakravorty Spivak.
The author invokes this term, which connotes non-
dominant groups that are separated from the elite
by social practices of exclusion, in contradicting
the conviction shared by architects like Martin

rufen Gefühls der Fragilität, Unsicherheit und Unterlegenheit manifestierte sich, so Akcan, unter den Künstlern und Intellektuellen in Istanbul in einem Zustand der Melancholie, die im folgenden Kapitel thematisiert wird. Die dem Verfall überlassenen alten Holzhäuser der osmanischen Zeit werden als kostbarer letzter Überrest einer verlorenen Zivilisation aufgefasst und beim Entwurf herangezogen, wie die Autorin am Beispiel der Bauten des Architekten Sedad Eldem zeigen kann.

Im dritten Abschnitt arbeitet Akcan mit dem an Antonio Gramsci und Gayatri Chakravorty Spivak orientierten *subaltern*-Begriff, mit dem nicht-dominante, durch soziale Exklusionspraktiken nicht zur Elite zählende Gruppen bezeichnet werden, um der von Architekten wie Martin Wagner, Wilhelm Schütte oder Ernst Egli vorgebrachten Überzeugung, dass die europäischen Normen des Modernismus reibungslos übersetzbar seien, zu widersprechen. Dabei dient ihr als Gegenbeispiel für eine doppelte – geopolitische und ökonomische – Benachteiligung die an der Schwarzmeerküste liegende Bergbau-Stadt Zonguldak. Das vierte Kapitel handelt vom „originalen türkischen Haus". Statt eine eigene Definition des aus verschiedenen Einflüssen entstandenen Hybrids zu geben, fokussiert die Autorin auf die Geschichte der Konstruktion und Definition eines „Originals" vor dem Hintergrund von Ziya Gökalps Vorstellung von der Unübersetzbarkeit der Kultur als authentischem Wert der Nation und der Übersetzbarkeit der Zivilisation als wissenschaftlich-technischem Fortschritt. Bruno Tauts im japanischen und türkischen Exil entwickelte Kritik an der sich über die ganze Welt verbreitenden europäischen „Allerweltsarchitektur" und seine damit verbundene Suche nach einer das Dilemma der Modernisierung überwindenden Universalität und „kosmopolitischen Ethik" mutet schließlich im letzten Kapitel fast wie eine erlösende Vision der aus der kulturellen Übersetzung resultierenden Probleme an.

Architecture in Translation ist als wichtiger, theoretisch fundierter Beitrag zu einem postkolonialen Verständnis der Architekturentwicklung in einer globalisierten Welt zu werten. Esra Akcan wendet sich mit ihrem methodischen Ansatz den höchst komplexen Vorgängen innerhalb kultureller Transmissionsbewegungen zu. Wünschenswert wäre dabei gewesen, dass die Autorin die Vorzüge ihres Übersetzungskonzeptes gegenüber (älteren) Versuchen, die Übertragungsprozesse mit Begriffen wie Rezeption, Akkulturation, Kulturtransfer oder kulturellem Austausch zu beschreiben, erörtert hätte. So wäre eine Abgrenzung in Bezug auf das seit den 1990er Jahren diskutierte Kulturtransfer-Konzept interessant, vor allem in Bezug auf das 2008 erschienene Buch *Kulturtransfer und nationale Identität* von Burcu Dogramaci, bei dem es – wie der (bei Akcan übrigens im Literaturverzeichnis nicht angeführte) Untertitel besagt – ebenfalls um deutschsprachige Architekten und Stadtplaner in der Türkei geht.[2] Auf ein wichtiges Argument für den Übersetzungsbegriff geht Akcan lediglich in einer Fußnote (S. 291) ein: Anders als bei Begriffen wie Transfer, Import, Export oder *flow* sei beim Terminus Übersetzung der Akt der Veränderung während dieses Prozesses inbegriffen.

Auch wenn der Wert der ansonsten sehr überzeugenden und für künftige Architekturforschun-

---

2   Burcu Dogramaci, *Kulturtransfer und nationale Identität. Deutschsprachige Architekten, Stadtplaner und Bildhauer in der Türkei nach 1927*, Berlin 2008.

Wagner, Wilhelm Schütte, or Ernst Egli that the European norms of modernism can be seamlessly transferred to other regions. As a counter-example for twofold (geopolitical and economic) disadvantagement, she cites the mining town of Zonguldak situated along the Black Sea coast. The fourth chapter, in turn, deals with the "original Turkish house." Instead of providing her own definition of this hybrid created from various influences, the author focuses on the history of its construction and the definition of an "original" against the background of Ziya Gökalp's idea that culture as an authentic national value is untranslatable while civilization may indeed be translated into scientific, technical advancement. In the last chapter, the critical commentary developed by Bruno Taut while exiled in Japan and Turkey on the European "everyday architecture" spreading across the entire world—and the related quest for universality and "cosmopolitan ethics" to address the dilemma of modernization—ultimately almost seems like a redemptive vision of the problems resulting from cultural translation.

Architecture in Translation may be considered an important, theoretically substantiated contribution to a postcolonial understanding of architectural development in a globalized world. With her methodological approach, Esra Akcan investigates the highly complex processes found in cultural transmission movements. Here it would have been beneficial for the author to have discussed the merits of her translation concept vis-à-vis (more dated) attempts at using terms like reception, acculturation, cultural transfer, or cultural exchange to describe such transfer processes. For instance, it would have been interesting to have the concept of cultural transfer that has been discussed since the 1990s delimited here, especially in relation to Burcu Dogramaci's book *Kulturtransfer und nationale Identität* (Cultural Transfer and National Identity), which was published in 2008 and likewise pursues the topic of German-speaking architects and urban planners working in Turkey[2]—as the book's subtitle indicates (which is, by the way, not found in Akcan's reference list). However, Akcan does touch on an important argument for the translation concept solely in a footnote (p. 291): in contrast to expressions like transfer, import, export, or flow, the term "translation" implies the act of change during this process.

Without intending to devalue of the book's analysis, which is otherwise very convincing and will surely prove seminal to future architectural research, it is important to note that only vague differentiation between Germany and Austria is made. In the beginning, only the relations between Germany and the Ottoman state or, later, Turkey are mentioned, as well as and the state of discourse on architecture and settlements in the Weimar Republic. In the next chapter, however, the Austrian architect Clemens Holzmeister enters the discussion, along with the Vienna-based Swiss architect Ernst Egli, as protagonists of housing modernization, yet without any thematic discussion of the

---

2   Burcu Dogramaci, *Kulturtransfer und nationale Identität: Deutschsprachige Architekten, Stadtplaner und Bildhauer in der Türkei nach 1927* (Berlin, 2008).

gen fruchtbaren Analyse nicht geschmälert werden soll, sei hier doch noch auf eine Unschärfe
in der Differenzierung zwischen Deutschland
und Österreich hingewiesen. Eingangs ist lediglich von der Beziehung zwischen Deutschland
und dem osmanischen Staat bzw. der späteren
Türkei und den Bedingungen der Architektur-
und Siedlungsdebatte in der Weimarer Republik
die Rede. Im folgenden Kapitel werden aber als
Protagonisten der Modernisierung des Wohnens
auch der Österreicher Clemens Holzmeister und
der in Wien ausgebildete Schweizer Ernst Egli
in die Argumentation einbezogen, ohne aber die
Diskrepanz zwischen den durchaus unterschiedlichen Haltungen und Ausdrucksformen zu thematisieren – wohl zugunsten eines homogene-
ren Bildes. Dadurch wird nochmals deutlich,
dass Übersetzung – hier die von der Autorin in
ihrer Studie geleistete – nicht ohne Bedeutungs-
veränderungen abläuft.

Antje Senarclens de Grancy

discrepancy between the quite different approaches
and forms of expression—likely in favor of a more
homogeneous picture. This once again shows how
translation—in this case undertaken by the author
in her study—does not transpire without alteration
of meaning.

Antje Senarclens de Grancy
(translation Dawn Michelle d'Atri)

Monika Schlager

* 7. Juli 1972 | † 14. November 2013

Viel zu früh, sehr bald nach Ihrem 41. Geburtstag, hat uns Monika Schlager (12) am 14.11.2013 verlassen. Der plötzliche Tod von Monika hat ein Loch im Kreise der Kolleginnen und Kollegen der Fakultät hinterlassen, das noch immer spürbar ist. Wir haben eine Kollegin verloren, die immer einfühlsam, hilfsbereit und mit heiterer Gelassenheit auch stressige Arbeitssituationen bewältigt hat. Ihr Kampfgeist und Optimismus, auch im Umgang mit der schweren Erkrankung, wird uns in Erinnerung bleiben. Menschen, die uns begegnen, hinterlassen Spuren, die durch uns wieder sichtbar werden. Liebe Monika, Dein Optimismus bleibt unvergessen.

Barbara Herz

Birgit Schulz (2013), *Wirkung chromatischer Lichträume im Kontext der Architektur*, Institut für Raumgestaltung; 1. Gutachterin: Irmgard Frank, 2. Gutachter: Maximilian Moser; 145 Seiten, Deutsch.

Stefan Siebenhofer (2013), *Hausmühlen in Murau – Analyse von Form, Funktion und Potential dezentralisierter Energiequellen am Bauernhof*, Institut für Architekturtheorie, Kunst- und Kulturwissenschaften; 1. Gutachter: Holger Neuwirth, 2. Gutachter: Hans Gangoly; 278 Seiten, Deutsch.

Ida Pirstinger (2013), *Gründerzeitstadt 2.1 – Die Nachverdichtung von Gründerzeitquartieren – ein Modell zur inneren Stadterweiterung*, Institut für Gebäudelehre; 1. Gutachter: Hans Gangoly, 2. Gutachter: Christoph Luchsinger; 265 Seiten + Aufstockungskataster 165 Seiten + 2 Pläne, Deutsch.

Obituary

Doctoral Theses 2013

Monika Schlager

b. July 7, 1972 | d. November 14, 2013

Much too early, soon after her forty-first birthday, Monika Schlager left us on November 14, 2013. Monika's (12) sudden passing has left a gap in the circle of faculty colleagues, one that is still being felt. We lost a colleague who was always empathetic and helpful, who mastered work situations, even the difficult ones, with such cheerful composure. Her fighting spirit and optimism, even in the face of severe illness, will long be remembered. The individuals we encounter leave behind traces that become visible through us once again. Dearest Monika, your optimism remains unforgettable.

Birgit Schulz (2013), *The Effect of Chromatic Spaces of Light in the Context of Architecture*, Institute of Spatial Design; 1st reviewer: Irmgard Frank, 2nd reviewer: Maximilian Moser; 145 pages, German.

Stefan Siebenhofer (2013), *Household Mills in Murau: An Analysis of the Form, Function, and Potential of Farm-Based Energy Sources*, Institute of Architectural Theory, History of Art and Cultural Studies; 1st reviewer: Holger Neuwirth, 2nd reviewer: Hans Gangoly; 278 pages, German.

Ida Pirstinger (2013), *The Retrospective Densification of Gründerzeit Districts: A Model for Inside Urban Expansion*, Institute of Architectural Typologies; 1st reviewer: Hans Gangoly, 2nd reviewer: Christoph Luchsinger; 265 pages + cataster 165 pages + 2 blueprints, German.

Publikationen/ Forschung

Faustformel Tragwerksentwurf

Philippe Block/Christoph Gengnagel/Stefan Peters
unter Mitarbeit von Marcel Aubert/Eva Pirker/
Ines Prokop
München: DVA Architektur, 2013
Deutsch, 240 Seiten, klappenbroschiert
ISBN 978-3-421-03904-0
EUR 41,20

Das Buch (13) bietet dem Architekten und Bauingenieur ein ideales Werkzeug für Studium und Praxis. Es erläutert anschaulich und komprimiert komplexe Zusammenhänge und befähigt den Nutzer, die wichtigsten Entwurfsparameter schnell und überschlägig zu ermitteln. Ziel ist es, die Aspekte von Strukturform, Lastabtragung, Material und Fügung von Anfang an in den Entwurf einfließen zu lassen. So wird das Tragwerk zum integrativen Bestandteil des Gesamtkonzepts.

Stefan Peters ist Professor für Tragwerksentwurf und seit 2013 Dekan der Fakultät für Architektur der Technischen Universität Graz. **Eva Pirker** ist Universitätsassistentin am Institut für Tragwerksentwurf der Technischen Universität Graz.

Publications/ Research

Faustformel Tragwerksentwurf

Philippe Block/Christoph Gengnagel/Stefan Peters
Assisted by Marcel Aubert/Eva Pirker/Ines Prokop
Munich: DVA Architektur, 2013
German, 240 pages, paperback with flap
ISBN 978-3-421-03904-0
EUR 41.20 [A]

The book (13) offers architects and building engineers a simple tool for study and practice. It explains complex relationships in a clear and concise manner and enables the user to determine the most important planning parameters quickly and roughly. The aim is to allow aspects of structural form, load transfer, material, and transition to enter into the architect's plan from the very beginning, allowing the structural design to become an integrative component of the overall concept.

Stefan Peters is Professor of Structural Design and since 2013 dean of the faculty of architecture at Graz University of Technology. Eva Pirker is a Research and Teaching Associate at the Institute of Structural Design at Graz University of Technology.

Ortsentwürfe: Urbanität im 21. Jahrhundert

Bastian Lange/Gottfried Prasenc/Harald Saiko (eds.)
Berlin: Jovis, 2013
German, 224 pages, softcover
ISBN 978-3-86859-229-0
EUR 25.00

From an urban historical perspective, Graz has always had a "good" shore and a "bad" one. A

Ortsentwürfe – Urbanität im 21. Jahrhundert

Bastian Lange/Gottfried Prasenc/Harald Saiko (Hg.)
Berlin: Jovis, 2013
Deutsch, 224 Seiten, broschiert (Softcover)
ISBN 978-3-86859-229-0
EUR 25,00

Stadthistorisch gab es in Graz schon immer ein „gutes" und ein „schlechtes" Ufer. Um den Schlossberg herum entwickelte sich ein bürgerliches Zentrum, während entlang wichtiger Han-

delsstraßen auf der anderen Murseite ein Scherbenviertel entstand. Im Stadtteil Lend, dessen Charakter lange zweifelhaft schien, konnte sich so im Verborgenen ein kreatives Potenzial entwickeln, welches heute offen auf den Straßen ausgelebt wird.

Über dieses Spannungsfeld aus halbseidenem Image und nachbarschaftlicher Vitalität berichten Experten und Erzähler unterschiedlicher Disziplinen in dem Buch *Ortsentwürfe – Urbanität im 21. Jahrhundert*, welches aus einer Reihe von Symposien der Stadtforscher und Architekten um Gottfried Prasenc und Harald Saiko entstanden ist.

Ortsentwürfe (14) sucht in Graz nach Spuren urbaner Veränderungen, die eine neue Haltung in der Stadt im 21. Jahrhundert vermuten lassen. Nicht als isoliertes Phänomen, sondern im Kontext europäischer Entwicklung werden hier die mittlerweile auch architektonisch sichtbaren Neuformatierungen des städtischen Raums gelesen.

Konkret beziehen sich die Texte immer wieder auf das Stadtteilfest LENDWIRBEL. Nachbarschaftliche Strukturen, Ortsaneignung und alternative Lebensformen werden mit diesem Fest jährlich im Lend greifbar und erfahrbar gemacht.

with fellow collaborating urban researchers and architects.

Ortsentwürfe (14) surveys Graz for traces of urban changes that show indications of a new urban stance in the twentieth century. Such reformatting of city space, now also visible in architecture, is read not as an isolated phenomenon, but rather in the context of European development.

The texts make concrete reference to the local festival LENDWIRBEL. Neighborhood structures, appropriation of local space, and alternative ways of life are made tangible and experienceable each year in Lend during this festival.

With contributions by **Christoph Twickel, Christoph Laimer, Peter Mörtenböck, Robert Kaltenbrunner, Rainer Rosegger, Philipp Schmidt, Claudia Gerhäusser, Elke Krasny,** among others.

Co-editor **Gottfried Prasenc** served from 2005 to 2013 as aResearch and Teaching Associate at the Institute of Spatial Design at Graz University of Technology.

middle-class area came to form around the Schlossberg, while on the opposite side of the Mur River a lower-class "slum district" developed along important trade routes. The Lend quarter, the nature of which had long seemed dubious, saw the dawning of creative potential, which still today openly plays out along the streets.

Experts and narrators from a range of disciplines report on this ambivalent realm of shady imagery and neighborly vitality in the book *Ortsentwürfe: Urbanität im 21. Jahrhundert* (Municipal Designs: Urbanity in the 21st Century), which originated from a series of symposia organized by Gottfried Prasenc and Harald Saiko, along

Mit Beiträgen von **Christoph Twickel, Christoph Laimer, Peter Mörtenböck, Robert Kaltenbrunner, Rainer Rosegger, Philipp Schmidt, Claudia Gerhäusser, Elke Krasny** u.a.

Der Herausgeber **Gottfried Prasenc** war von 2005 bis 2013 Universitätsassistent am Institut für Raumgestaltung.

Staub. Eine interdisziplinäre Perspektive

Daniel Gethmann/Anselm Wagner (Hg.)
Schnittstellen. Wissenschaft und Kunst im Dialog 2
Wien/Münster: LIT Verlag, 2013
Deutsch, 192 Seiten, broschiert (Softcover)
ISBN 978-3-643-50491-3
EUR 19,90

Staub umgibt uns überall und alles wird auch irgendwann zu Staub – ob wir wollen oder nicht. Staub nicht nur zu bekämpfen, sondern zu untersuchen, bildet den Ausgangspunkt zahlreicher Forschungen in den Natur-, Ingenieur- und Kul-

Staub: Eine interdisziplinäre Perspektive

Daniel Gethmann and Anselm Wagner (eds.)
Schnittstellen: Wissenschaft und Kunst im Dialog 2
Vienna and Münster: LIT Verlag, 2013
German, 192 pages, softcover
ISBN 978-3-643-50491-3
EUR 19.90

Dust completely surrounds us, and one day, like it or not, everything will inevitably turn to dust. Not only the combating of dust, but also its exploration, provides the point of departure for numerous research endeavors in the fields of natural science, engineering, and cultural studies. The publication (15) *Staub: Eine interdisziplinäre Perspektive* (Dust: An Interdisciplinary Perspective) links such contributions made to dust research with artistic projects. Analyses and insights from science and art, as related to dust's ability to blend, circulate, and spread, foster an interdisciplinary perspective on this element

ISBN 978-3-86859-216-0
EUR 24,80

turwissenschaften. Der vorliegende Band (15) verbindet solche Beiträge aus der Staubforschung mit künstlerischen Projekten. Analysen und Einblicke aus Wissenschaft und Kunst in die Fähigkeiten des Staubs zur Vermischung, Zirkulation und Verteilung eröffnen eine interdisziplinäre Perspektive auf dieses so verbreitete wie unbeachtete Element unserer Umwelt.

Mit Beiträgen von **Julia Feldtkeller**, **Daniel Gethmann**, **Anna A. Gorbushina**, **Andrés Gutiérrez Martínez**, **Sabine Kacunko**, **Slavko Kacunko**, **Roland Meyer**, **Bertl Mütter**, **Ursula Sorz**, **Ernst Stadlober**, **Wladyslaw W. Szymanski**, **Klaus Torkar**, **Bettina Vismann**, **Anselm Wagner**, **Monika Wagner**.

Daniel Gethmann und **Anselm Wagner** lehren am Institut für Architekturtheorie, Kunst- und Kulturwissenschaften der Technischen Universität Graz.

Das Solarhaus Zankel im französischen Prévessin bei Genf, ab 1976 vom Grazer Architekten Konrad Frey geplant und 1978–85 vom CERN-Physiker Karl Zankel für dessen Familie errichtet, ist das Produkt einer kongenialen Partnerschaft, wie sie in der Architektur nur höchst selten vorkommt: Architekt und Bauherr vereinte dieselbe Freude am risikoreichen Experiment, durch die ein Projekt zum Lebensinhalt und ein Bauwerk zum Kunstwerk werden kann. Das Ergebnis lässt sich nur in Gegensätzen beschreiben: experimentelles Solarlabor und vernakulärer Landsitz, expressive Raumskulptur und ökologische Versuchsstation, repräsentative Gesellschaftsbühne und alternatives Kinderhaus, postmoderne Collage und technoide Wohnmaschine, manieristische „folie" und mönchische Zelle. Umso verwunderlicher, dass dieses einzigartige Gebäude bislang keine nennenswerte Rezeption in der Architekturkritik gefunden hat – es ist das unbekannte Meisterwerk der „Grazer Schule". Das Buch (16) ist im Rahmen eines Masterstudios der TU Graz zur Dokumentation des vom Abriss bedrohten Hauses entstanden.

Konrad Frey: Haus Zankel. Experiment Solararchitektur

Anselm Wagner/Ingrid Böck (Hg.)
architektur + analyse 2
Berlin: Jovis, 2013
Deutsch, 160 Seiten, broschiert (Softcover)

ISBN 978-3-86859-216-0
EUR 24.80

from our environment that is so pervasive yet so often unheeded.

With contributions by **Julia Feldtkeller**, **Daniel Gethmann**, **Anna A. Gorbushina**, **Andrés Gutiérrez Martínez**, **Sabine Kacunko**, **Slavko Kacunko**, **Roland Meyer**, **Bertl Mütter**, **Ursula Sorz**, **Ernst Stadlober**, **Wladyslaw W. Szymanski**, **Klaus Torkar**, **Bettina Vismann**, **Anselm Wagner**, and **Monika Wagner**.

Daniel Gethmann and **Anselm Wagner** teach in the Institute of Architectural Theory, History of Art and Cultural Studies at Graz University of Technology.

Konrad Frey: Haus Zankel. Experiment Solararchitektur

Anselm Wagner and Ingrid Böck (eds.)
architektur + analyse 2
Berlin: Jovis, 2013
German, 160 pages, softcover

The solar house Zankel in the French town of Prévessin near Geneva was designed by the Graz-based architect Konrad Frey starting in 1976 and was built in 1978–85 by CERN physicist Karl Zankel for his family. The structure is the product of a congenial partnership that occurs only very rarely in the architectural world: architect and client were united by the same joy in adventuresome experimentation that can turn a project into a life purpose and a building into a work of art. The result can only be explained through contrasts: experimental solar laboratory and vernacular country estate, expressive spatial sculpture and ecological research station, representative societal stage and alternative children's home, postmodern collage and technoid housing machine, Mannerist backdrop and monastic cell. It is indeed astonishing that this unique building has not yet received a noteworthy reception in architectural criticism—for it is the unknown masterwork of

the "Graz School." This book (16) was created in the context of a master studio at Graz University of Technology with the aim of documenting this building that is faced with potential demolition. **309**

Die Herausgeberin **Ingrid Böck** war von 2008 bis Ende 2012 Universitätsassistentin am Institut für Architekturtheorie, Kunst- und Kulturwissenschaften der Technischen Universität Graz. **Anselm Wagner** ist Professor an selben Institut.

Is There (Anti-)Neoliberal Architecture?

Ana Jeinić/Anselm Wagner (Hg.)
architektur + analyse 3
Berlin: Jovis, 2013
Englisch, 160 Seiten, broschiert (Softcover)
ISBN 978-3-86859-217-7
EUR 24,80

Die neoliberale Ideologie hat in unserer politisch-ökonomischen Realität ihre unverkennbaren Spuren hinterlassen. Aber welcher Zusammenhang besteht zwischen dem Neoliberalismus und der Produktion der gebauten Umwelt? *Is There (Anti-)Neoliberal Architecture?* (17) versucht die bislang vorwiegend von einer stadt-soziologischen und geografischen Perspektive geprägte Analyse um einen im engeren Sinne architekturtheoretischen Blickwinkel zu ergänzen. Die im Band versammelten Beiträge nehmen verschiedene Dimensionen des gegenwärtigen Architektursystems in den Blick: die architektonische Praxis, den Status der Disziplin, den Diskurs, exempla-

Is There (Anti-)Neoliberal Architecture?

Ana Jeinić | Anselm Wagner [eds.]

17

rische Projekte, theoretische Konzepte usw. Damit zeichnet der Band ein vielschichtiges Bild von Architektur in der Epoche des Neoliberalismus und dessen Krise.

Mit Beiträgen von **Gideon Boie (BAVO)**, **Ole W. Fischer**, **Maria S. Giudici**, **Rixt Hoekstra**, **Ana Jeinić**, **Tahl Kaminer**, **Ana Llorente**, **Olaf Pfeifer**, **Andreas Rumpfhuber** und **Oliver Ziegenhardt**.

Die Herausgeber **Ana Jeinic** und **Anselm Wagner** forschen und lehren am Institut für Architekturtheorie, Kunst- und Kulturwissenschaften der Technischen Universität Graz.

Identität Politik Architektur. Der „Verein für Heimatschutz in Steiermark"

Antje Senarclens de Grancy (Hg.)
architektur + analyse 4 (18)
Berlin: Jovis, 2013
Deutsch, 272 Seiten, broschiert (Softcover)

Co-editor **Ingrid Böck** has served as a Research and Teaching Associate at the Institute of Architectural Theory, Art History and Cultural Studies at Graz University of Technology from 2008 to 2012. Co-editor **Anselm Wagner** teaches at the same institute.

Is There (Anti-)Neoliberal Architecture?

Ana Jeinić/Anselm Wagner (eds.)
architektur + analyse 3
Berlin: Jovis, 2013
English, 160 pages, paperback (softcover)
ISBN 978-3-86859-217-7
EUR 24.80

Over the last three decades, neoliberal ideology has irreversibly changed our political and economic reality. Assuming that the built environment both expresses and shapes social processes, there must be a profound relationship between neoliberalism and the architecture of our time. But

what relationship is it? Until now, the approaches to this question have been mostly borrowed from various disciplines of the *urban*, such as urban sociology, urban geography, and urbanism. The book *Is There (Anti-)Neoliberal Architecture?* (17) seeks to complement these approaches by addressing the subject from the more specific angle of architectural theory. Offering a broad range of perspectives on the subject, this volume describes the historical origins of neoliberalism and its impact on architecture and on the spatial organization of labor and learning; it discusses the end and possible return of utopia and critique; and it examines certain cases of *neoliberalization* of architectural practices and discourses, while simultaneously reflecting on the possibility of anti-neoliberal engagement through architecture.

With contributions by **Gideon Boie (BAVO)**, **Ole W. Fischer**, **Maria S. Giudici**, **Rixt Hoekstra**, **Ana Jeinić**, **Tahl Kaminer**, **Ana Llorente**, **Olaf Pfeifer**, **Andreas Rumpfhuber**, and **Oliver Ziegenhardt**.

The editors, **Ana Jeinić** and **Anselm Wagner**, teach and conduct research at the Institute of Architectural Theory, Art History and Cultural Studies at Graz University of Technology.

Identität Politik Architektur: Der "Verein für Heimatschutz in Steiermark"

Antje Senarclens de Grancy (ed.)
architektur + analyse 4 (18)
Berlin: Jovis, 2013
German, 272 pages, softcover
ISBN 978-3-86859-218-4
Euro 29.80

"Good" and "bad," "wrong" and "right": such juxtapositions are characteristic of many publications by *Heimatschutz* (home protection), an international cultural reform movement that also took root in Austria around 1900 as a reaction to the changes befalling both land- and cityscape. In

ISBN 978-3-86859-218-4

Euro 29,80

„Gut" und „schlecht", „falsch" und „richtig":
Solche Gegenüberstellungen charakterisieren
viele der Publikationen des Heimatschutzes,
jener internationalen Kulturreformbewegung,
die als Reaktion auf die Landschafts- und Stadt-
bildveränderungen um 1900 auch in Österreich
rasch Fuß fasste. In Graz besteht der 1909 gegründete „Verein für Heimatschutz in Steiermark" –
wenn auch inzwischen in „BauKultur Steiermark"
umbenannt – bis heute. Ein interdisziplinäres

Team von Autorinnen und Autoren untersucht
am Beispiel dieser lokalen Vereinigung die sich
im Laufe des 20. Jahrhunderts wandelnden Heimat-
schutzagenden im Kontext nationaler und regionaler Identitätssuche und (kultur-)politischer Kooperationen, aber auch historischer Verstrickungen sowie internationaler Architekturdiskurse.

Antje Senarclens de Grancy lehrt und forscht
am Institut für Architekturtheorie, Kunst- und Kulturwissenschaften der TU Graz.

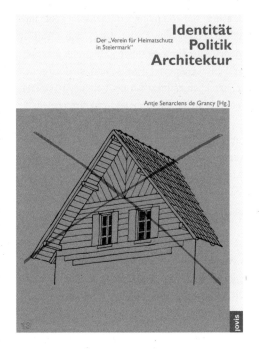

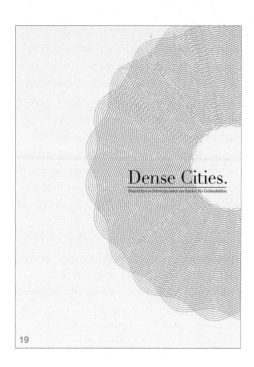

 ## Dense Cities. Forschung und Lehre zu Architektur und Nachverdichtung 2009–2012 mit Projekten im Grazer Stadtgebiet

Markus Bogensberger/Hans Gangoly/Andreas
Lechner/Ida Pirstinger (Hg.)
Materialien zu Schwerpunkten des Instituts für
Gebäudelehre
Graz: Verlag der TU Graz, 2013
Deutsch, 399 Seiten, kartoniert

ISBN 978-3-85125-265-1

EUR 55,00

Das Institut für Gebäudelehre stellt mit seiner
Publikation *Dense Cities – Forschung und Lehre
zu Architektur und Nachverdichtung 2009–2012*

Dense Cities: Forschung und Lehre zu Architektur und Nachverdichtung 2009–2012 mit Projekten im Grazer Stadtgebiet

Markus Bogensberger, Hans Gangoly,
Andreas Lechner, and Ida Pirstinger (eds.)
Materalen zu Schwerpunkten des Instituts
für Gebäudelehre
Graz: Verlag der TU Graz, 2013
German, 399 pages, paperback
ISBN 978-3-85125-265-1
EUR 55.00

With the publication *Dense Cities: Forschung
und Lehre zu Architektur und Nachverdichtung
2009–2012* (Dense Cities: Research and Teaching of Architecture and Retrospective Densification, 2009–2012), the Institute of Architectural
Typologies introduces projects on the topic of urban density which were carried out or worked on
from 2009 to 2012 in the institute. Besides offer-

ing extensive overviews of workshops, symposia,
publications, and third-party-funded research,
the book focuses on designs, course results, and
theses that deal with the highly relevant economic and ecological question of spatial densification
potential by example of the provincial capital of
Graz. The approach pursued originates from a
programmatic-functional, infrastructural, socially
acceptable, and, not least, design-related vantage
point using concrete architectural means. Here
architecture plays a research-informed role in that
it illustrates the theses on the sustainable density
of cities by example of projects—citing specific
design proposals, from business premises to city
districts—and renders the retrospective densification scenarios in urban space explicable.

*Dense Cities: Forschung und Lehre zu Ar-
chitektur und Nachverdichtung 2009–2012* (19)
was funded by the Regional Government of
Styria – Department of Science and Research.

Markus Bogensberger, **Hans Gangoly**, **Andreas
Lechner**, and **Ida Pirstinger** conduct research and

Graz the "Verein für Heimatschutz in Steiermark"
(Association for Home Protection in Styria),
founded in 1909, still exists today—though it has
since been renamed as "BauKultur Steiermark"
(BuildingCulture Styria). An interdisciplinary
team of authors cites this local association in exploring the home protection agendas that changed
over the course of the twentieth century. This
transpired in the context of a national and regional quest for identity and (cultural-)political cooperative relationships, but also of historical entan-
glements and international architectural discourse.

Antje Senarclens de Grancy teaches and conducts research at the Institute of Architectural Theory,
Art History and Cultural Studies at Graz University
of Technology.

Projekte vor, die zum Themenkreis städtischer Dichte von 2009 bis 2012 am Institut durchgeführt und bearbeitet wurden. Neben ausführlichen Überblicken über Workshops, Symposien, Publikationen und Drittmittelforschungen fokussiert die Publikation Entwürfe, Lehrveranstaltungsergebnisse und Diplomarbeiten, die anhand der Landeshauptstadt Graz der wirtschaftlich und ökologisch hoch relevanten Frage nach räumlichen Verdichtungs-Potenzialen aus programmatisch-funktionaler, infrastruktureller, sozialverträglicher und nicht zuletzt gestalterischer Sicht mit den konkreten Mitteln der Architektur nachgehen. Die Architektur ist hier forschend tätig, indem sie die Thesen zur nachhaltigen Dichte von Städten mit Projekten – vom Geschäftslokal bis zum Stadtquartier – im Rahmen konkreter Entwurfsvorschläge illustriert und Nachverdichtungsszenarien im Stadtraum nachvollziehbar macht.

Dense Cities – Forschung und Lehre zu Architektur und Nachverdichtung 2009–2012 (19) wurde durch das Land Steiermark – Wissenschaft und Forschung gefördert.

Markus Bogensberger, **Hans Gangoly**, **Andreas Lechner** und **Ida Pirstinger** forschen und lehren

teach in the Institute of Architectural Typologies at Graz University of Technology.

Stadthäuser: Ein Segment von Eisenerz als Möglichkeitsraum

Alexandra Isele
Materialien zu Schwerpunkten des Instituts für Gebäudelehre (20)
Graz: Verlag der TU Graz, 2013
German, 270 pages, paperback
ISBN 978-3-85125-285-9
EUR 49.00

The mining city of Eisenerz in Upper Styria sparks a gamut of questions usually reduced to the topic of shrinkage in this Austrian municipality that has been most strongly impacted by this situation. Not until the negative coverage has been dissolved can these questions also be viewed as a basal search for identities and characteristic

features. The author invokes the *Kastenhäuser*

ám Institut für Gebäudelehre der Technischen Universität Graz.

Stadthäuser. Ein Segment von Eisenerz als Möglichkeitsraum

Alexandra Isele
Materialien zu Schwerpunkten des Instituts für Gebäudelehre (20)
Graz: Verlag der TU Graz, 2013
Deutsch, 270 Seiten, kartoniert
ISBN 978-3-85125-285-9
EUR 49,00

Die obersteirische Bergbaustadt Eisenerz spannt ein Feld von Fragen auf, das meist auf den Umstand der von Schrumpfung am stärksten betroffenen Gemeinde Österreichs reduziert wird. Erst durch die Entflechtung der Negativberichterstat-

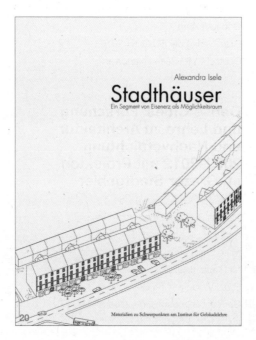

(box houses) as a building structure in Eisenerz of urban-planning and historical significance. She goes on to analyze, evaluate, and narratively develop this form further: structural interventions are varied by way of adaptations to the living and working conditions of their potential inhabitants and are illustrated in scenarios as multifaceted opportunities for both the individual and the collective appropriation of spatial resources. The the-

tung können diese Fragen auch als basale Suche nach Identitäten und Besonderheiten verstanden werden. Mit den „Kastenhäusern" identifiziert die Autorin eine stadträumlich und historisch signifikante Gebäudestruktur in Eisenerz, die sie analysiert, bewertet und erzählerisch weiter entwickelt: Bauliche Eingriffe werden durch die Anpassung an die Lebens- und Arbeitsumstände ihrer potenziellen Bewohnerschaft variiert und als vielschichtige Möglichkeiten zur individuellen ebenso wie kollektiven Aneignung räumlicher Ressourcen in Szenarien illustriert. Mit persönlichem Engagement, Interviews, detaillierten Illustrationen und hochwertigem Bild- und Anschauungsmaterial kommuniziert die Arbeit dabei ihre Vision ebenso in die Breite, wie sie durch Aufbau, thematische Entwicklung und Literatur ihre politische Relevanz und gesellschaftlichen Anspruch im aktuellen Kontext der tiefgreifenden Transformationsprozesse regionaler Strukturen belegt.

Die als Diplomarbeit am Institut für Gebäudelehre unter der Betreuung von Andreas Lechner verfasste Arbeit wurde durch Unterstützung vom Amt der Steiermärkischen Landesregierung Abteilung 16, Verkehr und Landeshochbau veröffentlicht.

sis employs personal involvement, interviews, detailed illustrations, and high-quality image and visual material to broadly communicate the author's vision. Moreover, the book's structure, thematic development, and selected references attest to its political relevance and demands on society in the current context of profound processes of regional structural transformation.

This thesis was written by Alexandra Isele with advising by Andreas Lechner in the Institute of Architectural Typologies. It was published with the support of the Office of the Regional Government of Styria, Department 16 (Transport and Building Construction).

The Ancient Monastic Complex of Dangkhar

Holger Neuwirth/Carmen Auer (eds.)
Buddhist Architecture in the Western Himalayas (21)
Graz: Verlag der TU Graz, 2013
English, 328 pages, paperback

The Ancient Monastic Complex of Dangkhar

Holger Neuwirth/Carmen Auer (Hg.)
Buddhist Architecture in the Western Himalayas (21)
Graz: Verlag der TU Graz, 2013
Englisch, 328 Seiten, broschiert

ISBN 978-3-85125-297-2
EUR 88.00

Dangkhar is located within the Spiti valley in Himachal Pradesh, India, a region inhabited by a Tibetan-speaking population for more than thousand years. The ancient monastic complex, situated in the village of the same name, is nested on a vertiginous cliff at the impressive altitude of 3,850 m overlooking the meanders of the Spiti-Pin river confluence.

The origin of this fortified site is believed to go back to the 10th-11th century when a powerful dynasty of royal patrons and kings initiated a Buddhist renaissance in the Western Himalayas.

It gradually assumed the double function of a political centre and a religious establishment and witnessed the various influences from the neighbouring states (e.g. Ladakh, Tibet) which competed for political supremacy and religious hegemony. Despite the lack of historical sources and archaeological evidence available, the monastery of Dangkhar is intimately linked to the history of

ISBN 978-3-85125-297-2
EUR 88,00

Dangkhar liegt im Spiti-Tal im indischen Bundesstaat Himachal Pradesh, einer Region, die seit über tausend Jahren von einer tibetisch sprechenden Bevölkerung besiedelt wird. Die alte Klosteranlage in dem gleichnamigen Dorf sitzt auf einem steilen Felsvorsprung in der schwindelnden Höhe von 3.850 Metern und blickt auf die Mäander der Spiti-Pin-Mündung hinab.

Der Ursprung der befestigten Anlage soll ins 10.–11. Jahrhundert zurückreichen, als eine mächtige Dynastie königlicher Schirmherren die buddhisische Renaissance im Westhimalaya einleitete.

Nach und nach wuchs dem Kloster eine Doppelfunktion als politisches und religiöses Zentrum zu und es war allerlei Einflüssen aus den Nachbarstaaten (z.B. Ladakh und Tibet) ausgesetzt, die hier um die politische und religiöse Vorherrschaft rangen. Trotz des Mangels an verfügbaren historischen Quellen und archäologischen Belegen steht fest, dass das Kloster von Dangkhar eng mit der Geschichte des Spiti-Tals verbunden ist, welches ein bedeutendes Zentrum für Handel, Kommuni-

the Spiti valley which was an important centre for trade, communication and religious ideas between the Indian subcontinent, Central Asia and West Tibet.

Holger Neuwirth and **Carmen Auer** teach and conduct research at the Institute of Architectural Theory, Art History and Cultural Studies.

verMESSEN: Franziszeische Grundkataster von Graz

Bernhard Reismann/Marion Starzacher/
Elisabeth Seuschek/Ramona Winkler
Archiv und Bibliothek der TU Graz 3
Graz: Verlag der TU Graz, 2013
German, 94 pages, paperback
ISBN 978-3-85125-274-3
EUR 42.00

Embedded in an exciting, interdisciplinary discourse between historians, art historians, geode-

kation und religiöse Ideen zwischen indischem Subkontinent, Zentralasien und Westtibet war.

Holger Neuwirth und **Carmen Auer** lehren und forschen am Institut für Architekturtheorie, Kunst- und Kulturwissenschaften.

verMESSEN. Franziszeische Grundkataster von Graz

Bernhard Reismann/Marion Starzacher/
Elisabeth Seuschek/Ramona Winkler
Archiv und Bibliothek der TU Graz 3
Graz: Verlag der TU Graz, 2013
Deutsch, 94 Seiten, kartoniert
ISBN 978-3-85125-274-3
EUR 42,00

Eingebettet in einen spannenden, interdisziplinären Diskurs zwischen Historikern, Kunsthistorikern, Geodäten und Architekten werden in diesem Buch (22) der Franziszeische Kataster der Stadt Graz – die Urmappe von 1820 – und das

sists, and architects, in this book (22) the Land Register of Francis I of the City of Graz (the original map of 1820) is juxtaposed with the complete resurveying of the same region (dated 1829) in direct comparison for the first time. The

komplette Neuaufmaß derselben Region – datiert mit 1829 – erstmals in einem direkten Vergleich gegenübergestellt. Dieses sogenannte „Zweitaufmaß" von 1829 stellt eine Besonderheit dar, da bis dato kein weiteres vollständiges Zweitaufmaß eines anderen Kronlandes der Habsburger Monarchie im Zuge der Zweiten Landesaufnahme bekannt ist. Es werden neben den Exponaten der Ausstellung *verMESSEN. Franziszeische Grundkataster von Graz*, die als Auftakt zur öffentlichen Präsentation der ersten Forschungsergebnisse zum Franziszeischen Kataster in Graz im GrazMuseum stattgefunden hat, die Intention des Forschungsprojektes „verMESSEN", Studierendenarbeiten aus aktuellen Lehrveranstaltungen der Fakultät für Architektur, sowie Auszüge des Nachlasses von Franz Allmer, persönliche Gedanken zu seinem Wirken und die wissenschaftlichen Beiträge der TeilnehmerInnen an der Podiumsdiskussion „vermessen, verwalten, versteuern" publiziert.

Bernhard Reismann ist Leiter des Archivs der Technischen Universität Graz. **Marion Starzacher**, **Elisabeth Seuschek** und **Ramona Winkler** gründeten die Initiative ARCHelmoma und lehren bzw. studieren an der Technischen Universität Graz.

so-called *Zweitaufmaß* (second survey) of 1829 was a special case considering that, as per our knowledge today, during the second land survey no other known complete second survey was undertaken of another Habsburg monarchy crownland. Besides the exhibits shown in the exhibition *verMESSEN: Franziszeische Grundkataster von Graz*, which was initiated at GrazMuseum as a prelude to the public presentation of the first research findings on the Franziszeische Kataster in Graz, the research project "verMESSEN" seeks to publish work by students from current classes in the Faculty of Architecture, as well as excerpts from the Estate of Franz Allmer, personal reflections on his work, and scholarly contributions written by participants in the panel discussion "vermessen, verwalten, versteuern" (surveying, administrating, taxing).

Bernhard Reismann is the director of the archive at Graz University of Technology. **Marion Starzacher**, **Elisabeth Seuschek**, and **Ramona Winkler** are the founding members of the ARCHelmoma initiative and teach/study at Graz University of Technology.

Architectural Scale Models in the Digital Age. Design, Representation and Manufacturing

Milena Stavrić/Predrag Šiđanin/
Bojan Tepavčević (Hg.)
Wien: Springer, 2013
Englisch, 260 Seiten, Hardcover
ISBN: 978-3-99043-526-7
EUR 54,99

Die Erstellung physischer Modelle komplexer geometrischer Formen mit einer Vielzahl struktureller Verbindungen ist eine der großen Herausfor-

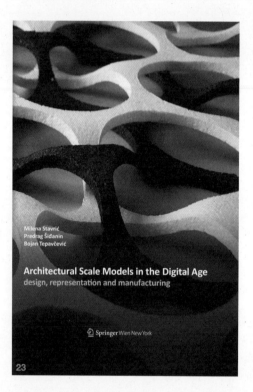

Architectural Scale Models in the Digital Age. Design, Representation and Manufacturing

Milena Stavrić/Predrag Šiđanin/Bojan Tepavčević (eds.)
Vienna: Springer, 2013
English, 260 pages, hardcover
ISBN: 978-3-99043-526-7
EUR 60.49

Making physical models of complex geometric shapes and their multiple structural connections

derungen im Zeitalter moderner Computertechnik und parametrischer Konstruktion in der Architektur. Das Buch (23) behandelt die für diese Arbeitsweise erforderlichen neuen Modellierungsstrategien, -technologien und -methoden. Komplexe geometrische Formen, die in virtuellen Arbeitsumgebungen entstanden sind, können nur mittels physischer Modelle auf ihre Praxistauglichkeit geprüft und validiert werden. Zeitgenössisches Architekturdesign erfordert aufgrund seiner Komplexität die Beherrschung neuer Methoden in der Herstellung von maßstabsgetreuen Modellen. Das vorliegende Buch legt den Schwerpunkt auf diese neuen Möglichkeiten im Bereich der Modellierung. Zusätzlich zu den traditionellen Techniken als Basis der Modellierung geht das Buch auf die Grundlagen der digitalen NURBS-Modellierung, der parametrischen Modellierung, der digitalen Modellierungshilfen und auf Modellerzeugung ein, ergänzt durch zahlreiche Anleitungen, praktische Lösungsvorschläge und Beispiele aus der zeitgenössischen Architekturpraxis.

Milena Stavrić forscht und lehrt am Institut für Architektur und Medien der Technischen Universität Graz.

is a major challenge in the age of advanced digital technology and parametric design in architecture. This approach requires new modeling strategies, technology and methods which are introduced in this book (23). Complex geometric forms generated by using virtual media can be tested and validated only by means of physical models, which also make it possible to assess their practical application. The complexity of contemporary architectural design requires the mastery of new methods of producing scale models, which opens a new chapter in the field of modeling. Along with the traditional methods that provide the basis for modeling, this book presents the principles of digital NURBS modeling, parametric modeling, digital modeling support, and model creation, in addition with a number of tutorials, practical advice and examples found in architectural practice today.

Milena Stavrić teaches and conducts research in the Institute of Architecture and Media at Graz University of Technology.

Preise

GAD-AWARDS 2013.
Grazer Architektur Diplompreis

Zum 11. Mal wurden die besten Diplomarbeiten des vergangenen Studienjahres mittels Jury gewählt, prämiert und zur Diskussion gestellt. Ausgerichtet wurde die diesjährige Veranstaltung vom Institut für Städtebau der TU Graz.

Jurymitglieder: Vorsitz: Arch. **Christian Rapp**, TU Eindhoven; Dipl. Ing. Arch. **Bernd Vlay**, Studio Vlay Wien; Dipl. Ing. DDr. techn. **Claudia Yamu**, TU Wien; Dipl. Architekt **Mathieu Wellner**, LFU Innsbruck; Dipl. Ing. **Danijela Gojic**, GS architects Graz.

1. Preis: **Claudia Kresser/Diane Brachtenbach**: *Die Brise. Heuristische Erkenntnisschleifen einer Stadtplanung für Szczecin.* 2. Preis: **Martin Slobodenka**:

Refill Radkersburg. Eine zeitgemäße Wellnessarchitektur zur Erweiterung des touristischen Konzepts. 3. Preis: **Martin Grabner**: *Pirgos Peiraia. Die Reparatur von Stadt und die Wiederherstellung von Urbanität mittels der räumlichen und ikonischen Aktivierung einer vertikalen Brache.*

Hollomey Reisepreis: Thomas Untersweg: *Seoul Megacity – Best Before?*

Tschom Wohnbaupreis: Felix Zankel: *Die Zeile der 50er – Vitalisierung einer 50er Jahre Siedlung*

Ausstellung der eingereichten Arbeiten: 11.–17. Oktober 2013, Foyer & HSII

Susan Kraupp

„OCCUPY:ROOFSCAPE".
HERBERT EICHHOLZER STUDIERENDEN-PREIS 2013
„OCCUPY:ROOFSCAPE".
Performativer Urbanismus GRAZ

Der nach dem Grazer Architekten Herbert Eichholzer benannte studentische Förderungspreis wird alle zwei Jahre durch die Stadt Graz an begabte ArchitekturstudentInnen vergeben.

Im Fokus des Wettbewerbs stand diesmal die soziale Performanz und verantwortungsvolle Bezugnahme zur gebauten Umwelt, die bekanntermaßen auch im Schaffen des Architekten Herbert Eichholzer eine zentrale Rolle einnahm. Für Eichholzer waren bereits in den 1930er Jahren Architektur und politisches Engagement untrennbar miteinander verbunden. „Er vertrat die mutige Vision der Moderne in Verbindung mit sozialer Verantwortung" (Margareth Otti).

Im Titel des diesjährigen Studierendenpreises „OCCUPY:ROOFSCAPE" klingt die Aufforderung an, politisches Engagement und Architektur gemeinsam zu denken – nicht vorrangig architektonisch formbezogene Räume zu schaffen, son-

Awards

GAD AWARDS 2013.
Graz Architecture Diploma Award

For the eleventh time, the best diploma theses of the past academic year were selected by a jury to receive the Graz Architecture Diploma Award and have thus been put up for discussion. This year's event was hosted by the Institute of Urbanism at Graz University of Technology.

Jury Members: Chair: Arch. **Christian Rapp**, Eindhoven University of Technology; Dipl. Ing. Arch. **Bernd Vlay**, Studio Vlay, Vienna; Dipl. Ing. DDr. techn. **Claudia Yamu**, Vienna University of Technology; Dipl. Arch. **Mathieu Wellner**, University of Innsbruck; Dipl. Ing. **Danijela Gojic**, GS architects, Graz.

1st Prize: **Claudia Kresser** and **Diane Brachtenbach**, *Die Brise: Heuristische Erkenntnisschleifen einer Stadtplanung für Szczecin* (The Breeze: Heuristic Loops of Cognizance in Urban Planning for Szczecin). 2nd Prize: **Martin Slobodenka**, *Refill Radkersburg: Eine zeitgemäße Wellnessarchitektur zur Erweiterung des touristischen Konzepts* (Refill Radkersburg: A Contemporary Wellness Architecture for the Expansion of the Tourist Concept). 3rd Prize: **Martin Grabner**, *Pirgos Peiraia: Die Reparatur von Stadt und die Wiederherstellung von Urbanität mittels der räumlichen und ikonischen Aktivierung einer vertikalen Brache* (Pirgos Peiraia: The Repair of a City and the Restoration of Urbanity through the Spatial and Iconic Activation of a Vertical Wasteland).

Hollomey Travel Award: Thomas Untersweg, *Seoul Megacity – Best Before?*

Tschom Housing Award: Felix Zankel, *Die Zeile der 50er: Vitalisierung einer 50er Jahre Siedlung* (The Row of the 1950s: Vitalization of a 1950s Housing Settlement)

Exhibition of the Submitted Works: October 11–17, 2013, Foyer & HSII

Susan Kraupp

"OCCUPY:ROOFSCAPE":
HERBERT EICHHOLZER STUDENT AWARDS 2013
"OCCUPY:ROOFSCAPE":
Performative Urbanism GRAZ

The student sponsorship award named after the Graz architect Herbert Eichholzer is bestowed on talented architecture students every two years by the City of Graz.

This year the competition was focused on social performance and responsibly made reference to the built environment, which is also known to have played a central role in the architectural work of Herbert Eichholzer. In his eyes, architecture and political commitment were already inseparably linked in the 1930s. "He represented

dern vor allem das soziale Gefüge der Nachbarschaft im Bezug zu Bildung und gelebter Umwelt zu diskutieren.

Als Ort mit hohem Potenzial, um ökologisch wie sozial nachhaltiges Handeln in unserer Gesellschaft zu entfalten, wurde für dieses Vorhaben die von TEAM A Architekten in den 1970er Jahren entwickelte Schule BG/BRG & MG Dreihackengasse in Graz mit besonderem Augenmerk auf die brache Dachlandschaft der Anlage gewählt.

Jury: **Eva Guttmann**, Architektin, Leiterin des HDA Graz; **Marie-Therese Harnoncourt**, Architektin, the next enterprise Wien; **Bernhard Inninger**, Leiter des Stadtplanungsamt Graz; **Andreas Lichtblau**, Architekt, Leiter des Instituts für Wohnbau TU Graz; **Klaus K. Loenhart**, Architekt und Landschaftsarchitekt, Leiter des Instituts für Architektur und Landschaft TU Graz; **Petra Petersson**, Architektin, Leiterin des Instituts für Grundlagen der Konstruktion und des Entwerfens, TU Graz.

Preisträger 2013: 1. Preis: **Theresa Reisenhofer**; 2. Preis: **Fabian Fitzner, Janosch Webersnik, Martin Ziegerhofer**; 2. Preis: **Wolfgang Windisch**,

Anna Kickingerder; Anerkennung: **Selina Mirkovic, Georg Siegfried**.

Lisa-Maria Enzenhofer

Piranesi Award

Seit 1983 finden jährlich die Piran Days of Architecture statt. Im Rahmen der internationalen Architekturkonferenz wird alljährlich der renommierte Piranesi Award für praktizierende Architekten sowie für Studierende der Architektur vergeben. Auch dieses Jahr wurden die Studierendenbeiträge der TU Graz zum Piranesi Award vom Institut für Architekturtechnologie ausgewählt (Selector: Prof. Roger Riewe, Co-Selector: Armin Stocker).

Benannt nach dem im 18. Jahrhundert wirkenden Architekten und Architekturtheoretiker Giovanni Battista Piranesi ist es das Ziel der Konferenz, neue Richtungen in der Architektur aufzuzeigen und innovative Ideen und Ansätze in Architektur und Raumproduktion auszuloten und zur Diskussion zu stellen.

Es erörterten das diesjährige Thema „Ethik in der Architektur" unter anderem Kevin Carmody und Andrew Groarke (London, GB), Taisto H. Mäkelä (Denver, USA) sowie Špela Videčnik und Rok Oman (Ljubljana, SI).

Parallel zur Konferenz fand die Ausstellung der eingereichten Projekte aus Slowenien, Kroatien, Slowakei, der Tschechischen Republik, Italien, Ungarn, Griechenland und Österreich statt. Im Rahmen der Ausstellung wurden die mit dem Piranesi Award 2013 prämierten Beiträge bekanntgegeben und die Auszeichnungen vom Bürgermeister der Stadt Piran, Peter Bossman an die Preisträger überreicht.

Die Beiträge der TU Graz zum Piranesi Award 2013 stammen von Stefan Nuncic und Isabel Janka. Stefan Nuncics Arbeit wurde von Prof. Roger Riewe und Marcus Stevens im Zuge der Projektübung des Masterstudiums am Institut für Architekturtechnologie betreut. Sie setzt sich mit dem „Neubau der Neuen Zentral- und Landesbibliothek Berlin" am Rande des Tempelhofer Flugfeldes auseinander. Das Projekt „Übernachtung im Hotel am Park" von Isabel Janka thematisiert die alte Basteimauer in Graz als Bauplatz und wurde von Prof. Hans Gangoly

the courageous vision of modernism connected with social responsibility" (Margareth Otti).

The title of this year's student prize "OCCUPY: ROOFSCAPE" reads like a challenge to consider political commitment and architecture in a joint context—with a focus not merely on creating architectural spaces based on form, but rather especially on discussing the social fabric of neighborhoods as relates to education and an animated environment.

As a site with high potential for the unfolding of both ecologically and socially sustainable agency in our society, the school called BG/BRG & MG Dreihackengasse in Graz (developed in the 1970s by TEAM A Architekten) was selected for this undertaking, with a special focus on the uncultivated roofscape of the grounds.

Jury: **Eva Guttmann**, architect, Director of HDA Graz; **Marie-Therese Harnoncourt**, architect, the next enterprise, Vienna; **Bernhard Inninger**, Director of the Urban Planning Office, Graz; **Andreas Lichtblau**, architect, Director of the Institute of

Housing, Graz University of Technology; **Klaus K. Loenhart**, architect and landscape designer, Director of the Institue of Architecture and Landscape, Graz University of Technology; **Petra Petersson**, architect, Director of the Institute of Construction and Design Principles, Graz University of Technology

Award winners 2013: 1st Prize: **Theresa Reisenhofer**; 2nd Prize: **Fabian Fitzner, Janosch Webersnik, Martin Ziegerhofer**; 2nd Prize: **Wolfgang Windisch, Anna Kickingerder**; Appreciation: **Selina Mirkovic, Georg Siegfried**

Lisa-Maria Enzenhofer

Piranesi Award

Since 1983 the Piran Days of Architecture have been held annually. In the scope of this international architecture conference, each year the renowned Piranesi Award is bestowed upon both practicing architects and students pursuing a

degree in architecture. This year contributions by students from Graz University of Technology were selected to compete for a Piranesi Award by the Institute of Architecture Technology (selector: Prof. Roger Riewe, co-selector: Armin Stocker).

Named after Giovanni Battista Piranesi, an architect and architectural theorist who was active in the eighteenth century, the conference sets out to herald new directions in architecture and to fathom and incite discourse on innovative ideas and approaches related to architecture and spatial production.

This year's topic, "Ethics in Architecture," was debated by Kevin Carmody and Andrew Groarke (London, GB), Taisto H. Mäkelä (Denver, US), as well as Špela Videčnik and Rok Oman (Ljubljana, SI), among others.

In parallel to the conference there was an exhibition of the submitted projects originating from Croatia, Slovakia, the Czech Republic, Italy, Hungary, Greece, and Austria. The contributions honored with the Piranesi Award 2013 were announced in the scope of the exhibition, and the

als Projektübung am Institut für Gebäudelehre betreut.

Von der Jury unter der Leitung von Olga Felip (Girona, ES) wurde am 23. November 2013 bei den diesjährigen Piran Days of Architecture das Projekt von **Stefan Nuncic**, „Neubau der Neuen Zentral- und Landesbibliothek Berlin" ausgewählt und mit der „International 2013 Student's Honorable Mention" ausgezeichnet.

Die Jury charakterisierte das Projekt in ihrer Begründung als mutigen und radikalen Beitrag zur Entwicklung einer neuen Typologie der Bibliotheksarchitektur und als kraftvollen Ausdruck der Speicherung und des Konsums von Wissen.

Wir freuen uns über diese wichtige Auszeichnung und gratulieren dem Preisträger!

Armin Stocker

Auszeichnungen beim Bauhaus Solar Award

Seit dem Aufkommen der Wegwerfgesellschaft in der westlichen Welt gegen Ende der 1940er Jahre wurde eine nicht enden wollende Vielfalt an unterschiedlichen Materialien produziert, um wenig später auf Mülldeponien zu landen. Die Stadt New York hatte sich zur gleichen Zeit entschlossen, das Areal der Fresh Kills auf Staten Island – ein ursprünglich artenreiches Feuchtbiotop – mittels einer temporären Mülldeponie trockenzulegen und als Bauland zu entwickeln.

In der Folge wurde Fresh Kills Landfill jedoch die weltgrößte Mülldeponie. Täglich gelangten neun Millionen Liter Deponiesickwasser in Grundwasser und umliegende Gewässer und etwa zwei Prozent der weltweiten Methan-Emission als Deponiegas in die Atmosphäre. Seit 2001 ist die Deponie geschlossen und wird zu einem zwölf Quadratkilometer großen Park umgebaut.

25

awards were conferred on the winners by the mayor of the City of Piran, Peter Bossman.

The contributions from Graz University of Technology that were submitted for a Piranesi Award 2013 were developed by Stefan Nuncic and Isabel Janka.

Advising on Stefan Nuncic's project was carried out by Prof. Roger Riewe and Marcus Stevens in the scope of Master's degree project development in the Institute of Architecture Technology. The project deals with the "New Construction of the New Main Regional Library in Berlin" next to Tempelhof Airport.

The project "Overnight Stay at a Hotel near the Park" by Isabel Janka thematizes the old bastion wall in Graz as a building site, with Prof. Hans Gangoly serving as advisor for project development in the Institute of Architectural Typologies.

On November 23, during this year's Piran Days of Architecture, the jury headed by Olga Felip (Girona, ES) selected **Stefan Nuncic's** project to receive the "International 2013 Honorable Mention."

In the jury statement, the project was characterized as a courageous and radical contribution to the development of a new typology for library architecture and as a powerful expression of the retention and consumption of knowledge.

We are very pleased about this important distinction and extend our congratulations to the award winner!

Armin Stocker

Distinctions, Bauhaus Solar Award

Since the emergence of the throwaway society in the Western world, around the late 1940s, a seemingly never-ending variety of different materials has been produced, only to land in garbage dumps shortly thereafter. During the same period, the city of New York decided to drain the Fresh Kills area on Staten Island—originally a wetland habitat with a diversity of spe-

cies—by turning it into a temporary landfill site before developing it as real estate. Instead, the Fresh Skills landfill ended up becoming the world's largest garbage dumb. Each day, nine million liters of landfill leachate drained into the ground water and into nearby atmosphere as landfill gas. The disposal site has been closed since 2001 and is presently being converted into a twelfe-square-kilometer park.

In the master studio and design class 4 at the Institute of Architecture and Landscape, scenarios and designs for a future Fresh Skill park landscape were developed in summer 2012. Considering the generous dimensions of the area and the processes that will continue to evolve over decades underground, it stands to reason that the site could additionally be used for power generation. The student project "Atmospheres" by **Christoph Walter Pirker** and **Carmen Bakanitsch** (25) was distinguished by the Bauhaus Solar Award 2012 for its groundbreaking implementation of photovoltaic technologies. Their design proposes a linear and strongly elevated lighted space that is formed

Im Masterstudio und Entwerfen 4 am Institut für Architektur und Landschaft wurden im Sommer 2012 Szenarien und Entwürfe für eine zukünftige Parklandschaft in Fresh Skills entwickelt. Aufgrund der weitläufigen Dimensionen des Areals und der noch über Jahrzehnte im Untergrund stattfindenden Prozesse ist eine zusätzliche Nutzung des Ortes zur Energiegewinnung naheliegend. Für ihren wegweisenden Einsatz von Fotovoltaiktechnologien wurde die studentische Arbeit „Atmospheres" von **Christoph Walter Pirker** und **Carmen Bakanitsch** (25) beim Bauhaus-Solar-Award 2012 ausgezeichnet. Ihr Entwurf sieht einen linienförmigen und deutlich überhöhten Lichtraum vor, der durch zwei parallel verlaufende Vorhänge aus OPV-beschichteten Kunststofffäden gebildet wird. Dieses Lichtband soll das Areal als Erschließungsachse und Lichtskulptur durchqueren.

Karin Pramstraller und **Sarah Lena Tribus** erhielten eine Anerkennung für ihr zurückhaltendes und atmosphärisches Projekt „ePlant-Fields".

Bernhard König

Auszeichnungen für das Architekturbüro .tmp architekten

Uli Tischler, Universitätsassistentin am Institut für Gebäudelehre der TU Graz und **Martin Mechs**, die das Architekturbüro .tmp architekten leiten, sind Preisträger der GerambRose 2012 zum Thema „Gemeinschaftliche Räume" für die Volksschule Hausmannstätten (26/27 © Paul Ott). Im Jahr 2013 wurde das Schulgebäude Hausmannstätten vom Bundesministerium für Unterricht, Kunst und Kultur mit einer Auszeichnung beim „Award Bessere Lernwelten" prämiert und erhielt den Architekturpreis des Landes Steiermark unter der Kuration von Nathalie de Vries (MVRDV). Bei diesem Preis werden herausragende zeitgemäße Architektur-Projekte der vergangenen drei Jahre in der Steiermark ausgewählt und prämiert.

Die besondere Qualität des Außenraums der neuen, zwölfklassigen Volksschule mit großen Freiflächen, die die Belichtung der Innenräume einerseits und Ausblicke andererseits sicherstel-

26

len, soll im Gebäude als Lernlandschaft weitergeführt werden.

Den großzügig bemessenen Bewegungsflächen kommt innerhalb des Projekts besondere

27

by two parallel-running curtains made of synthetic fiber coated with organic photovoltaics (OPV): This band of light is designed to span the grounds as a central axis and light sculpture.

Karin Pramstraller and **Sarah Lena Tribus** received an honoralbe mention for their reserved and atmospheric project "ePlank-Fields."

Bernhard König

Awards for the architectural firm .tmp architekten

Uli Tischler, Research and Teaching Associate at the Institute of Architectural Typologies at Graz University of Technology, and **Martin Mechs**, who jointly run the architectural firm .tmp architekten, were the GerambRose 2012 award winners for the topic "Communal Spaces" for the primary school Volksschule Hausmannstätten (26/27 © Paul Ott). In the year 2013, the Hausmannstätten school building received the Bessere Lernwelten (Im-

proved Learning Worlds) award from the Austrian Federal Ministry for Education, the Arts and Culture and also the Architecture Award of the Province of Styria under the curatorship of Nathalie de Vries (MVRDV). The latter prize selects and

distinguishes outstanding contemporary architectural projects from the previous three years in Styria.

The exterior space of this new primary school designed to accommodate twelve classes em-

Bedeutung zu. Die Funktionsüberlagerung von Erschließungs- und Pausenflächen soll die informelle Kommunikation der Kinder, aber auch die Interaktion mit ihren LehrerInnen fördern. Die Mehrfachnutzung dieser Bereiche als Arbeits-, Spiel-, Lern- und Verkehrsflächen wird durch das Angebot an Freiräumen unterstützt.

Räumlich und konzeptuell sind diese Bereiche einer neu interpretierten Pausenhalle mit ihren Treppen, Galerien, Nischen, Sitzzylindern und Übergängen zu den Loggien, nicht nur der zentrale Teil des Gebäudes, sondern als Lernlandschaft auch der Versuch, eine Pädagogik des 21. Jahrhunderts zu ermöglichen, die sich vom Frontalunterricht im Klassenzimmer löst und den Raum – neben den Lehrenden und MitschülerInnen – als „dritten Pädagogen" versteht.

Uli Tischler und Martin Mechs wurden 2013 außerdem mit dem Architekturpreis „Das beste Haus" für das Projekt „Haus SH" (28/29 © Paul Ott) ausgezeichnet.

Das Projekt umfasst die Renovierung eines Einfamilienhauses am Stadtrand von Graz und die Erweiterung um einen Wintergarten.

Der Zubau nimmt die Form des vorhandenen steirischen Gegengiebels auf, verzieht ihn

aber soweit, dass das gesamte Gebäude durch seinen L-förmigen Grundriss einen Gartenabschluss zur Straße bildet. Der Wintergarten öffnet sich nach Süden und über seine Längsseite nach Westen in die Tiefe des Gartens, zur Straßenseite ist er vollkommen geschlossen. Im Inneren führt eine neue, zweite Treppe ins Obergeschoss, das über dem bestehenden Flachdach

bodies a special quality characterized by large open spaces. This serves to facilitate a strong sense of light inside the building while simultaneously allowing for excellent views. The exterior space extends inward to foster a landscape for learning.

The generously dimensioned spaces for movement were assigned special meaning within the project. The functional layering of areas for access and recess is meant to promote informal communication among the children, but also interaction with their teachers. The multiple-use design of these areas as space for working, playing, learning, and socializing is supported by the range of open spaces.

In terms of space and concept, the areas that make up the newly interpreted assembly foyer—with its stairs, galleries, niches, seating cylinders, and transitions to the loggias—represent the central part of the building, but it is also a learning landscape. This design reflects an attempt to facilitate a twenty-first-century pedagogical approach, one that departs from the tradition-

al classroom-based teaching style and instead considers space to be a "third educator," next to the teachers and the classmates.

Uli Tischler and Martin Mechs of.tmp architekten were also awarded the architecture prize Das beste Haus (The Best House) for the project Haus SH (28/29 © Paul Ott).

The project involves the renovation of a single-family home in the outskirts of Graz and includes an extension taking the form of a conservatory. The annex seizes upon and reinterprets the existing Styrian gabled roof, shaping it in such a way that the entire building, with its L-shaped outline, shelters the yard area from the street. The conservatory has southern exposure, with its long side facing west toward the depths of the yard; it is completely closed off on the street side. Inside the building, a new second stairway leads to the upper level, which was added to the former flat roof to create a view-sheltered roof terrace. The stairs give rise to new paths within the building and a change in utilization patterns. Small interventions have served to modernize the existing building, to improve interaction with the yard, and to implement sources of daylight.

um eine vor Einblick geschützte Dachterrasse erweitert wurde. Die Treppe ermöglicht innerhalb des Gebäudes neue Wege und eine veränderte Nutzung. Mit kleinen Eingriffen wurde das Bestandsgebäude modernisiert, der Bezug zum Garten verbessert und Tageslichtquellen implementiert.

Das Büro .tmp architekten erhielt außerdem den Steirischen Holzbaupreis 2013 in der Kategorie „Innovation" für den Umbau und die Erweiterung der VS Gabelsberger Graz (30/31 © Paul Ott).

Die Volksschule in der Gabelsbergerstraße erhielt einen Zubau im nebenstehenden historischen Gebäude. Die Intention, beim Umbau mit möglichst geringen Eingriffen möglichst hohe räumliche Qualität zu erreichen, führte beim hofseitigen Verandabau dazu, dass sich die gesamte Fensterfront zum grünen Innenhof des Gebäudeblocks öffnet. Die Schulkinder haben freie Aussicht, gleichzeitig ergibt sich eine klar strukturierte Raumerweiterung, verbunden mit einer konstruktiv gelungenen Kombination von Holz- und Massivbauweise.

Eva Sollgruber/Uli Tischler

The architectural firm .tmp architekten was granted the Styrian Timber Construction Award 2013 in the category "Innovation" for the renovation and extension of VS Gabelsberger Graz (30/31 © Paul Ott).

The primary school along Gabelsbergerstraße received an annex to the adjacent historical building. The intention of using minimal interventions to achieve a maximum of spatial quality led to an opening of the entire window front of the court-facing veranda structure toward the green interior courtyard of the building complex. The school children are given an open view, while at the same time a clearly structured extension of space could be linked with a structurally successful combination of wood and solid-construction methods.

32

Interviews/Projekte/
Ausstellungen/
Öffentliche
Veranstaltungen

Grundlagen-Lehre

Petra Petersson (PP/32) im Gespräch
mit **Daniel Gethmann** (GAM)

GAM: Sie sind im Wintersemester 2013 als Professorin an das neu gegründete Institut für Grundlagen der Konstruktion und des Entwerfens an der Technischen Universität Graz berufen worden. Bevor wir über Ihre Pläne und Konzepte für die Grundlagen-Lehre in Graz sprechen, geht es mir zunächst darum zu erfahren, welche Grundlagenausbildung Sie selbst durchlaufen haben?

PP: Ich hole ein bisschen aus, weil ich glaube, dass viel von dem, wie ich arbeite und wie ich denke, auch damit zu tun hat, wo ich herkomme. Ich bin eigentlich Schwedin, habe aber den größten Teil meines Lebens nicht in Schweden ver-

bracht. Als Kind lebte ich lange Zeit im Ausland und bin jedes zweite Jahr umgezogen; ich war in Frankreich, der Schweiz, Finnland, Deutschland, Amerika, bis ich dann irgendwann wieder zurück nach Schweden gekommen bin, mein Abitur gemacht und angefangen habe, Architektur zu studieren.

GAM: Wie ist es denn zu dieser Entscheidung für die Architektur gekommen?

PP: Ich habe angefangen, Architektur zu studieren, weil meine Mutter das wollte. Und meine Mutter wollte das, weil ihre Großmutter bereits um 1900 Architektur studiert hat. Das ist schon sehr ungewöhnlich. Der Vater meiner Urgroßmutter war Baumeister in einer kleinen Stadt in Schweden und hat seine zwei Kinder nach Berlin geschickt, um dort Architektur zu studieren. Meine Urgroßmutter Ruth Svensson ist wieder zurückgekommen, hat dann in dem Büro von ihrem Vater gearbeitet und in Karlshamn mehrere Bauten geplant, die durchaus von der Architektur Berlins Anfang des 20. Jahrhunderts inspiriert sind. Meine Mutter ist teilweise bei ihr aufgewachsen und hat durch sie diese Liebe zur Architektur entwickelt und an uns Kinder weitergegeben. Die Mutter meiner Mutter hat Kunst studiert

und Ihre Cousine Tutti Lütken gehörte zu den ersten selbständigen Architektinnen in Dänemark. Also war ich nicht ganz unbelastet, als ich angefangen habe, Architektur zu studieren und habe das Glück, von einem etwas anderen Frauenbild als viele meiner Kolleginnen und Kollegen geprägt worden zu sein.

GAM: Wo haben Sie denn Architektur studiert?

Interviews/Projects/
Exhibitions/
Public Events

Teaching Design Fundamentals

Petra Petersson (PP/32) in conversation with
Daniel Gethmann (GAM)

GAM: You moved to Graz in the winter term 2013 to serve as a professor in the newly founded Institute of Construction and Design Principles at Graz University of Technology. Before we discuss your plans and concepts for teaching design fundamentals in Graz, first I would be interested in hearing about the foundational education that you received during your study period.

PP: I am going to give a somewhat tangential answer, because I feel that the ways in which I work and think are related to where I come from. I am actually a Swede by birth but have

spent very little time in Sweden during my life. Much of my childhood was spent living abroad, and we moved every two years. I lived in France, Switzerland, Finland, Germany, and the United States before finally returning to Sweden at one point, where I completed secondary school and started to study architecture.

GAM: How did you arrive at the decision to study architecture?

PP: Initially, I started to study architecture because it was what my mother wanted. And my mother wanted this because her grandmother had already studied architecture around 1900. This was very unusual of course. My great-grandmother's father had been a master builder in a small Swedish city, and he sent his two children to Berlin to study architecture there. My great-grandmother, Ruth Svensson, later returned to Sweden and worked in her father's firm. She designed a number of buildings in Karlshamn that were inspired by the Berlin architecture of the early twentieth century. My mother spent part of her childhood with her grandmother and thus developed this love of ar-

chitecture, which she then passed on to her own children. My mother's mother studied art, and her cousin Tutti Lütken was one of the first independent architects in Denmark. So when starting my architectural studies, I had a whole history behind me and was fortunate to have been influenced by a somewhat different picture of women than many of my colleagues.

GAM: Where did you study architecture?

PP: I spent two years in Sweden at the technical university in Lund, but I felt called to go elsewhere. This may have been because Lund was immersed in something of a transition phase during the mid-1980s—people there were stuck in the programmatic discussions of the 1970s and had moved away from architecture. So then I took a year off and spent time working in Stockholm and New Zealand. There was an exchange program between the Mackintosh School of Architecture at Glasgow School of Art and Lund University, so I ended up in Glasgow. I stayed there for three years and earned my degree from the Glasgow School of Art. As opposed to Lund, in Glasgow there was

321

PP: Ich war zwei Jahre in Lund an der Technischen Universität und hatte das Gefühl, dass ich irgendwo anders hinmusste. Vielleicht, weil Lund Mitte der 80er Jahre in einer Art Übergangsphase war – eigentlich steckten sie in den programmatischen Diskussionen der 70er Jahre fest und hatten sich von der Architektur entfernt. Dann habe ich mir erst mal ein Jahr freigenommen, habe in Stockholm und Neuseeland gearbeitet. Es gab ein Austauschprogramm zwischen der Glasgow School of Art, Mackintosh School of Architecture und Lund und so bin ich in Glasgow gelandet. An der Glasgow School of Art bin ich drei Jahre geblieben und habe da mein Diplom gemacht. Im Unterschied zu Lund gab es dort sowohl bei den Studenten als auch bei den Lehrenden eine unglaubliche Leidenschaft für die Architektur. Glasgow hat nur 40 bis 50 Studierende pro Jahrgang und es ist ein intensives Studium gewesen.

GAM: Und nach dem Diplom haben Sie erst mal in Architekturbüros gearbeitet und dann Ihr eigenes gegründet?

PP: Genau. Ich bin nach dem Diplom kurz nach Schweden gegangen. Das war ein bisschen schwierig Anfang der 90er Jahre. Da kommt man aus der Universität und denkt, man bekommt einen Job, aber es gab eine Finanzkrise. Und deswegen bin ich nach Berlin gegangen. Zehn Jahre habe ich dort in Büros gearbeitet und mich dann selbstständig gemacht mit meinem Büro: Realarchitektur.

GAM: Die Anfänge in der Selbstständigkeit waren vermutlich ein harter Weg?

PP: Die Selbstständigkeit war und ist richtig hart. Berlin ist toll zum Leben, aber es gibt dort einfach nicht genügend Arbeit, doch unglaublich viele Architekten. Es gab zehn Jahre lang kaum öffentliche Wettbewerbe, weil die öffentliche Hand kein Geld mehr hatte. Die Projekte, die gebaut wurden, waren die Riesenprojekte und die Architekten haben eher etwas für sich selbst oder mit Baugruppen gebaut. So haben manche die Chance gehabt, ihre ersten Bauten zu realisieren.

GAM: Bekannt geworden ist Ihr Büro mit dem Umbau eines ehemaligen Reichsbahnbunkers für den Kunstsammler Christian Boros in Berlin.

PP: Interessant an dem Projekt war, dass wir uns im Inneren des Bunkers mit einer Schaffung des Raumes durch Subtraktion auseinandergesetzt haben. Das Gebäude setzt sich aus fünf axialsymmetrischen Geschossen mit ungefähr 240 Räumen zusammen, doch jetzt sind es halt viel weniger. Wir haben einfach entnommen. Und durch diese Entnahme, dieses Abreißen und Herausnehmen von Decken, sind neue Räume entstanden und eine Verbindung über die Geschosse. Das hat eine eigene Komplexität innerhalb des Gebäudes geschaffen, die vorher nicht da war. Durch diese Löcher gibt es eine neue Orientierung in dem Gebäude, wobei die Kunst der Hauptfokus ist. Man sieht ein Kunstwerk von einer Ebene und dann wieder von der nächsten. Das hat zwei Effekte: zum einen versteht man das Gebäude besser und wo man sich darin befindet, und zum anderen tritt die Kunst viel stärker hervor als in einer normalen Galerie. Das ist ein interessanter Aspekt, der inspiriert ist von einem Ausstellungsraum mit Giacometti-Skulpturen im dänischen Louisiana-Museum, einem meiner absoluten Lieblingsräume. Da kommt man von oben hinein, sieht dann diese Skulpturen von Giacometti, die wie Schatten vor der Landschaft stehen, geht hinunter und betrachtet sie aus der Nähe.

Schließlich war unsere Arbeit ein Versuch, an dem weiterzubauen, was wir vorgefunden haben: Wir benutzen die gleichen Materialien und die gleiche Struktur und haben versucht, das in die-

---

an unbelievable passion for architecture among both the students and the instructors. The school has only forty to fifty students per year, so it was an intense academic experience.

GAM: And after earning your degree, you worked in architectural firms before opening your own office?

PP: Exactly. After completing my studies, I first went to Sweden for a while. That was a bit difficult in the early 1990s. Upon graduating from university, one expects to find a job, but it was a time of economic crisis. That's why I moved to Berlin. I spent ten years working at firms there before founding my own company: Realarchitektur.

GAM: The initial stages of self-employment were presumably difficult?

PP: Self-employment was, and still remains, truly difficult. Berlin is a wonderful place to live, but there is simply not enough work there, especially considering the incredible number of architects. During these ten years hardly any public competitions were held because the public sector had run out of money. The projects that were actually built were very large, and the architects involved either took them on individually or in building groups. So some architects did have a chance to realize their first buildings.

GAM: I first heard of your office in connection with the conversion of the former German National Railway bomb shelter for the art collector Christian Boros in Berlin.

PP: What was interesting about this project was that on the inside of the bomb shelter we explored the creation of space by means of subtraction. The building is made up of five axial-symmetrical stories with approximately 240 rooms total, but now the number is much lower. It basically involved removal. And through this removal—this act of demolishing and pulling down ceilings—new spaces emerged along with a connection between the different stories. This fostered a unique complexity within the building that had not been present before. The gaps lent the structure a new orientation, with art being the main focus. For instance, an artwork may be visible from one level, but also from another.

This has two effects: for one, it helps convey a better understanding of the building and one's place in it, while at the same time allowing the art to stand out much more strongly as compared to a normal gallery. This is an interesting aspect that was inspired by an exhibition space that houses Giacometti sculptures in the Louisiana Museum in Denmark—one of my absolute favorite spaces. You enter from above and then see these sculptures by Giacometti standing there like shadows against the landscape before descending to view them from up close.

Ultimately, our work on the bomb shelter was an attempt to continue building what we found there: we used the same materials and the same structure, and we tried to integrate them throughout the building. Ceasing to celebrate old and new and instead just continuing to build is also a quite popular approach among our colleagues right now. I try to change the existing architecture in a way that results in the creation of a completely new whole.

GAM: How does the concept of continued building correlate with constructive structure?

sem Gebäude weiterzuziehen. Mit dem Zelebrieren von Alt und Neu aufzuhören und stattdessen weiterzubauen ist auch zurzeit bei den Kollegen beliebt. Ich versuche das, was da ist, so zu verändern, dass es letzten Endes ein neues Ganzes ergibt.

GAM: In welchem Zusammenhang steht das Konzept des Weiterbauens mit der konstruktiven Struktur?

PP: Mein Empfinden für Konstruktion liegt im Inneren des Gebäudes: Zu verstehen, wie es zusammengesetzt wird, worin seine Erdung besteht. Diese Wahl steht ganz am Anfang: Wie erde ich mein Gebäude? Was für ein Material benutze ich? Wie lasse ich mich von dem, was das Material kann, inspirieren? Was für ein Material und welche Bauart sind auch im Kontext relevant? Denn das Kontextuelle des Projekts beeinflusst die Konstruktion. Was ich mache, ist Erdung: Wie, warum, wieso setze ich ein Haus so und nicht anders zusammen.

GAM: Seit Herbst 2013 leiten Sie in Graz das Institut für Grundlagen der Konstruktion und des Entwerfens, wo auch die früheren Kurse zur Grundlage der Gestaltung zusammengeführt werden. Aber ist die Spaltung zwischen Entwerfen

und Konstruieren noch zeitgemäß oder werden diese beiden architektonischen Schwerpunkte im Institutsnamen programmatisch enger zusammengeführt? Wie sehen Sie das Verhältnis zwischen Konstruktion und Entwerfen?

PP: Die Schaffung dieses neuen Institutes, die bestimmt mehrere Jahre gedauert hat, ist ein großer Luxus und einer der Hauptgründe für meine Bewerbung. Sehr wichtig ist das Ziel, Konstruktion und Entwerfen näher zusammen zu bringen. Darin liegt wahrscheinlich auch teilweise der Grund, warum gerade ich auf die Professur berufen wurde, da beides in meiner Arbeit sehr nah beieinander liegt. Die Projekte, die wir machen, sind ganz „reale" Projekte – auch konstruktiv – denn es gibt doch eigentlich keine richtige Trennung. Die Zielstellung der Grundlagenlehre, die wir jetzt Stück für Stück aufbauen, ist einfach folgende: Konstruktion und Entwerfen einander näherzubringen. Jede Konstruktionsvorlesung enthält einen Teil, in dem es darum geht, Gebäude zu zeigen, die ganz klare konzeptionelle Ausdrücke für die jeweiligen Konstruktionsweisen zeigen. Der Hauptfokus im Konstruktionsunterricht liegt im Moment darauf zu zeigen, inwieweit der Kontext bei der Wahl der Konstruktion

eine Rolle spielt – es geht nicht nur um einen unmittelbaren urbanen Kontext, sondern auch um den kulturellen, sozialen und konzeptionellen Kontext.

GAM: Ich glaube, es ist unstrittig, dass u.a. durch digitale Technologien die beiden fast 200 Jahre getrennten Bereiche Entwerfen und Konstruieren wieder zusammenkommen, dass Entwerfen häufig auch bedeutet, bestimmte Fertigungsdaten zu erstellen usw. Die für Sie vielleicht relevantere Frage ist dabei: Wie reflektiert man diesen Zusammenhang in der Grundlagenlehre? Es gibt zu dieser Entwicklung eine sehr lange, spannende und ergiebige Vorgeschichte in Graz, weil hier seit den 60er Jahren aus einem konstruktiven Zugang heraus entworfen wurde; daher erscheint es mir sehr logisch, das hier in der Architekturlehre noch stärker zu betonen.

PP: Was wir deshalb zunächst betreiben, ist eine Art Grundlagenforschung. Wir beschäftigen uns mit der Frage, wie die Grundlagen in Graz bislang unterrichtet worden sind. Wir nutzen dieses erste Jahr, um das zu bewerten, parallel auch zu sehen, was es woanders gibt, wie woanders gelehrt wird, um dann daraus die besten Bestandteile herauszunehmen. In der Arbeitsweise bin ich an

PP: My sense of construction lies in the inside of a building: understanding how it is put together, how it is grounded. This choice arises at the very beginning: How should I ground my building? What material will I use? How might I draw inspiration from the capacities of this material? Which material and what building style are appropriate to this particular context? Because contextual factors do influence the construction process. Here I focus on grounding, on how and why I compose a house this way instead of a different way.

GAM: Since the fall of 2013 you have been heading the Institute of Construction and Design Principles in Graz, where previous courses in design principles are also being consolidated. But is the divide between design and construction still in keeping with the times, or are these two core architectural themes being more closely consolidated on a programmatic level as initiated by the institute? And what is your take on the relationship between construction and design?

PP: The founding of this new institute, a process that surely took a number of years, is a great luxury and one of the main reasons I submitted an application. The goal of bringing construction and design closer together is a crucial one. This is probably one of the reasons that I was granted the professorship, for both areas are closely linked in my work. The projects that we work on are very "real" projects—also structural—for there really is no separation between the two. The objective of design fundamentals that we are working to establish step by step is simply the following: bringing construction and design closer together. Each lecture on construction includes a section where buildings are shown that display very clear conceptual expressions for the respective construction methods used. The main focus of construction classes is to show the extent to which context plays a role in selecting a construction method—and by context I mean not only an immediate urban context, but rather also the cultural, social, and conceptual contexts.

GAM: I think it is undisputable that digital technology, among other influences, has brought the areas of design and construction back together after a separation period of nearly two hundred years, and also that design frequently entails a compilation of certain production data, etc. Yet the more relevant question for you here is perhaps: How can we reflect on this reciprocal relationship in design fundamentals? There was a very long, exciting, and productive history leading up to this development in Graz, for starting in the 1960s the process of design has been based on a structural approach. Therefore, it seems logical to me that this aspect would be even more strongly emphasized here in the context of architectural education and theory.

PP: That is why we have started out by conducting some basic research. We are concerned with the question of how design fundamentals have been taught in Graz up until now. We are using this first year for evaluating and, in parallel, also seeing what exists elsewhere, what is taught where, in order to pinpoint the best ele-

den Seminaren und Vorlesungen mit meinen beiden Assistenten beteiligt, wir arbeiten gemeinsam in der Gruppe.

GAM: Welche weiteren Schwerpunkte über die Grundlagenausbildung oder -lehre hinaus würden Sie gerne innerhalb der Lehre setzen?

PP: Unsere Aufgabe ist es zunächst, dass die Grundlagen funktionieren. Unsere nächste Aufgabe ist es dann, die ersten Entwurfsprogramme anzubieten und wir betreuen auch Diplomanden. Und dann ist es naheliegend, dass wir letzten Endes ein neues Lehrprogramm für die Grundlagen aufbauen und dazu erforschen werden, was es derzeit für architektonische Lehrprogramme gibt.

GAM: Es wäre ja naheliegend, dass sich die Forschung am Grundlageninstitut hauptsächlich auf die Grundlagenlehre richten würde, oder gibt es ganz andere Bereiche, die Sie für die Forschung für hochgradig relevant halten und am Institut entwickeln möchten?

PP: Es gibt bei mir grundsätzlich das Interesse des Kontextes, das mir sehr wichtig ist. Ich finde, dass es auch zu den Grundlagen gehört, dass man den kulturellen Kontext, in dem man agiert, ernst nehmen muss. Das andere, das im-

mer wichtiger wird, sind Projekte, in denen es wieder um die Menschen geht – um eine humanistische, kulturelle, kulturpolitische Richtung. Was wir jetzt versuchen, ist, die Art zu finden, die uns dies ermöglicht und einen Prozess oder eine Methodik zu entwerfen, in der wir diese Forschung ausüben und letzten Endes hoffentlich zu etwas kommen werden, von dem wir noch gar nicht wissen, was es ist.

STELA: Smart Tower Enhancement Leoben Austria

Das Siegerprojekt „STELA" (33) gewann die 3. Ausschreibung für sichtbare „Smart City" Demo- und Pilotprojekte des Klima- und Energiefonds der Österreichischen Bundesregierung. Die genehmigte Fördersumme beträgt 950.000 Euro. Das Institut für Gebäudelehre war als Initiator des Projektes für die Erstellung des Förderantrags verantwortlich und wird in Zukunft die Koordination des Gesamtprojektes übernehmen. Neben der Stadtgemeinde Leoben als Konsortialführerin

und Antragstellerin sind unter anderem das Institut für Tragwerksentwurf der TU Graz, die Montanuniversität Leoben, die Energie Steiermark AG und Gangoly & Kristiner Architekten ZT-GmbH weitere Projektpartner.

Das Projekt befasst sich mit der umfassenden thermischen und technischen Sanierung und gleichzeitig grundlegenden Aufwertung von Wohnquartieren, die in den 70er Jahren konzipiert wurden, am Beispiel einer Wohnanlage in Judendorf Leoben. Des Weiteren soll ein Mobilitätskonzept getestet werden, das sich als integrativer Teil des Energiesystems des Gebäudes darstellt.

ments. In terms of working approach, I am involved in teaching seminars and giving lectures together with my two assistants; we work together in a group.

GAM: Aside from foundational education, which other areas would you like to focus on in teaching?

PP: First, it is our job to ensure that the foundational principles are conveyed. Then our next task is to offer the first design programs, and we also advise degree candidates. Ultimately, our objective is to create a new program for teaching principles, so we will be ascertaining which programs for teaching architecture already exist.

GAM: One would naturally assume that the research conducted at the Institute of Construction and Design Principles is primarily geared toward design fundamentals, or are there entirely different areas that you consider highly relevant to research and would like to develop at the institute?

PP: I am fundamentally interested in context; that is very important to me. In my mind,

taking seriously the cultural context in which one is moving counts among the foundational principles. Something else that is becoming increasingly important are projects that deal with people—with a humanist, cultural, cultural-political orientation. What we're trying to do is to find a path that makes this possible for us and to design a process or methodology where we can carry out this research—in the hope of ultimately arriving at something without knowing which form it will take yet.

STELA: Smart Tower Enhancement Leoben Austria

The winning project "STELA" (33) topped the list of the 3rd competition for visible "Smart City" demo and pilot projects by the Climate and Energy Fund of the Austrian Federal Government. The approved funding sum amounted to 950,000 euros. As initiator of the project, the Institute of Architectural Typologies was re-

Ökologischer und ökonomischer Hintergrund ist der Umstand, dass zentrumsnahe verdichtete Siedlungsformen Ressourcen schonen und die Belastung der Umwelt verringern.

Im Rahmen dieses Projekts werden Ansätze formuliert, wie sich nachhaltige Alternativen zum Einfamilienhaus am Stadtrand denken lassen. Es werden Räume für Wohnen, Arbeit und Erholung vorgeschlagen, deren Umräume nicht mehr vornehmlich für Autos, sondern wieder für Menschen gestaltet werden. Außerdem sollte aus stadtplanerischer Sicht das Wohnangebot die gewünschten Lebensstilkonzepte bedienen und somit einen ausgewogenen Benutzermix unter Berücksichtigung der demografischen Entwicklungen ermöglichen.

Markus Bogensberger, Gernot Reisenhofer

34

Aquatopia: Das Forschungs-U-Boot

Ein Projekt des **Instituts für Zeitgenössische Kunst** (34/35) der TU Graz und des Kinderbüros Graz in

Zusammenarbeit mit dem **ZOOM Kindermuseum Wien**
www.aquatopia.at
Künstlerisches Konzept und
Koordination: **Daniela Brasil**;
Architekturassistenz: **Thomas Kalcher** und **Patricia Wess**; Kunstassistenz: **Lola Anna Seibt**

Im Sommer 2013 ging ein U-Boot auf dem Grazer Karmeliterplatz und im Museumsquartier Wien vor Anker – und brachte eine Atmosphäre spielerischen Experimentierens in den öffentli-

35

sponsible for preparing the project application and in future will coordinate the entire project. In addition to the municipality of Leoben as consortium leader and applicant, other project partners include the Institute of Structural Design at Graz University of Technology, Montan University of Leoben, Energie Steiermark AG, and Gangoly & Kristiner Architekten ZT-GmbH.

The project involves the extensive thermal and technical renovation and concurrent basic upgrading of residential neighborhoods that were designed in the 1970s based on the example of a housing complex in the Judendorf district of Leoben. Furthermore, a mobility concept is to be tested, which represents an integral part of the building's energy system.

The ecological and economic background of the project is based on the circumstance that centrally located settlement forms conserve resources and minimize the negative impact on the environment.

During this project, approaches are conceptualized for creating sustainable alternatives to

the suburban single-family home. Developed here are spaces for living, working, and leisure that are surrounded by space no longer dedicated primarily to motor vehicles but rather now designed for people. Moreover, from an urban-planning perspective, the housing market should meet the desired lifestyle concepts and thus facilitate a balanced blend of inhabitants in consideration of demographic developments.

Markus Bogensberger, Gernot Reisenhofer

Aquatopia: The Children's Research Submarine

A project by the **Institute for Contemporary Art** (34/35) of the TU Graz & Kinderbüro in cooperation with **Zoom Children's Museum, Vienna**
www.aquatopia.at
Artistic concept and coordination: **Daniela Brasil**;
Architecture Assistants: **Thomas Kalcher** and **Patricia Wess**; Art assistant: **Lola Anna Seibt**

In the summer of 2013, a submarine docked at the Karmeliterplatz, Graz and the Museumsquartier, Vienna, bringing an atmosphere of experimental research and playfulness to the public space. Its extradisciplinary crew merged artistic and scientific processes to observe, record, and discuss our daily relation to water and the related plastic waste production.

Preparations were made in a research project and in teaching activities throughout the academic year. Excursions followed the paths of fresh water supplies and the sewage systems of the cities of Graz and Vienna. Out of field notes, artistic installations were developed and an illustrated logbook, displaying the water cycles of Graz and Vienna in a comprehensive and child-appropriate way, was pro-

chen Raum. Seine außerdisziplinäre Crew beobachtete, dokumentierte und erörterte mit künstlerischen und wissenschaftlichen Verfahren unsere Alltagsbeziehung zum Wasser und zur damit verbundenen Produktion von Plastikabfall.

Vorbereitet wurde das Ganze in einem Forschungsprojekt und in Unterrichtsaktivitäten während des gesamten akademischen Jahres. Auf Exkursionen erkundeten wir die Wasserleitungs- und Kanalnetze von Graz und Wien. Aus den Feldstudien entstanden künstlerische Installationen und ein illustriertes Logbuch, das die Grazer und Wiener Wasserkreisläufe ausführlich und kindergerecht darstellte. Parallel dazu wurde die Universität zu einer Werft: In einem partizipatorischen Entwurfsprojekt bauten Studierende der Architektur das 11 × 5 × 4 Meter große U-Boot aus Abfallmaterialien. Seine Außenhaut bestand aus 2.000 in Kooperation mit Schulen und dem Reinigungspersonal der TU Graz gesammelten Einweg-Plastikflaschen. Das Innere war mit Arbeiten von 12 internationalen KünstlerInnen, u.a. der New Yorker Künstler Catherine Grau, bestückt.

Daniela Brasil

duced. At the same time, the university became a dockyard: within a participatory and collaborative design, architecture students built the submarine (11 × 5 × 4 m) from materials sourced in junkyards. Its outer skin was made out of 2,000 disposable plastic bottles, collected and prepared in cooperation with local schools and the TU Graz cleaning staff. The interior was furbished with works from 12 international artists, such as New York based artist Catherine Grau.

Daniela Brasil

Capacity Building for Rural Development in Occupied Palestinian Territory

A project by the **Austrian Partnership Program** in **Higher Education and Research**
www.appear.at

Rural areas in the occupied territories of Palestine are suffering from substantial development pres-

Capacity Building for Rural Development in Occupied Palestinian Territory

Ein Projekt des **Austrian Partnership Program** in Higher Education and **Research for Development**
www.appear.at

Der ländliche Raum in den besetzten Territorien Palästinas leidet unter erheblichem Entwicklungsdruck. Die zwei wichtigsten Ursachen für die aufkommenden Umweltprobleme sind das rapide Bevölkerungswachstum und die fehlenden In-

sures. The two most significant causes of the nascent environmental problems are the rapid population growth and a lack of instruments for spatial order. Palestinian rural environments are in need of evaluation and profile definition but also require the identification of dangers resulting from environmental degradation and the establishment of development strategies.

Cooperating on this project (36/37 © Johann Zancanella) are the Department of Architecture at Birzeit University (BZU) in Palestine (coordinating institution), the Institute of Urbanism at Graz University of Technology (partner institution), and the BOKU and Vienna University of Technology (associate partners). The project pursues the implementation of specialized knowledge for

strumente für die Raumordnung. Der ländliche Raum Palästinas bedarf einer Evaluierung, einer Definierung des Profils sowie der Erkennung der Gefahren, die aus der Umweltzerstörung resultieren und der Etablierung von Entwicklungsstrategien.

Am Projekt (36/37 © Johann Zancanella) kooperieren die Abteilung für Architektur der Birzeit University (BZU) in Palästina als Koordinator und das Institut für Städtebau der TU Graz als Partnerinstitution bzw. die BOKU und die TU Wien als assoziierte Partner. Das Projekt verfolgt die Implementierung von Fachwissen für die Planung ländlicher Räume, die Förderung des

planning measures related to rural spaces and promotes knowledge transfer between BZU and municipalities as well as international networking with BZU. The project involves the development

Wissenstransfers zwischen BZU und Gemeinden sowie die internationale Vernetzung der BZU. Das Projekt beinhaltet die Entwicklung eines Curriculums für Raumordnung an der BZU, Postdiplomkurse für Fachleute aus der Praxis und den öffentlichen Institutionen, Intensivprogramme mit Studierenden und eine internationale Konferenz. Die Aktivitäten werden von den österreichischen Universitäten mit deren Expertisen in Naturressourcen, Umwelt und Raumordnung unterstützt. Das zweijährige Projekt läuft seit September 2012.

Grigor Doytchinov, Johann Zancanella

Objects, Daily Grind and Architecture

Möbelentwürfe der Studierenden am
Institut für Raumgestaltung im
Salone Mobile 2014

Der Begriff „daily grind", der tägliche Abschliff, wird im Englischen verwendet, um eine alltägliche Arbeitsweise, eine Routine zu beschreiben. Der Begriff ist schillernd, zeigt er doch zum einen

die Kontinuität der Arbeit, aus der heraus Expertise und Knowhow erwachsen. Zum anderen erinnert er daran, dass Routine sich einschleift, dass in der Arbeit, die man im Schlaf beherrscht, auch immer wieder Brüche geschehen müssen.

Die Prototypenwerkstatt für Möbelbau des Instituts für Raumgestaltung (38 © Manfred Stocker)

in den Händen von Diplomingenieur Matthias Gumhalter und dem Tischlermeister Rainer Eberl lotet in Möbelentwürfen (39 Entwurf Caroline Puchleitner „3-Bein" © Manfred Stocker) seit geraumer Zeit den Zwischenraum zwischen robuster Alltäglichkeit und aufgebrochener Routine aus. Das wurde bereits 2013 in einer Ausstel-

of a curriculum for spatial order at BZU, postgraduate classes for experts from both the private sector and public institutions, intensive programs with students, and an international conference. The activities are supported by the participating Austrian universities with their expertise in natural resources, environmental issues, and spatial order. The two-year project started in September 2012.

Grigor Doytchinov, Johann Zancanella

Objects, Daily Grind and Architecture

Furniture design by students from the **Institute of Spatial Design** at **Salone Mobile 2014**

The English phrase "daily grind" is used to denote everyday working life or routine. Though the term is somewhat dubious, it does convey a certain work-related continuity that gives rise to expertise and know-how. Also, it reminds us of how routine grinds on and how work that we can carry out

blindfolded may benefit from disruptions again and again.

The prototype workshop for furniture construction in the Institute of Spatial Design (38 © Manfred Stocker), headed by graduate engineer Matthias Gumhalter and master carpenter Rainer Eberl, has been exploring for some time now the intermediate space between robust everyday occurrence and disrupted routine through furniture design (39 "3-Bein" by Caroline Puchleitner © Manfred Stocker). This was already evident in an exhibition at Haus der Architektur in 2013. Objects

made in the workshop that are suited to everyday life, such as a side table or wardrobe, will be exhibited in April 2014 at the Milan Furniture Fair, the most influential furniture design fair worldwide, after successfully passing through an international jury-based selection process. Prototypes that have been developed, calculated, and executed in university seminars on a scale of 1:1 offer insight into the approach taken in the classes taught in the Institute of Spatial Design under the guidance of Prof. Irmgard Frank. Here, the priority was placed on the objective of fostering a realistic full-scale experience whenever possible—moving from drawing to material, from idea to performance, from a sociopolitical position to an architectural design.

The "daily grind" is being exhibited in a workshop, packaged as fifteen small pieces of furniture made of solid wood, whose semblance is a product of routine artisanship while likewise reflecting its potential diversity.

Claudia Gerhäusser

lung im HdA deutlich. Mit alltagstauglichen Objekten wie Beistelltisch oder Garderobe wird die Werkstatt im April 2014 auf der Mailänder Möbelmesse, der weltweit einflussreichsten Messe im Möbeldesign, nach erfolgreich absolviertem Auswahlverfahren durch eine internationale Jury ausstellen. Prototypen, die in den Seminaren im 1:1 Maßstab von den Studierenden entworfen, kalkuliert und handwerklich umgesetzt werden, geben einen Einblick in die Haltung, die in den Lehrveranstaltungen des Instituts für Raumgestaltung unter der Leitung von Frau Prof. Irmgard Frank vertreten wird. Der Schritt aus der Zeichnung heraus zum Material oder aus dem Gedanken hin zur Perfomance, aus einer sozio-politischen Position in den architektonischen Entwurf, mit dem Ziel, wann immer es möglich ist eine realmaßstäbliche Erfahrung zu vermitteln, hat hier Priorität.

Ausgestellt wird der „daily grind" in einer Werkstatt, verpackt in 15 kleine Möbelstücke aus Massivholz, deren Erscheinungsbild sowohl ein Produkt der Routine handwerklichen Arbeitens ist, als auch deren mögliche Vielfalt spiegelt.

Claudia Gerhäusser

heimat/los: Explorations among Identity, Politics, and Architecture

The symposium co-organized by the Institute of Architectural Theory, History of Art and Cultural Studies (akk) at Graz University of Technology on October 18, 2013 was based on the architecture-relevant field of tension between global networking, the new formation of political-national borders, and local claims to exclusivity. Two questions emerged from this: In the context of "building culture," who considers something their "own" and according to which criteria and collective models, that is, which "foreign" elements not associated with this are ruled out? And in the context of societal and political upheaval, how do shifting identities attain visible expression?

It was with a plea for a pluralistic concept of home that is not tied to specific space that contemporary historian Helmut Konrad opened the symposium. Subsequently, the first panel, which featured author Olga Flor and architectural theo-

heimat/los. Erkundungen zwischen Identität, Politik und Architektur

Das vom Institut für Architekturtheorie, Kunst- und Kulturwissenschaften (akk) der TU Graz am 18. Oktober 2013 (co-)veranstaltete Symposium ging von dem auf Architektur wirkenden Spannungsfeld zwischen globaler Vernetzung, Neuformierung politisch-nationaler Grenzen und lokalen Ansprüchen auf Exklusivität aus. Daraus ergaben sich zwei Fragen: Von wem und nach welchen Kriterien und kollektiven Leitbildern wird im Bereich der „Baukultur" etwas als das „Eigene" in den Blick genommen bzw. als das „Fremde", nicht Dazugehörige ausgeschieden? Und wie erhalten im Kontext gesellschaftlicher und politischer Umwälzungen sich verändernde Identitäten einen sichtbaren Ausdruck?

Mit einem Plädoyer für einen pluralen und nicht an den Raum gebundenen Heimatbegriff eröffnete der Zeithistoriker Helmut Konrad die

rist Oliver Ziegenhardt, explored the "politics of fading in and out," both in public space and in relation to the term "building culture," which has enjoyed a boom for years now. A second panel comprised of geographer Xénia Havadi-Nagy and architect Ursula Faix focused on the theme of "architecture and fluid identities" by example of Roma architecture in Romania, yet also with a view to the urban interventions by architecture students in the Kosovan captial, Priština (40 bus stop © Christoph Grill, edited by Toni Levak).

The topical point of departure for the event was Antje Senarclens de Grancy's presentation

Veranstaltung. Daran anschließend erkundete das erste Panel mit der Schriftstellerin Olga Flor und dem Architekturtheoretiker Oliver Ziegenhardt „Politiken des Ein- und Ausblendens", zum einen im öffentlichen Raum, zum anderen in Bezug auf den seit Jahren boomenden „Baukultur"-Begriff. Im zweiten Panel untersuchten die Geografin Xénia Havadi-Nagy und die Architektin Ursula Faix das Thema „Architektur und fluide Identitäten" am Beispiel von Roma-Architektur in Rumänien bzw. im Hinblick auf städtische Interventionen von Architekturstudierenden in der kosovarischen Hauptstadt Priština (40 Bushaltestelle © Christoph Grill, bearbeitet von Toni Levak).

Aktueller Ausgangspunkt der Veranstaltung war die Präsentation des von Antje Senarclens de Grancy am akk herausgegebenen Buches *Identität – Politik – Architektur. Der ‚Verein für Heimatschutz in Steiermark'* (Berlin: Jovis, 2013), das den Blick auf die Kontinuitäten und Brüche der „baukulturellen" Themenstellungen dieser 1909 in Graz gegründeten Vereinigung richtet und

of the book recently published by akk called *Identität – Politik – Architektur: Der "Verein für Heimatschutz in Steiermark"* (Identity – Politics – Architecture: The "Association for Home Protection in Styria," Berlin: Jovis, 2013). It hones in on the continuities and fractures of the thematic "building-cultural" issues related to this Graz-based association founded in 1909, and it also thematizes the association's (identity-)political positions, usurpations, and enmeshments in the twentieth century.

Antje Senarclens de Grancy

deren (identitäts-)politische Positionen, Vereinnahmungen und Verstrickungen im 20. Jahrhundert thematisiert.

Antje Senarclens de Grancy

„Architektur begeistert!"
Ball der Technik am **25. Jänner 2013**
im **Grazer Congress**

„Herausbrechende Säulen", „hölzerne Kristalle" und „fallende Fenster": Verschiedene Kunstinstallationen und architektonische Illusionen transportierten das Motto „Architektur begeistert" des letztjährigen Ball der Technik (41 © IAM/TU Graz) im Grazer Congress.

Der traditionsreiche Ball der Technik zählt zu den Höhepunkten der steirischen Ballsaison. Den Ball der Technik 2013 haben verschiedene Institute der Architekturfakultät mit Projekten, die im Rahmen von Lehrveranstaltungen von Studierenden entwickelt und gebaut wurden, gestalterisch bereichert. Bei schmalem Budget mit großer Gestaltungs- und Innovationsfreude sowie

hohem Improvisationstalent haben die ArchitekturstudentInnen eine faszinierende Fülle von Installationen und Objekten erarbeitet und damit dem Ball einen einmaligen Charakter gegeben. Hier können nur ein paar Projekte stellvertretend herausgegriffen werden.

„Herausbrechende Säulen" – Robert Damm und Philipp Loibl inszenierten eine historische Säule durch einen transparenten Schatten. Das Projekt „Schattensäule" funktionierte mittels Doppelung und Verschiebung. Bei Andrea Zalesak und Daniela List bildeten Bewegungsrichtungen die Entwurfsbasis: Der Strom der Ballgäste ins Gebäude und die Bewegungen im Inneren. Die Rahmen des „fallenden" Fensters leiteten die innere Bewegung nach Außen. Im Treppenhaus erwartete die Besucher die größte Installation des Balles, das Projekt „Neuronen" von Alma Wimmer, Evelyn Anvidalfarei und Lisa-Maria Gantschacher: ein aus transparenten Pneufolien mit einem Ultraschallschweißgerät in viel Handarbeit erstelltes Neuronenmodell, welches, mit Luft gefüllt, das gesamte Treppenhaus überspannte.

Die genannten drei Projekte und sechs weitere wurden gemeinsam vom Institut für Zeit-

41

genössische Kunst unter der Leitung von Hans Kupelwieser und vom Institut für Tragwerksentwurf unter der Leitung von Stefan Peters betreut, welche die Gestaltung des Balles zum gemeinsamen Thema in ihren Masterstudios gemacht hatten.

Im großen Ballsaal hing neben den traditionellen Lustern ein hölzerner Kristall über den Tanzenden. Kann man aus Holz einen Kronleuchter bauen? Das war die Fragestellung des Masterstudios, welches sich am Institut für Architektur und Medien unter der Leitung von Urs Hirschberg, Richard Dank und Christian Freißling in Zusam-

"Architektur begeistert!"
Ball der Technik (Ball of Technology)
on **January 25, 2013**
at **congress|graz**

"Burgeoning pillars," "wooden crystals," and "falling windows": various art installations and architectural illusions convey the motto of last year's Ball of Technology (41 © IAM/TU Graz) at congress|graz: "Architecture Excites."

The Ball of Technology, which enjoys a rich tradition, counts among the highlights of the Styrian ball season. The Ball of Technology 2013 was enriched by design projects developed and built by students in the framework of classes at various institutes within the Faculty of Architecture. Working on a meager budget but with great joy in design and innovation, as well as high talent for improvisation, the architecture students created a fascinating wealth of installations and objects, which in turn lent the ball a very unique character. It is only possible to outline several of these projects here.

"Burgeoning pillars"—Robert Damm and Philipp Loibl staged a historic pillar using a transparent shadow. The project "Schattensäule" (Shadow Pillar) functions by way of doubling and shifting. In the case of Andrea Zalesak and Daniela List, by contrast, directions of movement formed the basis for design: the flow of ball guests entering the building and the movement evolving inside. The frames of the "falling" window channeled the inner movement toward the outside. In the stairwell visitors encountered the largest installation of the ball, the project "Neuronen" (Neurons) by Alma Wimmer, Evelyn Anvidalfarei, and Lisa-Maria Gantschacher: a neuron model made of transparent tire foil that was painstakingly handcrafted using an ultrasound welding apparatus. The model was filled with air and spanned the entire stairwell.

The three projects cited here and six additional ones were developed by the Institute of Contemporary Art and the Institute of Structural Design under the advising of Hans Kupelwieser and Stefan Peters, respectively. They made the

designing of the ball a collaborative topic in their master studios.

Hovering above the dancers in the large ballroom next to the traditional chandelier was a wooden crystal. Can a chandelier be fashioned from wood? This was the question explored using parametric production methods in the master studio at the Institute of Architecture and Media under the guidance of Urs Hirschberg, Richard Dank, and Christian Freißling in collaboration with the Wood Innovation Center in Zeltweg. The answer arrived in the form of the project "Pallantis" by Paul Frick, which was collaboratively implemented through the teamwork of all involved master studio students. The use of LED lighting technology (Prof. Leising, Institute of Solid State Physics) allowed the chandelier of wood veneer to become "enflamed" with light. The support structure of the "wooden crystal" was generated according to the Voronoi principle: no two parts of the structure are alike, and all were precisely wrought by a robot. The individually controllable lights illuminated the ball-

menarbeit mit dem Holzinnovationszentrum in Zeltweg mit digitalen und parametrischen Fabrikationsmethoden auseinandergesetzt hat. Die Antwort war das Projekt „Pallantis" von Paul Frick, welches in Teamarbeit von allen Studierenden des Studios gemeinsam umgesetzt wurde. Durch die Verwendung von LED Lichttechnologie (Prof. Leising, Institut für Festkörperphysik) bringt der Kronleuchter die „Flammung" von Furnierholz zum Leuchten. Die Tragstruktur des „hölzernen Kristalls" wurde nach dem Voronoi-Prinzip generiert – keine zwei Teile der Struktur sind gleich, alle passgenau vom Roboter gefertigt. Die einzeln ansteuerbaren Leuchten erhellten den Ballraum in unterschiedlichen Mustern im Takt mit der Musik.

Urs Hirschberg

South East Europe Research Project Cultema

Cultema (Cultural Value for Sustainable Territorial Governance and Marketing) ist ein Forschungs-

projekt am **Institut für Städtebau** an der **Technischen Universität Graz**.

Das Ziel des Projektes Cultema ist es, eine gemeinsame Marketing-Strategie für Investitionen in kulturelles Erbe zu entwickeln, neue institutionelle Kapazitäten zu schaffen und innovative Governance-Muster umzusetzen, die in der Lage sind, administrative, soziale und wirtschaftliche Barrieren zwischen kulturellem Erbe und potenziellen Investoren zu verringern. Unter Berücksichtigung kultureller Werte als regionale nachhaltige Wachstumsfaktoren, wurden spezifische Projektziele definiert, um das kulturelle Erbe und dessen Werte in Regionalentwicklungsstrategien aufzunehmen und administrative, technische und politische Kapazitäten zu verbessern. Das Institut für Städtebau hat ein kreatives Modell für kulturelles und regionales Governance Marketing entwickelt und konzentriert sich darauf, Wissen und technische Werkzeuge zu implementieren. Die Nachhaltigkeit des Projektes wird auf lange Sicht durch das Cultema Labor Netzwerk an der TU Graz gewährleistet.

Kersten Christian Hofbauer

Besseres Licht im Krankenhaus

Lichtgestaltung zur **Verbesserung** der **Allgemeinbeleuchtung** in **PatientInnenzimmern**.

Die vorgestellte Studie „Besseres Licht im Krankenhaus" ist Teil eines in Kooperation mit der Firma XAL, der steiermärkischen Krankenanstaltengesellschaft m.b.H. (KAGes) und dem Institut für Raumgestaltung an der TU Graz durchgeführten FFG Forschungsprojektes.

Anliegen der Studie ist es, mittels wissenschaftlicher Messmethoden die Gesamtzusammenhänge des persönlichen Erlebens von Licht und den Einfluss auf die Wahrnehmung von Raum zu untersuchen.

Vergleichend untersucht wurden zwei unterschiedliche Situationen von Allgemeinbeleuchtung im PatientInnenzimmer. Im Fokus der Betrachtung stehen Lichtqualität, Lichtfarbe, Leuchtendesign und Oberflächenmaterialien und deren Wirkung auf den Raumeindruck des Menschen.

Die Dokumentation der Studie umfasst einen allgemeinen Thementeil, der einen Ausblick auf die Komplexität der Aufgabenstellungen in der

---

room with different patterns aligned to the rhythm of the music.

Urs Hirschberg

South East Europe Research Project Cultema

Cultema (Cultural Value for Sustainable Territorial Governance and Marketing) is a research project at the **Institute for Urbanism**, **Graz University of Technology**.

The aim of the Cultema project is to develop a shared marketing strategy, to increase cultural heritage investments; to establish new institutional capabilities; to implement innovative governance patterns, able to reduce administrative, social and economic barriers between cultural heritage and potential investors. Considering cultural values as a territorial sustainable growth factor, specific project objectives are developed to include cultural heritage values into territorial development

strategies and to improve administrative, technical, and political capacity, ensuring the project sustainability in the long run, when a Laboratory Network located at the Graz University of Technology is operative. The Institute of Urbanism developed a creative model of cultural governance and territorial marketing and focuses on the need to implement knowledge and technical tools.

Kersten Hofbauer

Improved Hospital Lighting

Lighting Design for **Improving General Lighting** in **Patient Rooms**.

The study introduced here, "Besseres Licht im Krankenhaus" (Improved Hospital Lighting), is part of a Austrian Research Promotion Agency (FFG) research project cooperatively carried out by three parties: the lighting company XAL, the hospital company Steiermärkische Krankenanstaltengesellschaft m.b.H. (KAGes) and the

Institute of Spatial Design at Graz University of Technology.

The study is concerned with using scientific methods of measurement to investigate the overall context involved in the personal experience of light and also the way the perception of space is influenced. A comparative approach was taken in looking at two different situations where general lighting was found in patient rooms. The focus was trained on light quality, light color, lamp design, and surface materials, as well as on the effects thereof on different individuals' perception of this space. The documentation of the study encompasses a general thematic section which offers an overview of the complexity of the conceptual formulation related to lighting design for patient rooms. In order to establish the relation between space, material, and light reflection, in the first stage empirical studies were carried out on the surface appearance and general impression of the materials involved. Subsequently, mock-up rooms (42 © XAL GmbH, Paul Ott, Graz) at a scale of 1:1 were used for test-

Lichtgestaltung für PatientInnenzimmer gibt. Um den Zusammenhang zwischen Raum, Material und Reflexion von Licht nachzuweisen wurden in einer ersten Stufe empirische Studien zu Oberflächenbild und Gesamteindruck von Materialien durchgeführt. Abschließend wurden in 1:1 aufgebauten Mock-up Räumen (42 © XAL GmbH, Paul Ott, Graz) Lichtkonzepte mit unterschiedlichen Lichtqualitäten und diese bedingende Leuchten getestet und durch eine ExpertInnenrunde aus MedizinerInnen, Pflegepersonal, ArchitektInnen und LichttechnikerInnen evaluiert. Aufbauend auf die Recherchen und Studien zur Allgemeinbeleuchtung und Materialwahl wurden Empfehlungen für ein exemplarisches PatientInnenzimmer abgegeben.

Der Bereich der Forschung von Licht in Realräumen ist beispielhaft. Es sind wenige Studien im architektonischen Kontext bekannt. Deshalb verlangt es angesichts einer sich schnell entwickelnden Lichttechnologie nach Folgeuntersuchungen in diesem Feld.

Institut für Raumgestaltung

„Rurban City. Design your free local menu!"

Seit 2012 entwickelt und veranstaltet das Institut für Architektur und Landschaft „Design your free local menu!" – gemeinschaftliche öffentliche

---

ing lighting concepts of differing light quality and also these conditional lamps. The results were evaluated by a panel of experts comprised of medical doctors, nursing staff, architects, and lighting engineers. Moreover, recommendations for an exemplary patient room were given based on the research and studies of general lighting and material selection.

The area of light research as applied to real spaces plays a model role since only very few studies in an architectural context exist. As such, follow-up investigations are called for in this field, especially considering how quickly lighting technology is developing.

Institute of Spatial Design

"Rurban City: Design your free local menu!"

Starting in 2012, the Institute of Architecture and Landscape has developed and organized "Design your free local menu!" The event is a public cooking action where fruit, vegetables, greens, and blossoms—whatever is currently available in public space or in local communal gardens—can be harvested for use in culinary experiments. The special organization of these actions sets out to show mindfulness and appreciation for public greenery and spaces open for free utilization.

By uniting joint action and ecological, social, and political initiatives, new strengths form that facilitate the development of our urban living environments. Landscape and natural contexts can thus once again become an active part of urban culture.

In the fall of 2013, the project was invited to celebrate the ten-year birthday of the Kunsthaus Graz and, shortly thereafter, to participate in the 10th Architecture Biennale in São Paulo. At the Biennale opening, on the roof terrace of the main event building, the Centro Cultural de São Paulo, cooking took place in collaboration with local urban gardening initiatives (43/44 © Bernhard

König). "Rurban City: Design your free local menu!" became a meeting place and point of

Kochaktionen, bei denen Obst, Gemüse, Grünzeug und Blüten, das, was aktuell im öffentlichen Raum oder in lokalen Gemeinschaftsgärten geerntet werden kann, für kulinarische Experimente verwendet wird. Durch bewusstes Gestalten dieser Aktionen soll öffentlichem Grün und nutzungsoffenen Freiräumen Aufmerksamkeit und Wertschätzung entgegengebracht werden.

Mit dem Zusammenbringen von gemeinsamer Handlung und ökologischen, sozialen und politischen Initiativen formen sich neue Kräfte für die Entwicklung unserer urbanen Lebensumgebungen. Landschaft und natürliche Zusammenhänge können so wieder aktiver Bestandteil urbaner Kultur werden.

Im Herbst 2013 wurde das Projekt zur zehnjährigen Geburtstagsfeier des Kunsthauses Graz eingeladen und kurz darauf zur Teilnahme an der 10. Architekturbiennale in São Paulo. Dort wurde zur Eröffnung der Biennale auf dem Dachgarten des Hauptveranstaltungsgebäudes, des Centro Cultural de São Paulo, gemeinsam mit lokalen Stadtgärtner-Initiativen gekocht (43/44 © Bernhard König). „Rurban City: Design your free local menu!" wurde Treffpunkt und Ausgangspunkt für Debatten über urbanes Grün

und innerstädtische Landwirtschaft in São Paulo. So fand in der Folge u.a. das Gründungstreffen von MUDA-SP (Movimento Urbano de Agroecologia de São Paulo) in der Gemeinschaftsküche von „Rurban City: Design your free local menu!" statt.

Ein weiteres dieser Gemeinschaftsprojekte im Innenhof der leerstehenden Dominikanerkaserne in Graz-Gries, welches in Kooperation mit dem Garden Lab Graz, GemeinschaftsgärtnerInnen in Graz und Lendlabor entstand, wurde mit dem Umwelt-Preis Graz 2013 ausgezeichnet.

Bernhard König

Überlegungen zur Stadtwahrnehmung beim Gehen

Die Ausstellung *Gehversuche* im **GrazMuseum**.

Von 22.3.–3.6.2013 war im ebenerdigen, zur Straße hin „offenen" Franz Ferdinand Raum des GrazMuseums (46 © Brigitte Kovacs) die von Christina

Töpfer und Brigitte Kovacs kuratierte Ausstellung *Gehversuche. Überlegungen zur Stadtwahrnehmung beim Gehen* zu sehen. Gezeigt wurden zwölf teils interaktive künstlerische Projekte von Studierenden des Instituts für Zeitgenössische

Gehversuche
Überlegungen zur Stadtwahrnehmung beim Gehen
Ausstellungsdauer: 22.03. bis 03.06.2013

departure for discourse on urban greenery and inner-city agriculture in São Paulo. It thus followed that the founding meeting of MUDA-SP (Movimento Urbano de Agroecologia de São Paulo), among other events, was held in the communal kitchen of "Rurban City: Design your free local menu!"

Another such community project—which took place in the inner courtyard of the empty Dominican barracks in the Gries district of Graz and was founded in cooperation with the Garden Lab Graz, communal gardeners in Graz, and Lendlabor—was honored by receiving the Environmental Prize Graz 2013.

Bernhard König

Reflections on Urban Perception While Walking

The Exhibition *Gehversuche* at **GrazMuseum**.

From March 22 to June 3, 2013, the exhibition *Gehversuche: Überlegungen zur Stadtwahrneh-*

mung beim Gehen (Walking Endeavors: Reflections on Urban Perception while Walking), curated by Christina Töpfer and Brigitte Kovacs, was shown in GrazMuseum's ground-level Franz Ferdinand Room (46 © Brigitte Kovacs) which "opens up" to the street. Presented there were twelve artistic projects, some of which were interactive, by students from the Institute of Contemporary Art; the works were developed during the summer semester 2012 as part of a class called *Stadtspaziergänge: Gehen als künstlerische Praxis* (City Strolls: Walking as Artistic Practice). A pivotal moment in all works was the

Kunst, die im Sommersemester 2012 in der Lehrveranstaltung *Stadtspaziergänge. Gehen als künstlerische Praxis* entstanden. Zentrales Moment aller Arbeiten war der Versuch, das Gehen als Medium der Stadtraumerforschung einzusetzen und damit eine neue Raumwahrnehmung zu provozieren.

Neben der Ausstellung (45 Ausstellungsposter © Brigitte Kovacs) wurde von den Kuratorinnen ein umfassendes Rahmenprogramm konzipiert. Ein Vortrag von Dieter Spath und Bernd Vlay über ihr spektakuläres Diplomprojekt *City Joker* an der TU Graz aus dem Jahr 1995 sowie dessen filmische Inszenierung durch Gerald Straub waren Inspiration für einen eigenen Stadtspaziergang „der Sonne entgegen" im Sinne der Situationistischen Internationale.

Mit Arbeiten von **Nadin Bierbauer, Horia Daniel Brad, Miroslava Denina, Denise Erhardt, Luis Pedro Hurtate Caceres, Christoph Walter Pirker, Hannes Pramstraller, Alexander Pucher, Daniel Tolpeit, Cordula Weitgruber, Marco Wenegger** und **Zerina Dzubur**.

Brigitte Kovacs

attempt to use walking as a medium of urban-space exploration and thus to provoke new spatial perception.

Accompanying the exhibition (45 exhibition poster © Brigitte Kovacs) was a comprehensive events program conceptualized by the two curators. A lecture by Dieter Spath and Bernd Vlay on their spectacular diploma project *City Joker* at Graz University of Technology from the year 1995 and its filmic staging by Gerald Straub proved inspirational for a joint city walk "into the sun" along the lines of the Situationist International.

With works by **Nadin Bierbauer, Horia Daniel Brad, Miroslava Denina, Denise Erhardt, Luis Pedro Hurtate Caceres, Christoph Walter Pirker, Hannes Pramstraller, Alexander Pucher, Daniel Tolpeit, Cordula Weitgruber, Marco Wenegger**, and **Zerina Dzubur**.

Brigitte Kovacs

Freiräume – Freuräume
**GrazMuseum,
12. Juni–2. September 2013.**

Einen Sommer lang standen die Türen des GrazMuseums hin zur Sackstraße weit offen. *Freiräume – Freuräume* quartierte sich nach umfangreichen Vorarbeiten der vergangenen Jahre – Ausgangsmaterial ist die Untersuchung „Lücken im urbanen Raum", sowie eine Erkundung des sich quer durch den Stadtraum hindurch schlängelnden Mühlgangs – in den Franz Ferdinand Raum des Erdgeschosses im GrazMuseum (47/48 © Nicole Pruckermayr) ein.

Freiräume – Freuräume
GrazMuseum, June 12–September 2, 2013.

One whole summer long the doors of GrazMuseum were opened wide on the Sackstraße side. The exhibition *Freiräume – Freuräume* made itself at home in the ground-floor Franz Ferdinand Room at GrazMuseum following extensive preparatory work over the previous years—with source material from the study "Lücken im urbanen Raum" (Gaps in Urban Space) and an exploration of the Mühlgang path (47/48 © Nicole Pruckermayr) which meanders all the way across town.

Order, security, cleanliness, and a well-designed environment are important factors in keep-

Ordnung, Sicherheit, Sauberkeit und eine durchgestaltete Umgebung sind wichtig, um eine komplexe Welt am Laufen zu halten. Sie können aber auch zu Überregulierung führen. Wer hat nicht romantische Bedürfnisse nach dem Nicht-Geordneten – den Freiräumen, den Gstettn[1] und anderen Nischen der Stadt? Zwischen den Orten des Konsums, des beschleunigten Durchzugsverkehrs und den Zonen der Res-

1 Freiraum, Restfläche, Leerstand, Baulücke, Brache … Dieser Ort innerhalb einer geplanten Stadt wird umgangssprachlich als Gstettn bezeichnet. Er könnte das Gegenteil gestalteter Plätze bzw. Räume sein. Was auf einer Gstettn geschieht, mag unbeabsichtigt sein, der Platz selbst kann aber gewollt sein.

ing a complex world running. But they can also lead to overregulation. Who does not have a romantic desire for less order—for open spaces, the *Gstettn*[1] and other niches within the city? Open spaces keep popping up between sites of consumption, areas of accelerated through traffic, and zones of restriction. Exemplary of such physically experienceable spaces are the *Gstettn*. They are spaces of projection and places that can be perceived differently depending on the perspec-

1 Open space, surplus land, vacancy, empty building site, fallow land, and more. This place within a planned city is called Gstettn in the colloquial German spoken in Austria. It could be the opposite of designed places or spaces. While the happenings at a Gstettn may be unintentional, the place itself can indeed be deliberate.

triktion tun sich immer wieder Freiräume auf. Diese physisch erlebbaren Räume sind zum Beispiel Gstettn. Sie sind Projektionsflächen und Räume, die von jeder Perspektive aus anders wahrgenommen werden. Auf der Gstettn trifft sich so manches.

Innerhalb des Ausstellungszeitraumes wurden durch sieben gemeinsam erfahrbare Erkundungen in der Stadt – Gstettntouren – unterschiedlichste Perspektiven auf das Flüchtige und Ungreifbare dieser urbanen Räume erprobt. Künstlerische Arbeiten wie die Wandillustration „Spielwiese der Wahrnehmung" oder die Videoinstallation „Sehnsuchtsort Freiraum: Visionen, Grenzen, Praktiken" illustrierten die unterschiedlichen Blickwinkel.

Konzept: **Nicole Pruckermayr**; Mitarbeit: . **Reni Hofmüller**; Gestaltung: **Renate Mihatsch**

Nicole Pruckermayr

November Talks. Positionen zur zeitgenössischen Architektur

Vortragsreihe am **Institut für Architekturtechnologie** in Kooperation mit der **STO-Stiftung**.

Im Rahmen der „November Talks", einer Veranstaltung mit dreijähriger Tradition an der TU Graz, werden internationale Architekten eingeladen, ihre Positionen zur zeitgenössischen Architektur vorzustellen. Jede Veranstaltung findet an einem Montagabend im November statt und besteht aus einem 45-minütigen Werkvortrag und anschließender Podiumsdiskussion, in der man auf einzelne Aspekte der Arbeiten, deren Hintergründe und die Arbeitsweise der Gastarchitekten eingeht. Die Vortragsreihe wird vom Institut für Architekturtechnologie unter der Leitung von Prof. Roger Riewe organisiert und moderiert.

Durch das einzigartige Format der November Talks – eine Kombination aus Vortrag, Interview und Diskussionsrunde – wird eine intensive öffentliche Auseinandersetzung mit den

November Talks: Positions on Contemporary Architecture

Lecture Series at the **Institute of Architecture Technology** in Cooperation with the **STO-Foundation**.

Within the framework of November talks, an event with a three-year tradition at the Graz University of Technology, international architects are invited to expose their positions on contemporary architecture. Each event takes place on a Monday evening in November and consists of a 45 minute work presentation, followed by an equally long panel discussion where specific aspects of the guest's work and its backgrounds become topic. The lecture series is organized and moderated by the team of the Institute of Architecture Technology under the supervision of Prof. Roger Riewe. The unique format of the November talks—a combination of lecture, discussion and interview—generates

tive you take. Many different things meet at the *Gstettn*.

Over the course of the exhibition, seven collectively experienceable excursions through town—*Gstettn* tours—fostered a wide range of perspectives on transient and intangible facets of these urban spaces. Artistic works like the wall mural *Spielwiese der Wahrnehmung* (Playing Field of Perception) or the video installation

Sehnsuchtsort Freiraum: Visionen, Grenzen, Praktiken (Open Space, a Site of Yearning: Visions, Boundaries, Practices) illustrated the various vantage points.

Concept: **Nicole Pruckermayr**; Collaboration: **Reni Hofmüller**; Design: **Renate Mihatsch**.

Nicole Pruckermayr

Werken der Architekten und ihren Architektur-
haltungen erzeugt. Gäste der November Talks
2013 (49) waren Go Hasegawa (Japan, Tokio),
Spela Videčnik (Slowenien, Ljubljana), Jordi
Badia (Spanien, Barcelona) und Felix Claus
(Holland, Amsterdam). Aufzeichnungen der Vor-
träge können auf der Homepage des Institutes
für Architekturtechnologie (www.iat.tugraz.at)
gefunden werden. Ebenfalls sind am Institut die
Broschüren der November Talks 2011 (Bostjan
Vuga, Xiaodu Liu, Angela Paredes und David
Adjaye) und der November Talks 2012 (Bernard
Khoury, Brigitte Shim & Howard Sutcliffe,
Jonathan Sergison und Dorte Mandrup) erhält-
lich. Diese ausführlichen Publikationen enthal-
ten die Transkriptionen der Interviews mit den
Architekten sowie einen Überblick über deren
Werke und Biografien. Eine weitere Auflage
der Broschüre für 2013 befindet sich in Vorbe-
reitung. Besonderer Dank geht an die STO-
Stiftung für die finanzielle Unterstützung.

Sorana Radulescu

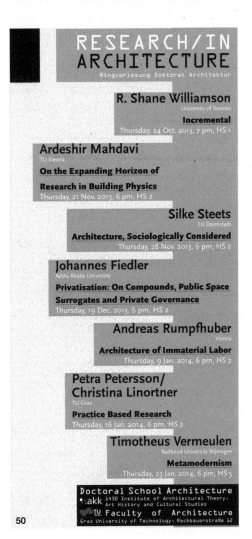

---

an intensive public debate of the architects' works
and their approach. Guests of the November 2013
talks (49) were Go Hasegawa (Japan, Tokyo),
Spela Videčnik (Slovenia, Ljubljana), Jordi Badia
(Spain, Barcelona) and Felix Claus (Netherlands,
Amsterdam). Recordings of the presentations
are available on the website of the Institute of
Architecture Technology (www.iat.tugraz.at).
Brochures of the November Talks 2011 (Bostjan
Vuga Xiaodu Liu, Angela Paredes and David
Adjaye) and the November Talks 2012 (Bernard
Khoury, Brigitte Shim and Howard Sutcliffe,
Jonathan Sergison and Dorte Mandrup) are also
available at the Institute. These publications
contain detailed transcriptions of the interviews
with the architects, as well as an overview of
their works and biographies. Another edition
of the brochure for 2013 is in preparation. Very
special thanks go to the STO-Foundation for the
financial support.

Sorana Radulescu

High Density and Living Comfort // China – Austria 2013

An international symposium on
contemporary requirements for
dense housing areas.

In China there are already eighty-six cities of
over five million inhabitants each, and the rapidly rising population numbers present great challenges to urban planning and housing development. In the scope of the three-day conference
High Density & Living Comfort, experts thematically explored how to reconcile energy efficiency and living comfort in the most limited of
spaces in Asian cities (51 © Benny Lam for the
Society for Community Organisation, Hong Kong).
The symposium, which was held at Graz University of Technology and involved 450 participants and international speakers, was organized

High Density and Living Comfort // China – Austria 2013

Ein internationales Symposium zu
zeitgenössischen Anforderungen
an **dichte Wohngebiete**.

In China leben bereits in 86 Städten jeweils über
fünf Millionen Menschen: Die rasant steigenden
Einwohnerzahlen stellen die Stadtentwicklung
und den Wohnbau vor große Herausforderungen.
Im Rahmen der dreitägigen Konferenz „High
Density & Living Comfort" thematisierten Ex-
pertinnen und Experten, wie sich Energieeffizienz und Wohnkomfort in asiatischen Städten
auf engstem Raum in Einklang bringen lassen
(51 © Benny Lam für die Society for Community
Organisation, Hong Kong). Die Fachtagung mit
450 Teilnehmenden und internationalen Vortragenden, die an der TU Graz stattfand, wurde vom
Institut für Architekturtechnologie (Wissenschaft-
liches Komitee: Roger Riewe und Ferdinand
Oswald) mit dem Konfuzius-Institut der Uni
Graz veranstaltet.

Die Qualität von urbaner Dichte stand in diesem Kontext ebenso zur Diskussion wie der tech-

by the Institute of Architecture Technology (academic committee: Roger Riewe and Ferdinand
Oswald) together with the Confucius Institute at
the University of Graz.

In this context, the quality of urban density
was discussed, as was the expenditure of technology and energy necessary for even attaining

nische und energetische Aufwand, mit dem eine hohe und verträgliche Bebauungs- und Bevölkerungsdichte überhaupt erreicht werden kann. Dieser Diskurs über die Verträglichkeit von hoher Dichte und Wohnkomfort muss folglich zu einer Übereinkunft über die Qualitäten von Dichte führen.

Im Zuge der Konferenz wurde die Ausstellung „Structure & Facade" eröffnet, in der Ergebnisse aus Forschung und Lehre des Instituts für Architekturtechnologie unter Leitung von Ferdinand Oswald gezeigt wurden. Die ausge-

stellten Arbeiten zeigten innovative Fassadensysteme und architektonische Konzepte, welche Lösungsansätze zu den Themenfeldern Nachhaltigkeit, Energieeffizienz und Behaglichkeit im Innenraum darstellen (52 Wohnungsbau in Hong Kong © Hong Kong Housing Authority).

An der Konferenz nahmen zwölf Doktoratsstudierende aus Australien, China, Deutschland, Indonesien, Iran, Italien, Japan, Nepal, Österreich, Saudi Arabien, Spanien und den USA teil. Die zehn Vortragenden kamen aus China, Deutschland,

Großbritannien, Kanada, der Schweiz, Singapur und Südkorea.

Die Konferenz ist die zweite ihrer Art und wird als Konferenz-Serie zukünftig regelmäßig vom Institut für Architekturtechnologie (IAT) veranstaltet .

Nachdem DETAIL Research offizieller Forschungspartner vom IAT geworden ist, veröffentlichte die DETAIL mehrere Artikel über die Konferenz im *DETAIL Magazin* und online in der DETAIL Research.

Eine Publikation der Konferenzergebnisse wird 2014 erscheinen.

Roger Riewe/Ferdinand Oswald

52

Chinesisch-österreichischer Ökopark in China

Im Juni 2013 hat Roger Riewe im Namen des *team styriA*, das vom Institut für Architekturtechnologie initiiert wurde, den Vertrag zur Planungsbeteiligung der Eco City in Nantong,

Chinese-Austrian Eco Park in China

In June 2013, in the name of the *team styriA* initiated by the Institute of Architecture Technology, Roger Riewe signed a contract to participate in the planning of the Eco City in Nantong (53 signing the contract at Graz University of Technology © Institute of Architecture Technology), China. The idea is to integrate Austrian know-how and sustainable building technology into the planning of the new city Su-Tong, and also to give Austrian companies a chance to establish new enterprise locations in China.

The Su-Tong Eco Park is situated in the Chinese provincial capital of Nantong (54 master plan Su-Tong-eco-park, Nantong, China © Su-Tong-Ökopark Bauprojekt Holding Co. Ltd.). It is projected that in approximately ten years there will be 300,000 residents living and working here. The bridge from Shanghai across the Yangtze River to the new Su-Tong city has already been built, which now positions the planned city with

a building and population density that is both high and acceptable. This discourse on the compatibility of high density and living comfort was intended to result in an agreement on the qualities of density.

During the conference, the exhibition *Structure & Facade* was opened, which displayed research and teaching results presented by Ferdinand Oswald from the Institute of Architecture Technology. The exhibited works showed innovative façade systems and architectural concepts that reflect approaches to developing solutions in the thematic fields of sustainability, energy efficiency, and comfort in interior space (52 housing area in Hong Kong © Hong Kong Housing Authority).

Twelve doctoral students took part in the con-

ference from Australia, Austria, China, Germany,

Indonesia, Iran, Italy, Japan, Nepal, Saudi Arabia, Spain, and the United States. The ten presenters harked from Canada, China, Germany, Great Britain, Singapore, South Korea, and Switzerland.

The conference was the second of its kind and will be regularly held by the Institute of Architecture Technology (IAT) as a conference series in the future .

Since DETAIL Research has become the official research partner of IAT, DETAIL has published several articles about the conference in *DETAIL Magazin* and on the DETAIL Research website.

A publication on the conference results will be released in 2014.

Roger Riewe/Ferdinand Oswald

China, unterschrieben (53 Vertragsunterzeichnung an der TU Graz © Institut für Architekturtechnologie). Die Kooperation sieht vor, österreichisches Knowhow und nachhaltige Bautechnologien in die Plaung der neuen Stadt Su-Tong zu integrieren und Unternehmen die Möglichkeit zu geben, neue Unternehmensstandorte in China zu gründen.

Der Su-Tong-Ökopark liegt in der chinesischen Provinzhauptstadt Nantong (54 Masterplan Su-Tong-Ökopark, Nantong, China © Su-Tong-Ökopark Bauprojekt Holding Co. Ltd.). In rund zehn Jahren sollen hier 300.000 Einwohner leben und arbeiten. Die Brücke von Shanghai über den Jangtse-Fluss zur neuen Su-Tong-Stadt wurde bereits realisiert, wodurch die geplante Stadt schon jetzt an die 23,5-Millionen-Einwohner-Metrophole Shanghai hervorragend angebunden ist. In der neuen Stadt sind zehn von insgesamt 50 Quadratkilometern für österreichische Firmengründungen reserviert worden.

Steirisches Knowhow. Das *team styriA* dient als Plattform, um Instituten, Unternehmen und Planungsbüros den Einstieg in dieses Milliardenprojekt zu ermöglichen. Die Leitung des *team styriA* hat Roger Riewe, Vorstand des Instituts für Architekturtechnologie (IAT), übernommen. Zusammen mit dem IAT bilden folgende Institute bzw. Unternehmen den Kern des *team styriA*: das Institut für Gebäude und Energie der TU Graz, das Ingenieurbüro Wörle Sparowitz, Riegler Riewe Architekten ZT-GesmbH sowie KLH Massivholz GmbH.

Asien Experte. Das Institut für Architekturtechnologie hat bereits in den vergangenen Jahren intensive Kontakte und Kooperationen mit chinesischen Hochschulen und Büros aufgebaut. Einer der Forschungsschwerpunkte des IAT sind nachhaltige Fassaden- und Gebäudetypologien in tropischen und subtropischen Regionen. Das Grazer Institut leistet nicht nur Entwicklungsarbeit, sondern koordiniert Unternehmen und Fachplaner bis zur Zertifizierung und Markteinführung von Fassadensystemen.

Roger Riewe/Ferdinand Oswald

53

an excellent connection to the metropolis of Shanghai with its population of 23.5 million. In the new city, ten of the available fifty square kilometers have been reserved for the formation of Austrian companies.

Styrian Know-How. The platform *team styriA* is designed to provide institutes, companies, and architectural firms with access to this multibillion venture. The directorship of *team styriA* has been assumed by Roger Riewe, Chair of the Institute of Architecture Technology (IAT). Together with IAT, the following institutes and companies represent the nucleus of *team styriA*: Institute of Buildings and Energy at Graz University of Technology, the engineering firm Wörle Sparowitz, the architectural office Riegler Riewe Architekten ZT-GesmbH, and the wood company KLH Massivholz GmbH.

Experts on Asia. In recent years, the Institute of Architecture Technology has intensively forged contacts and cooperative relationships with Chinese universities and architectural firms. One of the IAT research priorities is focused on sustainable façade and building typologies in tropical and subtropical regions. The Graz-based institute is involved not only in development efforts, but also in advising both companies and planning specialists throughout the certification process, including the market launch of façade systems.

Roger Riewe/Ferdinand Oswald

Exhibition
verMESSEN. Franziszeische Grundkataster von Graz

The idea, concept, and implementation for this exhibition originated with curators **Marion Starzacher**, **Elisabeth Seuschek**, and **Ramona Winker**. The project was supported by the **Graz-Museum** team in cooperation **Graz University of Technology**, the **university archive**, and the **Faculty of Architecture**.

This exhibition took place as a first historical excursion in the scope of a permanent exhibition

54

Ausstellung *verMESSEN: Franziszeische Grundkataster von Graz*

Idee, Konzept, Umsetzung und kuratiert von **Marion Starzacher**, **Elisabeth Seuschek** und **Ramona Winker** unterstützt vom Team des **GrazMuseum** in Kooperation mit der **TU Graz**, dem **Archiv der TU Graz** und der **Fakultät für Architektur TU Graz**.

In dieser Ausstellung, die als erster historischer Exkurs im Rahmen der Dauerausstellung *360 GRAZ | die Stadt von allen Zeiten* im GrazMuseum stattfand, wurden einerseits durch historische Exponate die Geschichte der Franziszeischen Landvermessung in Graz und Umgebung veranschaulicht und andererseits der Schritt in die Jetztzeit durch die Transkription der historischen Pläne in eine zeitgemäß lesbare Form sichtbar gemacht.

Franz Allmer, Geodät, Sammler und Lehrender der Vermessungsgeschichte an der TU Graz, der immer mit Begeisterung jungen Menschen historisch bemerkenswerte Sachverhalte aus seiner Profession in anschaulichen Vorlesungen, Ex-

kursionen und Stadtrundgängen präsentiert hat, begleitete die BesucherInnen als virtueller Erzähler. Er führte sie mittels einer Zeitreise durch die Ausstellung; für die jüngste Generation auch mittels Büchern, Kartenpuzzles und Suchspielen altersgemäß verständlich gemacht. Erstmals wurden Exponate und Texte aus dem persönlichen Nachlass Franz Allmers, wie auch Blätter der Franziszeischen Kataster, datiert mit 1820 und 1829, und historische, sowie zeitgenössische Messgeräte im Zusammenhang mit studentischen Arbeiten der Fakultät für Architektur einer breiten Öffentlichkeit zugänglich gemacht.

Franz Allmer erzählt – und wir setzen seine Erzählungen fort – mit der Transformation der

historischen Planinhalte in eine nach heutigen Maßstäben erarbeitete, lesbare daher klar definierte Form.

Im Rahmen der Ausstellung (55 © Andreas Untersteggaber) fand die Podiumsdiskussion „vermessen, verwalten, versteuern" moderiert von Dr. Monika Stromberger statt (56 © Andreas Untersteggaber). In den unterschiedlichen Impulsvorträgen beleuchteten die RednerInnen die Intention, die hinter der großangelegten Landesvermessung des 19. Jahrhunderts stand, die mit dem Grundsteuerpatent vom 23. Dezember 1817 von Franz I. verordnet wurde, in Relation zu ihren Disziplinen, brachten so manch wenig Bekanntes sehr humorvoll und anschaulich ans Tageslicht

at GrazMuseum called *360 GRAZ | die Stadt von allen Zeiten* (360 GRAZ | The City of all Ages). It featured historical exhibits that illustrated the history of Franziscean land surveying in Graz and the surrounding areas, while also using a contemporarily readable approach in visualizing the steps to the present through a transcription of historical maps.

The exhibition visitors were accompanied by a virtual narrator, Franz Allmer—a geodesist, collector, and teacher of the history of land surveying at Graz University of Technology who has been known to enthusiastically present young individuals with historically noteworthy facts from his profession through vividly descriptive lectures, excursions, and city tours. He took exhibition visitors on a journey through time, which for the youngest generation included books, map puzzles, and hidden-object games for conveying age-appropriate information. Exhibits and texts from the personal estate of Franz Allmer were made accessible to the public for the first time, as were pages from the

Franziscean Cadastre (dated 1820 and 1829), historical and modern surveying instruments, and Faculty of Architecture student projects.

Franz Allmer told of the translation of historical map content into a form that complies with today's measurement criteria and hence is readable and clearly defined.

In the framework of the exhibition (55 © Andreas Untersteggaber), the podium discussion "vermessen, verwalten, versteuern" (surveying, administrating, taxing) was held, moderated by Dr. Monika Stromberger (56 © Andreas Untersteggaber). The various keynote speakers shed light on the intentions behind the large-scale land surveying measures

und regten im Anschluss daran zur intensiven Diskussion mit dem Publikum, das sich aus Geodäten, Kunsthistorikern, Architekten und grundsätzlich an der Thematik Interessierten, an.

„Raum ist eine zentrale Kategorie der Wahrnehmung, der Wirklichkeitsdeutung, des individuellen Agierens. Insofern ist die Auseinandersetzung mit seiner Vermessung ein wichtiges Moment, dem hier eine kleine, feine Ausstellung gewidmet ist." (Zitat Monika Stromberger, Ausstellungsrezension auf gat.st)

Exkurs No 1 – verMESSEN.
Franziszeische Grundkataster von Graz
6. März–22. April 2013
(www.archelmoma.at)

Marion Starzacher

57

temporär_wohnen_kinder

„Kinder haben ein Recht auf Selbstbestimmung des Lebens und ein Recht, ernst genommen zu werden und zu nichts verpflichtet zu werden, was die Kraft und das Alter eines kleinen Menschen übersteigt." (Janusz Korczak 1878–1942)

Jenseits von Zielen bloßer „Kindertauglichkeit" durch das Ausschalten möglicher Gefahrenquellen bedeutet die Schaffung von Lebensraum für „kleine Menschen" in der Stadt eine

conducted in the nineteenth century, which were prescribed by the property tax commission of December 23, 1817 under Emperor Francis I of Austria. The speakers related this to their respective disciplines, bringing some little known information to light with much vividness and humor. An intensive discussion with the audience followed, which was comprised of geodesists, art historians, architects, and those sharing a general interest in the topic.

"Space is a main category of perception, of interpreting reality, of individual action. It follows that the analysis of its measurement is a critical moment, to which this small but excellent exhibition is dedicated." (Quote: Monika Stromberger, exhibition review at www.gat.st)

Exkurs No. 1 – verMESSEN:
Franziszeische Grundkataster von Graz
March 6 – April 22, 2013
(www.archelmoma.at)

Marion Starzacher

temporär_wohnen_kinder

"Children have a right to self-determine their lives and a right to be taken seriously and to not be bound to anything that would exceed the power and age of a young person." (Janusz Korczak, 1878–1942)

Extending beyond the goals of mere "childproofing," such as the elimination of possible sources of danger, the creation of living space

58

besondere Herausforderung: Welche Freiräume brauchen Kinder in einer Wohnung in urbaner Lage? Wie erfahren und deuten Kinder Raum – und wie unterwandern und besetzen sie die hochspezialisierte „erwachsene" City mit ihren alternativen Bedürfnissen und ihren eigenen Bauvorhaben? Wie flexibel kann, soll und muss Wohnraum auf unterschiedliche Entwicklungsstufen der Kindheit (Baby, Schulkind, Jugendlicher …) reagieren?

Im Rahmen des Sommersemesterthemas „temporär_wohnen_kinder" des Instituts für Wohnbau unter Leitung von Prof. Andreas Lichtblau gewährte der Impulstag am 21. März 2013 im Forum Stadtpark den StudentInnen erste Einblicke in die Thematik (57/58).

Die ReferentInnen Andreas Lichtblau, Monika Keplinger, Rainer Rosegger, Bertram Werle, Ali Seghatoleslami (PPAG), Michael Tatschl (breadedEscalope) sowie Susanne Fritzer und Wolfgang Feyferlik erzählten von verschiedenen Aspekten und unterschiedlichen Positionen zum Leben mit und von Kindern in der Stadt, von Ansprüchen, Möglichkeiten, Entwicklungsprozessen und den daraus entstehenden Architekturen.

Als atmosphärischer Abschluss dieses Impulstages sorgte der von Dominik Kamalzadeh (*Der Standard*) vorgestellte französische Kinderfilmklassiker „Krieg der Knöpfe" (1962) nicht nur inhaltlich, sondern auch aufgrund der höchst unterschiedlichen Rezeptionen für Konfliktstoff. Angeblich finden verwunderte Spaziergänger rund ums Forum immer noch lose Knöpfe …

Sigrid Verhovsek

Frey_denken. Architektur als Experiment
HDA Graz,
21.–27. Februar 2013

Im Rahmen einer Projektübung am Institut für Architekturtheorie, Kunst- und Kulturwissenschaften wurde eine Ausstellung über Konrad Frey, einen der wichtigsten Vertreter der „Grazer

4 INNENTASCHEN
_Stauraum
_USB-Anschlüsse für Handy, GPS, etc.

2 SOLARPANEELE
_Lithium-Ionen Akku
_U=5 Volt
_3000 MWp Leistung
_Ladezeit: 2 Stunden

2 AUSSENTASCHEN
Stauraum

2 RÜCKENTASCHEN
zum Verstauen von
_Zeltstangen _Schnur
_Heringen _Ärmeln
_unterer Zeltteil

59

for "young people" in an urban context presents a special challenge: What free space do children need in an apartment located in an urban setting? How do children experience and interpret space? And how do they infiltrate and occupy the highly specialized "adult" city with their alternative needs and their own building ideas? How flexibly can/should/must living space react to different developmental stages of childhood (baby, pupil, youth, etc.)?

On March 21, 2013, an "impulse day" was held at Forum Stadtpark—organized as part of the summer semester topic "temporär_wohnen_kinder" (temporary_housing_children) in the Institute of Housing under Prof. Andreas Lichtblau—with an aim to offer students initial thematic impressions (57/58).

Contributors were Andreas Lichtblau, Monika Keplinger, Rainer Rosegger, Bertram Werle, Ali Seghatoleslami (PPAG), Michael Tatschl (breadedEscalope), Susanne Fritzer, and Wolfgang Feyferlik. They spoke of different aspects and positions related to city life with and by children, of aspi-

rations, opportunities, developmental processes, and the resulting architectural forms.

A spirited closure to this impulse day was provided by the French children's film classic *War of the Buttons* (1962), introduced by Dominik Kamalzadeh (*Der Standard*)—not only in terms of content, but also due to the highly varied reception of the conflict-laden material. Apparently, surprised passersby are still finding random buttons near the Forum …

Sigrid Verhovsek

Frey_denken: Architektur als Experiment
HDA Graz, February 21–27, 2013

Frey_denken: Architektur als Experiment (Thinking Frey-ly: Architecture as Experiment), an exhibition on Konrad Frey, one of the most important representatives of the "Graz School," was produced in the framework of a master studio in the Institute of Architectural Theory, Art History and Cultural Studies. In addition to Frey's experimental projects, which are still considered visionary today, the work of students was also on show, where Freyian thought had been experimented with in their own design projects. As Ulrich Tragatschnig noted in his review on www.gat.st: "Considering similar efforts, one must appreciate how these student explorations do not attempt to overtrump the master on thin ice with their own creativity. Indeed, they approach Frey's work with great precision and sensitivity, already taking up an idea in their design that was never executed due to cost factors: the construc-

Schule", produziert. Neben Freys experimentellen, noch heute visionären Projekten waren auch Arbeiten der Studierenden zu sehen, die das Frey'sche Denken in eigenen Entwurfsprojekten erprobten. Ulrich Tragatschnig urteilte in www.gat.st: „Dass die studentische Auseinandersetzung nicht den Versuch unternimmt, den Meister so eigenkreativ wie auf dünnem Grund zu übertrumpfen, versteht sich eingedenk verwandter Bemühungen nicht von selbst. Tatsächlich geht sie sehr genau und einfühlsam mit dem Werk von Frey um, greift bereits in ihrem Design eine aus Kostengründen nie umgesetzte Idee zur Konstruktion eines Hauses aus Wellpappe auf. Sie liefert präzise Analysen, die an einer Stelle auch aneignend weitergesponnen werden: Claudia Horneber und Bernadette Prinz nehmen den Faden bei Freys ‚Kuhwickel' auf und entwickeln mit ‚Tentsuit' (59) einen weniger modischen als nützlichen Mantel, der sich zum Zelt umbauen lässt."

Leitung: **Anselm Wagner**, **Ingrid Böck**, **Margareth Otti**, **Konrad Frey**.

Studierende: **Katharina Ackerl**, **Alfred Angerer**, **Nadin Bierbauer**, **Sonja Brandstetter**, **Andreas Bretter**, **Thurid Coll**, **Irene Heinrich**, **Kathrin Hirsch**, **Claudia Horneber**, **Sarah Mair**, **Regina Monetti**, **Bernadette Prinz**, **Katharina Puck**, **Olivia Purkarthofer**, **Lisa Schex**.

Anselm Wagner

tion of a house from corrugated board. Precise analyses are presented before being appropriated and even carried further in one case: Claudia Horneber and Bernadette Prinz take the rope in Frey's 'Cowcicle' and create 'Tentsuit,' (59) which is a less fashionable than useful coat that can be turned into a tent."

Organized by: **Anselm Wagner**, **Ingrid Böck**, **Margareth Otti**, **Konrad Frey**.

With works by: **Katharina Ackerl**, **Alfred Angerer**, **Nadin Bierbauer**, **Sonja Brandstetter**, **Andreas Bretter**, **Thurid Coll**, **Irene Heinrich**, **Kathrin Hirsch**, **Claudia Horneber**, **Sarah Mair**, **Regina Monetti**, **Bernadette Prinz**, **Katharina Puck**, **Olivia Purkarthofer**, **Lisa Schex**.

Anselm Wagner

GAM.
ARCHITECTURE MAGAZINE **11**

http://gam.tugraz.at

Archiscripts

Das Architekturmagazin GAM beschäftigt sich in seiner nächsten Ausgabe mit der Frage, auf welchen Ebenen Architektur und Schreiben miteinander verbunden sind. Nicht nur die enorme Zahl der Architekturzeitschriften, wissenschaftlicher Journals und weiterer architekturrelevanter Printmedien, sondern auch die den Architekturprojekten zugehörigen textlichen Beschreibungen organisieren einen vielfältigen Architekturdiskurs, der die Aufmerksamkeit der architektonischen Öffentlichkeit steuert. Im Lauf seiner langen Geschichte entstanden dabei viele spezifische Formen des architektonischen Schreibens; der Architektur der Gegenwart liefert dieser Diskurs „ihr Medium des Austauschs und konstruiert ihr System der Rechenschaftslegung. Es gibt – einfach gesagt – ohne Schreiben keine Architektur", wie Jeffrey Kipnis feststellt. Denn sich von den rein konstruktiven Baupraktiken zu unterscheiden, konnte innerhalb der modernen Architektur nur durch Wertschätzung ihrer Reflexion geschehen, wodurch das Schreiben und Publizieren in einem stetig zunehmenden Maße zum Kennzeichen ihrer Autonomie geworden ist. In diesem Diskurs erfährt Architektur ihre Bewertung und Anerkennung, ihre Weiterentwicklung oder Beendigung einer überkommenen Entwicklung. Über diese Funktion als Grundbedingung der Architektur hinaus besitzt der geschriebene Architekturdiskurs aber noch weitere Bedeutungen – so gelten viele Publikationen auch als sensible Indikatoren für Trends einer zukünftigen architektonischen Entwicklung. Ging man vor nicht allzu langer Zeit noch von den architekturspezifischen Textfunktionen der Beschreibung, der Reflexion und Neuformulierung ihrer Grundsätze, sowie der Verständigung über die Ziele architektonischen Handelns aus, so treten in zahlreichen Publikationen die architektonischen Faktoren inzwischen in den Hintergrund. Vielmehr vermitteln viele Texte in Architekturjournals und -blogs eher atmosphärische Impressionen, die die sensationellen Bilder der Bauprojekte veranschaulichen.

Diese gegenwärtige Situation einer merkbaren Veränderung des Architekturdiskurses nimmt GAM zum Anlass, um eine Bestandsaufnahme der unterschiedlichen architektonischen Praktiken des Schreibens und ihres aktuellen Stellenwerts vorzunehmen: das Schreiben besitzt für die Architektur nicht nur analytische, deskriptive, projektive oder imaginäre Funktionen: Essays, Traktate, Manifeste, Utopien oder textlich orientierte Entwürfe verhandeln auch die architektonischen Leitlinien und gültigen Paradigmen; Texte ermöglichen Raumkonzeptionen, die über rein geometrische, technische oder funktionale Anforderungen hinausgehen, da sie die Architektur einem subjektiv Imaginären öffnen.

GAM.11 interessiert sich dafür, welche eigenständigen Publikations-, Diskussions- und Schreibformen sich in der grundlegenden Verbindung von Architektur und Schreiben herausgebildet haben und fordert dazu auf, die Eigenständigkeit des architektonischen Schreibens zu analysieren und in den Beiträgen zur kommenden GAM-Ausgabe selbstreflexiv weiterzuentwickeln. Willkommen sind jegliche innovativen Formen solcher Archiscripts: theoretische Reflexionen und Entwicklungsanalysen, selbstreflexive Konzepte und Architekturmanifeste, literarisch-architektonische Spekulationen, aber auch eigenständige Entwurfexperimente, die Schrift zu ihrem primären Entwicklungs- und Darstellungsmedium machen.

GAM.11 lädt Sie ein, ein Abstract (max. 500 Wörter) zum Thema „Archiscripts" bis zum **4. Mai 2014** einzureichen. Der Abgabetermin für den finalen Beitrag ist der **31. August 2014.**

GAM.
ARCHITECTURE MAGAZINE 11

http://gam.tugraz.at